Ireland's Holy Wars

Ireland's Holy Wars

*The Struggle for a
Nation's Soul, 1500–2000*

Marcus Tanner

Yale University Press
New Haven and London

For information about this and other Yale University Press publications, please contact:
U.S. Office: sales.press@yale.edu   www.yale.edu/yup
Europe Office: sales@yaleup.co.uk   www.yaleup.co.uk

Set in Adobe Garamond by Northern Phototypesetting Co. Ltd, Bolton, Lancs.
Printed in Great Britain by The Bath Press

Library of Congress Control Number: 2001093662

A catalogue record for this book is available from the British Library.

ISBN: 0–300–09072–2

1 2 3 4 5 6 7 8 9 10

Contents

Illustrations and Maps

23. Ian Paisley at an anti-Catholic protest, Canterbury, 7 July 1970 (© Hulton–Deutsch Collection/CORBIS).
24. Pope John Paul II on his way to Drogheda, September 1979 (© Vittoriano Rastelli/CORBIS).
25. Bishop Eamonn Casey, when Bishop of Kerry, *c.* 1971 (RTE).
26. St Peter's, Drogheda (author photo).
27. Dan Winters' Cottage, Loughsall, Co. Armagh (author photo).
28. Apprentice Boys' Parade, Derry (author photo).
29. Protestant mural, Waterside, Londonderry (author photo).
30. Protestant paramilitary mural in Shankhill area of West Belfast (author photo).
31. 'Priest on Duty', Drogheda (author photo).

Preface

In the summer of 2001 I was dispatched by a British newspaper to cover the Drumcree 'stand-off' in County Armagh, Northern Ireland. At the nearby town of Portadown, most things are as you would expect. The church and war memorial stand in the town centre, flanked by an ordered high street. Beneath the railway bridge a road leads past new housing developments towards the village church of Drumcree. Hanging baskets of fuchsias decorate front doors.

And yet there is a madness to the place. Each July, thousands of British troops pour into Portadown to erect 20ft-high metal sheeting between the road of hanging baskets and the cosy high street. Thousands of protestors, never otherwise seen in the vicinity, clamour behind the metal barrier against the British government's refusal to let them walk that particular road into Portadown.

I have always been fascinated by the Drumcree dispute and the light it cast on Catholic-Protestant tensions in Northern Ireland. But it was only when I went there as a journalist that I realised it had turned into a media carnival. Vast white container lorries of broadcasting companies thundered down the lanes around Drumcree church, planting cranes, watchtowers and searchlights in expected 'flash-points'. All the houses nearby, except for the rectory, appeared to have been commandeered by television crews posting notices reading 'no entry except to TV personnel' on the gates. It proved almost impossible to interview the 'angry locals'. Few were to be found among the ranks of Spanish-speaking journalists, shouting into mobile phones about the 'build-up' of the crisis, while an army spokesperson crisply briefed anyone with a notebook: 'You see, what we are trying to achieve here, Mr Tanner, is . . .'

What the media circus in Drumcree did not do was explain why any of this was taking place. I have written this book to answer the questions the endless media coverage of Northern Ireland fails to address, in particular the role the churches have played in building up – and breaking down – confessional battle lines. Much of my research was done in libraries, museums and exhibitions, poring over the voluminous memoirs of the bishops, priests and ministers whose lives – especially in the nineteenth century – were either recorded by their own hand or by their progeny and fellow clerics. But I spent just as much time on the road, crossing and re-crossing the thirty-two counties of Ireland, trying to match places to dates, searching for ruined abbeys and cathedrals and talking wherever possible to priests, ministers and their congregations.

This research-odyssey is indelibly etched on my memory: chancing upon the medieval tombs in the ruins of Gowran church, Co. Tipperary, of the Butler family; wading through the knee-deep weeds in a forgotten quaker churchyard in Ballitore, Co. Kildare; hearing a service of Gregorian chant at a Cistercian abbey outside Roscrea, Co. Tipperary; and making up the numbers at a sad, empty Protestant service in Dingle, Co. Kerry.

I have sought to give a sense of the country's landscape because only by seeing it in County Armagh was I able to make sense of the historic division between Catholic and Protestant, native and settler. As I traversed the border of the Protestant north of the county, with its fecund plum orchards, and moved south through gorse and heather, the link between the struggle for land and the conflict over religion in Armagh became real.

In Bosnia in the mid-1990s, a young Serb farmer – an Orthodox Christian – had explained to me why he hated the Muslim inhabitants of the town along the river Drina. 'We've always hated them', he said. 'Ever since the seventeenth century, when the Turks invaded Bosnia, they gave the Muslims all the best land along the riverside. Now we're going to get it back.'

Ireland and the former Yugoslavia are separated by more than geographical distance but their histories have certain common elements. After spending long periods in each, I concluded that Ireland was what Yugoslavia could have been in a best-case scenario, while it was also an awful warning of what Northern Ireland might have become if the 'peace process' had totally failed. In both countries the connection between land, religion and foreign invasion is intimate and – more importantly – still prominent in popular consciousness. The Bosnian farmer insisted on calling all Muslims 'Turks' and 'settlers', even though they had inhabited the area three centuries earlier. In Drumcree an elderly man, observing a BBC lorry outside his garden, said life in Portadown used to be much better – before the English invaded Ireland under Henry II in the twelfth century.

Irish history – Protestant or Catholic – is like a great shrine. The shamans guarding the doors are nervous about allowing the uninitiated to stroll through the sacred precincts, let alone a foreign historian trample through with his muddy boots. I hope my foreignness has been an advantage: to see one's own country through another's eyes can yield a fresh perspective. Then again, I hope my family background – half Welsh-speaking and very Celt, half English and very Anglo-Saxon – has given me a more nuanced outlook than some might anticipate. This book will undoubtedly offend at certain points; the Northern Protestants, by using the more common 'Derry' rather than 'Londonderry', and Catholics by employing 'Ulster' for Northern Ireland (or the north of Ireland) and failing to expound the idea that a United Ireland is the holy grail towards which all history leads.

I want to thank all the people who spoke to me, from the Apprentice Boys of Derry who shared their burgers on their big day; to the housewives of the Garvaghy Road who, though bored by the same questions from journalists year after year, patiently went over everything again; to the (unnamed) priests of the Dublin diocese who shared robust stories about life under the Archbishop. I thank also the many librarians who helped me understand the history of their country, in particular the staff of the National Library in Dublin, the Cardinal Tomas O'Fiaich Memorial Library in Armagh, the Armagh Robinson Library, the Linen Hall Library in Belfast, the Union Theological College Library in Belfast and the Representative Church Body Library in Dublin. I especially enjoyed the Catholic Central Library and Marsh's Library in Dublin. Finally, I want to thank Willie Hayes of Roscrea, a former priest at Holy Cross abbey, whose knowledge of, and interest in, the lives of the priests and people of Co. Tipperary over generations is inexhaustible. The view from his house over the moody, undulating hills of that county is moving and awesome. If anyone understands the connection between land and faith, it is he.

NORTHERN IRELAND

County	County town		County	County town
1. ANTRIM	Antrim		20. MAGHERAFELT	Magherafelt
2. ARDS	Newtownards		21. MOYLE	Ballycastle
3. ARMAGH	Armagh		22. NEWRY & MOURNE	Newry
4. BALLYMENA	Ballymena		23. NEWTOWNABBEY	Ballyclare
5. BALLYMONEY	Ballymoney		24. NORTH DOWN	Bangor
6. BANBRIDGE	Banbridge		25. OMAGH	Omagh
7. BELFAST	Belfast		26. STRABANE	Strabane
8. CARRICKFERGUS	Carrickfergus			
9. CASTLEREAGH	Cregagh			
10. COLERAINE	Coleraine			
11. COOKSTOWN	Cookstown			
12. CRAIGAVON	Portadown			
13. DERRY	Londonderry/Derry			
14. DOWN	Downpatrick			
15. DUNGANNON	Dungannon			
16. FERMANAGH	Enniskillen			
17. LARNE	Larne			
18. LIMAVADY	Limavady			
19. LISBURN	Lisburn			

Map 1   Ireland

RAPHOE

DERRY

DOWN & CONNOR

ARMAGH

CLOGHER

DROMORE

KILLALA

ACHONRY

KILMORE

ARDAGH & CLONMACNOISE

TUAM

ELPHIN

MEATH

GALWAY

GALWAY

TUAM

KILMACDUAGH

CLONFERT

KILDARE & LEIGHLIN

DUBLIN

KILFENORA

KILLALOE

OSSORY

CASHEL & EMLY

LIMERICK

FERNS

WATERFORD & LISMORE

KERRY

CLOYNE

CORK

ROSS

0 10 20 30 40 50

km

Map 2   Church of Ireland Dioceses

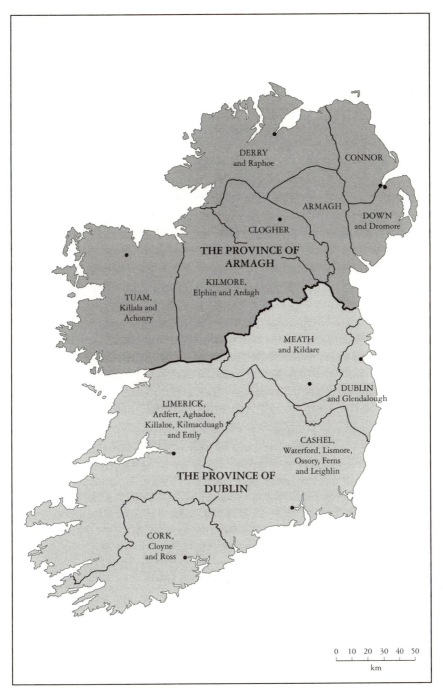

THE PROVINCE OF ARMAGH

DERRY
and Raphoe

CONNOR

ARMAGH

DOWN
and Dromore

CLOGHER

TUAM,
Killala and
Achonry

KILMORE,
Elphin and Ardagh

MEATH
and Kildare

DUBLIN
and Glendalough

LIMERICK,
Ardfert, Aghadoe,
Killaloe, Kilmacduagh
and Emly

CASHEL,
Waterford, Lismore,
Ossory, Ferns
and Leighlin

THE PROVINCE OF DUBLIN

CORK,
Cloyne
and Ross

0 10 20 30 40 50

km

Map 3   Catholic Dioceses

INTRODUCTION

If Stones Could Speake

First let me tell you that in Ireland, Protestantism is really Protestant.
(Bernard Shaw, *John Bull's Other Island*)[1]

The road to Derry started in Dublin. After disembarking at Dublin port I drove through the capital and headed north. It was high summer but in this chilly corner of north-western Europe the evenings were already tinged with damp and swirls of mist rose up in front of the car headlamps. The hedgerows and villages on the road north from Dublin recalled the English countryside I was brought up in. It was not hard to recall that this was once the 'Pale', the name given to the narrow strip of land around the capital that was densely populated by English settlers in the Middle Ages.

There were slight differences between this landscape and England's. There were far fewer lights and houses. About an hour's drive north of Dublin I reached Drogheda, the epitome of an English Pale town, with its banks of decaying Georgian mansions tumbling down to the River Boyne and the spire of the parish church of St Peter's rearing up in the evening light behind elaborate wrought iron gates.

The real shock was not Drogheda and the south with all its echoes of England, but Belfast, capital of British-ruled Northern Ireland. From the border between the Republic of Ireland and Northern Ireland, which is unmarked save for a flurry of currency exchange shops and a change in road markings, there is a dramatic change of mood and pace. As in the former Yugoslavia, before the outbreak of war in the early 1990s, there is an explosion of flags. Just north of the border on the road to the town of Newry, it is the green-white-and-gold Irish tricolour that flutters from every pub, lamppost and lawn. From then on, the red-white-and-blue British flags hold sway with ever increasing intensity on the main road to Belfast.

Even that does not prepare the visitor for the riot of colour in the Sandy Row area of south Belfast. There, entire streets look like a film set for a coronation. Kerbstones painted in the red-white-and-blue of the Union Jack, bunting in similar colours hanging from roof to roof and vast murals, festive and brilliant, proclaim the fervent allegiance of the local population to the symbols of the Protestant religion and the British crown.

If Protestants historically have banished art from their churches, the suppressed impulse has certainly found its natural outlet in the iconography on these Belfast streets. And for a religious community that has traditionally disdained allegory, it is ironic that of the two communities in Ireland, it is the Protestant murals that are the more symbolic and mystical. The wall paintings in Catholic areas in Northern Ireland are straightforwardly political in their message and entirely realistic. They portray communities in resistance in contemporary clothes.

The most famous in Northern Ireland dominates the view of the Bogside from the city walls in Derry: YOU ARE NOW ENTERING FREE DERRY, it reads. There is no trace of religious imagery in this scene and no appeal to tradition. The central figure, the civil rights politician, Bernadette Devlin,[2] is shown in a grey jersey and baggy jeans, shouting through a loudspeaker in front of a barricade. Behind her another woman in a 1960s-style short skirt, kneels on the ground, banging a dustbin lid. It is a photograph rendered in paint.

The Protestant counterparts of this mural are executed on quite different lines. The colours are surprisingly sensual – vivid scarlets picked out against moody aquamarine. Many contain no words at all. If they have them, they are phrases in Latin or sentences from the Bible. These are works rich in allegory. Non-human symbols – crowns, wreaths and red hands[3] – dominate the picture. Some feature a warrior figure holding a shield. The titan with the long blond hair, distinguishable from a 1970s rock singer only by his axe and toga, is Cuchulain, a mythical Gaelic hero who defended Ulster against the forces of Queen Maeve[4] of the south. Cuchulain was an inspiration to the mainly Catholic nationalists who rebelled against British rule in Ireland in 1916. Now he serves a different purpose, defending the northern Protestants against the southerners who they believe are trying to overwhelm them. Likewise the Protestants' favourite symbol, the Red Hand, was once the emblem of Ulster's Gaelic Catholic aristocracy, the very people who were expropriated in the 1600s to make way for Protestant settlers. The Protestants have rummaged through Ulster's Gaelic past in the search for symbols that will service their own community's view of the world. The Red Hand is really theirs, now. They have plundered the collective memory of the enemy.

This may be Britain but it is certainly not England. Confirming the change of pace and atmosphere, I switched on the car radio to hear a BBC Radio Ulster report on an outbreak of inter-Protestant violence in the Waterside district, Derry.[5] The report said paramilitary gangs had forced a number of Protestant families to flee from the area. It seemed like a bout of Balkan-style 'ethnic cleansing'. But in this case, Protestants were being attacked by their own people. The reporter spoke to a former Lord Mayor of the city. 'The only community suffering as a result of this is the Protestant community,' he said.

Away from the bunting-covered ghetto of Sandy Row, and its much larger Catholic counterpart, the Falls Road, Belfast is a shiny, mercenary city. The fruits of lavish subsidies, both British and European, are on display in a city centre that has been carefully restored since the devastating IRA bombing campaigns of the 1970s and 1980s, when the violence drove out most of the old businesses. Down the so-called 'Golden Mile' that stretches from the vast City Hall, that gaudy Versailles of the Protestant *ancien régime*, to Queen's University, cars are piled bumper to bumper in the evenings, full of people heading out to pubs, bars and restaurants. There is a good life to be had here. Salaries are much the same as they are in Britain or the Irish Republic but, in most places, property costs a fraction of the price. The average professional in Belfast ends up with far more disposable income than his or her counterpart in London or Dublin. These days you have to be in love with the tribal atmosphere of the ghetto, or spectacularly unsuccessful, to be living in the densely packed streets of the Catholic Falls or the Protestant Shankill. Why stay in those throbbing little hothouses with their poisoned history when even a low salary can deliver a mortgage large enough to transport you to the mock-Georgian suburban bliss of Holywood, Newtownbreda or Glengormley? Most Protestants have taken the hint. The Shankill and Sandy Row have become half-empty Protestant theme parks. There are plenty of boarded-up windows. Even the old curse of Ireland, unemployment, is now low. The clatter of tills has not conquered Ulster's tribal divisions but it has helped to drown them out.

The next day I headed west across the River Bann to Derry. The countryside was a patchwork of flags that reminded me of the landscape of eastern Croatia and Bosnia in 1991 and 1992 in the run-up to the recent Balkan wars. In lush, lowland areas, Union Jacks flapped from the telegraph poles along the roadside. As my car climbed uphill into the heathery moors of County Tyrone, they gave way to Irish tricolours. As I moved west from the Protestant heartland of County Antrim and County Down towards County Londonderry, there was a general tendency for Irish flags to gain ground.

Derry is the Jerusalem of Northern Irish Protestants, or the Protestant Kosovo. It is the holy city, or as they call it, the Maiden City, whose walls were never breached by the Catholic enemy. But like the Serbs in Kosovo, the Derry Protestants have lost the demographic battle. The Orthodox Serbs had lost the baby race in Kosovo to the Albanians, most of whom are Muslim, in the eighteenth or early nineteenth century.[6] The English and Scottish Protestants of Derry lost their majority in the city towards the end of the nineteenth century.[7] The Serb pilgrims to Kosovo's Orthodox monasteries are now strangers in a land they still think of as holy. They move among people who resent their presence and who deny that the land forms part of the Serb state. The Protestant marchers in Derry's annual Apprentice Boys parade are equally unwelcome in a population that is now 70 per cent Catholic. For a day they make Derry a Protestant city once again. Only in the Waterside area, separated from the old walled city by the River Foyle, does the landscape recall the Protestant streets of south and east Belfast. There are the same bunting and murals as in Belfast, though the walls bear a different, more local, slogan: '300 years and still under siege'.

A striking mural shows a skeletal figure striding with tattered Union flag and sword in hand through a sulphurous inferno of gunshot and corpses. The ghoulish apparition crushes underfoot a broken tablet that reads: YOU ARE ENTERING FREE DERRY, a macabre case of one mural copying another. It is an apocalyptic scene, and one that hardly corresponds to the efforts of Derry's City Council to portray a community engaged in reconciliation. They would much prefer visitors to look at the sculpture on the outskirts of the city centre that depicts two people, standing on separate walls, stretching out their hands to one another across the divide.

The Apprentice Boys parade was due to take place the day after I arrived. There were rituals to be observed. The ritual of the Orangemen in their bowler hats and sashes, holding their banners and trudging down the streets with impassive faces. And the ritual of Catholic youths in balaclavas, skipping into the air to hurl their rocks and home-made petrol bombs over the sheets of corrugated iron erected by the police to separate the marchers from their opponents.

On the evening before the march the atmosphere was palpably sullen on the Catholic Bogside, and in the neighbouring nationalist Creggan estate. The grid-work of grey council houses that is home to the majority of the city's population looked empty. On the Waterside and in the tiny Fountain estate, a blob of Protestant territory on the city side of the River Foyle, there was a corresponding air of glee. Children scurried through the tatty lanes as light fell, shovelling sticks, bits of wood and furniture on top of huge bonfires. Later these would be lit to celebrate the end of the Catholic siege of the city in 1689, when Protestant King Billy saw off Catholic King James. We were hours away from the high point of the Protestant liturgical calendar.

The Fountain estate nestles under the walls of the city, hugging the grey bulk of St Columb's cathedral. This was the first cathedral built by Protestants in Ireland,[8] its grey stone walls and soaring spire a warning to the Irish natives that the British Protestants were here to stay. St Columb's is a cathedral of the Church of Ireland, the Church that the English colonists brought to Ireland after the Reformation.[9] The name hints at the Church's attempt to link itself to an older, Gaelic Irish past. It proclaims the Church of Ireland's desire to be seen as a successor to something that went before.

The interior of the cathedral belies this token gesture to the Gaelic past. Everything in it announces this to be a church of conquerors and settlers who have narrowly survived repeated attempts by the older race to get rid of them. It is the message of the cannonball, fired by King James's army in the siege, which still lies in the cathedral. It is the message of the British regimental flags, ghostly and threadbare, that hang from the gloom of the cathedral roof, and of the silken flags above the altar that the besieged garrison seized from James's French troops. It is the message of the dedication plaque, dated 1633, which recalls the role of the guilds of London in the Jacobean Plantation of Ulster: 'If stones could speake then Londons prayse should sounde Who built this church and cittie from the grounde.'

Above all, it is the message of the great stained-glass window to the right of the cathedral entrance. Here in brilliant colours, is the Protestant story of the siege. In one panel we see the famous apprentice boys of legend shutting the gates of Derry against the King's Catholic army.[10] In the central panel we see three British ships, led by the *Mountjoy*, which sailed into Lough Foyle on 1 August 1689 to relieve the 105-day siege after breaking the boom that the Jacobite army laid across the river. In the foreground, looking out to the Lough, stands the Reverend George Walker,[11] the Protestant governor of the city. His left hand points out to the British ships. His right hand points up to heaven. Behind his head a crimson banner flutters in the wind, while two apprentice boys lean over the walls. The sun is sinking behind the hills of Inishowen, for the relief took place around sunset. There are two women in the tableau. One cradles a dying man, representing the Protestant community's past sacrifices for its survival. The other holds a baby – the Protestant generation of the future.

The window is based on an 1861 picture entitled *The Relief of Derry*,[12] but it draws on far older folk memories among the Ulster Protestants. The theme is deliverance. The besieged city stands for the entire Protestant community, eternally ringed by hostile and more numerous forces. Salvation comes, but only after endurance and suffering. The immediate agents are the Protestant British, but salvation flows ultimately from a right relationship with God. This is the sacramental relationship of Unionism to Protestantism.

The Protestants have left Derry in large numbers since the Catholic civil rights movement shook the old order in the late 1960s. For generations it was an overwhelmingly Protestant, English-speaking settlement. The minority of Catholic merchants and artisans was forced to live beyond the city walls in the area that became the Bogside. Industrial expansion in the nineteenth century changed this. As workers poured in from the overwhelmingly Catholic countryside, the Protestant community shrank in relation to the whole. By the turn of the twentieth century the Catholics were in the majority.

Derry was incorporated into Northern Ireland because a Protestant state without the holiest Protestant site was unthinkable, in spite of the fact that a plebiscite would have resulted in Derry's incorporation into the new Irish Free State. Partition failed to reverse what was already a pronounced demographic trend. The Protestants kept control of the city government only by massaging the boundaries of the wards that elected local councillors and by manipulation of the voting qualifications. The Protestant percentage of the population continued to decline. But it was only during the disturbances of the late 1960s and 1970s that Catholic, Irish Derry finally swamped Protestant, British Londonderry. By the 1990s, only about 21,000 of the 95,000 inhabitants were Protestant.[13] The Maiden City had been breached after all.

The outgoing Protestant tide in Derry has left the old shrine of the cathedral beached on an Irish Catholic shore. Few of the 200 or so regular worshippers now come from the surrounding area. It is the same for all the surviving Protestant churches on the city side of the Foyle. Most worshippers in St Augustine's, which overlooks the Bogside, used to live in what is now 100 per cent Catholic territory. The parishioners were driven out to the Waterside during 'the troubles' but still return to their former neighbourhood for Sunday services, marriages and burials.

A woman who attends the church told me she had grown up near the Bogside. Peering over the city walls towards the spires of the Catholic St Eugene's cathedral, I asked her if she ever visited her old Catholic acquaintances, living only yards away from where we stood. She said she did not as she felt unwelcome in streets decked with Irish tricolours, although she had no qualms about standing underneath the same tricolour on visits to the Irish Republic. There was no vehemence – merely surprise that anyone should even think of crossing into hostile territory. 'Take away religion and the Irish are a pretty friendly people,' she added. It was an odd comment from a committed Christian.

The Fountain estate, that small and shabby remnant of Londonderry's once powerful Protestant working class, is separated by a main road from the Bogside. It is easily marked out by the Orange, English and Union flags fluttering from the roofs and lampposts. Barricades of sofas, beds and boards marked a recent protest against the decision of the government-appointed Parades Commission to forbid Protestant marches along the stretch of the city wall beside Butcher's Gate that overlooks the Bogside.[14]

In contrast to this battered enclave, the Bogside wears a confident and unruffled air. A rash of murals facing the (Protestant) east proclaim: NO CONSENT, NO PARADE, and 'Disband the RUC'.[15] But most of the streets that climb up towards the cathedral and the Milltown cemetery are free of graffiti. There is no need to mark out territory here. It is all Catholic. The Protestant businesses that dominated the commercial heart of the city 30 years ago have all gone. Many were bombed out by the IRA. Both sides in the city have engaged in ethnic cleansing; the Clooney estate on the Waterside was once a mixed area. Now it is more than 90 per cent Protestant. But in the struggle for territory in Derry the Protestants have been by far the biggest losers.

On the night of the Protestant bonfires I switched on the radio news. There was a discussion involving survivors of the Real IRA bomb planted in the town of Omagh in County Tyrone one year before, which killed 29 people.[16] The news then moved on to a report from the Lower Ormeau Road, in central Belfast. A nationalist pressure group, the Concerned Residents,[17] was organising a sit-down protest against a decision by the Parades Commission to allow an Orange march through their street. Northern Ireland was bracing for trouble. I headed out into the night.

The first port of call was the Orange disco. It wasn't called that. It was a social evening held in the Orange Lodge headquarters in the old city. A man I met in the cathedral earlier that day had offered to take me along. I went to his home, a mock-Georgian house in a new estate on the Waterside, to wait for him. The house was immaculate; the garden waist high in weeds. He lived alone and talked in a fanatical fashion of the purgatorial existence of the Protestants of Londonderry and the endless snubs and persecutions to which they were exposed. I asked whether he had ever thought of turning to gardening to relax from all the communal tension in the city? No he had not, he said, making it clear that he regarded this as a frivolous contribution to the debate. Did he not think some of the British flags in the cathedral ought to come down, to make the building more attractive to the Catholics who lived around it? Under no circumstances. The flags had been blessed and were sacred. It seemed a curious notion for a Protestant, to treat a flag as a kind of reliquary. When he was ready to die, he said, he wanted to go out whirling a sword around his head through a large crowd of Catholics and decapitating as many of them as possible.

We had Orange business to carry out before the dance. My new friend had contacted a fellow-thinker from Antrim on the internet and we were to meet him on a corner in town. In the event, the Orangeman from Antrim never turned up, so we headed off for the Orange lodge.

Getting into the Orange club was a tricky business. There was a lot of shouting through keyholes and clanking of locks before the iron gates swung open and we were allowed in. I expected a lot of people talking like my friend about whirling swords around and slicing off Catholic heads. But if there was such talk I missed it. It seemed like a working men's club anywhere in the north of England, the same musical hits from the 1980s, the same stiff hairdos and 'best night out' clothes on the women and the same beery *bonhomie* among the men. Only the frosted glass image on the mirror behind the bar of William and Mary[18] – the forgotten Orange queen – reminded me where we were.

Soon it was time for the bonfires. The fires at the Fountain, at New Buildings, Irish Street and the Lincoln Court estate were all to start at different times to allow people to visit several in the course of the evening. At New Buildings, on the outskirts of the city, the traffic lights on the road blinked red, amber, green in a pointless fashion, as there was no traffic to direct. The only headlamps from approaching cars belonged to people coming to watch the fire and catch a beer. A large crowd milled around in the middle of the empty highway drinking from plastic cups and jiggling a little to the tunes pumping from the improvised disco rigged up on the edge of the road.

Every so often a car drew up and disgorged a family. Mum and Dad clambered out, sleepy-headed children lolling over their parents' shoulders. Some of them, long in the future, would surely remember that night as the night when they were inducted into the mysterious world of their parents' innermost beliefs – the unique cosmos of the true-believing Ulster Protestants. Perhaps they would carry away memories of Mother's scent, Father's sweat, the warm night air, the blinking traffic lights on the empty road, the heads of the crowd silhouetted against the crimson flames and their deep, orgasmic roar as the fire licked the tricolour on top of the pile.

The fires were for the local people. Few of the following day's marchers were to be seen wandering around the New Buildings or the Lincoln Court estate that night. They had come in their cars and buses from home, some from as far as Scotland and Liverpool,[19] with their sashes and their uniforms. I was told they were tucked up in bed, saving their energy for the following day.

The Ulster Protestants have reinvented church art through the means of the mural. They have reinvented the Catholic procession through the march. Uniquely among the world's Protestant communities, they have transferred faith from the church buildings to the street. The Orange Order functions, in fact, like a Catholic guild or confraternity, offering brotherhood, rituals, uniforms and a form of liturgical calendar that revolves around the life and acts of King William. The medieval Catholic guilds were devoted to different saints. The Orange movement is similarly subdivided, with a number of offshoots, such as the Apprentice Boys or the Royal Black Preceptory. The Apprentice Boys are particularly devoted to the cult of the siege of Derry.

A medieval pilgrim might feel quite at home in this procession of faith, accompanied by relics and banners. The Orangeman, like the ultra-Orthodox Jew, has adopted a European urban costume from a specific era as his distinctive uniform. It is the dress worn by the British middle classes and 'respectable' working classes in the late nineteenth and early twentieth centuries, comprising black suit, white shirt, tie, shiny polished black shoes and – most distinctively of all – a black bowler hat. It is that black hat, long since vanished from the City of London, which is the trademark. Any cartoonist wanting to depict an Orangeman will seize on the hat. So will Catholic nationalist opponents of the marches. Placards depicting a bowler hat with a red line through it are a common way of expressing hostility to marches in an area.

The Orange parade is conducted like a Catholic procession. Instead of relics, the Orangemen often carry an open Bible on a scarlet cushion in the front of the procession. And whereas Catholics – and still more, the Orthodox – carry icons or cloth banners embroidered with images of the Virgin Mary and of saints, the Orange procession's most distinctive feature are the large banners embroidered with images of King William, the Reverend George Walker, the *Mountjoy*, or the shutting of the gates.

The marcher may smile occasionally or call out the odd greeting, but talking or facial gestures are not encouraged. The conscientious marcher wears a grave expression, eyes fixed on the swaying banner up front. He may not amble, talk or stare at the crowd. This is a procession of faith to which certain military touches have been added.

The service was due to start in the cathedral at 11.30 a.m. Once, this would have been a great civic affair, graced possibly by the Northern Ireland Prime Minister, members of his cabinet, Church of Ireland bishops and a fair sprinkling of the Protestant gentry. Now the politicians and ministers stay away. The presence of the city's Catholic mayor in 1999 was hardly to be expected. But there was no bishop either and we had to make do with the Dean. Even the cathedral's bells did not peal. Broken, I was told. Most of the shops had shut in anticipation of 'trouble' from the Bogside and it soon became clear that only a token force of Apprentice Boys was going to make it across the river to the service.

They were smartly dressed when they came. Three young men marched at the front with shiny cheeks and oiled hair, carrying their flags, followed by a couple of men with swords. They came clattering into the church with their flags and a banner of the Apprentice Boys of Derry General Committee and for a while there was some confusion, after the verger insisted they had to leave their swords in the umbrella stand. But there were not many of them and the service was an anticlimax. There was no fiery Orange sermon but an inaudible, almost incomprehensible lecture on some Old Testament prophet and the Orangemen were shifting in their seats before it ended.

It was a relief to join the real action down on the Waterside, where the rest of the Apprentice Boys, tens of thousands of them, were being marshalled behind their banners and drummers for the grand procession. The discordant sound of a thousand pipes and drums being tested filled the air. Along the route, stall holders had set out their wares, mainly beefburgers, fried onions and Coca-Cola. There were Orange music cassettes for sale and T-shirts with pictures of the Pope saying: I SUPPORT THE DRUMCREE MARCHERS, making light of the annual controversy over the Orange march to Drumcree church near Portadown in County Armagh.[20]

In spite of the spitting rain, local people had filled all the spaces along the route. It would take about four hours for the marchers to pass by and the older people had set out their chairs beside the road to get the best view.

The purple banners engraved with MOUNTJOY AT THE BOOM, or SHUTTING THE GATES and REVD GEORGE WALKER, stretched as far as the eye could see. Some of the companies were from Scotland, from Glasgow and Motherwell, a faint echo of the once tight bonds between the Ulster Protestants and the Scottish Presbyterians. But most of the clubs came from towns and villages all over the six counties of Northern Ireland, with a handful from the Protestants in Donegal, Cavan and Monaghan, the three Ulster counties that joined the independent Irish state in 1922. The marchers took no notice of the rain. They marched regardless, ignoring the water bouncing off their bowler hats and streaming down their faces. The drummers were the real athletes. The parade demanded an enormous effort from all of them as they squirmed and gyrated with barely concealed sexual energy behind their huge instruments, arms rotating like helicopter blades and raining down blows on to drums labelled PRIDE OF THE BANN or SONS OF ULSTER.

Not much has changed in this march, except the route, for generations. The Ulster Protestant community presents an unchanging face. The procession is old fashioned, unfashionable and quite rigid compared to the St Patrick's Day parades I had seen in Dublin and New York. In Dublin, gay and lesbian marchers have been included in an increasingly flexible itinerary since the early 1990s. It is hard to imagine the Orange sash and the pink ribbon ever walking together. Even women still seem to occupy a very subordinate position in the Orange pantheon. On the march they were like modest peahens beside the strutting Orange peacocks. The Orange people have not updated their culture. While Republicans have always given women a high profile in the movement, no Unionist party seems even to have considered giving a woman a leading job. Orange Protestant culture remains unrepentantly white, middle aged and male.

By about 4 p.m. the deckchairs had been folded and taken away, the crowd drifted off, and red-white-and-blue bunting hung limp in the drizzle. The empty pavements echoed to the clatter of thousands of beer cans being blown around by the wind. Debris from the previous night's bonfires had left a blackened mess around the Fountain and the Lincoln Court estates. In the distance, helicopters buzzed in the threatening sky. They were the only hint that not all was well that day in the city of Derry.

The Apprentice Boys' parade might be for Derry what Gay Pride is for Sydney and the Notting Hill Carnival is for London. It ought to be a big advertisement for the city, a money-spinner for the local businesses, an excuse for the whole community to join in a party and a draw for tourists around the world. It is, after all, a unique cultural folk festival.

But it is not so. The parade generates neither money nor community goodwill but Molotov cocktails and an annual eruption of communal hatred that invariably leaves the police and insurance companies footing a large bill. The 1999 parade triggered a night of rioting by a section of the city's Catholic youth in which more than 100 petrol bombs were thrown and eight police were injured. Shops were smashed in the commercial heart of the city and the Kentucky Fried Chicken store – inexplicably – was set on fire. In the Creggan estate, a lorry delivering food to a local supermarket was hijacked and set ablaze in what appeared to be a failed bid to lure the police into the Republican stronghold.

The animosity in Derry is replicated in dozens of towns in Northern Ireland in the so-called 'marching season' during July and August. Drumcree and the Lower Ormeau Road are only the most famous. The roots of this conflict long predate the civil rights movement, the IRA campaigns, or the partition of Ireland after the First World War. They go back to a religious struggle for the soul of Ireland which itself stretches back to the Reformation.

To understand this hatred one has to go beyond the partition of Ireland, back to the failed attempt of the English authorities to impose the Protestant religion on Ireland in the sixteenth century. There was nothing unique in some Irishmen rejecting the faith that crown and parliament had ordained for their use. It was the scale of rejection that was astonishing. In spite of the fact that the Protestant state Church was endowed with all the lands and buildings of its Catholic predecessor, its services were shunned by all but a handful of officials and crown dependants. The religious conflict between Ireland's governors and the people endured for more than three centuries, from the passage of the Reformation Acts in the Irish parliament in the 1530s to Gladstone's disestablishment of the Church of Ireland in 1869. Even then, the Protestant landed gentry remained the owners of most of the soil of Ireland for another generation. It was only after the agitation of the 1870s and 1880s that the British government reluctantly passed Acts that finally gave the land to the peasants who worked it.

Ireland's failed Reformation injected a religious element into a still older conflict between the English settlers who had colonised Ireland in the Middle Ages and the Gaelic natives. Resistance to authority became clothed in the white of martyrdom, and rebellion took on the colours of a crusade.

The Reformation set the English in Ireland against each other. The 'Old English', as the original settlers were called, remained overwhelmingly loyal to the Catholic Church. Protestantism estranged this deeply conservative community from the English motherland. The people of the walled towns and the Pale had always looked to England to defend them against the 'wild' or 'mere' Irish around them. Now religion engineered a historic realignment in Ireland, binding former enemies, under the banner of Catholicism, against the New English as the new generation of Protestant settlers was called.

If the English had adopted Lutheranism, the religious struggle might have taken a different course. But English Protestantism took a radical and Calvinist turn. Elizabeth I's Anglican bishops looked to the 'pure reformed churches' of Switzerland for inspiration and guidance,[21] not to Germany or Sweden. They did not gently nudge Catholic patterns of worship in an evangelical direction. They demanded a radical break with the past and engaged in deliberate campaigns of iconoclasm, destroying altars, shrines and statues.

In Ireland, the conservative Catholicism of the Old English and the radical Protestantism of the New English met in head-on collision. The failure of the Protestant authorities to induce either the Old English or the native Irish to accept the reformed Church ended in a massive experiment in social engineering, in which an entirely new Protestant community was transplanted into the north of Ireland. This great experiment in colonisation, known as the Ulster Plantation, was a religious, not a racial undertaking. The government of James I was not interested in adding to Ireland's considerable Anglo-Saxon gene pool. Their concern was to increase the number of Protestants.

James's Ulster Plantation differed from earlier English 'plantations' in Ireland in another crucial way. James I, who was James VI of Scotland,[22] was already in early middle age when he inherited his English kingdom in 1603. He had many Scottish supporters to reward. His predecessors on the English throne had tried to keep the Scots out of Ireland. The Scots had settled on Ireland's north-east coast in any case: the short distance between Antrim and south-west Scotland meant migration was impossible to control. But under James I, Scottish immigration received official sanction. Scots were now expressly encouraged to pour into the lands in Ulster that James had confiscated from the Gaelic chieftains. The injection of Scots into the least tamed and most Gaelic of all the Irish provinces in the

1600s permanently changed Ireland's ethnic and religious composition. Settling in dense communities in the counties nearest their homeland, the Scots were never absorbed by the native Irish, as countless English settlements had been. Four centuries on they remain a distinctive religious and ethnic community.

But the influx of Scots did not benefit the Church of Ireland, which James himself enthusiastically championed. The English Reformation had been managed by government. Kings and parliaments had directed and organised the changes, which were then imposed on the population. This left certain anomalies. The crown had no objection to the Calvinist theology that had filtered into the country through the universities, but was determined to retain the existing Catholic machinery of church government. Elizabeth I and James I both saw the desirability of controlling the new religion through bishops they appointed. The Church of England remained a church of archbishops, bishops, priests, deacons, deans and archdeacons.

The Scottish Reformation was very different. There, a genuine popular uprising in favour of Protestantism was carried out in opposition to the crown. The agent of the English Reformation, Thomas Cranmer, was the devoted servant of King Henry VIII. The father of the Scottish Reformation, John Knox,[23] had a very different relationship to Mary, Queen of Scots.

The sight of mobs destroying cathedrals with their bare hands disturbed the men whom Elizabeth I picked to staff the Anglican bishoprics. 'God keep us from such visitation as Knox have attempted in Scotland,' Archbishop Matthew Parker of Canterbury declared: 'the people to be the orderers of things.'[24] Elizabeth's successors were determined that the people would not become the 'orderers of things' in the Church of England. They could not reverse the course of events north of the border, where the Scottish Church remained stubbornly Presbyterian, composed of ministers, or presbyters, in company with lay elders. Lay elders, and not bishops appointed by the crown, 'called', or appointed, ministers to serve parishes. Ministers in synod governed the Scottish Church as a whole. It was incomparably more democratic than the Church of England.

The differences between the churches of England and Scotland affected the course of events in Ireland, too. The Scottish settlers in Ulster brought their anti-hierarchical notions and instincts with them. By the 1630s the Anglican Church of Ireland was aware that it faced two enemies – the Catholic Old English and native Irish on one hand and the Scottish Presbyterians on the other.

If the English had governed Ireland with greater constancy, the Church of Ireland might have gained a greater hold on the population. But the fortunes of all three churches rose and fell. The Catholics thought they had only to endure the reign of Elizabeth before enjoying liberty under the son of Mary, Queen of Scots. They were disappointed in James I. But the collapse of the crown during the English Civil War in the 1640s enabled them to seize power and for several years in the 1640s the Confederate Catholics of Kilkenny ran most of Ireland as an autonomous kingdom.[25]

Oliver Cromwell's victory over the crown's forces ended Catholic hopes. In the 1650s they were dispossessed on a scale never even contemplated by Elizabeth or her successors. The common ruin of Old English and Irish natives encouraged their union as a single 'Irish' nation. Cromwell, ironically, helped to forge it.

Now it was the turn of the Presbyterians to expect great things, as Catholicism and Anglicanism were driven underground. It was the first – and last – opportunity for Presbyterianism to claim the leading role in Ireland. But the Restoration in 1660 ended its hopes of supremacy and again the Anglicans saw their fortunes restored.

These constant convulsions in Church and state drew out the protracted struggle for the soul of Ireland. It was not until the 1850s, when the catastrophe of the great famine had laid waste the landscape, that it became absolutely certain that the Catholic Church had won this long battle. By then it was clear that neither of the main Protestant churches would ever be more than a Church of a relatively small minority. The Catholic Church emerged triumphant and its role as keeper of the nation's conscience seemed unshakeable. For 150 years, Irishness and Catholicism would be inter-linked. One seemed unimaginable without the other.

Naturally, political radicals in Ireland were never entirely happy with the conjunction of Irishness and Catholicism. Frequently drawn from the Protestant upper class themselves, they rejected a simplistic identification of faith and nationality. The Irish flag, which blends orange and green, is part of their ideological legacy. In the 1790s, the example of the French and American revolutions encouraged a radical secret society, the United Irishmen, to rise against British rule. However, the attempt to disentangle religion from politics and forge a new, secular Irish nationalism was a failure. The 1798 rising ended in sectarian massacres in County Wexford, with the burning alive of hundreds of Protestants in a barn in the village of Scullabogue.[26]

The legacy of Scullabogue dogged attempts in the following decades to build an Irish nationalist movement that was genuinely inclusive of both religions. In its place, Irishness became ever more strongly identified with Catholicism, while Protestants, both Anglican and Presbyterian, retreated into a British identity. For them, the Act of Union of 1800, which joined the British and Irish parliaments, took on an almost sacred significance. The politics of the United Irishmen were exchanged for the Orange Order, an exclusively Protestant organisation formed with very different goals.[27]

The link between Irishness and Catholicism, and between Protestantism and Britishness, meant that ecumenical gestures in Ireland were fraught with political significance. It also made the partition of the country almost inevitable once it was clear that the country's Catholic majority was determined to annul the Act of Union. There has been great reticence over the years to admit the religious dimension of partition. This is largely because the ideology of the Republican nationalists, the group most interested in talking about partition, will not admit it. Just as the Serbs invariably insisted that the Germans and the Pope, not the Croats and the Bosnians, broke up Yugoslavia, Irish Republicans have always maintained that partition was the work of the British, rather than the Irish Protestants. The Catholic Church generally has supported this interpretation, effectively denying that the northern Protestants were an independent party in the conflict. The conflict in the North, according to this rationale, is about imperialism, not sectarianism.

The political leaders of the Protestants have connived at this secular interpretation of Irish conflict for different reasons. Even since partition, Catholics have predicted that demographic changes in Northern Ireland mean there will eventually be a Catholic majority. The change has taken longer than they expected and the Northern Irish state has long outlived their calculations. But in the first decades of the twenty-first century, this prediction looks certain to come true,[28] and the knowledge of this makes Ulster's Unionist leaders reluctant to rest the claims to statehood on religion. Unionist leaders long ago stopped referring to Northern Ireland as a Protestant state, preferring a vaguer ethnic or political appeal to a wider 'British' or 'Loyalist' majority.

This shyness towards religion is illustrated by media coverage of the Drumcree conflict. From the mid-1990s the political life of the province has been shaken each July by the unresolved conflict over whether an Orange march should be allowed to pass up the Catholic and nationalist Garvaghy Road that links Drumcree parish church and Portadown. In 2001 I watched the British Army put up a twenty-foot-ish metal fence on the Drumcree Road which leads into the Garvaghy Road to stop the marchers even attempting the route. A group of Orangemen observed the proceedings from Drumcree churchyard with impotent fury. Nothing, it seemed, could be more symbolic of Ireland's division than that curious event. Year after year the conflict has been relayed by television to millions of homes in Britain, Ireland and the world. This massive coverage invariably presents the conflict as a political clash between Unionism and Nationalism. The Unionist Orangemen want to walk up the road. The nationalist and Republican residents of the Garvaghy Road want to stop them. Perhaps it is so obvious that Irish nationalists are Catholic and that Orangemen are Protestants that any further discussion of this issue is deemed unnecessary. But unless one examines the struggle for supremacy between the Catholics and Protestants of Ireland over almost 500 years, terms like Unionist and Nationalist are difficult to understand. It was Ireland's religious struggle that forged the political and national identities of the Irish people, or peoples. It is a struggle that resulted purely from Ireland's position as England's first and oldest colony.

CHAPTER ONE

The Hart of the English Pale

The plottes for reformacion of Irelande are of two kyndes. One which undertake to procure it by Conqueste and by peopling of Contres with English inhabitantes . . . another kynde is of those wherein is undertaken to make reformacion by publique establishment of Iustice.
(Anon., *A Treatise of Irelande*, 1588)[1]

In the spring of 1556 a ripple of excitement spread across the city of Dublin, capital of England's ancient but far from flourishing colony. A new Lord Deputy was about to arrive by sea from England, in the shape of Thomas Radcliffe, Viscount Fitzwalter, later ennobled as the Earl of Sussex. It was true that Lord Deputies came and went from Dublin with bewildering speed,[2] and that some came, went and then returned again.

In 'The Irish London',[3] as Dublin was called, the inauguration of a Lord Deputy was an occasion for Church, state and citizens to unite in a display of common Catholicism and loyalty to the English crown. Lords, bishops and burgesses would have the chance to rival each other in finery donned for the processions to and from High Mass in the Cathedral of Christ Church and at the celebrations held in Dublin Castle, the Archbishop's palace and the mayor's residence. There would be feverish speculation about the new governor's intentions. The size of the city lent itself to such intrigues, for the Dublin of Queen Mary was cramped. Practically every inch of space within the walls was let out for accommodation, often so flimsy that the tenements collapsed. Fever in those crowded apartments could spread like wildfire and the sickness of 1575 would carry away perhaps a third of the city's five- or six-thousand-strong population.

The River Liffey, which now bisects the city, then formed the city's northern frontier. Beyond, the road crossing the city's sole bridge led to a small suburb that had sprouted between St Mary's Abbey and Oxmantown Green, whose name recalled the former settlements of Norse 'Ostmen' in Dublin. The name of one of the main streets, Hangman Lane, indicates what grim sight confronted travellers heading into Dublin on the northern highway from Drogheda.

South of Dublin Castle, which now stands nearly in the centre, the roads leading from Polegate and St Nicholas Gate[4] led out of the city to the bustling ecclesiastical suburb clustered round the extra-mural cathedral church of St Patrick[5] and the adjacent palace of St Sepulchre, the residence of the archbishops of Dublin. With five parish churches, two friaries and the lepers' hospital of St Stephen, the southern suburb had seen the greatest expansion outside the walls. In the west, Newgate and Gormands' Gate led to a residential suburb that fanned out along the roads running to another of the great religious houses of Dublin, the Victorine abbey of St Thomas. In the south-east of the city, relatively little had developed between the battlements of Dublin Castle and the salt marshes that edged the sea. The main activity taking place on what is now St Stephen's Green, then called Hoggen Green after the Norse *haugar*, or burial mounds on it, was archery practice, other sports and outdoor performances of plays. Trinity College had to wait for the closing years of Queen Elizabeth for its foundation. The site was still occupied by the demolished ruins of the monastery of All Hallows, desolate since Mary's father, Henry VIII, had ordered the suppression of the religious orders almost twenty years previously. To cross the city from Newgate in the west, passing the High Cross near the cathedral and on past the stocks to Dames' Gate in the east would have taken only about a quarter of an hour.

The labyrinth of lanes running off the bigger thoroughfares of High Street, Winetavern Street and Fishamble Street, and the alleys circling Christ Church, made for an atmosphere that was both incestuous and intimate. The intimacy was heightened after sunset, when the gates of the city clanked shut after the tolling of a curfew bell in St Andrew's church.[6] Comings and goings were easily observed, faces quickly recognised and a stranger would be spotted almost immediately.

Most of the city's prying eyes focused on arrivals and departures from the Castle. The largest and most important building in the city, it was the seat of the Lord Deputy and of the Irish Council. It was the nerve centre of the English administration in Ireland. Here new officials from England arrived, full of bustling self-importance as they took up their posts in the colonies. It was here that proud embassies of native Irish lords dismounted, alien figures to the citizens with their long hair, sweeping cloaks and billowing, saffron-dyed shirts, charging into the city to treat with the representative of the English monarch whose right to rule Ireland they barely recognised. Traitors and criminals were dragged here with less ceremony, thrown in the dungeons beneath the state apartments. The problem of buildings such as the Castle was poor maintenance and the citizens were often concerned about its dilapidated state. Nevertheless, it was an imposing building with 'four goodlie and substantiall towers' in Mary's time that under Elizabeth would be 'much beautified with sundrie and gorgeous buildings',[7] when Sussex's successor, Sir Henry Sidney, was Lord Deputy.

The Castle's only rival in town was the palace of the Archbishop of Dublin. Officially he ranked as the second ecclesiastic of Ireland, after the Archbishop of Armagh, the Primate of all Ireland. In fact, he was by far the more important figure, just as Dublin was infinitely more important than the half-forgotten village of Armagh, in the heart of Gaelic Ulster. Lying just beside St Patrick's, the palace of 'Saint Pulchers' was stately rather than spectacular, 'as well pleasantlie sited as gorgeouslie builded'.[8] Perhaps too much so, for when Archbishop George Browne returned from a preaching tour of south-west Ireland at the beginning of 1539, he found the Lord Deputy, Lord Leonard Grey, had moved in and seized the property for himself.

The Castle and the palace were the great fixtures of the city. The Tholsel, the town hall, was the business centre and an invaluable source of gossip. Dubliners were famous for their hospitality, both for distributing it and for taking advantage of it. No one was expected to be more liberal in dispensing free food and drink than the mayor during his annual term of office. 'The maior, over the number of officers that take dailie repast at his table, keepeth for his year in manner open house,' the Catholic writer, Richard Stanihurst noted in the 1580s. 'In tearme time his house is frequented as well of the nobilitie as of other potentats of great calling . . . they that spend least in the maioraltie make an ordinarie account of five hundred pounds for their viand and diet that yeare, which is no small summe to be bestowed in house-keeping.'[9] The mayor in 1554, Patrick Scarsfield, claimed he gave out 20 tons of claret during his year of office, not including white wine, sack and muscatel, while his buttery and cellars had been full of guests on most days from five in the morning until ten at night.[10]

To the *habitués* of the mayor's crowded cellars, all the great officers of the colony, starting with the Lord Deputy, the Archbishop of Dublin and the Lords Justices, would have been well known figures. Their policies, private lives and suspected vices were the object of hilarious gossip and scurrilous reports. Would the new Lord Deputy favour English-born arrivals over the native-born colonists in his distribution of posts? Who would be chosen for the prestigious offices of parliament (if he summoned one) such as the Speaker for the Commons? Would he repel the native Irish from the borders of the Pale? And if he did, who would pay for such an expedition?

Lord Deputies of Ireland were notorious for abruptly cancelling the policies of their predecessors and throwing them into reverse. As the Tudor burgess and sheriff of Waterford, Edward Walshe, despairingly noted: 'Every niewe deputy shulde begyn where the former deputy made an ende and so some goode shulde be done, whereas hitherto it hath ben otherwyse, and eveiry newe Deputy setting a singular waye, muche confusion hath happened.'[11]

Edmund Spenser, the poet and Elizabethan Planter, thought the merry-go-round of Lord Deputies in Ireland was one of the chief causes of the island's administrative chaos. 'For this ... is the common order of things,' he wrote in 'A View of the State of Ireland', in the 1590s, 'that who commeth next in place will not follow that course of government, how ever good, which his predecessor held ... but will straight take a way quite contrary to the former'.[12]

The pageantry of the Lord Deputy's installation was rich in symbolism. After Mass in Christ Church the Earl of Sussex received the sword and patent of his office from Archbishop Hugh Curwin. The Archbishop solemnly read out the Lord Deputy's oath, which the Earl in turn intoned over a mass book. 'That done, the trumpets sounded, the drums beat and the Lord Deputy kneeled down before the altar until the Te Deum was ended.'[13] The following day there was more drama as the Earl returned to the cathedral, processing in under a canopy held aloft by his attendants. At the door of the great church he was received by Archbishop Curwin and his clergy and this time the priests were on their knees. He was, after all, now the living embodiment in Ireland of their Catholic majesties of England and Ireland, Queen Mary and her Spanish consort, King Philip.

The Lord Deputy would be their temporary King, Prime Minister and Defence Minister, rolled into one. It was he, after consultation with London, who would summon Irish parliaments, and ensure that the sometimes wayward assembly of bishops, lords, knights, burgesses and citizens contained the kind of men who could be counted on to expedite the royal will. His remit was almost limitless, and the responsibilities were correspondingly awesome. The Earl of Sussex's commission from Queen Mary ordered him, among other things, to

> punish all persons offending, to ordain ordinances and statutes, to make procla-
> mations and demand the due execution thereof, to chastise and incarcerate all
> offenders, to receive all rebels to the king's allegiance, to grant pardon to all
> desirous of obtaining it . . . to do justice to all persons according to the laws and
> customs aforesaid, to punish all persons invading or intending to plunder or lay
> waste the kingdom . . . to conquer and chastise rebels . . . pardon all treasons
> and other offences . . . to nominate all officers . . . to summon and hold one
> parliament only, when most expedient, the King's consent in that behalf being
> first had, to prorogue and adjourn that parliament as there should be necessity
> and fully to determine, dissolve and end it within two years from the time of
> its beginning . . . to exercise and ordain everything which by right use or
> customs belongs to the office of Deputy and necessary for the good government
> and custody of the peace of the land.[14]

The responsibilities were enormous. The remuneration was not inconsiderable. After Mary's death, Elizabeth confirmed the Earl of Sussex's terms of office: an annual stipend of £1,000, a discretionary fund of an extra £500 a year, the use of the house, mills and fishing rights at the dissolved priory of St John at Kilmainham and the use of castles south-west and south of Dublin, at Carlow and at Wicklow. He was to maintain a retinue of 50 horsemen and 50 footmen.[15] But the fees on the table were only half the story. At his disposal was every crown office in the land, save those of Chancellor, Treasurer, Vice-Treasurer, Receiver, Marshal, Master of Ordnance, Chief Justice, Justices of the Bench, Justices of Common Pleas, Baron of Exchequer, Master of the Rolls, Sergeant-at-law, Attorney, Solicitor and Chief Engrosser.

The possibility of glittering rewards tempted many to try their hand, but the

Irish post was the ruin of many an ambitious statesman. As Sir John Perrot despondently reflected at the end of his term of office in 1586, after receiving another stinging letter from Queen Elizabeth: 'I was once in a hope to have returned (to my mother's fame and comfort) with a taber and pipe careieng a Trophe before me but nowe must come home trailing a black ensign of despaire after me . . .'[16]

It so easily became a poisoned chalice from which many a Lord Deputy wished he had never drunk. Such thoughts probably drifted through the Earl of Sussex's mind as the priests with thurifers sent clouds of incense billowing over his head towards the end of the service, and as he knelt forward to kiss the cross the Archbishop tendered to his lips and was solemnly blessed. As he proceeded slowly to the high altar, while the choir of priests sang the Te Deum, he must have scanned the faces of his chief officers and wondered if he would follow those of his predecessors who had stumbled and been recalled to London in disgrace.

Many of the men on his Council at that cathedral service were insatiable plotters, wily and ruthless survivors of the regimes of Henry VIII, Edward VI, and now Mary. Their intrigues and dark whispers about treason had helped bring down two of Sussex's predecessors and almost destroyed a third. Accused of aspiring towards a crown of his own, Gerald, 9th Earl of Kildare,[17] and thrice Lord Deputy between 1513 and 1534, had been summoned to England and had died in the Tower of London. His hot-headed son, Thomas, Lord Offaly, had risen in revolt against his father's mistreatment and he and five of his uncles paid with their lives, executed at Tyburn in 1537. The 9th Earl's dismal end was not unique. Fresh whispers of treason from the Lord Deputy's 'colleagues' helped to send Kildare's English-born successor to his death seven years later. Lord Leonard Grey was also recalled in disgrace in 1540. Charged with conspiring with the disgraced Kildares, he too was executed in London.

Lord Grey's successor, and the Earl of Sussex's immediate predecessor, Sir Anthony St Leger, had fared better. He survived three separate terms in Dublin and returned to England with his head securely on his shoulders.[18] Yet the malice of his colleagues on the Council had threatened him at times. 'Manie slanderous informations were made and inveighed against him,' Stanihurst recalled. It was, he remarked sadly, 'a fatall destinie, and inevitable to everie good governour in that land, for the more paines they take in tillage, the worse their harvest.'[19]

As the Te Deum ended, the Earl offered a piece of gold to the high altar, as was customary for all new Lord Deputies, and left. The following day there was entertainment of a more convivial kind: a dinner with the Archbishop at his palace. There was much real business to discuss, after the exchange of gifts and pleasantries. Like the Earl, Archbishop Curwin was English born. The former Dean of Hereford he was a relatively recent arrival, having been sent over in 1555 following the deprivation of his disgraced – and married – Protestant predecessor, Archbishop Browne. Like the Earl, Curwin had been dispatched with the express command to restore the Catholic Church in Ireland in all its pre-Reformation splendour. In that, the Queen of England had been absolutely specific, ordering her Lord Deputy

> to advance the honour of God and the Catholic faith, to set forth the honour and dignity of the Pope's holiness and the see apostolic from Rome and from time to time to be ready with our aid and secular force, at the request of the spiritual ministers and ordinaries there, to punish and repress all heretics and Lollards and their damnable sects, opinions and errors.[20]

Curwin and the Earl had key parts to play in the business of the Catholic Church's restoration. Like England, Ireland had spent 20 years out of communion with the see of Rome, ever since the Irish parliament of 1536–37 obediently followed the example of England in passing the Act of Supremacy, giving Henry VIII the title of Supreme Head of the Church. The Irish had never embraced the principle of Royal Supremacy with anything like the enthusiasm of a section of the English. But by the early 1540s even the more distant Irish bishops had taken oaths acknowledging the King's new title and abjuring the Pope.

As the two Englishmen dined at St Sepulchre's, they would have discussed the strategy they were intending to adopt in the forthcoming parliament to be held in Dublin in June the following year. Queen Mary trusted Curwin, and had followed the established custom of making the Archbishop of Dublin Lord Chancellor of Ireland. In that, she showed herself a poor judge of men. While Earl and Archbishop discussed their plans to restore Catholicism in Ireland, neither she nor they can have guessed that in less than three years both men would be supervising the reintroduction of Protestantism under Elizabeth.

The discussion would have taken place over an excellent meal. English standards of hospitality were maintained at the table of the archbishops of Dublin. The city had an excellent supply of fish and oysters; herring and salmon were both cheap and plentiful. The quality of meat was less reliable and sometimes needed a spiced sauce to disguise the fact that it had gone off. But there was no excuse for lack of variety. Ireland abounded in wild game. There were 'numberless big birds', wrote the Elizabethan Jesuit, and papal legate David Wolfe,

> such as cranes both tame and wild, geese tame and wild, ducks, peacocks, partridges, pheasants and other domestic birds. There are fair and great rivers, many streams and springs of water limpid and most pure. There are also numberless lakes and huge ponds full of fish, such as eels, great pike, trout and other like fish. There is such an abundance of herring and salmon in Ireland that every year many ships are laden with these fish for England, France and other countries.[21]

Irish colonial fare was much the same as English food, although English visitors pulled long faces and sneered at it. Fynes Moryson thought the meat served in Dublin acceptable. 'The English-Irish after our manner serve to the table joints of flesh cut after our fashion with geese, pullets, pigs and like roasted meats,' he wrote.[22] Pork was the cheapest and most plentiful meat available in Dublin. Many of the city's inhabitants – too many, according to the city fathers – kept hogs inside the walls where they broke into other people's gardens, rooted around in cellars, died and created a terrible stink, or created mayhem by wandering into the streets. The urban pig problem was a regular item on the City Council's agenda, and in 1492 it led to a ban on keeping inner-city pigs.[23] The law was ignored: the nuisance created by urban hogs was back on the council agenda in 1541 and 1558, when citizens were empowered to arrest and make off with any pig found in the city without a ring in its nose.

Out on the road, among the native Irish, the quality of the fare deteriorated. Modern Ireland has become synonymous with high-quality dairy products but Tudor visitors did not share our enthusiasm. Rudolf von Munchhausen,[24] a German traveller in Ireland in 1591, said Irish butter was amongst the worst he had seen, 'full of dirt and hair because they never strain it'.[25] He was equally offended by the manners of his Irish host, who shocked his prudish guest when he casually warmed his naked buttocks by the fire.

Moryson thought the native Irish cooking was 'barbarous and most filthy'.[26] 'They devour great morsels of beef unsalted and they eat commonly swine's flesh, seldom mutton and all these pieces of flesh and also the entrails of beasts unwashed, they seethe in a hollow tree, lapped in a raw cow's hide and so set over the fire and therewith swallow whole lumps of filthy butter,' he reported. 'It is strange and ridiculous but most true that some of our carriage horses falling into their hands, when they found soap or starch carried for the use of our laundresses, they thinking them to be some dainty meats did eat them greedily.'[27]

We need not worry retrospectively on behalf of the Earl of Sussex's stomach. Accounts of the Christ Church archiepiscopal dinners suggest the archbishops were certainly not dining on hairy butter or unwashed entrails wrapped in hide. They ate a wholesome diet, with plenty of vegetables, seasoned their meals with imported mustard, pepper and olive oil and washed it all down with the Spanish wine that was so plentifully imported through the ports of Dublin, Cork, Waterford and Galway. The price list of ingredients for Archbishop Browne's Christmas dinner in 1542 suggests a meal that was destined to be rather meaty. 'For ther standinge dynner – a pece of bef, ivd [4 pence]; porke, ivd; three hennes; brede, ivd; drinke, ivd; wine, iiid. The second supper – a pece of bef, ivd; a pece of porke, ivd; two hennes, ivd; wyne, iiid'.[28]

Drinking was heavier on the far side of the Irish Sea than it was at home. English visitors to the colony were struck by the quantity of alcohol the Dubliners consumed. The Jacobean Puritan, Barnaby Riche, complained that practically every householder in Dublin ran a pub where ale was served by 'young ydle huswives that are both verie loathsome, filthie and abomnible . . . the most of them known harlots'. He added: 'There is almost never a householder in Dublin (whatsoever trade he otherwise useth) but hee have a blinde corner in his house reserved for a taverne and this (if he have not a wife of his owne to kepe it) shall be set out to one of these women taverne keepers.'[29] Moryson was less squeamish. He considered the local whiskey first class: 'The Irish aqua vitae, commonly called usquebaugh, is held the best in the world of that kind.'[30] But Moryson agreed that the level of alcohol consumption was too high among both the English colonists and the native Irish. 'The English-Irish drink largely and in many families, especially at feasts, both men and women use excess therein,' he said. 'Some gentlewomen were so free in this excess as they would, kneeling upon the knee and otherwise, carouse health after health with men, not to speak of the wives of Irish lords who often drink till they be drunken, or at least till they void urine in full assemblies of men.'[31]

This view of the Irish as binge drinkers was common among English visitors. Local writers drawn from the English colonial community took a subtler line. The native Irish 'usually only drink milk and water', wrote Rowland White, in his book *The Dysorders of the Irissherye*, in 1571, 'which seldome maketh them dronke. But when they have anie wine theie ar never sober.'[32]

The Archbishop's dinner in honour of the Earl of Sussex would not have witnessed the vulgar excesses Moryson and Riche claimed to have observed. In any case, the new Lord Deputy had little time to savour his first Irish whiskey or worry about the meat. From Dublin he set out on the road to Drogheda, northern outpost of the little English colony and seat of the Archbishop of Armagh, the Primate of all Ireland. In the great parish church of St Peter's he would have to go through exactly the same ceremony he had undergone in Dublin, kissing the cross and being censed by the Archbishop and sprinkled with holy water. After that followed a progress round the kingdom.

In the towns and cities that the Earl of Sussex visited over the next two years he found the same grave determination to maintain the customs of their English ancestors that he saw in Dublin. The further away from Dublin, the pricklier the colonial English became on the subject of their English blood and lifestyle. They hated it when foreigners confused them with the more numerous Gaelic natives and took perverse pride in the fact that the Irish hated them. 'They do not depart by a hairs breadth from the customs of their English ancestors,' Stanihurst said of his fellow colonials. 'They differ little or nothing from the ancient customs and dispositions of their progenitors, the English and Welsh men, being therefore as mostallie behated of the Irish as those that are borne in England.'[33]

When the Earl of Sussex visited Limerick in June 1558, accompanied by a great phalanx of lords, both English and Irish, the mayor and his aldermen came out to meet them dressed in scarlet gowns for the ceremonial presentation of the key and mace of the city. In the churchyard of the cathedral, the embassy encountered Hugh Lacey, Bishop of Limerick, and his clergy, arranged in procession. The Earl knelt down, was censed and kissed the cross before proceeding into the gloom of the church to repeat the same rite before the figures of Christ, Mary and John on the rood screen.[34] At Galway, in July, the same spectacle was repeated. After being escorted into the city under a canopy he was met by the Archbishop of Tuam, Metropolitan of Connacht, and the bishops of Clonfert and Cork and Cloyne, dressed in rich copes, with their clergy arranged in procession behind them. Again, the Earl was censed, kissed the cross and was ritually sprinkled with holy water. Proceeding into the town he was met at the gates of the churchyard by an armed company who fired cannons 'as the like was not heard in Galway'.[35]

The mystical rites of censing and kissing crosses disappeared under Elizabeth's Protestant regime. But the visit of Lord Deputy Sir William Pelham to Waterford in 1580 held echoes of the old splendour:

The bulwarks, gates and curtains of the city were beautified with ensigns and several cannon were discharged in a warlike manner, which were answered by all the ships in the harbour and a great number of pieces on the quay. The soldiers also fired several volleys. The mayor and aldermen received his lordship in their scarlet gowns and presented him the city sword and keys of the gates, which were immediately returned; and the mayor carried the sword before him to the cathedral. There were two orations made by him in Latin by the way and at his return from church a third speech was made by him at the door of his lodging.[36]

Such grand receptions were ways in which the English colony in Ireland celebrated their civic pride and their English loyalty. For the Lord Deputy, these imposing ceremonies had another purpose, too: to dazzle the local native Irish lords with the grandeur of the English crown.

The military resources at the command of the English colonial government in the fifteenth and early sixteenth centuries were small. They were woefully insufficient to the task of actually bringing to heel the leaders of the septs,[37] as the native Irish clans were called. When the Earl of Surrey had landed in Ireland with a force of only 700 men in May 1520, his army seemed so vast and impressive that it caused a sensation.[38] The native Irish, as Stanihurst remarked, were 'pliable', and the object of these gaudy displays of English flummery was to attract them into surrendering their Irish titles and accepting English ones instead. It was more than a question of titles. To become an English earl, rather than leader of a sept, implied recognition of English sovereignty and law and the English tradition of primogeniture. It implied recognition of the jurisdiction of the crown's sheriffs and of crown courts and abandonment of the culture, traditions and independence of native Irish society.

Such was the business of the Earl of Sussex in Limerick in 1558 when he attended a solemn service in St Mary's cathedral with the head of the powerful O'Brien sept. 'After High Mass in the great church of Limerick,' it was recorded, 'the Earl of Thomond and all the freeholders of the county of Thomond were sworn upon the sacrament with all the holy relics of the church as book, bell and candelight. The Earl of Thomond was sworn to forsake the name of O'Brien and use the name and style of Earl of Thomond and be faithful and true to the King and Queen.'[39]

The Earl of Sussex had to rely on such deceitful displays of pomp, complete with trumpets, swinging thurifers and the intoning of curses, because he administered a kingdom that was a kingdom in name alone. In 1541 Henry VIII had upgraded his lordship of Ireland to a kingdom.[40] The act signalled a determination to reinforce his claim to be Supreme Head of the Church in both England and Ireland, and to bring both the colonial English and the native Irish lords into his orbit. The event had been presided over by the unfortunate Lord Grey with as much solemnity as the colony could muster. A special session of parliament was held, and church services to which the lords of the parliament rode in splendid procession. Grey ordered an amnesty for all prisoners not in debt, or accused of rape or murder, and the delighted ex-prisoners no doubt availed themselves fully of the fountains of wine erected for the day in the streets. But after the wine was drunk, the crowds had dispersed and the incense had drifted out of the cathedral window following the end of the High Mass, Ireland remained a kingdom without much substance. As Sir John Davies,[41] the Jacobean Attorney General for Ireland, later complained: 'Though the prince doth bear the title of sovereign lord of an entire country, as our kings did of all Ireland . . . there be two-third parts of the country wherein he cannot punish treasons, murders or thefts unless he send an army to do it.'[42] In other words, whether he was a king of Ireland or just a lord, the colonial Englishman still had little control over the island's native Irish majority.

The Englishmen of Queen Mary's time were aware that this had not always been the case. They recalled that after the Anglo-Norman invasion of Ireland in 1169, the settler lords had gained control of most of the ancient provinces of Leinster, Munster, Ulster and Connacht, and that only since the fourteenth century had territory under crown control contracted to a small patch of land around Dublin. In Connacht, the English presence had never meant much more than an occasional castle, inhabited by a single, powerful family. But English settlers had densely settled most of Leinster, the counties of Cork, Waterford, north Kerry and Tipperary in the southern province of Munster and the eastern portion of Ulster, round what are now the counties of Down and Antrim. For several generations they were a New England, not merely possessing garrison towns but ruling what one modern historian has called an 'occupying, cultivating population of small free tenants of English or occasionally Welsh origin who in some districts probably outnumbered the native Irish'.[43]

By the sixteenth century this English presence had largely evaporated, commemorated only by empty towns, ruined castles and churches and forgotten villages. The passage of time, the distance from England, the preoccupation of the English with their civil wars, the Scottish invasion of 1315, the Black Death in the 1340s (which affected the urban English more than the rural native Irish), a gradual tendency towards intermarriage with the native Irish, all subverted and at last buried the gains of the conquest. As the English sea receded, it left only scattered pools, of which the largest was the territory that in the fifteenth century became known as the Pale. By the early decades of the sixteenth century the Pale did not even encompass the whole of the county of Dublin. The 'obedient shires', as they were called, were reduced to a strip of land about 40 miles long and about 20 wide. South of Dublin the Pale extended no further than a few miles, to the village of Dalkey. North of Dublin it encompassed the busy trading port of Drogheda, before reaching the northern extremity of Dundalk, which by then was very much decayed. Heading west into the interior, the Pale extended to the castle of Trim.

Outside the Pale, English civilisation and the authority of the crown ebbed and flowed, depending on a combination of geography, communications, trade links and the local interests. In the Irish interior, about 70 miles south-west of Dublin, the Butler family, headed by the Earls of Ormond,[44] presided over a bastion of English culture and loyalty from their castle in Kilkenny, whose battlements reared high over the River Nore. Kilkenny was the only city of any size and the surrounding land 'hath the moste of cyvillitie of any other border counties, being well replenished with fayre castles, howses and estates, with English manner of enclosing their groundes', according to a description in the 1590s.[45] The marble houses of Kilkenny's merchant princes and the luminous stained-glass windows of St Canice's cathedral, the glory of the city until Cromwell's soldiers smashed them, were testaments to wealth gained by supplying the port of Waterford with wool, corn, skins and leather for export.

The Butlers made Kilkenny and the town of Carrick-on-Suir their principal seats. They also ruled a semi-independent palatinate to the west in neighbouring County Tipperary. Together, their possessions comprised a little kingdom whose English character was so pronounced that it was sometimes called the 'second Pale'. The loyalty of the Butlers was vital to the crown and the Dublin government. Their possessions lay on a strategically crucial junction in the interior between Munster and Leinster and controlled the flow of the Nore and Suir, which in the absence of roads, were important routes of transport and trade. The Butler lands also abutted the territory to the south-west of the Fitzgerald Earls of Desmond, who were far less reliable.

The Butler lordship was not the only outpost of English culture beyond the Pale. The port of Wexford, in the south-east, lay close to the site where the Anglo-Norman invaders of Ireland first landed in the twelth century. Here 'the auncientest gentlemen descended of the first conqueror doe inhabite', as an Elizabethan writer put it.[46] By the sixteenth century it was another isolated oasis of English culture. The Wexford English were cut off from their compatriots in the Pale by the wooded mountains of what was later called Wicklow, which was the domain of the O'Tooles and O'Byrnes. Trading ties between Wexford and Bristol in the west of England were strong. Like Kilkenny, the county 'serveth to be [both] an Inglish Pale and an Irish countie'.[47]

The southern port of Waterford was another enclave of English culture and loyalty, a town that 'hath continued to the crowne of England so loiall that it is not found registered since the conquest to have beene distained with the smallest spot or dusted with the least freckle of treason'.[48] As for Limerick, that was 'a wonderous proper city and strong and standeth environ'd with the river Shannon, and it may be called little London for the situation and plenty'. To David Wolfe, admittedly a Limerick man, it was the 'mightiest and most beautiful of all the cities of Ireland' and was 'fortified by great walls of vivid marble'.[49]

Most of the western province of Connacht was a lost world as far as Tudor England was concerned. But, lashed by the Atlantic, the little town of Galway preserved the English culture of the ancient colonists. A Jacobean visitor, Sir Oliver St John, was struck by his discovery of a prosperous, if old-fashioned microcosm of English urban society, so far from home. 'The town is small but all is faire and statelie buildings,' his account began.

> The fronts of the houses (towards the streets) are all of hewed stone uppe to the top, garnished with faire battlements in an uniform course, as if the whole towne had been built uppon one modle . . . The merchants are rich and great adventurers at sea . . . they keep good hospitalitie and are kind to strangers and in their manner of entertainment and in fashinninge, and apparellinge themselves and their wives do most preserve the ancient manner and state as much as any towne that ever I saw.[50]

The walled seaports and cities of Ireland were essentially self-governing republics, preserving only a vestigial connection to the mother country. For all their loyalty to the crown, they had long since developed into introverted societies where local power was drawn into a web of old families who intermarried. In Galway, St John noted, 'Their commonaltie is composed of the descendants of the ancient English families of the towne and rarelie admit any new English amonge them, and never any of the Irish.'[51] Galway's elite comprised 14 families, later nicknamed the 'tribes', who had settled there between the Conquest and the fifteenth century: the Lynches, Martins, Athys, Blakes, Bodkins, Brownes, Deanes, D'Arcys, Ffonts, Ffrenchs, Joyes, Kirwans, Morrises and Skerrets. The Lynches held the post of mayor in almost uninterrupted succession from 1484 to 1654. In Waterford, the dominant families were Sherlocks, Walshes, Comerfords, Dobbyns, Lombards and Waddings. The Sherlocks and Walshes provided the city with most of its mayors. The 10 'tribes' of Kilkenny were the Archers, Archdekins, Cowleys, Langtons, Lees, Knaresboroughs, Lawlesses, Roggets, Rothes and Shees,[52] of whom only the Shees were of Irish origin. Between them the Archers, Shees and Rothes shared out the post of mayor, known locally as the sovereign; the Rothes held the office 10 times from 1494 to 1537.[53]

The walled cities of Ireland had a strong sense of racial consciousness and constantly enacted and re-enacted by-laws aimed at keeping the native Irish outside. The by-laws of Galway in 1518 imposed a 12 pence fine for any man who 'should bring any Irishman to brage or boste upon the towne' and ordered 'that no man in this towne shall ost or receive into their houses at Christemas, Easter, nor feast elles, any of the Burks, M'Williams, the Kellies . . . without license of the mayor and councill on payne to forfeit 5 pounds, that neither O ne Mac shall strutte ne swaggere thro the streets of Gallway'.[54] Saffron clothes, long hair and moustaches were forbidden, as was the Irish sport of hurling, or as they put it, 'horlinge of the litill balle with hockie stickes or staves'.[55]

In Dublin in 1454 the Council ordered the expulsion of 'al maner of men of Iryshe blode and women' who had been resident there for less than 12 years, and 'gyf eny of this Irysshe blode, men or women, may be founde within the said cite or frauncheis after the said iiii wekys day they shal forfete gode catel, and to be put in prisone'.[56] The Dublin Council returned to the subject the following year, apparently to clear up a misunderstanding over whether the ban applied to Irish clerics and nuns as well as laymen. It certainly did. The Council ordered 'Irysche begeryes, Yrische nonys [nuns], Irysh ermyntys [hermits], Irysch clerkys, Irysch frayerys and al maner of oryr begerys that ben cum out of strange parties [to] avoyde the Kynges cytte of Dyvelyng'.[57] In theory, the penalty for disobedience was a life sentence.

The civic elites were determined to maintain the English character of their towns. Outside the walls, it was another matter. Far from England and unable to call on the enfeebled government of the Pale for help, the councils of Cork, Waterford and Galway treated with the neighbouring septs as if they were tiny independent states. Some survived centuries of encirclement by paying the septs annual bribes, known as 'black rents'. That was the route chosen by Cork, Limerick and Wexford, to the tune of about £40 a year in the mid-sixteenth century.

The Pale, the Butler lands and the walled towns were embattled English boats, tossed around on choppy, shark-infested Irish waters. Beyond the desolate, tree-less vista of the Pale[58] and outside the walls of the towns, in the woods of Munster, which as late as the sixteenth century were still home to packs of wolves, in the lonely damp glens of Ulster and the bogs and moorlands of Connacht, Irish law, Irish language and Irish culture were again supreme. A briefly conquered race had come back down from the hills, reclaimed the plain and was now ensconced right outside the wall of the English towns. The double ditch that ran round the edge of the Pale was a dismal admission that the English had lost the racial war with the Irish and that the English crown no longer seriously claimed to rule all Ireland.

The native Irish resurgence had been most complete in the north and west. There, outside Galway, English language, law and 'civility' were almost extinguished. When the Lord Deputy Sir Henry Sidney visited the borough town of Athenry in 1576 he discovered it had a fine set of walls but was 'totally burned – college, parish church and all that was there'.[59] In the north, Ulster had returned, or succumbed, depending on how you looked at it, to the Gaelic order, the Irish language and the Irish traditions of justice, known as Brehon law.[60] Only parts of County Down held out, along with the garrison town of Carrickfergus on the coast of County Antrim, which the English could easily reinforce by sea. In County Tyrone, there was nothing to recall the English presence in 1598 but 'divers ruined castles'.[61]

In the south-west, Counties Kerry and Tipperary had once been studded with English settlements. But when Sidney visited Limerick and Waterford in 1575 he did not even attempt to extend the tour south-west to Kerry. The reason, he said, was that by now 'the Queen's writ is not allowed any currency' there.[62] In the southern city of Cork, the inhabitants were so troubled with 'evill neighbours' that they were 'faine to watch their gates hourlie, to keep them shut at [church] service times, at meales, from sun to sun',[63] a state of affairs that suggests virtual siege conditions.

English rule remained strongest in the eastern province of Leinster. But even there it was patchy and the use of English was in decline. Leix, on the western border of the Pale, was colonised and renamed Queen's County after Queen Mary in the 1550s. By the 1590s, the English settlement there had collapsed. It was reported that 'the new planted inhabitants hath bene so molested continuallie with the multitudes of the first natives thereof . . . as that they have in a manner recovered the countrie againe and expelled all the Inglysh inhabitants, saving 3 or 4'.[64] County Kildare lay only a few miles east of Dublin and once had been 'Englyshe, as the countye of Dublyn now is'. In 1537, however, Sir James Luttrell complained that the English-speaking community of Kildare had disappeared within his own lifetime: 'ther is not one husbondman, in effect, that spekeith Englyshe ne useith any English sort ne maner and ther gentylmen be after the same sort.'[65]

Further south, the ancient town of Ross, in the hinterland of County Waterford, had crumbled away. Ross was an old borough town, with representatives in the Irish parliament. It had been one of the most important trading centres in Leinster and a close rival to Waterford as the richest English city in the southeast. By the sixteenth century Ross was a shell. The town was 'in maner utterlie decaied and wasted and so hath bene theis many yeres,' according to a depressing report filed by the Irish Council in 1539.[66] Waterford was more prosperous but, like Cork, was virtually cut off by land from the rest of Ireland by hostile Irish neighbours. In 1368 the mayor of Waterford was killed in a pitched battle between the citizens and the neighbouring sept of O'Driscoll[67] who attacked the city repeatedly in the fifteenth century. In 1474 the town was so exhausted with this conflict that they complained to the crown that they no longer had the money to repair their own city walls.

Even Dublin was unsafe, menaced by O'Byrnes and O'Tooles who lurked in the wooded mountains to the south. 'Those that dwell even within the sight of Dublin are not subject to the laws,' Sir George Carew complained in 1590.[68] 'The very gall of Ireland, the flame from which all other rebels take their flame, is our next neighbour, Pheaghe McHugh, who like one absolute within himself with his den of thieves ruleth all things in his own country, at his own will.' A description of Ireland written in 1598 estimated that the rebel stronghold was located no further than four miles distant from the walls of Dublin, and said that for that reason 'the cittie is constreyned to keep strong watch, least on a sudden these rebells that lurke in these mountains do set the suburbs on fire, which hath heretofore been done by them in the government of the late Lord Grey'.[69] The writer lamented that 'All the gents betwixt Dublin and these mountains do daylie susteyn great losse in their goods, and sometimes lose their lives.'[70]

On-off warfare with the O'Tooles and O'Byrnes had been a fact of life for the Dubliners for at least three centuries, when the septs were first displaced by Ireland's Anglo-Norman invaders from Kildare, west of the city, and forced into the hills south of Dublin which since then had remained a 'land of war'. Today, County Wicklow is 'the garden of Ireland' and its unspoilt woods provide the city with its green lung and some of its most delightful countryside. The medieval Dubliners saw nothing charming in that dense forest. The fear of Irish raiders was so intense at harvest time that in 1344 the canons of Holy Trinity in Dublin paid watchmen to stand on the hilltops at the abbey's estate at Clonkeen for two nights while the crops were brought in.[71] The fear was not just of robbery. The labourers at Clonkeen would have retained grim memories of the notorious attack on the English settlement of Freynestown 12 years previously, when the Irish burned down the church with the parish priest and 80 of his congregation inside.[72]

Englishmen serving in the Irish colonial administration, and the colonists themselves, put pen to paper to bewail the collapsed fortunes of the great imperial experiment. Almost every Englishman who set foot in Ireland seemed unable to resist the temptation to write his own diagnosis of 'the Irish problem' and propose a stack of remedies. The poet Edmund Spenser, who came to Ireland in the 1580s in the baggage train of the Lord Deputy Lord Arthur Grey of Wilton, Fynes Moryson, Sir William Pelham, Barnaby Riche, Sir William Herbert and Sir John Davies were only some of those who promoted their own unique plans for reducing Ireland to obedience, or who compiled 'descriptions' of Ireland, complete with colourful comment on the cultural shortcomings of the natives and what needed to be done to bring them to the blessed state of 'civility'.

They looked back with nostalgia to an imagined golden age in the late twelfth and thirteenth centuries, when the Anglo-Norman knights had first subdued Ireland, followed by a rapid fall from grace under Edward II and Edward III in the fourteenth century.[73] They blamed external causes, such as the Scots invasion in 1315 and the Hundred Years War, which drew the colonial aristocracy out of their Irish estates and on to the battlefields of England. They blamed certain individuals or key families, such as the Geraldine earls of Desmond in south-west Munster and the De Burgos, or Burkes, of Connacht, as the apostles of disloyalty to the crown among the Anglo-Irish aristocracy. They excoriated the English landowning class for succumbing to the Irish tradition of 'coign and livery', which meant quartering private armies on their tenants' land and at their tenants' expense. 'They bringe into the hart of the English Pale Irishe tenants,' read one complaint from 1537 at the expense of the landowners, 'which neither can speke the Englishe tonge ne were cappe nor bonet and expulseth ofte the auncient good Englishe tenantes . . . by that meanes the pore Englishe tenantes are dryvin into Englande and Wales'.[74]

There were heralds of the divided opinions in Britain four centuries later to the troubles in Northern Ireland in the split between 'liberals' who advocated concil-iating the natives and blamed the authorities for undue harshness, and conserva-tives who insisted the colonial crisis demanded a tougher stand against the natives. As the anonymous author of the *Treatise of Irelande* of 1588 wrote, 'the plottes for reformacion of Irelande are two kyndes. One which undertake to procure it by Conqueste as by peopling of Contres with English inhabitantes . . . another kynde is of those wherein is undertaken to make reformacion by publique establishment of Iustice.'[75]

The authors of 'The Supplication of the Blood of the English Most Lamentably Murdered in Ireland', written in 1598, belonged to the former camp. Failed colonists[76] who were driven out of Munster in the Irish rebellion of the late 1590s, they rounded on weak-kneed liberals in England and howled for genocide. 'Lett the feete of yore forces treade and trample downe these bryars that will not suffer yore plantes to prosper,' they urged Elizabeth. 'Lett them weare with theire heeles the very rootes out of the earth that they springe no more: soe shall you make Ireland a flourishing nursery for England.'[77]

The line between the advocates of 'Iustice' and the shrill supporters of 'Conqueste' often fell between the old settlers and the new colonists. It fell between those who had lived in Ireland for several generations and those who only came over to make a buck and who could afford to sound harsh. But the lines were blurred. Sir John Davies was an odd man to be described as a liberal. The English-born Solicitor-General and then Attorney-General for Ireland under James I played a leading role in one of the most exploitative land grabs in history, the Jacobean 'Plantation' of Ulster. Yet he belonged to the camp of those who saw 'Iustice' as the key to England's Irish problem. Davies drew closer to the views of local-born colonial Englishmen, seeing the alienation of the Irish from the law as the root of the evil. Back in the 1550s Edward Walshe had predicted that 'without Iustice evin englishe bloodes wax [turn into] wylde Yrishe and the kinge, where no Iustice is, looseth his right and revenue.'[78]

Davies took the same line. It was 'this oppression', he insisted, which 'did of force make the Irish a craftie people, for such as are oppressed and live in slavery are ever put to their shifts'.[79] As a legal man he had spent time examining case histories in Dublin Castle, and was critical of the system of legal apartheid which for centuries had placed the native Irish literally outside the operation of the law. He condemned the 'heavy penal laws' imposed on the native Irish, 'whereby it is manifest that such as had the government of Ireland under the crown of England did intend to make a perpetual separation and enmity between the English and the Irish, pretending no doubt that in the end the English should root out the

Irish, which the English not being able to do did cause a perpetual war between the nations'.[80]

English writers did not differ much in their views on Irish culture. It was barbarian and utterly redundant. But they admired the brute strength and virility of the native Irish. The Lord Deputy, Sir Anthony St Leger, told Henry VIII in 1543 that they made excellent soldiers and 'be of suche hardnesse that ther ys no man that ever I sawe that will or can endure the paynes and evill ffare that they will sustayne . . . at all tymes they eate such meate as ffew other could lyve with'.[81]

Otherwise, they were contemptuous. The opinions of generations of Englishmen on Ireland had been shaped by the *Topographia Hibernica* and *Expugnatio Hibernica*, the work of the twelfth-century Welsh monk Giraldus Cambrensis,[82] the enthusiastic biographer of the first generation of Anglo-Norman conquerors. When the thirteenth-century Bishop of Cork, Philip of Slane, travelled to the papal court to explain to His Holiness why the Irish were best entrusted to English rule, he carried the *Topographia* in his luggage for the Pope to read.[83] The works of Giraldus were still doing the rounds centuries later. The only reason so many Englishmen thought the Irish went around in the nude was because the sharp-tongued Welshman had told them so.

Sir John Davies, for all his misgivings about the system of justice to the Irish, was in no doubt about the inferiority of their culture and morals. He voiced disgust at 'their common repudiation of their wives, their promiscuous generation of children, their neglect of lawful matrimony . . . and their contempt and scorn for all things necessary for the civil life of man'.[84] Sir John Perrot was similarly shocked by the ease with which the native Irish 'put away theyre wives uppon any slight occasion without lawfull cause and more redie to take on any new [wife] than to be constant in theyr old choyse'.[85] Fynes Moryson reported that an Irishman might dump his wife merely for farting.[86]

What was to be done with these savages? Sir William Herbert,[87] an Elizabethan planter in Munster who got out before the catastrophe of the revolt in the 1590s, advocated respect for the Irish as persons. 'Towards the Irish the English should show kindness and affability. They should set an example of all that is best not just by words but also by deeds, without insults, mockery, affront or contempt,' he wrote. 'This would work powerfully on the minds and hearts of the Irish.'[88] But he thought that personal kindness ought to be accompanied by root and branch annihilation of Irish customs. The Irish were 'barbarous' and their culture 'ought to have been destroyed and stamped out altogether, with their religious usages, their pomps and their wicked and rude customs'.[89]

Herbert and Davies were English-born colonists who only spent a portion of their lives in Ireland. Local men like Stanihurst and Walshe also saw the contest between English and Irish culture as a battle between 'civility' and barbarism. On that point they did not disagree much with the newer English settlers, even if they shied away from their strident racism. 'The Yrishe lordes and al they that enbrace Yrishe rule have alwaye abhorred the cominge of englishe order in Yrlande,' said

Walshe in his *Conjectures* on the state of Ireland of 1552, 'and even yet unto this daye they wolde have no englishe man come within their countreyes bicause they feare at any tyme to lose there vile absolute power'.[90] Stanihurst believed as fervently as any imported bureaucrat in the intrinsic right of the English to rule the Irish, and in the need 'to reduce them from rudeness to knowledge, from rebellion to obedience, from trickerie to honestie, from savagenesse to civilitie, from idlenesse to labour, from wickednesses to godlinesses'.[91]

The native Irishman was seen as a brute. But his beastliness in English eyes was redeemed in part by innocence. There was always the hope that the native might be taught to cut his hair, learn English, keep to one wife, take to the plough; in short, be 'reduced to civilitie'. The English were far more horrified by the spectacle of their own kith and kin gone to seed. This was the phenomenon of the Gaelicised, or as they put it, 'degenerate', Englishman. His crime was infinitely worse than that of the native, and it aroused feelings of shame and anger, not pity.

What was one to make of an Englishman who had drunk from the cup of 'civilitie' only wantonly to throw the precious gift away? The sight of the degenerate Englishman was frightful and disgusting in a way that no Irish native could ever be. The natives' barbarism was observed with a lazy eye, which is why many Elizabethan and Jacobean accounts of the Gaelic Irish are vague and uninteresting. The sight of the Gael was not mentally challenging. The Irishman or woman was 'savage', inclined to rob, was promiscuous, ate foul food, drank too much, exposed his or her private parts without shame, fought well, urinated in public and that was just about that. The degenerate Englishman, with his smattering of mangled English and crazy dress sense, was an altogether more frightening spectacle. In that 'savage', but recognisably English face, his refined Tudor counterpart read a terrifying parable on human nature and a living example of the possibility of his own fall from grace.

Davies compared the degenerate English to those who had 'metamorphosed like Nebuchadnezzar, who although he had the face of a man had the heart of a beast'. They were 'like those who had drunk of Circe's cup who were turned into very beasts and yet took such pleasure in their beastly manner of life as they would not return to their shape of men again . . . they did not only forget their English language and scorn the use thereof but grew to be ashamed of their very English names, though they were noble and of great antiquity'.[92]

Sexual contact between the two races was widely seen as the root of the evil. 'What hath made the Geraldins, the Laceyes, the Purcells to alter the nature of themselves from the nature of theire names but their former Irishe matches? What hathe turned them from English which they sound in name to Irish which appeare in nature? from men to monsters but their Irishe matches, . . . the blood of their Irishe mothers hath wasted away the naturall love they bare to theire mother England.'[93]

The sheer number of these reprobates was England's dirty secret, for they greatly outnumbered the 'civil' English of the towns and the Pale. A report on the state of Ireland in 1515 listed 13 shire counties originally settled by the English, but noted the high incidence of rural degeneracy among the colonists. 'All the Englyshe folke of the saide countyes be of Iryshe habit, of Irish language and of Irish condytions, except the cyties and the wallyd tounes,' it said.[94]

The decay of English culture was a trend that repeated Acts of parliament, forbidding the English to marry Irish spouses, speak Irish, wear Irish clothes or resort to Irish law, had palpably failed to stem. The result was the Gaelicised Burkes, or De Burgos, of Connacht, the Breminghams of Athenry, the Geraldine earls of Desmond, the Condons and Powers of Waterford, the Savages and the Russells of Ulster, many of the Dillons and the Daltons of County Meath, the Roches of Munster, some branches of the otherwise loyal Butlers of Tipperary and Kilkenny and, unfortunately, many others. To Lord Deputy Sidney they belonged to a strange twilight world, and when he visited the Cork region in 1575 he reported: 'There came to me also many of the ruined reliques of the ancient English inhabitants of this province as the Arundells, Rochfords, Barretts, Flemings, Lombards, Terries and many others whose ancestors . . . did live like gentlemen, knights some of them, and now all in misery.'[95]

The English inhabitants of Ireland during the reigns of Henry VIII, Edward VI, Mary and Elizabeth I were convinced, correctly, that their world was shrinking day by day. On the borders of the Pale, the Protestant Bishop of Meath, Alexander Craik, complained in 1561 that no one in his diocese spoke English any longer.[96] Perhaps he was exaggerating the problem to explain why no one attended his Protestant services, but it is entirely possible that even in Meath and Kildare, in spite of their proximity to Dublin, English had died out by the sixteenth century.

In Elizabethan County Wexford Stanihurst detected the same decay. He recalled a time when the people of the county were

> so quite estranged from the Irishrie as if a traveller of the Irish, which was rare in those days, had pitched his foot within the Pill [Pale] and spoken Irish the Weisfordians would command him forthwith to turn the other end of his toong and speake English . . . but in our days they have so acquainted themselves with the Irish as that they have made a mingle mangle or gallimanfrie of both the languages, as commonlie the meaner sort speake neither good English nor good Irish.[97]

The 'mingle mangle' now spoken by the 'meaner sort' in County Wexford was an ominous sign, and suggested that by the middle of the sixteenth century the more isolated pockets of Englishry were lapsing into a patois. Later in the century Moryson noted a separate development among the Old English outside Dublin: a reluctance to speak English even when they knew the language. 'The English Irish and the very Cittizens (excepting those of Dublin where the Lord Deputy resides) though they could speake English as well as wee, they commonly speake

Irish among themselves, and were hardly induced by our familiar conversation to speake English with us'.[98]

Even inside the little Pale there was a perception in the sixteenth century that the region's English character was collapsing in the face of Irish immigration and the flight of English peasants and tenant farmers back to England and Wales. It is possible that the Gaelic-speaking Irish were the majority population in the Pale at this time and that they made up the overwhelming majority of tenant farmers, servants and labourers. In 1536, King Henry was warned that his colony faced the imminent prospect of sinking without trace into an Irish sea. 'Your Highnes muste understande that the Inglishe blodde of the Ynglish conquests ys in maner worne out of this land,' the Council wrote to him, 'and contrarywise the Irish blodde ever more and more without such decaies, encreasith'.[99]

The feeling of defeat lay heavy on the English in Ireland in the sixteenth century. A manifestly inferior culture and race, as they saw it, was overpowering a superior one. The mood among many was close to desperation and it explains why the prospect of the Reformation at first aroused enthusiasm in the colony. At last, it seemed, England was taking some notice. That – at first – seemed preferable to slow death.

CHAPTER TWO

It is Necessary that we Eradicate Them

Not only their laymen and secular clergy but some also of their regular clergy dogmatically assert the heresy that it is no more sin to kill an Irishman than to kill a dog.

(Irish remonstrance to the papacy, 1317)[1]

The tomb of James Rice, Catholic mayor of Waterford, lies in Waterford's Protestant cathedral. One of the finest pre-Reformation funerary monuments in Ireland, it commemorates the life and death of a devout Christian, a great philanthropist and a local statesman. The tomb is difficult to see. Waterford's Protestants are few in number and the church is closed outside the tourist season except for a Sunday morning service. The tomb was built in the morbid late Gothic fashion, for a world turned sorrowful in the aftermath of the Black Death; Mayor Rice's decomposing cadaver is represented in stone on top, the corpse lying in a shroud tied in a knot above his head, his disintegrating flesh being gnawed and devoured by frogs or toads and other crawling things. The pleading inscription that runs around the figure was almost obliterated by years of exposure to the elements before it was repositioned inside the building. But we know what it says, for it was copied down long ago: 'Whoever you are that pass by, stand, read, weep,' the mayor urges from his tomb. 'I am what you will be and I was what you are.'[2]

Rice was a remarkable man. Mayor of the city 11 times between 1467 and 1486 he made two pilgrimages from his home in the south-east of Ireland to the great Spanish shrine of St James the Great at Santiago de Compostela in 1473 and 1483.[3] It was an immense round trip, entailing a journey of about 1,400 miles. Apart from the sheer length of the sea journey from Waterford to La Coruña, from where he would have travelled by land to the shrine, such a journey was fraught with danger. In 1473 the pirates who infested the waters between Ireland and the Continent kidnapped 400 pilgrims returning to Waterford.[4] It was not unusual for the victims of such outrages to disappear for ever, or return home only after years spent as slaves in Africa or Arabia. Fortunately the Waterford pilgrims were spared, and were released at Youghal, County Cork after the payment of a ransom. Rice must have heard all about their experience. Yet in that same year he also set off to join the great concourse of pilgrims heading to the shrine from all over Europe.

Mayor Rice was a devout Christian, a model specimen of the impeccably orthodox Catholic piety of the colonial English in Ireland. Before embarking on his second voyage to Compostela he had a side chapel housing his tomb constructed in the cathedral and dedicated to the saint of his favourite shrine, St James, and to St Catherine. It became known as Rice's chapel. He had a second chapel built in the cathedral, which was dedicated to St Saviour. Rice was a great benefactor of his local cathedral but he was not the sort of man who was so busy saving his soul that he did not notice the plight of his fellow man. Like any good Christian, Rice believed that faith and works marched together. The relief of his soul and that of his beloved wife Catherine Brown went hand in hand with the business of relieving the poverty of the men in Waterford, for whom he built a poorhouse, known as the Good Men's House. To make it a going concern, the charity was endowed with the rents of houses and lands donated by the merchants of Waterford.[5] Much of this came from Rice, on condition that the men prayed three times daily for the repose of his soul and that of his wife: at 8 p.m., midnight and at sunrise.

But Rice was no saint. In 1480, the elderly Bishop of Waterford, John Bulcoup, decided to resign his see. The Archbishop of Cashel, as Metropolitan of Munster, appointed Nicholas O'Hennessy as his successor. Rice was outraged. He complained to Rome that the new appointee did not understand English properly, or speak it intelligibly.[6] The problem, as far as Rice was concerned, was that O'Hennessy was an Irishman. Rome was not impressed by the complaint. Sixtus IV approved O'Hennessy's appointment and ordered the Archbishop of Cashel to make sure he was received by the city. In spite of his Catholic orthodoxy, Rome's ruling did not deter Rice. Instead, he seems to have persuaded the retiring Bishop to revoke his resignation, while the campaign to find an alternative English candidate for the diocese resumed in earnest. Rice got his way. Although the Pope was still pressing O'Hennessy's claims on the Archbishop of Cashel in 1482, he was never received into Waterford, and in 1483 Thomas Purcell, a canon of Ferns diocese and a man of English blood, got the job instead.[7] Mayor Rice probably felt that the prayers he had offered during the final work on the chapel of St James and St Catherine had been answered.

James Rice, Nicholas O'Hennessy and Thomas Purcell were all members of the same Irish Church. But their tangled, crotchety relationship is a reminder that while the two nations of Ireland shared a common devotion to the Catholic faith, the Church groaned under the strain of the bouts of racial antagonism that it had to absorb. It was a conflict that had rumbled along ever since the Anglo-Norman invasion of Ireland in the 1170s. Monasteries were at the centre of this tug of war. Take the Cistercian Order. Founded in Cîteaux in northern France in 1098, they reached Ireland more than a quarter of a century before the Normans arrived. The Order's mother house at Mellifont, in County Louth, was an Irish foundation. So were the houses of St Mary, in Dublin, at Newry in Ulster, at Bective, Baltinglass and Jerpoint in Leinster, and at Holy Cross, Maigue, Abbeydorney, Fermoy, Maure, Chore, Kilcooley, Corcomroe and Kilshane in Munster. So when the Cistercian General Chapter in 1226 and again in 1227 empowered an English abbot to reform their houses, the Irish naturally interpreted his mission as a move to place their monasteries under foreign control.

Stephen de Lexington was a respected academic who had cut short promising secular career prospects to enter the Order. The Church saw him as a catch and his tour of Ireland proved only one step on the fast track of promotion that would culminate in his becoming the Abbot of Clairvaux.[8] Lexington had talent. But he was also a harsh, impatient, doctrinaire man and it is no wonder his reputation triggered panic in the Irish houses he was about to visit. 'The order does not intend to exclude any race but only the inadequate, the useless and the uncivilised,' he said smoothly.[9] But there was no doubt that he thought those adjectives applied most often to native Irish rather than English Cistercians, and that the whole Order would benefit if the Irish were weeded out of their old monasteries. 'You should be surprised that we did not apply ourselves to expel the Irish as some considered we would do,' he confided to the Abbot of Furness, in Lancashire, 'because this would be completely against your interests and that of the order. For it is necessary that we eradicate them little by little, and by stages.'[10]

Abbot Stephen went about his visitation busily, touring most of the houses between March and November 1228, removing Irish abbots and confirming English appointees 'little by little', dispersing Irish monks and replacing them with English ones. He insisted on a basic knowledge of French and Latin as a precondition for any new professions. It might have seemed a logical step in Cîteaux, Clairvaux or Stanley, but in an Irish context this hurdle was effectively a device to ethnically cleanse the country's monasteries. The Abbot was outraged to discover Irish monks blending the Cistercian rule with the older traditions of the Celtic Church. The Irish, he gravely informed the mother house at Cîteaux, were daily committing crimes of 'abominable gravity'. Instead of living in the community they slept in their own wooden cottages, 'miserable huts outside the cloister, in groups of three or four'.[11] They retained servants, galloped around on horseback, talked to women, did not keep the rule of silence and went to the local shops instead of living off the produce of the monastery. He found that one abbot's seal had been pawned to a local tavern for 18 pence.[12]

The Abbot of Stanley bustled around Ireland, hiring and firing, but the Irish monks did not go gently into that good night. At Mellifont, they tried to murder the newly appointed abbot. At Baltinglass they pulled him off his horse and ripped up his seal of office. At Inishlounaght in County Tipperary, Stephen encountered the Irish abbot wielding a sword and a lance with his monks armed for battle. At Maigue, near Limerick, the monks expelled their new abbot along with all the other English brothers and 'strongly fortified the dormitories of the monks and lay brothers with great stones, slates and palings and weapons according to the custom of their people'.[13] The revolt was only put down with bloodshed by the intervention of an armed force under the Bishop of Limerick, which stormed the building. The Irish houses were still resisting 'reform' three years after Abbot Stephen had left Ireland for his new post at Savigny, when Inishlounaght again refused to admit a visitation, along with Fermoy, in County Cork and Corcomroe, in Clare.

Racial conflict dogged the newer Religious orders in Ireland at the end of the thirteenth century. The Franciscans reached Ireland in the 1230s. By the 1280s their order was also divided on ethnic lines. Nicholas Cusack, Franciscan Bishop of Meath, wrote to Edward I complaining of the seditious machinations of members of his own Order 'of the Irish tongue', accusing them of attending meetings of the native Irish septs and of stirring up hatred against English settlers.[14]

The crown's suspicions about Irish friars were heightened after a Scottish army under Robert the Bruce's brother, Edward, invaded Ireland in 1315, in a campaign that lasted until 1318. Most of the native Irish clergy looked on the invaders as liberators. Edward II was furious. On 20 August 1316 the King sent a sharply worded letter concerning the Irish Franciscans to the Order's minister-general, Michael of Cesena, saying 'they do not cease from daily inciting the Irish laity to rebel against us in every way possible and join up with the Scots who have illegally entered that country'.[15] A similar letter was dispatched to the papal curia, demanding the appointment of English candidates to the vacant archbishoprics of Dublin and Cashel.

The stream of complaints flowing from England to Avignon did not go unanswered. From Bruce's base in Ulster, his Irish supporters under Domnal O'Neill filed their own fierce indictment of English rule to the Pope in 1317 in which they virtually accused the English of genocide. This remonstrance had an agenda, which was to tilt John XXII in the direction of recognising Bruce, not Edward, as Ireland's King. But the Irish grievances were not imaginary. 'They have striven with all their might and with every treacherous artifice in their power to wipe out our nation entirely and utterly extirpate it,' the letter read: 'bishop and dignitaries are summoned, arrested, taken and imprisoned without respect by the king of England's ministers in Ireland . . . not only their laymen and secular clergy but some also of their regular clergy dogmatically assert the heresy that it is no more sin to kill an Irishman than to kill a dog.'[16] The last complaint appears to have been well founded, as Archbishop Richard Fitzralph of Armagh felt it necessary to tell the people of his home town of Dundalk that killing Irishmen was a sin in the eyes of God, even if was sanctified by local custom.[17] As the leading Franciscan historian Francis Cotter says: 'The importance of the remonstrance lies in the fact that it confirms from an Irish source how divisive the race issue had become within Ireland and among the religious and not just among the friars minor.'[18]

The racial feud in the Irish Church went on. Several years later Edward II was still groping for new mechanisms to control the Irish clergy, sending a mission to Avignon under Philip of Slane, Bishop of Cork, in 1324 with recommendations that the Pope 'reform' the Irish Church by cutting the 30-plus bishoprics to 10, and locating them all in the English-held cities.[19] At the same time he urged the Holy Father to publicly condemn rebels against royal authority, along with Irish monasteries that were holding out against English monks.

With the collapse of the Scots campaign in the autumn of 1318, English victory was inevitable. John XXII told Edward II to deal more justly with his angry Irish subjects, but he declined to answer the Irish remonstrance directly and agreed to the King's request to send two Englishmen, Alexander Bicknor and William Fitzjohn, to manage Dublin and Cashel. The Pope congratulated the English King on crushing the Irish rebels and threatened the rebellious Irish clergy with excommunication. When the next Franciscan provincial chapter assembled in Dublin in 1324, it met under express orders from the Pope to deal harshly with Irish troublemakers. He empowered commissioners, led by the English Dean of St Patrick's, in Dublin, to order the dispersal of the Irish monks from eight offending houses and their replacement by Englishmen.

Unfortunately for the Irish, the interests of the papacy usually dovetailed nicely with those of the English crown. The popes needed England's support as a counterweight to the influence of France. John XXII took seriously his paternal role as feudal overlord of England which was ceded to the papacy under King John. The reform of the Irish Church on English lines was a project in which crown and papacy had a joint interest. The idiosyncratic practices Stephen de Lexington had criticised held no attraction for the papacy: the papal machinery hankered for uniformity, not particularism, and the replacement of Irish abbots with Englishmen was a device to advance it. Against such vast vested interests, the muffled squeals of the Irish scarcely counted. Until the English break with Rome in the 1530s created an entirely new ecclesiastical constellation, the papacy was not concerned with Ireland. In 1531 the Carmelite General Chapter noted: 'The Irish province has many monasteries and many friars but because it is so far away little or nothing is known of it.'[20] That attitude of neglect, even if it was benign, encouraged the 'Rome runners', the Irish clergy who travelled to Rome or Avignon to lobby for their own ecclesiastical promotion. The popes were so casual about the Irish church appointments that one insistent Rome-runner, Tomas Mathghamhna, in 1360 secured nomination to a non-existent bishopric located on an island in the Shannon.[21]

When the popes did act in Ireland, it was usually to carry out some request of the English crown that hurt the Irish. In 1312, the papacy rescinded the Franciscan Irish chapter's right to elect its own Provincial. The Franciscan General Chapter meeting in Lyons in 1325 divided the Irish houses into five blocks, or 'custodes', but granted four of them to the English nation and only one – grouping together the eight houses of Nenagh, Athlone, Ennis, Claregalway, Galway, Armagh, Cavan and Killeigh – to the Irish. The Irish Dominicans also lost their autonomy in the fourteenth century. Boniface IX granted them their own province in 1378, but a prompt appeal against the decision by Richard II resulted in that decision being reversed.

Racial power struggles were particularly difficult to manage in those orders where the friars were not sedentary but moved around. The Cistercian houses were semi-independent corporations and once they had been allocated to one nation or another, it was possible to achieve a kind of stability. It was less easy to find a *modus vivendi* in the mobile preaching orders. In these orders, according to Father Cotter, 'when the race issue surfaced, the whole province became an arena of conflict and the aim of the power struggle between the two groups of friars centred on control of the government of the province'.[22]

The language and practice of apartheid in the Irish Church became harsher as the fourteenth century progressed, as the English colony suffered numerical and economic decline. Irish parliaments repeatedly passed legislation aimed at keeping the commanding heights of the Church in English hands. In 1310 the Irish parliament banned the profession of Irish monks in any houses in 'territory at peace, or in English hands'.[23] The parliament of 1366 in Kilkenny dealt with this subject in greater detail. In 36 chapters, this assembly proposed what amounted to a sweeping code of ethnic separation in Church and state. The Statutes of Kilkenny[24] bear comparison with anything attempted under the apartheid laws of twentieth-century South Africa. English settlers were forbidden to take Irish spouses, speak Irish, take Irish names, use native Brehon law, foster children out to Irish families, wear Irish clothes, ride on horses without saddles, grow long hair or moustaches or play hurling (they should shoot bows and arrows and hurl lances). In the realm of the Church, it was ordained that 'no Irish . . . be admitted . . . to any benefice of Holy Church among the English of the land . . . and that no house of religion which is situate among the English, be it exempt or not, henceforth receive any Irishmen'.[25] The parliaments held in 1380 and 1402 confirmed the statutes.

The Statutes of Kilkenny were enacted under the guiding hand of Edward III's son, Lionel, Duke of Clarence, but the pressure to erect racial barriers in the Irish Church came as much from the colonists as from the English government. They were the ones who most keenly felt the gains of the Conquest being rolled back and wanted a line drawn in the sand.

The towns and cities undertook their own initiatives to keep the Irish out of their churches. In Waterford, Mayor Rice and his friends opposed the appointment of an Irish bishop to their town. In Galway, the struggle took a slightly different turn. Unlike Dublin, Cork, Limerick and Waterford, Galway was not the centre of the local diocese. Instead, the city was subject to the Archbishop of Tuam. It was not the distance from Galway to Tuam that was the problem but the nationality of the archbishops. Of the four archbishoprics in Ireland, Tuam alone was usually occupied by an Irishman. That was an insult to the English inhabitants of Galway and in 1484 the mayor, Stephen Lynch successfully petitioned Richard III and Pope Innocent VIII to win ecclesiastical independence from Tuam and set up a collegiate church whose vicars would be appointed by the local corporation. It was an extraordinary concession. The Warden of the college in Galway became a kind of locally elected bishop. As one historian remarked, 'a new form of ecclesiastical government which had no counterpart in Ireland sprang into existence'.[26] Donough O'Murray, Archbishop of Tuam, made no objection, even though the townsmen did not conceal the fact that their quarrel centred on the issue of race. The Irish, they said, were 'a wild and mountainous population . . . unpolished and illiterate by whom they were often disturbed in the exercise of their religion'.[27] Galway people were unable to receive the sacraments from their clergy 'according to English decency'.

The Irish bishoprics were also carved up on ethnic lines. After the death in the 1170s of Lawrence O'Toole, the last native Irish Archbishop of Dublin, the bishoprics of the eastern dioceses of Dublin, Kildare and Meath went to Englishmen. But if the English appropriated the lion's share of the Leinster and Munster bishoprics, it was equally uncontroversial that the poorer bishoprics of Connacht and Ulster would go to the Irish. This was not the fruit of a conscientious policy of nominating Irish candidates to western sees. The decline of the English colony in the fourteenth century placed the region beyond the crown's reach. In the previous century the crown had insisted on its right to nominate candidates even for the most distant bishoprics. The King sent a mandate to the chapter of the vacant diocese, giving them permission to elect a candidate. This protocol, known as the *congé d'élire*, gave the crown power to nominate the candidate of its choice and take possession of the temporalities of the see until the new bishop had sworn fealty. The papacy's role was minimal. The Pope had only to confirm the election, give the local archbishop permission to consecrate the new bishop and send a pallium if the new man was an archbishop.

The decline of the crown in Ireland meant the protocol broke down in the fourteenth and fifteenth centuries. Irish dioceses in the west ceased applying for a royal *congé d'élire* and dealt with the papacy directly.[28] The papacy usually agreed to the choice of the diocese, but there was an increase in the number of papal-appointed candidates, often bureaucrats in the curia who remained absentees.

One diocese was divided openly on ethnic lines, an emblem of the state of the Irish Church as a whole. This was Armagh, see of the Primate of All Ireland, which was split into two administrative blocks known as Ecclesia inter Anglicos (the Church among the English) and Ecclesia inter Hibernicos (the Church among the Irish). The Irish zone covered the three deaneries of Armagh, Tullaghoge and Oritor, the lands of the O'Neills, O'Hanlons and O'Donnells, and held its synod in Armagh. The 'Church among the English' covered the three deaneries in the Pale of Dundalk, Ardee and Drogheda and held its synods in St Peters' church, Drogheda.

The medieval archbishops of Armagh were nearly all of English nationality,[29] and normally resided at the northern tip of the Pale, at Termonfeckin, near Drogheda. These men had to be diplomats to manage their unusual diocese, moving to and fro between the Pale and the Irish bastion of Ulster and employing a mixture of threats and blandishments to maintain some sort of control over their property in Armagh. But in the fifteenth century they experienced such difficulty in retaining any hold over church lands in Ulster and getting rents that they rarely ventured into Armagh itself, where the O'Neill clan had installed themselves on much of the archbishops' property.[30]

In Armagh, religious apartheid was on display. But many of the 30 dioceses in the Irish Church were divided in a similar fashion. Ardfert, in Kerry, straddled a racial frontline. Among the English colonists, who had settled heavily in northern Kerry in the thirteenth century, the Fitzmaurice and Stack families were prominent. The south of Kerry was solidly Irish. The diocese reflected the division in its two archdeaconries: the northern covered the Anglo-Norman stronghold around the see town of Ardfert, while the other covered Gaelic south Kerry, and was based in Aghaboe, near Killarney. North of the line, men with English names held almost every ecclesiastical post in the fifteenth century, including five of the six bishoprics, three of which were held by the Stack family.[31] By the sixteenth century, the Old English community of Kerry was 'degenerate'. But in previous centuries the diocese had functioned much like Armagh, almost as if there were two separate churches, one 'among the English' and the other 'among the Irish'.

In practice, the Statutes of Kilkenny were only partially enforced. Many older Cistercian and Augustinian houses upheld the ban on Irish monks, which was why many became empty. But it was impossible to keep all the 'benefices of Holy Church among the English' in English hands when there were no longer enough Englishmen to fill them. After the ravages of the Black Death, the Irish Church could not function without an increasing number of Irish staff. In Armagh diocese, the appearance of a church 'among the English' was maintained by reserving the richer, urban posts for the English and giving the poorer, rural posts to the Irish. By the sixteenth century almost a third of the 19 known parishes 'inter Anglicos' were held by Irishmen,[32] and the Irish probably made up the bulk of unbeneficed curates whose names have not been recorded.

The racial chasm in the Irish Church had much to do with money and status. It was a fight for control over the church machinery. It did not involve deep and serious disputes over matters of faith and devotion. English settler and native Irishman held in common a deep devotion to the same relics and shrines. They did not divide up their sacred spaces. The gentry of the Pale and the Irish knelt together in front of the relics in Holy Trinity in Dublin, and at Marian shrines in Cavan and Trim. Holy Trinity was the centre of pilgrimage in Leinster, possessing hundreds of sacred souvenirs, including the stone altar of St Patrick, a portion of St Peter's chains and his cross, St Sylvester's sandals, and pieces of the hair, nails and bodies of scores of lesser saints. The prize possessions, the Staff of Jesus, Bacula Jesu, also known as the staff of Patrick, was supposed to have passed from Christ to Ireland's patron saint via an angel in the Mediterranean. Descriptions of it are vague, but it may originally have been an iron-clad walking stick with a spike, that was embellished over the centuries into the shape of a crozier, plated with gold and inlaid with jewels.[33] Removed from Armagh to Dublin for safety in the eleventh century, it was kept in a chest. Everything went on display to the pilgrims on 31 July, the feast day of the relics. Many must have been on permanent display, as the cathedral drew pilgrims all year round and pilgrims formed such an important source of the income that the city government passed a by-law in 1493 to make sure they travelled 'without any impedyment, molestacion or grevaunce' to the church.[34]

Relics and shrines bound the English and Irish together. The most powerful were used to seal treaties and oaths between the two communities. In 1529, Sir Gerald MacShayne was examined, or tried, in Christ Church, after he swore on 'the Holie masboke' and on 'the great relicke of Erlonde called Baculum Christi', in the presence of the Lord Deputy, the Lord Chancellor, Lord Treasurer and a great crowd of officers of state.[35] In 1533 the Earl of Desmond made a solemn promise over the relic before the mayor and justiciar in front of the high altar.[36]

In Munster, the relic of the True Cross, kept at Holy Cross Cistercian abbey, near Thurles, performed the same function. In 1517 it was transported to the capital of the Butlers' palatine territory in Tipperary at Clonmel for the swearing of a truce between Sir Piers Butler and his Butler cousins of Cahir.[37] It also cured the sick and was escorted on pilgrimage under a white pall decorated with a purple cross. A seventeenth-century account of the miracles attributed to the relic records three instances of blind people recovering their sight in 1607 in Granard, County Longford. These were a nine-year-old girl, cured in front of a crowd of 200, a man named Thady Byrne, from Roscommon and another girl aged eight or nine, Sadhbh Donecan, of Walterstown, Meath.[38] The relic cured Anastasia Sobechan of affliction by 'magic spells' in 1609, restored a woman's speech in 1611, and in 1623 cured the deafness of Edmund O'Ryan, aged 22, of Ballychalatan, Tipperary, which was fortunate, as he was a flute player. A poor man brought to the relic in a cart, 'entirely wasted away, nothing but skins and bone, dreadful to look at, shouting continually owing to the great tortures he had endured', was up and eating heartily with the Abbot after only an hour's contact.[39]

The True Cross could ward off natural disasters, such as crop failure. In 1608 it saved the oat and wheat crop near Urlingford, County Tipperary, after being dipped in water that was sprinkled on the afflicted fields. It demonstrated its crime-busting function in 1611, when Diarmid McShane attempted to steal a bag of wheat from the abbey and was rooted to the spot with the offending sack on his back, 'having become a warning and a laughing stock to all his neighbours'.[40]

Brother Malachy's *Triumphalia Chronologica Monasterii Sanctae Cruciae* was written in 1640 as a comfort to Catholics and a rebuke to Protestant scoffers. But there is no reason to suggest the relic's functions had changed greatly in the century in which he was writing. Like the Staff of Jesus, the relic of the True Cross was in English possession, for Holy Cross abbey lay on the outskirts of the Butler town of Thurles and the abbey passed to the Earl of Ormond under Elizabeth. But it was used and revered by the Irish as much as the English.

The important shrines did not all lie in English towns. The old monastic complex at Glendalough, south of Dublin, a centre of the cult of St Kevin, was one of Leinster's ancient pilgrimage sites.[41] The warfare between Dublin and the O'Byrnes and O'Tooles in the nearby hills made Glendalough dangerous territory for English travellers. A thirteenth-century Archbishop of Tuam claimed the shrine was nothing more than a pit of robbers.[42] But the stream of Irish pilgrims continued, and long after the Reformation it was reported that on St Kevin's Day, 'an infinite number of people and great store of friars and priests resort to Glendalagh to go in pilgrimage and there offer unto the priests and friars'.[43]

Monaincha, the *Insula Viventium*, was a popular pilgrimage site located in the marshlands of County Tipperary, near the Butler town of Roscrea. Called 'the island of the living' because it was reputed that no one who visited it could die a natural death, the trees and plants there possessed magical properties. The wood from the trees could be used to ward off poisonous beasts.

Ulster boasted the shrine of St Patrick's Purgatory, in the middle of Lough Derg in Donegal. The centrepiece was a cave that Christ had revealed to St Patrick, in which any pilgrim who completed due penance might see the joys of the saved and the horrors of the damned. In spite of its remote location it was well known in Europe. English pilgrims ventured to Lough Derg, even though it was deep inside solidly Irish territory. Theft was said to be common, as the Irish, 'though very religious', according to Francesco Chiericati, the papal nuncio, 'do not regard stealing as sinful nor is it punished as a crime'.[44] Lough Derg was still sufficiently prestigious and glamorous for Chiericati to consider it worth making the trek in 1517, travelling from London to Chester and then by boat to Dublin. To reach the shrine, he told his friend Isabella d'Este, wife of the Marquis of Mantua, he blew on a horn and waved a white flag on a pole, after which a boatman rowed him across the lake for a small fee. There he met the three canons who resided on the island and ran the site. After a bit of bureaucracy – pilgrims rather ominously had to make out a will before they started – the penance began.

The spiritual rewards for completing a pilgrimage on Lough Derg were huge but the schedule was exacting. The penitents spent nine days fasting on bread and water, confessing to the canons and visiting the three cells on the island dedicated to Saints Brigid, Patrick and Columba. They had to say an enormous number of Ave Marias and Pater Nosters and conduct regular acts of mortification, such as standing in the freezing water up to their necks.

Chiericati was a child of the Renaissance who saw himself more as a tourist than a pilgrim. But his companions underwent the whole thing and after Mass at dawn received communion and were escorted to the door of 'the purgatory'. This was a grotto, locked with an iron door and with enough standing room for about 12 people. 'They enter it naked and the door is not opened until the same hour on the following day,' he said.

A hole has been made in one side of the rock and through this a vessel is passed in and out to serve their needs. One of the canons keeps vigil beside this opening all the time, exhorting those inside to be faithful and firm in not allowing themselves to be overcome by diabolical temptations. The reason given for this is that there are many apparitions and several pilgrims emerge suffering from loss of memory or even raving because they yield to the devil's temptations.

Among those who entered while I was there, two had such visions. One who came out almost insane was interrogated in various ways. He said he had been terribly beaten, by whom he had no idea. The other told of having seen many voluptuous and beautiful women who invited him to eat with them and showed him good cheer. They offered him all kinds of fruit and food and because of the great languor that overcame him he nearly let himself be vanquished. The others declared that they neither saw nor heard anything but experienced cold, hunger and great weakness. They were half dead when they came out . . . [45]

The 'rounds' Chiericati saw pilgrims making on Lough Derg were a feature of devotional practice at Irish shrines, where the goal usually was to circle the holy object a set number of times, complete a number of prayers and keep moving clockwise. The legacy of pre-Christian cults in the emphasis on numbers and clockwise motion was clear. At Monaincha in 1591, that unsympathetic Lutheran visitor, Rudolf von Munchhausen, watched pilgrims removing their shoes and making eight rounds of the church. After that they crawled on their knees to the altar of the small chapel beside the church, and then to the stone cross inside the church, which they had to hug with their backs pressed against the cross.[46]

It was the same at holy wells, many of which were linked with cults of early Irish saints. Lough Derg and the big English-run shrines were the five-star hotels of Irish Catholicism. The humble holy well was the corner pub from which no one was barred and where there was no entrance fee. The rewards too were on a humbler scale. There were no great indulgences or promises of remission from purgatory, merely a good chance of curing a bad leg. The pilgrim usually approached the well from the north side, completed a set number of rounds, usually three or nine, always moving clockwise and following the movement of the sun. At the end, the pilgrim embraced or kissed the holy object, drank the holy water or washed the red eye or sore leg. Moving anticlockwise, against the sun, risked invoking negative energy and was a way to put a curse on one's enemies.

At St Patrick's well, near Killeevan, County Monaghan, John Richardson witnessed pilgrims carrying out a ritual in the 1720s which had probably not changed in generations. 'The pilgrims to this place first kneel at the north side of the well, salute St Patrick, say fifteen Paters and one Credo,' he wrote.

They rise up, bow to him, walk thrice round the well and drink of the water every round at a place where they began. From thence they go to the heap of stones, bow to the cross, kiss the print of St Patrick's knee and put [into it] one of their knees, always kissing the stone that hath the print of St Patrick's knee when they come to it. They rise up and bow to it and walk thrice round, bowing to the said stone when they come before it, and the last time kiss it. From the heap of stones they go to the alder tree. They begin at the west side with bowing to it, they go thrice round and bow to it from east and west and conclude their great superstition and folly with fifteen Paters and one Credo.[47]

Making the rounds of local shrines and wells long survived the Reformation in Ireland. The Munster shrine in Ballyvourney, dedicated to the sixth-century Irish nun St Gobnet, was going strong in the early eighteenth century, and Richardson saw pilgrims making 'rounds' of the 2-foot high statue of the saint in the now ruined church. 'The pilgrims resort to it twice a year, viz on St Valentine's eve and on Whitsun Thursday,' he noted. 'It is set up for their adoration on the old ruinous walls of the church. They go round the image thrice on their knees, saying a certain number of Paters, Aves and Credos . . . they conclude with kissing the idol and making an offering to it, everyone according to their ability.'[48] Many of the wells drew large crowds making 'rounds' on their patronal feast days well into the nineteenth century. There were holy wells everywhere. County Wicklow had at least a hundred, which suggests a rough total in the country of about 3,000. Not all, however, had even a vestigial connection with a saint, though in Wicklow about 60 per cent were named after saints.[49]

The seventeenth-century Irish chronicle, the *Annals of the Kingdom of Ireland*,[50] attests to the devotion of the Irish to all the country's shrines, English or Irish, and to the popular revulsion at their destruction. 'A new heresy and a new error in England,' the *Annals* for the year 1537 noted, 'so that the men of England went into opposition to the Pope and to Rome . . . they broke down the monasteries and sold their roofs and bells so that from Arran of the saints [the islands in Galway Bay] to the Iccian Sea [English Channel] there was no monastery that was not broken or shattered, with the exception of a few in Ireland of which the English took not notice or heed. They afterwards burned the images and shrines and relics of the saints of Ireland and England. They likewise burned the celebrated image of Mary at Trim, which used to perform wonders and miracles, which used to heal the blind, the deaf and persons affected with all kinds of diseases; and the staff of Jesus, which was in Dublin, performing miracles.'[51]

As the *Annals* paid little attention to most acts of the English authorities, unless it was a military offensive, the arrival of a new Lord Deputy or a coronation, it is significant they devoted so much space to the destruction of the Pale shrines. Clearly they saw it as an assault on the common religious patrimony.

The condition of Hibernica Ecclesia before the Reformation is difficult to judge at this distance. Irish Protestant writers before the later twentieth century conducted a long propaganda war against the old Church. They took their cue from Henry VIII's agents and hangers-on who had justified the Reformation by describing the fabric of the Church as ruined and the clergy as vile and vicious.

Although English motives in besmirching the Catholic Church are transparent, not all their accusations were necessarily false. Many contemporaries described the pre-Reformation Church in Ireland as a Church in decay. Buffeted by the long contest between the English and Irish for supremacy, its infrastructure was damaged by the decline in the crown's power. The proliferation of minor border wars between the English and the Irish, between the Irish septs and Old English lords, left many churches in ruins. Christopher Bodkin, Archbishop of Tuam from 1536 to 1571, told David Wolfe in the 1540s that he was the first archbishop to minister in Tuam cathedral for three centuries,[52] and that for generations it had been used by the gentry as a fortress and a stable. Wolfe later reported that the cathedral at Achonry was also used as a fortress 'and does not retain one vestige of the semblance of religion'.[53] That report to Cardinal Moroni in Rome was made in 1561, but it seems quite likely that Achonry had ceased to be a working church a long time before that. Several of the smaller cathedrals in the west had all but collapsed by the early decades of the sixteenth century. Clonmacnois, near Tuam, had no roof by then. Ardagh was also a ruin. A description of Clogher from 1517 found in the papal archives said the cathedral had stone walls but was only roofed 'partly with wood, partly with straw'.[54]

Decline was most evident in the English monasteries of the Pale, where numbers had dropped in most houses probably as a result of the ban on Irish monks. The English alone could not fill the great Gothic edifice of Jerpoint, near Kilkenny, or the big religious houses of the Dublin area. On the eve of the dissolution of the monasteries the two biggest Irish Cistercian houses, St Mary's abbey in Dublin and Mellifont contained 18 and 21 monks respectively.[55] In the thirteenth century, Mellifont had housed several hundred professed monks, and that figure did not include an even larger number of lay brothers. Elsewhere, numbers were even smaller. There were only seven monks at Jerpoint, six at Abbeylara, five at Hore, five at Inishlounaght, three at Newry and two at Kilcooley.

Even the most prestigious houses 'among the English' seem to have been half empty, or completely empty, by 1500. Grace Dieu, north of Dublin, was the most important convent in the Pale and had won a reputation as the best boarding school for girls in Ireland. In 1539 there was an outcry when it became clear it would be closed with all the rest of the religious houses. But when Alison White surrendered the Augustinian convent in October there are records of pensions being paid only to herself and to four other nuns, all with English names.[56] The hospital of St John's outside Newgate in Dublin once contained beds for 150 of the city's sick. By the time of the dissolution it was only capable of caring for 50.[57] Dublin's population had not dropped by two-thirds, nor had the number of sick people shrunk. It can only mean the number of potential carers had melted away.

The trend was the same outside Dublin. The ruins of the Augustinian house at Bridgetown, near Mallow, north of Cork, suggest that a substantial community was in residence in its thirteenth-century heyday. But from the 1400s onwards it became increasingly difficult for Bridgetown to supply priors from its own dwindling ranks of canons and by the time William Walshe surrendered it in 1541 the building was partly in ruins.[58]

The moral state of the English houses on the eve of the Reformation is harder to assess. It is significant that the Commission empowered to oversee their surrender attacked the monks' loyalty to the Pope and not their morals. They were 'addicted partly to their own superstitious ceremonies, partly to the pernicious worship of idols and to the pestiferous doctrine of the Roman Pontiff'.[59] In some, we know, discipline was feeble. When the authorities moved against the Irish religious, it was easy for them to find members of the public willing to make embarrassing charges. In 1537 local juries were induced to complain that at Athassel, County Tipperary, 'there was no divine service, but few masses with four canons and some of them using and having wives and children'.[60] The Abbot of Inishlounaght, James Butler, was accused of having a concubine, and of 'using her openly by day and night to his pleasure'.[61]

Clerical concubines and priests and abbots with sons who took over the family business were often the rule by the sixteenth century. Irish society had no bias in favour of clerical celibacy.[62] Historians have traced many professional clerical families from the time, such as Art MacCawell, Bishop of Clogher from 1390 to 1432, whose son became a canon and whose grandson and great-grandson both became bishops of Clogher.[63] Lochlainn O'Gallagher, Bishop of Raphoe, in Donegal from 1442 to 1478 had at least two concubines and seven sons, some of whom were priests, and when he was induced to go to Rome in 1476 to seek absolution it was not for incontinence but for alienating church land to his mistresses' families.

When John Bale, the first Protestant Bishop of Ossory, attacked clerical incontinence in his diocese in 1553 he was attacking an almost universal condition. If it had once been a feature of the Irish community, it had definitely spread to English bastions like Kilkenny. Bale took the clergy of Kilkenny to task over their mistresses. 'Muche were the prestes offended also for I had in my preachinges willed them to have wyves of their owne and to leave the unshamefast occupienge of other mennes wyves doughters and servauntes,' he recalled.[64]

It was difficult to expect chastity from the clergy in Butler country after the example set by the leading family. James Butler, the miscreant Abbot of Inislounaght, was the son of Sir Piers Butler, as was Edmund Butler, Archbishop of Cashel from 1524 to 1551.[65] Alexander Devereux, Abbot of Dunbrody in Wexford and Bishop of Ferns from 1539 to 1566, was an orthodox Catholic who left several children in priests' cures. The Lord Deputy Sidney complained that he 'left his see so vacant as his bastards, the token of his incontinency, have at this day in manner the whole of his livings'.[66]

Clerical concubines and illegitimate children were accepted in Irish society. In his *The Dysorders of the Irissherye* (1571) Rowland White remarked that the Irish as a whole 'dyd not so comonly comitt adulterye not for that they doo professe or keepe such chastyty but for that they seldoom or never marrye, therefore fewe of them [have] lawfull heyres'.[67] To be the illegitimate son of a priest was a point in one's favour. As Bishop Bale angrily recalled, a priest in Knocktopher told him it was 'an honour in this lande to have a spiritual man as a Byshop an Abbot a Monke a Fryre or a Prest to father'.[68]

Englishmen like Bale and Lord Deputy Sidney were genuinely outraged because their native society not only expected continence from the clergy but often got it. The pre-Reformation bishops of England were chaste men. The first generation of Protestants hated men like Cuthbert Tunstall of Durham, William Warham of Canterbury and Stephen Gardiner of Winchester for their religious conservatism. There was never any suggestion that they fathered illegitimate families. Against an English background, the morals of the Irish Church seemed shocking. There was a marked difference between England and Scotland, where clerical dynasties flourished in the Irish fashion. The Chisholms, James, William and William II, ran the see of Dunblane as a family firm for about a century while David Beaton, Cardinal Archbishop of St Andrews, fathered at least eight children.[69] The mores of the Irish clergy seem to have been part of a Celtic pattern.

While the ecclesiastical commissioners plodded round the English-speaking convents of Ireland, searching for signs of 'incontinence' among elderly nuns and among wheezing abbots, the future of the Irish monastic orders was being forged among people whose language they barely understood.

The Observant movement was the last great wave of reform to reach the religious orders before the dissolution. Reformers reacted against the secular values of the older conventual houses, with their landed estates, by demanding close 'observation' of the apostolic vow of poverty and of the monastic rule, be it Franciscan, Dominican, Augustinian or Carmelite. But the Observants were not only concerned with tightening up discipline. They claimed freedom for themselves from local provincials and demanded to be subordinated to prior-generals of their own in Rome. The special significance of the Observants in Ireland was that, for once, the interests of the Irish and the papacy appeared to converge against those of the English government. Rome could hardly object to a reform that increased its direct control over the religious orders. The demand for prior-generals was conceded to the Irish Observant Franciscans in 1460 and the Dominican Observants in 1484, though the English Dominicans spoiled this achievement by successfully demanding that the province be reduced to a vicariate.[70]

One has to beware of seeing the Observants as a purely Irish force, pitted against the older English conventual houses. The racial boundaries were not so clear. In 1469 a native Irishman, William O'Reilly, was appointed Provincial of the Irish conventual Franciscans, while Richard Nangle, an Englishman, was made Provincial-General of the Observant Augustinians in the 1530s. But in the charged atmosphere of Hibernica Ecclesia, the Observant movement had unmistakable racial undertones. It promised immeasurably greater freedom to Irishmen who had chafed for centuries under the rule of English provincials. As one historian has put it, 'the Observant reform meant that the Gaelic, as well as the

Anglo-Irish, friars were given an opportunity which had been denied to them for at least a century and a half'.[71]

Not surprisingly, the Observant movement spread fastest and furthest among the native Irish. In 1420, just before the movement reached Ireland, there were about 35 Franciscan houses in Ireland. A century later there were 54, of which 30 were Observant and most of the patrons of these foundations were Irish.[72] It was the MacNamara family who brought them to Quin, County Clare, in 1430, the Macarthys who brought them to Muckross, County Kerry, in 1448 and the O'Neills who founded at least three houses in County Antrim. The O'Donnells brought them to western Ulster, both Aedh rua O'Donnell and his wife Nuala being buried in the house they founded in Donegal. The fifteenth-century foundations at Ballynassagart in Tyrone in 1489 and at Bunamargy, Dungannon and half a dozen sites in Donegal were also native Irish houses.[73]

The Dominicans also experienced most growth in the fifteenth century in the Irish heartlands of the west, founding new houses at Portumna in 1414, Longford in 1420, Toombeola in 1427, Urlaur in 1434, Tulsk in 1448 and Balindoon in 1507.[74] Some of these houses were Observant, others were conventual, but they were all Irish. It was the final reversal of the legacy of Stephen de Lexington. In the Irish Church, the Irish were no longer going to be hewers of wood and drawers of water for the Old English.

The monks and nuns of the English Pale had resigned themselves to a life of drowsy good behaviour and civic duty. They had become the governesses and hoteliers to visiting English businessmen and politicians. The connection between their houses and England was so old that they could not conceive of a world in which their religious calling and the demands of the crown could ever conflict. In their remote fastnesses, the Observants were never hostages to the world in the same degree. Obedient only to the Pope and drawing their strength from the 'mere Irish', they would provide Rome with the shock troops in the coming struggle against the English Reformation.

CHAPTER THREE

Myn Auctoritie is Litle Regarded

The Proctours of the Spiritueltie somewhat doo stick in diverz of theis Actes and lothe thei are that the Kinges Grace shuld be the Supreme Hed of the Church . . .
(William Brabazon to Thomas Cromwell, 1538)[1]

Behind high and ornate wrought iron gates in Drogheda stands the stately, steel grey parish church of St Peter's. An elegant Georgian reworking from the 1750s of a much older parish church, it has an imposing, almost magnificent aspect, which owes much to its geographical position, crowning the town. From the top of a hill it commands views of the River Boyne that sweeps through the valley below.

In the cemetery, the headstones beside the porch attest to the wealth and prestige of past worshippers in the parish. If it were in England, the church door would almost certainly be open and the porch noticeboard choked with fluttering announcements of fêtes, festivals, musical performances, interesting talks, the inevitable appeal for funds as well as information about forthcoming services. The church would hum, even in a secular generation that has little time for religion, with that low but constant level of activity that characterises the life of principal churches in large English country towns.

But this is not England. It is the east coast of Ireland and St Peter's, Drogheda does not hum with any kind of activity. On a summer's afternoon there is nothing to disturb the eerie stillness of the forecourt and mine are the only footsteps to crunch across the unweeded gravel. The town is busy with shoppers on a Saturday but the activity stops dead outside the church gates as if hermetically sealed off by an invisible glass wall. On closer examination it can be seen that the superb iron gas lamps on the steps are rusted, twisted and broken and that a buddleia is growing out of the church roof, swaying in the breeze. The church is locked and a small notice informs visitors that it has been closed due to a recent fire. Potential worshippers can arrange for transport to services at Termonfeckin if they inform the vicar.

Drogheda is a very English looking town. The character of the steep and narrow streets that tumble down towards the Boyne evokes vague recollections of a number of towns in the English West Country. It is not difficult to recall

Drogheda as a centre of the English Pale with strong trading ties to England and to Bristol in particular. What is utterly un-English is the visible, palpable divorce between the town and its ancient church. Once the fulcrum of Drogheda's civic life, the seat of diocesan synods, the object of triumphant processions, decorated with many altars and side chapels and crowned with a famously tall steeple, it now seems marooned and forgotten by the society that hurries around it.

Its successful rival is visible from the graveyard. From a gap in the iron railings, across the other side of town can be seen the mid-nineteenth-century Gothic revival tower of the other St Peter's. It is to this building, the Catholic St Peter's and not its Protestant Church of Ireland counterpart, that all but a handful of the town's Christians resort for prayer and worship. Here is a very different scene, one of quiet but pulsating activity. Overlapping posters in the porch advertise trips to the pilgrimage centres of Knock and Lourdes, offer advice for depression and urge women to consider joining the Presentation Order. There is less interest now in the little bronze statue of St Peter, beside which reads an Indulgence of Pope Pius X from 1907, for anyone who kisses the statue's feet. No one going in or out takes any notice of it. But the building reverberates with the combined movement of tourists, worshippers and cleaning ladies preparing for the next Mass. The eye is drawn to the shiny tall reliquary that houses the blackened head of Oliver Plunket, saint and Catholic Archbishop of Armagh, put to death in England in 1681 in the anti-Catholic hysteria surrounding the 'Popish plot' to kill Charles II. The martyr's eyes are closed. His lips, however, are drawn back slightly, as if to reveal a tight, ironic smile.

The state of play between the two St Peter's of Drogheda is repeated throughout Ireland. In Armagh there are two cathedrals of St Patrick. There is a Church of Ireland Archbishop of Dublin and a Catholic Archbishop of Dublin. There is a Church of Ireland Primate of All Ireland and a Catholic Primate of all Ireland. There is a Church of Ireland Bishop of Cork and a Catholic Bishop of Cork, a Church of Ireland Bishop of Limerick and a Catholic Bishop of Limerick. Once there was one. Now there seem to be two of everything, bishop and counter-bishop, church and counter-church, the names held in common begging the question of which is the 'real' one.

The era of duplication and confusion was inaugurated with a series of blows to the old order. First came the destruction of the apparently invincible Geraldine earls of Kildare, those semi-regal subjects who ruled as Lord Deputies, 8th Earl and 9th Earl, father and son, from the reign of Henry VII in 1496 well into the reign of his son Henry VIII in 1519. The Kildares had straddled the world of English and Irish with apparent ease, marrying into great English and Irish families alike, and so becoming neither wholly 'degenerate', as the Munster earls of Desmond, nor as English as the Ormond Butlers. The 9th Earl had grown up at the English court, a contemporary of the king who would later annihilate him, before leaving at the age of 16. Like his father he brought home an English wife, Elizabeth Zouch. On the 8th Earl's death in 1513 he inherited all his father's lands, the biggest estate in the Pale, as well as his position as Lord Deputy. Cardinal Wolsey, Henry's chief minister, had long plotted to get rid of this aristocrat whose power and popularity hinted to him, at least, at an ambition to kingship and from 1520 a succession of Lord Deputies was appointed to Ireland as Henry and Wolsey attempted to run Ireland on the cheap and without the Kildares. Deputies came and went as if through a revolving door. The Earl of Surrey was followed by Sir Piers Butler; Butler was followed by the Earl of Kildare again; the Earl was then followed by Richard Nugent, Lord Delvin; Delvin gave way to Sir William Skeffington; Skeffington gave way to the Earl of Kildare again in 1532. But although it was Wolsey who encouraged the King's suspicions about the Kildares, Wolsey was disgraced and dead before the Earl received his final, terrifying summons to England in 1534. By then Wolsey had been succeeded by Thomas Cromwell.

Under Cromwell's guiding hand the 'King's Great Matter', concerning his projected divorce from his Spanish Queen, Catherine of Aragon, assumed a course Wolsey could never have contemplated. In place of the gentle Catholic humanist, William Warham, Thomas Cranmer – a crypto-Lutheran – was inserted into the see of Canterbury. The entire clerical order was humbled and its legislative powers taken away by the Act of Submission. Papal authority was repudiated by the Act of Supremacy. England was about to produce its first Catholic martyrs in 1535 as the King's former Lord Chancellor, Sir Thomas More, and John Fisher, Bishop of Rochester, chose death rather than submit to Henry as Supreme Head of the Church of England.

By 1534, the legislation of the parliament in England had already left the Church in Ireland in an anomalous position. The Acts of Supremacy and Restraint of Appeals had made Henry VIII a virtual pope in England. He could hardly continue to co-operate with the other Pope in running the Church in Ireland. What untied the knot was the desperate throw of the dice by the Kildares in the form of a rebellion by the Earl's 21-year-old son, Lord Offaly, known famously as 'Silken Thomas'. Furious over his father's departure to England in the spring of 1534 and convinced he had been put to death, he raised the standard of revolt on 11 June, hunting down and murdering his father's great enemy in Ireland, Wolsey's former chaplain, John Alen, Archbishop of Dublin.

The revolt was destined to fail, or succeed, absolutely. Henry had either to withdraw from Ireland or find the money to send a serious army to Ireland and crush it totally. In October, Sir William Skeffington landed with a force of 2,300. Support for Kildare melted away. The rebellion was effectively over, though Silken Thomas did not surrender until August the following year. The failure of the revolt was not surprising. The 'wild' Irish and the 'civil' English had no tradition of combining against the crown. Even a cause as popular as the house of Kildare did not tempt the English of the Pale to shake off their allegiance. 'Silken Thomas' claimed desperately to be fighting for Ireland and Catholicism, but his plea fell on deaf ears in a country where national identity was fractured and the Church had scarcely felt a tremor from the ecclesiastical earthquake in England. The revolt did not unite the English to the Irish or the Irish to each other. The O'Neills supported the revolt but their rivals, the O'Donnells, did not. Some of the Pale gentry supported the revolt as did the Desmonds, but the Butlers did not. Neither did the citizens of Dublin or Waterford.

The destruction of the Kildare family and the murder of Archbishop Alen opened the way for new political and ecclesiastical arrangements. It left room for the Kildares' conspicuously loyal rivals, the Ormond Butlers, relatives of Henry's new Queen Anne Boleyn. Just as Warham's timely death had allowed Henry to intrude Cranmer into Canterbury with the minimum of fuss, Alen's messy exit enabled Henry and Cromwell to bring Hibernica Ecclesia into harmony with its English counterpart.

The man they chose was George Browne. No picture survives of Archbishop Browne to allow comparisons with Ficke's famous portrait of Cranmer in his magpie rochet, cap and chimere. Browne's nineteenth-century Protestant hagiographer, Bishop Mant of Down and Connor,[2] said he was 'a man who has been handed down to posterity as of cheerful countenance, in his actions plain and downright, to the poor merciful and compassionate, pitying the state and condition of the souls of the people'.[3] Mant was writing in the 1840s, when the Protestant church establishment was under attack. He clearly felt an obligation to defend every moment of his church's history. But some modern church historians have largely concurred, one describing Browne's 'distinguished service in the Irish administration while occupying archepiscopal office'.[4]

None of Browne's contemporaries remarked on any of these qualities. At least one thought he was a swine.

A more realistic guess is that he was a shortish man, portly and undistinguished. His face was perhaps one that twisted easily into a look of rage, or of furtive greed. It is a fanciful picture and one assembled only by a process of negative selection. Comeliness and height, even when it came with a character as repulsive as that of Browne's successor but one in Dublin, Adam Loftus, was always remarked on in a society as prone to physical disfigurement. And John Bale, Browne's fellow Protestant Bishop of Ossory, has left a sharp and unflattering portrait of the Archbishop. After he was refused permission to preach in Browne's archdiocese in 1553, he wrote: 'As the Epicurous archebishop had knowledge of my beinge there [in Dublin] he made boast upon his ale benche with cuppe in his hande, as I hear the tale tolde, that I shude for no mannis pleasure preache in that cytie of his. For (however) I thought nothinge lesse at that time than to poure out the preciouse pearles of the Gospell afore so brockenish (beastly) a swine as he was'.[5]

Bishop Bale's words were intended to convey his contempt for Browne's moral fibre. They are not a literal commentary on his looks. But the picture of the 'epicurous' foodie on his ale bench with his tankard in hand is not necessarily false. He bequeathed his personality in his writings. They have a querulous tone. There is a discernible whine in his communications with London and he continually sneaked on his colleagues in government. Then there is the secretive nature of his marriage, and the outbursts of temper which made it impossible for him to work with almost all his colleagues. Taken together they evoke a small, bustling figure, perhaps red-faced, and furtive, and a larger than appropriate belly.

It is remarkable that after 18 years as archbishop no one liked Browne. At best he gained the wooden approbation of fellow conspirators against the Lord Deputy, Lord Grey. That he should have earned the contempt of loyal papists was understandable; what is striking is the utter dislike felt for him by his two fellow Protestant bishops, a feeling shared by two Lord Deputies. This was the man on whose shoulders the success or failure of the first phase of Reformation in Ireland devolved.

Browne's background is obscure. Like Cranmer, though without Cranmer's intellectual or literary gifts, he belonged to that class of people who would have floated in the middle or near the bottom of the ecclesiastical pool had it not been for the stirring of the waters in the 'King's Great Matter'. It was in 1532 that the Prior of the Augustinian house in Throckmorton Street in London came to the hostile notice of the imperial ambassador and the approving gaze of Cromwell, who desperately needed clergy to preach in favour of Henry's divorce from Queen Catherine and the Royal Supremacy.[6] In Browne he found an eager partner. In April 1534 Browne was made Provincial of the Augustinian Order in England and that summer, along with another monastic reformer, John Hilsey, he was entrusted with undertaking a rapid visitation of the Augustinian houses to make sure they signed their assent to the Supremacy. Browne moved fast. By July he was in Yorkshire; after that, Newcastle. In the autumn of 1534 he was heading south through London and the southern counties. In January 1535 Browne was a special preacher before the King at Richmond.

By now Browne had a reputation as an advanced reformer, a member of the faction in the Church which was not openly Protestant, but wanted to go further than simply proclaiming Henry Supreme Head of the Church. Some members of the reform movement had visions of building a new society out of the Church's expropriated income. They dreamed of schools sprouting from the foundations of ruined monasteries. Others simply advanced themselves by noisily championing the King's divine right to do what he wanted. Browne undoubtedly belonged in the second category. His reputation for religious radicalism stemmed purely from his extreme Erastianism. In the summer of 1535 he raised his profile after a sermon in which he declared that the spiritual functions of bishops derived from the King, and that the bishops, in consequence, needed to exchange all their papal bulls of appointment for royal ones.[7] It earned him the deep hostility of the more conservative bishops and when Cromwell promoted him to preach at St Paul's Cross in London that summer, Bishop Stokesley tried in vain to have the permit withdrawn.

Cromwell's belief that Browne was constructed from unusually pliant material was well founded. As the stock of the ecclesiastical conservatives waned in the

1530s, Browne found himself on the short list for promotion. He must have hoped for an English see, especially after his former colleague, Hilsey, was rewarded with Rochester after the execution of John Fisher. But Cromwell had had a vacancy to fill in Ireland since the untimely death of Archbishop Alen. On 28 December 1535 Henry issued the *congé d'élire* for Browne to become Dublin's next Archbishop and on 19 March 1536 he was consecrated in Lambeth by Cranmer, Hilsey and Nicholas Shaxton of Salisbury.

Browne missed the opening phase of the Irish Reformation parliament that the new Lord Lieutenant Lord Leonard Grey summoned for May Day in Christ Church. He did not reach Dublin until July and did not preach in his cathedral until the end of November.

After the revolt of the Kildares, the Irish parliament met in a contrite mood and offered little resistance to the package of ecclesiastical laws prepared in England and brought over for a rubber stamp. The principal item on the agenda, naturally, was the Act of Attainder against the Kildares, which would forfeit their estates to the crown. The Acts concerning the Church were copies of the English Acts passed from 1532 to 1534. The Act of Supremacy, as in England, declared Henry Supreme Head on earth of the Church of Ireland. An Act in restraint of appeals redirected all pleas for bulls of appointment, dispensations and adjudication from Rome to the King. The Irish Act of Succession was untimely. Like the English bill, it fixed the succession on the heirs of Henry and Anne Boleyn. The loyal men of the Irish parliament had no idea that back in England the Queen had rapidly fallen from favour and was about to be executed.[8] As a result, the Act had to be rewritten. The Act of First Fruits and Twentieths assigned the King the value of all ecclesiastical promotions for the first year and an annual income tax of a twentieth of the value thereafter.

The Irish parliament was being asked to nod through an ecclesiastical revolution. Yet in spite of the magnitude of the issues, it went without a hitch. There was opposition from the clergy, as there had been in the early stages of the Reformation parliament in England under Warham and Stephen Gardiner of Winchester. But there was support from the knights, burgesses and citizens in the Irish House of Commons. There was none of that virulent lay anticlericalism which Henry was able to train with deadly effect on the clergy in England. And there was a wave of enthusiasm in the Pale for what looked like a clear sign that England was at last taking an interest in its neglected colony. The Pale had been dispirited by the relentless decline of 'civil' English society, the steady implosion of the Pale and the turf wars between various 'degenerate' great lords. The Palesmen had long demanded a 'reformation', in the sense of a drastic overhaul of the system of government. William Brabazon, Master of the Rolls, summed up the split in the two houses of the Irish parliament when he wrote to Cromwell on 17 May 1536, weeks after the parliament opened: 'The Proctours of the Spirituelتie somewhat doo stick in diverz of theis Actes and lothe thei are that the Kinges Grace shuld be the Supreme Hed of the Church . . . [but] the Common

House is merveilous good for the kinges causez and all the lerned men within the same be verie good.'[9]

Exactly who the 'spirituality' were in the 1536 parliament is hard to pin down. The Irish House of Lords comprised a floating contingent of bishops and abbots whose numbers varied. Ware listed 14 abbots and 10 priors who were entitled to sit in parliament, though he thought only 3 abbots and 1 prior attended regularly. They appear to have played no noticeable role in the 1536 assembly. The 30 or so Irish bishops were also only partly represented. Even in the high days of English rule, no one expected the native Irish bishops of the tiny Kilfenora, Killala or Kilmacdaugh to trek to Dublin or Drogheda for a parliament.

The Archbishop of Tuam was usually enough for Connacht. Nor would many Ulster bishops have been summoned, except for the Archbishop of Armagh and the Bishop of Down. The bishops of Meath, Kildare and Ferns certainly attended in 1536, most probably augmented by the Archbishop of Cashel, the bishops of Ossory and Waterford from the south, and the Archbishop of Tuam and the Bishop of Limerick from the west.[10]

The traditional rivalry between the two primates of Ireland, the archbishops of Dublin and Armagh meant the northern primate was represented by proxy. In England, the meeting of the two houses of parliament was often accompanied by convocations of the clergy. These were separate clerical parliaments representing the two ecclesiastical provinces of York and Canterbury, which drew up ecclesiastical legislation and voted the crown clerical subsidies. In Ireland the set-up was slightly different. There were no convocations of the four provinces of Dublin, Armagh, Cashel and Tuam but a single assembly of clerical proctors, comprising two clergymen for each of the 30 dioceses. Like the convocation, it sat at the same time as parliament and claimed the right to veto any legislation concerning the Church. The result was that in 1536 and 1537 the Irish clergy had two avenues of defence against the crown; with the bishops and abbots in the House of Lords, and through the House of Proctors.

At the end of May, parliament was adjourned after passing the Act of Attainder against the Kildares, the Act of Supremacy, and the Acts concerning the succession, the restraint of appeals to Rome and the first fruits of the clergy. So far, so good for the government. The Lord Deputy then set out on a military progress throughout the south-east, an expedition aimed at showing the flag in those parts of Leinster and Munster that acknowledged English rule and publicising the decrees of the parliament to the townsmen and the heads of the septs. As was the custom, parliament followed in the Lord Deputy's wake and held a few symbolic sessions in Cashel, Kilkenny and Limerick.

Thus far the Irish 'Reformation' had gone like a dream. It was only when parliament reassembled in September in Dublin that the trouble began. Even then, resistance did not come from the expected quarters of the bishops. Instead it came from the lay members of the House of Commons who had appeared so enthusiastic for the King's cause in May. Three new bills stuck in the craw of the laymen.

In March the English parliament had passed an Act suppressing the smaller religious houses. It was clearly a test measure, pending a large scale suppression, though it was not yet certain that all the English monasteries were to be closed. In September, the Irish confronted a similar proposal involving the suppression of 13 religious houses in the Pale and in Wexford. The list comprised five Cistercian houses at Bective in Meath, and Baltinglass in Wicklow, Duiske in Kilkenny and Dunbrody and Tintern in Wexford, the Augustinian houses at St Peter's in Trim in Kildare, Duleek, Ballylogan, Holmpatrick, Teac-Noling and Ferns in Wexford and the convents of St Mary del Hogges in Dublin and the convent of Grane, in Kildare. That was unwelcome in itself. But along with this bill were two financial proposals, requiring the Irish parliament to grant the King additional customs taxes and a new income tax.

The smooth passage of the Irish Reformation stopped immediately while the Lord Deputy and the small band of committed reformers, with Browne at the head, confronted a solid block of bishops and laymen, united in defence of their purses and their religious houses. The spokesman for the rebels was not an outraged abbot but Sir Patrick Barnewall, a pillar of the loyal gentry of the Pale and the King's Sergeant-at-law. Barnewall insisted the Royal Supremacy empowered the King to amend existing abuses in religious houses, not close them down. As Robert Cowley, Master of the Rolls, told Cromwell at the height of the deadlock in October, Barnewall 'wolde not graunte that the Kynge as Hedd of the Churche had soo large power as the Bysshop of Rome and that the Kinges jurisdiccion therein was but a spirituell power to refourme or amende the enoormyties and defaultes in rreligeous housez but not . . . dissolve abbayes or to alterate the foundacion of theyme to any temporal use.'[11] The colonial English might welcome the Royal Supremacy in the Church as an instrument of long-awaited 'reformation' of the Pale. They were not a push-over when it came to Acts that affected their pockets.

Parliament adjourned after achieving nothing, at the end of September. It reassembled and was adjourned again in January 1537. Barnewall was sent to explain himself to Henry in England in February but if his enemies had expected the King to turn the full force of his fury on the obdurate MP they were disappointed. When it came to Ireland, Henry was shrewd enough to take half a loaf rather than insist on the whole and end up – possibly – with nothing. He used Barnewall to offer the Irish parliament a compromise. In exchange for the suppression of the 13 monasteries, one of the proposed new taxes was quietly shelved while the income tax of the twentieth was made applicable only to the clergy. In a stroke, the revolt of the Irish laity in the Commons was defused.[12]

A year after it first opened, parliament reassembled in Dublin. The Commons now ceased resistance. But the fight had not yet gone out of the clergy: they took up the baton by wielding the veto of the proctors, the clergy's representatives in parliament. Again the proceedings ground to a halt. Lord Deputy Grey, suspecting a co-ordinated plot between the proctors and 'their masters the Bishoppes',[13] adjourned parliament again in May. In the meantime he sought a royal declaration to have the proctors' powers quashed under the authority of the King's Great Seal. While commissioners were sent over with the Great Seal, Henry's irritation with the filibustering tactics of the Irish parliament boiled over. It was 'much to our marvail', he complained to the Irish Council in February, 'that you have not yet proceded [sic] to the suppression of the monasteries'.[14]

In July 1537 royal anger over the muddle in Ireland vented itself in a highly threatening letter to Archbishop Browne. The tone revealed how his opinion of Browne had deteriorated since the days when Browne had done so much useful work on behalf of the royal divorce. It was intended to be a crushing rebuke to an *arriviste* who had become overexcited about his stunning rise from the role of obscure monk to Prince of the Church. 'The good opinion we had conceyved of you is in maner utterly frustrate,' it began; 'for neyther doo ye geve your self to the instruction of our people there in the Worde of God, ne frame yourself to stande Us in any stede for the furtherance of our affaires such is your lightnes in behaviour and suche is the elation of your mynde in pride that glorieng in follishe ceremonies and deliting in "we" and "us", in your dreame companying yourself soo nere to a prince in honour and estimation that all virtue and honestie is almost banished from you.' It concluded with a tart reminder that the Royal Supremacy gave the King ample powers to make and unmake bishops at will.[15]

The fourth session of the Dublin parliament opened in October, in an atmosphere of exhaustion. The proctors' teeth had been drawn. By December, the Act of Suppression had been passed along with two additional Acts, ordering a working knowledge of the English language to be the precondition for any new clerical appointment unless no English candidate was available and penalising anyone maintaining the Pope's authority. Every lay and ecclesiastical official was ordered to take a loyalty oath, undertaking 'that he from henceforth shall utterly renounce, refuse, relinquish and forsake the bishop of Rome and his authority . . . and that from henceforth he shall accept, repute and take his Majesty to be the only supreme head on earth of the Church of England and of Ireland'.[16]

Henry's letter shook Browne to the core and the Archbishop wrote a grovelling reply in September. He said he was busy preaching against the Pope in spite of the fact that sentimental loyalty to Rome in Ireland was 'a thing not a litle rated amonges th'inhabitantes here'.[17] The problem, he told Cromwell in January 1538, was that it was proving impossible to translate the reformation of the Irish Church from parliament to the real world. Parliament might have passed the Act of Supremacy, but as the Archbishop was finding out, that meant little in Ireland. It was impossible to get anyone to preach in favour of the Royal Supremacy, even among the minority of clergy who were known preachers.

Neither by gentill exhortacion, evangellicall instruccion neither by oathes of theym solemply taken, nor yeate by threates of sharpe correccion can I persuade or induce anye, either religious or secular sithens my commyng over ons [once] to preache the Worde of God or the juste title of Our moste illustrious Prince . . . And yet before that Our moste dreade Soverayne was declared to be (as he was ever in deade) Supreme Hed over the Church commytted unto his princely care, they that then could and wolde, very often even till the right Christians were wery of theym, preache after thold soarte and facion, will not now ons open theire lippes in any poulpett.[18]

The clergy were not only boycotting the Supremacy. They were also refusing even to alter their mass books to remove references to the Pope. Browne grumbled that he had been forced to send his own officials to scrub out the Pope's name in the missals in Dublin's churches, 'whereby your Lordship may perceyve that myn auctoritie is litle regarded'.[19] He made two further observations about his difficulties. One was that the Observant friars – those pillars of Irish resistance to English domination – were at the centre of the campaign of opposition to the Royal Supremacy. The other was that almost every bishop nominated by the King found himself in competition with a rival appointed by Rome. The process of duplication that would culminate in the establishment of two mirror Churches and two hierarchies had begun.

Browne made no progress as the months passed. The year 1538 was crucial for the progress of Protestantism in England. The authorities began a wholesale attack on pilgrimages, shrines, monasteries and the cult of saints. Parish churches were ordered to purchase the new English Bible. This was the year when 'reform' shaded into revolution. But in Ireland, Browne and Edward Staples of Meath were solitary apostles of the new order. The other bishops assented to the King's new title but did nothing. Edmund Butler of Cashel ceased to communicate with Rome but until his death in 1554 he did nothing to promote any changes in religious practice.[20] In Armagh, George Cromer also assented to the Royal Supremacy, prompting Rome to appoint Robert Wauchop as its new Archbishop of Armagh in 1539. But passive assent was as far as Cromer went. As Browne complained to Cromwell, 'George my brother of Armagh . . . is not active to execute His Highness's orders in his diocese.'[21]

In Dublin, Browne hit a glass wall when he tried to emulate recent changes in England and have images and relics removed from churches. The move threatened to deprive Dublin's cathedrals of an ancient and valued source of income from pilgrims and the clergy dug in their heels. The 'Romish reliques and images of both my cathedrals' stayed where they were, Browne said in April, because the Prior of Holy Trinity and the Dean of St Patrick's 'find them so sweet for their gain that they heed not my words'.[22] In June, Browne wailed about his unpopularity to Cromwell: 'There goeth commen brewte amonges the Irish men that I intende to ploke down Our Lady of Tryme with other places of pilgramages as the Holy Crosse and souche like, which indeade I never attempted, although my conscience wolde right well serve me to oppresse such ydolles.'[23]

The progress of the Reformation in Ireland was hindered by the open divisions in the ranks of the Irish Council, pitting Browne and a clique of 'advanced' reformers against the Lord Deputy. In October, Grey and Browne had a public spat outside the abbey church at Trim. The Lord Deputy insisted on hearing Mass in front of the Marian shrine; Archbishop Browne, Robert Cowley, Master of the Rolls and William Brabazon, the Vice-Treasurer refused to set foot inside the building and so signify support for 'Romish reliques' at a time when in England all the shrines were being dismantled. Grey brazened it out. Much to their horror, he showed the world he still revered 'the ydoll of Trym' and 'very devoutly kneeling before hir heard three or four masses'.[24]

The assault on relics in Ireland would have to wait until February 1539, when Browne, Brabazon and John Alen, the Lord Chancellor, received a commission from Cromwell in England to hunt them down. Not surprisingly, the Lord Deputy was omitted from the list of those officials charged with locating 'notable images and reliques at which the simple people of the said Lord the King were wont superstitiously to meet together and wandering as on pilgrimage to walk and stray about them or otherwise to kiss, lick or honour them, contrary to the honour of God'.[25]

While the assault on relics and shrines hung fire, the Archbishop tried his hand at reforming the liturgy. The avenue he took was through the 'beads', as the bidding prayers in the mass were called. In the spring of 1538 Browne drew up a set form of beads for the diocese. As he could not persuade his clergy to preach on the Royal Supremacy in their sermons, he redrew the prayers to insert an antipapal tirade into the liturgy. The new beads consisted of a wordy defence of the Royal Supremacy, including the rather irrelevant information that it had been endorsed by the University of Oxford, and a vehement exhortation against the Pope, in which the congregation was urged to 'have from henceforth no confidence nor trust in him nor in his bulls nor letters of pardon'.[26]

The beads ran into the same defiance as the attack on relics and images, once again exposing the Archbishop's pitiful lack of authority. On 8 May Browne told Cromwell of a revealing incident with James Humfrey, a canon prebendary of St Patrick's cathedral who had openly shown contempt for the new beads at St Audoen's by refusing to read them. The church was the city's principal parish church, situated practically next door to Browne's cathedral. Browne took up the story. 'Thys man synging Hyghe masse as that daye because he is there parson, att the tyme when that the beades is customably redd, after the forme and maner as I have devysed and set them forthe for all curates, he hym sellff thought scorne to reade them. Wherfor hys paryshe preiste accordyng unto hys othe went up yn to the pulpitt and there began to reade them unto the people; he hadd unnethes [only] redd a 3 or 4 lynes butt [when] the parson began the preface and the quyer sange, yn so much that the beades were unbidden.' Browne ended the letter with a grouse against the city's clergy, none of whom apparently supported him. 'They be all in maner att the same poynt with me,' he said. 'There is an 28 of them and amongst them all therre is not three learned off them, nor yet scarse one that favoreth Goddes Worde . . . where they rule Godd and the Kynge cannott justlie reign'.[27]

Browne had Humfrey flung into jail. But if thought he could frighten the recalcitrant papists, the following 10 days revealed just how ephemeral an archbishop of Dublin's authority could be when it was not bolstered by powerful alliances within the Pale. As he told Cromwell soon after, no sooner had he put Humfrey in jail than the Lord Deputy released him, humiliating the Archbishop in front of the small gossipy city. As he explained: 'I committed one Humfrey, a prebendarye of Sanct Patrikes unto ward tyll tyme that I know ferder the kynges pleasour yn correctyng off soche obstinate and sturdye papistes, thynckyng that yn so doyng I shold have ben ayded and assisted off my Lord Deputi and the Consell. Howbeyt . . . to my grate rebuke . . . mye Lord Deputie hath sett hym att lybertye (so doyth hys Lordship ayde me yn my Princes causes).' Browne closed with a thoroughly unconvincing threat to resign. 'I thyncke the symplest holy water clerke ys better estemed then I am,' he said. 'I beseche your lordship yn the way of charite, other cause mye authorytye to take effect, or els lett me returne home agayne unto the cloyster. When that I was att the worst I was yn better case than I am now, what wyth my Lord Deputi, the Bisshop of Methe and the pecuniose prior of Kylmaynam.'[28]

The Lord Deputy, the Bishop of Meath, the Prior . . . they were all at loggerheads. Browne's plight, and the plight of the Irish Church reform party, was that although they were a small minority, they were a house divided along lines that were as much personal as political. Grey and Rawson, Prior of the crusading Order of Knights Hospitaller of St John of Jerusalem, were military men, uninterested in doctrine and no doubt contemptuous of civilians like Browne. Staples was a convinced reformer but unlike Browne he was a Palesman and had a natural inclination to see reform put through with the consent of the community. From the start of Browne's archiepiscopate, Staples found himself in an acutely uncomfortable position. His views ought to have placed him on the side of the Archbishop, but he seems to have felt uneasy about Browne's reliance on coercion. It was a typical dispute between an imported colonial boss and the local man with his ear to the ground. 'In the Iryshry,' he complained in 1538, 'the commyn voyce runyth that the [royal] Supremecy of our Soveran Lord is meantenyd only by power, and not reyseoned by lernynge.'[29] Out in Meath, Staples felt early on that religious reform was being mishandled. He thought that instead of trying to inculcate the new religion with terror, the native Irish clergy should be granted safe conduct to come to Dublin and attend disputes on the new learning on the understanding that they could speak freely and return home without hindrance. He found Browne arrogant and coarse.

In the summer of 1538 the dispute between the only two convinced Protestants among the bishops in Ireland blew up into a pulpit war. Browne was sure that Canon Humfrey was a stalking horse for the Bishop of Meath. The dispute began two weeks after Lent, when Staples preached at Humfrey's church and in his sermon told the congregation to beware of the new breed of 'seditious and false preachers' who were reinterpreting Holy Scripture. Browne had no doubt the false preacher referred to was himself, and blasted back from his own pulpit a hundred yards away in the cathedral in a sermon to the Irish Council that vigorously defended the right of preachers to discuss the scriptures. That ought to have been the end to it. But according to Browne, Staples had stayed in communication with Humfrey on new ways to render the Archbishop's position uncomfortable. He had sent the canon an encouraging letter, 'whereof in parte was that the saide Busshop of Mythe wolde prove the Archbusshop of Dublin to be an heretike'. [30]

Staples then publicly attacked the Archbishop. Browne's subsequent report to Cromwell was highly coloured, but there was obviously something in his complaint when he said the Bishop of Meath had 'rayled and raged ayenste me, calling me heretike and begger with other rabulouse revilinges'. [31] Matters reached a climax on Palm Sunday at Kilmainham, when Browne claimed he was in church to hear Staples preach. He was most surprised when after the sermon, Staples dallied in the pulpit, begged the congregation's patience and

therewith ploked out of his bosom a leter the which, though it were not trew, he appertely asseuered to be sent hym from Dublin from a servante of his that harde me preache, comprehending certen poyntes of my sermon invehyed ayenste him. The truthe is Humfrey of St Patrikes wrote the leter signifying unto hym ferr otherwise than I spake. Nevertheles he made them at his pleasure a comment on the saide letter without all honest shame even before my own face, present at his sermon with souche a stomake as I think the three mouthed Cerberous of hell could not have uttered it more viperiously. And all this he dothe . . . to plocke away the credence of the people from me . . . he exorted them all . . . to give no credence unto me whatsoever I saide, for afore God he wolde not. [32]

Was the Archbishop really sitting in the front row at Kilmainham while the Bishop of Meath denounced him to his face? That may have been artistic licence on Browne's part. More likely he heard of the sermon from another source. But it was a bad Easter for the church reform party in Ireland.

While the tiny group of Protestant clergy fought like ferrets in a sack, the split inside the administration widened between Grey on one side and Browne, Alen, Brabazon, Cowley and the Butlers on the other. Cromwell received a stream of letters denouncing the Lord Deputy as a papist and an intriguer with the Kildares. To show their independence of the Lord Deputy, while he was on progress in December 1538 in Galway, Browne, Alen and Brabazon set off on their own tour of the south-east as guests of the Butlers. The Munster tour wound through Kilkenny, Ross, Wexford, Waterford and Clonmel and was an occasion for the church reformers to prove their worth to the King. At New Year 1539 Sir Piers

Butler publicly entertained the party in Kilkenny while Browne hammered away at every opportunity on the Royal Supremacy. At the end of January the bishops of Munster were summoned to a meeting in Clonmel and told to take the oath of loyalty to the Royal Supremacy then and there. Browne used the occasion to advance liturgical reform by disseminating copies of the English versions of the Ave Maria, the Credo, the Pater Noster and the Ten Commandments.[33] He also handed the bishops 10 'articles of faith', which were probably copies of the 10 Articles[34] published in England in 1536, which promoted a distinctly Lutheran interpretation of the major points of Christian doctrine.[34] The Munster bishops listened gravely, nodded, signed, took the English prayers and articles, went home and probably threw them all in the bin. There is no sign that these directives had any effect anywhere. But Archbishop Browne was seen to be about the King's business and the party cheerfully reported their success back to England. At every stop, it appeared, 'my lord of Dublin preached, having a very great audience'. At Clonmel, they added, 'was with us twoo Archebusshops and eight Busshops in whose presence my Lord of Dublin preached in advauncing the Kinges supremacy and thextinquishement of the Busshop of Rome. And his sermon fynyshed, all the said Bisshops, in all thoppen audience, toke the othe mencioned in thActes of Parliament, bothe touching the Kinges Succession and Supremacy befor me, the Kinges Chaunceller.' [35] Alen did not name the bishops and archbishops who took the oath.

The assembly probably included Milo Baron of Ossory, Nicholas Comyn of Waterford,[36] John Coyne of Limerick, Dominick Tirrey, the royal nominee for Cork, and Butler of Cashel. The only other archbishop could have been Christopher Bodkin of Tuam.[37] Alen may have been exaggerating the numbers.

The Archbishop's preaching tour widened the split between Browne and the Lord Deputy. When Browne returned to Dublin in February 1539, weary but triumphant, he discovered that the Lord Deputy had spitefully moved into his palace, forcing him to shift his digs to an out of town manor at Tallaght, where he moaned he was in danger of being murdered.[38] The split between Grey on one side, and Browne, Alen, Brabazon and Cowley on the other, widened in 1539. As the Protestant party gained strength in England, pressure mounted on the Irish administration to attack traditional devotions by dissolving the remaining monasteries and removing shrines and relics. After the test suppression of 13 houses in 1537, Browne, Alen, Brabazon, Cowley and Thomas Cusack received two commissions, on 3 February and 7 April 1539, empowering them to receive the surrender of the rest of the Irish houses. They were told to offer benefices to heads of religious houses who surrendered without a fuss, and to 'apprehend and to punish such as adhere to the usurped authority of the Roman pontiff and contumaciously refuse to make such surrenders'.[39] On 21 May the Lord Deputy again revealed his conservative instincts by sending a plea to Cromwell on behalf of six of the most prestigious houses, a letter which Browne and his allies ostentatiously refused to sign. Grey argued strongly for the preservation of St Mary's abbey and the priory of Holy Trinity in Dublin, for Grace Dieu, in County Dublin, for Connel, in County Kildare, and for the houses at Kells and Jerpoint, in County Kilkenny. The Lord Deputy defended their retention strictly on grounds of public utility, not religion, though that argument hardly concealed his obvious aversion to the whole course of church reform. They were the only good hotels and schools in the country, he said.

> For in those houses commenly and other suchelike, in defaute of comeninnes [common inns] which are not in this land the Kinges Deputie and all other His Graces counsaill and officers, also Irishmen, and others resorting to the Kinges Deputie in their quarters is and hath bene moste commenlie loged at the coasts of the said housez. Also in them yong men and childer, bothe gentilmen childer and other, bothe of man kynde and woman kynde be brought up in vertue, lernyng and in the English tonge and behauior, to the great charges of the said houses.[40]

Other threatened priors wrote in a similar vein. In a climate of such religious uncertainty they also shunned the dangerous whirlpools of theology and clung to safe appeals about the public good. Richard Weston, Prior of St Wolstan's in Kildare, warned that the suppression of his house, lying on the borders of the Pale, would harm the English cause. It 'would be greatly to the decay and hinderance of the common weale, the decrease of certain English order and speech,' he said.[41] The Abbot of St Mary's abbey in Dublin begged for his house to be saved because 'Verilie we are but stewards and purveyours to other men's uses for the Kinge's honour, keping hospitalitie and many pore men scoler and orphans'.[42] Cromwell was deaf to such artful claims, even when the Pale's English character was apparently at stake.

Holy Trinity was spared after an outcry from the city of Dublin, which made a sterling defence of the priory on patriotic grounds. The City Council said the priory was where 'honourable Parliaments and Counsailles ar kepyn, all sermons are made, and where as the congregacions of the said citie, in processions and station daies, and at all other tymes necessarie, assemblith, and at all tymes of the birth of our mooste noble princes and princesses, and othir tymes of victorie and triumphe, processions are made, and Te Deum Laudamus customabilie is songe, to the laude and praise of God, and the honour of the said Princes and Princesses.'[43] But the conversion of the priory into a secular cathedral, and of the prior and canons into a dean and chapter, was not remarkable. Cromwell wanted the support of civic leaders in the assault on the Church and in England and Ireland normally handed abbeys and priories located within city walls to the local councils.

The government's lack of power beyond the Pale meant it was not possible to carry out a general visitation and valuation of all the religious houses in Ireland. No one even knew exactly how many the country possessed. Outside the Pale the government had to rely on those local lords who could be co-opted into suppressing monasteries in their areas. In Kilkenny and Tipperary that was not a problem. The Butlers had already demonstrated their enthusiasm for the reform programme when they entertained Browne and his party in the winter of 1538. But in the south-west, the west and the north, the process of suppression was patchy. As a result, those regions of Ireland that saw the most dynamic expansion of the religious orders under the Observant movement in the late fifteenth and early sixteenth centuries were the least touched by the campaign of suppression. Almost half-way through the reign of Elizabeth I, a 'Rentall of Mounster and Connaught' dated February 1577,[44] lists many Franciscan houses still occupied by friars in the counties of Roscommon, Mayo and Galway. Athenry friary was 'in the tenure of William McKennye and other friers',[45] according to the rental, as were houses at Burrishole, Urlaur, Moyne, Ballinasmall, Ardnaree, Kilkonnelp, Elphin and Rossreilly. Several other houses were still standing and in the hands of various 'priests' who were clearly not Protestant ministers.

The houses that survived longest usually lay in remote regions, far from passing traffic and the prying eyes of English troops and officials. But in 1616 the Franciscan Provincial of Ireland, Donough Mooney, found the Order's house at Kilkonnel, on the road between Athlone and Galway, still inhabited by six friars, in spite of a seemingly perilous position near a main road. 'It is a remarkable fact which must be attributed to the divine power,' he wrote, 'that though the convent of Kilkonnel stands in an exposed position in the open country close to the open thoroughfare along which pass day by day numbers of the English who now occupy Connacht, though detachments of soldiers have often been stationed there and turned it into a fortress in time of war, yet the convent and church remain to this day complete in all their parts, the glass in the windows unbroken, the ceilings uninjured and the paintings in good condition.'[46] At Quin, in County Clare, he found most of the roofs had fallen in but the choir and chapel were still occupied by two or three brothers. Intriguingly, the friary at Ennis, the principal town in County Clare, was also still in use. The building was 'entirely in good repair'[47] thanks to the O'Brien earls of Thomond whose ancestors had founded it. The house had been officially suppressed and converted decades ago into a county court and was even used to lodge visiting English officials. Unofficially, however, the friars remained within. In 1616 one was still there, and was dressed in his habit.[48] The fudge over the friary at Ennis was repeated elsewhere. An easy deceit was to transfer ownership of an abbey or priory to secular hands but leave the religious in day-to-day occupation of the premises.

Before Lord Deputy Sidney built a bridge across the Shannon at Athlone in 1566, there was little road traffic between the eastern and western seaboards. This isolation enabled an English Catholic enclave like Galway to ignore the order to suppress the monasteries for decades. The Observant Franciscan friary on the north side of Galway underwent the same phoney suppression as the house at Ennis. The building was handed over to the town council in the 1540s, but it was still a functioning friary in the 1560s when pious citizens continued to leave legacies to the friars.[49] It was only after the Lord Deputy's visit to Galway in 1567 that religious change reached the town and mass was belatedly suppressed in the collegiate church of St Nicholas. Nevertheless, little else seems to have been done in Galway, because in 1572 the Franciscans held a provincial chapter there without disturbance.[50] By 1617 the old Franciscan friary had been converted into a court for judges on circuit and the friars had moved.[51] It had taken about 70 years for the suppression of monasteries in 1539 to reach the Atlantic coast.

The religious houses in Ulster also seem to have survived until the end of the century, outside County Down. The Carmelite house at Rathmullen, in Donegal, founded by the MacSuibhne family, survived with its furnishings until the 1590s, when the English governor of Connacht, Sir George Bingham, was accused of making off with 24 sets of eucharistic vestments.[52] Religious houses in the south-west, in Kerry, also survived into the second half of Elizabeth's reign. At Muckross, the Observant Franciscan friary seems to have been more or less untouched until English soldiers raided it and killed two of the friars in 1589.[53]

An approximate estimate is that fewer than half the monasteries in Ireland were closed in the reign of Henry VIII. The seventeenth-century historian James Ware thought there had been at least 362.[54] A surviving manuscript in the Public Record Office in London, detailing the extent of monastic possessions in Ireland in 1540–41 lists 172 houses that had been closed and whose possessions had been sold.[55] They give an idea of the reach of the government in Ireland. The houses are all in the counties of Dublin, Meath, Kildare, Carlow, Kilkenny, Tipperary, Wexford, Waterford, Cork and Limerick. According to this list, most houses in the Pale surrendered to the commissioners between May and November 1539 while the other counties and cities followed in 1540 and 1541.

Of the bigger houses, the monastery of the Blessed Virgin at Trim closed on 15 May 1539,[56] which is probably when the 'ydolle of Tryme' that the Lord Deputy revered so much was dismantled. The Crutched friary of St John's, Newtown, Meath, surrendered on 18 July.[57] The Marian shrine at Navan, Meath, surrendered to the commissioners the next day. The famous Cistercian abbey of Mellifont, scene of the dramatic confrontation between Stephen de Lexington and the Irish monks in the 1220s, followed on 23 July. St Thomas Court, outside Newgate, in the western suburbs of Dublin, surrendered on the 25th. St Mary's abbey in Dublin surrendered on 21 October, while Grace Dieu, County Dublin, followed on the 28th. Kells, County Meath, surrendered on 18 November and Kilmainham four days later.

The houses in the Ormond territory of Kilkenny and Tipperary surrendered in 1540 and 1541. Jerpoint was handed over on 18 March 1540. The Carmelite house in Thurles surrendered on 28 March. The Carmelites of Knocktopher and Horetown followed in January 1541, Clonmel at some time in the same year. The Augustinian houses of Tipperary town and Fethard and the Franciscans of Cashel closed at some point in 1541, as did the Cistercians of Hore Abbey and Kilcooley. In spite of the Butler clan's vocal support for the royal campaign of reform in the Church, they shielded the pilgrimage abbey of Holy Cross from the rigours of the suppression. The last pre-Reformation Cistercian abbot, Philip Purcell,[58] was reincarnated as the first provost. It appears there was no move to remove the relic of the True Cross in Elizabeth's reign because in 1600 the Archbishop of Dublin was complaining that the abbey was still being used to consecrate oaths, 'afore that idol whom the Irish nation do more superstitiously reverence than all the other idolatries of Ireland'.[59]

Suppression of the monasteries in the Pale was thorough. The list of 1540–41 details the fate of each building, down to the orchards, pigeon lofts, eel weirs and bells. There was no room for the kind of obfuscation that was going on in the far west and the north. However, even in the eastern counties the business was still bungled by delays and corruption. News of the suppression of the religious houses in England in 1538 reached Ireland months before the surrender in Ireland got under way. In the interval, lands were leased and valuables spirited away. The treasure was appropriated or hidden from the officials, much like the magnificent set of sixteenth-century Flemish mass vestments discovered in Waterford when the old cathedral was knocked down, though they were most likely hidden in the reign of Edward VI.[60] By the time the King's men came to receive the surrender of the religious houses at the front door, the moveable goods had all too often disappeared out the back. At the Carmelite house in Ardee the commissioners noted that everything but the bricks and mortar had vanished before their arrival.[61] Browne had warned Cromwell to hurry the whole business in 1538. He said the monks were continually selling their moveable goods 'and also alienate theire jewelles and other theire templarr ornamentes with setting forthe leases after soache an soarte that I fear the Kinges Grace shall have small commoditie'.[62] The Archbishop was correct. The sale of Irish monastic goods yielded a disappointing sum. The jewels and ornaments of the Irish religious houses, including the shrines of Trim, Navan and Holy Cross, yielded only £326 2s. The goods and chattels of Irish friaries yielded £487 16s. 8½d. while the other monastic houses yielded £1,702. The grand total came to £2,544 1s. 7½d. After the payments of debts, the net gain came to £1,693 19s. 2½d.[63] As Brendan Bradshaw, author of a study of the dissolution of the Irish houses, has remarked, things had gone seriously awry if the famous shrine of Trim yielded only £40 of jewels and Holy Cross £24, when St Swithin's shrine in Winchester yielded £1,333 in silver alone. The commissioners had come too late and were effectively reduced, in Bradshaw's words, to 'rifling the oblations box and confiscating the candles'.[64]

The suppression of 172 houses, some of which came with thousands of acres and hundreds of shops and other properties, caused an explosion on the property market as the biggest sharks, the members of the government, snapped up the juiciest items while the gentry, like minnows, nibbled away at the rest. Once it was clear that all the religious houses were to go, conservative Catholics fought as hard as reformers for the properties. The Lord Deputy had pleaded for six monasteries to survive in May 1539. In October he made off with the best of those six, St Mary's in Dublin.[65] The largest of all the Irish houses came with 5,000 acres and 134 properties in the city. The abbey of St Thomas Court was another glittering prize: it came with 2,197 acres and 67 houses. After Abbot Henry Duffe surrendered the house in July, Brabazon and John Alen fought over the spoils, with Brabazon emerging triumphant.[66] St John's hospital, in Naas, was bought by Thomas Alen.[67] The Dominican friary at Trim went to Sir Thomas Cusack.[68]

The members of the Irish administration got the best prizes, but the land grab was not an exclusive party for government ministers and would-be Protestants. Families like the Dillons, Plunkets, Barnewalls and Stanihursts, all of which within a generation were to become well known for their Catholic sympathies, took part. Archbishop Browne put in a desperate plea to Cromwell for Grace Dieu convent, saying he was homeless after Grey had thrown him out of St Sepulchre's palace. But he lost out to the same Patrick Barnewall who had defended the monasteries in parliament in 1536, and who also took St John's Newtown.[69] The Barnewalls in the next century would be archetypal Counter-Reformation Catholics. Nevertheless, their house at Turvey was built out of the stones of a demolished convent.

The Carmelite house of the White Friars in Dublin went to Nicholas Stanihurst,[70] grandfather of the Elizabethan Catholic apologist Richard Stanihurst. So did the nunnery at Odder. The Dillons and Plunkets helped themselves to the Victorine priory at Newtown and to Kells in Kildare, while in Waterford, the mayor, or recorder, James White, bought the Dominican house.[71] In Tipperary and Kilkenny, various Butlers made off with the lion's share. Cahir priory went to Sir Thomas Butler, Mothell, in County Waterford, to Lady Katherine Butler, while Earl James got – among others – the Carmelite house in Thurles and Kilcooley, Bective and Duiske abbeys, Jerpoint,[72] and most of the lands that belonged to Kells.

There was no opposition from the clergy within the Pale. The houses were too weak and the monks and nuns too steeped in the tradition of obedience to the crown to imagine resistance. There were strong positive inducements in the form of pensions and future jobs. Richard Nangle, Provincial of the Augustinian Observants in Ireland, was offered a bishopric, though it was only little Clonfert, and the powerful Burkes, the future earls of Clanricard, intruded their own candidate instead. The Prior of Holy Trinity, John Lockwood, and the canons slipped off their old habits and emerged without a hitch as the Dean and chapter of Christ Church. The battle with Archbishop Browne over their collection of 'Romish reliques' was now forgotten. Sir John Rawson, last Prior of Kilmainham, continued to sit on the Irish Council after he surrendered his priory, in return for a munificent pension of £500 and the title Viscount of Clontarf.[73]

Most abbots and priors were awarded pensions of between £6 and £40. James Butler, the errant Prior of Inishlounaght, got £10 6s. 8d.[74] Patrick Dongan of

St John's Newtown was awarded £10,[75] Geoffry Dardice of the Blessed Virgin Mary of Trim got £15[76] as did Thomas Wafre of Navan.[77] The women received the worst pay-off: Margaret Sylke, of Odder, County Meath, was awarded only £6[78] and Egidia Wale of Graney just £4.[79] Margaret Harte,[80] of Termonfeckin, near Drogheda, got only 26s. 8d.[81] The other canons, friars and nuns had to shift for themselves with payments of 20 shillings or so.

Writing in the 1860s, the Catholic clerical historian of the diocese of Meath, Father Cogan, delivered his eulogy to the fallen of the monasteries from a distance of more than two centuries.

> When standing amongst graves, tombstones and mouldering walls we reflect on the past, how in years gone by the holy sacrifice was offered with incense and ceremony, how the divine office was chanted there by night and by day and the benedictions of heaven invoked on a sinful world by hearts dedicated to the service of God, when we think of the merry laugh of the young student, the holy aspirations and resolves, the religious ceremonies, the ordinations, the last farewell of generation after generation of young missioners to their alma mater before entering on perilous warfare and the generous and cheerful welcome by which the young aspirant was greeted by the good old monks; when we think of the easy and indulgent landlords, the happy and contented peasantry, the board of hospitality spread at all hours for the indigent and the infirm, for the traveller and the stranger, architecture, painting and the fine arts patronised; when we think on the past and look on the crumbling walls, the ivy clad ruins, the silent graves, the loneliness and solitude and desolation of a once populous and frequented abbey . . . assuredly we will have no great reason to eulogise English rule or feel grateful for the boasted blessings of the so-called Reformation.[82]

Cogan took a rosy view of the Irish monasteries before the Reformation. Most likely, the 'merry laugh' in Inishlounaght in the 1540s came from Abbot Butler's girlfriend, not from keen students or sturdy beggars. But he was right to describe the suppression of the monasteries as a national trauma. The dissolution brought home the reality of those Acts the Irish parliament had passed so casually a few years earlier. Suddenly it became clear that the academic notion of the Royal Supremacy involved drastic changes in religious practices.

The shock was felt more in the English towns than among the Irish. The skyline changed out of all recognition within months as familiar landmarks disappeared. The old buildings were not left to quaintly moulder and gather ivy. As the inventory of monasteries compiled in 1541 shows, a large proportion of the buildings were simply demolished. Those in the countryside had a better chance of survival. Many had a double function as the local parish church, and their chancels were saved for the use of the community. The urban churches often vanished. Towns like Trim were mutilated as the sale and demolition of several friaries left nothing in their place. Drogheda lost a hospital of Crutched Friars of

St John, a Crutched Friary of St Mary de Urso, a Dominican house of Friars Preachers, an Augustinian friary, a Carmelite house, a Franciscan friary and a priory of St Lawrence. That was a lot of change within the space of a single year in 1540, and it was a negative change. The old buildings became the barns,[83] granaries, quarrying yards[84] or the new homes of the rich, not the hospitals or schools of the many.

Henry VIII died in 1547 having moulded the Church in Ireland into the Church of Ireland. Though the far reaches of Kerry, Mayo, Clare and Ulster were beyond his grasping hand, he subdued the rest and enforced compliance to his new role as head of the Irish Church. The raft of Reformation legislation was completed in June 1541 when a parliament in Dublin proclaimed him King of Ireland; the assembly was attended by an unusually large number of bishops and lords, including numerous Irish chiefs and 'degenerate' English lords not usually seen at such gatherings. The recalcitrant Earl of Desmond attended with the reliable Earl of Ormond and 'dyverse other Lordes of Munster . . . all presente at the saide Masse, the moste parte of them in their robes and rode on procession solemply in suche sorte as the like ther of hath not bene sene here of many yers'.[85] The King's new title was announced in parliament on Friday the 18th, passed both houses on Saturday, while on Sunday 'all the Lordes and gentilmen rode to your Chirche of Sent Patrikes wher was songe a solempe Masse by the Archbisshop of Dublin and after the Masse the said Acte proclaymed ther in presens of 2000 parsons and the Te Deum song with grate joy and gladnes to all men'.

Between 1541 and his death in January 1547 the King pursued a policy with the Irish of surrender and re-grant. In return for the Irish chiefs surrendering their lands to the crown they received confirmation of ownership and English titles. It was an attractive package, and in the early 1540s a steady stream of Irish chiefs signed indentures with the crown and headed off to England to receive their titles from the King. By the end of 1541, many of the septs, including the O'Briens of Leinster, the Kavanaghs of Wexford, the O'Donnells of Ulster and even Conn O'Neill, who had not attended the 1541 parliament, had joined the MacWilliam Burkes of Connacht in submitting and receiving back their lands along with English titles. A group of new Irish peerages was created as Ulick MacWilliam Burke was reincarnated as the Earls of Clanricard, Murrough O'Brien became Earl of Thomond,[86] while Conn O'Neill took the earldom of Tyrone.

The policy of 'surrender and re-grant' is often attributed to the skill and emollient tactics of Lord Grey's successor, Sir Anthony St Leger, Lord Deputy until 1548. The little stampede of Irish chiefs to England to collect their new titles brought a clutch of Ulster bishops into Henry's hands. The indentures that the Irish chiefs signed with the Lord Deputy in Ireland before setting off for England included a religious clause requiring them to recognise Henry's role as Supreme Head of the Church.[87] None of the chiefs appears to have made any objection.

The rural bishops followed their chiefs. Cromer of Armagh had submitted back in 1539. Edmund Nugent, Bishop of Kilmore since 1530, submitted in 1540.

Florence Kirwan, papal appointee in 1535 to Clonmacnoise, took the oath of allegiance in September 1541. Eugene McGuinness, papal appointee to Down and Connor in 1539, was confirmed by Henry in his bishopric in September 1541. Aodh O'Cearbhallain, or O'Cervallen, the papal appointee to Clogher, surrendered his bulls to Henry in person when he accompanied O'Neill to London in September 1542.[88] O'Neill's other chaplain on that visit was George Dowdall,[89] a Drogheda man and Rector of Killeavy. His deportment so impressed Henry that he made sure Dowdall became the next Archbishop of Armagh after Cromer died in 1544. The Irish lords expressed no more interest in church reform after they recognised Henry as Supreme Head of the Church than they did before. But their submission was not without effect on church policy. It was significant that when in 1542 Rome sent a small mission to Ireland of the newly founded Jesuit Order, the O'Donnells and O'Neills felt bound to snub them.[90]

Rome appointed more shadow bishops to northern sees. A precedent had been set in 1539, when Wauchop began shadowing Cromer in Armagh. After Dowdall succeeded Cromer in 1544, Wauchop continued as papal archbishop until the latter's death in Paris in 1551. Edmund Nugent of Kilmore had a papal rival in John McBrady from 1540. O'Cervallen of Clogher had a rival in Raymond McMahon from 1546. After Henry appointed Richard O'Ferral to Ardagh in 1541, Rome nominated Patrick MacMahon.

In contrast to the mirror church that Rome set up in Ulster, the papacy appointed no rivals to the royal bishops of the Pale. Browne and Staples faced no competition in Dublin and Meath. Rome seemed nonplussed at the prospect of appointing bishops who had no chance of gaining physical possession of their dioceses. As yet, Rome was no more ready to start a catacomb church in Ireland than it was in England.

Royal policy succeeded where it respected local channels of patronage. The King did not make the mistake of foisting English Protestants on sees beyond the Shannon. When local lords pressed for their clients to be made bishops, their wishes were accommodated. After the see of Clonfert became vacant, Browne clamoured for the appointment of Richard Nangle, former Provincial of the Augustinian Observants in Ireland and a committed Protestant. He duly became the royal candidate. But when Nangle was ejected from his new diocese by Roland Burke, or De Burgo, the candidate and relative of the Burke Earls of Clanricard, who simply threw away Nangle's seal of office,[91] this rough justice was accepted as a *fait accompli*. In England, bishops were expected to preach energetically against the papacy, pilgrimages, the religious orders and 'superstition'. In Ireland, acceptance of the Royal Supremacy meant just that. The conformity Henry successfully imposed did not include any doctrinal price tag. The oath that the bishops had to take obliged them 'to utterlie renounce, refuse, relinquishe and forsake the bushope of Rome and his unjustlie pretended auctoritie power and jurisdiccion'.[92] It did not require them to agree with Luther.[93] Archbishops Bodkin of Tuam, Butler of Cashel, Cromer and Dowdall of Armagh did not promote evangelical teaching. On the contrary, Dowdall, Henry's personal choice, emerged as a most formidable defender of Catholic orthodoxy in the reign of Edward VI.

While Henry lived, Hibernica Ecclesia remained the Church of the entire land. It still bound the English inhabitants of the 'civil towns' and the Irish who lived outside them in one heaving framework. The process of duplication and creating rival hierarchies competing for the loyalty of the people had hardly begun. The testing time would come in the next reign, when the attempt was made to go beyond the demolition of monasteries and the signing of indentures to the construction of a truly Protestant society.

CHAPTER FOUR

The Kings Most Godlie Procedings

Go to, go to, your matters of religion will marr all.'
(Lord Deputy St Leger to Archbishop Browne)[1]

The city of Kilkenny is perhaps more anchored to its past than any other in Ireland. In no other city is it so easy to imagine oneself back in the Ireland of the Old English under the Tudors or the Stuarts. From Dublin, the visitor sweeps into the city across the Nore and confronts the battlements of the castle, home of the Butlers until 1967. From Kilkenny castle it is a short walk past the rows of merchants' houses in the high street to the other great citadel of authority in the city, the massive, squat cathedral of St Canice. So many Irish cathedrals have fallen into ruin, been demolished, like Holy Trinity in Waterford or St Fin Barre in Cork, or been restored beyond recognition, like Christ Church in Dublin and St Patrick's in Armagh. But St Canice is still visibly a church built by the Anglo-Norman conquerors in the twelfth and thirteenth centuries. The slabs and effigies of the Butler lords, Piers Butler among them,[2] lie scattered in the sepulchral gloom of the interior; the men dressed in knight's armour and the women, hands clasped together, shrouded in long cloaks and the archaic horned head-dresses of the colonial Irish aristocracy.

Kilkenny lay at the centre of a web of Butler towns whose nodal points were Roscrea, Fethard, Nenagh, Thurles and Carrick. Many of these towns preserve portions of ancient castles. Lying on fertile agricultural land by the banks of the Nore and the Suir, these settlements grew wealthy on the export of wool and hides to Waterford; the goods then were transported to England and Europe, from where wines and other luxuries were imported. A bastion of English culture, even at the height of the Gaelic resurgence in Ireland in the fourteenth and fifteenth centuries, the city remained English in language and loyalty and resistant to the Gaelic culture to the south and the west. Here, if anywhere, the English Reformation might have expected a hearty welcome.

The ecclesiastical reformers could rely on the support of the most powerful local family. As the hereditary rivals of the Geraldines of Kildare, the Butlers allied themselves naturally with the Kildare clan's great enemy, Thomas Cromwell. They embraced the Royal Supremacy from the start. It was Sir Piers Butler who had put on a show of great hospitality for Archbishop Browne when he toured the southern counties in the winter of 1538, preaching on the Supremacy. After Sir Piers died the following year, his son and heir, James, became a pronounced supporter of the Royal Supremacy and Protestant church reform.

James Butler died in 1546. His heir Thomas, the famous 'Black Tom', attracted Elizabeth I with his virile good looks, and obviously many others, for he littered the Ormond country with bastard children before his death in 1614. He did not share his father's convinced Protestantism but he was not a recusant, even if he shielded many who were. In short, the lords and patrons of Kilkenny throughout the sixteenth century were men who favoured royal policy in Church as in state.

Yet the 'second Pale' rejected the Reformation. Its first Protestant bishop, John Bale, was in office for less than a year before the death of Edward VI. The succession of the Catholic Queen, Mary, terminated the evangelical experiment. But the episcopate of Bale in Ossory was a template of the popular reaction to Protestantism in the other 'English' walled towns. It was expected that these oases of English speech and loyalty would be the channels through which the new religion might flow into the rest of Ireland. Instead, the English towns became not channels but dams, blocking the progress of Protestantism. Nationalist historians would later obfuscate this point, stressing the role of Gaelic Irish society in resisting Protestantism. In fact, it was the most English elements in Ireland – in political terms the Loyalists of their time – who played the crucial role in rejecting Protestantism. And it was the English of the walled towns who brought the Counter-Reformation to Ireland. At the time, the native Irish were far less decided in their opinions.

Bishop Bale's arrival in Kilkenny marks the time when Protestantism was seriously introduced into Ireland. After the campaign against monasteries and images in the 1530s, the 1540s had been a period of relative quiet in Ireland. Archbishop Browne did not stir out of Dublin. We glimpse him presiding at the great ceremonies marking Henry's proclamation as King of Ireland. By then he was married and had started a family. Lord Grey's successor as Lord Deputy, Sir Anthony St Leger, was a moderate man by temperament and less prone to quarrel with his colleagues than his ill-fated predecessor.

While the Irish Reformation halted in its tracks in the 1540s, in England it hurried on, in spite of the fall of Cromwell and the passage of the conservative Six Articles in 1539. The eclipse of Bishop Gardiner and arrest of the Duke of Norfolk shortly before Henry's death in January 1547 removed the two most important conservatives from the scene and left the reformers in pole position to command events after the King's death. As it was, the succession of Edward VI enabled them to attack freely what remained of traditional worship.

The uncle of the new nine-year-old King, the Duke of Somerset, known as the Protector, moved in concert with Archbishop Cranmer to alter the mass and introduce a new liturgy which was in English, not Latin, and which expressed Protestant theology. A set of ecclesiastical injunctions that Somerset released in

August 1547 paved the way for serious change, ordering the removal of remaining images and even lighted candles, saving two on the altar. They also ordered the reading of the Gospel and Epistle in English.

In March 1548 England lurched further in the direction of continental Protestantism when a new Order of Communion was published that inserted English translations of the exhortation, the confession and the blessing into the liturgy, while parliament permitted communion to be taken in both kinds. The Chantries Act of December 1547 was just as important a move. Chantries were where priests said mass for the dead. Their existence was an expression in bricks and mortar of the Catholic doctrine of purgatory. The suppression of chantries was a sign that Edwardine England was moving into the camp of advanced Protestant countries. The Order of Communion was clearly a holding operation. Even while it was being introduced a team of bishops was working under Cranmer to draw up an entirely new liturgy. That was complete by Christmas and on 21 January 1549 parliament passed the Act of Uniformity, enjoining the compulsory use of the new Book of Common Prayer, by Whit Sunday, 9 June. England had broken with the mass and apart from a brief interval under Mary and an even briefer one under James II it would not be said in public for centuries.

The conservative bishops were expelled and their places taken by supporters of root and branch reform. Gardiner of Winchester and Edmund Bonner of London were jailed for public opposition to the changes. Nicholas Heath of Worcester, George Day of Chichester and Cuthbert Tunstall of Durham were deprived of their sees. London went to Nicholas Ridley and Gloucester to an ultra-radical, Nicholas Hooper. The new men held religious opinions well to the left of Luther. They did not believe in the Real Presence of the body and blood of Christ in the Eucharist, but, like the Swiss reformer, Ulrich Zwingli, looked on the service as a memorial. Also, like the Swiss reformers, they were iconoclasts who fiercely rejected Luther's tolerant attitude towards visual aids in worship. In England, unlike Germany or Sweden, vestments, statues and pictures were now fit only for destruction. It was of enormous importance for the course of the English Reformation that its chief supporters were disciples of the radical theology emerging from the Swiss and south German towns. And it was of equal importance for Ireland.

The alteration of the English episcopate was so rapid and drastic that by the time the 1549 Book of Common Prayer had arrived, it already seemed old-fashioned and was subjected to criticism by the advanced continental reformers to whom Cranmer deferred. It was more Lutheran than Zwinglian, and even before it was out, Cranmer was at work on purging the book of traces of popery and producing a more radical Book of Common Prayer, released in 1552.

While Anglicana Ecclesia tilted rapidly in a Protestant direction, Hibernica Ecclesia remained much where it was. In the west, nothing changed at all. In the east, the monasteries had been dissolved and the Dublin cathedrals purged of statues and relics. The Royal Supremacy functioned throughout the island.

Bishops were selected without reference to the Pope and without seeking bulls from Rome. But the Supremacy was only a cold, juridical fact in Ireland: it evoked no warm feeling of loyalty and carried no doctrinal baggage. In the primatial see of Armagh, although Dowdall was the King's archbishop and a schismatic in the eyes of Rome, he was an orthodox Catholic in every other respect.

In 1547 the period of limbo came to an end. Suddenly, it became difficult for men like Primate Dowdall to find their way. Only a few months into the new reign, the peaceable and conservative Lord Deputy St Leger was withdrawn. His replacement in the summer of 1548, Sir Edward Bellingham, was a convinced Protestant, the prototype of the kind of man who would become known as the 'New English' – different from the Old English not only in the length of time they had spent in Ireland, but in their religious beliefs.

Bellingham began his term of office with an aggressive military tour of the Ormond territories. His arrival alerted Archbishop Browne to the need to be seen to be promoting religious reform once again. After Cranmer began to circulate the Order for Communion in the spring of 1548, Browne dispatched copies of a similar Book of Reformation to his own suffragan bishops in November. The spurt of energy on Browne's part did not convince everyone, after at least seven years of doing nothing. An anonymous document of November 1548 charged the Archbishop with gross neglect,[3] which suggests that a powerful member of the new administration did not think much of Ireland's Cranmer.

Browne got nowhere with his brother of Armagh. In spite of the pressure of the Lord Deputy and of Browne, Dowdall refused to introduce any liturgical changes into the north. The distance of Ulster from the Pale forced a measure of caution on the authorities and in December 1548 Lord Deputy Bellingham did no more than appeal for the Archbishop to show discretion in his opposition to the government's religious policy. 'I pray you Lovyngly and charytably to be circumspect in yor doings', he wrote, passing a reluctant tribute to the Primate's 'reputacyon amongst the pepoll whyche requirythe a great consyderacyon at all thymes'.[4] The confusion in Ireland was heightened when Bellingham was abruptly withdrawn in December 1549 and replaced with St Leger again. To Archbishop Browne of Dublin it was highly vexing. One moment he was being charged with neglect. He had then swung into action, distributing his Book of Reformation and locking horns with the Archbishop of Armagh. Now the ground had shifted from under his feet as an old Lord Deputy returned and put the programme of church reform on hold.

Browne resorted to his usual methods of sending poisonous letters to London denouncing his colleagues. In St Leger's case, he claimed he had spotted the papist in him as soon as he unpacked for his second tour of duty in September 1550 and headed for the cathedral. Civic ceremonies informed the people which way the wind was blowing in religion. Browne must have recalled with irritation how Lord Grey had ostentatiously heard masses at the Marian shrine in Trim when Browne had been engaged in a campaign to have such images removed. Ten years on, another Lord Deputy was making a show of himself in front of the people with a display of old Catholic ceremonies, including the custom of offering a piece of gold at the high altar of Christ Church cathedral. 'Upon his last arrival in authority [he] went to the chief church of this realm Christs Church in Dublin,' the Archbishop told the Earl of Warwick, 'and there, after the old sort, offered to the altar, then of stone, to the comfort of his too many like papists and the discouragement of the professors of God's word.'[5]

St Leger, the Archbishop claimed, lay behind the resistance of the Irish bishops to Reformation. He had winked at Primate Dowdall's flagrant use of abolished ceremonies and 'neither sent for any of the offenders nor yet caused punishment nor redress to be executed in this behalf'. He had lent the Archbishop of Dublin a package of books which Browne found to be 'poisoned to maintayne the Mass with Transubstantiacion and other naughtiness . . . clean contrarie the sincere meanings of the worde of God and the Kings most godlie procedings'.[6] Browne, so he assured Warwick, had manfully defended the King's rights against the treacherous Lord Deputy. 'I said to his Lordship the King could not be taken in good part to be totally proclaimed and the deeds so apparent contrary unpunished. At time the said deputy said to me and others: "go to, go to, your matters of religion will marr all."'[7]

It is curious that the Lord Deputy should have shown Browne his secret and very contraband collection of theological books. He can hardly have imagined that Browne would wink at the contents. One is left with the impression that Browne was a man people loved to tease and that his habit, as Henry VIII put it, of 'comparing himself unto a prince' made colleagues long to deflate him. Did Lord Grey really need to move into the Archbishop's palace of St Sepulchre when Browne was away on his great preaching tour in Munster, or did the old soldier cackle at the thought of seeing the expression on Browne's face when he returned to find his furniture in the street? Perhaps St Leger showed Browne his indiscreet literature for the same reason.

The Lord Deputy may have had a private collection of 'poisonous' books for night time reading, but St Leger was a civil servant by day, and a very cool headed one, which explains why he survived several terms in the dangerous hot seat of Ireland. His commission from the King and Council before he arrived on his second term of office in Dublin included an order to 'set forth God's word in English'. Whatever his private thoughts on the matter, he proceeded with plans to introduce the first Book of Common Prayer into Ireland. At Easter 1551, the new English liturgy was performed in Christ Church when the mayor and aldermen of Dublin attended the first service, which Archbishop Browne conducted.

Evidence of use of the Book of Common Prayer outside the capital is patchy. It was obviously a useless liturgy in the vast majority of parishes where the population spoke only Irish. The lack of provision for an Irish liturgy was typical of the way the Reformation was imposed on the country, almost as an afterthought that took no heed of different conditions. The programme underlined the extent to which the authorities imagined that Reformation and Anglicisation would converge. The talk of 'Gods word' obscures how little interest there was in making Irish people Protestants if it did not involve turning them into Englishmen and women at the same time.

The new liturgy was confined to the Pale and some of the towns. We know it was used in Waterford, because John Bale saw it performed there in January 1553,[8] almost certainly in the cathedral. It seems to have been used in Limerick. It was not used in Galway, where the mass remained in use until the mid-1560s. The Book of Common Prayer may not have penetrated into County Meath, even though the diocesan was Edward Staples, a convinced Protestant. Bishop Staples's problem was that he had no cathedral to act as an example for the diocese. Meath was unusual in that it had no ecclesiastical centre. The diocese was composed of small market towns where the English element was in decline. Meath's rural and Irish-speaking population did not take to the changes coming out of Dublin. At the end of 1548 Staples told the Lord Deputy the local people were boycotting his services and that he feared for his life.[9] He said the women refused to let him confirm their children because he was a heretic. Already an all-important alliance between Catholicism and women in Ireland was emerging.

The new liturgy was not used in Armagh diocese. Much of it was Irish-speaking territory but it included the Pale towns of Dundalk and Drogheda. In spite of the fact that the new liturgy was supposed to come into general use, Archbishop Dowdall refused to act. Browne said Dowdall blatantly maintained all the old forbidden rituals and that 'the same notwithstanding, the massing, holy water Christmas candles and such like continued under the Primate'.[10] Browne was certain that it was the Lord Deputy's visible dislike of Protestantism that encouraged Primate Dowdall to keep up the mass. As was so often the case, the steady drip of Browne's malicious whispering had an effect. A month after the new English liturgy was first performed in Dublin, St Leger was recalled and a more robust Protestant sent over. Sir James Crofts's arrival sapped Dowdall's will to resist. In October, the authorities humiliated him by stripping him of his status as Primate of All Ireland and bestowing it on Browne. In England, the imprisonment of the Catholic bishops for opposing religious change hinted at what might befall him. The ex-Primate sniffed the wind and left Ireland for exile on the Continent.

Under Crofts, the business of appointing English Protestants to augment Browne and Staples began in earnest. Now Dowdall was out of the country, Hugh Goodacre was nominated for Armagh, although he never got there, dying shortly after his arrival in Ireland. The other key vacancy was in the south: it was the see of Ossory. This now went to Bale. A Suffolk man, John Bale was born in 1495. Educated at Cambridge, he was a near contemporary of Cranmer's. He emerged from his studies unaffected by the ideas being passed around by the Protestant clique at the White Horse tavern in Cambridge. Clearly, not everyone at Cambridge in the 1520s left the university a Lutheran. As the Carmelite Prior of Maldon and then of Ipswich, Bale showed no enthusiasm for Protestant theology.

It was only in the mid-1530s, through his contact with a local landowner, that he underwent a dramatic change of heart. Bale's was a Pauline conversion. Overnight the conservative monk and enthusiastic chronicler of saints and miracles metamorphosed into a Protestant zealot. Resigning from his Order, he took up parish ministry as Rector of Thorndon, in Suffolk, where he gained a reputation as a fanatic, so much so that his advanced views earned him a brief spell in jail in 1537.

Bale did not linger there. In the topsy-turvy environment of the 1530s, a jail sentence one day could be followed by a bishopric the next. Cromwell soon spotted the potential worth of such a militant opponent of the papacy, and the enthusiastic chronicler of the Carmelite Order now devoted his talents to the service of the reformers, staging an anti-papal play before the King and court at Canterbury in September 1538.[11] But the next few years were hard for men with Bale's convictions. The fiasco over the King's marriage to the Lutheran Anne of Cleves ended in the disgrace and execution of Cromwell, the reformers' great patron. The passage of the Six Articles then reaffirmed orthodox Catholic teaching on transubstantiation and silenced the most exteme preachers. Cranmer stayed in Canterbury but the most radical bishops resigned their sees. Bale fled abroad to Basle where at least he could continue to write.

By the time Edward ascended the throne in 1547 and it was safe to return to England, Bale was in his early fifties. He was an old man by sixteenth-century standards and more than a little embittered by the way his services to the Protestant cause had gone unnoticed. But in August 1552, when Edward had been on the throne for five years, he finally succeeded in gaining a brief interview with the King at Southampton, a few miles from Bale's parish at Bishopstoke. Bale remembered bitterly the way he had been shunted aside. 'It had bene tolde hym a lytle afore that I was bothe dead and buried,' he grumbled.[12]

As Bale was approaching 60, his frustration was understandable. But what was to be done with a man whose advanced years and uncertain temper rendered him unsuitable for promotion in the Church of England? One can see the idea forming in royal councillors' heads while they stifled their yawns as the old man rambled on about his sufferings. A bishopric, yes, but not at home. Ireland, the perfect dumping ground! Bale's nomination to Ossory followed within days. He left Bishopstoke in December and took ship from Bristol to Waterford on 21 January 1553.

Bale was locked into one controversy after another from the moment he set foot on Irish soil. He had more than a few arguments in Waterford. He had some more in Dublin with Browne, whom he loathed from the first. And that was nothing in comparison to the conflict he stirred up in Kilkenny.

The disappointment started in Waterford. On his arrival, Bale found that the town's old Henrician bishop, Nicholas Comyn, had introduced the second Book of Common Prayer into his diocese, but that the theology it contained had sunk somewhere in the Irish Sea. The 1552 liturgy had purged itself of any remaining recollections of the old mass and anything that suggested the Catholic notion of a sacrifice offered to the living and the dead. But in Waterford Bale found the congregation struggling with the new service while attempting to recreate the old ceremony and doctrine of the mass. The communion service, Bale recalled, 'was there used altogyther lyke a Popysh masse with the old apysh toyes of Antichrist in bowynges and beckynges, knelinges and knockinges'.[13]

Bale's merciless, shrill tone sheds light on why so much went wrong with the English Reformation in Ireland. It was not simply that it was English. It was the way that English clerical leaders like Bale assumed the only way to achieve progress was to advance like a steamroller over all opposition. A more discerning pastor would have seen the pathos of a community battling to make sense of the unfamiliar. But Bale was absolutely characteristic of English Protestant imports to Ireland under Edward VI and Elizabeth I. At Dublin, he insisted on the new English standards being applied at his consecration. There was another clash. In England, the new liturgy in 1552 had been accompanied by a new ordination service. Out went the old symbols of priestly sacrifice and Catholic episcopacy, the chalices, patens and croziers. But in Ireland, nothing had been done about the new ordinal. As a result there was furious quarrel in Dublin before Bale's ordination service between the new Bishop of Ossory, Dean Lockwood of Christ Church and Browne. The Bishop-elect insisted on being consecrated under a reformed rite; the Dean and Archbishop demanded adherence to the law. Bale got his way at the cathedral owing to the support of one of the more convinced Protestants on the Council, the Lord Chancellor, Sir Thomas Cusack. But the affray was just the beginning of his troubles. Browne, never a man to leave a score unsettled, got his revenge later that year.

In Kilkenny, Bale found the clergy of the 'second Pale' united in their determination to resist the imposition of any religious change beyond the Royal Supremacy. At least in Waterford they had used the new service book. In Kilkenny, Bale's clergy would not touch the new service. Bale blamed Browne for failing to enforce it outside his own cathedrals, claiming that Browne's example had encouraged the Kilkenny clergy to snub his orders, 'allegynge for their vayne and ydle excuse the lewde example of the Archebysshop of Dublyne, whych was always slacke in thynges perteyninge to Gods glorie'.[14]

The clergy of the Ossory diocese brazened it out, probably because a reasonable guess suggested the regime of Edward VI might not have the last word in religion. Why should it, when they had already observed several changes in direction? Bale blamed Browne for his failure in Kilkenny; Browne blamed Dowdall of Armagh for his problems in Dublin. Again, the cause of the Irish Reformation was undermined by the almost hopeless divisions in the ranks of the reformers.

The Edwardian Reformation in Kilkenny never extended beyond the precincts of the cathedral. There Bale had his way, suppressing services on the saints' days and keeping a stern eye on clergy offering up 'whyte goddes of their makinge'[15] for worship, as he called the host. Even in the cathedral he made powerful enemies. He thought Sir Richard Rothe, the cathedral treasurer and member of one of the most powerful local Old English families, wanted to kill him. He was probably right.

The death of Edward VI revealed how little progress Protestantism had made in this most loyal, English and 'civil' of Irish towns. The King died on 6 July 1553. Two weeks of confusion followed while Somerset's successor as Protector, the Duke of Northumberland, marshalled his supporters behind the Protestant candidate, Jane Grey. It was not until 20 July that the English Council wrote to their Irish counterparts instructing them to proclaim Catholic Mary, not Protestant Jane, as Queen.

Significantly, before this news even reached Kilkenny, the citizens treated Edward's death as a cause for celebration. There were scenes of almost hysterical rejoicing over the death of the boy King upon whom the fate of the English and Irish Protestant project depended. Bale recorded the proceedings in vivid colour in his short autobiography, *The Vocacyon of John Bale to the Bishoprick of Ossorie*. He described how his clergy descended 'by heapes from taverne to taverne'[16] the moment they heard Edward was dead. Between the King's death and Mary's belated proclamation in Kilkenny on 20 August, Bale was in a cold war with his diocese. After the new Queen's proclamation, Kilkenny reverted to Catholicism spontaneously, without waiting for permission from their bishop or from the Irish parliament. When Bale processed to Kilkenny's market cross to preach an accession sermon for the new Queen, his clergy humiliated him by processing in front of him with the hated papal symbols of mitre and crozier. The old grump went down fighting. At the market cross he preached on Paul's epistle to the Romans, taking as his text: 'I am not afraid of the Gospel'. It was Bishop Bale's last hurrah.

At the end of August 1553 Kilkenny took to the streets to celebrate the restoration of Catholic worship. Bale detested what he saw but the old journalist in him was too professional not to do some justice to the mood he witnessed. 'They ronge all the belles in the cathedral minstre and parish churches, they flonge up their cappes to the battlement of the great temple with smylinges and laughinges most dissolutely,' he wrote. 'They brought fourth their coupes, candelstickes, holy waterstockes, crosse and sensers. They musterd fourth in generall procession most gorgiously all the towne over with Sancta Maria, Ore Pro Nobis and all the rest of the Latine Letanie. They chatred it, they chaunted it with great noyse and devocion. They banketted all the daie after to that they were delivered from the grace of God into a warme sonne.'[17]

The great street party marked the end of the stand-off between Kilkenny and the Bishop. Since Edward's death Bale had retreated to his manor at Holmes Court, trusting in the goodwill of the mayor, Robert Shea, for his physical protection. But now the Catholic reaction had begun, a settling of scores could not be postponed. Bale was already convinced his enemies were plotting to have him assassinated. After several of his servants were murdered in the fields, while working on one of the saints' days Bale had tried to stamp out, the Bishop determined to quit. Escorted back to Kilkenny under an armed guard of the mayor,

Bale left shortly after for Dublin. There, he was promptly forbidden from preaching by the Archbishop. Browne must have relished the opportunity to snub his fierce critic, though by then he would have been anxious for his own future under the daughter of Catherine of Aragon.

Might Bishop Bale have built up a party of convinced Protestants in Kilkenny in time, enough to hibernate during the brief interlude of Mary and spread forth under Elizabeth? He was the Ian Paisley of his day, a man with a certain bizarre charisma. Not everyone hated him, for on his return from Holmes Court to Kilkenny he remembered the comforting sight of 'yonge men syngynge psalmes and other godly songes all the waye in rejoyce of my deliveraunce'.[18] But what happened to those young men singing psalms? They appear to have grown into middle-aged men who sang responses to the mass instead. By the time Kilkenny got another convinced Protestant as bishop in Hugh Walshe in the 1570s, when Bale's 'yonge men' would have been in their forties, there was no sign they had ever existed.

The restoration of Catholicism was celebrated with such vigour in Kilkenny because it was one of the few towns in Edwardian Ireland that had had a real taste of what Protestant worship was like. Elsewhere there was less excitement because so little had changed. It might have been thought that a Catholic bastion like Ireland would have loomed large in the calculations of Queen Mary. It was not so. Like all the Tudor monarchs, Mary spent her life in London and the eastern counties. She made no attempt to visit those parts of her kingdoms, the north and west of England and Ireland, where her presence might have galvanised an overwhelmingly Catholic population.

In Ireland she was concerned only to see justice done to Dowdall and to restore the title of Primate of All Ireland to Armagh. He was restored with honour to his see in March 1554.[19] She saved St Patrick's cathedral, which had been threatened with dissolution in the closing months of Edward's reign; Mary promptly reversed the order.[20] Yet the business of reconciling the Irish kingdom to Rome was subjected to insulting delays. The Earl of Sussex did not summon a parliament in Ireland until 1 June 1557. While England was reconciled to Rome and absolved from schism on 30 November 1554, Ireland had to wait another two and a half years before Pope Paul IV's bull absolving Ireland from schism was received by Archbishop Curwin in the Irish parliament 'and read upon his knees in open parliament deliberately and distinctly in an high voice'.[21]

Sussex's commission from the Queen ordered him 'to advance the honour of God and the Catholic faith, to set forth the honour and dignity of the Pope's holiness and See Apostolic from Rome and from time to time to be ready with their aid and secular force at the request of all spiritual ministers and ordinaries there to punish and repress all heretics and Lollards and their damnable sects opinions and errors.'[22]

It was an unnecessarily terrifying order. There was little need to prosecute heretics in Ireland as there were so few. In London and the south-east of England there was popular resistance to the Catholic restoration, which showed itself in outbursts of iconoclasm and attacks on religious processions. In Ireland no heretics were burned and nothing disturbed the return of Catholic worship.

There were only two bishops to get rid of. It was the end of the road for Browne and his old rival, Staples of Meath. Enemies throughout their careers, they were condemned together. Browne had risen from nowhere to an archbishopric by attacking the Queen's beloved mother. He was also married. But there was no question of Browne or Staples following Cranmer, Latimer and Ridley to the stake.[23] Even their expulsion from office was a leisurely affair. In November 1553, six months into the new reign, the two men were still receiving orders to consecrate new bishops.[24] The Archbishop of Dublin was expelled from office the following year for breaking his vow of celibacy. He was never accused of heresy and eked out the rest of his life, presumably without Mrs Browne, as a canon of St Patrick's. Ever the pliant Tudor bureaucrat, he survived even this latest change – just.

Mary's Archbishop of Canterbury was her ailing, pious cousin, Reginald Pole. Her man in Ireland was a weary cynic, Hugh Curwin. Pole at least had a certain personal holiness, a quality no one even dreamed of attributing to Curwin. But for very different reasons neither was the man to inject Counter-Reformation fire into the belly of their churches. Both men relied on Henrician veterans to restore Catholic worship, old men who knew the ropes but who had changed their minds so often they no longer knew what they ought to believe. The new Archbishop of Dublin was an odd choice of Mary's, as his stock had risen – like Browne's – owing to his support for Henry's divorce and the Royal Supremacy.[25] Curwin was no more wedded to Mary's brand of Catholicism than Browne had been to Edwardine Protestantism. He died in 1567, a year after leaving Dublin, as Elizabeth's first Protestant Bishop of Oxford. William Walsh was one of the few more imaginative appointments.[26] Unlike Curwin, the new Bishop of Meath was the harbinger of a type of Catholic bishop who would vigorously uphold the Roman obedience.

The new Queen was ill, prematurely old and cannot be blamed for failing to anticipate the devotional revolution unveiled at the Council of Trent. It was only under her half-sister that the Council's decrees would filter back to Ireland. The Queen's face was turned resolutely towards the past. She had lived in virtual seclusion for the six years of her half-brother's reign. Her instincts were to restore the world she had known in her youth, before her parents' hideous, protracted divorce, before she was exiled from the splendour of court to live in dark, dank houses with her vanquished, embittered mother. She made no move in either of her kingdoms to revitalise the Church by encouraging the establishment of seminaries, or diocesan synods. There was no more attempt in Ireland than there was in England to revive the monasteries. In Ireland they had never closed in the north and west, but the gentry of the eastern counties remained firmly in possession of the lands they had gained under Henry VIII. In England, the only monastic revivals were at Westminster Abbey, Syon and Greenwich. In Ireland, Kilmainham was restored as a priory. That was all.

Mary's death on 17 November 1558 marks a watershed in English religious history. Several of her bishops died within weeks of her own passing, including Archbishop Pole. The cull of clerics meant Elizabeth I confronted a weakened bench of only 10 bishops when the first parliament of the new reign met on 25 January 1559 to reintroduce a modified version of the Edwardine liturgy and the Acts of Uniformity and Supremacy. Catholics in England paid dearly for Mary's penchant for appointing as bishops elderly friends of her mother.

Among the surviving English bishops, resistance to another religious revolution was almost total. Only two Marian bishops acknowledged the reintroduced Royal Supremacy and the Book of Common Prayer, the insignificant bishops of Llandaff in Wales and the Isle of Man. Just one, Owen Oglethorpe of Carlisle, could be induced to crown Elizabeth as Queen. The display of collective stubbornness was not evidence of the new spirit of the Counter-Reformation coursing through the veins of the English hierarchy. It was old age and weariness. Tunstall of Durham and Heath of York were simply beyond publicly renouncing once more what they had just upheld. The refusal of the English bishops to conform suited Elizabeth well enough. It enabled the new government to deprive them of their sees and install a set of men who were totally committed to the Queen, the Royal Supremacy and the restored Book of Common Prayer. The Swiss theology and Puritan leanings of several of them were not to the Queen's taste but that, for the moment, was a minor problem.

Mary's death and Elizabeth's accession had far less impact on the Irish Church. In England the Act of Supremacy made it compulsory for all 'ecclesiastical persons' to take the Oath of Supremacy, which declared Elizabeth 'the only supreme governor of this realm . . . as well in all spiritual or ecclesiastical things or causes as temporal'. The oath was not pressed on parish clergy, many of whom retained their benefices, but it was certainly pressed on bishops and deans. No bishop in England of conservative instincts could have survived long in the altered religious climate. Even convinced but moderate Protestants like Matthew Parker,[27] the Queen's first Archbishop of Canterbury, felt highly uncomfortable in a Church dominated by radical bishops.

The coercive clauses in the Acts of Supremacy and Uniformity in 1559 laid the foundations for a raft of penal legislation that would make life increasingly dangerous for English Catholics as the reign went on. Parliaments in 1571 and 1581 massively increased the penalties for dissent, imposing a swingeing £20 a month fine for absentees from church, and the death sentence for actively withdrawing the Queen's subjects from her obedience. A total of 123 priests and more than 60 lay people went to their deaths during the 43 years of Elizabeth's reign for 'withdrawing' subjects from their obedience and harbouring those who did. It was half the number burned under Mary's brief reign, but it was enough to frighten most traditionalists into swallowing their principles and taking the Protestant communion.

There was no corresponding pressure on the Catholic clergy or laity in Ireland. This was not altogether surprising when it is recalled that for the first few years of the reign, the two main instruments of government, Curwin and Sussex, were the same two men who had laboriously supervised the reintroduction of Catholicism two and half years previously. But even when very different men occupied Dublin Castle and the see of Dublin, there was no attempt to recreate England's penal legislation. Only the most senior office holders in the country were expected to take the Oath of Supremacy. The passage of Reformation legislation in Elizabeth's Ireland was trouble free. Elizabeth's first Irish parliament assembled under Sussex's authority in January 1560, a year after the English parliament opened at Westminster. There were fewer delays in importing the Reformation than there had been in 1536–37. After the opening session on 12 January, business was concluded by the first of the following month. The first Act restored the Royal Supremacy. The second restored the old Act of Uniformity, and included a minor concession to local feeling in permitting the use of the liturgy in Latin. The clergy's first fruits and twentieths again were annexed to the crown. It was a revealing little provision, highlighting the new regime's basic lack of interest in the success of Protestantism in Ireland. A preaching church in Ireland needed every penny it could get.

The Irish bishops put up less opposition to the reintroduction of these laws than had their English counterparts the previous year. They must have noted that the most determined of their English colleagues, like Tunstall, Heath and Bonner of London, were now languishing in prison.[28] The parliament of 1560 were essentially an assembly of the Pale.[29] Most of the writs went out to boroughs and shires in Leinster. There is no record of which of the 30 or so Irish bishops were present, although most would have made an effort to be in Dublin for such an important occasion at the start of a new reign.

Their voting record has not survived. But three days after parliament closed the authorities summoned three bishops, Bodkin of Tuam, Walsh of Meath and Thomas Leverous of Kildare, to take the Oath of Supremacy.[30] It is clear they had caught the eye of the Lord Deputy as active opponents of the legislation. Bodkin backed down and took the oath, so the number of active dissidents among the Irish bishops can be reduced to only two. David Wolfe confirmed the figure. He travelled round the country and spoke to several bishops who had taken the oath, such as Bodkin and in a letter on the state of the Irish Church in the 1570s described the Irish hierarchy as 'hirelings'[31] with the exception of Walsh, Leverous, the former Dean of St Patrick's and Richard Creagh,[32] the new papal-appointed Archbishop of Armagh.

What caused such a failure of will in Ireland? Writing in the 1630s, David Rothe, Catholic Bishop of Ossory, decided that the laws must have been passed when the Catholics were absent from the chamber at their devotions and that the Lord Deputy and the speaker, James Stanihurst, had perpetrated the trick. 'The statutes were laid before the parliament covertly and bit by bit, through the extreme skill and worldly wisdom of the governor, to whom the sly or rather the ambitious speaker sang second and pandered,'[33] he claimed. Rothe was writing in a sterner religious climate, when fudging a matter like the Royal Supremacy seemed incomprehensible. The theory was designed to salve his conscience about the behaviour of his predecessors. But it is most unlikely that the Lord Deputy would have tried to pass crucial legislation when the chamber was virtually empty, while the fact that three bishops were summoned to account for their behaviour in parliament strongly suggests the Acts were passed in a straightforward manner.

Walsh and Leverous were deprived of their sees. Their Protestant successors, Thomas Craike and Hugh Brady,[34] did not enjoy successful careers. The rest of the bishops were left in place and the reintroduction of the Book of Common Prayer was patchy. In Dublin, where there was no escape, the ever-compliant Archbishop Curwin had the cathedrals whitewashed, and removed the images he himself had so recently restored to their old places. But in the west of Ireland, no convinced Protestant bishops were appointed until the second half of Elizabeth's reign. Hugh Lacey, a Marian Catholic, remained in position in Limerick until 1571, when he was deprived. Limerick was an important see and a major port, but his replacement, William Casey, held much the same conservative views.

In the smaller sees of Connacht the government displayed even less interest in altering the religious complexion of the bishops. Those two ancient Henrician relics, Bodkin of Tuam and Roland Burke, or De Burgo of Clonfert, hung on for decades. Both men were appointed in the 1530s and died in undisturbed possession of their sees, in 1572 and 1580. Neither made the slightest effort to wean their flocks off Catholicism.

In the north, the Queen and a succession of Lord Deputies turned a blind eye to the old religious order. Elizabeth did not even attempt to exercise the Royal Supremacy in Ulster by appointing bishops to the sees of Derry, Kilmore or Clogher. In the east, Down and Connor remained under Eugene Magennis, a man of no known religious convictions who probably attended the 1560 parliament and took the Oath of Supremacy. There was no attempt until 1562 to fill Armagh, vacant since Dowdall's death in August 1558. Even then it seemed possible that the archbishopric might be offered to the Dean, a native Irishman and the representative of the old Gaelic order. In the end Armagh went to Adam Loftus, an ambitious young Englishman whose principal commendation in the eyes of Elizabeth was his good looks. He may have been good looking at 28 when he got Armagh, but he turned out to be a greedy bigot and a dubious ornament to the Protestant Church. For more than 40 years, until his death in 1605, Loftus exercised a baneful influence over his adopted country as Archbishop of Armagh and then Dublin. Nevertheless, the appointment of Loftus was not a sign that the Queen had suddenly resolved to fill the Irish bench with hard-line Protestants. Men of ambivalent religious convictions continued to rise in Elizabeth's Irish Church.

The papacy made no systematic attempt to fill Irish sees with Catholic candidates either. In 1563, Rome appointed Creagh as Primate in Armagh, but no

Catholic archbishop or bishop was appointed to any Pale diocese during Elizabeth's lifetime. There were few appointments outside Ulster and Connacht. Rome was still unwilling to appoint bishops to sees when they had no prospect of gaining physical possession of their dioceses. Armagh was a special case. Loftus probably never even visited his cathedral town; he remained safe in the southern periphery of his diocese at Termonfeckin inside the Pale.

Ten years into Elizabeth's reign, Ireland was not yet a land with two separate Churches, duplicating, mirroring and competing with each other. The great silent withdrawal of the people, both the native Irish and the Old English, from parish worship was yet to come. As in England, men with conservative religious convictions continued to attend the churches and cathedrals for the first decade of the new reign.

They may have attended infrequently and behaved irreverently. The northern Catholic students who misbehaved during the singing of the British National Anthem on graduation day in Queen's University Belfast in the 1970s had their antecedents in the Dubliners of the 1560s, who, according to the Earl of Sussex, attended the new liturgy as if it were a game.[35]

The parish churches and cathedrals were staffed with the same clergy after 1560 as before. The changeover from Catholic priest to Protestant minister was slow and did not gather pace until the foundation of Trinity College in the 1590s. Until then the Church of Ireland had no seminary and the cause of reform depended on a handful of preaching ministers. The bulk of the clergy, where it used the new service, probably used it like the clergy Bishop Bale had observed in Waterford in 1553.

By 1565 there were Protestant bishops who acknowledged Elizabeth's supremacy in position in Dublin, Kildare, Meath and Armagh. In Limerick, Cork, Ferns, Tuam and Clonfert the bishops acknowledged the Royal Supremacy but were traditionalists in doctrine. Papal-appointed bishops enjoyed the run of most of Ulster and Connacht, in Killaloe, Kilfenora, Achonry and Derry.

The Elizabethan Church of Ireland was the Wild West of the Anglican Communion in every sense. It was a dangerous borderland that attracted adventurers, scoundrels and violent thugs – men who could not possibly have found employment as pastors in a controlled environment. The worst of the clerical cowboys was Miler Magrath, the flamboyant but scandalous Archbishop of Cashel who terrorised several dioceses and charmed Elizabeth for decades, dying aged over 100 in 1625. First appointed by the Pope to Down and Connor in 1565, he switched to the Queen's Church when he sought her appointment to Clogher and then Cashel. Magrath was a double agent. As a native Irishman he was a useful spy to a government which was increasingly alienated from the general population. Magrath was about as far from the image of a preaching bishop as could be imagined. He was little better than a gangster who galloped round his diocese wearing armour,[36]surrounded by outriders and preceded by a man carrying a skull on a tall pole. Sincere Protestants detested this bastard child of the Reformation, but to Elizabeth, his services as a listening post in the strategic border region of Cashel rendered him invaluable. As a result, the authorities overlooked the way he enriched his clan. They also overlooked the fact that he had his own children baptised as Catholics.[37]

Men like Magrath inhabited a twilight world between the native Irish and the New English. Such men were not unusual in the first half of Elizabeth's reign. But by the time he died in 1622, having alienated most of the assets of Cashel, as well as the dioceses of Waterford, Lismore and Emly, he was an anachronism and an embarrassment. In a Church that was now self-consciously Protestant, and rather more fastidious about its chief officers than it had been under Elizabeth, he represented a fast-diminishing type of ecclesiastical trimmer.

Most Irish people simply ceased to attend church in the early 1570s. The Pope's belated decision to end the cold war with Elizabeth by excommunicating the Queen drew a line in the sand. The papal bull *Regnans in Excelsis* did more than place Elizabeth beyond the pale of salvation. It dethroned her and released her subjects in England and Ireland from the obedience owed to a prince. The bull dealt a fatal blow to the hopes of 'Church papists' who wanted to attend the occasional Protestant service out of loyalty to the state. They were forced to decide. The vast majority of the Old English community in Ireland decided for the Pope. The vast majority of the people in England decided for the Queen. Like oil and vinegar, the Protestant Church of Ireland and the Catholic Church in Ireland began to separate. The fight for the soul of Ireland had begun, and so had the era of martrydoms.

CHAPTER FIVE

The Devil's Service

*The people of Munster are Spanish in heart, papist in religion
and most infinitely discontented*
(Sir Peter Carew, 1595)[1]

In the summer of 1569, the little world of the gentry families of the Pale was
enlivened by a distinguished visitor. The guest in the Stanihursts' Dublin home
was an Oxford graduate, Edmund Campion,[2] a youngish man whose exceptional
talents had already brought him to the attention of the Queen. Physically
imposing, tall, well-built, Campion later sported a thick beard. His host was
an old university friend Richard Stanihurst, a former student at University College while Campion attended St John's. Like him, he was a keen Greek
scholar.

The two men resumed their friendship in Ireland with some intensity, for
Campion was to spend seven months with the Stanihursts, from August that year
until the end of March 1570. He spent part of the time writing a tract on that
favourite humanist theme, the ideal student, *De homine academico*. But there were
also weeks spent with Richard, poring over the books in the Stanihurst library as
he worked on a history of Ireland, intended to be dedicated to that great patron
of the Puritans, the Earl of Leicester. Unfinished at the end of Campion's stay, but
completed by his friend, the text appeared under Stanihurst's name as the Irish
section of Holinshed's *Chronicles of England, Scotland and Ireland* of 1577.

There must have been a good deal of social activity alongside the hours spent
among the books in the Stanihurst library, and especially with the Barnewalls of
Turvey. Richard had a particular interest there, for within a few years Sir
Christopher's daughter, Janet, was to become his first wife. The Barnewalls liked
and esteemed Campion: when he finally left the Stanihurst household in a hurry
it was to spend his last weeks in Ireland at the Barnewalls' home at Turvey, about
10 miles from Dublin.

The discussions between Campion and his new friends were not about their
student days. Campion was deeply troubled by the widening chasm between
England and Catholic Europe. So were his hosts. As autumn turned into winter
and walks in fields gave way to discussions around the fire, everyone's mind was

drawn to the sudden outbreak of rebellion in northern England and the Pope's excommunication of the Queen.

In the north, the feudal earls of Westmorland and Northumberland rose against the crown's centralising policies and the new religion. In Durham cathedral the rebels tore up the Protestant service books and mass was said at the high altar. The government crushed this last desperate revolt of the old order. But then the Pope unleashed his bull. For a decade, Rome had bowed to Spanish pressure and refrained from firing thunderbolts against the heretical Queen. Locked into struggle for supremacy with France, Philip II of Spain wanted no immediate conflict with his dead wife's half-sister – yet. The papacy had sat quiet and done nothing to bolster the English Catholics, but as news of the revolt reached Rome, Pius V shrugged off Spain's concerns and damned the Queen anyway. *Regnans in Excelsis*, published in February 1570 and impertinently nailed to the front door of the Bishop of London's palace, outraged Protestant opinion in England. When parliament assembled that year MPs clamoured for harsher penalties against the Catholics and their priests.

In the worsening struggle between the supporters of the Queen and those of the Pope, Campion found his conscience pulling him inexorably towards the latter and it was in Ireland that he decided to jump. His embryonic history of Ireland had been dedicated in fulsome terms to the Earl of Leicester, the Queen's favourite and the patron of the Puritans. Campion was already in Anglican orders, though only as deacon.

Campion finally chose Counter-Reformation over Reformation in the home of a family distinguished for generations of service to the crown and intimately connected to the first phase of the Irish Reformation. Richard Stanihurst's great-grandfather, Richard, had been mayor of Dublin in 1489.[3] His grandfather, Nicholas, had been clerk to the 1541 parliament, which proclaimed Henry VIII King of Ireland. Grandfather Nicholas had not scrupled to get his share of the dissolved monasteries, buying the Carmelite house of the White Friars and obtaining a lease of the lands of the nunnery at Odder. He had been mayor of Dublin in 1543. James Stanihurst, Richard's father, had been the Speaker of the 1560 parliament, which reintroduced the Acts of Supremacy and Uniformity and put down the mass. Other old Pale families might have 'degenerated' into mixed or confused loyalties, but the Stanihursts and the Barnewalls had lived and died serving the crown and the English interest. If Elizabeth could depend on anyone in Ireland to act as her loyal lieutenants it was such families as these.

But the Stanihursts and the Barnewalls had turned. They had built new homes out of the bricks and mortar of the dissolved monasteries and had championed the Royal Supremacy. But by the 1570s, they were disappointed and felt cheated. 'Reformation' had not brought about the ordered, humanist society they expected. The sale of the monasteries had not resulted in the establishment of new schools or a university. Greater interference by England had not created a society in which 'civility' was recognised and rewarded. It had brought English carpet-baggers who took the jobs that once went to Pale families and destructive changes in religion almost no one in Ireland had sought. The alteration of the Church had become the focus of discontent with England's Irish policy. As the Church took on a more visibly Protestant character, the Stanihursts and Barnewalls instinctively sympathised with the resistance of the northern English earls. It was not a national protest and was not anti-English. They saw themselves, as Richard Stanihurst did for most of his life, as members of an anglophone Catholic community.

Campion clearly knew the Stanihursts shared his views, for in a letter of thanks to James Stanihurst from the Barnewalls' home he referred revealingly to the danger he had been in from 'the heretics of Dublin'.⁴ The casual use of such a phrase told much. Perhaps Campion had resolved their doubts, too, before departing for the Continent and eventual martyrdom.

When Campion left the Stanihurst household at the end of March or early in April he knew the 'heretics' were watching him. He was damned by his own fame, after impressing the Queen and Leicester with his orations on the royal visit to Oxford in 1566. Before leaving for Ireland, he had engaged himself as tutor in the household of a notoriously Catholic peer, Lord Vaux. He was known to be closely linked to several men who had joined the exodus of English dons and students to the Catholic universities of France and the Netherlands. Among them was Gregory Martin, a former tutor to the crypto-Catholic Duke of Norfolk and now ensconced at the new English seminary at Douai. He had written to Campion from Douai, urging him to jump ship and in 1577 Campion recalled the effect that letter had had on him. 'I remember how earnestly you called me from Ireland to Douay, and how effective were your words,' he wrote.⁵

After Campion had stayed for seven months with the Stanihursts the authorities in Dublin were keen to interview him. It was then, possibly tipped off by the Lord Deputy, Sir Henry Sidney, that he decamped to the Barnewall home at Turvey. He remained there for a few weeks in seclusion, closeted in the library. By the time he was spirited out of Drogheda to England in June 1571, Campion had decided his future course. Within months of leaving Ireland he had broken with the England of Elizabeth and joined his friends at Douai.

The secession from the Church of Ireland that began in 1570 split the tight little world of the Pale gentry. They were almost all related to one another. While Richard Stanihurst married Janet Barnewall, his sister, Margaret married Arland Ussher, a member of the even smaller world of Dublin Protestants. Her son, James, would become the Protestant Archbishop of Armagh under Charles I and the greatest apologist the reformed Church in Ireland possessed.

Archbishop Ussher's uncle, Richard, did not follow the well-trodden Stanihurst path into government. Instead, he withdrew from contact with Protestantism by entering the service of the disgraced family of the Earl of Kildare, as a mere tutor. It was the common ruse for many English Catholics, lay or clerical. A 'tutor' in a great family could enjoy a gentleman's lifestyle without coming near the Oath of

Supremacy. Within a decade Stanihurst was living abroad. He ended his career a pensioner of Spain, as chaplain to the Habsburg Archduke and Archduchess of the Netherlands. The lives of the Kildares, the Barnewalls, the Stanihursts and the Usshers were interwoven. Through Campion, the fate of the Old English was linked to that of the Catholics of England.

But there was a big difference. Campion represented an end and not a beginning in England. The Catholic England of 1570 encompassed much of the north and west, the Midlands, and pockets in the south, like Sussex. At the beginning of Elizabeth's reign her ecclesiastical commissioners reported that 'a greate parte of the sheres of Stafford and Derbye are genrally evill enclyned towardes religion and forbear comying to church'.[6] A report by the English bishops to the Privy Council in 1564 on the religious feeling among the Justices of the Peace, said that a majority opposed the new religion in the dioceses of Carlisle, Chester, Chichester, Exeter and Hereford, as well as many in York, Worcester, Coventry and Peterborough.[7]

But if England was half-Catholic at the start of her reign it was not half-Catholic at the end. By the 1590s the last Marian priests had died and their places had been taken by committed Protestants. An increasing percentage of the clergy were university graduates who were able to argue the case for the reformed Church.

Campion and his fellow seminarians were hunted down and killed off by a ruthlessly effective policy of containment. Campion went to his death at Tyburn in December 1581. The laity were worn down by a mixture of jail terms and horrendous fines for non-attendance at church, which, at £20 a month, could bankrupt even the wealthiest gentlemen in a short time. As one historian of Elizabethan Catholicism has put it: 'During the last 19 years of Elizabeth's reign the Roman church dwindled to a leaderless and powerless minority.'[8]

In Ireland the current ran in the opposite direction. The slow death of English Catholicism eroded the centuries-old links between England and the Old English of Ireland. The Stanihursts made the same decision as the majority of Old English families in Dublin, the Pale and in the walled towns. Parents who had conformed yielded their place to children who were resolutely Catholic. In collective disobedience they found a certain safety.

Why the Catholics in England dwindled, while the Old English Catholics held firm, is not a mystery. The law in England was entirely in the hands of the Protestants and was used with increasing ferocity as the reign went on. At first the Acts of Supremacy and Uniformity had ordered the Oath of Supremacy to be tendered only to 'ecclesiastical persons', university graduates and members of parliament. In the 1560s it was increasingly tendered to Justices of the Peace. The strict penalties to be inflicted on Catholics did not gather dust on the statute books. Ecclesiastical commissions with wide powers were established to summon and imprison dissenters. They reached into the furthest corners of the realm. Nowhere was the result of this policy more obvious than in the north of England, a Catholic bastion well into the second decade of the reign. The Ecclesiastical Commission based in York, under Edmund Grindal, Archbishop of York from 1570 to 1576 and the Earl of Huntingdon, president of the Council of the North, broke the back of the gentry's resistance to the reformed Church over the decade by ruthlessly pursuing, interrogating and punishing Catholic traditionalists.[9]

The Church of Ireland had no such sturdy pillars to rest on. The Oath of Supremacy was never forced on Irish members of parliament and as a result, the Elizabethan parliaments of 1560, 1569 and 1586 had a Catholic majority in both houses. It is not surprising that they declined to adopt any of the English parliament's anti-Catholic laws. So Irish local government remained in Catholic hands. Judges, lawyers, mayors, aldermen and schoolteachers, even in Dublin, did not take the Oath of Supremacy. There was no attempt to force people into their parish churches. The law imposed no fines for attending mass, or for saying it. The assault on Catholicism depended on hunts for papal-appointed bishops, who could be accused of treason. Ecclesiastical commissions periodically sprang to life in Dublin under Archbishop Loftus; as in England, these could summon, fine, jail and even torture suspects. But such an arbitrary, violent and inconsistent system failed entirely to halt the exodus of the Old English community from the cathedrals and parish churches that they had raised up and embellished over many generations.

The precise date when people stopped attending services in the state church varied from city to city. Fynes Moryson thought the publication and dissemination of *Regnans in Excelsis* the decisive moment. 'Generally all the Papists in Ireland (as allso in England) came ordinarily to the church service of the Protestants till about the yeare 1572,' he wrote. But after the publication of the papal bull, 'it was more easy . . . to bring a Beare to the stake than any one of them to our Churches'.[10] Dublin, the Pale and the walled towns defected first. In Galway, the withdrawal from public worship in the parish churches was slower and did not take place until the turn of the century. Most communities muddled along as 'church papists', attending the Protestant liturgy in the parish church and then mass at home, until the influx of continental-educated seminary priests persuaded them otherwise.

A letter from an English Protestant schoolteacher in Waterford in 1585 describes a city that was obviously several years into a near-total boycott of the official Church. John Shearman's letter to Archbishop Long of Armagh was accusatory. Long had not told the Englishman the real state of affairs in Waterford when he persuaded him to take the job. Shearman said the mayor of Waterford had pulled the wool over the Protestant Archbishop's eyes. Few marriages now took place in the Protestant parish churches, and no christenings or burials. There were remnants of an earlier phase of 'church papistry', in that the people were occasionally induced to attend the odd service. But they behaved with such calculated irreverence that it was an insult to the minister and sheer torture for the minority of Protestant believers seated up in the chancel.

'When they come there they walk around like mill horses, shopping and changing and talking merchandise and in such a manner that they who are in the choir and willing to hear, through their babbling, cannot hear a word,' he said.[11] Most of Shearman's pupils had left his school because he was a Protestant, and had decamped to a papist school. He complained: 'Even the mayor himself of whom you made such great account hath dealt but strangely with me.'

Life in Waterford for his few remaining Protestant pupils, including his landlord's boy, was a grim diet of ostracism. 'They called a son of Peter Strange's where I stop, turncoat, traitor and Protestant because he used to go to the English service,' he said. 'These speeches and far worse are in their children but if your honour did but dwell amongst the parents, to see their villainy in Massing at home and murmuring at God's word in the church, I know you could not abide it.' Shearman was like a character in an old horror movie. The fresh-faced English graduate arrives in town to find that behind the façade of normality, something sinister is going on. Behind walls and through keyholes he can hear the whispering and murmuring of forbidden services. But when he goes to the mayor, who is outwardly a conformist, he behaves 'strangely'. The scene can be imagined. The young man earnest and angry, demanding action; the mayor vague, shifting his gaze, professing total ignorance of what is going on under his nose. And this was in Waterford, a city which prided itself on its loyalty to the crown.

The disastrous state of the reformed Church in Waterford could be ascribed to the abortive activity of a latter-day Bishop Bale. Marmaduke Middleton, the city's first Elizabethan bishop from 1579 to 1582, was a confrontational Protestant who had the city's much-loved statue of St Dominick burned at the town cross in 1578 'amidst the great lamenting of the people'.[12]

Middleton's ministry was a fiasco. The City Council brought charges against him for sacrilege, which the Protestant Lord Deputy naturally threw out, but he was moved out of harm's way to St David's in his native Wales in 1582. His replacement was the appalling Miler Magrath, Archbishop of Cashel, a man of no known religious opinions who embezzled property in all the dioceses and livings he held.

By the end of the century, the cathedral James Rice had loved, worshipped in and embellished, was deserted. William Lyon, Bishop of Cork, complained in 1596 that the city had rejected the reformed religion in its entirety. 'The mayor of Waterford, which is a great lawyer, one Wadding, carrieth the sword and rod for Her Majesty,' he said, 'but he nor his sherrifs never came to the church sithence he was mayor . . . nor none of the citizens, men nor women.'[13] The people of Cork withdrew from the established church services around 1594, according to the Bishop. Cork had a better pastor than Waterford in the shape of Bishop Lyon, which may explain why the citizens appear to have attended reformed services several years after the people of Waterford had stopped. However, even Lyon's flock deserted him in the end. 'The young merchants,' he wrote in July 1596, 'going to their masses with their daggers and pistols ready prepared . . . generally are mighty drawn away from their loyalty to Her Majesty's godly laws now within these two years so far, that where I had a thousand or more in church at sermon, I now have not five, and whereas I have seen 500 communicants or more, now there are not three and not one woman either at divine service or at communion.'[14] He went on: 'The best name that they give unto the Divine service appointed by Her Majesty in the Church of England and Ireland is the devil's service and the professors thereof devils and when they meet one of the profession they will cross themselves after the Popish manner and any that accompany us or receive any living of me or the like being appointed by Her Majesty, they excommunicate him.'

The defection of the children in Cork was complete. To his 'great grief' Bishop Lyon found that all references to the Queen's Supremacy had been torn out of the primers in the local school. Like Shearman, Bishop Lyon was aware that the local authorities discreetly supported the Catholics. He knew of at least 10 Catholic clergy in the city 'and when I am out of town they walk openly and commonly in the streets accompanied with the aldermen'.

Kilkenny had demonstrated its conservative Catholic instincts under Bishop Bale's regime. As in Waterford, the people of Kilkenny appear to have boycotted Church of Ireland services in the 1570s. The Bishop of Ossory, Nicholas Walsh, told the Privy Council in 1578 that he was completely isolated in his diocese. 'Not only the chiefest men of that town (as for the most part they are bent to popery) refused obstinately to come to the church and that they could by no means be brought to hear divine service there with their wives and families,' he said, 'but that almost all the churches or chapels or chancels within that his diocese were utterly ruined and decayed and that neither the parishioners nor others that were bound to repair them and set them up could by any means be won or induced so to do.'[15] The Bishop's dolorous career ended abruptly with his murder in 1585.

Reports of church attendance in Limerick in the 1570s are scarce. But David Wolfe, the papal legate, provided a brief description of the city's religious complexion. Wolfe was a Limerick man, and very proud of his home town. He was precise about the relative strength of the denominations in an account from 1574. The city of some 5,000, he said, was 'Catholic all save for seven or eight young men who embrace the Lutheran heresy more to please the Lady Elizabeth than for any other reason'.[16]

Seven or eight Protestants? If these accounts from Cork, Kilkenny, Limerick and Waterford are correct, the Reformation had ground to a halt in those English towns where it might have been expected to find a foothold. Unless the reports are wide of the mark, the number of Protestants in the four cities towards the end of Elizabeth's reign could be comfortably seated in one small chapel. It makes a total of about 20 or 25 Protestants out of a population of perhaps half a million.[17] The Old English had totally rejected Protestantism.

The Dublin government had more influence in the Pale. But here, too, the Protestant Church was ailing. Meath possessed a dynamic Catholic bishop in

William Walsh, who was deprived for refusing the Royal Supremacy in 1560 but remained at liberty until his arrest in 1565. His Protestant successor, Hugh Brady, like William Lyon, was a local man and might have been expected to enjoy local credit. Instead, the diocese decayed so badly that the Lord Deputy, Sir Henry Sidney, wrote to the Queen in 1576 citing Meath as an awful example of what had gone wrong with the Reformation in Ireland.

Of 224 parochial livings, Sidney said, 165 had been leased out, with

> no parson or vicar resident upon any of them and a very simple or sorry curate for the most part appointed to serve them, among which number of curates only 18 were found to be able to speak English, the rest Irish priests or rather Irish rogues . . . in many places the very walls of the churches down, the chancells uncovered, windows or doors ruined or spoiled . . . if this be the state of the churche in the best peopled diocese and best governed country of this your realm, as in truth it is, easy it is for Your Majesty to conjecture in what state the rest is.[18]

Sidney's pen sketch of a diocese in crisis touched on the Church of Ireland's desperate economic plight. Before the Henrician Reformation, two-thirds of the livings in Meath had been in the gift of the monasteries. But when the religious houses were dissolved, the laymen who bought or leased the abbeys also got their hands on the livings of the churches. In England a large percentage of livings also fell into the hands of laymen. But those laymen in England were usually Protestant. In fact, the problem of the Anglican bishops was that they were often Puritans, bent on setting up a parallel Church within the official structure. But whatever they thought of stained-glass windows, even Puritans wanted a roof over their head when they went to divine service. Parish churches in Elizabethan England did not simply fall down.

In Ireland, the percentage of livings in the hands of the religious houses was larger than in England, rising to 80 per cent in Connacht. But the 'farmers' of livings cited by Sidney in Meath included very few Protestants, and although they collected the tithes, they made no attempt to supply the churches with clergy or repair the roofs. The Church in Ireland found itself caught in a trap. Conscientious bishops struggled to repair the material fabric of dioceses over which they had little control. There were proposals for the crown to confiscate all the livings and start again. But these plans never got beyond the drawing board. Elizabeth was unwilling to confront the Irish gentry head on with such an incendiary proposal.

Dublin was a special case. Here the Lord Deputy could at least ensure a degree of outward conformity. There was more money available and the livings in the gift of the city's two cathedrals were sufficient to enable Archbishop Loftus to plant Protestant ministers in key parishes. But Loftus was able to harry the Dubliners to church only through a series of ecclesiastical commissions that were licensed to fine, jail and even torture suspects. And these commissions were temporary. The authorities in London or Dublin were unwilling to maintain such unpopular coercive machines permanently. When they lapsed, conformity collapsed. When Lord Burghley asked Loftus in 1590 to account for the poor state of church attendance in Dublin, the Archbishop could only fall back on the old policy of blaming the Lord Deputy. 'This general recusancy is of but six years continuance at the most,' he complained, 'and began in the second year of Sir John Perrot's government.'[19] Loftus claimed the Catholicism of the townsmen would inevitably create a climate of political disloyalty. 'It is to be feared (if some speedy remedy be not provided) upon pretence of religion they will shake off all obedience,' he said.

This was a questionable calumny. The Elizabethan towns in Ireland were not disloyal to the crown. They had shunned the revolt of the Kildares in 1535. They had also shunned the next great aristocratic rebellion, under Garret Fitzgerald, which erupted in November 1579.

The Earl of Desmond's semi-independent palatinate had long been earmarked for destruction. His huge territory, which he inherited in 1558, encompassed 800,000 acres spread over the three counties of Kerry, Cork and Waterford and stretched from the Dingle peninsula to the River Blackwater. The Desmonds resembled that other doomed, aristocratic family, the Percy Earls of Northumberland. Like the Percies, they were old-fashioned feudal lords and old-fashioned Catholics in religion. They bitterly resented attempts by central government to encroach on their rights by intruding judges, sheriffs or reformed preachers into their lands. Descended from Anglo-Norman stock, the Desmonds had long since 'degenerated'. They were Gaelic in lifestyle, so much so that when the Earl escaped from Dublin Castle in 1573 it was said he slipped off his English dress as soon as he reached Desmond territory. Whereas their Butler neighbours and rivals attached themselves to every project of the Dublin government, the Geraldines sat apart. When it came, the revolt was no surprise. The Queen had expected it since 1574 at least and had regularly written to Desmond's wife, the Countess Eleanor, urging her to keep her husband on side.

The Earl's cousin, James Fitzmaurice, precipitated the final cataclysm. In April 1575 he left Ireland for Spain, where he made contact with Nicholas Sanders, an exiled English Catholic controversialist. Sanders, theology professor at Louvain University, was a militant Catholic, convinced that only foreign invasion could restore the faith to his English homeland. That meant supporting Spain. For men like Sanders, Ireland was not an end but the means. The expulsion of Elizabeth's government from Ireland was just the first stage. Sanders filled Fitzmaurice with talk of a Desmond kingdom in Munster and the help their crusade might attract from Rome and Philip II.

The plotters were disappointed in all their grand schemes. 'Unarmed, without a fleet and without men,'[20] Fitzmaurice complained, the little invasion force did not sail from Galicia until 27 June 1579, landing at Smerwick, near Dingle, on 18 July. The invading armada consisted of six craft, reported the Attorney for Munster,

James Goldie, who added that two friars and a bishop in mitre and with crozier,[21] probably Donnchadh O'Gallagher of Killala,[22] preceded Fitzmaurice off the boat. This small band of men triggered events that were to plunge southern Ireland into a disastrous three-year war. By the end, there were 30,000 dead, mostly victims of famine. The other great casualty was the 300-year-old Desmond earldom.

The Earl was probably not behind the Fitzmaurice invasion as he had earlier handed his son and heir over to the Dublin government as a hostage for his own good behaviour. But he was carried away by events. His two brothers, John and James, joined the revolt within a fortnight, and at an inn in Tralee John murdered two government agents, Arthur Carter and Henry Davells, the Constable of Dungarvan castle. The Constable had been sent into Desmond country with articles to present to the Earl, demanding he account for his suspected disloyalty.

The original invasion was now almost a sideshow. Within a month of its landing Fitzmaurice had been killed, near Limerick, in a squalid dispute over cattle rustling. The government's real foe now was the Earl's brother, Sir John Desmond. Sir William Drury, now President of Munster,[23] ordered the Earl to join him in hunting down his brother and the Earl at first co-operated, rounding up the recently returned Bishop of Mayo, Patrick O'Healy and handing him over to the authorities, who executed him in August.[24] But Drury died suddenly and the Earl declined to offer the same co-operation to his temporary substitute, the President of Connacht, Nicholas Malbie, whom he accused of desecrating the Desmond family tombs at Askeaton, near Limerick.

As the Earl withdrew his support from the government, the revolt spread. The new acting Lord Deputy, Lord Justice Pelham, panicked. He intemperately ordered the Earl to appear before him immediately or hand over Dr Sanders, whom he believed was hiding in the Earl's entourage. Pelham received what he considered an evasive answer and rushed to proclaim Desmond a traitor on 2 November 1579. A long war began. Elizabeth was furious with Pelham for committing her to such an expensive conflict but by now the stakes were too high for the crown to back down.

A horrifying description of the ensuing slaughter and famine in Munster has come down from Edmund Spenser, who arrived in the entourage of the next Lord Deputy, Arthur Lord Grey of Wilton, in 1580. Desmond and the Earl of Ormond, Elizabeth's commander in Munster from January 1580, both pursued scorched earth policies, seizing cattle and burning corn and castles. By the summer of 1580, famine stalked the south. 'Out of every corner of the woods and glens they came creeping forth upon their hands,' Spenser wrote, 'for their legs could not bear them. They looked anatomies of death, they spake like ghosts crying out of their graves . . . the very carcasses they spared not to scrape out of their graves and if they found a plot of water cress or shamrocks, there they flocked as to a feast.'[25]

With the help of Dr Sanders, who died in Ireland in 1581, Desmond presented the revolt as a Catholic crusade against a heretical government. It was a war 'in defence of our Catholicke faithe and the overthrowe of my contrie againste Englishemen which had overthrown the Holy Churche'.[26] Yet the Catholic towns held aloof. Later generations would mourn the fate of the Earl of Desmond, a semi-regal figure, pursued to his death like a wounded stag. To later generations, the story of the Earl's murder on 11 November 1583 by Owen Moriarty and Daniel O'Kelly was so wrenching and bathed in pathos that it summed up the whole horror of their country's subjection to alien rule. But it would be some time before the people of Cork or Limerick would sing laments about the bloodstained spot on the ground where Desmond was slain, or curse Moriarty and O'Kelly as 'The two base felon hearts / That planned that deed of blood'.[27]

To the embarrassment of later generations of nationalists, the Gaelic chroniclers of the *Four Annals* also took a decidedly unromantic view of the Desmonds. The Catholic and crypto-Catholic officials Shearman and Lyon encountered in Cork and Waterford combined religious loyalty to Rome with political loyalty to Ireland's Protestant Queen. It was an uncomfortable arrangement but not an impossible one. Catholicism did not propel the Old English townsmen into the arms of the Desmonds, whom they saw as emblems of an overmighty feudal order they could well do without. The world of the Desmonds was the world of coign and livery, forced exaction, private armies and turf wars that left villages burnt, churches desecrated and trade in ruins. The townsmen groaned at the expense of quartering thousands of the Queen's soldiers while the campaign dragged on,[28] but that was a different issue. The foot soldiers of the revolt were the Desmonds' feudal retainers. Their supporters were not urban merchants but the kind of 'degenerate' country lords Sir Henry Sidney had met on his visit to the south-west in 1576.

In the summer of 1580 the revolt spread to Leinster, when James Eustace, Viscount Baltinglass, joined the uprising. The Viscount took his stand equally on the abominable government of the Queen's 'New English' officials and their religious policy. It was a scandal, he told the Earl of Ormond, 'that a woman, uncapax of all holy orders, should be the Supreme governor of Christ's church, a thing that Christ did not grant unto his own mother.'[29] When it came to the listing of indicted rebels, only a handful of merchants in Dublin and Cork were accused of aiding the Desmonds. The bulk of the Old English of the towns were not disloyal – yet.

Nevertheless, Archbishop Loftus was right to detect a trend, even if he failed to see that it was his policy of persecution that was driving the Old English and native Irish together. Elizabethan Ireland was still one land with two nations. But by the end of reign, a common allegiance to Catholicism had awakened the idea among some Old English intellectuals that it was the 'wild Irish' who held the key to the restoration of true religion in the country. Suspicion would bedevil relations between them until the end of the seventeenth century. But in the last and most serious revolt against Elizabeth's rule, which began in the 1590s, there were distinct signs that a common hatred of Protestantism was forging a new constellation of political forces in Ireland, indeed, a new nationalism.

There was startling evidence of the decline in loyalty to the crown in 1588, after the failure of the Spanish Armada. The invasion force was the most serious threat to England's independence since the Battle of Hastings and in England even the persecuted Catholic community clamoured to be allowed to demonstrate their loyalty to Queen and country. In Ireland, Archbishop Loftus complained that the citizens of the capital refused to attend services held in honour of the Queen's deliverance. 'Even in Dublin itself, the lawyers in term time took occasion to leave the town of purpose to absent themselves from that godly exercise,' he said.[30] The authorities in Munster were in no doubt that loyalty was shifting in the direction of Catholic Spain. It was the attempt to settle English colonists on the expropriated estates of the Desmonds that appeared to have driven Old English and native Irish together. In a *Discourse on Ireland* in 1595, Sir Peter Carew said the plantation of settlers in Munster had given rise to great feelings of alienation. 'The people of Munster are Spanish in heart, papist in religion and most infinitely discontented since the traitors' lands were divided,' he asserted.[31]

The last revolt of Elizabeth's reign, which first flickered to life in Ulster in 1592 and then exploded three years later, did not require an alliance of Old English and native Irish. Ulster was by far the least settled of the Irish provinces and the descendants of Anglo-Norman families there had long since been absorbed into Gaelic Irish society. The leader of the rebellion, Hugh O'Neill, grandson of Conn, first Earl of Tyrone, found his supporters in the Church among the native Irish clergy. Long before O'Neill revolted, the bishops of Ulster had been agitating for a Spanish invasion. Edmund MacGauran, Bishop of Ardagh and then Archbishop of Armagh, visited Spain in 1585 and Rome in 1587 to whip up support for the venture. Intercepted letters showed he was still hoping for an invasion in 1591.[32] When the Ulster chiefs began to stir in 1592, MacGauran, Archbishop of Armagh since 1587, summoned a council of the northern bishops that dispatched James O'Healy of Tuam to take their appeal personally to Philip II. MacGauran was killed by the English soon after on the battlefield. But the Archbishop of Tuam continued his mission, reaching the Spanish court in September.

The Irish bishops got little for their effort. Philip was old, dying of cancer and broken by the failure of the Armada. O'Healy was escorted home in the spring of 1594 without the thousands of soldiers he had asked for. To cap the failure of his efforts, he drowned in a storm.

The Earl of Tyrone did not join the Ulster revolt until 1595, when he broke with the government and destroyed the strategic bridge over the River Blackwater. The revolt that lasted until the end of the Elizabeth's reign was a native Irish uprising, and as always, the Old English towns held aloof. Nevertheless, there were ominous signs for the English of the beginnings of a seismic shift in Ireland. The reaction of Richard Stanihurst to the rebellion was illuminating. The young man who had defended Old English colonial culture against Irish barbarism with such passion, by 1600 appeared to see Ireland through new eyes. There was no more talk of ancient ties to the crown dating back to the Norman Conquest, or of 'Irish lordlings' as 'O's and Macs'.[33] Instead, he offered to act as O'Neill's ambassador at the Habsburg court in Brussels. Peter Lombard, MacGauran's successor in Armagh and an Old Englishman, also supported the Ulster revolt. There was an element of pragmatism here. O'Neill's stunning military victories over the government at Yellow Ford on 14 August 1598 suddenly raised the extraordinary prospect that Elizabeth's rule in Ireland might be overthrown. After the news of Yellow Ford reached Munster, the new settlers – Spenser among them – were driven off their lands.

But there was more to Stanihurst's change of heart than mere adjustment to changed circumstances. It reflected a level of disenchantment with English rule among the Old English, which had reached such a pitch that the ancient quarrel with the native Irish appeared redundant. The Old English took little pleasure in the defeat of the last of the old Gaelic chieftains in 1603. On the contrary, it was the news of Elizabeth's death that triggered an outburst of popular rejoicing. In Munster, the townsmen proclaimed the Habsburg Archduchess Isabella their next Queen instead of Elizabeth's designated successor, James of Scotland. That in itself was a triumph of hope over experience as even the Pope had made no ruling on the English succession. James was proclaimed King in Dublin on 5 April. But by then the Irish cities were caught up in the tide of popular sentiment in favour of Isabella. At Waterford, the crowds prevented the Chief Justice, Sir Nicholas Walsh, from proclaiming James king at the town cross.[34] Their passions were inflamed further by a sermon on the Queen's death by James White, vicar apostolic for Waterford, in which he likened her to the Old Testament Queen Jezebel, whose body was thrown to the dogs. At Cork, the local council also refused to proclaim James. Mass was restored, adding to the woes of Bishop Lyon, and at Easter long-concealed images and statues reappeared to take their places in the first outdoor religious procession the city had seen since the 1560s. Crowds broke open the Royal Ordnance and attacked the town's fortifications. Mayor Sarsfield later coyly excused this, suggesting it was done to prevent the native Irish from seizing them and causing mischief. The real intention was to make it less easy for the authorities to block a Spanish invasion.

The revolt against Protestantism in Cork and Waterford was repeated in Kilkenny, where the citizens reclaimed the former Dominican 'Black Abbey' for Catholic worship. The Earl of Ormond tried to rein in the tumult and in April arranged a conference between a delegation from the city and the Lord Deputy, Sir Charles Blount, Lord Mountjoy. As a result, the authorities took no reprisals against Kilkenny. In Waterford, the religious rebellion lasted until the first week of May. All hopes of Isabella's succession had been dashed but the townsmen still hoped for toleration from James, as did all the old English Catholics.

Francis Bryan, Mayor of Wexford told the Lord Deputy on 23 April that his community wanted pragmatic recognition of the fact that they had long since rejected the Protestant religion. 'Long before the death of our late sovereign Queen Elizabeth and since, Mass was said and openly in certain houses whereunto all the inhabitants of this town (with few exceptions) did resort,' he wrote. 'Since the Queen's death, without . . . opprobrious words used towards the said [Protestant] Lord Bishop or any others [they had] entered with a priest unto the churches and in one church which was ruinous, named St Patricks, Mass is said, which the people think will be graciously accepted of his most royal Majesty.'[35]

Waterford remained obstinate, even after Lord Mountjoy, the Earl of Ormond and Archbishop Loftus's ally, the Bishop of Meath, arrived outside the city with an army of 14,000. The Lord Deputy was fresh from crushing the last embers of the Ulster rebellion and had just secured O'Neill's submission, ending a Nine-years War that almost expelled the English from Ireland. The city fathers demonstrated nerves of iron by defying Mountjoy at that stage. For two days they wrangled over the terms of their surrender, making matters worse by sending the vicar apostolic who had insulted the memory of the late Queen to negotiate terms.

Waterford surrendered on 3 May. Once again the images and crosses were stored away, the vestments hidden in chests and cupboards and the churches handed back to become the half-empty chapels of the Protestants. But the turmoil was slow to die away and in Kilkenny, the Protestant Bishop, John Horsfall complained in June 1604 that mass was still being celebrated in the Black Abbey.[36]

The religious disturbances in 1603 were a watershed in the history of the Irish Reformation. Catholics briefly tasted religious liberty. They saw for themselves how strong they really were. On the other side, the Protestants had experienced public humiliation. The authorities went on the offensive after this débâcle, forcing the Oath of Supremacy on mayors of the corporations and in 1605 issuing the first proclamation in Ireland that ordered Jesuits and other foreign-educated seminarians to leave the country. But the measures did not crack the new confidence of the Catholics. Mountjoy's secretary, Fynes Moryson, said the mayor and aldermen of Dublin continued to attend service in Christ Church cathedral with the Lord Deputy, as custom dictated. But now they 'stopp their eares with woll or some like matter so as they could not heare a worde the Preacher spake'.[37] What kind of a state Church was it where in the main cathedral the principal officers of the city covered their ears rather than hear the sermon?

When the Oath of Supremacy was forced on the mayor, John Shelton, in 1604, he resigned office rather than take it.[38] His example was repeated in Clonmel, where John White was removed as sovereign (mayor) for refusing to attend the parish church; this was not surprising, as he was the cousin of Archbishop Lombard, the Catholic Primate of Armagh. The Irish Privy Council in 1608 reported that most of the mayors and principal officers of the cities and corporate towns and justices of the peace refused to take the Oath of Supremacy. The Catholics who had grudgingly attended church, clattering around like mill horses, gave way to a generation that would not enter a Protestant church in any circumstances whatever.

By the middle of James's reign, the authorities were literally reduced to dragging people into Protestant churches. A letter of 1611 from Drogheda described how 'one William Kairhe being takein wase brought to the church against his will. When he came to the church doore he would not goe in by anie mens; he that carried the great Mace before the Lord Deputy seinge the man he would not go in he struck him with his mace on the hed and mad him stombill on the ground with madness; by this mens he was carried into the churche.'[39] It was a bizarre state of affairs. The author of the letter claimed the Lord Deputy tricked one of the aldermen in Drogheda into attending a Protestant service by asking him to accompany him to the door of the parish church. When they got there, five of the Lord Deputy's men grabbed hold of the man and dragged him in to the service.

The era of the church papist, of the temporiser and the trimmer, was over. A new generation of priests educated in foreign seminaries was streaming back into Ireland, bringing the teachings of the Council of Trent with them. The struggle for religious supremacy was entering a newer and more dangerous phase.

CHAPTER SIX

Seminaries beyond the Seas

No street, no corner, no Cabbin without a seminarie priest. They swarme
everywhere. They tickell the eares of the comon sort whoe are the easelyest wonne to
any desperate attempte because they have least to loose.
(The supplication of the blood of the English, 1598)[1]

In a quiet side street of the rue des Carmes, off Montmartre in Paris, stands the
Syrian Catholic church. A noble building, the very closed looking iron gates and
the damaged arms over the portico give it a mournful appearance. The arms were
defaced during the French Revolution and we cannot be sure what was there. But
it is likely that they were either an Irish harp and crown, or the coat of arms of one
of the great Irish continental dynasties[2] that flourished in France, Spain, Portugal
and the Low Countries. For this was once an Irish church, the chapel of the Irish
College from 1737 until 1927.

Round the corner, naturally enough in the rue des Irlandais, the Irish College
in Paris still stands. The Scots College that once stood nearby has gone. The
English College in the rue des Postes has gone. Only the Irish remain. On the eve
of the Revolution this was one of two Irish colleges in the French capital. The first,
founded by John Lee in 1578, was sited in the former Collège des Lombards in
the Impasse des Boeufs. The building is still there though it now consists of
private apartments. The second foundation, which remains today, was established
in the 1770s, in what used to be called the rue du Cheval Vert.

Lee was a Waterford man, child of a city that was fast emerging as one of the
centres of the Counter-Reformation in Ireland. It was important that Waterford
was a port, linked by trade to Spain and France. As the Old English inhabitants
became increasingly alienated from the English, it was natural that they should
strengthen their ties with their continental trading partners. Lee belonged to a
network of Old English mercantile families from the south-east who were to
emerge as fervent agents of the Counter-Reformation in Ireland. In the same
company were Thomas White of Clonmel, founder of the Irish College in
Salamanca in 1592, John Howling who performed the same service in Lisbon in
1593 and Christopher Cusack, founder of a series of Irish colleges in Douai,
Anvers, Tournai and Lille. Cusack, ironically, was the grandson of the staunchly
Protestant politician, Sir Thomas Cusack.

The need for diocesan seminaries had been strongly urged at the Council of Trent, the final sessions of which closed in 1563. It was a key item on the agenda of the Council fathers, who rightly thought only a more educated and aggressive clergy could confront the Protestant challenge. In England and Ireland, Protestant persecution rendered this impossible. Lee, Howling and Cusack begged and borrowed from the courts of Europe to realise the command of the Fathers of Trent overseas. In the sixteenth and seventeenth centuries colleges sprang up all over Europe, from Seville to Prague, at Madrid, Alcala, Santiago, Toulouse, Bordeaux, La Rochelle, Nantes, Rouen, Rome, Charleville, Antwerp and Aix-la-Chapelle.

The splendid portals of the Irish chapel in Paris and the grand *palazzo*-like exterior of the college buildings belong to the last phase of this era of continental educational expansion. By then the Irish community in Europe had expanded, augmented by thousands of exiles who fled the country for a mixture of religious and political reasons in the seventeenth century. They became an integral part of the hierarchical and aristocratic world of the *ancien régime* courts of Europe. They produced a Rector of the University of Paris and royal chaplains to, among others, the Polish court. It is a side of their history that the modern Irish, overly keen on selling their 'rebel' image, do not care to dwell on. It does, however, explain why the coat of arms over the door of the Irish chapel was scrubbed out by the French Revolutionaries.

The movement to establish Irish seminaries was hugely successful. In 1608 the Irish Privy Council reported that the influx of seminarians from Spain, France and Flanders had turned into a torrent.

The priests land here secretly in every port and creek of the realm (a dozen together sometimes as we are informed), and afterwards disperse themselves into several quarters in such sort that every town and country is full of them and most men's minds are infested with their doctrines and seditious persuasions.

They have so gained the women that they are in a manner all of them absolute recusants. Children and servants are wholly taught and catechised by them . . . they withdraw many from the church that formerly conformed themselves and other of them of whom good hopes had been conceived, they have made altogether obstinate and disobedient and contemptuous . . . the people in many places resort to Mass now in greater multitudes both in town and country than for many years past . . . such as are conformed and go to church are everywhere derided, scorned and oppressed by the multitude.[3]

The first Irish seminaries were not intended to be permanent foundations. They were just houses of refuge and study. It was only after the passage of time when that it became clear the Elizabethan settlement was no temporary phenomenon that they matured into seminaries.

The strong trading ties between Ireland and the Iberian peninsula dictated that many of the new houses would be located in Spain and Portugal, near the seat of the Spanish court, and around existing colonies of Irish businessmen. They were also founded in university towns, where groups of Irish students had already collected in informal associations and where Irish bishops and priests were living in exile. In Alcala, for example, many Irish priests had collected. William Walsh, the energetic Marian Bishop of Meath, died there in 1577. The Irish colleges in Douai and Rome were formed by hiving off the Irish students from existing English colleges.

The founders and first students were drawn from the Old English community of Dublin and the other cities, and it was urban Ireland that first felt the full effect of their ministry. They were slower to penetrate the native Irish countryside in the west and in Ulster. In the remote dioceses, uneducated native clergy of the old school continued to serve in nominally Protestant parishes well into the reign of James I. Even at that late stage, if the Church of Ireland had made a determined assault on the hearts and minds of the Gaelic population, Ireland's religious history might have followed a different course. The Welsh, after all, were brought into the Protestant fold and without sacrificing language or national identity. It is conceivable that Ireland might have been split on very different lines from the ones we know today, dividing the English-speaking Catholic Pale from an Irish-speaking Protestant west and north. Instead the influence of the Tridentine east spread slowly west. The result was a unified, hybrid culture – half Pale, half Gael. In some ways it was also a less Irish one.

The seminarians transformed the religious life of the country. Slowly they replaced the uneducated 'Irish rogues' Lord Deputy Sidney had encountered in Meath in the 1570s with persuasive advocates of Tridentine teaching. Church papists fell away as they ordered people to withdraw from all contact with the parish churches.

Under their influence, the laity took a more combative line with the authorities on religion. The Jesuit, Richard Field, reported with satisfaction on the truculent stand his people took towards Archbishop Loftus's Ecclesiastical Commission in 1603.

They fix a day in each week when the Catholics, (whom they style recusants) must appear before the commissioners. The gentry are asked in the first place, and then the common people, whether they will frequent the churches and assist at the sermons. The general answer is that they will not enter those profane places of worship or listen to the false doctrines of the preachers, and that by the faith of their forefathers and by the Catholic religion they are prohibited from communicating with them in sacred things . . . commitments for jail are made out for disobeying the queen's laws; fines of ten pounds are ordered for each offence or absence from the church on the Lord's day. The imprisonment thus imposed is patiently endured but the citizens will not pay the fines.[4]

Sir John Davies found the same mood in Clonmel. He attributed the stubbornness of the townsmen to the large number of Jesuits now resident there. It was
the Jesuits who made 'the burgesses more obstinate here than elsewhere', he said.
'For whereas my Lord President did justly offer to the inhabitants that he would
spare to proceed against them if they would yield to a conference for a time and
become bound in the meantime not to receive any Jesuit or priest into their
houses, they peremptorily refused both.'[5]

The seminaries generated a new type of Irish priest, and a new type of Irishman.
Richard Stanihurst had lamented that with the exception of the irritating 'Rome
runners', his fellow countrymen never travelled. Among the Pale gentry, a few
years at Oxford or Cambridge was likely to be the most cosmopolitan experience
they had.

Persecution created a new type of cosmopolitan Irishman, who commuted
between Rome, Louvain and Spain. Take David Rothe, Caroline Bishop of
Ossory. Born in Kilkenny in 1573, he studied at Douai, was ordained in
Salamanca and went on to Rome to work for seven years as secretary to Peter
Lombard, the exiled Archbishop of Armagh. By the time he returned to Ireland at
the age of 36 he had seen more of Europe than any of his Anglican counterparts
in England and Ireland had dreamed of.

Then there is the remarkable Wadding family. Luke Wadding,[6] born in 1588 in
Waterford, entered the Franciscan Order near Oporto in Portugal at the age of 16.
He studied at Lisbon and Coimbra and then at Salamanca and Leon in Spain. By
1618, he was so well known that Philip III of Spain included him in a royal
embassy sent to Rome to argue the case for the definition of the Immaculate
Conception. It was there that he founded the College of St Isidore for Irish
Franciscans, and there that he spent the rest of his life until his death in 1657.
Wadding's cousin, Peter, became Chancellor of the Charles University in Prague.
Of his other cousins, Michael became a missionary in Mexico, Luke a professor at
Salamanca and Ambrose became a professor at Dillingen, in Germany. Another
cousin, Richard, became an Augustinian hermit in Coimbra in Portugal. The
parents of the great historian and founder of St Isidore's died when he was only
14. Had they lived, what pride they must have felt in their sons and nephews,
spread over half a dozen countries and two continents.

To the new generation of Old English intellectuals like the Waddings, England
was the one country that was no longer a home from home. It was land to hurry
through on the way to the Continent, or to be avoided. As the English Catholic
community contracted, the bonds of blood that had linked the Old English to the
mother country withered away. This vanishing of old ties was the foundation of a
new 'Irish' identity, based on Catholicism. As the English became more anti-
European and ever more conscious of their separation from the continent, the
Irish became more self-consciously European.

The word 'college' conjures up images of solid stone buildings, endowments,
funds, bursaries, halls of residence and tutors. Most Irish colleges led a humbler

and more precarious existence. As Thomas Massingham, Rector of the Paris college wrote in the 1620s, they were communities 'exiled for faith and religion, lacking means, living in obscure places'.[7] Lack of money meant even the prestigious college at Salamanca, which basked in the favour of Philip II, could not feed, clothe and educate more than about 30 students at a time. Salamanca sent forth 370 students in the first 50 years of its existence, which suggests an annual intake of about half a dozen men. Lisbon sent out 124 priests in the first 25 years of its existence.[8] Douai from 1594 to 1613 produced 149 priests. The college at Bordeaux educated 212 students from 1602 to 1617, and the resident number there fluctuated between 12 and 40. Richard Conway, Rector of Seville from 1619 to 1624, said his college was able to send only 2 mission priests back to Ireland each year,[9] with a total student body of about 12, though his successor, Thomas O'Brien, Rector from 1631 to 1637, said he had raised the total student body to 24.[10] Alcala's benefactor, Baron Jorge de la Paz intended his college to house about 30 students. In fact, the numbers ranged from 13 to 29, as late as the eighteenth century.

Some establishments were very small. The endowment of the Irish College in Rome allowed for only six students, though in the early 1630s the money was stretched to cover 11. The college at Antwerp housed only about half a dozen students at any one time.[11] Finances were always a problem for such small institutions, especially as few of the students could afford to pay for their upkeep; however, they could help out by being ordained priests early on. The chronic shortage of money meant it was not possible for all of them to delay ordination until the completion of their studies. There was money to be earned, saying masses and working as chaplains to the Irish soldiers fighting in the Spanish army.

The colleges were sustained by the joint effort of the Habsburgs, local colonies of Irish businessmen and by pious Spanish, Portuguese and Flemish merchants and gentry, who endowed the Irish with property. In Seville, a large Irish merchant community helped the Irish College by donating a percentage of the profits on their wine trade.[12] Philip III, King from 1598 to 1612, was a sympathetic benefactor, awarding a grant to the college at Salamanca and instituting a travel allowance for every priest about to return to Ireland, known as the viaticum. Bordeaux was named the college of St Anne la Royale after its benefactress, Anne of Austria. The Irish College in Rome was funded by the Cardinal Protector of Ireland, Ludovico Ludovisi.[13]

Some colleges crumbled under the strain of tight budgets and had to be taken under the wing of the municipal authorities. Santiago and Alacala were absorbed into the Salamanca college in the eighteenth century. Madrid changed its purpose. Founded in 1629, it performed poorly from the start and its fate was sealed after a visitation by the Archbishop of Toledo in 1652 produced a deeply critical report. 'Grave damage has been caused to the Irish nation by the foundation of this seminary because the young men who have come to it to begin their studies have not attained the required level of knowledge,' it said. 'A contributory factor to this is the poverty of this seminary, for in all these years it has acquired no income whatever.'[14] Madrid did not close but changed into a hostel for Irish seminarians who had already completed their studies at Salamanca, Alcala and Santiago and were waiting to receive their viaticum from the King. As such it survived, under the auspices of the city of Madrid, but with its own Irish rectors, until the Revolutionary wars swept it away.

Most Irish colleges, with the exception of Nantes, did not educate the seminarians themselves. They did not have the staff or facilities, so they arranged the students' education at the local Jesuit or Dominican colleges, or the university, and provided a home, meals and a structured devotional life.

The Irish seminarians were kept under strict control. They were far from home and it was essential that they did not take to drink or fight with the local population. In Antwerp, the vicar-general of the diocese drew up rules in 1650 which ordered all Irish students travelling in the city to report to the Archpriest on their arrival. Seminarians attending courses at the Antwerp Jesuit college had to show the Archpriest their study notes every three months. They had to be indoors by 8 p.m. in summer and by 5 p.m. in winter.[15] They might not go to the pub or beg in the streets. The colleges themselves instilled a sense of corporate discipline by enforcing oaths on the students and dressing them in distinctive uniforms. At Seville, the Irish students wore blue cassocks and brown tippets.[16] The resident staff of the Irish colleges was small, usually just a rector, a couple of other staff and some servants.

The Jesuit influence on the colleges was enormous. Thomas White, founder of Salamanca, and John Howling, the founder of Lisbon, were both Jesuits. Several colleges started out as secular establishments and switched to Jesuit control. The Order took over Seville in 1619 and Rome in 1635.

Rome was a case study in the tensions that could beset such institutions.[17] Funded by Cardinal Ludovisi, its future was thrown into doubt when he died prematurely at the age of 37 in 1632. The Cardinal left money for the college to continue but ordered that the college, hitherto run by Franciscans, should now be placed under the Jesuits. Luke Wadding vigorously contested the will, only to become embroiled in a vicious racial intrigue between the Old English and native Irish students, one of whom, an Ulsterman, Terence Kelly, accused him of favouring Old English candidates from Wadding's home region of Munster. Rome's decision to award the college to the Jesuits was not simply an act of homage to the late Cardinal's will. It reflected Rome's fear that Irish secular colleges were prone to damaging outbreaks of ethnic tension and could not be trusted to run themselves.

Alcala remained a secular college in which students elected their own rectors. As a result of that dangerous experiment in democracy, 'it was the constant scene of disorders from the beginning'[18] and retained a reputation for turbulence into the eighteenth century. The last Rector, Patrick Magennis, barricaded himself into the building when Patrick Curtis, the future Archbishop of Armagh, then Rector of Salamanca, came to take possession in 1785, after it was decreed that the two colleges would merge. The police had to break down the door to get the Rector and his accomplice, a student, out of the premises.

Many priests serving in rain-sodden corners of Jacobean Ireland must have looked back with nostalgia to the balmy nights spent in good company over a flagon of Spanish wine in Salamanca or Madrid. Equally, there must have been terrible loneliness among the younger arrivals as they made the painful adjustment to life so far from home. Some mothers' sons never returned to regale their parents and siblings with tales of life in Spain, Portugal or Rome. Their colleagues had the dismal business of watching ageing parents' faces go white as they broke the news that their son had died, alone, in a foreign bed.

For many Irish lads, raised on cool summers and mild winters, the scorching heat of the Mediterranean was unbearable. Of the 157 students who passed through the portals of the Irish college in Lisbon, 33 never returned home.[19]

The English government and Dublin Castle were well aware of the dangerous consequences of foreign education. Compulsory passports were introduced in 1583 and the port authorities were ordered to search in-coming and out-going ships in 1593. The government's powers to search and detect were formidable. When they really wanted to find someone they usually succeeded, helped by a network of informers, double agents and reward-seekers.

The English authorities could pounce with lightning speed. Richard Creagh was appointed Catholic Archbishop of Armagh in 1564.[20] Arrested in Drogheda that Christmas, days after he landed in Ireland, he escaped, and returned to Ireland in July the next year. This time it took eight months, but he was caught again and spent the rest of his life in the Tower of London, until his death in 1585. Patrick O'Healy, Catholic Bishop of Mayo, practically walked off the boat and on to the scaffold. He landed at Smerwick in July 1579. He had three days of liberty in Ireland at the most before arrest and imprisonment in Limerick, after which the President of Munster, Sir William Drury, had him executed in mid-August. Creagh's counterpart in Cashel, Dermot O'Hurley, was caught on 7 October 1583 in Carrick on Suir after only a few weeks in Ireland.

Bishops and archbishops were in worse trouble than priests, especially if they failed to take the hint after being allowed to escape once. After Creagh was caught for the second time in 1567, he was sent to London, an infinitely more dangerous destination than Dublin, where the population was ferociously anti-Catholic. 'The Archbishop of Armesch is kept in the stocks in a subterranean place', David Wolfe reported to Rome in 1573, 'and though he is but 44 years old, he has already lost all his teeth. Much might be said of the spirit and holy life of this great man, but it were not meet at present. It will be said in due time and place, cos these things cannot remain hidden since in him God has shown the world a servant of His of so grand a type.' He died in prison in London, in 1585.[21] Wolfe, himself had been caught in 1567 but escaped in 1572 to Spain. William Walsh, the Bishop of Meath, who died at Alcala, was arrested in 1565 but escaped some time in the 1570s.

To be arrested in the panic-stricken atmosphere of a rebellion was the worst disaster that could befall a returning seminarian or bishop. O'Healy was arrested at the start of the Desmond wars in 1579. Dermot O'Hurley was arrested in October 1583 at the tail end of the revolt, while the Earl was still a fugitive. Both bishops were seen as Desmond clients. There was no second chance for O'Hurley and Archbishop Loftus had him savagely tortured in June 1584 with 'hot boots' made of molten iron that tore the man's skin off. On 19 June this vile ordeal ended. Loftus crowed with satisfaction over his success in murdering the Catholic Archbishop: 'We gave warrant to the Knight Marshal in Her Majesty's name to do execution upon him which was accordingly performed upon him and thereby the realm well rid of a most pestilent member.'[22]

The native Irish chief, the eager priest, the Old English Catholic gentleman sitting next to you at dinner – any of them might be an English spy. O'Hurley had been betrayed into the outstretched claws of Archbishop Loftus by two fellow Catholics, Christopher Barnewall and Thomas Fleming. One reason why the greed and closet Catholicism of Archbishop Magrath of Cashel were indulged for so many decades was because he ran a highly effective listening post in Cashel. As a native Irishman with a strong local power base he was well placed to know who was moving in and out of his diocese. Like a giant spider he would pounce and deliver his victims to the authorities. Magrath was rather obviously a double agent, and almost got into deep trouble when his friendly letters to Dermot O'Hurley were intercepted. However, he trapped enough priests and offered up enough information to keep the Queen on his side.

But if the big fish found it hard to slip through the net, the minnows swam through the mesh easily. The English had no problem noting which candidates Rome had appointed as bishops to the few dozen Irish sees; they could not keep track of thousands of priests. Periodic searches of boats did not stop the toing and froing of schools of anonymous seminarians whose names were not known to the authorities. The seamen were nearly all Catholics and their searches cursory.

In the nineteenth century, the Catholic Church dwelt lovingly on the image of priests living in holes when they were not swinging from gibbets. But the Catholic seminary priests did not all live miserable lives on the run. Henry Fitzsimon,[23] a Dublin-born Jesuit who returned to Ireland in 1598 in the middle of the Ulster rebellion, lived very comfortably. The Fitzsimons were a reputable Pale family who had supplied Dublin with mayors. The returnee priest became the darling of the local gentry and, so he told his superiors, never rode around the countryside without an escort of at least three or four.

Elite priests like Fitzsimon did not celebrate the sacraments out in the hills but in the homes and outhouses of the gentry, to which the local population were invited. A survey of the Protestant archdiocese of Dublin in 1630 pinpointed the growth of this domestic Catholicism. Although the survey was from the reign of Charles I, when conditions had eased greatly since Elizabethan times, the system it described would have been familiar to Fitzsimon. At Malahide, north of Dublin, it said, 'all the parishioners are Recusants and go to Mass now at Mr Talbot of Mallahydes house more usually than heretofore. The said Mr Talbot of Mallahyde is farmer to the tithes.'[24] At Monkstown, 'when the gentelmen thereabout, viz Mr Henry Chievers of Mounctowne, Mr James Goodman of Laghnanston Mr Henry Walshe of Dalkey be pleased to have Mass said in their own houses and castles, they have it, and that not seldom'.[25] At Bray, a few miles south of Dublin, there were 16 Protestant church-goers, while 'every gentleman thereabout hath a priest or a friar for a domestic chaplain and maintains and abetts them'.[26]

These clergy, the pampered pets of the local gentry, could be lured into a sense of false security. Fitzsimon led a highly indiscreet life during the brief, five-month Lord Deputyship of the Earl of Essex, when Essex's mind was preoccupied with the Earl of Tyrone's revolt. This was dangerous because the Old English gentry were not masters of their own situation. They dominated the Irish parliament, but that assembly met rarely and did no more than veto the application of England's anti-Catholic laws to Ireland. The daily administration of Ireland was in the hands of the Lord Deputy and his coterie of New English Protestant officials. In 1599 Fitzsimon was arrested and flung into jail in Dublin Castle, by which time the dashing Earl of Essex had left Ireland and been replaced by the sterner figure of Sir Charles Blount, Lord Mountjoy.

Even then, there was no certain outcome. Jailed priests were rarely freed but often 'escaped' with such monotonous regularity that it was obviously done with the collusion of the authorities. Fitzsimon spent five years in Dublin Castle and complained that during that time, one bishop, three Franciscans and six secular priests had been released as a result of fines, bribes and exchanges.[27]

In England, the mere fact of being a Jesuit would have been enough to send Fitzsimon to his death at Tyburn surrounded by a screaming crowd. Of all the Pope's battalions, the English most feared and hated the Jesuits. But in Ireland, the fate of a trapped priest, even a Jesuit, was less obvious. Fitzsimon's regime in Dublin Castle was not that appalling: in a letter he sent to the head of the Order in April 1603 he said he at least had liberty to read books and had refuted an article written against him by John Rider, the Protestant Dean of St Patrick's. Indeed, he boasted to his superior of his triumph in the field of religious controversy and begged to have his pamphlet published. 'My antagonist is considered, even in the opinion of Protestants, as a fellow who should be hissed and stamped off the stage,' he chortled.[28]

The main restriction Fitzsimon resented was the ban on the celebration of mass. The prison governor kept an eye out for that kind of activity and on one occasion even rushed into his cell when he was in the middle of the liturgy. Fitzsimon managed to gobble down the host but in the tussle the consecrated wine flew everywhere and the governor stormed off clutching his vestments.[29] But the relations between prisoners and jailers in Dublin Castle could be curiously intimate. It wasn't all squealing rats, rattling chains, thumbscrews, dripping walls and the rack. A priest could expect an easier time than O'Hurley if he had no record of political activism and no known family ties to rebel leaders. It also helped if you were upper class and Old English. The Fitzsimons were a Pale family and friends and relations kept up a steady stream of requests to the authorities for Henry Fitzsimon's liberation. The pleas eventually reached the top, and James I personally ordered his release in 1604. When Fitzsimon finally left Dublin Castle in that year, the governor presented him with 200 Flemish florins and burst into tears.

The expansion in foreign seminary education had an enormous impact on education at home in Ireland. Except for a handful of university-trained men, the older Irish clergy learned the liturgy and the sacraments in their localities. Edmund Tanner described the condition of the Irish clergy – and laity – before the arrival of the seminarians in almost apocalyptic terms. 'A pious Catholic is hardly to be found and no wonder since the clergy are the most depraved of all,' he told Ireland's Cardinal Protector Moroni in 1571. 'Moreover there is so little instruction to be had in the Christian faith, or the commandments and fewer still understand them. Sermons are so uncommon that there are many who have not heard so much as one; the sacraments are so rarely administered, so much more rarely understood, that the ignorant people know not whether they were appointed by God or man.'[30]

That changed over the next 30 years. The seminarian of the 1590s needed to arrive at his college with a working knowledge of Latin, the language in which his courses were conducted. The demands of the new seminaries in Spain, France and Flanders fuelled an education boom throughout Ireland, from basic hedge schools to real academies of excellence, often run by priests who had been expelled from their parish livings under Elizabeth or who had resigned in the 1560s. Richard Creagh, the future Archbishop of Armagh, ran a school in Limerick in 1560 before leaving for Rome in 1562. In Kilkenny, a former Marian Dean of Waterford, Peter White, ran a school that educated the children of many established Old English families from Munster, such as the Archers, Shees, Comerfords, Dormers, Butlers and Strongs. Richard Stanihurst and the future Archbishop of Armagh, Peter Lombard, were among White's pupils.

White's school attracted the cream of Munster, but there were many other local schools that supplied the seminaries with recruits. A royal visitation of Waterford diocese in 1615 found a school operating under a Mr Flahy which the visitors suspected existed to supply seminaries with students. Mr Flahy had conveniently left town before the visitors rode in, 'whereupon we left a L[ett]re with the Lord President of that province under our hands, praying and requiring him in His Ma[jes]ties name to take order to suppresse him from the exercise of his teaching and instruccion of youth, for he traynes up schollers to become seminarians beyond the seas'.[31]

It is unlikely that the school closed for very long, if at all. Visitors came and departed for Dublin. Mayors and aldermen remained. They were entrusted with closing Catholic schools: some hope, when they were sending their own sons to the same establishments. The local authorities were skilled in talking to Dublin Castle in one tone and acting otherwise. In Galway, the Lord Deputy Sir Henry Sidney first urged the local council to found a school when he visited the city in 1575. What Sidney envisaged was a Protestant academy. When the mayor, Dominick Lynch, did found a school in the 1580s under Alexander Lynch, the headmaster for the next 30 years, it was strongly Catholic. As in Waterford, an ecclesiastical visitation ordered the authorities to close it down in 1615. It may have shut its doors temporarily but it was still going in 1627 when the council was so irritated by outsiders posing as students that it ordered 'beggars and all pretended schoolers' to be 'whipped out of this towne'.[32] When Alexander Lynch's successor, John Lynch, retired as headmaster in 1638 the council that was supposed to be persecuting his establishment awarded him a pension.

These schools educated future mayors and merchants as well as priests. But the teachers inculcated a high Catholic ethos that exalted the role and the status of the priesthood. The school in Galway taught a new generation of fervently Catholic aldermen and mayors. In the 1570s, the Protestants had great hopes of Galway. After the very belated suppression of the mass in 1567 the town conformed to the Book of Common Prayer and attended the parish churches well into the 1590s. The hopes of the Protestant authorities were raised by the support they received from the O'Briens, the dominant Irish family, belted by Henry VIII as the earls of Thomond. Donough O'Brien, the 4th Earl from 1581 was a convinced Protestant whose kinsman, Murtagh, was sent to Cambridge and presented with the see of Killaloe in 1576. The Old English community in the city meanwhile produced a clutch of Protestant ministers like Roland Lynch, presented with the tiny see of Kilmacdaugh in 1587. Nehemiah Donnellan, a native Irishman from the Galway area, was made Archbishop of Tuam in 1595. This little hive of Protestant activity among the native Irish on the west coast attracted admiring notice from Sir Richard Bingham, President of Connacht, who boasted to Sir Francis Walsingham in 1581 that Galway was 'very well affected in religion . . . and 'more given to embrace the doctrines of the Gospel generally than any people in Ireland'.[33]

The governor was putting a good deal of 'spin' on the religious climate of Galway. Over the next decades, the generation that emerged from Alexander Lynch's school entirely rejected the Protestant conformity of their parents. The influence of the earls of Thomond counted for little, nor did the promotion of local men like Donnellan or Lynch to bishoprics. It was a fantasy in Dublin or England that the occasional token Irish-speaking bishop could check the collective influence and activity of hundreds of seminarians. The Protestant bishops' once-weekly sermons in church were more than counteracted by the daily lessons that the children received from their Catholic teachers in the classrooms.

Supporters of the reformed Church were uncomfortably aware that the seminary priests were raising the standard of the Catholic clergy to a level above that of their own ministers. Spenser delivered a critique of the two sets of clergy in Ireland: 'It is a great wonder to see the oddes which is betwen the zeal of the Popish priests and the ministers of the Gospell,' he wrote,

> for they spare not to come out of Spain, from Rome and from Remes, by long toil and dangerous travelling hither, where they know peril of death awaiteth them and no reward or riches is to be found . . . whereas some of our idle ministers . . . having the livings of the country offered unto them without pains and without peril will neither for the same, nor for any love of God nor any zeal of religion nor for all the good they may do by winning souls to God, be drawn from their warm nests.[34]

Sidney had alerted the Queen in the 1570s to the fact that the well-off Irish families were sending their children abroad to be educated and that she had better take action. Unfortunately for the Church of Ireland, the promised university was delayed repeatedly. The Irish parliament of 1569 pondered suppressing Dublin's second cathedral at St Patrick's and creating a university out of the revenue. Nothing came of it. In 1577, Elizabeth responded to Sidney's warning by suggesting the creation of a university in Clonfert, to be funded by dissolving the small sees of Elphin and Clonfert. The Queen understood the threat posed by the Irish seminaries. She told Sidney that 'we find that the Runagates of that nation which under the pretence of study in the universities beyond the seas do returne freight with superstition and treason and as the instruments to stirre up our subjects to undutifulness and rebellion.'[35] But the University of Clonfert remained a dream. It is hard to imagine the Queen was remotely serious about it. Clonfert was – and still is – a village in Connacht and, in the miraculous event of being endowed with a university, would never have attracted the gilded youth of the Pale. In a choice between Clonfert and Salamanca it is not hard to imagine where most Irish students would have ended up. It was no more difficult to get to one than the other, given the appalling state of the roads.

Sidney's successor, Sir John Perrott, returned to the fray in the 1580s. A convinced Protestant, he urged the government to set up a university while he was President of Munster in the 1570s. Translated to Dublin, he resurrected the old plan to endow a college out of St Patrick's. That scheme ran up against the vast bulk of Archbishop Loftus, who held the revenues of the cathedral and was using them, so he claimed, to fund the ministry of preachers in the archdiocese. Perrott thought that Loftus wanted to hold on to St Patrick's to finance the future of his army of 20 children. 'The ungodly gain that this archbishop doth suck out of that church to pump up himself, his children and friends as well in that realm [England] as in this, is so sweet that he cannot endure any man to look towards it,' he warned Burghley in 1585, 'for by that church and his covetous (I will not say corrupt) dealings therein and in his offices of chancery and high commissioner, he hath so well feathered his nest.'[36]

The battle over the university underpinned a profound difference of outlook between the Lord Deputy and the Archbishop. Loftus believed in conversion via the rack and the underground dungeon. He had hurried Dermot O'Hurley to his agonising death only days before Perrott was due to take the oath as Lord Deputy in June 1584, knowing that the new governor of Ireland would never have countenanced his gory methods. Perrott thought religion 'would rather be taught than forced', and as he explained in September 1585, 'to that end I was desirous of an university, whereof I can see no hope without St Patricks'.[37]

Perrott lost his battle with the Archbishop. St Patrick's survived for Dean Swift and posterity thanks to the phenomenal greed of Archbishop Loftus, who certainly did not care for its architectural value. Perrott returned to England in 1586. However, the Archbishop was now sufficiently rattled to join the campaign to establish a college on an alternative site.

The site agreed between Loftus and the Dublin corporation was the old monastery of All Hallows, near Hoggen Green, east of the city walls, which had been handed over to the council at the dissolution. Perrott's successor, Lord Henry Fitzwilliam, solicited funds from the local gentry and at a cost of just over £2,000 the building went up. The warrant for the licence to incorporate a university was signed on 29 December 1591, followed by a charter under which the college was styled the College of the Holy and Undivided Trinity of Queen Elizabeth, near Dublin. Lord Burghley was appointed the first Chancellor while the visitors included the Archbishop of Dublin, the Chief Justice and the mayor of Dublin. The first students were admitted in January 1593.

Trinity College was launched. Its ideological purpose was crystal clear. The Queen had said in her letter of December 1591 that she had founded Trinity 'whereby knowledge and civility might be encreased by the instruction of our people there whereof many have usually heretofore used to travel into France, Italy and Spain to get learning in such universities, where they have been infected with popery and other ill quality and so become evil subjects.'[38] Loftus made the same point to the aldermen and mayor of Dublin: 'You need not hazard them [your children] abroad for the acquiring of foreign accomplishments, having a well endow'd university at your door.' The new college, he predicted, 'will in this tyme of Reformacon dazle the eyes of the Papists'.[39]

Many Irish Catholics took this propaganda all too seriously. A petition of Irish exiles from around that time complained that while former kings had tried to suppress education in Ireland altogether, Queen Elizabeth was undermining their faith by luring the nation's youth into a Protestant seminary. 'Within the last two or three years the English have opened a college in Dublin to make the Irish the slaves of heresy by handing over our youth to be instructed by English heretics,' they said.[40]

They need not have worried. Ireland's Protestant college was a pathetically inadequate response to the challenge of the Catholic seminaries. The first generation of students produced a great Protestant thinker in James Ussher, but the number of students attending Trinity in the early years was minute. Even if every one became a preaching minister in Ireland – an unlikely prospect – it was a drop in the ocean compared to the hundreds of seminarians streaming back each year from France, Spain, Portugal, the Netherlands and Rome. Elizabeth wanted a college to wean the Pale gentry off their Catholicism. She was disappointed. By the time Trinity appeared, Dublin had already given its allegiance to Catholicism and the pronounced Calvinist tone of the new foundation made it even less popular with the community. From the day it opened, Trinity was seen as the college for the New English, not the Pale.

The impression was confirmed by the appointment of a succession of ultra-Calvinist provosts, Walter Travers, Luke Challoner, Henry Alvey and William Temple, men so hostile to the spirit and letter of the Book of Common Prayer that they could scarcely be considered Anglicans. By the 1590s such men were virtually unemployable in the Church of England. But they got top jobs in England's Irish dustbin, where any Protestant crank was taken as an ally.

James I looked on Elizabeth's Protestant Irish seminary with a cold, sceptical eye. He held out little hope for converting the Old English of the Pale and complained that Trinity College was not even attracting the native Irish. 'The simple natives . . . [who] we hear are found to be far more tractable . . . than amongst the uncomfortable English are still kept in darkness,' he said in 1620. 'We have reason to expect that in all this long time of our peaceable government some good numbers of the natives should have been trained up in that college.'[41]

The Catholic Church in Ireland in the 1620s was not a garden of the virtues. There were turf battles between the secular and religious clergy. The ancient struggle between the Old English and the native Irish was simply exported to a new background on the Continent. The organisation of the Church was lopsided and by the 1620s the Church in Ireland faced the problem of too few bishops and too many clergy. Bishop Patrick Comerford of Waterford complained to Luke Wadding that 'ere it be longe we are like to have one against every house'.[42] He feared that the surplus of clergy might stimulate anti-clericalism, 'beinge so many in a poore beggarlie country'.

A *Note of Archbusshoppes and Busshoppes of Ireland Consecrated and Authorised by the Pope* in 1618 reported that most of the Catholic hierarchy was still outside the country. Of the four archbishops, Lombard of Armagh was in Rome, Owen McMahon of Dublin was in Louvain and Flaithri O Maolchonaire (Florence Conry) of Tuam was in Spain. The one archbishop actually in Ireland was David Kearney of Cashel, who was reported to be in Tipperary. The only other bishop in the country was David Rothe, recently elected to Ossory. Once Rothe was in place, he consecrated Maurice Hurley to Emly and Richard Arthur to Limerick in 1623. Soon after, William Therey was consecrated to Cork in Brussels. In 1624, the three new bishops presided over a synod in Kilkenny. And it was at such synods, at Drogheda in 1614, at Armagh in 1618 and at Kilkenny in 1624, that Tridentine teaching was disseminated on marriage, baptism, confession and preaching and some attempt made to suppress the neo-pagan bawdiness at funerals and wakes.

By the 1620s the Church of Ireland was beginning to recover from the hammer blows inflicted on it in the latter half of Elizabeth's reign. As Bishop of Meath, James Ussher produced the first academic defence of the Church of Ireland, the *Discourse on the Religion Anciently Professed by the Irish and British*, in 1623. This weighty volume, the fruit of Ussher's extensive trawls through the country's libraries and church annals, challenged Rome's claim to the allegiance of the Irish by arguing that the Protestant Church was doctrinally truer to the Church of St Patrick than its papal rival. 'This country was heretofore, for the number of holy men that lived in it, termed the iland of Saints,' he wrote, before posing the rhetorical question: 'What one received any solemn canonization from the Pope before Malachias Archbishop of Armagh? . . . we reade of sundry Archbishops that have beene in this land betwixt the dayes of Saint Patrick and of Malachias, what one of them can be named that ever sought for a pall from Rome?'[43] Ussher's conclusions sounded very authoritative. 'As farre as I can collect by such records of the former ages as have come into my hands,' he wrote, 'the religion professed by the ancient bishops, priests, monks and other Christians in this land was for substance the very same with that which now by publike authoritie is maintained therein.'

Ussher did a great deal to revive interest among both Catholics and Protestants in the cult of Patrick and the old Celtic Church. The sheer novelty and boldness of his claim was striking. Before Ussher appeared, it had occurred to no one that the collection of crooks, cranks, adventurers and torturers who staffed the upper echelons of the Church of Ireland were the heirs of St Patrick. The Church of Ireland had been dumb in the face of Rome's taunts. Ussher's insistence that it was the true descendant of the church of the ancient Celts gave it a new self-confidence and a belief in itself that the vicissitudes of history have never quite shaken.

Ussher made some order out of the Church of Ireland's hopeless doctrinal clutter. He also introduced a new note of charity into its controversy. Loftus dealt with his rival archbishop by having his fleshed burned off. Ussher was the hammer of the Catholics in public but in private he conducted a fruitful correspondence with Catholic intellectuals. The Franciscan, Thomas Strange, told Wadding in Rome in 1628 that he had struck up a curious relationship with 'the man that can do us more mischief than all else in the kingdom'. He added: 'I keep up a good correspondence with him . . . and he makes much of me and of others on my account. He has a famous library; let me know whatever you have me search out in the said library, for he allows me access to it.'[44] Ussher had the grace to acknowledge the help of Bishop Rothe in his book, *The Antiquities of the British Churches*, which he published in 1539.

If Ussher injected a little thought into the Church of Ireland, some of his contemporaries tidied up its externals. William Bedell, Provost of Ussher's alma mater from 1626–9 moderated the college's ultra-Calvinist ethos and introduced a new dignity into college worship. In 1629, when he was translated to the diocese of Kilmore, he was succeeded by Robert Ussher, the first Irish-born provost. James I encouraged the Church of Ireland to recover alienated land. Slowly, the Church began to repair the fabric of its ruined cathedrals. The number of preaching ministers edged up. In Bishop Lyon's old diocese of Cork there were 39 clergy by 1615, of whom 16 were listed as preachers. Significantly, four had Irish names.[45] But the Protestant recovery was limited. It could not now loosen the hold of the Catholic Church on the faith of the majority. John Rider, the Dean of St Patrick's who had sparred with Henry Fitzsimon at the turn of the century, expressed the Church's continuing dilemma when he presented a report on the state of his diocese of Killaloe in 1622. Rider was one of the more energetic Jacobean bishops. In the 10 years he had been in Killaloe he had sent several bilingual clergy to Trinity, such as the wonderfully named Neptune Blood, 'a student in ye colledge at Dublin, a good scholar and reades ye Irishe tongue'. His cathedral was 'in very good repaire and adorned with a new pulpit and with many new, faire and convenient seates'. He had raised the number of clergy in the diocese from 7 to 47, of whom 24 could be classed as preaching ministers.

It had come too late to alter the religious loyalty of the majority of people in Killaloe. The Counter-Reformation got to Killaloe before the real Reformation and in the 1620s Rider's flock was continuing to withdraw from the parish churches and go to the priests for burial, marriage and christening, much to the detriment of the parish clergy, whose 'maintenance is nowe made lesse than formerly; yea, much less than is given to ye popish preists'. Bishop Rider complained of 'ye despising of my jurisdiction to wch very few are obedient at this day, occasioned partly by ye negligence of sherrifes . . . [and] partly through ye multitiude of priests and popish lawyers who still hold ye people in hand'.[46]

If this was true of Rider's diocese, it is not difficult to imagine the situation in a less well run diocese. In Kilmacdaugh and Clonfert, the royal visitors in 1615 found Bishop Roland Lynch's affairs in chaos. The local man of whom great hopes had been conceived in the 1580s was a broken reed by 1615. Lynch's task was not eased by the enormous number of livings impropriated to the Earls of Clanricard and other laymen, none of whom supplied these parishes with curates. But what were the ecclesiastical visitors to make of a Protestant bishop whose own family, not to mention his servants, were all Catholics? The diocesan finances were in such confusion, they reported, that 'we are unable to ascertain the value of these bishoprics with any kind of certainty'. The Bishop, they added, dealt 'perversely and fraudulently with us'.[47]

William Lithgow toured Ireland in 1619 and presented a very poor picture of the average Church of Ireland clergyman. Their 'bruised Latin' was 'seldom or never expressed unless under the force of quaffing', he said. 'The ale house is their Church, the Irish priests their consorts . . . their text, Spanish Sack; their prayers, carousing . . . their blessing, aqua vitae'.[48]

The Old English were lost to the Protestant cause under Elizabeth I. The native Irish slipped away under James I, as the seminarians infiltrated the countryside. Having failed to convert the existing population, the English began work on a more drastic solution to the Irish problem. They would import a whole new population of ready-made Protestants to serve as permanent watchmen on the rest. The location for this vast experiment was Ulster, the lands of the exiled earls.

CHAPTER SEVEN

The Scum of Both Nations

The King had a natural love to have Ireland planted with Scots as being, beside
their loyalty, of a middle temper between the English tender and Irish rude breeding
and a great deal more like to adventure to plant Ulster than the English.
(Andrew Stuart)[1]

The road from Belfast to the Ards peninsula in the east of Ulster passes through the
most densely populated part of the six counties of Northern Ireland. As far as the
coastal town of Bangor, the land has been absorbed into Belfast's suburban sprawl.
South-east of Bangor the road along the peninsula runs into quieter territory. Here
the traces of an older settlement pattern start to emerge. Banks of Edwardian villas
and mock-Tudor suburbs melt away, and in Ballywalter the clapboard fishermen's
cottages that line the main street run parallel to mudflats, which at dusk echo to
the mournful call of thousands of sandpipers feeding in the tidewater.

The feel and look of Ballywalter's single-storey wooden cottages recall villages
of about the same vintage on the other side of the Atlantic Ocean. There is a faint
reminder of New England here. The principal difference is wealth. The villages on
Cape Cod ooze self-confidence and an almost monumental prosperity that has no
echo on the Ards peninsula.

There is another difference. The villages on Cape Cod take visible pride in the
dates of their foundation. The painted sign proclaiming the year the settlement
was incorporated in the 1620s and 1630s is the first thing that greets the visitor.
The villages of the Ards peninsula remember only one date – 1690, the Protestant
year of miracles. In Ballywalter a triumphal arch bisects the main street. It is decorated with a series of coloured panels. The central panel depicts William of
Orange on his white horse. The two side panels both show the red hand of Ulster
on a white background. The inscription above reads NO SURRENDER and REMEM-
BER 1690. On the top fly two flags, the Union flag and a more recent composition,
the Drumcree flag, consisting of a crown, an Orange sash and the words HOLY
BIBLE. On the bottom is written 'Drumcree, Here we stand, we can do no other'.
Beneath it: 'Civil and religious liberty'.

The villages of Cape Cod and the Ards peninsula were founded at much the
same time by much the same kind of adventurers and disputatious Puritans. But

their destinies were different. The villages of New England spawned a phenomenally successful colony, which within a century and a half would break free of Britain and emerge as a Protestant superpower, dwarfing the motherland in size and strength.

The villages of the Ards peninsula were the start of something much less successful. The population of the United States today is about 280 million, of whom about 130 million belong to mainstream Protestant denominations. The Protestant population of Northern Ireland is less than one million, smaller now than 150 years ago. And while the United States shrugged off its colonial era generations ago, the descendants of the Ulster settlers have rarely had the luxury of imagining an independent existence. The triumphal arch in Ballywalter, decorated with the picture of the Protestant British King, is not a quaint historic relic like the stagy Puritan settlements which have been reconstructed for the benefits of tourists in New England. It is a reminder to everyone entering the town that the great issues at stake in 1690 remain unresolved 300 years later.

In the 1600s it was not at all clear which would be the more successful colony of the two, the Plantation of America, or the Plantation of Ulster. Many put their bets on the latter. Ulster had about 30,000 colonists in the 1630s. Virginia and New England had only about 8,000. The journey to America was extremely dangerous and the first harvests in the New World were disastrous. The dangers posed by the indigenous American population threatened them with annihilation. Ulster was a few hours by boat from Scotland and a brief spell of seasickness was the main hazard. The first harvests of the colonists in the Ards in 1606 and 1607 were fruitful. After the flight of Ulster's Gaelic chiefs in 1607, the danger posed by the native Irish was minimal. So it seemed.

The Plantation of Ulster, like the colonisation of America, was a Protestant undertaking. There was to be no repeat of the failed Munster Plantation, in which English Catholics had also taken part. The Munster Plantation had collapsed in 1598, when the Ulster rebellion spread to the south. It had structural weaknesses that the managers of the new enterprise were determined not to repeat. The estates, averaging 12,000 acres each, had been too big. The existing tenants were not moved off their land: they merely exchanged one landlord for another. This time the 'undertakers' who undertook to plant the land were forced to import English and Scottish tenants.

The colonisation of Ulster was not a single enterprise. In the eastern counties, on the Ards peninsula and in Belfast, the settlements were the private enterprise of a couple of adventurers. The Belfast settlement in County Antrim was the work of the future Lord Deputy, Sir Arthur Chichester, who was granted a patent to 'the castle of Bealfaste or Belfest with the Appurtements and Hereditaments Spiritual and Temporal, sitaute in the Lower Clandeboye'[2] in November 1603. The new owner thanked Lord Cecil for the grant, though he artfully suggested the gift was not worth much. 'Tuching a Pattent for the Government of Knockfergus and landes of Belfast . . . I will gladly sell the whole landes for the which others sell, five poundes in fee simple . . . yet I must acknowledge myselfe much bound to your lordshipe for procuringe the same for me'.

The settlements in County Down were the work of two Scots buccaneers from Ayrshire, Hugh Montgomery and James Hamilton, who gained their lands in 1605 from Con O'Neill, Lord of Upper Clandeboye, in a dubious exchange. O'Neill had been imprisoned: after his escape from jail in Carrickfergus, Montgomery offered to interpose with the King to secure his restoration in return for half his land. James I endorsed the deal but forced Montgomery to share the spoils with Hamilton, then the bursar of Trinity College. Hamilton took the west of Down. Montgomery took the east. The King's blessing on the enterprise was a significant sign of the new esteem the Scots enjoyed in Ulster.

The crown Plantation had nothing to do with these settlements in County Down and Antrim. It rose from the ashes of the rebellion of 1598. After O'Neill's capitulation in 1603, the northern earls of Tyrone and Tyrconnell hung on to their possessions for a few years. But as it became clear that the old Gaelic order they represented had been irrevocably defeated and that their only possible future was one of continual harassment and arrest, they left the country. The flight of the earls and their retinues in 1607 left a huge vacuum in Ulster, which James was determined to fill as soon as possible. The counties of Coleraine, Tyrone, Armagh, Fermanagh, Cavan and Donegal were forfeited to the crown and a commission promptly set up to survey the lands, which completed its task in September 1608.

The crown outlined its plan for this large territory in *A Collection of Such Orders and Conditions as are to be Observed by the Undertakers upon the Distribution and Plantation of the Escheated Lands in Ulster*. The plan set out to avoid the errors of the Munster Plantation. Instead of blocks of 12,000 acres, the land in Ulster was divided into holdings of 2,000, 1,500 and 1,000 acres. The holders of the bigger estates were to be obliged to build a castle, or bawn, within two years. They had to take the Oath of Supremacy. They were to reside on their new estates for at least five years. They were forbidden to alienate any of the land to the Irish. The crown would allocate some land to its Irish clients and supporters, but the rent of more than £10 per 1,000 acres was double the amount charged to British settlers.

A comparison between the two plantations, the government one and the private one, reads like a capitalist parable. The state-controlled enterprise, from the point of view of the Protestants, was a relative flop. It was corruptly managed, riddled with inefficiency and ruinously expensive. The private enterprise was a Protestant success.

In the crown Plantation, many of the undertakers sold their plots almost immediately, or left Irish tenants on their lands. The cost of the enterprise was so enormous that the King was forced to drag in the City of London and squeeze the City companies. Reluctantly, they offered £15,000 to settle 4,000 acres around Derry and another 3,000 acres around Coleraine. The agreement between the City and the King to this effect was signed on 28 January 1610. Under its terms, the City undertook to build 200 houses in Derry, of which 60 were to be completed by November that year. A further 100 houses were to be built in Coleraine. A governing board was set up, the Society of the Governor and Assistants, London, of the New Plantation in Ulster, later known as the Honorable the Irish Society. This was the body that was responsible for ordering the work and channelling funds. In 1613 Derry was renamed Londonderry in recognition of the connection between the English capital and the new city rising on the banks of the Foyle. Yet the City had never wanted to get involved in Ireland. After the bad business in Munster, English businessmen looked on Ireland as a very dodgy investment.

The Plantation turned into an ethnic and religious patchwork quilt. Hamilton and Montgomery peopled their holdings in Down with tenants from their home towns in south-west Scotland. The inhabitants of north County Down are very largely the descendants of emigrants from Ayr, Renfrew, Wigtown, Dumfries and Kircudbright. In Belfast, Chichester mingled Scots and Manx settlers with families from his native Devonshire. The settlers of the crown Plantation were both Scottish and English. In Londonderry and County Fermanagh, English immigrants were in the majority, which explains the strongly Anglican character of County Fermanagh even today. But the crown Plantation was far more corruptly managed than the private settlements and repeated many of the errors of

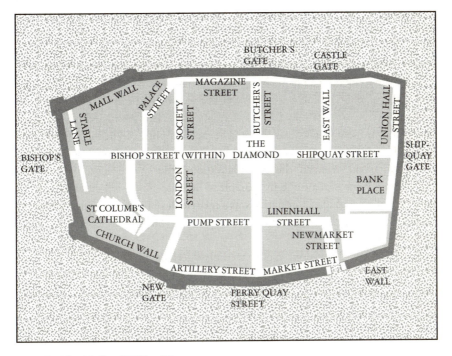

Map 4   The Medieval Walls of Derry

Elizabeth's experiment in Munster. As in Munster, the native Irish were frequently left on their lands, especially where the land was poor, in the uplands of Tyrone, in south County Armagh, in much of Donegal and in Cavan. The contours of Ulster's modern political and religious conflicts were fixed in the 1600s.

Reports of 1611 and 1619 expressed the mingled feelings of satisfaction and disappointment in government circles over the enterprise. Commissioners in 1611 found that on Chichester's land, 'the towne of Bealfast is plotted out in good forme, wherein are many famelyes of English, Scotch and some Manksmen already inhabitinge, of which some are artificers who have buylte good tymber houses with chimneys after the fashion of the English palle [Pale] and one inn with very good lodginge w[hi]ch is a great comforte to the travellers in those partes'.[3] By 1619 it was reported that there were at least 8,000 British settlers in Ulster as a whole, and that they had built 107 castles and 1,879 new dwellings 'of stone and timber after the English manner'.[4]

The Londonderry Plantation was in a worse condition. There were fewer settlers and too many Irish natives on the City of London's land, according to the commissioners, a state of affairs they blamed on unscrupulous estate agents who 'finding the Irish more profitable than the Brittish tenants are unwilling to draw on the Brittish, persuading the company that the land are mountainous and unprofitable'.[5] A report in 1622 underlined the small scale of immigration: 'The whole number of Brittishe men inhabyteinge and now found resident in the Citty of London Derry, the towne of Coleraine, Fort of Culmore and upon the whole 12 proporcons planted by the Londoners doth contain 979', it said.[6] They were very much outnumbered in the area, the report added, by at least 4,000 natives.

From the start the Scots felt more affinity with the land than the English. America might be a New England but Ulster never would be. The Scots felt they were tougher and better suited to the terrain than the English. Andrew Stuart, minister at Donaghadee, in County Down, from 1645 to 1671 and an early historian of his little tribe, viewed the English in a friendly but patronising way. 'Being a great deal more tenderly bred at home in England, they were very unwilling to flock hither except to good land such as they had before at home', he wrote: 'besides that the marshiness and fogginess of this island was still found unwholesome to English bodies, more tenderly bred and in a better air, so that we have seen multitudes of them die in a flux called here the country disease, at their first entry'.[7] Stuart went on: 'The King had a natural love to have Ireland planted with Scots as being, beside their loyalty, of a middle temper between the English tender and Irish rude breeding and a great deal more like to adventure to plant Ulster than the English'.[8]

The first generation of colonists in Ulster was Protestant but they were not God fearing. Like many recent Australian historians, Stuart took a perverse pride in the base material from which the colony was constructed. They were 'all of them generally the scum of both nations', he said, 'whom for debt or breaking and fleeing from justice or seeking shelter came hither, hoping to be without fear of man's justice'.[9]

Stuart's message was not democratic but theological. Like any good preacher he knew God could create great things out of dross. And if the first settlers were fleeing civilised society, God's self-appointed agents in the Scottish reformed Church were hot in pursuit of them. Within 15 or 20 years of their arrival the 'scum' of the Plantation would undergo an enormous religious revival that would transform Ulster into a citadel of zealous Protestantism.

The men behind the first great awakening were Scots Presbyterians with little time for the Anglican Protestantism of the Church of Ireland. Take Robert Blair, a former professor at Glasgow invited to Ulster by Hamilton, now ennobled as Viscount Clandeboye. He arrived in Bangor in 1622 and soon found clerical allies for the ministry he envisaged among fellow Scots immigrants, in particular Robert Cunningham, minister at Holywood and John Ridge, minister at Antrim.

The kind of ministry Blair intended to conduct in Ulster was shaped by his experience in the Church of Scotland. The Scottish 'Kirk' had been Calvinist since the Reformation. However, James I had succeeded in forcing bishops back into the system, where they formed a crypto-Anglican element, locked in a state of almost permanent conflict with Presbyterian purists. At a church assembly held in Perth in 1618 Blair had found himself ranged against the bishops, led by Archbishop Spottiswoode of St Andrews, who were fighting for the introduction of five Anglican practices, including kneeling at communion, confirmation ceremonies and the observance of saints' days and holy days. Blair was bitterly hostile to the entire programme and the struggle at Perth sharpened his hostility to the bishops. 'Yea, then I perceived that prelacy itself was the worst of all corrupt ceremonies', he recalled, 'and was then fixed in my judgement never to approve their way, it being destructive to the purity of the Gospel'.[10]

Anglican writers trawled the writings of the early Church Fathers for ammunition against their Catholic opponents. When Blair retired from the fray at Perth to consider questions of church government he never gave a thought to those Fathers on whom the Anglicans set such store. He took his stand on the Bible and passed his private judgement. As he wrote: 'In searching the scriptures I did find that our saviour upon several occasions did forbid . . . lordship and domination, even to his extraordinary commissioners and consequently to all that shall bear office at any time in his kirk'.[11] It simply never occurred to a man like Blair that a bishop ought to know any more about church doctrine than he did. An instinctive distrust of hierarchy affected Presbyterian attitudes to the state as well. In spite of the fact that Lord Clandeboye had invited Blair to Bangor, the minister bluntly told the Viscount he had no intention of using the corrupt and papistical Anglican liturgy, or of submitting to Anglican ordination. He was 'very plain with the noble patron who had given me the invitation', he said, 'that I could not submit to episcopal government, nor any part of the English liturgy which was there in use'.[12]

Far from being rapped over the knuckles for impertinence, Clandeboye flattered Blair into submitting to a form of ordination at the hands of the Bishop of Down that was so modified in the direction of Presbyterianism that even his tender principles were not affronted. It was the Anglican Bishop who submitted to the Presbyterian minister, not the other way around. Bishop Echlin confessed in almost grovelling terms that he was 'old and can teach you ceremonies and you can teach me substance'. Knowing what a low opinion Blair had of 'ceremonies', it was a strange admission. But Blair was not satisfied yet. 'I told him that [episcopal ordination] was contrary to my principles to which he replied both wittily and submissively "whatever you account of episcopacy, yet I know you account a presbyter to have divine warrant. Will you not receive ordination from Mr Cunningham and adjacent brethren and let me come in amongst them?" . . . This I could not refuse and so the matter was performed'.[13]

It was a shoddy compromise. A minister who detested and despised bishops had agreed to a form of episcopal ordination; an Anglican bishop had ordained a minister who scorned his Church's liturgy and doctrine. It was an uncomfortable arrangement, which reflected the peculiar circumstances of the Anglo-Scottish Plantation. Within a decade it would come under harsh scrutiny.

For the moment, all was well. Inside the Church in Ireland, the Scots built up a network of congregations in Ulster which were effectively Presbyterian. At Bangor there was Blair, and at Holywood there was Cunningham. James Glendinning ministered at Oldstone, John Knox's grandson, Josias Walsh, served at Templepatrick and John Livingston was at Killinchie.

The religious awakening they led was named the Five Mile Water revival, after the river which connected many of the towns and villages that were affected. Initially, it was the work of the weakest link in the ministerial chain. James Glendinning was more or less a lunatic and it was worries about his mental health that prompted Blair to persuade him to move from the populous port of Carrickfergus to the backwater of Oldstone. Buried in this hamlet outside Antrim, Glendinning declined to sink into hoped-for obscurity. He began preaching in a manic, hysterical way, concentrating almost exclusively on the topic of divine punishment. Glendinning had the kind of madness that attracts rather than repels the crowd. The pastor's frantic tone soon electrified the godless 'scum of both nations' who had drifted into Ulster in the first phase of the Plantation.

The revival was a natural human response to the Plantation's anarchic conditions, where the values of a more stable world seemed lost in the chaos of a frontier society. Glendinning's pitiful cries tapped a vein of suppressed anxiety and emotion. But he was a loose cannon – a man who in the wonderfully terse estimation of a later Scottish Church historian 'would never have been chosen by a wise assembly of ministers'.[14] At Bangor, Blair was deeply concerned by the news coming out of Oldstone. He was appalled by the general air of hysteria and by the idiosyncratic theology.

A lively understanding of the Holy Spirit was the cornerstone on which Protestant doctrine was built. But with no Pope to set limits, what was to stop every Christian from appealing to his or her own understanding of the Holy Spirit? Luther had encountered this problem in the 1520s, when the Reformation in the German city of Münster famously developed into a shocking revolt against traditional sexual morality. Glendinning was not as dangerous as that. But his preaching was dangerously idiosyncratic. He harangued people on 'nothing but the law, wrath and the terrors of God for sin'.[15] When Blair visited him at his home he was disgusted to find that that minister had 'begun to vent other conceits . . . that whosoever would join with him in a ridiculous way or roaring out some prayer, laying their faces on the earth, would be undoubtedly converted and saved'.[16]

Glendinning's ministry was a little bizarre. But he was a catalyst. His sermons set the string of settlements along the Five Mile Water in turmoil and created a hunger for preaching, which Blair's colleagues were eager to satisfy. It was in the aftermath of Glendinning's preaching that Walsh was sent to Templepatrick, next door to Oldstone, in order 'to heal them whom the other by his ministry had wounded'.[17] James Hamilton, the nephew of Lord Clandeboye, was sent to Ballywalter. George Dunbar went to Larne.

The 1620s and the early 1630s became a golden age for the Scottish ministers of Ulster as they forged a new identity for the Ulster Protestant community. Some of Blair's colleagues were English, like Mr Hubbard of Southwark, who ministered in Carrickfergus in the early 1620s, and John Ridge, the Oxford-educated minister at Antrim. But the dominant note was Scottish, not English, Presbyterian not Anglican, and was strongly influenced by the Presbyterian understanding of the doctrines of Predestination and Election. The sense of separation was strong from the start. Unlike earlier waves of English settlers who intermingled with the native Irish, the Scots community in Ulster kept resolutely apart.

The Scottish ministers were helped by the fact that both the Protestant bishops in Ulster in the 1620s, Echlin of Down and Knox of Raphoe, were Scotsmen, inclined to favour their compatriots and turn a blind eye to their blatant nonconformity. Blair enjoyed the favour of men in high places. It was Lord Clandeboye who introduced him to James Ussher, the Archbishop of Armagh. Blair's fervency and certitude brought out the Archbishop's latent sympathies for the ideological left wing of the Reformation. Primate Ussher was as deferential to Blair as Bishop Echlin had been, even when Blair bumptiously informed him that he could not dine again in the Archbishop's house because the Anglican liturgy was used there. Portentously, Blair told the Archbishop of his disappointment at having 'met with the English liturgy in his [Ussher's] family', because he had 'expected another thing in the family of so pious and learned a man'.[18] It was a pretty mean compliment to pay to an archbishop who had shown him nothing but courtesy but

Ussher remained emollient and assured Blair in gushing terms at a later meeting that he would never surrender to political pressure to prosecute the Scottish ministers for nonconformity. 'They think to cause me to stretch forth my hand against you', he said, 'but all the world shall never make me to do so'.[19]

But the good times were soon over. Even by the standards of a Church that accommodated Magrath in one archbishopric and Loftus in another, the state of affairs in Ulster was an intolerable anomaly. The Scots had tugged the entire province in the direction of nonconformity. Belfast was a good example. It was not a predominantly Scottish settlement, but it grew into a centre of religious dissent where the inhabitants practised what the bishops called a 'very refractory' version of Anglicanism, including burying their dead without prayers and coming into church with their hats on.[20]

When John Livingston came over to Ulster in 1630, at Lord Clandeboye's invitation, his ordination by Bishop Knox was like Blair's. The Bishop was only one of several to ordain presbyters and again the liturgy was doctored to suit Presbyterian consciences. In Livingston's case it was a kind of ordination *à la carte*. 'He gave me the book of ordination and desired that anything I scrupled at I should draw a line over it on the margin',[21] the minister recalled with satisfaction. 'But I found it had been so marked by others before that I needed not mark anything; so the Lord was pleased to carry that business far beyond anything I had thought or almost ever desired'.

The lax regime in the Ulster Church survived until James I's death in 1625 and continued under Charles I. Change was delayed by the fact that the new King had to put up with George Abbot, his father's Calvinistic Archbishop of Canterbury, until 1633. After that, the brakes came off. William Laud, standard-bearer of the anti-Calvinist faction in the Church of England, moved to Canterbury. The remodelling of the Church of England could begin in earnest. And both Laud and Charles were determined to export their version of High Church Anglicanism to Ireland.

The instrument in Ireland was a forthright Yorkshireman, Thomas Wentworth. After his appointment as Lord Deputy in 1632 he reached Ireland, following many delays, in 1634. Ulster was not Wentworth's only problem in sorting out the Church of Ireland. The glaring nonconformity of Catholic Dublin also demanded attention. Above all, there was the huge problem of the alienation of church property, which had wrecked the Irish Church's finances since the Reformation. The Lord Deputy terrorised bishops whom he discovered in the act of disposing of yet more of the Church's patrimony. He boasted to Laud of the effect he had had on the Bishop of Killaloe, caught signing away church lands worth £500 a year to Sir Daniel O'Brien for an annual rent of £26. He informed Laud he had told the Bishop 'he had deserved to have his rochet . . . pulled over his ears'.[22]

Wentworth's Irish policy was deservedly nicknamed 'thorough' and Ulster could not escape his hostile scrutiny for ever. Laud dealt carefully with Primate

Ussher. He genuinely respected Ussher's learning, while the Irish Primate respected Laud's determination to rebuild the Church's fortunes and political muscle. However, the Primate was sidelined progressively as Laud arrogated to himself control over Irish church appointments.

The English Archbishop even took over the management of the Church of Ireland's doctrine. Ussher had played a key role in drawing up the Church of Ireland's formularies in 1615. Though similar to the Church of England's own doctrinal standard, the Thirty-Nine Articles, they were an independent work and tilted in the direction of Calvinism on the questions of Predestination, Sunday observance and the Pope as the Antichrist.[23] Laud and Wentworth were determined to erase even these minor differences and quash Irish particularism. The Irish Church Articles were ceremonially scrapped in July 1634, when Wentworth convoked a joint session of the Irish parliament and a convocation, at which the clergy were instructed to adopt the Anglican articles and canons. It was a humiliating event for Ussher. The nominal President of the Church's convocation had to oversee the destruction of his own handiwork. In effect, the Church of Ireland was forced to rescind any claim to think for itself. Like so many generations of Catholic English churchmen before him, Laud believed that everything good in Ireland had come from England. In 1634 he rammed that message down the Irish Church's throat.

Empty posts were reserved to men of Laud's stamp, who shared the English Primate's fierce hostility to Calvinist theology and Puritanism. When Bishop Echlin of Down died in 1635, he was replaced by another Scotsman. But the new man, Henry Leslie, the former Dean of Down, was as determined as his mentor to see the Anglican liturgy, vestments and ceremonial applied in full.

Leslie's appointment was of importance only to Ulster. Richard Bramhall, the new Bishop of Derry, had a wider brief. Bramhall was Wentworth's former chaplain and a member of what one historian has called Wentworth's 'Yorkskire mafia'.[24] A high flyer in Laud's Counter-Reformation in the Anglican Church, Bramhall acted as Laud's eyes and ears in Ireland. He was, as his Scottish enemies said in 1640, 'a man prompt for exalting Canterbury'.[25]

Regularly he reported back to the Archbishop on the dismal state of the Irish Church. He expressed indignation at the state of the Dublin churches, some of which had been turned into tennis courts or stables. In Christ Church cathedral he found that 'the vaults from one end of the minster to the other are made into tippling rooms for beer wine and tobacco, demised all to popish recusants'.[26] The affairs of St Patrick's were even worse. There, the bishop discovered that the holiest spot in the church, the choir, had recently been purloined for an enormous monument for the Earl of Cork.

Richard Boyle's £400 black marble multi-storey edifice is still an imposing sight beside the west door. In its original position by the high altar it took over the building. Bramhall sputtered that when the Dublin clergy turned to the east in the liturgy, as the cathedral statutes bound them to do, they seemed to worship the

Boyles. The Earl had flung up his glorious essay in Jacobean kitsch in honour of his dead wife's family. The news that this huge black blob occupied what once had been the high altar acted like a red rag to the famously hot-tempered Laud. To the English Primate it was a symbol of the outrageously unequal relationship that had grown up between the clergy and the laity since the Reformation – a relationship he was determined to alter. No amount of special pleading from the Earl about all his charitable works and church-building activities in Munster could deflect the flow of sarcastic letters from the Archbishop on the subject. 'It is true I have taken exceptions to the monument which you have built in St Patrick's church', he told the Earl on 21 March 1634, 'and therefore whereas your lordship writes that you . . . never heard any mouth opened against it, it seems some mouths that durst not open there did open fully here . . . '.[27]

It was the kind of struggle Laud, Wentworth and Bramhall relished, and they savoured their symbolic victory over the overmighty gentry when Boyle was forced to shift his monument down to the cathedral's west end.

With Bishop Bramhall circling over Ulster like a hawk, it was the end of the experiment of Presbyterianism within episcopacy. Ussher's pledges were ignored and Blair and his colleagues weeded out of their parishes. Blair had a final furious interview with Bishop Echlin, after which Echlin died, 'in fearful dumps of conscience',[28] it was said, gleefully. But there was no escape. The ringleaders, including Cunningham and Hamilton, were silenced at a synod held in Belfast on 10 August 1636 where the atmosphere of drama was heightened by Bramhall's personal appearance and a sermon from Bishop Leslie, who took as his text the line from Matthew 18:17: 'But if he neglect to hear the church, let him be unto thee as an heathen man'. It was not difficult to determine the synod's outcome. At 9 a.m. the following day, Bishop Bramhall read out a sentence of perpetual silence on the dissenting pastors. For a minister of the Word, a gagging order was the end of the road. In September, Blair and Livingston attempted to set sail for New England, now the only suitable destination for men with tender Puritan consciences. The weather defeated them, however and they returned to Scotland. If the New Scotland in Ulster was not quite destroyed, Wentworth and Bramhall stunted its growth. It was the beginning of the decline of the Ulster Plantation.

The plight of the Scots in Ulster worsened over the next few years. In 1637 the King and Laud overreached themselves with an ambitious plan to foist the Anglican liturgy on the Church of Scotland. Although James I had intruded bishops on to the Kirk, he had wisely left its liturgy and doctrine alone. The new service – an advance in High Church terms on the Book of Common Prayer – was spectacularly unpopular north of the border and the Scots began to circulate a covenant binding the nation to resist the reintroduction of Catholicism. The Ulster Scots suffered most from the Scottish revolt. They were more vulnerable.

After the ringleaders of the Scottish rebellion solemnly signed the covenant in Edinburgh in March 1638, Bishop Leslie detected a rapid decline in obedience among the Scottish community in Ulster. In September, he warned the Lord

Deputy that events in Scotland had raised expectations in Ulster of the imminent victory of Presbyterianism over episcopacy. 'All the Puritans in my diocese are confident that the arms raised against the king in Scotland will procure them a liberty to set up their own discipline here,' he told him.[29] By the following month the Bishop feared for his life. 'As for those who contemn and oppose my process and oppose my jurisdiction, they are more in number than would fill all the gaols in Ireland', he reported. 'As in Scotland, they are entered into a bond to defend one another by arms', he told the Lord Deputy on 18 October. 'They do threaten me for my life, but by the grace of God all their brags shall never make me faint in doing service to God and the King'.[30]

For a time, Bishop Leslie could afford to mock his disobedient flock. The Scots had a parliament and an army. The Ulster Scots had neither. 'Deceive not yourselves', Leslie warned his clergy at Lisburn in the turbulent autumn of 1638, 'for howsoever some in Scotland think themselves strong enough to resist their prince, yet, I thank God, you are not so many here but the King's law and authority is well able to overtake you'.[31]

In May 1639 the Lord Deputy resolved to stop the contagion from spreading into Ulster by forcing the local Scots to take an Oath of Abjuration against the covenant. The Black Oath, as it was called, was more far-reaching than the Oath of Supremacy, which had touched only officials. It was forced on every male of Scottish descent aged over 16 and commissioners were appointed to each parish to ensure its execution. Thousands of settlers gave up and left the country. It was a huge blow to the colony, but a greater one followed. The struggle between the Ulster Scots and the Anglican authorities was a dispute between two sets of Protestants. It took no heed of the four-fifths of the Irish population who were enemies equally of both. As royal authority collapsed first in Scotland and then England, the Irish Presbyterians and Anglicans discovered their position was like that of two prize boxers fighting on the edge of a volcano that was about to erupt.

There had always been seers who had sensed the precarious position of the Protestant colony in Ulster. In 1634, one of Blair's close colleagues had experienced just such a vision. Among the beneficiaries of Glendinning's strange ministry on the banks of the Five Mile Water, was Andrew Stewart, minister of Donegore, near Templepatrick, from 1627 to 1634. As he neared death in June that year he was seized by an apocalyptic vision of the Ulster colony being cut to shreds. 'My hair stands to behold what I see coming on these lands,' he told those around his bedside. 'The bloody wars of Germany shall never be balanced with the wars of these three kingdoms. The dead bodies of many thousands who this day despise the glorious gospel shall lie upon the earth as dung unburied'.[32] The dark words of the dying minister terrified the godly folk assembled round the minister's deathbed. 'Is there no remedy?' one of the incredulous company asked. The minister's last recorded words were prophetic. 'No remedy, no remedy, no remedy', he shouted.

For the settlers of the Ulster Plantation, 1641 was year zero. The fury of the displaced native Irish Catholics boiled up and exploded and the settlers' descendants never forgot the torments to which their community was exposed that year. They turned it into a biblical parable in which they were the Israelites, the chosen people, while the natives assumed the role of the Old Testament tribes whose destiny, it seemed, was to make trouble, rise up and be crushed and slaughtered in an inevitable divine settling of accounts. This is how Charles Hanna, the nineteenth-century historian of the Scots-Irish, described 1641:

> Neither woman nor infant was spared, the brains of the children were dashed out before the eyes of their mothers, some were thrown into pots of boiling water and some were given to the pigs that they might be eaten.
>
> A Protestant minister was crucified. Many had their hands cut off or their eyes put out before their lives were taken. Others were promised protection on condition of their becoming executioners of their own nearest and dearest relations; but if they accepted these terms they themselves were afterwards murdered.[33]

Protestant historians competed to pile horror upon horror and geared their accounts to the susceptibilities of their audience. Macaulay dwelt on the outrages inflicted on the family in tones calculated to inflame the outraged decency of his mid-Victorian, middle-class readers.

> In vain did the pious son plead for his devoted parent, in vain did the tender mother attempt to soften the obdurate heart of the assassin in behalf of her helpless child; she was reserved to see them cruelly butchered and then to undergo a like fate. The weeping wife, lamenting over the mangled carcass of her husband experienced a death no less horrid than that which she deplored . . .
>
> Women, whose feeble minds received a yet stronger impression of religious frenzy, were more ferocious than men, and children, excited by the example and exhortation of their parents, stained their innocent age with the blackest deeds of human butchery.[34]

The great Presbyterian historian, James Seaton Reid, writing in 1867, concentrated on the martyrdom of the Protestant clergy. He recorded the fates of

> Mr Mather, of Donoughmore, cut to pieces and left unburied; Mr Blythe, minister of Dungannon, hanged; Mr Fullerton of Loughgall . . . stripped and murdered, Mr Matchet, minister of Magherafelt, after a long imprisonment . . . murdered . . . Mr Hudson, minister of Desertmartin, taken between two feather beds out of Mrs Chapell's house, where he had been long fed and concealed, was discovered and murdered . . . Mr Paulmaster, that once lived at

Carrickfergus, minister there, as his wife informed me, hanged at his church door; Mr Flack, of Fermanagh, a minister of special note, was with his two sons taken out of castle Crevenish and also offered up to God as a sacrifice.[35]

It was no accident that some of the goriest accounts were published when Irish nationalist agitation for home rule was growing. The message was stark: look what happened to us before, when the Irish Catholics had the upper hand.

Among Protestants, the events of 1641 were burned into the collective memory as an awful warning of the price exacted on earth for being chosen by God. In spite of their often privileged status, the folk memory of Ulster Protestants was henceforth dominated by the idea that they were victims.

Catholics remembered 1641 very differently, as the start of an inspiring revolt against English Protestant domination, which resulted in eight years of near-freedom for the Catholic majority until Cromwell's invasion. For the Catholics, the events of 1641 were a milestone on the road towards the creation of a new Irish nationalism composed equally of Anglo-Saxon and Celt, Gael and Pale, glued together by common allegiance to Catholicism.

The bloody stories repeated by the Protestant historians were drawn from 32 volumes of survivors' testimonies. Known as depositions, they were collected on the orders of the Irish Lords Justices and the English parliament. The first batch was compiled in 1642 when the first reports of the killings reached London, and a second group was compiled in 1651. They sprang out of a climate of Protestant hysteria in England over what was going on across the Irish Sea. Events had been relayed to the English public through pamphlets such as *Bloody Newes from Ireland*, printed in London in 1641. This was the tabloid journalism of the day – short on detail, and sensational. *Bloody Newes from Ireland* breathlessly reported how the Irish papists were 'deflowring many of the women, then cruelly murdering them and pulling them about the street by the haire of the head and dashing their childrens brains out . . . and tossing their children on pikes . . . saying that those were the pigs of the English sowes'.[36]

The depositions were compiled to flesh out these wild reports and justify an agenda of retribution that Cromwell had prepared for Ireland. They paved the way for the wholesale seizure of Catholic land in the 1650s and the transplantation of the expropriated Catholic landowners to Connacht.

Catholic historians, until the mid-twentieth century often belittled the depositions as fabricated accounts. Their scepticism was enjoined by some non-Catholic writers who in the relatively civilised environment of the nineteenth century thought descriptions of mutilation and mass murder incredible. Later historians, working in the aftermath of the Holocaust, the genocide of Tutus in Rwanda, or the mass killings of Muslims in Bosnia, look on the depositions with a less sceptical eye. The numbers of victims, however, remains open to question. The English parliament in 1643 decided at least 150,000 Protestants had been killed. *The Appeal of the Protestants of Ireland*, written at the time of the second Protestant crisis of the century, in 1689, asserted that 150,000 'British Planters' were massacred in 1641 alone. Patrick Adair, author of *A True Narrative of the Rise and Progress of the Presbyterian Church in Ireland*, written in the 1690s, thought the number of victims was about 300,000.[37] Sir John Temple, whose *Irish Rebellion* of 1646 became a standard Protestant text on the event and was reprinted almost every time the Irish Protestants were in a crisis in the eighteenth century, produced a similar figure.

In the calmer waters of the eighteenth century the figure was scaled down. When William Hamilton, Archdeacon of Armagh, preached the annual sermon on 'The Dangers of Popery'in Armagh cathedral on 5 November 1723, he said that 'above an hundred thousand persons were inhumanely butchered in a short time'.[38] More recent historians have pushed the figure much lower. One authoritative recent account of the rising in Ulster says the depositions suggest that between 527 and 1,259 people were killed in County Armagh between November 1641 and May 1642.[39] If this figure is multiplied by nine, a maximum figure of about 12,000 is reached for the nine counties of Ulster. The Protestant population of Ulster is believed to have been about 34,000 at the time,[40] so by this reckoning, up to one-third of the settler population was massacred. This is the absolute maximum possible death toll; as most of the bloodshed appears to have occurred around Armagh, it may be unrealistic to calculate a figure in this way.

While Protestant apologists claimed hundreds of thousands were put to the sword, other Protestant accounts suggest that the majority of settlers lived to see the Scottish army land in Carrickfergus, County Antrim, in 1642. According to Seton, the exiled ministers Reid, Blair and Livingston returned to Ulster in September that year to huge popular acclaim, which suggests the community was far from liquidated: 'Old and experienced Christians declared that they never saw the like nor ever heard the Gospel so powerfully preached and pertinently applied with such variety of threatenings and promises, exhortations, motives, comforts and cordials and that they never saw such commotion and heart-melting among hearers, both guilty and innocent'.[41] Blair and Livingston were experienced pastors who had vehemently opposed Glendinning's alarming ministry in Oldstone. They would not have embarked on such 'threatenings' if the community was as shattered as some later Protestant historians made out.

But a great many Protestants undoubtedly had been killed. Ulster in 1641 resembled Bosnia in 1992. It was the scene of frenzied pogroms that were often the work of local people turning on their neighbours. The depositions contain stories so vivid that it is unlikely they were manufactured. Honora Beamond, 'relict of William Beamond, innkeeper in Clouness, country Monaghan', may have got the number of bodies wrong when she claimed 'she herself saw the corpses of 16 Protestants, nearly all women and children, near the common mill, after the rebels had drowned them'.[42] But was she making the whole event up?

The depositions are 'true' in the same sense that the accounts of Albanian refugees fleeing from Serb-ruled Kosovo in 1999 were 'true'. The number of victims was exaggerated and eyewitness accounts were amplified by rumour and hearsay, but what remained in such accounts was a solid core of reportage. Lady Charity Staples provided a chilling first-hand relation of her time at Moneymore as 'a prisoner with the rebels'. While she was there, 'she looked out of the window where she was kept . . . and . . . saw the rebels cutting and slashing the poor British as they passed by her window, amongst whom there was one Archy Laggan, miserably cut, his two arms being cut half off, his head cut and one of his ears half cut off and hanging down . . . '.[43]

There is grim verisimilitude in the account of Joan Constable, of Drummada, County Armagh, who said she saw Protestants burned to death in a house in Kilmore by Jane Hampton, 'formerly a Protestant woman, but a mere Irish woman, lately turned to Mass'. Mrs Constable said: 'The outcry, lamentations and shriekings of those poor murdered persons were exceeding loud and pitiful, yet did nothing prevail nor mollify the hardened hearts of their murderers but they most boldly made brag thereof and took pride and glory in imitating their cries and in telling this deponent and her husband how the little children gaped when the fire began to burn them'.[44]

Another clue to the reliability of the depositions is that many unexpectedly testified to acts of kindness by the Catholic Irish 'enemy'. This would not have occurred in manufactured accounts. Michael Harrison, who was forced to act as secretary to the principal leader of the uprising, Sir Phelim O'Neill, related the courage of a Dominican friar in December 1641 at O'Neill's headquarters in Charlemont, County Armagh. According to Harrison, 'a soldier under the command of the said Sir Phelim, having killed an English Protestant, was apprehended by a friar called Father Gynan, guardian of the Dominicans near Coleraine, and brought by the friar with his sword bloody to Sir Phelim. The friar then told Sir Phelim if he would not punish the soldier for killing such as he had protected, God Almighty would not prosper his undertakings, to which the said Sir Phelim made answer 'Go about your business, it doth not concern you!'[45]

John Kerdiff, Protestant Rector of Diserteragh, near Dungannon, County Tyrone, was 'treated with a great deal of humanity' by a friar called Malone, even if the friar did cut up his Bible and throw it on the fire.[46] Edward Slack of Gurteen, Fermanagh, said that his Catholic neighbours 'took his Bible, opened it and laying the open side of it in a puddle water, leapt and trampled on it, saying "A plague on't, this Bible hath bred all the quarrels".' It was a revealing little anecdote, which points at feelings of regret among the Catholics for the 'quarrels' rather than pure malice against the Protestant immigrants.[47]

William Skelton's deposition denied there was an atmosphere of sectarian tension on the eve of the revolt in Kinard, County Antrim. Skelton, a servant, recalled being at his plough on Friday, 22 October when the revolt broke out. He thought the Protestants of Kinard 'lived plentifully and peacefully and were to this examt's apprehension well beloved by their neighbours of the Irish and differed not in anything, as this examt doth remember, save only that the Irish went to Mass and the English to the Protestant church . . . '.[48]

Thomas Taylor, of Clanbressil, County Armagh, a tanner, examined at Lisburn on 24 February 1642, lost two uncles and three sisters in the mayhem. They were drowned at Portadown in the single most infamous and widely documented atrocity. Taylor was nearly executed at Loughgall, County Armagh, 'but it pleased God he escaped out of their hands and hid himself and got back to the tan-house after three days and the said Hugh O'Neill kept him safe till a party of the English came over the [river] Ban about lamas 1642'.[49]

To the survivors of the Ulster killings, the murder of Protestant prisoners at Portadown stood out as one of the worst atrocities committed in the conflict. Whether it was premeditated or the result of panic will never be known. Nor will the death toll, which ranged from a few dozen to several hundred in the minds of those who survived. But there is no doubt that something dreadful happened on the bridge at Portadown in the autumn of 1641.

Elizabeth Price of Armagh city was one of a party of Protestants kept prisoner with five of her children in Armagh cathedral and was offered safe conduct to England by Sir Phelim after about a fortnight's captivity. She recalled that the safe passage was entrusted to a captain, Manus O'Caine. It was then that the nightmare began.

> His soldiers having brought or rather driven like sheep or beasts to a market these prisoners, being about 115, to the bridge of Portadown, the said captain and rebels then and there forced and drove all those prisoners and amongst them this deponents' five children by name Adam, John, Anne, Mary and Jane Price off the bridge and into the water and then and there instantly and most barbarously drowned the most of them.
>
> And those that could swim and came to shore they knocked on the head and also drowned them or else shot them to death in the water.

Mrs Price said she was eventually released by the intervention of the leader of the rebellion, Owen Roe O'Neill, who having landed in Ireland from Spain 'and [was] informed of their miserable torments and sufferings and what multitude of people the said Sir Phelim and his confederates had murdered or put to death . . . He did not only enlarge and set at liberty this deponent and the other prisoners that survived . . . but gave all who asked for it a convoy to or near Dundalk'.[50]

The drowning of the English prisoners at Portadown was corroborated by several other depositions, although the details of the number of survivors vary. William Clarke, a tanner, claimed he was the sole survivor and that the number of victims was 100. James Shaw, of Market Hill, County Armagh, examined in August 1643 was not a witness to the drowning but his report throws an interesting if gruesome light on the event.

Shaw said the rebels kept him prisoner for six months until he was exchanged for a priest being held by the English. 'Many of the mere Irish rebels in the time of this deponent's staying in restraint amongst them told him very often . . . that all those that lived about the bridge of Portadown were so affrighted with the cries and noise made there by some spirits or visions for revenge that they durst not stay there', he said. One of the Irish rebels, he added, 'said within this deponent's hearing and swore he was present when a bloody villain attempting after he had drowned many others to drown a Mrs Campbell, a goodly proper gentlewoman and a Protestant and for that offering violently to thrust her into the water, she suddenly laid hold of and caught him in her arms, that wicked rebel, and they both falling into the water, she held him there fast until they were both drowned'.[51]

Good men were swept away with the not so good. William Bedell, the former Provost of Trinity and Bishop of Kilmore since 1629 was the nearest thing the Church of Ireland possessed to a saint. A stickler for the Book of Common Prayer, Bedell was a fierce opponent of corruption and a man with such a naive understanding of his mission that he never understood why the native Irish should be treated like a conquered race. At Trinity he had engaged a native boy to teach him Irish, declaring: 'My first endeavour shalbe to understand the toung of this Country which I see (although it be accounted otherwise) is a learned and exact language'. 'I have taken a little Irish boy, a Minister's Sonne of whom I hope to make good use',[52] he told his old friend Dr Ward at Sydney Sussex, Cambridge. Bedell took this attitude to the natives to Ulster, where he busied himself publishing catechisms in Irish and converting several native Irishmen to his Church.

His ministry created an uproar. Primate Ussher might claim in his writings that the Church of Ireland was the heir of St Patrick and the true Church of the Irish people, but no one had seriously tried to put this theory into practice. When Bishop Bedell did so, he unwittingly exposed the absurdity at the heart of Ussher's assumption. The planter gentry of Ulster were not interested in a brand of Protestantism that included the natives and posed a threat to their monopoly on the Church's power and patronage. A test case arose when Bedell ordained Murtagh King, one of his native Irish protégés, to the ministry. The authorities threw King into jail. Bishop Bedell bravely excommunicated the settler clergyman who intruded himself into King's living, but then found he was being threatened with the crime of praemunire, or contempt of the crown. Bedell was distraught, travelling down to Dublin to try and get King out of jail and bombarding Bramhall, Laud and Wentworth with letters of protest. 'Surely the man who translated God's word into Irish deserves better treatment,' he told the Lord Deputy in December 1638. 'I pray you do him justice.'[53]

Bedell's admiring biographer wrote that the Bishop had laid bare a deep contradiction between the political interests of the settlers and the demands of the Gospel, and had chosen the latter.

When this indulgence of My Lord of Kilmore to get Irish natives in, preferring them and encouraging them to the ministry was noised abroad, the bishop was secretly checkt by some statesmen, as if he had only acted contrary to the English interest and policy all this while by his endeavouring to make the conquered and enslaved Irish capable of preferment in church and state . . . as no man did ever so much as once attempt before His Lordship.[54]

Bedell perished in a whirlwind he had done nothing to raise. He died in rebel captivity in February 1642, although his name was apparently good enough among the Catholics to ensure him a decent burial in the precincts of his cathedral.

Ulster was the eye of the storm. But the position of Protestants in the other provinces was not much more secure. Decades of concealed frustration with the new religion burst out in acts of iconoclasm all over the south and east. Henry Palmer of Fethard, County Wexford, recorded how the local Catholics 'went into the church and cut the Pulpit cloth and the Ministers Books in pieces and strewd them about the church-yard and caused the piper to play whilst they danced and trampled them under their feet and called the Minister dog and stript him out of his clothes'.[55] At Powerscourt, County Wicklow, Henry Fisher recorded: 'Bryan Lynch of Powerscourt revolted and fell from the Protestant religion to Masse, and the said Lynch, with severall other Rebells, entered the parish church of Powerscourt, called Staggonnell, and burnt up pues, pulpits, chests and Bibles belonging to the said church, with extreme violence and triumph and expression of hatred to Religion'.

Dublin remained in English hands throughout but was flooded with refugees. 'Multitudes of English came up in troop, stripped and miserably despoiled out of the north', Temple wrote. 'Thus was the town within the compass of a few days after the breaking out of this rebellion filled with the most lamentable spectacle of sorrows, which in great numbers wandered up and down in all parts of the city, desolate, forsaken'.[56]

Protestants in other towns were in greater danger. The Catholic majority took advantage of the collapse of the crown's authority to open their gates to the rebels. The Old English of Munster were less aggressive towards the New English Protestants than the native Irish of Ulster. There was no racial element to the quarrel. But they stripped many of them of their property and turned them out. Richard Boyle, Laud's old enemy, wrote at Christmas 1641 from his castle at Lismore, County Waterford, of the 'miserable estate whereunto this kingdom is reduced. And particularly this poor province of Munster . . . every day bringing us Job's messengers of killing, preying, burning and spoiling the English and Protestants'.[57] The Earl of Cork added that Kilkenny, Cashel and Fethard had surrendered to the rebels

and all the English Protestants stripped naked . . . the walled town of Clonmell, being the shire town, hath opened her gates and let in the rebels to pillage and spoil the English Protestants and that town is within twelve miles of my house

... the city of Waterford hath no guard upon the fort or city but the townsmen and every day we look to hear when it will be given up ... for the priests rule there and flock into this kingdom, especially into this province from all foreign parts, insomuch as it is creditably certified me that there is a whole army of ecclesiastics gotten into Munster ...

And therefore even upon the knees of my soul I beg and beseech you to supplicate His Majesty and the Lords and Commons of both Houses of Parliament that this fruitful province of Munster and the English subjects that are therein may not for want of timely supply of men, money and ammunition, be lost.[58]

Boyle died in 1643. By then Scottish forces had landed in Ulster. But outside Ulster and Dublin the Catholic Old English and native Irish took control of the island. For the dispossessed Catholic clergy it was a new dawn. Cathedrals, churches and abbeys which had not seen a celebration of mass since the turmoil of 1603 were reclaimed and the townspeople could enjoy the panoply of Catholic worship, including the long-forbidden outdoor processions.

David Rothe, the scholarly Catholic Bishop of Ossory, played a decisive role, in spite of his age – he was 70 in 1643 – because his diocese was the seat of the provisional government. With Dublin in hostile hands, Kilkenny emerged as the natural alternative capital, wealthy, Old English and located in the middle of the country. Rothe had close ties to the aristocratic Old English leaders of the Confederate Catholics, as the new government was called. Lord Mountgarret, the principal leader in the uprising in Leinster, was an old ally of Rothe's who had helped get his work, the *Analecta Sacra*, published in Cologne between 1617 and 1619. It was Rothe who summoned a national synod of the Church in Ireland in May 1642 that pronounced the Catholic revolt a just war and recommended the summoning of a general assembly.

Relations between the Old English and Irish were not easy. That they operated together at all marked a phase in the slow unification of the two peoples. Catholicism was the glue that held this new Irish nationalism together. When Giovanni Battista Rinuccini, the new papal nuncio, landed in Ireland in 1645 he enjoyed a triumphal reception in Kilkenny in November. The kind of treatment that used to be accorded to the representatives of the English crown was now bestowed on a Prince of the Church. 'Outside the city gates in the church of St Patrick were assembled the clergy, secular and regular who upon my arrival proceeded towards the city in solemn procession', he recorded.

At the gate the corporation of the city were drawn up and with them the vicar general in his robes who presented me with the crucifix to kiss and when I mounted on horseback, wearing the cappe and episcopal hat, the poles of the canopy were borne by some of the chief citizens who, notwithstanding the rain, walked uncovered.

The whole way to the cathedral . . . was lined with soldiers on foot . . . at the church door the bishop of the diocese [Rothe], the ordinary of the diocese, though advanced in years, was vested in cope and awaited me; he presented the aspersorium and incense and conducting me to the high altar recited the prayers prescribed in the ceremonial after which I gave the solemn blessing and published the indulgences.[59]

Few among the crowds could have imagined they would live to see Protestantism restored in the city within only five years and the Catholic Church forced underground again. Nor could they have realised how much trouble Rinuccini was about to cause. He had not been Rome's first choice. Francesco Scarampi was selected by Urban VIII and arrived in Ireland in June 1644. A Francophile, he had a keen sympathy for Charles's French Queen, Henrietta Maria, and through her, the Anglican royalist party in England. But Urban died a month after Scarampi arrived and the next Pope, Innocent X, was less friendly to the French Queen. Scarampi was withdrawn and in his place came the 53-year-old Florentine.

The collapse of the New English brought the struggle for supremacy between the Old English and native Irish into the open. Shared Catholicism may have blurred the division between the two racial groups but it did not abolish it. The Old English harboured sentimental ties of loyalty to the crown: they liked to think they had revolted on behalf of a king threatened by his Puritan foes. The native Irish saw the struggle much more as a revolt against the very existence of the English connection. The difference meant they had different agendas. The Old English wanted to see the New English humbled. They were loath to see them wiped out.

Both sides had conservative aims, but while the Old English wanted the clock turned back to the 1530s, the native Irish seemed to hanker after a return to the days before the Anglo-Norman invasion of the 1170s.

After the initial euphoria faded, the Irish Catholic Church found it shouldered the enormous responsibility of reconciling very different recollections of the past – and visions of the future. Its policy was to be more Roman than Rome and submit all controversies to the Pope or – after his arrival – to the papal legate. It suited the instincts of a generation of clergy trained in continental seminaries to exalt the Pope's authority and it also offered the best chance of avoiding the charge that the Church was siding with either the Old English or the Irish community. But a policy of handing over vital decisions to Rinuccini could succeed only while the legate cut an impartial figure. Unfortunately for the Old English, Rinuccini soon decided the Church's interests were best served by aligning with the native Irish under Owen Roe O'Neill. It was logical enough. The Old English advocated concessions to the Protestants while the native Irish did not. The Old English were reluctant to press the Anglican king too hard on religious matters in case it cut the ground from under his feet in Protestant England. The Irish had no such scruples.

The new nuncio was instructed to consider his mission in strictly ecclesiastical terms. 'His Holiness has no other object in this mission than the salvation of souls by means of the public exercise of the Catholic religion in Ireland,' he was told.[60] The nuncio interpreted this brief in very elastic terms. He sneered at the Irish Catholic bishops, who had endured hardships he knew nothing of. The Archbishop of Dublin was too fat. The Bishop of Ossory was too old and feeble. The Bishop of Meath was a heretic. They knew nothing about vestments and liturgy and celebrated mass on ordinary tables. 'To all ceremonies, to ecclesiastical decorations . . . they scarcely lend a thought,' he sniffed.[61] Within months of his arrival he was devoting himself to fratricidal intrigues against the Ormond party which consumed the rest of his stay. He threw his entire weight against a proposed compromise over religion that Ormond offered in the King's name, but which the nuncio feared would leave the Protestants in control of urban churches in towns like Cork and Youghal. In August 1646 the nuncio denounced the 'Ormond Peace' as 'contempt of the Holy Church' and threatened to excommunicate its supporters. The clergy backed Rinuccini's hard line at a church assembly in Waterford in September 1646, a stance that was popular among both the Old English and the native Irish, neither of whom felt any desire to conciliate the Protestants at this stage. At Clonmel the gates were closed in the face of heralds sent to proclaim the deal and remained shut even against the Earl himself. The newly elected General Assembly of the Confederate Catholics on 2 February 1647 took the same line. The nuncio's tough approach to the Protestant royalists did the Catholic cause little good in the long term. After the General Assembly endorsed his rejection of the Ormond Peace on 2 February 1647, the Earl surrendered Dublin Castle to parliamentarian forces on 17 July.

Common opposition to the Ormond Peace did not stop the fissures widening between the Old English and the native Irish. After O'Neill gained a stunning victory over the English at Benburb, County Tyrone, in June 1646, the Ulster leader considered attacking the Confederate capital and wiping out his Old English opponents. To his credit, the nuncio acted as a mediating force. It was O'Neill's avarice, the nuncio wrote, that 'induced him under pretext of religion to despoil that opulent city and revenge himself on his enemies the Butlers'. He added: 'If I had not sent my confessor to dissuade him from so unjust a resolution, the city would have been sacked'.[62] However, the nuncio used the crisis to position himself even more closely at the centre of political events, assuming overall control of Confederate Catholic affairs. The nuncio blocked any settlement between the crown and the Irish Catholics that would have enabled them to confront jointly the English parliament. Rinuccini made it plain that Ireland would accept the aid of Charles I only if Catholicism was Ireland's only tolerated religion. No Protestant king could agree to those terms.

When the Confederates' Supreme Council in April 1648 agreed to a truce with the royalist General Murrough O'Brien, Lord Inchiquin, a native convert to Protestantism, Rinuccini left Kilkenny for O'Neill's camp at Kilminchy, near

Maryborough in Leix, where he excommunicated the truce's supporters and placed all towns that accepted it under an interdict.

Lord Inchiquin was, admittedly, a difficult ally for a conscientious Catholic to stomach. He had fought for both parliament and King and in the September of the previous year had presided over an infamous massacre of Catholics in Cashel cathedral. 'We killed above seven hundred men', he boasted, 'whereof many were priests and friars, besides some women that perished in the action . . . they lay five or six deep in many places'.[63] It was not difficult for Rinuccini to rouse clerical opinion against Lord Inchiquin.

The nuncio's interventions had reduced the Catholics to fratricidal warfare. By the summer of 1648 the strain began to tear the Church apart. Priest preached against priest, pulpits attacked one another and the bishops strove vainly to maintain the façade of unity. There were tragicomic scenes in Galway where the nuncio's excommunication was announced in some churches but not in the collegiate church of St Nicholas, where John Burke, the Archbishop of Tuam, overruled it.

Old English descent was not a guide to opinions on the nuncio. Patrick Comerford, the Bishop of Waterford, one of the many former pupils of Peter White's famous school in Kilkenny, came from the great Old English clans of Clonmel but remained a resolute supporter of the nuncio to the finish. In obedience to the interdict on towns that supported the truce, he closed Waterford's churches.

The Confederate Catholics appealed to Rome against its own nuncio and enlisted a clerical agent, Peter Walshe, a Franciscan, to draw up seven queries to be submitted to the clergy, one of which asked whether the excommunication and interdict were not contrary to the laws of the Irish Kingdom.

Bishop Rothe must have hated the dispute. In 1646 he had supported Rinuccini against the Ormond Peace, but by 1648 even he had turned against the nuncio as a divisive force. The nuncio, for his part, obviously despised him, and in his communications with Rome referred slightingly to the old scholar as bedridden. Along with Thomas Dease, the Bishop of Meath, Rothe sided with the Old English on the Supreme Council against the nuncio, as did Archbishop Burke of Tuam, Andrew Lynch of Kilfenora and most of the Jesuit clergy. Luke Wadding, the Confederation's agent in Rome since 1642, was a friend of Comerford's, yet he opposed the nuncio's excommunication.

The final peace between Ormond and the confederation was signed on 17 January 1649 by Rothe and 10 Catholic bishops. The nuncio left Ireland on 23 February, escorted to his ship by large crowds in Galway. The nuncio wrote that they were all in tears. He signed off on a wonderfully self-congratulatory note. 'The future must be uncertain', he told the authorities in Rome, 'but at any rate I shall leave the country with consciousness of having done all in my power to save the kingdom from the heretics.'[64] By the time the Confederates formed an alliance with Ormond it was far too late to do anything. The King had been beheaded in

January and parliament was now free to turn its attention to Ireland. The Catholic cause unravelled fast. Cromwell had arrived in Ireland in August. By November, O'Neill had died. The calculated massacre of about 2,600 members of the Old English garrison at Drogheda on 11 September had the intended effect of persuading other Catholic strongholds to cease resistance.

Rinuccini died in 1657. Bishop Comerford died in exile in Nantes in 1652; Wadding in Rome in 1657. Bishop Rothe lived just long enough to witness the virtual annihilation of everything he had worked for in more than 40 years. Cromwell reached Kilkenny in March 1650 and on 27 March the 82-year-old Bishop was among the Catholics ordered to leave the city. Even the Cromwellians were moved by the spectacle of an aged and internationally renowned intellectual being forced into exile when he was dying. He was allowed back the next month, and died on 20 April. It was a rare act of charity, for Cromwell had resolved to solve the Irish problem on lines no English king or queen had contemplated. James I's Ulster Plantation was dwarfed by the plans prepared by the English republican regime, which involved the entire property-owning class of Catholics being transported west of the River Shannon to the waste land of Connacht.

The human misery involved probably equalled anything inflicted on Russia or Poland in the 1940s by Nazi Germany. A Protestant writer in the 1670s confidently declared that Cromwell's campaigns and the subsequent transplantation did away with seven-eighths of the population and left vast tracts of the country deserted.

> For ten, sometimes twenty or thirty miles together, nay indeed, almost all the kingdom over (except about the English garrisons) one should not behold man, bird or beast; the very wild fowls of the aire and the wild beasts of the field being either dead or having departed out of those desolations and thousands of Irish daily starving for want of food did in this extremity ordinarily feed on the Souldiers horses . . . the Irish did not only feed upon horses but upon dead corps taken out of the graves.[65]

The author of *The Present State of Ireland* thought there was nothing wrong with this slaughter. On the contrary, it was a 'just judgement of God inflicted on them for their notorious barbarisme committed in their massacring the English'.

The scale of the transplantation was awesome. Of Ireland's 7.5 million profitable acres, 5.2 million were forfeited for redistribution among Irish Protestants, New English settlers and Cromwell's soldiers. About 2 million of these acres found their way back into Catholic hands after Cromwell's death. But a sea change had taken place. For the next 300 years, the land of Ireland was mostly in Protestant hands. Catholics would no longer struggle against Protestant settlers grouped in plantations, but against what came to be called a Protestant 'Ascendancy' over the whole country.

The native population, slashed to about 800,000 by 1650, survived the Cromwellian regime because of their great fertility. Within 50 years their numbers had doubled to about 1.5 million. The Catholic Church survived with them, because the soldiers and adventurers rewarded under Cromwell never became the majority population in any of the country's parishes. A survey in Limerick in 1659 showed the Irish were still in the majority in the county's parishes by a factor of at least 10 to one. In Croom there were 14 new settler residents and 458 old ones. In Adare there were 4 English settlers and 245 Irish residents. Many baronies had no English settlers at all living in them.[66]

Ironically, it was not the Irish but their old enemies the Old English who were broken. Always a minority in Ireland, they had maintained a cohesive culture through their control of property and the commercial life of the towns of the eastern and southern counties. The old colony was a casualty of Cromwell's totalitarian experiment in confiscation and transportation. Uprooted from the lands they had held for almost half a millennium, they lost their identity. The Old English had survived as a distinct community where they dominated the lives of the towns, but from 1650 their connection with the towns was broken. Families which had supplied the corporations of Dublin, Kilkenny, Clonmel, Cork and Waterford with mayors and other officers for centuries were uprooted.

The list of the transplanted families of 1655 to 1659 reads like a death notice of the Old English of Ireland: Archer, Arthur, Aylmer, Barry, Bellew, Bermingham, Blake, Bodkin, Bourke, Browne, Butler, Cusack, Dillon, Dowdall, Fitzgerald, French, Kirwan, Lynch, Nugent, Plunkett, Prendergast, Rice, Stack, Stafford, Wadding, Walshe, White. And so it went on. Most left in the summer of 1656. There was no escape. Even the meanest landowners had to pack up and head for Connacht. Katherine Quirten of Galway's date of final settlement was listed as 16 May 1656. Mrs Quirten owned two acres.[67] Anne Birmingham, and her daughters Jane, Katherine and Mary, owned 47 acres.[68] A few left-wing Puritans protested. One such was Walter Gostelow, who published a pamphlet about the divine revelation he experienced in Broad Street, London, which informed him that the transplantation was an immoral undertaking. Gostelow wanted the Irish converted by 'brotherly love and unity' to the reformed faith. 'I am ashamed', he wrote. 'I will not call it an Act of Parliament. It was so contrary to God's good pleasure, or brotherly compassion. 'The poor Irish whom wicked men would have transplanted upon the same principles as obdurate Pharoah . . . God doth continue in their own land'.[69] Gostelow's vision took him to Youghal, County Cork, where he got up in church in the middle of the service and informed the mayor that the Irish were a 'poor and oppressed nation' who 'should not be removed but possess their own just rights'. As he noted before his arrest and imprisonment for six weeks, 'my congregation grew very thin in the end'.

Gostelow's was a rare voice of conscience raised in protest against a gigantic experiment in social engineering. He was only half right. God did 'continue the Irish in their own land'; the poor remained in place, exchanging one landlord for another. But the property owners and the Old English did not. In their place came new Protestant families from England who were imposed on all the towns. In

Clonmel, the Whites had dominated civic life at least since the 1420s. Their names now disappeared from the list of notables. In their place came the Moores, Hacketts, Mitchells and Bagwells, families which were prominent in corporate life in Clonmel until Catholic Emancipation and the reform of the corporations in the early nineteenth century.

The Old English were reduced to poverty or exile. Nicholas White, head of the family in 1650, was the son and grandson of an MP. But after the Commissioners of Transplantation reached Clonmel in December 1653, he joined the column of refugees heading for the commissioners' headquarters in Connacht, at Loughrea, clutching his certificate and waiting to see where he would be told to live. In 1656 he was granted 1,004 acres in west County Clare. He never returned to Clonmel.[70]

'The English race in Ireland' either forgot their own distinctive myths and traditions or repudiated them. In 1600 it was still common for the Old English to boast of 'the blood of the Conquest' in their veins. By 1700, their descendants were unaware of that blood or, more importantly, ashamed of it.

This was a sea change with enormous consequences. Since Elizabeth I's reign, Ireland had contained three distinct communities: the native Irish, the Old English and the New English. James I added a fourth element, the Ulster Scots. Under Cromwell, these divisions were simplified. In Ulster, the differences between English and Scottish communities were submerged in a common British Protestant identity. In the rest of Ireland, the chasm between Old English and Irish was effaced as both communities were reduced to the same low level. In place of the complicated old divisions, two remained: Protestant and Catholic, British and Irish. Quite unknowingly, Cromwell had become the midwife of modern Irish nationalism.

CHAPTER EIGHT

Such Dangerous Persons

The papists being already five or six to one, and a breeding people, you may imagine
in what condition we are like to be
(Archbishop William King to Archbishop Wake of Canterbury,
6 February 1717)[1]

In 1660, Griffith Williams, the Protestant Bishop of Ossory, journeyed from
Dublin to Kilkenny. He had been waiting to make the journey for almost two
decades. Appointed to Ossory just before the outbreak of war in Ireland, it was
only now Cromwell was dead and the monarchy and Church of England restored
that he was free to go home.

The cathedral of St Canice was an architectural treasure. Only a few years
before it had been the scene of the rapturous reception of Cardinal Rinuccini. In
contrast to almost every other Irish cathedral, those of the capital not excepted, it
had not decayed under Protestant control and had been re-roofed as recently as
1597. But when the Bishop reached Kilkenny he was appalled. 'The great, and
famous, most beautiful cathedral church of Saint Keney they have utterly
defaced,' he moaned, 'and ruined, thrown down all the Roof of it, taken away the
great and goodly Bells, broken down all the windows and carried away every bit
of the Glass . . . and all the doors of it, that Hogs may come and root and Dogs
gnaw the Bones of the Dead.'[2]

Bishop Williams found the Church's assets had been virtually liquidated
throughout the county. 'They had beheaded most of the Churches of Christ
within my Diocess,' he wrote, 'the Roofes of them, both Slates and Timber, being
quite taken off . . . and the walls of very many of them thrown down. Of above
an hundred parishes, I saw not ten Churches standing.'[3]

The dismal scenes quelled any feeling of euphoria among the returning clergy
as they regained their bishoprics and rectories. The restoration of the Anglican
Church under Charles II had been surprisingly swift. The Cromwellian regime
had faced no serious external or internal threats. Charles I was dead and his son
was in exile, a penurious pensioner of France. Anglicanism had been forced underground and the Presbyterians disappointed. They had hoped to inherit a national
Church and run it on the same exclusive lines as their Anglican predecessors, but

by the time Presbyterian establishment had reached the statute book in 1646, power was passing to the army, which was dominated by Congregationalists, known as Independents. From then on they had had to jostle with all the other denominations under a system of toleration that excluded only Anglicans, papists and some of the more radical sects.

Cromwell's sudden death changed everything. But as the army tilted rapidly towards a royal restoration, the fact that the exiled King's fortunes were rising did not automatically mean the Church of England would rise with him. Charles I had been a devout Anglican. It was obvious Charles II was not. His mother and favourite sister were Catholics, and his brother and heir James would soon become one. But in exile, Charles II's initial hopes had been focused on Presbyterian Scotland. Even in 1660 there was nothing to exclude the possibility that he would make a pitch towards that religious constituency.

The hopes of the anti-episcopalian party were boosted by a royal declaration on religion issued from Breda in Holland on 4 April 1660. It was vague and left the key decisions to parliament but it did pledge 'liberty to tender consciences' and promised no man would be 'disquieted, or called in question' for differences in religion so long as these did not threaten the peace. That spring, it seemed possible that the new King would continue the Protector's policy of religious toleration, extending it to include Anglicans, and even Catholics.

What transformed the situation was the intransigently Anglican mood of the new parliament that met on 8 May 1661. The King's chief advisers, Edward Hyde, ennobled as the Earl of Clarendon and the Marquis of Ormond, now elevated to a dukedom, were strong Anglicans, determined to achieve more for their Church than mere toleration. Parliament wrecked the last hopes of the Presbyterians and Independents. A reaction in favour of the Church of England had been expected, yet even Clarendon was disturbed by the aggressively Anglican tone of the new assembly. The sons of the men who had voted to abolish bishops in 1643 had more than repented of their parents' convictions. They were convinced that only a hierarchical Church stood between them and social revolution and they were determined to enact punitive laws against dissenters. It was no longer a question of how the Church of England would be restored, but whether any accommodation would be made to those outside its fold.

For the Anglicans it had been a close call. Like the Catholic Church, their communion depended for its survival on the succession of bishops. But the Catholic Church was a vast international organisation and no amount of persecution in any one country endangered its overall survival. The Anglican hierarchy existed only in England, Wales and Ireland. There were no bishops in the American colonies. The fact that no bishops had been consecrated in Britain or Ireland since the early 1640s, therefore, posed a real threat to the continuity of the Anglican hierarchy. It is a moot point what would have happened if Cromwell had survived another few years, outliving the last of the old bishops. As it was, the Restoration occurred just before several sank into the grave. Richard Juxon, the new Archbishop of Canterbury, was 78 at the Restoration, tottered through Charles's coronation and died in 1663. His Irish counterpart, Bramhall, was another extinct volcano and died in the same year.

The Irish Primate lived long enough to oversee the mass consecration of a dozen new bishops. The Irish hierarchy, like its English counterpart, was depleted by the Restoration. Apart from Bramhall and Henry Leslie, the old foes of Blair and the Presbyterians in Ulster in the 1630s, only the bishops of Raphoe, Kilmore, Clonfert, Clogher and Ardfert survived, along with Williams of Ossory, who had never yet been able to occupy his see.

The consecration of the new bishops on 27 January 1661 in St Patrick's was the most splendid liturgical occasion the Church of Ireland had ever staged. Ireland was not to see a coronation, so in a sense, the Anglican Church had to stand in and supply the glamorous, symbolic event that buried the old era and inaugurated the new. On that January morning the Church of Ireland basked in a wave of popular adulation it had never seen before and would never experience again. Dubliners lined the streets to watch the grand procession of prebendaries, canons, minor canons, vicars-choral, choristers, the Vice-Chancellor of Trinity and doctors of divinity. The city had been a parliamentary stronghold. But those memories were wiped away as mayor and aldermen in scarlet robes marched at the head of the long column that processed towards the cathedral in silence, the Speaker of Convocation having the mace carried before him. At the west gate the vicars and choristers burst into a Te Deum and in the service chanted an anthem specially composed by the Dean:

Now that the lord hath readvanced the crown,
Which thirst for spoyle and frantick zeal threw down
Now that the lord the miter hath restored
Which with the crown lay in dust abhorr'd
Praise him ye kings.

'The multitude of people in the streets . . . seemed so great as to deny Rome for a regular and solemn proceeding,' Dudley Loftus, the Vicar-General of Ireland exulted. 'Yet so much respect did they show that they did with an extraordinary reverence open so wide a passage for the entire proceeding that there was no interruption given from first to last, nor any noise heard in the streets, save that of eulogies and benedictions from the people of all sorts to the Lord Primate.'[4]

It was a glorious new beginning. But once the bunting was down, the new bishops confronted the same problems Williams had found in Kilkenny. The physical fabric of the Church, poor before the war, was now immeasurably worse. All the steps that Wentworth and Bramhall had taken in the 1630s to rectify the mess had been undone. Laud's great project had been to make the Protestant Church as rich, powerful and independent a corporation as its Catholic predecessor. Their concern had been to humble the gentry as much as the Puritans. Now the Church's credit and its fortunes lay in the dust, along with shattered masonry and the shards of broken glass from the cathedral windows.

Then there was the question of restoring conformity. Over the previous 20 years, first the Irish Catholics and then the nonconformists had rebuilt congregations and tasted real, if temporary, liberty. Now the Anglican bishops were charged with reintroducing absolute compliance to a system of worship that only the middle-aged could even remember.

The situation was worst in the north, where the re-established Anglican Church had to be imposed on a popular local Presbyterian establishment, which had been in place ever since the Scottish army landed in 1642. The handful of ministers Blair and Livingstone brought with them had grown. They numbered 24 in the early 1650s and 80 by the Restoration, organised into five presbyteries.

The Irish authorities left no room for manoeuvre. On 25 March 1660, parliament pronounced the Solemn League and Covenant to be against the laws of God and ordered it to be burned in each town by the public hangman. The mayor of Carrickfergus had to be threatened with a fine of £100 before he would carry it out.[5] The ejection of Presbyterian ministers followed. The Irish Anglicans outdid their English counterparts in zeal, expelling the Presbyterian ministers in Ulster before they were ejected in England by the St Bartholomew's Day deadline in 1662.[6] Sixty-one Ulster ministers gave up their parishes, the majority from the Presbyterian heartland in Counties Down and Antrim. Presbyterianism was suppressed but its spirit was not broken, as Jonathan Swift discovered when he was sent to the parish of Kilroot in County Antrim in 1695 and found himself almost the only Anglican in the area. Strong popular attachment to Presbyterianism hindered the Church of Ireland's recovery in the north. 'Some parishes have not ten, not six, that come to church,' Bishop William King of Derry was warned, 'while the Presbyterian meetings are crowded with thousands covring all the fields'.[7]

The Anglicans had fewer worries about the Catholics, who had been destroyed by the transplantation as a political and economic force. A few favoured Catholic families had their estates returned to them in the 1660s, but the adventurers and Cromwellian soldiers were left with two-thirds of their Irish lands. No Catholics were restored to the corporations or parliament. In the 1650s only one Catholic bishop remained in the country. There were still only three bishops by 1660, and all were in Ulster.

Their fortunes improved only briefly after 1669, when Lord Berkeley replaced Ormond as Lord-Lieutenant. For three years the Catholics were unmolested, but in 1672 Arthur Capel, Earl of Essex, replaced Berkeley and the old policy of harassment was revived. By then, the King's attempt to introduce official toleration for Catholics without parliamentary sanction through a royal Indulgence had aroused Protestant opposition. In England, parliament began pressing for a renewal of persecution and in September 1673 the Irish Council was informed that it was 'His Majesty's express pleasure and command' that the authorities expel

Peter Talbot, Catholic Archbishop of Dublin, and all the other bishops, abbots and lesser holders of ecclesiastical discipline.

This caused chaos as shipowners argued with Dublin over the fees they were entitled to demand for transporting hundreds of banned clergymen to the continent. It was not an efficient operation. Many clerics got on board ships in one port only to disembark a few miles downwind. The Earl of Essex was aware of the problem. On 25 January 1674 he complained of the

> new inventions of the priests to evade the execution of the Proclamation. As particularly from [New] Ross I hear that there several friers being there putt on board some shippes in order to their transportation into forreign parts were by the Owners of the ships sett on shoar within ten miles of the place . . . I perceive plainly that unless His Majestie send some ships or orders to hire them here on purpose to transport these people we shall not be able to gett the country cleared of them.[8]

The drive to expel the clergy continued in 1674, with a fresh proclamation in April. At first the campaign did not touch Archbishop Oliver Plunkett of Armagh, who went into hiding. The authorities in Dublin had no strategic interest in expelling him. Lord Essex considered Plunkett 'a wise and sober man' and a great deal preferable to his colleague in Dublin, Archbishop Talbot. 'Plunket was for their [the Catholics] living quietly and in due submission to the government without engaging into intrigues of state.'[9]

Plunkett's subsequent martyrdom had little to do with circumstances in Ireland and did not reflect sectarian tensions in that country. Of Old English stock, Plunkett was a resolute enemy to the rebels against the Cromwellian land settlement known as Tories, and a fanatical royalist: 'The poor man hath an ecstasy of passion for the king's service,' the authorities noted approvingly in 1670.[10] This earned him the hearty hatred of many of the native Irish clergy in Ulster, who bitterly resented his imposition on Armagh. Their enmity went so deep that they were more than ready to play ball with the ex-Republicans in England to secure his death.

The leader of this group, Anthony Ashley Cooper, Earl of Shaftesbury, was anxious to play the ultra-Protestant card against the court to flush out the Catholics round the King, humiliate the crown and reverse the trend towards arbitrary government. As a Catholic bishop and a devoted royalist, Plunket's destruction became convenient to two entirely separate parties, the anti-court party in England and the anti-English party in Ulster.

The tool that the King's opponents had been looking for presented itself in September 1678, when a deranged clergyman named Israel Tonge produced a stream of accusations that became known as the 'Popish Plot'. Tonge was followed by an ambitious former Catholic seminarian named Titus Oates. The rising hysteria over the supposed plot gathered steam in October, when Sir Edmund Berry

Godfrey, the magistrate to whom Oates had made his deposition, was mysteriously killed. In November, Shaftesbury demanded the exclusion of the King's Catholic brother, James, Duke of York, from the succession. The crisis lasted until 1681, when Charles dissolved parliament for the last time in his reign.

It was an English political drama, but inevitably it sucked Ireland and the Irish Catholics into its entrails. In October 1678 Ormond, now in his second term as Lord-Lieutenant, was informed that Archbishop Talbot was the ringleader of a conspiracy aimed at murdering him. The killing was to be the signal for a Catholic revolt, backed by the Pope and the French. Talbot was arrested and on 16 October there was another proclamation ordering the expulsion of bishops and the religious orders followed by two more anti-Catholic proclamations forbidding papists from bearing arms and barring them from garrison towns, including Drogheda, Wexford, Limerick, Youghal, Waterford, Cork and Galway. In March of the following year new rewards were offered for anyone discovering a Catholic priest: £10 for archbishops, bishops or Jesuits; £5 for anyone lower down the hierarchy.

Plunkett hoped he might ride out the storm. But in the following year the Shaftesbury faction established fortuitous contact with Plunkett's enemies among the clergy in Armagh. Presented with fresh accusations of treason, Ormond ordered the Archbishop of Armagh's arrest in December.

Even then it seemed highly unlikely that the Irish Primate would come to lasting harm. Ormond himself was convinced of Plunkett's innocence. The testimonies of Plunkett's enemies among the Irish clergy in Ulster did not move him. They were 'such creatures that no schoolboy would trust them with a design for the robbing of an orchard'.[11] One was a 'silly drunken vagabond'; another was 'debauched'. His low opinion of Plunkett's accusers dovetailed with that of the Protestant jury in Dundalk that was first charged with hearing the accusation.

Plunkett would never have suffered if the case had remained in Ireland. Unhappily, Shaftesbury's agents were determined to have it transferred to England. Plunkett sailed over on 24 October 1680 and was examined before the House of Lords on 4 November. The Archbishop's dignity was striking but already his position was hopeless. The Shaftesbury faction wanted his scalp and so did a large party of the native Irish in Ulster. Twenty-five were brought over in January 1681 as witnesses. They 'swore against Plunkett that he had got a great bank of money to be prepared, and that he had an army listed and was in correspondence with France, to bring over a fleet from thence'. No one except Shaftesbury and his allies pretended to take this stuff seriously, and their testimony did not tally. In spite of it, Plunkett was brought to trial on 8 June. He sent a petition to the King, remarking that under Irish law he ought to have been tried in Ireland and he reminded Charles that many witnesses against him were proclaimed outlaws. But there was no reprieve. The King would not sacrifice his brother but he did sacrifice his two loyal Irish Archbishops. Plunkett was executed at Tyburn on 1 July In his last testimony, he begged God to grant the royal family 'long life and all prosperity in this world'.[12] Talbot, a former chaplain to Charles's Portuguese Queen, Catherine of Braganza, languished in jail until his death in October 1682.

Plunkett's death was the result of political intrigue in England between the court and an emerging Whig party. Ireland was a sideshow, and as the Dundalk jury showed, most Irish Protestants were far less worried about their security than were their English counterparts. The Church of Ireland in the early 1680s did not see the Catholics as a threat to their regime. As the Munster squire Sir Robert Southwell told his son-in-law Sir John Perceval on 16 May 1682, 'It is plain, as things stand, that the Protestants, having the authority of the government, the garrisons and arms in their hands, could drive the Irish in to the sea if that were fit and thought convenient . . . the Protestants owe their quiet and their security to their power.'[13] While the Duke of Ormond remained in control, the Anglican regime in Ireland looked impregnable. As Sir Robert said, it was supported by 'all the old and English proprietors . . . all the churchmen . . . also such of the Irish as were restored to their estates – which were about 500.'

That 'eternal peace' was only upset in 1685 when the Catholic Duke of York ascended the throne. In England, the accession of a Catholic monarch stirred vague memories of the fires at Smithfield under Queen Mary. In Ireland it awoke far more recent memories of 1641. The new regime of James II made no attempt to allay such fears. Ormond was abruptly dismissed as Lord-Lieutenant and as in England, though with far more potential effect, the corporations were remodelled to enable the election of Catholics. Power moved rapidly into the hands of the late Archbishop Talbot's brother, Richard Talbot, whom the King made Lieutenant-General of the army and ennobled as Earl of Tyrconnell. In 1687 he was made Lord-Lieutenant, the first Catholic to hold the post since Queen Mary's reign.

The dramatic shift in power in Ireland towards the Catholics brought them a few fair-weather friends. Peter Manby, Dean of Derry, and Alexander Moore, Precentor of Down cathedral, converted to Rome. But the crisis facing the Church of Ireland was not individual defections but how a Catholic king might exercise the Royal Supremacy over the Church as a whole. The mere fact of James's Catholicism did not preclude him from exercising the Royal Supremacy. Several generations of Anglican apologists had elevated the doctrine of the divine right of kings to the status of a dogma. If the new King had kept his religion a relatively private matter, the dominant High Church faction would have continued to preach energetically on the duty of loyalty and passive obedience. But James was not content that his faith should be a private matter. He quickly revealed his unfriendly intentions to the Protestant Church by refusing to appoint new bishops and archbishops, a course that strongly suggested he intended to put Catholics into the vacant sees. In Ireland, the archbishopric of Cashel and the see of Elphin were left empty.

The Churches of England and Ireland had no precedent for dealing with a monarch who refused to appoint bishops. The discourse of Anglican divines held that kings and queens were the Church's 'nursing mothers'. Now the Church had to deal with a mother bent on infanticide. As in the 1650s, there was a danger that the succession of bishops might be terminated.

The slow strangulation of the hierarchy was a long-term problem. The short-term problem was financial collapse. The Church of England could call on the active sympathy of a large proportion of the population even when it was out of sympathy with the government. The Church of Ireland had no such advantage. It was the Church of a minority, and depended for its day-to-day survival on the coercive machinery of the state to secure its tithes from Catholics in the south and Presbyterians in north-east Ulster. As soon as James ascended the throne, people in Ireland stopped paying. 'Truly the condition of the Church at this time is contemptible', William Moreton, Bishop of Kildare, complained to Ormond. 'Not only the church dues but the very tithes are now withheld or like to be so.'[14]

With the memory of 1641 hanging over them, the Protestant bishops began to slip out of Ireland. Seven remained – Anthony Dopping of Meath, Primate Boyle and the bishops of Ossory, Cork, Killaloe, Limerick and Waterford. William King, then the Dean of St Patrick's, rallied the Anglicans in Dublin, attacking defectors, such as the Dean of Derry, in pamphlets.

In England, the Anglican establishment tasted real danger only briefly. In May 1688 six bishops and William Sancroft, the Archbishop of Canterbury, were imprisoned for refusing to sanction another royal Indulgence to Catholics, which the King wanted to be read out in all the parish churches. The bishops were taken to the Tower of London and sent for trial. For a few weeks it looked as if the Church of England might be decapitated, just as the Marian establishment had been after the accession of Elizabeth I. But in June the bishops were released after the jury found them not guilty of seditious libel. The King now backed down, dismissing the newly appointed Catholic Lords-Lieutenant and restoring the corporations. On 5 November 1688, James's son-in-law, William of Orange, landed in Devon, triggering the almost immediate collapse of the regime and the King's flight to France. The Church of England had passed through the dark night of the soul. It now had only the minor problem of fending off schemes to reward the Protestant dissenters for their support.

In Ireland, the Established Church's troubles were just beginning. After James fled to France he landed in Ireland on 12 March 1689 at Kinsale, County Cork, on the first leg of a campaign to recover his English throne. After being met by Tyrconnell, he proceeded via Cork to Dublin, which he entered on 24 March.

The parliament that James summoned, which met on 7 May, saw the last concerted effort by the broken remnants of the Old English to undo the effects of Cromwell's transplantation. Lords who had been deprived of their places in parliament were restored once more to the House. The Act of Settlement, confirming the Cromwellian Protestants in their estates, was repealed. As the bulwarks of Protestant domination were dismantled, one by one, the Protestant Church stood out alone as the last sentinel. In the House of Lords, Dopping of Meath cut a lonely figure when he spoke against the Act of Settlement's repeal. Most of the churches were seized in September 1689 under the claim that they were being used to store arms. 'The manner of doing it was this,' William King recalled. 'The mayor or governor in the towns with the priests went to the churches, sent for the keys to the sexton and if they were found, forced them from them; if not they broke open the doors, pulled up the seats and reading desks and having said mass in them lookt upon them as their own.'[15]

In 1641, Irish Protestants had had the comfort of hanging on to the capital. They were never cut off and connections remained open between Dublin and England. There was no equivalent sanctuary in 1689. In the north, Derry and the town of Enniskillen, in County Fermanagh, held out against the King. But they were surrounded and were no substitute for the loss of Dublin where Christ Church was locked up on 6 September and Catholic worship restored on 27 October. Once again the cathedral that had echoed to the sound of so many liturgical experiments resounded to the Latin mass.

If the Protestants of Ireland feared a rerun of the anarchic slaughter of 1641 their concerns were misplaced. The Catholic revolution of the late 1680s in Ireland was relatively peaceful and although Protestant leaders, including King, were imprisoned, there was no relapse into sectarian violence. After the King's Catholic army was crushed by William of Orange in July 1690, the Protestants had difficulty recalling any particularly horrifying episodes apart from the outrage of seeing those who lost their lands under Cromwell being restored to their estates.

Protestant services were disrupted and clergymen were assaulted. Nathaniel Foy, the Rector of St Bride's, was manhandled by soldiers while conducting a funeral service in a churchyard and forcibly prevented from preaching a sermon. Alexander Allen, the minister in Wexford, told King that the mayor, Edward Wiseman, had personally encouraged a mob to attack his church and 'break down and demolish all the Pewes and Altar'.[16] George Prowd had a similar experience in Trim, though he had the satisfaction of noting that the man who broke his communion rails went completely mad soon after, 'tore all the Cloaths off his back and ran naked about the Streets and . . . dyed in a sad and deplorable manner'.[17]

It was the elevation of the lower classes that most affronted King when he came to write his account, *The State of the Protestants of Ireland under the Late King James's Government* (1691). King trained his hostility on the low social status of the Catholics rather than on their beliefs. It was not the return of the mass to Dublin's cathedrals that outraged him so much as the promotion of 'the scum and rascallity of the world'.[18] The plebeian character of James's Catholic army struck him as unnatural; they were turning the social order on its head. 'Hundreds of them had been cowherds, horse boys and footmen,' he snorted. 'One that was a few days before no other than a cowherd to his Protestant landlord perhaps was set before him on the Bench as Justice of the Peace.'[19]

King's charge reflected a subtle change in the nature of the debate between Anglicans and Catholics since the Restoration. Ussher had looked on the Early Church as the final court of appeal on questions of doctrine, and had defended

Anglicanism above all as the religion 'anciently professed by the Irish'. The new generation defended Anglicanism as the religion not so much of saints as of gentlemen. Where Ussher claimed the Church of Ireland was the successor of the old Celtic Church, King asserted that the Established Church was the spiritual organ of the New English. There was no appeal to antiquity or St Patrick. To King, the Church of Ireland was like the army: it existed to maintain the settlers and suppress the natives.

The Protestants in the southern counties endured the brief reign of James II with little more than bruised pride. It was not the same for the descendants of the Ulster settlers. The size of the Protestant population in the north emboldened them to oppose the Catholic Counter-Revolution proceeding in Dublin. Their defiance over the next few months provided material for the legend that was to become the core folk memory of the Protestant population for at least the next three centuries, overshadowing and absorbing the memory of the bloodshed of 1641.

That the siege of Derry became the favourite symbol of the history of the entire community is not surprising. The Ulster Protestant imagination was informed by the Bible and the story of the siege contains many of the great themes of the New Testament. There was the theme of betrayal, with the governor of Londonderry, Colonel Robert Lundy, taking the role of the traitor, Judas Iscariot. There was the theme of suffering for the sake of righteousness. There was the theme of endurance to the end. And there was the theme of eventual deliverance. The setting was symbolic. Londonderry was a walled city. To anyone versed in the Old Testament, the image of the kingdom of God as a city on a hill acted powerfully on the imagination.

Of course, dry facts had to be massaged and enlivened to bear the interpretation that the Protestant community chose to see in the events of 1689–90. In reality, the siege involved a confusing array of actors, including an English Catholic king and a Catholic army composed of Irish Catholics and French troops. On the other side was a force of Anglicans and Presbyterians, sworn enemies at the Restoration who had put aside their differences to support the claims of a Dutch Calvinist prince allied to the Catholic Habsburgs and the Pope, who was claiming the throne in the name of his Anglican wife, daughter of the English Catholic king. Militarily, it was not much of a siege by continental standards of warfare. As one recent expert has written, 'Militarily, we cannot make a case for a siege [although] psychologically there was one, and that cannot be ignored'.[20]

The drama in Londonderry began in December 1688, when Tyrconnell sent a Catholic regiment to the city under the control of Lord Antrim. The Bishop of Derry, Ezekiel Hopkins, true to the Anglican doctrine of passive obedience, favoured submission. Majority opinion in the city, especially among the younger aldermen, urged resistance. As Lord Antrim's troops approached the city the gates were closed in their face by the group of young men history remembers as the 13 Apprentice Boys. Tyrconnell tried to defuse the dispute by offering to send a garrison that was Protestant led but loyal to James. After a certain amount of haggling, the terms were agreed. Lord Mountjoy and Colonel Lundy were allowed to bring in two companies instead of the proposed six and the city was permitted to retain its own arms. Lundy was appointed governor of the city.

The uneasy compromise lasted until James reached Ireland in the New Year. The King had to subdue Ulster if he was to preserve his Irish kingdom from a Williamite invasion so he marched north to deal with the recalcitrant city, reaching Omagh, in County Tyrone, on 14 May. Four days later he arrived at the walls of Derry and demanded the city's surrender. Lundy presided over a council that recommended 'timely capitulation' to the King's army 'in hopes that the inhabitants . . . may make better terms'. But the garrison refused. Their answer, 'No surrender', supposedly bellowed over the walls, was a shout that entered the history books. The phrase became the key to the Ulster Protestant identity.

James returned to Dublin, confused and disappointed. The garrison in Londonderry now dispensed with Colonel Lundy, whose behaviour had raised suspicions about his ultimate sympathies. He was replaced by Major Baker and George Walker, Church of Ireland Rector of Donaghmore, in County Tyrone, who had been arguing with Lundy over strategy since he reached Londonderry in mid-April.

The siege began. The summer months were a crucial test of the city's resolve. William was preoccupied with prosecuting his war against France and was not yet in a position to help. Londonderry was perilously isolated. The garrison numbered just over 7,000. The city had a normal peacetime civilian population of only 2,000, but the influx of Protestant refugees from other parts of Ulster had increased the number. About a third left before the siege began. That still left a large civilian population, all of whom needed food, water and shelter from Ulster's wet and cool summer weather. Everything hinged on timing and on whether the city would starve before aid arrived from the new Protestant government in England.

The sight of several British ships in nearby Lough Foyle on 13 June raised false hopes of prompt redemption. But the Ulstermen were forcibly reminded that while they prized the British connection above all others, the feeling was not reciprocated with quite the same ardour. The deliverance of Ulster was not a priority for the English parliament or the new English King.

The siege went on. The Catholic army laid a barrier, called a boom, of twisted metal and wood across the River Foyle, which stopped ships in the Lough from sailing upriver to the city walls. The bombardment continued while the ships remained tantalisingly close.

George Walker's account of the siege, even if he greatly exaggerated the size of the Jacobite army,[21] remains a thrilling piece of reportage about conditions in the city during the summer months of bombing and mounting hunger. Naturally, he dramatised his own heroic role to ensure that William recognised his services, much to the irritation of the Presbyterians, who furiously contested his version of affairs. Walker's account still makes a harrowing dispatch. By 27 July, he wrote, a quarter of dog 'fattened on dead Irish' was going for five shillings; a dog's head was sold for 2s. 6d.; cat was worth 4s. 6d., a rat fetched a shilling and a mouse sixpence. How many people in Londonderry in the summer of 1689 truly dined out on roast mouse? This was Walker indulging in poetic licence. But there is no reason to doubt that pets like cats and dogs did have to be sacrificed. Walker had a gallows sense of humour; he hinted that some of the fleshier human inhabitants of the city had good reason to worry about their fate. 'A certain fat gentleman conceived himself in the greatest danger and fancying several of the garrison looked on him with a greedy eye thought fit to hide himself for three days,' he wrote.[22]

At times, the bombardment was relentless. 'They plied the Besieged city so close with great guns in the day time and bombs in the night, and sometimes in the day, that they could not enjoy their rest,' Walker wrote, 'but were hurried from place to place and tir'd into faintness and diseases, which destroyed many of the garrison.'[23]

The longed-for relief depicted in stained glass in Derry cathedral came on 28 July when the three British ships in Lough Foyle moved out of the Lough and chanced the boom, hitting the iron chains and twisted cable and cruising downriver under heavy gunfire.

Walker watched the events leading to the city's delivery unfold.

The Mountjoy of Derry, captain Browning commander, the Phoenix of Coleraine, captain Douglas master, being both loaden with provision, were conveyed by the Dartmouth frigate. The enemy fired most desperately at them from the fort of Culmore and both sides of the river; and they made sufficient returns and with the greatest bravery.

The Mountjoy made a little stop at the boom, occasioned by her rebound after striking and breaking it, so that she was run a-ground; upon this the enemy set up the loudest huzza's and the most dreadful to the besieged that ever we heard; fired all their guns upon her and were preparing their boats to board her:

Our trouble is not to be express'd at this dismal prospect, but by great providence firing a broadside the shock loosened her so that she got clear, and passed their boom. Captain Douglas all this while was engaged, and the Dartmouth gave them very warm entertainment.[24]

The *Mountjoy* brought the first relief to the city in more than 100 days. The besieging army melted away. The price of victory was high. Battle casualties during the siege numbered about 80, but hunger, fatigue and disease, which spread as a result of malnutrition, took away far more lives. By mid-June, according to Walker, the garrison had lost at least 1,000 men. By the end of July, when the siege was lifted, 2,800 members of the garrison had died of starvation and disease.

The deliverance of Londonderry did not end the war. The Jacobite armies fought on. It was not until the Battle of the Boyne, on the outskirts of Drogheda, on 1 July 1690 and the Battle of Aughrim, near Galway, on 12 July 1691 that James lost his hope of regaining the English throne.

The Boyne, though the less significant of the two battles, also entered Protestant mythology. The waters of the river became holy, and the tradition of making toasts of 'Boyne water' sprang up. But the siege of Londonderry was more significant to Ulster Protestants. It developed over several centuries into the focal point of an alternative religion with a calendar of events that could be re-enacted annually. The physical debris left behind by the siege was lovingly collected and guarded as if it was as precious as any flask of saint's blood. The apprentice boys became The Apprentice Boys, alternative saints of this new religion. The names of William Cairns, Henry Campsie, William Crookshanks, Alexander Cunningham, John Cunningham, Samuel Harvey, Samuel Hunt, Alexander Irwin, Robert Morrison, Daniel Sherrard, Robert Sherrard, James Spike and James Steward were inscribed on the popular imagination. The images of George Walker and of the *Mountjoy*, crashing through the boom, were standardised and turned into icons, to be reproduced on thousands of the banners held aloft each July in commemoration of the events of 1689 and 1690.

Ulster Protestants came to canonise William of Orange. His icon pictures him on the famous white horse which he rode on landing at Carrickfergus in County Antrim in June 1690. Although he had not even been present at the siege, memories of William, the white horse, Derry, the Boyne and Aughrim merged into one event. The elevation of the King to supernatural status began while he was alive. When Ormond's chaplain, Edmund Arwaker, preached on the anniversary of the Treaty of Limerick at Dungannon in 1698 he compared James to wicked King Ahab and William to Solomon. There was no doubt in Mr Ardwaker's mind that William's victory was the result of divine intervention, for just as a bad king provokes God 'to shut up the windows of heaven', a good one releases the flow of divine blessings. It was the 'certain evidence of God's favour' to William that had brought the circumstances of the Irish Protestants 'to resemble Israel's in his [Solomon's] days when every man dwelt safely under his vine and under his fig tree'.[25]

Kilmurry, in County Clare, was unusual in the early 1690s. Both the Church of Ireland rector and the Catholic priest remained in the village throughout the Jacobite war, at a time when most of the Church of Ireland clergy felt it unsafe to remain in the countryside. But the Protestant vicar, Reverend Barclay, was a hardy animal who declined to join the exodus to England. Ejected from his cure by the priest, he stayed on, holding a farm under a lease from the see of Killaloe. Now he was paying his tithes to a Catholic clergyman in direct reversal of earlier practice. Relations between the representatives of Ireland's two great confessions were correct in Kilmurry, if distinctly chilly. According to an account of the episode recorded in *The Diocese of Killaloe from the Reformation to the Close of the Eighteenth Century*, written in 1878: 'The priest was particularly severe in exacting tythes from the ejected vicar and always required security for their payment.'

It went on:

> In the summer of 1691 he was unusually hard to be pleased in the security and Mr Barclay, despairing of being able to procure it was returning in low spirits to his residence at Ballyartney when he met Captain O'Brien of Ennistymon, with the news of the utter defeat of the Irish army at Aughrim. He returned immediately to the house, where the intruder was setting the tythes to his parish, surrounded by a great number of people. 'Have you got security, Sir?' said the priest in a loud imperious voice.
>
> 'I have' said Barclay. 'My security is the great king William. And if you don't deliver up the security in ten minutes I will have you hanged on the high road to Kilmurry.' The priest turned pale and trembled in his seat of office. Mr Barclay's tythe-books were submissively returned to him and the Protestants of Clare for fifty years after drank to 'Barclay's security' in a bumper toast.[26]

The tale of the ejecter ejected, cherished by generations of Clare Protestants and no doubt embellished along the way, shows how the radical swings of fortune between the Irish Churches affected one small community. The story is presented in almost humorous terms. Priest and vicar perch on either end of a see-saw. One moment the vicar goes up and priest comes down. In the next, the situation is reversed. Behind the dry humour lurks a sour little tale. The representatives of the two great religious communities of Ireland are shown as bodies that lack charity towards each other. There is intimacy here, but no affection, or even respect. There seems to be no threat of bloodshed, either. Ireland in 1691 was not the Ireland of 1641. But the two churches are represented as mutually exclusive organisations. It is axiomatic that the triumph of one spells the ruin of the other.

The Treaty of Limerick, signed on 3 October 1691, almost three months after Aughrim, ended the Jacobite war. It comprised 52 articles, and offered honourable terms to a Catholic army that was defeated but never destroyed. Thousands of soldiers were permitted to sail out of Ireland to France and the civilian population was promised the same degree of religious freedom they had enjoyed under Charles II and the right to retain their property.

It is always easy to say history might have followed an entirely different track if such and such had been done. But there are points in Irish history where the possibility of a break in the cycle of revenge that had dogged confessional relations appear tantalisingly close. This was one. The new King was far more intelligent than his father-in-law. William was not a bigot. The Dutch Reformed Church in which he was reared was doctrinally more rigidly Calvinistic than the Church of England. But the Dutch were immeasurably more tolerant than the English. Amsterdam was notorious as the haven of freethinkers, a place where censorship was so feebly enforced that almost anything might be printed there. Dutch Catholics had to worship behind closed doors and their clergy were forbidden to appear in public in ecclesiastical dress, but the Dutch never hunted down their priests and nuns, let alone tortured them. The notion of being boiled alive in 'hot boots' like Archbishop O'Hurley was alien to the whole tenor of the Dutch Reformation.

William's instincts were to apply this same cool and pragmatic spirit to English and Irish ecclesiastical affairs. Before the Battle of Aughrim he had seemed ready to offer Irish Catholics far better conditions for a speedy end to the conflict than they had ever extracted from the Stuarts, including the use of half the country's church buildings. He was wary of becoming the tool of ultra-Protestant Whigs and had an important Catholic ally in the Emperor Leopold of Austria.

The Limerick articles were less favourable than the hazy terms mentioned before Aughrim. But they still pointed towards a resolution to the Irish religious imbroglio on Dutch lines, a solution that favoured the Protestants but restrained them from vindictive triumphalism. However, the spirit of Reverend Barclay gained the day. The gloating priest of Kilmurry was replaced by the noisy triumphalist vicar. Ireland returned to the familiar regime of victorious but nervous Protestants taking a high hand over bitter, humiliated Catholics. Bishop Dopping set the tone, delivering a furious tirade against the Irish Catholics at the thanksgiving service in honour of the peace treaty in November 1692, using language that shocked and disgusted the authorities. 'We have particular reason to complayne of the behaviour of the Bishop of Meath', the Irish Lords Justices wrote to London on 30 November, 'who . . . upon that occasion did make the most bitter invectives against the whole books of the Irish that could be invented, stirring up the people . . . to continue their animosities against them.'[27].

The Irish parliament echoed with views similar to those of Bishop Dopping, rather than William III. It did not attemp to honour the promise of isolation but, instead, passed a series of laws during the 1690s that progressively increased the disabilities placed on the Catholic community and which in time came to be known as the Penal Laws. The phrase was not one used by contemporaries, who generally insisted on their defensive character as 'restraints' on popery. The 'restraints' began with the extension to Ireland of an English law of 1691, confining membership of parliament to Protestants, by means of an oath tendered to all MPs in which they had to abjure belief in transubstantiation and the deposing power of popes. The parliament of 1695, encouraged by a strongly anti-Catholic new Lord-Lieutenant, Lord Capel, then passed the 'Act for the better securing the government by disarming Papists', which forbade Catholics to bear arms or own horses worth more than £5. Another Act effectively outlawed foreign Catholic education by imposing a £200 fine on anyone sending children abroad to be educated in a foreign seminary, abbey or convent. The parliament of 1697 was even more energetic. 'An act for suppressing all friaries, monasteries nunneries and other Popish convents and for banishing all regulars of the Popish clergy out of Ireland' was extended to include the bishops as well, by including 'all papists exercising ecclesiastical jurisdiction'. The cut-off date for leaving the country was set for 1 May 1698. The bill further forbade any bishops, archbishops, deans or vicars-general then outside Ireland from entering the country after 29 December. Heavy fines were ordered for any laymen concealing such persons from the authorities.

The Banishment Act of 1697 directly contravened the promises William had made to his continental Catholic allies. But it provoked only fitful protests from the Emperor Leopold. The Austrians were confused about what was going on in Ireland and had no idea the original bill, banishing only monks and friars, had been extended to encompass bishops. The English misleadingly informed the Habsburg ambassador in London that 'the banishment of the regular priests will relieve the seculars . . . [as] the former were all the agents of France and will work only for our common enemies'.[27] The following year the ports were kept busy with the business of transportation. Some 153 priests were transported from Dublin, 190 from Galway, 75 from Cork and 26 from Waterford. Most sailed to France. Others sailed to Cadiz, Lisbon and other ports in Spain. In France the destitute exiles were thrown on to the charity of the exiled James II at St Germain near Paris and the Catholic Church in France, which ordered that collections be raised on their behalf. Some made their way to Rome and presented their plight to the Pope.

There were few bishops to deport. Of the 16 surviving Catholic bishops five were already in exile at Tournai and Louvain, or with James at St Germain. The Catholic bishops of Kildare and Ossory left Ireland before the deadline. A few stayed, as Edward Comerford of Cashel put it, hiding in 'the cellars and cisterns, in mountains and caves'.[28] John Sleyne, Bishop of Cork, was arrested in 1698, imprisoned, and eventually transported in 1703. The Bishop of Clonfert stayed but was caught in the same year. The Bishop of Dromore, Patrick Donnelly, remained at large until he was run to ground in 1706. After that there was only Archbishop Comerford, who died at the end of Anne's reign without being caught.

Two further attempts were made to squeeze out the remaining Catholic clergy and detect those in hiding. In November 1701 a proclamation 'for the better encouragement of such person or persons who shall be active in the discovering of such offenders' offered a sliding scale of rewards to informers. The price on the head of an archbishop or bishop was £100. The discovery of a dean or vicar-general was worth £30, a Jesuit or a monk £10.

After the banishment of the bulk of the bishops and the regular clergy, the authorities hoped the secular clergy would die off. Determined to cut the supply of replacements by forbidding priests who had been ordained abroad from entering the kingdom, the 1703 parliament passed an Act that forbade Catholic clergy from entering the country after a deadline of 1 January 1704. At the same time, clergy who converted to the Church of Ireland were offered a solid financial inducement in the form of pensions worth £20 a year; later this was increased to £40.

There remained the business of establishing how many secular priests the preceding laws had left in place. In 1703 parliament passed an Act for Registering the Popish Clergy, which ordered all the remaining clergy in the country to register their names, parishes and place of ordination along with the names of the bishops who ordained them, so that 'the government be truly informed of the number of such dangerous persons as still remain among us'.[29] Most of the clergy complied, as a result of which the authorities compiled a list of 1,089 priests still serving in Ireland. The order for the remaining secular clergy to register in 1704 revealed a parish structure that was remarkably intact. The names were spread evenly over Ireland, with 352 in Leinster, 289 in Munster, 259 in Connacht and 189 in Ulster. Although the Catholic population had increased from about 800,000 in the 1650s to between 1.5 and 1.75 million, the number of clergy still allowed for a tolerably comprehensive system of parish ministry.

It was a disappointment to the authorities and in 1709 the Irish parliament passed the Popery Act, which ordered all the priests who had registered in 1704 to take an oath renouncing loyalty to James II's heir and swearing to uphold the Protestant succession. The deadline was 25 March 1710. This time there was resistance. A derisory 33 priests took the Oath of Renunciation. From a practical point of view it was impossible for the clergy to take it. After James II's death in 1701, Rome had recognised James III as the rightful King of England, Scotland and Ireland and the exiled King continued to enjoy the right to nominate Catholic bishops to Irish sees. It was never likely that priests would question the legitimacy of their own bishops by abjuring the exiled Stuarts under oath. It was even less likely that they would swear to uphold the Protestant succession. As a result, the priests who had volunteered so many details about their whereabouts and their background in 1704 now found the information used against them to secure their banishment.

A decade later, when it became clear many clergy had slipped back into the country and that they were not dying out, there was renewed pressure for another legislative offensive. In 1719, the Irish parliament even mused over a draconian proposal to hound priests out of the kingdom by branding their cheeks, while the Irish Privy Council suggested castration. The heads of a bill were sent over to England for approval but ran into opposition in the English Privy Council and no more was heard of it.

While some laws pinned down the Catholic clergy, others aimed to break the remnant of the Catholic gentry. The 1703 parliament outlawed primogeniture among Catholics, effectively breaking up the remaining Catholic estates. Catholics were forbidden to purchase new land or to take out long leases. This ensured that the percentage of land held by Catholics dropped steadily for the next century. They owned 22 per cent of Ireland at the start of William's reign, 14 per cent at the beginning of Anne's reign in 1703 and 5 per cent by the 1770s. Dean Swift noted the collapse of the Catholic gentry with satisfaction: 'The estates of the Papists are few, crumbling into small Parcels and daily diminishing,' he wrote in 1733. 'The common people are sunk in Poverty, Ignorance and Cowardice and of as little consequences as women or children. Their Nobility and Gentry are at least by one half ruined, banished or converted.'[30]

The destruction of the Catholic property-owning class ran concurrently with the abolition of their remaining political rights. As the right to elect was tied to the value of land, the number of Catholics who could vote fell steadily until 1728, when the last Catholics lost the vote.

An occasional appearance at the parish church was not enough to secure relief from the anti-Catholic laws. The onus lay on the victim to prove his conformity to the Church of Ireland. The 'Act to Prevent the Further Growth of Popery' in 1703 laid down the procedure. Disabilities ceased only after the convert's name had been enrolled in the High Court of Chancery. The convert had to take an oath that was precisely worded, in which he swore 'that in the sacrament of the Lord's Supper there is not any transubstantiation of the elements . . . and that the invocation or adoration of the Virgin Mary or any saint and the Sacrifice of the Mass . . . are superstitious and idolatrous'. In addition he had to swear loyalty to the Queen and abjure loyalty 'to the person pretended to be the Prince of Wales.' Registration in the High Court of Chancery might only follow the reception of a Protestant bishop's certificate.' The negative character of the oath was obvious. It did not demand admiration for the Church of Ireland but the unambiguous rejection of key Catholic doctrines. In 1709 the Act was tightened up, so that the convert had to take the Anglican communion within six months of conversion and obtain a sacrament certificate that was then lodged in the courts.

The Church of Ireland clergy looked on the Penal Laws with ambivalence. Bishop Dopping supported persecution, but William King drew very different conclusions. As Bishop of Derry from 1690 and the Archbishop of Dublin between 1703 and 1729, he was never convinced of their worth, voted consistently against the most anti-Catholic Acts and considered the betrayal of the Treaty of Limerick a mistake. King was no liberal, as a book he published in 1691 after the Williamite revolution on the state of the Protestants under King James had showed. But his experience in Derry left him convinced that Presbyterianism was still as dangerous to the Establishment as Catholicism. He complained that in his part of Ulster 'the dissenters . . . have settled many of their ministers where none was before the troubles [and] they make it their business to obstruct and destroy the discipline of our Church . . . They pretend to be very encouraged by the government. In the meantime their people are very vicious and lewd.'[31]

King brought his distaste for Presbyterianism to Dublin. His was a 'northern' perspective on church affairs but many Church of Ireland clergymen shared it at least until the second decade of the century. The 'representation of the present state of religion', which the Irish clergy drew up in convocation in 1712 did not ignore popery, or infidelity. But the clergy insisted Presbyterianism was the greatest obstacle. It was Presbyterians, not Catholics, who had 'erected large piles of buildings in the form of churches in the midst of towns and cities and . . . even in the neighbourhood of our cathedrals'. And it was the fault of the dissenters that 'the clergy of the established Church have been openly insulted in the discharge of their office.'[32]

These fears of Irish Anglicans increased after Anne's death in 1714 and the failed Jacobite rebellion of 1715, which ruined the High Anglican party. The accession of the Lutheran Hanoverian dynasty caused the same flutter of nerves in the church dovecot that William III's accession had provoked in 1688. In 1716 Thomas Lindsay, Archbishop of Armagh from 1714 to 1724, complained of gangs of armed Presbyterians going around Ulster and searching Anglican houses under the pretext of uncovering Jacobite arms caches. He handed the Irish Lords Justices an official complaint about *The Insolence of the Dissenters against the Establish'd Church* in which he stated that Anglicans were 'terrified from coming to the Publick prayers and service' by these Presbyterian bullies.[33]

King's other worry about the popery laws was their purely negative spirit: they were concerned with keeping political power and property in the hands of the existing class of Protestants, and not with converting Catholics to the Reformed religion. The Archbishop sarcastically likened the laws to an 'Inquisition' and suggested that a few 'soft laws and strict execution'[34] on Dutch lines might be more effective than a stack of draconian laws that were badly enforced. King suspected the men behind the popery laws did not want a wave of converts to the Church of Ireland. 'There is a party among us that have little sense of religion and heartily hate the Church,' he told Jonathan Swift, his successor as Dean of St Patrick's. 'They would have the natives made Protestants but such as themselves are deadly afraid they should come into the Church because, say they, this would strengthen the Church too much . . . I am afraid that little would be done.'[35]

The Archbishop's fears were borne out by events. The convert rolls, listing the names of those who abandoned Catholicism, record only 5,500 names from 1703 to 1789, and unsurprisingly most converts were landowners. Very few were listed as members of the lower classes. The rolls list one fisherman, boatman, bricklayer, glazier and plasterer each.[36] John Cullen of Nenagh, Tipperary, was a lone 'perry-wigmaker' whose conversion was registered in 1770.[37] At the other end of the scale there were 33 peers. Occasionally an entire family converted together. Arthur, John, Meredyth, Valentine, Thomas and William Dines of Dromore all went over on 30 March 1768. It was more usual for sons or brothers to convert when they were about to inherit property, titles or be offered a job in the adminstration. Richard Nugent, eldest son of Lord Riverston, converted in 1704, as did William Nugent, the next Lord Riverston, in 1738. Robert Nugent, Vice-Treasurer, converted in 1762; Anthony Nugent, Lord Riverston, in 1765. There were few clerical converts; some 70 over the period. Overall, Archbishop King was right to be concerned. The popery laws were not designed to bring over the mass of the Irish Catholics.

Swift's friend, Archbishop Lindsay, was one of those foot-draggers who seemed reluctant to assist the process of conversion. Much to King's annoyance, Lindsay criticised moves to revive preaching in Irish on the ingenious ground that they contradicted the Acts of the Reformation parliament which had ordered the use of English 'in all places'. Nathaniel Foy had been King's clerical ally in Dublin under James II, as Rector of St Bride's. As Bishop of Waterford from 1691 to 1707 he also opposed King's support for Irish Bibles and Irish-speaking missionaries. Foy wanted the Irish language to die. 'To furnish the natives with Irish testaments . . . will not answer the end because there are not perhaps 500 persons in the whole kingdom who can read or write the Irish tongue,' he said, 'nor is it fit they should be taught.'[38]

If this was the attitude of the Protestant bishops, it is understandable that the calls made in the convocation of 1703 for Irish-speaking preachers to be sent to every diocese never got far. The Church of Ireland took no advantage of the enforced flight of so many Catholic clergy to evangelise the country. The effort was left up to individual dioceses and a few enthusiastic clergymen, such as John Richardson, Rector of Belturbet in County Cavan. Richardson was indefatigable in urging Ormond to support the printing of Irish Bibles and prayer books and the use of Irish missionaries. A disciple of Bishop Bedell, Richardson shared Bedell's conviction that assaults on Catholic worship were counterproductive. Richardson collected a great deal of information on pilgrimages and shrines for the book that he published in 1727, *The Great Folly, Superstition and Idolatry of Pilgrimages in Ireland*. He had no sympathy for Catholic shrines, but was critical of Protestants who demolished them. 'Where any superstitious place is defaced or demolished they repair it and seem more inclined to resort to it than formerly,' he remarked.[39]

Richardson engaged the interest of Ormond and King, but, like Bedell, he found that his ideas ran counter to the whole ethos of his Church. In theory, it existed to serve the Irish people as a whole. In practice, it was the Church of the 'New English' Protestants. King was pragmatic about his protégé's failure.

God sometimes blesses such endeavours . . . [and] if the bishops of Ireland had heartily and unanimously come into this work and the government had given it countenance, certain methods might in my opinion have been taken that . . . would have had great effect towards the conversion of the natives and making them good Protestants and sincere in the English interest. But what success it may have in the hands of a private man, without such evident encouragement, nay under the manifest disapprobation of those who are able to give it life, I believe it not difficult to guess.[40]

King was a contradictory man. A Whig in politics but not a Low Churchman, he opposed the various schemes to unite the Church of Ireland with dissenters by altering the liturgy and the ordinal. A strong supporter of the English connection, which his generation called 'the English interest', he rejoiced in the vast crowds who filled the streets of Dublin on the accession of George II in 1727. 'Surely His Majesty has not more obedient people . . . than the Protestants of Ireland,' he declared happily.[41]

At the same time, King anticipated the rise of a class of Protestant Irish nationalists. He was less pungent than Swift and never enjoyed the popular following of the author of the *Drapier's Letters*, but he could write in stinging tones to Archbishop Wake of Canterbury about the hostile actions of 'your parliament' and their effect on Irish manufacturers. Above all, he opposed the number of Englishmen being forced on the Irish Church by Whig ministries. The type of career Englishman that he detested was represented by Hugh Boulter, Bishop of Bristol, who followed Lindsay to Armagh in 1724. Boulter's subsequent reputation has usually rested on his edited letters. Published by his secretary in 1769–71 they cast a curious light on the Primate as a man concerned almost exclusively with promoting 'the English interest' and, as he put it himself in a letter to the Duke of Newcastle, with 'breaking the present Dublin faction on the bench'.

Boulter's letters portray a career prelate in the Age of Enlightenment in the worst possible light, obsessed with the minutiae of Whig politics and seemingly devoid of spiritual qualities. Boulter thought it his duty to inform his English connections of any episcopal illnesses among the 'Dublin faction' and to speculate greedily on their successors. He behaved like an angel of death, hovering over bishops' sickbeds and retiring in a huff when the patients recovered. In September 1724, shortly after his arrival, he told the Duke of Newcastle with excitement that the Archbishop of Cashel's wife had accidentally set fire to her husband and 'his life is thought to be in great danger. As his post is the third in the Church and has a good income belonging to it I thought it my duty to give Your Grace immediate notice.'[42] He did not conceal his disappointment when the Archbishop staggered on for another nine months. Archbishop King knew very well that Boulter was slavering over the idea of his death. Anxiously, Boulter monitored every reported stumble, gasp and hot flush, eagerly writing to London that the ripest of all the Irish episcopal plums was about to drop. Three years before King died, Boulter was already talking of him as if he was gone. 'The new Archbishop ought to be an Englishman,' he told Lord Carteret in February 1726. 'As for a native of this country, I can hardly doubt that whatever his behaviour has been or his promises may be, when he is once in that station he will put himself in the head of the Irish interest.'[43]

Boulter ensured that the Englishman John Hoadly succeeded King in Dublin but remained preoccupied with the number of Irishmen still lurking on the bench, complaining to the Lord-Lieutenant in 1734 that 'it will be very dangerous to let the majority of natives who are already twelve on the bench grow great and we cannot but be apprehensive that as they grow stronger they will grow more intractable.'[44]

Under Boulter, the Church of Ireland became more self-consciously English. Like Bishop Foy, he had no sympathy with schemes to evangelise the Irish through the Irish language in case it should prolong the language's existence. Instead, the Boulter camp looked to education to strengthen the Protestant interest.

The Charity School movement was the Primate's answer to those earlier schemes for converting the Irish through missions. It aimed not to increase social mobility by granting poor children access to a good education but to bolster the social order by teaching the poor to be good maids, servants and apprentices. For Boulter, as he put it, the goal was to 'teach the children of the papists the English tongue'. The very title of the society set up in 1733, the Incorporated Society for Promoting English Protestant Schools in Ireland, was instructive. The hope was that they would turn out young English men and women. In a sermon preached in Christ Church on the fifth anniversary of the society's foundation, Robert Howard, Bishop of Elphin, conjured up what was for him the delightful image of the schools churning out 'little colonies instructed in religion and inured to labour almost from their infancy.'[45] These industrious Protestant ants would then be 'sent out to improve the many barren and now neglected parts of this kingdom and raise a spirit of industry and activity in the natives and contribute even to their conversion from the barbarity of their manners and folly of their superstition'. In contrast to Richardson's plan for Irish-speaking ministers to trek into the hills, there was no danger of charity schools extending the life span of the Irish language.

George Stone, Bishop of Ferns, saw a direct link between the growth of popery and the need to set up charity schools when he preached before the society's board in Christ Church cathedral in 1742. The Reformation, he remarked, had 'made very little impression on the natives, the generality of whom did as they do to this day continue papists'.[46] What Stone described as a 'wise and effectual remedy' to this problem was a programme to seize as many children from the Catholics as possible and bring them up in the Protestant faith. Bishop Stone hastened to add that parents would have to hand over their children voluntarily. In this way the society would 'propagate the Protestant religion among the lower sort of people here by a rational and hopeful method; by taking the children of Popish parents who would willingly intrust them to our care'. Distance, Bishop Stone said, was a crucial factor. Previous experience showed that children educated in Protestant academies returned to their former religion if they remained in contact with their families. They had a tendency to 'revert to barbarity', the Bishop said. The remedy was 'removing the children at a distance from their parents and relations by which all intercourse is prevented, properly transplanting them out of the reach of the bad influence in which they were born'.

The Charity School movement was the first concerted attempt by the Church of Ireland to convert the poor to their religion as opposed to putting negative obstacles in the way of their preferred form of worship. But it failed to increase the percentage of Protestants in the population. If each school had numbered several hundred children, talk of 'little colonies' of Protestants reclaiming the countryside for industry and the reformed religion might have been realistic. But the 40 or so schools claimed by the society in the 1750s never contained more than a total of about 1,400 pupils. The regime was unattractive. A report on the school at Templetown, in County Wicklow, in 1740, found 10 boys and 10 girls who divided their time between reading, writing, learning the Church of Ireland catechism, digging potatoes and clearing land. The girls spent much of their time spinning linen. The children were marched to the parish church on Sunday where they sang psalms for the service.

Bishop Stopford of Clogher informed the society in 1758 that 'many persons with numerous families, distressed by poverty, choose rather to breed up their offspring in beggary, nakedness, idleness and vice than to send them to these seminaries'.[47] A visitor to a school in Athlone in the 1770s noted the same phenomenon. Even the most desperate Catholic parents did not want to send their children to the local Protestant free school. 'The children of Protestants are I presume received for want of other candidates for I am assured that a papist would suffer any loss except that of his child rather than send it to one of these schools.'[48]

The need for the schools to support themselves out of the income generated by their endowments condemned most of them to a grinding poverty that attracted increasingly hostile reviews in the 1780s. A parliamentary report in 1788 on the 28 remaining schools was damning. In one the inspectors found the windows filled with dung and the 18 girls and 14 boys 'most of them sickly, wretched looking creatures, covered with the itch'.[49] The schools had become an embarrassment.

The impetus behind the Charity School project was a dawning awareness among Boulter's contemporaries that Catholicism was a far greater danger than their predecessors had thought. Although churchmen had looked on Presbyterians as the strongest threat in Queen Anne's time, it was clear by the reign of George II that Catholics were the greater danger. Popery was 'still the same religion, the same that it was in the days of the powder plot', John Ryder, Bishop of Down and Connor, told an illustrious audience in Christ Church 1743, which consisted of the Lord-Lieutenant and the House of Lords. 'We are therefore under the necessity of being continually on our guard against it and [should] not . . . place our security in any imagined alteration of temper and disposition in papists towards Protestants'.[50] The Bishop reminded the congregation that the Williamite revolution had rescued them from 'the cruelties of the Inquisition, their burning of heretics and many other wicked methods in which they are allowed to endeavour the overcoming all opposers, murdering and massacring, privately or publicly . . . This is Popery! These the principles and practices of the Church of Rome!'

Ryder was preaching on 5 November, the anniversary of the Gunpowder Plot, a day set aside for reflections on the benefits of Protestantism and denunciations of the creed that had inspired Guy Fawkes. By the 1740s, such sermons were mining a growing sense of unease among Protestants that their earlier confidence regarding the slow disappearance of Catholicism had been misplaced. In several parts of the country, Protestantism appeared to be on the defensive, in spite of all the props laboriously erected by the laws. Several plantations of continental Protestants in the 1690s and 1700s had virtually disappeared within a generation through intermarriage with Catholics and, as Boulter remarked with dismay, the descendants of the Cromwellian settlers were turning Catholic.[51] Even in Ulster, the Protestant heartland, they were in visible retreat. As Bishop of Derry, King had complained at the turn of the century about an influx of thousands of Scots Protestants, bringing what he considered their libertarian Presbyterian ideas with them. Two decades later in Dublin, he and Archbishop Boulter were complaining of the rate at which the Protestants were leaving Ulster for the colonies. King told Archbishop Wake in 1717 that 'thousands of families are gone to the West Indies [while] no papists stir except young men that go abroad to be trained in arms . . . the papists being already five or six to one, and a breeding people, you may imagine in what condition we are like to be'.[52] The Archbishop of Armagh told the Duke of Newcastle in 1728 that 'we have hundreds of families (all Protestants) removing out of the north to America' and that several thousand had also left for the West Indies in the space of only three years.[53]

The campaign to drive the Catholic clergy out of Ireland had failed. A 1731 report on the state of popery in Ireland made grim reading for Boulter and his colleagues. In many dioceses, the number of Catholic clergy was reported to be twice the size of that of their Protestant counterparts. In Cashel and Emly there were said to be 62 Catholic priests and 31 ministers of the Church of Ireland. In Cloyne in County Cork there were 92 priests and 'stroling Fryers'[54] but just 47 ministers. In Leighlin in Carlow the proportion was 48 priests to 26 Protestant clergymen. In Ferns there were 53 priests and 27 Protestant clerics. Clogher had 46 priests, about 20 friars and 33 Protestant ministers.

The Catholic parochial network had never totally collapsed even at the height of the persecution. Bishops expelled in the 1690s often left vicars-general behind to keep the diocesan machinery ticking over. When the authorities forbade Catholic priests from keeping curates and set a maximum of one priest per parish, Catholics evaded the restrictions by passing off regular clergy and even bishops as ordinary parish priests.[55] Parishes that were defunct or had been united were listed as separate units to take up the slack. Patrick Donnelly, Bishop of Dromore, had been registered in 1704 as a parish priest in Newry. Archbishop Comerford of Cashel had been registered as a parish priest in Tipperary. As Comerford's presence in the district was known to most of the county, the failure to detect such an important figure can only be attributed to the complicity of the local authorities.

The gentry had often ignored orders to round up Catholic clergy, dreading the turmoil it involved. The more Protestant the area, the less enthusiasm there was for persecution. In Belfast, almost entirely Protestant by the early eighteenth century, the townspeople had no fear of Catholicism and looked on the order from Dublin to arrest the town's only priest as interference. A town like Belfast, with a large Presbyterian population, was ambivalent about helping the Anglican Church to persecute fellow dissenters. When George McCartney, the mayor, reported in 1708 that he had taken in Father Phelomy O'Hamill, he reminded the Lords Justices that the priest's record was 'so kind to the Protestants . . . that I had offered me the best Bail the Protest[ant]s of this Country afford'.[56] The arrest of the Catholic Dean of Armagh in 1712 was another blunder. The Dean was 90, senile and had to be fed like a baby. Thomas Dawson's decision to claim his £50 reward for grabbing this danger to Church and state did not meet with the approval of the county or his relatives. It 'brings such odium upon him and a reflexion to his family. For everyone does here cry out upon him for it,' Dawson's brother complained.[57]

In Munster and Leinster, the Protestant authorities were reluctant to arrest priests for the opposite reason. Adam Haycock, the mayor of Kilkenny, complained in 1708 that Protestants were such a small faction in the town that they would need troops to bolster any action against the priests.[58] Edward Tyrell, a notorious priest catcher made the same observation. On 10 January 1712 he told the Lords Justices he had spotted a bishop four days previously celebrating High Mass in a private house in Clonmel 'in a Bishops habit with a mighter on his head'. Arrest was out of the question, however, 'there being so vast a number of Popish mobbe in this towne'.[59]

As the campaign to capture Catholic priests ran out of steam in the 1730s, disbanded religious houses re-established themselves in the countryside. Abbots and monks often posed as farmers employing young farmhands. Their landlords were now Protestant. But the class of Protestants of the 1730s included a fair number of converts who had altered their faith to keep their land but retained frank sympathies for their former co-religionists.

There was a suspiciously large number of converted Protestant benefactors of religious communities on the list compiled in County Galway in 1731 for Boulter's attention. The friars at Portumna in Galway now lived two miles away from their old abbey at Buoly, 'which they rent from Edmund Dolphin, a convert'.[60] The friars at Kinallehin lived on an eight-acre estate purchased from the late Earl of Clanricard by Denis Daly of Rafort, a convert, 'and by him sett to those fryers . . . Mark Hickey, the Guardian of the Convent, often declared that they paid no rent to Daly but their prayers and that he was their great benefactor'. The report said the friars of Ross had moved to Kilroe, in County Mayo, 'on the estate of Martin Blake, a convert'. The friars of Kilconnell lived near their old abbey 'on the estate of Anthony Daly, a convert'. The report ended with a complaint about 'the power, influence and strength, the number and intolerable insolence of papists who possess entire parishes and not one Protestant family in some of them'.

In the 1730s, most of these re-established communities were discreetly positioned in rural areas. But the towns were changing their religious complexion, too, as dispossessed Catholic families turned to trade and moved back into former Protestant strongholds. The phenomenon was pronounced even by the late 1670s. 'How came the great number of Irish inhabitants and servants into those towns and garrisons?' Archbishop Boyle asked in March 1679. 'Were they not all expelled and thrust out? It is not therefore to be doubted but that the English themselves received them in again for their own advantage; they knew not well how to live without them.'[61] By the 1720s, Archbishop King was complaining 'that the Papists being made incapable to purchase lands have turned themselves to trade and already engrossed almost the trade of the kingdom'.[62] The Protestant-controlled guilds attempted to keep Catholic merchants out of the towns but the system was breaking down. By the middle of the century the guild system was in a state of collapse.

The Catholic resurgence was particularly pronounced in Galway. As in all the corporate towns, Galway's Catholic population had been expelled in the 1650s, but they had returned in force by the 1700s, after which the Protestant population went into free fall through a combination of emigration and intermarriage. By the 1730s, only about 350 of the 14,000 people in the town were Protestant. In 1747 Galway's Protestant governor remarked that the town housed 'six friaries and nunneries, two popish chapels, eight popish schools, above 30 papists to a Protestant and at least two hundred popish ecclesiastics within the town and suburbs'.[63] At this time, in some towns in Munster, Protestants began to feel encircled by the 1730s. The mayor of Cork, James Huleatt, said he had no exact figure for the number of priests in the diocese but was 'of the opinion that the number of Popish priests here are so great that they amount to one hundred (if not more) to the great prejudice of His Majesty's loyal Protestant subjects'.[64]

In the 1740s and 1750s there were constant complaints about the 'insolence' of the local papists as the once silent majority shrugged off the deferential manners of their predecessors. It manifested itself in increasingly aggressive protests against arrests of priests. When orders were sent in March 1754 for the authorities in Cashel to arrest a priest and transport him to Limerick, Jonathan Lovett, the County Sheriff of Limerick, complained that he and his sub-sheriff were overwhelmed by a mob pelting them with stones, in spite of the fact that he was accompanied by a guard of soldiers.[65] Even in Leinster the pretence that Ireland was a Protestant kingdom was becoming hard to maintain as demographic change and immigration eroded the Protestant character of the Irish towns. Dublin, a strongly Protestant city since the 1650s, lost its Protestant majority by the middle of the century as urban expansion drew in ever-increasing numbers of Catholic labourers and servants. Even in the 1700s Dublin had a substantial Catholic population, concentrated in the north-side parish of St Michan, who could make life hazardous for the paid informants known as priest catchers. On 24 March 1711 the *Dublin Intelligence* reported that 'some hundreds of the popish inhabitants of this city in a riotous and tumultous manner assembled in Fishamble Street and in other parts of the town in order to way-lay and insult one Henry Oxenard, on whose testimony several regulars and popish priests were lately convicted . . . [They] pursued the said Oxenard thru several streets . . . crying out a Priest-catcher, and thereupon threw stones, Brick Batts and Dirt at him in so violent a manner that his life was greatly endanger'd.'[66]

John Garcia – a Portuguese immigrant who was awarded £100 and a flat in Dublin Castle for landing a cargo of six priests and three nuns between 1717 and 1720 – complained in 1720 that he was involuntarily incarcerated in his apartment by the atmosphere of hostility on the streets 'and is forced to keep his room like a prisoner for the occasion of his great persecution'.[67] In a bid to squeeze more money from the authorities he claimed the following year that he was still stuck in his home and only able to emerge out to rush to attend church services on Sundays.

The 1731 report on popery listed 12 chapels in the city and three Catholic schools. From the 1720s, the existence of such institutions was so widely accepted that robbers of Catholic churches were prosecuted like any other criminal. Henry Watts was sentenced to transportation in 1723 for robbing the Francis chapel of its chalice and silver box.[68] In June the following year the regular clergy held their first assembly in the city since the Reformation when the Irish Augustinians presided over a general chapter meeting. The Dublin newspapers in the 1730s began to report on the deaths of the Catholic clergy in reverential tones. The *Flying Post* in June 1739 told its readers of the sad news that 'last Tuesday the Revd Mr Tallent, a priest belonging to Lithey-Street chapel, after having celebrated Mass twice that Day, went to his chamber, sate down on a chair and expir'd immediately'.[69] In August, the newspaper reported the death of Peter Mulligan, Bishop of Ardagh and former Provincial of the Augustinians – a man, the newspaper said, 'of the most profound Humility and unfeigned Piety'. A few days later there was the 'melancholy accident' of Father Charles Fleming's death. While giving absolution to man about to be executed, he was shot dead by mistake.[70]

The trend towards acknowledging the existence of Catholics and even treating them in a friendly manner did not mean Protestants were ready to share political power. The corporations clung to their rituals and observed the anniversaries with as much pomp as they could manage. In Dublin, the anniversary of the Gunpowder Plot in 1739 was marked by sermons, a dinner at the town hall, the Tholsel hosted by the Boyne Club and 'the ringing of bells, bonfires, illuminations'.[71] The corporation of Clonmel celebrated the anniversary of the Battle of the Boyne in 1767 in similar style. 'The morning was ushered in with ringing of bells', the *Freeman's Journal* reported on 1 July.[72] 'The Ensigns or Standards of the different Companies of the corporation were displayed from the Tholsel, and the mayor, Burgesses, Freemen and Gentlemen of the different Corporations with

Orange Cockades proceeded at Six o' Clock in the Morning to perambulate the Liberties and Franchises. The evening concluded with Bonfires, Illuminations and other Publick Demonstrations of Joy.'

'We the present Irish are a part and piece of ENGLAND,' the *Freeman's Journal* assured its readers in February 1764, 'her colony and her offspring, descended from the same stock, born and bred under the same influence of the same constitution with the same sense of religion and spirit of liberty.'[73] The Protestant writers of the *Freeman's Journal* were, indeed, convinced that 'the present Irish' were themselves. At the same time, they no longer spoke of the Catholics as a conquered, enslaved people, as Archbishop King had done. They admitted that the Catholics comprised the majority of the population and no longer seriously pretended it was possible, or even desirable, to undo this. They observed the Catholic society multiplying around them with a lazy, and occasionally approving, eye. To an extent, they wished to accommodate Catholic desires. They hoped Protestant domination could somehow be conjoined with the 'spirit of liberty' of which the *Freeman's Journal* spoke. It was, however, a false hope. There could be Protestant Ascendancy and there could be liberty but they could not coexist for ever in the same country. At the end of the century a rebellion erupted which exposed the fact.

CHAPTER NINE

Furious Demagogues of Rebellion

*The outrages of the Whiteboys in the south, supposed to be confined to tithes, do by
no means stop there. They extend to the persons of the established clergy who are
hunted from their parishes.*
(Bishop Woodward of Cloyne, 1787)[1]

North Armagh is Ulster's green orchard. The smaller roads running from
Portadown to the cathedral city of Armagh curl through prosperous, rolling countryside dotted with apple trees. These are the fertile lands that the eagle-eyed businessmen of the Ulster Plantation seized from the native Irish, forcing those they
dispossessed to relocate to higher ground. North Armagh is Protestant; South
Armagh is Catholic. The north is low, flat and lush, while the south is stony,
rugged moorland.

North Armagh was the scene of the some of the worst atrocities in 1641. At
Portadown, about 100 English settlers were drowned beside the bridge in an act
of senseless madness. Loughgall is where the hellish Jane Hampton, 'formerly a
Protestant', threw off her mask and herded Joan Constable, her friends and their
children into a burning barn, laughing madly as 'the children gaped when the fire
began to burn them'.

South Armagh is defiantly Catholic and bitterly anti-British. Drivers on the
road from Armagh city to Crossmaglen, near the border of the Irish Republic, can
hardly miss the slogans in support of the Irish Republican Army painted on
wooden boards and telegraph poles. More British soldiers were shot in the village
of Crossmaglen during the 'troubles' from 1967 to 1997 than anywhere else in the
province. For many people of the community, that grim tally is a badge of honour.

South Armagh's reputation as a rebel stronghold long predates the conflicts of
the 1960s. In the eighteenth century, the land round Crossmaglen, known as the
Fews, spawned Gaelic poets like Art Mac Cooey, who fought to keep the Irish
language alive in poetry and song at a time when it was crumbling under the pressure of relentless Anglicisation. They were artistic rebels, bucking the trend. The
lonely moorlands and undulating heaths were also perfect terrain for Tories, rebels
against the Cromwellian land settlement who preyed on the gentry occupying
their ancestors' homes.

The sympathies of South Armagh people instinctively lie with men and women who defy authority. That does not mean they do not bear a grudging respect for the lawmen who hunted down the Tories and their ilk. One of the most famous, John Johnston, 'Johnston of the Fews', who died in 1759, is buried in Creggan churchyard near Crossmaglen and the rhyme about the constable's exploits is still well known: 'Jesus of Nazareth, King of the Jews' it runs, 'Save us from Johnston, King of the Fews.'

Protestantism in south Armagh is the religion of the planter and the enemy. There were Protestant landlords in south Armagh but there was never a large Protestant population. The majority has pushed the minority out, so that the region is now almost ethnically and confessionally homogeneous. In such an isolated and rural community the concept of a multi-racial or multi-confessional society is not widely accepted. It would be seen as a Trojan horse of the British aimed at diluting the region's Irish character. The old Church of Ireland church at Creggan serves only about seven remaining Protestant families. It has survived by re-marketing itself as a visitors' centre, providing information and videos about the eighteenth-century Gaelic-speaking poets. Tomas O'Fiaich, late Cardinal Archbishop of Armagh and a stern critic of British rule in Ulster, features largely in several of them. He was, not surprisingly, given his political views, a great fan of the poets of the Fews. It is strange fare to be served up in an Anglican church, videos about men who opposed and despised Protestantism, but it may have saved a rare medieval parish church from the hostile attention of IRA sympathisers.

The ethnic border cuts through the county town. Armagh is not Beirut, Mostar or even Belfast, and no green line or peace line divides the town. But the roads leading north through Richhill towards Portadown are mostly Protestant, while it would be a brave Protestant who asked to be rehoused on the Windmill estate on the southern edge of the city. The estate is a Republican bastion, on a slope directly south of the Protestant cathedral. The small row of cottages once occupied by the cathedral canons marks the uneasy front line between the two worlds and its residents are usually the first to experience the wrath of the Windmill whenever sectarian tension has risen elsewhere in the province.

North of the neatly kept green in the centre of Armagh lie the more spacious suburbs of the Protestant residents. Most belong to the Church of Ireland, for we are out of the zone of Scottish settlement. Before the 'troubles' started, Protestants and Catholics lived together in the commercial heart of Armagh, in areas such as Scotch Street. A succession of IRA bombs in the 1970s emptied the area of its civilian population. Today, like so many towns in Northern Ireland, the centre of Armagh is almost deserted outside regular shopping hours. The ethnic and religious divisions in County Armagh that are now so stark – English versus Irish, English language versus Gaelic, Protestant versus Catholic, North versus South – were less fixed in the eighteenth century. There were more Catholics in the north and more Protestants in the south. For example, according to the parliamentary return of 1776, the population of Portadown comprised 514 Protestant families and 395 Catholic ones.[2] Although the border between the communities was fuzzier then in County Armagh, the tension was just as strong as it is today. This helps to explain why Armagh Protestants never embraced the anti-sectarian ideology of the Belfast Presbyterians and why the county gave birth to an organisation based on very different principles from the United Irishmen – the Orange Order.

The dramatist Richard Cumberland left a striking description of Richard Robinson, Archbishop of Armagh from 1765 to 1794, attending Sunday worship. 'I accompanied him on the Sunday forenoon to the cathedral,' he wrote.

> We went in his chariot with six horses attended by three footmen behind. At our approach the great western door was thrown open and my friend (in person one of the finest men that could be seen) entered like another Archbishop Laud, all in high prelatical state, preceded by his officers and ministers of the church, conducting him in files to the robing chamber and back again to the throne.
>
> After the divine service the officiating clergy presented themselves in the hall of his palace to pay their court. I asked him how many of them were to dine with us. He answered 'not one'. He did them kindness but he gave them no entertainments. They were in excellent discipline.[3]

Robinson presided over the Church of Ireland at the high noon of the Protestant Ascendancy. Towards the end of his life the shadows were lengthening. Within four years of his death Ireland would be engulfed by the 1798 rebellion and by bloodshed not seen since the 1640s. It brought the entire social order he had strained to defend to the brink of collapse. Mistrustful of their ability to control the Catholic population seemingly infected by the revolutionary doctrines of the French, the Irish Protestants voted their ancient parliament out of existence. The Act of Union of 1800 united the English and Irish legislatures and the English and Irish Church establishments.

Robinson arrived in Ireland in 1751 as chaplain to the Duke of Dorset. The Duke rewarded him almost immediately by securing him the modest bishopric of Killala. In 1759 he was promoted to Ferns and Leighlin. Two years later he was transferred to Kildare, a poor see but one customarily held in tandem with the lucrative deanery of Christ Church, Dublin.

His career path was a well trodden one. Of the 40 men appointed to Church of Ireland bishoprics between 1760 and 1780, 17 were formerly chaplains to Lord-Lieutenants. It was a contentious subject in Ireland. The jobbery in the Established Church was a favourite subject for the Protestant nationalists, who began to style themselves the 'Patriot' party in the 1750s, under the Lord-Lieutenancy of the Duke of Bedford. The Patriots pilloried a system of government that enabled men like the Robinsons of Rokeby Hall, in Yorkshire, to seize the most lucrative positions in the Irish Church. They complained that the Church of Ireland had fallen 'in the hands of strangers advanced to the mitre not for their virtues or their knowledge but quartered in this country through their own servility . . . and inclined naturally to oppress us.'[4]

The Church of Ireland was the victim of its own economic success. Englishmen in the seventeenth century had to be dragged to Ireland. Almost constant warfare and the locust-like activities of the first generation of Protestant bishops had rendered many Irish sees worthless. Peace and the steady rise in land values in the eighteenth century radically improved the Church's fortunes. Ambitious Englishmen now began to drool at the thought of an Irish bishopric, and the cry went up that the English were jumping the queue, taking jobs that might have gone to the Irish Protestant gentry. Dean Swift complained to the Earl of Peterborough that 'the bishops sent over to Ireland, having been without other distinctions than that of chaplains to the governors do frequently invite over ther old acquaintance or kindred, to whom they bestow the best preferments in their gift'.[5] The result, he added was that 'the whole body of the gentry feel . . . utterly destitute of all means to make provision for their younger sons either in the Church, the law, the Revenue or, of late, in the army.'

As the century progressed, the proportion of English to Irish-born candidates on the bishops' bench continued to increase. Under Anne, English imports made up less than a quarter of episcopal promotions, but by 1760 the 22 bishoprics were evenly divided, with the English holding three of the four archbishoprics. By the last quarter of the century, the majority of bishops were English. The cry went up that the Church of Ireland was too rich, as well as too English. Whilst the Irish Protestants in the previous century had moaned about their Church's poverty, by the 1730s their successors were fending off envious complaints about their wealth. The feeling that the Church was too fat and that English leeches were appropriating its incomes inspired the Protestant gentry to attack the system of tithes in parliament in the mid-1730s. Dean Swift rushed to defend his order, English-born or not, and in May 1736 fired off a counterblast, *Concerning that Universal Hatred Which Prevails against the Clergy*. But the mud stuck. As Boulter confessed to Sir Robert Walpole in 1737, 'most of the needy gentry here envy to see the bishops . . . easy in their circumstances'.[6] The idea that the Church of Ireland was too rich for its own good lasted at least until disestablishment in 1869.

Irish Protestants might call the imported English clergy oppressive, but Irish Catholics often preferred them, considering English Protestants less bigoted than the domestic variety. But Armagh Catholics were to be disappointed in Archbishop Robinson. His term as Primate coincided with the progressive relief of the anti-Catholic laws passed at the turn of the century. The Archbishop resolutely opposed the reforms. His one surviving sermon – he was no preacher – rang with denunciations of papal tyranny and claimed that any measures to relieve Catholic disabilities posed a mortal danger to the state. As the Patriots chipped gingerly at the foundations of the Protestant Ascendancy, Robinson shored them up in the only way he knew: by covering his diocese with massive monuments that exalted his Church's power and charitable largesse.

As the Catholics and their liberal Protestant allies agitated for land and voting rights, the Archbishop reinforced the tottering ramparts of the Ascendancy with piles of marble. Armagh is his epitaph. He dotted the city with buildings constructed in a simple classical style that has never gone out of fashion. In the process he made what had been an undistinguished village a gracious, substantial town.[7] The Archbishop's one great failure was the botched plan to transform St Patrick's cathedral in 1782 by remodelling the tower on the lines of the much-loved tower of Magdalen College, Oxford. After it showed signs of stress he had it dismantled. Archbishop Robinson's legacy is elsewhere. He built an observatory, which is still working and attracting scientists from all over the world. He constructed a huge, rather plain palace of local marble, which now provides an extravagant setting for the Armagh local government offices. Then there is the 14-foot obelisk which commemorates his patron, the Duke of Northumberland, and the delightful library outside the cathedral, which is still open and now also houses the deanery. He contributed generously to the foundation of a college and an infirmary. Finally he left £5,000 – a vast sum in his time – towards the establishment of a university. Sadly this magnificent bequest came to nothing. The terms of his will set a five-year limit for the completion of the project. It ran out in the aftermath of the turmoil of the 1798 rebellion.

As Robinson's projects show, a Protestant archbishop in the era of Ascendancy was much more than an ecclesiastical leader. He sat at the centre of the local economy and local politics. He was the manager of an estate, a source of welfare and employment, a military commander and a dispenser of justice.

When the new Archbishop, Power Le Poer Trench arrived in Tuam in 1819 he was serenaded by crowds who lined the route to the palace, burning bonfires of peat. 'We arrived here safely at 4 o clock on Friday,' he wrote. 'We were met by a large mob at the suburbs of the town and the crowd was so great from thence all through the town, cheering, that the carriage could hardly move.'[8] When John Jebb was made Bishop of Limerick in 1822, he, too, was met on his entrance to the city by crowds of peasants who unhooked his horses and drew his carriage for the last mile of the journey, 'preceded by a band of rustic music'.[9]

The cheering crowds were Catholics – the same people who indignantly rejected the right of Anglican Bishops to baptise them, marry them or catechise their children. The Irish Catholics had no problem in separating Trench's and Jebb's episcopal functions from those of a local magnate: when a Protestant bishop took up his see, there were jobs going. Cumberland recalled with some misgivings the sight of hundreds of farm workers on Robinson's estates in Armagh, scurrying over the fields 'like ants'. A man like Trench, the son of an earl, moved around with a princely retinue of gardeners, cooks, butlers, coachmen, valets, parlour maids, kitchen maids, not to mention the battalion of ladies' maids and wet-nurses required to wait on his wife and daughters.

Primate Robinson's time in Armagh coincided with an upsurge in agrarian violence among the Catholic peasantry that threatened this life of responsibility and privilege. The Whiteboys, who were active in Munster from the 1770s, directed their outrages above all against church tithes. They grew increasingly confident in the last decades of the century. In July 1786 *Saunders's News-Letter* reported 'tumultuous assemblies' of Whiteboys in County Cork and said that in Dunmanway they had opened fire on the troops.[10]

In the Established Church, opinion was divided over ways to confront this violence. Bishop Richard Woodward of Cloyne's account of the state of Ireland in 1787 portrayed the Whiteboy protests as the thin end of a wedge that could only end in the annihilation of Protestantism. 'The outrages of the Whiteboys in the south, supposed to be confined to tithes, do by no means stop there. They extend to the persons of the established clergy who are hunted from their parishes,' he said. 'On the whole, all the clergy in the extensive county of Cork . . . were under continual alarm and obliged to arm themselves in the best manner they could; and had they not yielded to the violence of the insurgents, I am persuaded, would have been . . . perhaps buried in those graves which were in many places dug (professedly) for their reception.'[11]

Robinson and Woodward represented conservative opinion in the Church of Ireland. Alarmed by the growing 'insolence' of papists, they argued for the retention of anti-Catholic laws and harsh punishments for lawbreakers. They were not a small body. James Butler, Catholic Archbishop of Cashel, noted that Woodward's book had gone through four editions in 12 days.[12]

On the other hand, *Saunders's News-Letter* reported that many parish clergy supported tithe reform – and any other reform that would lessen Catholic anger. 'What in the name of patriotism can so blindfold our government as not to give proper encouragement to the Irish Catholics, receive them in our army and navy and make them participate in the blessings they have a right to?' it asked.[13]

That was certainly the standpoint of Robinson's nemesis, Frederick Hervey, Bishop of Cloyne in 1767–68 and of Derry from 1768 to 1803. Like Robinson, Hervey was a product of a patronage system that was passing out of the hands of the monarch to government ministers. Hervey's patron was his brother, the Earl of Bristol, a title he himself inherited in 1779. Like Robinson he had floated into the Church by default, and without displaying much sign of a religious temperament. But that was where the similarity ended. Robinson strained every nerve to defend the settlement in Church and state. Hervey pulled in the opposite direction. He was that well-known phenomenon, the English upper-class revolutionary. Robinson thought he ought to have been arrested.

Hervey's lifestyle as a bishop invited condemnation. He abandoned his wife in the 1780s. He lampooned his own Church and was reported to have made his fattest clergy run a race for the best living in the diocese.[14] The winning post was placed in quicksand. From 1791 until his death in 1803 he was not seen in his diocese, or in Ireland, while he wandered through Italy, Germany and Switzerland. Towards the end of his life an English visitor to Rome spotted the Earl-Bishop in his adopted milieu. 'He is the patron of all modern artists whose wives he not only associates with as his only female company but has their pictures drawn as Venuses all over his house,' she wrote. 'His three favourite mistresses are represented as June, Minerva and Venus in the Judgment of Paris. Tho' he is one of the greatest curiosities alive, yet such is his notorious character for profane conversation and so great a reprobate is he in the unlicensed sense of the word that the English do not esteem it a very creditable thing to be much in his society.'[15]

In Londonderry, Hervey had ardently supported the removal of all remaining restrictions on Presbyterians and Catholics. A true radical, he derided the halting half-measures of the day. He claimed he wanted only to forestall a Catholic insurrection, but his English enemies said the Bishop's agitation contributed to the phenomenon he said he hoped to prevent. Horace Walpole thought him a dangerous lunatic and detested his intrigues with the Presbyterians. 'Think of a reformation of parliament by admitting Roman Catholics to vote at elections!' he sputtered in 1787. 'That it was sanctified by a Protestant bishop is not strange; he would call Mussulmen [Muslims] to the poll were there any in the diocese of Derry.'[16]

In their different ways, Robinson and Hervey were responding to the challenge of the Catholic revival, even though by the standards of the following century, the Irish Catholic Church was virtually invisible. Visitors to Armagh since the 1870s have been struck by the outline of two cathedrals, and the Catholic cathedral is the grander of the two. Robinson's Armagh had only one – his own. And just as the Archbishop's view was not spoiled by the sight of a rival cathedral, he was not offended by the presence of a rival Archbishop either. Robinson was the first Protestant Primate to reside in the city and he ruled the roost. The Catholic Primates did not live in Armagh and did not dream of living in the kind of cold magnificence Robinson surrounded himself with. Archbishop Michael O'Reilly lived in the 1750s in a cottage in Termonfeckin, near Drogheda. His successor, Anthony Blake, Archbishop from 1758 to 1787, spent most of the time in his native Galway, from where he unsuccessfully attempted to govern his archdiocese by correspondence.

Archbishop Blake's colleagues were grateful to the authorities for the fact that they were not beaten up, imprisoned or expelled. They were hardly assertive in their attitude to the Ascendancy. They lacked the confidence of their distant predecessors and their successors, were humble in their attitude to the Established Church and effusively loyal to the crown. The most condescending attention by English statesmen excited their fervent gratitude.

Archbishop Blake's time as Primate coincided with the removal of a stumbling block in relations between the British government and the Irish Catholic Church. In 1766 the exiled James III died in Rome. The papacy did not recognise his heir, Charles, the ageing 'Bonny Prince Charlie' of legend, and withdrew the right of the Stuarts to nominate Irish Catholic bishops. After the failure of the 1745 Jacobite rebellion it was not a burning topic. But it was an irritant. Now, at last, the ghost was exorcised and the Catholic bishops could no longer be accused of acting as the agents of a foreign power. With the business of the Stuarts gone, schemes were inevitably floated for the right of nomination to be transferred to the British crown and over the next half-century there was much enthusiastic talk of at least conceding the crown the power of veto. Nothing came of it, but the fact that it was discussed at all showed how much the climate had warmed between the Irish Catholic Church and the British state. The Catholic hierarchy was outwardly submissive in the age of Archbishop Blake. They were keen to break the connection in English minds between Catholics and insurrection and when the Whiteboys appeared in the 1760s, they denounced them. John Troy, Bishop of Ossory and later Archbishop of Dublin, excommunicated them in 1779, urging that 'their names be blotted out and let their memory perish from the earth'.[17]

The hierarchy's submissiveness did not mean they were slow to take advantage of the relaxation in the anti-popery laws. In Galway, Blake oversaw the construction in 1750 of the town's first purpose-built Catholic church since the Reformation, in the central location of Middle Street. As Archbishop, he presided over diocesan synods in 1761 and 1764 that were held in public and which called for Catholic churches to be built in every parish in the country.

Church buildings reappeared in Irish towns and cities, replacing the 'wretched cabins' that had been the standard setting for Catholic worship. Only parts of Ulster and Connacht were so poor that Catholics continued worshipping in the open air. According to the 1731 report on popery, mass in Derry diocese was still customarily said 'in the open fields or under some shed'. Raphoe's 26 priests had the luxury of choosing to say their services in 'one old Mass house, one Mass house lately built, one cabin where Mass is said publickly and two sheds'.[18] In Dublin, the Catholics of St Mary's parish had a church built in Liffey Street in 1729 that later served as a pro-cathedral. In Cork, the 'Bishops chapel', in the Shandon district, was built around 1730. Limerick Catholics rebuilt a chapel first constructed in the 1700s near St John's Gate at the same time. In Ennis, in County Clare, a Catholic church was built in 1735. Ballina, in County Mayo, got its first purpose-built Catholic church around 1740. Carlow and Cavan followed around 1750.

There are not many details of what these early to mid-eighteenth-century Catholic churches looked like. The mayor of Cork described the Bishop's Chapel in Cork as 'sumptious'.[19] If that was accurate, it was unusual, but thatched barns were giving way to more solid structures. The popery report of 1731 said the mass house in Clonmel had been a thatched building under Queen Anne but had received a slate roof under George I, since when it had also been fitted with galleries.[20]

By the 1770s the first generation of Catholic churches was giving way to larger, more dignified stone structures. Irish Catholics were not yet rich or confident enough to fling up cathedrals; that had to wait until the 1790s, when the baroque Italianate façade of Holy Trinity cathedral rose up in the centre of Waterford. But by the last quarter of the century Catholicism was no longer an invisible religion.

The days were now gone when worshippers disappeared down alleyways to perform their mysterious acts in closed courtyards, their chants heard only through keyholes and partition walls.

The champions of the Ascendancy could draw comfort from the fact that Dublin still looked like a Protestant city. While the Catholics were constructing their first humble chapels, the Dublin Protestants were beautifying the city with a string of elegant classical churches. St James in James Street was built in 1707. St Werburgh in Werburgh Street was rebuilt in 1715–19. St Ann's, Dawson Street, went up in 1720. Work began in 1729 on St Mark's, Great Brunswick Street (now Pearse Street). St Thomas, Marlborough Street, was built between 1758 and 1762. St Werburgh was rebuilt in 1759 after a fire; St Nicholas Within in 1767. St Catherine in Thomas Street went up in 1769. Construction on this scale sent out a message that Protestants intended to remain in control of the capital. The Catholics were still nervous of treading too heavily in the Ascendancy's citadel, and when Archbishop Troy built their cathedral in 1807, he passed up a prominent location in what is now O'Connell Street for a more discreet site.

Even in Dublin, the city's Protestant character was only really apparent in the afternoon, after the Protestants had got out of bed. The *Philosophical Survey of the South of Ireland* (1778) observed that the streets looked different when they were full of Catholic servants and labourers. It was then that the visitor was forced to notice the presence of 'two papists for one Protestant'. In the morning, the book commented, 'before the higher classes are up, you would imagine half the prisons in Europe had been opened and their contents emptied into this place'.[21]

In Cork the author remarked on the openly Catholic character of the kingdom's second city. Cork Protestants had only seven churches while the Catholics had 11 'mass houses' of various descriptions, and whereas one service a week in the parish churches was enough for Protestant needs, the mass houses held 'a succession of services on Sundays and holy days from early in the morning till late at night for the accommodation of their votaries'.[22] Outside the Catholic churches the sight of 'several elegant carriages standing before the door' bore striking witness to the growth of a wealthy Catholic middle class.[23] Cashel provided a still starker example of the decay of the Established Church. The magnificent Gothic cathedral on the rock still towered over the plain. But now it was deserted, the haunt of bats, mice and the odd curious tourist. The roof had been pulled off in the late 1740s, since when Church of Ireland services were performed in 'a sorry room where county courts are held'. There were very few worshippers in this dreary setting, which afforded a rather obvious symbol of the close relationship between the Church of Ireland and the civil power. It was 'a thin congregation composed of some well-dressed women, some half a dozen boys and perhaps half a score of foot soldiers'.[24]

The emergence of a Catholic middle class and the construction of Catholic churches did not alarm all Protestants. It was violence they most dreaded, not the spread of civility. Many Protestant gentry held the same sentiments as John Law, the gentle Bishop of Clonfert from 1782 to 1787, who decided that as he could not turn his Catholic flock into Protestants, he would be better employed making them 'good Catholics, good citizens, good anything'.[25] With that project in mind he paid for the circulation of 'improving' Catholic literature in his diocese.

The liberal Protestant middle classes and gentry gave the Catholics land and money to build churches. The Mathews family of Thomastown Castle who owned most of Thurles, converted to Protestantism in the eighteenth century to keep their land. But they still patronised the construction of the first new Catholic church in Thurles in the 1730s and encouraged the Catholic archbishops of Cashel to settle in the town from 1757.[26]

Waterford offered a striking example of co-operation between Protestants and Catholics. Two cathedrals were bestowed on the city in the late eighteenth century. The Protestants built their new cathedral in 1773–79, controversially demolishing the medieval cathedral to make way for it. The Catholics started building their cathedral in 1793. It could easily have become a source of petty confessional rivalry. Instead, both communities turned to the same local Protestant architect, John Roberts, who, if anything, lavished most care on the Catholic building. While the Protestant cathedral is an elegant construction, it looks as if it might have been assembled from a kit. The Catholic cathedral is a luxuriant essay in baroque which, as many writers have observed, introduced an unexpected blast of Mediterranean colour and warmth into Ireland's damp northern landscape.

There was another ecumenical episode in the construction of Waterford's two cathedrals. In the course of the demolition of the old structure, workmen uncovered a perfectly preserved set of rich eucharistic vestments, embroidered in the Flemish style and dating from the late fifteenth or early sixteenth century. They had been hidden away in the Reformation era and then forgotten. The Protestants had no need for mass vestments. But it was still a generous gesture of the Dean to donate them to his Catholic counterpart.

The American rebellion in 1776 brought the two confessions in Ireland together. Britain's protracted war with its Protestant colonies placed no strain on the loyalty of the Catholic population, as earlier struggles with France and Spain had done. Britain had, after all, provoked the quarrel in part by deciding to 'establish' the Catholic Church in Quebec. Irish immigrants to America supported the rebel cause to demonstrate their loyalty to their new homeland, but at home the Irish Catholic bishops were determined to prove their loyalty to the crown and ordered prayers to be said for the King's forces.

The sympathies of the Presbyterians of Ulster were much more actively engaged on the side of the American colonists. Many of the sons of the Ulster Protestant emigrants to the colonies in the 1730s became the rebels of the 1770s. At least 100,000 Ulster Presbyterians left Ireland for America in the eighteenth century before the outbreak of war and by the end of the century a quarter of a million people, one-sixth of the white population of the United States, claimed Scots-Irish descent. To many Ulster Presbyterians, the American Revolution was their revolution. The American Declaration of Independence was covered with their footprints. The document was in the handwriting of an Ulsterman, Charles Thompson of Maghera. It was first printed by an Ulsterman, John Dunlap of Strabane. It was first read in public by the son of an Ulsterman, Colonel John Dixon. And the only signature on it for a month was the name of a man whose ancestors were Presbyterians from County Down, John Hancock, the President of Congress and governor of Massachusetts. The American war emboldened the radicals in the Presbyterian Church. When the government allowed the Irish to form Volunteers in 1776 as a home guard to safeguard the island's defences after the withdrawal of much of the regular army, the Presbyterians were the most enthusiastic supporters. Many of their ministers joined the Volunteers, and their Convention in February 1782 was held in the Presbyterian meeting house at Dungannon, County Tyrone.

The radical Presbyterians found a close ally in the clownlike but dangerous Bishop of Derry who shared their enthusiasm for the Volunteer movement and attempted to use them as a battering ram against the Ascendancy system. Hervey was delighted by the downfall of the monarchy in America. It was the perfect occasion to break down confessional ties between Catholics, Anglicans and Presbyterians, which was the prerequisite for any political change on the island.

The progressive politics of the Ulster Presbyterians in the 1780s dovetailed with theological changes. Ulster Protestants had maintained close links with the Scottish universities, where Calvinist orthodoxy went into rapid retreat in the early eighteenth century. The Scottish Enlightenment inevitably affected Ulster. All the British churches were stressing the reasonable nature of religion. John Locke's book, *The Reasonableness of Christianity* of 1695 had been enormously influential in arguing that there were 'no facts or doctrines of the Gospel or the Scriptures which when revealed were not perfectly plain, intelligible and reasonable', but the Presbyterians went furthest in the direction of rationalism and vague deism. They had no equivalent to the Anglican Book of Common Prayer to anchor them in certain dogmas. All that held them in place was the Calvinist Westminster Confession of 1643, and this was an irritant the rationalist party longed to throw off. The rejection of the confession by some presbyteries in the 1790s split the Church into New Light and Old Light factions, echoing the theological division among the Anglicans between the High and Low Church parties. Old Light theological conservatives tended to be conservative in their politics as well, though not always. Some were Old Light in religion and radical in politics. But it was natural for the men of the New Light to take the lead in the campaign against remaining disabilities placed on Catholics. It was not simply a question of being reasonable. New Light men reacted against Calvinist pessimism with a studied optimism about human nature. They flourished most where there was a certain level of prosperity in the community and an absence of sectarian pressure. Belfast was their bastion, where the Protestant majority could afford to feel relaxed about Catholic emancipation and where Presbyterians looked on Catholics as fellow underdogs.

In his message to the Volunteers holding a review in Belfast on 12 July 1784, an Anglican sympathiser, William Todd Jones, MP for the manufacturing town of Lisburn, reminded them that parliamentary reform in Ireland would never occur unless Catholics and Protestants joined forces. He recalled that 'Protestant America receives its liberty by the interposition of the Catholic French', and added that there was a lesson in this for liberal Irish Protestants as they struggled for reform. 'When we are told by great authorities that a union with Catholics is a dangerous expedient we ought anxiously to enquire by what mode they propose to accomplish a reform of parliament without their co-operation.'[27]

The most ardent Protestant supporters of Catholic emancipation were often utterly unsympathetic to Catholic beliefs. Bishop Hervey hoped political freedom would result in Catholics discarding their 'silly religion'. A pamphlet entitled *Plain Arguments in Defence of the People's Absolute Dominion over the Constitution*, written in 1784, addressed Catholic emancipation in terms designed to appeal to Protestant progressives. Property qualifications would exclude most Catholics from the franchise, it said, while the author went on to blame Protestant bigotry for the survival of Catholicism. 'In our country it will wear out faster than the possessions of the Roman Catholics will accumulate, unless we prop their superstition with their resentment and keep their prejudices alive by maintaining our own.'[28]

The progressive Ulstermen had little contact with these Catholics whom they hazily imagined as their allies. At the beginning of the century, the mayor of Belfast, George McCartney had remarked that there were only seven Catholics in the entire town. There were more than that by the end of the century. A population of about 2,000 in the 1680s had quadrupled to 8,500 by 1750, rising sharply to more than 13,000 in 1782. Even then, Belfast remained a close-knit, almost entirely Protestant community. It was not bigotry but lack of a congregation that delayed the construction of a Catholic church until 1783. When mass immigration drastically altered the city's ethnic make-up in the first half of the nineteenth century, Belfast shed its reputation as a haven of tolerance.

The Volunteers fuelled an appetite for change that they could not satisfy. They emboldened the Irish parliament to demand – and receive – legislative independence from a distracted English government in 1782. But the conventions and parades did not move the Irish parliament to restore Catholic votes. Disappointed, Bishop Hervey gave up and left the country in 1791, never to return. His radical Presbyterian allies began to plot a more dangerous course with the creation, on 14 October 1791, of an overtly revolutionary and republican organisation, the Society of United Irishmen. The Volunteers were inspired by the American revolt of 1776; the ideals of the United Irishmen owed more to the French Revolution of 1789.

With a large, Presbyterian population, Belfast was the obvious place to found the United Irishmen. The Dubliner Wolfe Tone has generally been credited as the driving spirit behind the new society but several Presbyterian ministers were among the early leaders. William Drennan, a Scottish-trained doctor and son of a minister, was the leader in Belfast while several ministers were involved in the production of the United Irishman's newspaper, the *Northern Whig*, their mouthpiece until it was suppressed in 1797. They included William Steel Dickson, minister at Portaferry, Sinclair Kelburn of Belfast and James Porter of Greyabbey. About 30 ministers would later be implicated to some extent in the uprising that broke out in 1798, including Dickson, William Sinclair of Newtownards, David Bailie of Killinchy, Arthur McMahon of Holywood and John Glendy of Maghera.

The resolutions adopted by the United Irishmen in Belfast in 1791 reflected the extent to which revolutionary French and American nationalism had penetrated this Presbyterian stronghold. 'We have no national government,' they began. 'We are ruled by Englishmen and the Servants of Englishmen whose object is the interest of another country whose instrument is corruption and whose strength is the weakness of Ireland.' The first of the three resolutions declared: 'The weight of English influence in the government of this country is such as to require a cordial union among all the people of Ireland.' The second called for radical reform of parliament. The third said 'that no reform is practicable, efficacious or just which shall not include Irishmen of every religious persuasion'.[29] They called for Thomas Paine's *Rights of Man* to be distributed throughout all sects and denominations on the island.

The radicalism of the Belfast United Irishmen appealed to Tone, whose journal records frequent visits to Belfast and his impression of an almost millenarian fervour among the local Protestants. 'Curious discourse with a hairdresser (one Taylor),' he noted, 'who has two children christened by the priest though he himself a Dissenter, merely with a wish to blend the sects.'[30]

Such a chic approach to Ireland's ancient religious conflicts was only popular in that small corner of Ulster where Catholic Emancipation would have little impact on the local pecking order. After the 1798 rebellion ruined their dreams of the peaceful transformation of society, David Bailie embarrassed his colleagues in the presbytery of Bangor by reminding them of what most had professed a few years earlier. His sarcastic *Farewell Address to the Junto of the Presbytery of Bangor* was written after the revolt collapsed and his colleagues had expelled him from the ministry. He taunted them for their new-found timidity: 'Every one of you has both publicly and privately circulated republican morality that the will of the people should be the supreme law,' he wrote, 'and now from terror, to show your fatuous glow-worm loyalty, you have met as a military inquisition.'[31] It was stirring stuff and it had absolutely no effect. The outbreak of rebellion that year and reports of bloody assaults on the Protestants of Leinster awoke older, tribal memories among the Ulster Presbyterians. Half-forgotten tales of the siege of Derry and, before that, the massacres of 1641 were disinterred and dusted down. Glendy, Sinclair and Bailie ended up in the Protestant paradise of America, where their optimistic creed found its natural expression. The Protestants of Ulster followed an entirely different course and returned to Calvin and the crown. In place of the old Protestant–Catholic co-operation, they sought a united front against the Catholics. The quest was symbolised by the creation of an organisation that was destined to play an immense part in the political and religious shaping of Ulster long after the United Irishmen had been forgotten – the Orange Order.

The spot where the Orange Order sprouted is Loughgall. A scene of horror in 1641, it is now a neat, fastidious village. On a road just outside Loughgall stands a black marble column commemorating the bicentenary of the formation of the first Orange Lodge on 21 September 1795 after the Battle of the Diamond. Here is where Orangeism and the modern cult of 1688 and King Billy began.

The history of the Battle of the Diamond is bound up with a solid, white-washed farmhouse that stands only a few yards down the road from the black column. This is Dan Winter's cottage and it reminds the visitor of the small scale on which Irish history operates. The foundation of the Orange Order centres in this small marble column, a small grass meadow opposite, and a snug white cottage. Hilda Winter, farmer's widow and owner of the cottage, is the keeper of the flame in what has become an Orange shrine. Since the family moved out of the old homestead in 1953, the cottage has been turned into an Orange Order museum, housing a collection of bullets, pitchforks and government proclamations. The chair of Dan Winter, one of the founders of the Order, stands beside the hearth in the low-ceilinged living room. On the walls hang ancient muskets and a sword, which was discovered in the thatched roof, and which Mrs Winter believes saw action in the great battle.

The cottage and its sacred trophies bear witness to the Ulster Protestants' enthusiasm for collecting relics. The leaflet Mrs Winter has written for visitors places the Winter family in a kind of alternative Apostolic succession, linking Dan Winter through the French Huguenot settlers in Antrim (to whom they may be connected) to Luther and the Waldensians of pre-Reformation Italy who, as the leaflet informs the reader, 'were the first Protestants'. Mrs Winter makes no claim to be biologically descended from the Waldensians. What interests her is the transmission of faith across the generations. It is the notion of belonging to an unbroken succession of Christians that leads back to the first communities who protested against the 'errors from Rome' in the valleys of northern Italy. As Mrs Winter bustles round the cottage, an enthusiastic unpaid curator in her own museum, she points out the artefacts while minding her granddaughters. The two hills that figured the battle of the Diamond are visible from the house. Grangemore Hill rises up behind the house, covered in apple trees. Faughart Hill lies diagonally opposite the front porch.

The Orange Order is popularly associated with Protestant sectarianism. To Irish nationalists, the Orangeman is a bogeymen and an attempt to revive an Orange procession in Dublin in the year 2000 caused such protests it had to be abandoned. Hostile cartoons of the Orangeman, with his snarling face and a bowler hat jammed on his head, cover the walls of Belfast's nationalist Ormeau Road. Mrs Winter clucks with annoyance at this. Her late husband, Derek, was an Orangeman. Her sons are Orangemen. Mrs Winter feels Orangeism is all about Protestant liberty rather than supremacy. As she puts it in her leaflet: 'The people of over two hundred years ago had guide lines from the Bible which they wished to retain when they gathered in Daniel Winter's farm house home. The right to practise their Protestant faith and to be able to live by the Bible teaching.'

Dan Winter, the ancestor of Hilda's husband, flew on to the stage of Irish history on 21 September 1795. It was in this small room of the cottage, perhaps sitting in the old chair beside the hearth, that he, James Sloan, his neighbour, James Wilson and several others met after a fight in the nearby fields to discuss the formation of a new organisation to defend their community. The formal launch took place at Sloan's cottage in Loughgall. The battle that triggered the formation of the Orange Order was one of many sectarian skirmishes in rural County Armagh. These quarrels occurred only a few miles from the Belfast of the United Irishmen. But the Winters inhabited a different world from that of the New Light theologians. It was a more fearful environment, fiercely contested by two races and peopled by underground sectarian organisations that had arisen to protect each other and inflict violence on the their opponents. These organisations appealed to a lower, less literate social class than the United Irishmen. What attracted men to these fraternities (they were all male, naturally) were oaths, secret signs, code words and, of course, fighting.

Gang warfare was an integral part of eighteenth-century life in Ireland. The newspapers were full of references to bloody clashes between the rival Ormond Boys and Liberty Boys of Dublin. They reported in a world-weary tone on incidents of stomach-churning violence: a baby found in a churchyard, 'its brains dashed out';[32] women who murdered each other in brawls over the price of a drink; men who killed each other in fights over prostitutes. One reported on a boy whose eye was ripped out by an older man after he threw a snowball at him.[33]

The Battle of the Diamond grew out of this world of casual violence and bloodshed. The Peep o' Day Boys and the Defenders sprang out of one such fight at Portnorris (now Mountnorris) fair, County Armagh, on 14 July 1784.[34] The two farmers who were involved were both Protestants, but the gangs they created evolved along sectarian lines. The Break of Day, or Peep o' Day boys were Protestants. The Defenders were Catholic. By 1789, the Defenders had expanded into an organisation that covered most of Ulster, holding regular meetings and setting up lodges. At first they had no connection with the United Irishmen. They were rural Catholics, while the United Irishmen were dominated by urban radical Protestants committed to suppressing religious differences. The Defenders were labourers and small farmers. The United Irish were middle class. The Defenders were royalists and their oaths demanded loyalty to George III. Like the French and Americans they so much admired, the United Irishmen were republican.

By the end of the 1780s, tit for tat exchanges between the Defenders and the Peep o' Day Boys had raised the sectarian temperature in County Armagh. In 1789 the Catholic chapel in Portadown was burned down. In January 1791, the Defenders inflicted a horrible reprisal in south Armagh on the Barclay family. Alexander Barclay was a Protestant schoolteacher in Forkhill, a few miles east of Crossmaglen. On 28 January, Defenders stormed his cottage and cut out part of his tongue, inflicting the same torture on his wife and her 13-year-old brother, Nathaniel. The mutual assaults polarised the community and resulted in small-scale acts of 'ethnic cleansing'. The mutilation of the Barclays hastened the flight of south Armagh's Protestant minority and forced a Protestant charity to abandon its plans to endow the settlement of Protestant tenants in the area.

The Peep o' Day Boys drove out Catholics by 'papering and wrecking': they stuck pieces of paper on the doors of Catholic homes, ordering the occupants to go 'to hell or Connaught'. If they stayed put, the houses were stormed and wrecked.

Dan Winter, a tenant farmer, was typical Peep o' Day material. The Battle of the Diamond started after he hosted a dance in his cottage on Friday, 12 June 1795. The Peep o' Day Boys claimed they were returning to their homes after the dance finished when a group of Defenders attending a wake on Faughart Hill opened fire. Whoever started the shooting, the exchange continued all night, and on Sunday the authorities sent in the militia from Armagh. The troops arrested a few dozen Defenders but failed to suppress the conflict, which resumed at the July fair in Loughgall, and again in Loughgall in September. There, fighting between Defenders positioned on Faughart Hill and the Peep o' Day Boys on Grangemore Hill began on 16 September and continued for several days. After a truce, there was more action on 21 September, when the Defenders on Faughart Hill, now numbering several hundred men, opened fire on Winter's house at dawn. Winter and his men beat a retreat to the relative safety of the Peep o' Day camp on Grangemore, after which the Defenders followed them and overran the camp. Round one had clearly gone to the Defenders, who celebrated their victory with a lot of drinking.

But the battle was not over. Some landlords may have cast a benevolent eye on the prospect of sectarian struggles absorbing their tenants' energies, but Joseph Atkinson of Crowhill sympathised strongly with the Protestant side. He had already supplied the Peep o' Day forces with arms and as soon as he heard of their defeat he sent word to other Peep o' Day forces in the neighbourhood to move towards Grangemore. The reinforcements caught the Defenders off guard and with disastrous consequences they surrendered their high ground. As they retreated down Grangemore towards Faughart Hill, the Peep o' Day men picked them off, killing at least 30, though the toll may have been as high as 60. The fight led directly to the foundation of the Orange Order. As Winter's cottage was badly damaged, Winter and his companions met that evening at John Sloan's tavern in Loughgall, where the founders of the new society drew lots for the first lodges.

The Orange Order originated in the turmoil in a hamlet in County Armagh and quickly spread. Some of the more liberal gentry complained of gangs of 'lawless banditti' persecuting ordinary Catholics, but most were quick to spy the potential use of a militantly counter-revolutionary organisation and lent it active support. 'The Orange boys parade in great numbers in the vicinage of Lisburn', the Earl of Charlemont was told in August 1796. 'A clergyman of the Marquis of Hertford harangues them, tendering them the oath of alliegance and promising them, it is said, arms from Government.'[35]

The Orangemen sealed their initial success with a wave of terror directed against the Catholic community in north County Armagh in the autumn of 1795. They drove thousands of families out of the area and pushed hitherto uncommitted Catholics into the ranks of the United Irishmen. The pogrom helped bring about the union of the Defenders and the United Irishmen in 1796. One new convert was James Quigley, a priest from County Armagh who returned from France after the Irish College in Paris was closed in the Revolution. Quigley's contact with the Revolution had inoculated him against United Irish ideas. But he changed his mind after Peep o' Day Boys papered and wrecked his father's house just before the Battle of the Diamond, an act that sent his mother insane and forced the family to move to Dundalk. Quigley's baptism of fire into Armagh's sectarian politics could have prodded him into planning a grisly act of sectarian revenge along the lines of the atrocity inflicted on the Barclay family in Forkhill. Instead he took the revolutionary path, working with Presbyterian ministers to persuade both communities of the folly of attacking each other.[36] Quigley was arrested in 1798 and executed. He died bravely.

The oaths taken by Orangemen in the 1800s show how the organisation had grown from an Armagh into an all-Ireland force, committed to breaking the influence of the United Irishmen. The would-be Orangeman had to swear 'to the utmost of my power [to] support and defend the present King George III, his heirs and successors so long as he may support the Protestant Ascendancy, the Constitution and the laws of these kingdoms and that I will ever hold sacred the name of our glorious deliverer William the Third, Prince of Orange'. He had to swear 'that I am not nor ever was a Roman Catholic or papist, that I was not am not nor ever will be a United Irishman and that I never took the oaths of secrecy to that or any other treasonable society'.[37]

The wording of the oath makes it plain that the Orange Order was set up to defend Protestant privilege, not Protestant liberty. People who were born Catholics, even if they renounced their faith, were banned. The Orange Order defined Protestantism as a genetic inheritance rather than an intellectual choice. It was significant that the oath placed loyalty to the crown in conditional terms. Everything depended on the crown's continuing loyalty to Protestantism. It became a defining characteristic of Ulster Unionist politics which generated much confusion in England, where it became commonplace to complain of disloyal Orange Loyalists.

The foundation of the Orange Order coincided with the climax of Ireland's political crisis. The outbreak of war between Britain and Revolutionary France in 1793 stimulated and radicalised the United Irishmen, just as the earlier war in America had goaded on the Volunteers. In Ireland the authorities outlawed celebrations in honour of the Revolution but the growing pressure did not destroy the United Irishmen, it merely forced them underground. After a French fleet appeared off the west coast of Ireland in 1796 the tension increased sharply and the authorities launched a savage clampdown on the United Irishmen, arresting suspects and even burning their houses.

Repression continued the following year, when a swoop on the house of John Alexander in Belfast on 14 April resulted in the seizure of papers that contained details of an insurrection the United Irishmen were preparing to launch. They listed 2,639 supporters in Belfast alone, and arms including 526 guns, 399 bayonets, 88 pistols, six cannons, a mortar and a considerable quantity of ammunition.[38]

The unfolding crisis presented a terrible dilemma for those churchmen in Ireland who wanted peaceful reform of the Ascendancy. Since William III's reign Presbyterian clergymen had received an annual grant from the crown known as the Regium Donum. But their flocks could play no part in the political life of the country, were often tenants of Anglican landlords and had to pay tithes to the Established Church. Catholics were also impatient for representation in parliament, and for reform or abolition of the tithes. But after the outbreak of war, both Catholics and Presbyterians had to weigh their desire for further reform – desires that were not incompatible with loyalty to the crown – with the fear that they might be embroiled in a revolutionary conspiracy.

The Catholic hierarchy had only recently begun to bask in the tepid affection of the authorities. A relief Act in 1793 had lifted most remaining restrictions on Catholics with the exception of the right to sit in parliament and hold some of the top positions in the administration. In 1795 the government resolved to finance a Catholic seminary at Maynooth, County Kildare. The Prime Minister, William Pitt risked incurring the odium of outraged Protestants by actually paying for popery. So there was a great deal at stake and the Catholic bishops were determined not to see their precious gains ruined by a few hot-tempered priests.

Troy, who had excommunicated the Whiteboys with such vigour in the 1770s, dutifully excommunicated the United Irishmen after he became Archbishop of Dublin in 1786. He was not moved to denounce the United Irishmen out of a spirit of supine acquiescence. The rank atheism of the French Revolutionaries appalled him. The Irish bishops watched with dismay as the French Church – a Church many of them were deeply familiar with – was forced to bow to a 'civil constitution' in 1790 that resembled only too clearly the yoke placed by Henry VIII on the Church in the 1530s. Then there was the closure of the religious orders, waves of savage, iconoclastic attacks on church buildings, the execution of the royal family and finally, in 1794, the complete abolition of state Christianity and the transformation of French churches into 'temples of reason'.

The Irish Church was directly and adversely affected by the Revolution. Since Elizabeth's reign, persecuted Catholic clergy had been educated by the generosity of Catholic monarchs in France, Spain, Portugal and Austria. The system was, perhaps, past its prime. An anonymous letter sent to the Empress Maria Theresa in 1780 from a former seminarian in the Austrian Netherlands claimed the Irish Church's educational system was in deep decay. The colleges at Louvain, Antwerp and Tournai were in 'irreperable ruin', he said.[39] After 1789, the Irish seminaries in France, at Paris and Bordeaux, were closed and their property seized. When the French began exporting their revolution, the whole system of Irish seminary education was threatened. The colleges in the Low Counties closed in the 1790s. A few years later it was the turn of the remaining colleges in the Iberian peninsula. As the continental seminaries were broken up, the Irish bishops had every reason to be grateful for the establishment of Maynooth and very cautious about any indiscreet word or act that might jeopardise its future.

Troy set the tone in a pastoral letter he released in 1793 *On the Duties of Christian Citizens*. This reminded Catholics of their duty to obey the crown, and at the same time reminded the crown of the Catholic Church's utility in suppressing sedition. It was thanks to the Catholic Church, Troy said, that the government had been able to suppress the Whiteboys and the Defenders and it was thanks to the Catholic Church that most Irish Catholics had been loyal to the King's cause against the Americans. 'Beware then,' the Archbishop told his flock, 'of their insidious attempts to seduce you from the allegiance due and sworn to his Majesty under the specious pretext of reform.'[40]

The caution of the Presbyterian clergy also began to assert itself as ideological sympathy with France became increasingly identified with treason. Money always helps people feel loyal and in 1792 the government wisely bumped up the Regium Donum, prompting the dispatch of a particularly enthusiastic message to 'Your Majesty's illustrious family' from the annual synod, held at Lurgan.[41] In June 1793 the synod warmly congratulated Irish Catholics on the latest relief bill, which restored them to the franchise, and urged the King to reform the Irish parliament. The ministers also reminded the King that their Church rejected 'with abhorrence every idea of popular tumult or foreign aid'.[42]

The Church of Ireland was in a very different position from the Presbyterians and Catholics. With the exception of the eccentric Bishop of Derry, its leaders dreaded change and had no hesitation in damning the French Revolution and all its works. When Thomas O'Beirne, the convert Rector of Temple Michael, preached on the French Revolution in Longford on 28 February 1794, he used language that would have made most Presbyterians feel very uneasy. It was a 'confederacy of robbers and assassins collected together from the dregs of infamy and the sinks of vice'.[43] There was no attempt to distinguish between the good and bad here. To Anglicans, the peasants were indeed revolting. 'The most destructive ravages committed by the slaves of Lewis the Fourteenth were tender mercies compared with the horrors daily committed by the descendants of these same slaves,' O'Beirne said, 'now broken loose from their chains and in the insolence of their power indulging their servile, vulgar and ferocious nature.'

William Magee, a rising star and future archbishop, spoke in the same anathematising tone in Trinity College in February 1797. Magee conjured up the horrible spectre of 'the peasant even forgetting the source of his consolations . . . everywhere sweeping down the barriers and mounds of religion'.[44] He warned his upper-class audience that their neglect of religion had bred a 'contempt of all authority, and that in the too general rejection of the sovereignty of the Most High, the great principle of subordination being lost, the several parts of the community should be convulsed in mutual conflict – the arms of the lower orders turned against their superiors and the supporters of legitimate authority silenced and overborne by the furious demagogues of rebellion'.[45]

As the French fleet appeared off Cork in January 1797 and the likelihood grew of an invasion, Robinson's successor at Armagh, William Newcome, penned a pastoral epistle to both Catholics and Protestants, reminding both communities that their own laws and traditions forbade rebellion. Primate Newcome hoped his targeted Catholic audience would recall St Paul's injunction to the slaves 'to obey in all things your masters'.[46]

Some of the Catholics heeded official calls to publicly affirm their loyalty and took oaths of allegiance to the King. At Magherafelt, County Tyrone, all the Catholic tenants of the parish in January took the oath in front of the rector.[47] At Tarbert in County Kerry the Catholic priest, Michael O'Sullivan, was the first among his flock to swear on the Bible to 'use every effort to preserve peace and good order in the parish and assist the military in their operations against the enemy'.[48] In December the parish priest of Calfaghtrin, in north Antrim, Patrick Brennan, publicly pledged 'to support with our lives and our fortunes the blessed constitution of this country and His Majesty's happy government'.[49]

As the war continued and the crisis deepened, Catholic leaders competed in their professions of loyalty to Great Britain. In 1797 Thomas Hussey, Bishop of Waterford told the clergy to exert themselves constantly 'to keep the laity within the bounds of religion, morality and decorum'. Irish Catholics, Bishop Hussey went on, 'remained inflexibly attached to their king . . . even in the worst of times . . . when some of the most powerful men in the nation declared in the senate that they hoped to see the day when no Catholic would dare to speak to a Protestant with his hat on'.[50] In January 1798 Archbishop Troy ordered prayers of thanksgiving for the recent British victories and urged Catholics to 'prostrate yourselves on the occasion before our heavenly father and beseech him to continue his merciful protection'.[51]

Lower down the social scale the Catholics were less loyal. In the spring of 1798 there was an outbreak of attacks on the homes of Protestant clergymen in the southern counties. Some of it was rather harmless. At Lilliput, near Limerick, a band broke into the home of the Rector and stole his supply of bacon.[52] But at Schull, County Cork, in April, a crowd of 500 attacked the rectory and the incumbent was forced to flee for safety on to the roof.[53] At Castle Cooke County Cork, men broke into the Rector's home and demanded arms.[54] In Limerick, the authorities arrested a schoolteacher for 'damning the King, ministry and soldiery and saying that the United Irishmen were right'.[55] At Finglas, just north of Dublin, soldiers discovered a maypole 'seditiously decorated with the cap of liberty, alias the Jacobinical emblem'.[56] On 24 May soldiers were attacked outside Naas, County Kildare, and forced to retreat from the Crumlin–Tallaght road. The mail coach was stopped and the contents burned. Two days later more fighting was reported from Naas, Wicklow, and Hacketstown in County Carlow.

As the country slithered into disorder, Archbishop Troy put pen to paper again to denounce the United Irishmen. On 27 May he had a pastoral letter read out at every mass in Dublin, condemning the 'desperate and wicked endeavours of irreligious and wicked agitators' and damning 'the heinousness of violating the laws of our country and of attempting by insurrection and murder to subvert the government of our gracious King'.[57]

The bishops' exhortations dovetailed with the views of the Catholic gentry, who signed a petition on 25 May denouncing the radicals for aiming at the collective 'downfall of the clergy, of the ancient families and respectable commercial men of the Roman Catholic religion'.[58] But the bishops were unable to restrain those lower down. The day after Troy's pastoral was read out in Dublin, United Irishmen seized the town of Enniscorthy in County Wexford. Two days later their forces took up two positions, on Vinegar Hill, outside Enniscorthy, and at Three Rocks, on the main road from Wexford to New Ross. The following day government militia evacuated Wexford town and the United Irishmen moved in. Catholic Ireland was in revolt against the King, and against its own bishops.

The leaders of the Wexford rebellion included several members of the Protestant gentry. The first commander of the rebel army, Bagenal Harvey, was the grandson of two Church of Ireland clergymen and the nephew of two others. Another of the leaders, Anthony Perry, was a Church of Ireland landowner in the north of the county. Four of the eight members of the United Irishmen's government established in Wexford were from the Church of Ireland.

But while radical Protestants were thick on the ground among the intellectual leaders of the United Irishmen, they were thinly represented at the other end. The foot soldiers of the rebellion, the pikemen of '98 of legend, were inspired by older passions. They were the same people who filled the ranks of the Defenders and the Whiteboys and the other secret societies that flourished in the Catholic peasantry. The absorption of the Defenders into the United Irishmen gave the Wexford rising a distinctly sectarian colouring. The leaders might preach the secular nationalism of the French Revolution. The ordinary pikemen were motivated by an age-old hatred of Protestants of all classes. In Wicklow and Wexford it was noted that while the rebels attacked property indiscriminately, they burnt only the houses of the Protestants. And while they held Wexford town in the first three weeks of June, they killed Protestant clergymen whether or not they were magistrates, or associated with landlords. Five of the 57 clergymen in the Protestant diocese of Ferns were killed in the revolt,[59] and the victims included a 22-year-old curate, John Pentland of Killann, as well as Robert Burrowes of Oulart, the brother of a United Irishman and son of a Catholic mother. Samuel Heydon, Rector of Enniscorthy, was killed on the streets of his parish by a local butcher, in front of his wife. Bishop Eusebius Cleaver's palace was plundered and the library destroyed.

The Protestant laity suffered much more than the clergy. After the rebels seized Enniscorthy and Wexford town on 30 May, several hundred Protestants who had failed to get out by land or sea found themselves hostages. Some were shot and about 500 were jailed. It was ominous for the cause of the supposed revolution in Wexford that the rebels called their prisoners 'heretics'. But the worst nightmares were realised after the all but inevitable defeat of the rebel army by government forces on 5 June. A United Irish force attacked New Ross, was beaten off and many of the rebels were killed in the streets. As news of the slaughter filtered back to the rebel camp there was demand for reprisals. A group of at least 100 prisoners, overwhelmingly Protestant, and including women and children, was forced into a barn at Scullabogue, six miles east of New Ross, and burned alive. No one survived. Some of the victims are believed to have been Catholics and at least three of the 17 or so men who perpetrated the massacre were Protestant.[60] But there were strong echoes at Scullabogue of the sectarian slaughter of the 1640s.

There were more reprisals before General Lake broke the back of the revolt on Vinegar Hill on 21 June. According to a survivor, about 95 Protestant hostages were taken out of prison the day before the battle and stabbed to death by the pikemen on Wexford bridge. 'Beyond a doubt,' he told *Saunders's News-Letter* after the rising was crushed, 'religion was the object of the war that though they accepted the assistance of some Protestants in the beginning, they were latterly every day superceding them in command and appointing priests in their room who . . . declared from their pulpits that theirs was the religion of Irishmen and that none other was allowed.'[61]

Of the 85 clergy in the Catholic diocese of Ferns, 11 were directly involved in the 1798 uprising. Philip Roche was a key figure as commander of Wexford. Some were eccentric, like John Keene, the self-appointed chaplain to the rebels and 'blessed priest of Bannow' who rode into the rebel encampments on the back of a pony preceded by a crier shouting 'make away for the blessed priest of Bannow'.[62]

It was fortunate for the standing of Bishop Caulfield in the eyes of the authorities that some Catholic clergy in Ferns diocese took a very different stance. *Saunders's News-letter* on 20 June reported that at Dromain, County Wicklow, the rebels set houses on fire and 'would have committed further outrages were it not for the interference of the Revd Mr Lowe, the parish priest who exhorted and went upon his knees imploring them to desist'. John Broe, a Franciscan, was active in protecting Wexford's Protestants, while another Catholic priest, John Currin, prevented a massacre of Protestants on Wexford bridge by going down on his knees and begging the crowd to spare the Protestant hostages who were in danger of being killed. Such priests were not necessarily opposed to the United Irishmen, but they certainly opposed sectarian bloodshed.

Father James Doyle was in an altogether separate category. At the height of the insurrection he told the local Protestants of Davidstown to 'rest assured that this beautiful island will not long remain in the hands of rebels. King George will soon send over an army to defeat them.'[63]

On 23 August 1798 a French squadron sailed into the Bay of Killala in County Mayo and about 1,000 soldiers landed, much to the surprise of Joseph Stock, the Protestant Bishop who was eating his dinner when he was informed that the advancing French were exactly one mile away. The invasion force did not trigger the hoped-for uprising in Connacht and the French took pains to ensure that their presence did not occasion sectarian bloodshed. Stock's little cathedral was not occupied and the Bishop was politely offered a place on the proposed Directory of Connacht. The Catholic peasants discovered they had little in common with the French. Bishop Stock noted: 'the atheist despised the bigot, but the wonder was how the zealous papist should come to any terms of agreement with a set of men who boasted openly in our hearing that they had just driven Mr Pope out of Italy . . . it astonished the French officers to hear the [Irish] recruits, when they offered their service, declare that they were come to take arms for France and the blessed Virgin.'[64]

When their hopes of a general insurrection faded, the French surrendered on 8 September. Stock was deeply critical of the authorities' excessive reaction, as there had been little bloodshed. 'Fire and sword was the language of gentlemen whose loss by the war, though grievous and highly provoking, was only the loss of property.'[65] The year of tumults was over. The rebellion in Leinster had been crushed. The French in Connacht had surrendered. A small squeak of a revolt in June in Ulster, a tiny sideshow compared to events in Wexford, had been snuffed out. The churches had all been shaken to the core. Apart from Dominick Bellew,[66] Stock's opposite number in Killala, no Catholic bishop was implicated with the United Irishmen or the French invaders. Bellew was an unusual case. His brother, Matthew, had accepted a French commission with the rank of general in the Franco-Irish invasion force and after the French surrendered, he was executed. The Bishop was denounced to Dublin for 'training his clergy and diocese to rebellion,' though nothing came of the charge.

The rest of the bishops hastened to denounce the insurrection. Bishop Caulfield, whose diocese had been the epicentre of the earthquake, was savage in his criticism of his clergymen who had been involved. The 'blessed priest of Bannow' he described as a virtual idiot – an opinion shared by the government, who declined even to prosecute him. Another rebel priest, John Byrne, was 'a drunken giddy man'. Thomas Clinch was a 'beastly drunkard'.[67] Others were written off as fools and reptiles. If the Catholic bishops feared the uprising might throw all their gains into jeopardy their fears were unfounded. The British authorities noted the conservatism of the Catholic hierarchy with appreciation. The future of Maynooth was assured. Far from punishing the Catholics, the authorities began to entertain schemes to draw the Catholic Church closer to Dublin Castle.

The Church of Ireland was the most traumatised. From the 1790s its clergymen had been preaching in increasingly hysterical tones on the hydra of revolution that was threatening to demolish all social hierarchies. Now it had stared revolution in the face and several of its clergymen and many of its laymen had been killed. Bishop Stock had been taken hostage. Bishop Cleaver had lost his mind. He was transferred to Dublin but required the assistance of a coadjutor. The Established Church had been shaken to its foundations.

The Church of Ireland had supplied the United Irishmen with many of the movement's radical aristocratic leaders, including Tone, Lord Edward Fitzgerald, the younger son of the Duke of Leinster, and Bagenal Harvey, the first commander in Wexford. When the rising collapsed in Wexford, his successor, Father Roche was executed along with the town's Church of Ireland governor, Matthew Keugh.

The Church of Ireland did not lose much sleep over the treason of men like Lord Edward Fitzgerald. Nor was it the physical suffering of the clergy that mattered so much. It was the damage to morale. The rising demolished all the Church's lingering hopes that Catholicism might wither away. Its status as the Church of a hated minority had been exposed with humiliating clarity. In one important sense, the Church of Ireland learned absolutely nothing from 1798. The obvious lesson was that the Church's wealth and political privilege had contributed to a state of almost grotesque alienation from the population. But this was not a topic the clergy showed any willingness even to consider. Right up to Disestablishment in 1869 the Church battled to retain its privileged position.

What the Church was willing to do was to reconsider its pastoral mission. After 1798 there were no more colourful eccentrics like Bishop Hervey, with his mistresses and long sojourns in Europe. There were no more men like Archbishop Robinson either, expending all their energy and income on architectural projects. The Church of Ireland bishops of the next generation were a graver, duller but undoubtedly more spiritual bunch. God was more imminent to them and Christ – a rather distant and embarrassing figure to many eighteenth-century clergymen – was on their lips and in their hearts. The lesson they drew was not the need for Disestablishment but the need to unsheathe the rusty sword of the Establishment and forge it anew in the white heat of holiness.

The leadership of the Presbyterian Church felt utterly humiliated by the events of 1798. Over a few dramatic days in June the United Irishmen had attacked Ballymena and Antrim town in County Antrim and had even scored a victory over government forces at Saintfield in County Down on 8 June before being crushed five days later at Ballynahinch. The ministers suspected their liberal instincts on the slave trade and parliamentary reform had been harnessed to a very different cause by a handful of militants. It was a matter of deep shame that a few, such as Dickson, had been arrested for their involvement with the United Irishmen, still more that Thomas Birch, the minister of Saintfield, had preached to the rebels at Ballynahinch. One minister was executed for his role in the revolt: James Porter, hanged in front of his own meeting house in Greyabbey.

When the synod met a few weeks later at Lurgan on 28 August, having been forced to postpone the usual June date because of the fighting, they fired off a contrite message, informing His Majesty of their 'deepest humiliation that the most stable and sacred principles of many of our people and some of our members have been shaken by the convulsions of this sceptical and revolutionary era'. They ventured 'to entreat Your Majesty not to impute to a whole the transgressions of a part'.[68]

The Presbyterians rushed a similar note to the Lord-Lieutenant, Lord Cornwallis, expressing 'sorrow and indignation [over] the late attempts which have been made to subvert our government under the specious pretext of reforming it'. With Dickson, Birch and Porter in mind, the synod reflected 'with grief and indignation on the conduct of some members of this body . . . who have been lately implicated in seditious and treasonable practices'. They declared 'their most pointed abhorrence of a Deportment so inconsistent with the character of a minister of religion'.[69] The following year the synod felt the need to acknowledge yet again the 'scandal brought upon its reputation by the indiscretion and misconduct of a few misgided and unworthy individuals'.[70]

After his arrest, William Steel Dickson was held in a prison ship in Belfast Lough and in jail in Scotland. The conditions the Presbyterian minister experienced did not resemble a Russian gulag. 'We have very fine salmon twice or thrice a week,' he wrote from Scotland; 'latterly we had plenty of garden stuffs or salading – and some young ducks and peas . . . our wine and porter have all been uniformly good. And at supper we occasionally have very fine crabs and lobsters.'[71] He was released in 1802. To the end he retained the liberal, nationalist convictions that had led him to join the United Irishmen. At a Catholic dinner held in Dublin on 9 May 1811 he denounced 'the malicious rumours, industriously circulated, that Presbyterians had become enemies of their [the Catholics'] interests and at least lukewarm to their cause'.[72]

But Dickson was plain wrong. By the time he died in 1824 the type of Presbyterian he represented had virtually disappeared. Ulster Presbyterians remained political Liberals until the Home Rule crisis, but they were far more conservative than Dickson's generation had been. The future course of Ulster Presbyterianism was to be shaped to a large degree by a child baptised, ironically enough, by the United Irishman, John Glendy of Maghera. Henry Cooke was born in 1788 and after the age of 10 was haunted for the rest of his life by the memory of seeing Loyalist farmhouses burning against the night sky – victims of United Irishmen's terror. A deeply emotional man who seems never to have been far from a nervous breakdown, he devoted his life to leading a passionate crusade against what he saw as the hellish forces of disorder. When reasonable men spoke in calm tones of the benefits of Catholic emancipation, Cooke's mind rewound to the flames of Maghera, the sight of his gaunt mother, hands flung up towards the sky and the small terrified boy who hid from the rebels in the hedgerows. The boy was, of course, himself. 'For weeks together during the summer of '98 I never slept in my father's house,' he later recalled. 'To have done so would have been almost certain death. All loyal families were marked and watched by bands of assassins . . . it was then and thus I learned my principles. I was taught in a hard school – the school of care and suffering. Unceasing watchfulness made me prematurely old.'[73]

What Cooke spent his life watching ceaselessly was Irish Catholicism. And whereas the older Presbyterians had sympathised with Catholics as fellow victims of the Anglican Establishment, Cooke strained every nerve to reawaken buried memories of 1641 and the siege of Derry, when all Protestants stood shoulder to shoulder against Rome's legions.

He displayed many of the symptoms of manic depression. He was often crying, or lying sick and motionless on the couch. Periods of lethargy gave way to super-human bursts of energy. He shunned the measured style of the eighteenth-century preachers for fiercer imagery. His predecessors had treasured consensus and concord. Cooke revelled in discord and in the imagery of conflict.

Before the premature ageing process of which he spoke had reduced him to a shadow of his young self, he was an unforgettable preacher. A listener who heard him at the May Street church in Belfast remembered 'the power of that full-toned voice whose lowest whisper could be distinctly heard in the most distant seat of the gallery and whose thunder peals the moment after made the ceiling ring . . . the stream of irony, and eloquence, and argument that flowed that evening from the pulpit of May Street and blended together in one burning flood of fiery decla-mation, was as irresistible as a cataract from the hills.' It was irresistible even when the lights blew out in the chapel, and when, 'like a hurricane at midnight he thundered through the gloom'.[74]

The Presbyterians of Dickson's generation had looked on the Church of England as the spiritual wing of an oppressive Ascendancy. Cooke drew on all his intoxicating imagery to urge them, not entirely successfully, to love her 'sculp-tured minarets', her 'gothic windows' that 'drink in the sun through stained glass. Must I, therefore, collect pebbles to demolish those rainbow beauties?'[75]

What thrilled Cooke's many disciples was the way he positioned Ulster as a key player in the cosmic struggle between the forces of good and evil. The old Presbyterians had never imagined Ulster in such dramatic colours. Many had been in a hurry to leave for America. Cooke saw Ulster in a new light, as God's chosen vessel. Cooke's Ulster was lonely, but would have the awesome loneliness that accompanies true greatness and a knowledge of one's inspiring destiny. His Ulster was the great oak that mocked the raging storm, 'the battlefield of the constitu-tion . . . the Marathon where the invaded stand and conquer'.[76] Cooke delighted in being called illiberal and reactionary in his opposition to Catholic emancipation. 'I glory in the accusation,' he told the Belfast *Newsletter* in 1827. 'I was born the subject of a Protestant government, the original liberty of which my Presbyterian forefathers chiefly contributed to establish and maintain. Esto Perpetua is the fervent prayer which I breathe over it.'[77]

Ulster Presbyterianism did not switch overnight from radical, green nationalism to conservative, Orange Unionism, in spite of the best efforts of Henry Cooke. The battle was long and hard and it had to be waged on many fronts. To Cooke and his allies, theological and political conservatism went hand in hand. The sunny, rather bland creed of the Enlightenment had to be uprooted and replaced by the sombre creed of the Westminster Confession. At the same time the Presbyterians had to be taught how to 'forget about Laud and Wentworth'. 'Let our common faith and common dangers unite us for common protection,'[78] he told a vast meeting of 40,000 at Hillsborough, County Down in October 1834. Cooke succeeded very largely in his goals. He was the father of modern Ulster, much more so, at any rate, than the Presbyterians and New Light men of 1798. He urged the Presbyterians to merge as much as possible with the other Protestants of Ulster and separate themselves from the Irish nation. He urged them to believe that the Catholics were not their fellow citizens, still less their fellow underdogs, but, as he told the Hillsborough meeting, 'the powers of earth and the powers of darkness'. It was thrilling, dangerous, intoxicating stuff, and to a very great degree they heeded his call.

CHAPTER TEN

The Crash of a Great Building

It is encouraging to know that a large and powerful party in England has been convinced of the wisdom of disendowing the Protestant Church establishment in Ireland – the fruitful source of all our evils
(Archbishop Cullen, January 1867)[1]

Jane Prior died of inflammation of the bowels in Kilkenny on a Thursday night in the year 1810. She was a member of the Church of Ireland. Peter Roe, Vicar of St Mary's, Kilkenny, visited her on the night before her death and later published his conversation with the dying 15-year-old.

'Jane are you willing to die?'
　'Yes, I am willing to go now if God were to take me.'
　'What makes you so willing to die?'
　'Because I hope to go to heaven.'
　'Is it because you were always good and dutiful you hope to go there?'
　'No, because I have committed a great many sins and do not deserve heaven. But Jesus Christ is there and he died for me and intercedes for me, and I hope to be with him.'
　'What reason have you to hope this?'
　'He says that no one will come to the father but by him and that he will not cast out those that come to him.'

Roe visited her the next morning and found her struggling with death. 'As soon as she observed him she grew very restless and at last succeeded in getting out of bed. No sooner did she reach the floor than she fell on her knees and said with a distinct voice "Let us pray". She was quietly placed in bed and all present united in prayer and commended her soul into the hands of a faithful creator and most merciful saviour. In about half an hour her spirit departed from a frail body and an evil world, to join, we may trust, in that happy kingdom where the wicked cease from troubling and the weary are at rest.' Roe ended his recollection of Jane Prior's last moments with a warning to parents to watch out for their children, 'lest they experience the doom of Eli who saw his children making themselves vile'.[2]

Roe saw death as an evangelistic opportunity. When his sister developed an ominous cough he was quick to seize his chance. Three days before her death he told her: 'By your lingering illness, a gracious opportunity has been afforded you of looking for consolation to the fountain of living waters.' He did not record her response to his helpful remark.

Roe's average week went as follows:

On Sundays he gave a religious lecture at 8 a.m. and a catechism class at 10 a.m. before leading morning service in church at 11.30. In the afternoon there was a vestry meeting and a visit to the general hospital. Then he was back at church for the evening service at 6 p.m. Mondays started with a visit to the local lunatic asylum at 10 a.m., before a vestry meeting at midday. Roe then distributed blankets and other items to the poor in the afternoon and finished off by delivering a lecture from 6 p.m. until 7.30.

Tuesdays were given over to visits to a local factory, schools and the town jails. Wednesdays started with more prison visits before he held morning service in church at 11 a.m. and taught catechism from midday to 2 p.m. From 5.30 to 7 p.m. there was another lecture. Thursdays began with visits to the factories followed by visits to the charter school and the poorhouse. There was a lecture for men in the afternoon. Friday saw a return to the jails at 10 a.m., a service in church at 11 a.m. and two-hour catechism class from midday to 2 p.m. At 5.30 there was another hour-and-a-half lecture. Roe dined on bread and cheese. Before he went to bed, it was his custom to write down two questions: 'Whom did you intend to visit?' and 'Whom did you visit?'[3]

Roe was a model for the new type of Church of Ireland clergyman. They were the children of 1798, the year, incidentally, when Roe was ordained. The Established Church had brushed with death. Now it had been set on its feet again, they were determined to imbue it with a new sense of mission.

Roe's contemporaries obviously thought his lifestyle differed from that of his predecessors. That was why a book was written about him. His austerity struck them as remarkable, as did his concern for visiting the poor and preaching to prisoners and factory workers.

He was also more passionate than his father's generation in his opposition to Catholicism. The Church of Ireland clergy of the previous generation mostly opposed Catholic emancipation out of concern for its possible effects on the constitution. It was the danger to the state, not the Church, that worried Archbishop Robinson. Roe represented a new type of Protestant, or rather a very old type that had been revived. He did not attack Catholicism because it was a threat to the state but because Catholics were the congregation of Satan and the vehicle of the Antichrist. 'Depend upon it,' he wrote in the *Christian Guardian* in September 1812 on the subject of Catholic emancipation, 'the cloven foot and the double tongue will again appear – popery would lord it over the humble followers of Jesus and the scenes of Smithfield again presented to view.'[4]

Evangelicals like Roe were great formers of associations. They set up national institutions, like the London Hibernian Society and the Home Mission, to propagate the circulation of Bibles and finance missions. Others were local. Like the godly crypto-Presbyterian ministers of the seventeenth century, the evangelicals of the nineteenth century enjoyed forming local associations of like-minded clergymen to pray and preach together and formulate strategy. Roe had scarcely been ordained for two years before he set up a monthly club of this kind. Roe's association was evangelical and fiercely anti-Catholic. Men like Roe boldly confronted the fact that the Established Church had failed to win the souls of the vast majority of Irish people and were determined to remedy that fact. That meant taking the war to the enemy camp and adopting tactics that had scarcely been tried in Ireland. The causes of evangelism and anti-popery went hand in hand. It was hard to imagine the success of one without the other. When Roe's association met in Kilkenny on 7 September 1803, the subject of popery, and how to stop it, topped the agenda. Roe's clerical colleagues came up with the following explanations for Protestant failure: (1) lack of education; (2) lack of dissemination of the Bible; (3) lack of religious education in schools; (4) intermarriage; (5) absentee gentry; (6) the false liberality of Protestants; (7) the proselytising zeal of papists; (8) clerical neglect in visiting and teaching; (9) neglect of preaching against Catholic doctrine; (10) clerical non-residence; (11) neglect of family religion; (12) preaching 'justification by works'.

The background to Roe's frantic energy was the increasing gloom about the Catholic Church. The Act of Union had united the British and Irish parliaments and put four Protestant Irish archbishops in the imperial House of Lords. Pitt the Younger had gravely disappointed the Catholics in soliciting their support for the Union by dangling the promise of emancipation and then failing to carry it out. But the Church of Ireland could draw little comfort from the situation. Everywhere they looked Catholics were organising, combining and agitating. The Catholic Committee, founded in 1786, harnessed the energies of the 'respectable' classes to reform. At the other end of the social scale lurked those mysterious and shifting agrarian societies, the Threshers and Caravats – successors to the Defenders – which with their secret signs and combinations carried out acts of terror against landlords, their agents and the clergy of the Established Church.

The men of the Catholic Committee complained that the 'Catholic question' had not been discussed as they had hoped, during the first session of the newly expanded imperial parliament. They kept up the pressure and sent a petition to parliament in 1805, which drew vigorous support from the radical Whigs led by Charles James Fox. It contained 99 signatures, was headed by seven peers and included the name of Daniel O'Connell, whose election as MP for Clare would force the eventual repeal of the prohibition on Catholics sitting in parliament. The petition, phrased in unctuous terms, urged King and parliament to approve a measure that would 'annihilate the principle of religious animosity and animate all descriptions of His Majesty's subjects in an enthusiastic defence of the best constitution that has ever yet been established'.[5] It was a few years before O'Connell would start describing the British constitution in less glowing terms and agitating for the repeal of the Union.

In May 1805 the House voted by a comfortable majority against Fox's motion to consider the Catholic petition. But the Church of Ireland was not relieved, for Fox's stance was ominous. The Irish Church now depended on the support of a British parliament in which one of the two great parties of the state was deeply sceptical of its value. While the Tories held office, the Ascendancy and the Irish Establishment were safe. But what would happen to the Church of Ireland once the Tories lost power? They hardly dared consider.

Within 10 years of the Union, disappointment among Catholics had soured attitude. Opinion in Dublin began clamouring for repeal. At the same time the Catholic Committee assumed a new tone of almost belligerent self-confidence that made the Anglicans shudder. The committee's 'Statement of the Penal Laws which Aggrieve the Catholics of Ireland' in 1812 bragged that the Catholics

> have prodigiously increased and they are continually increasing beyond example in any other country. Already they compose the far greater part of the trading and manufacturing interests. The agricultural class, so powerful and influential throughout Ireland, is almost universally Catholic . . . numerically the Catholics constitute full five-sixths of the Irish population and compared with members of the Established Church they are in the proportion of at least ten to one, a proportion, be it observed, rapidly advancing of late years.[6]

The statement then reeled off the many instances of their second-class status. They could vote but they could not sit in parliament. They were rarely admitted to the corporations or to the rank of freemen. They were excluded from legal offices, from ranking positions in the army and navy and from strategically sensitive businesses such as the Post Office.

The British authorities hoped to channel this explosion of potentially dangerous energy by gaining the power to veto candidates for Irish bishoprics. It was one of the bargaining points floated in the discussions preceding the Union. The scheme would have given the crown prerogatives well short of those enjoyed by the exiled Stuarts, and the government would merely be able to examine the names of candidates for sees on their way from Ireland to Rome and delete the least favourable. They would not be able to intrude their own candidates. In 1807, Dr Milner, Vicar-Apostolic of the English Midlands district, was sent over to Ireland to canvass support in the Irish hierarchy. Ten bishops were thought to privately favour the project, but it fell through after the proposal was leaked. A furious public outcry followed. At a meeting in Kilkenny, speakers described the measure as 'a disgraceful barter of things spiritual for things temporal, which would destroy people's trust in the priests'.[7] A congratulatory address to one of the scheme's lay sponsors, Lord Fingal, prompted two huge counter-addresses with 5,000 and 40,000 signatures respectively. Pamphlets complained that the Anglican government would use the scheme to promote 'blockheads . . . as the least dangerous competitors your church would have'.[8]

The wave of indignation flushed out Troy and the other closet supporters of the veto. At a synod in Dublin on 14–15 September 1808 the bishops declared it 'inexpedient to introduce any alteration in the canonical mode hitherto observed in the nomination of Irish Catholic bishops'.[9] The resolution was backed at a bishops' meeting in Dublin on 24 February 1810.

The attempt to muzzle the Catholics with the veto had failed. More than that, it backfired on the Established clergy by raising a clamour over their privileged position. The moderate Catholic bishops and their aristocratic supporters were embarrassed, and the initiative among the Catholics passed increasingly into the hands of the radical middle-class lawyers led by a stalwart opponent of the Act of Union, the Kerryman, Daniel O'Connell. He was less gentle with the Ascendancy than the bishops. If England wished to save Ireland for the empire, the argument increasingly ran, the government would do well to kick away the tottering columns supporting Protestant Ascendancy and get rid of the old corporations, where the freemen were all Protestant. And then get rid of Church tithes, and then Trinity College. Were they not 'all organised accomplices of old errors and of old vices . . . ?'[10]

The evangelical movement reached Ireland largely through John Wesley, the founder of Methodism. Wesley was assiduous in visiting Ireland, touring the length and breadth of the country 21 times from 1747 until his death in 1791. He made very little lasting impact on the Catholics. As John Jebb, the clever Protestant Bishop of Limerick, remarked, Catholic lay fraternities in Ireland already satisfied the same energies and instincts that the Methodists had harnessed in England.[11] It was the Protestants who were touched by Wesley's message. The Low Church evangelical tone of the Church of Ireland in the early nineteenth century was essentially Wesleyan. It was not Calvinist, not interested in the doctrine of the predestination of the soul, not very intellectual.

Many sponsors of the evangelical movement were women. The role of patron of an evangelical salon was an important outlet for the energies of upper-class women in a Church that otherwise gave them nothing to do. In Dublin, it became the fashion to attend weekly prayer meetings held at the homes of pious aldermen and wealthy widows, like Mrs Johnson of Stephen's Green, remembered as 'a very accomplished old lady who had frequent evening assemblies of a divine character'. In the country there were women like Lady Powerscourt, of Powerscourt, in County Wicklow, who held meetings at her palatial home each Tuesday, 'when she filled her house with the most eminent divines of every denomination in England, Scotland and Ireland; topics were arranged for discussion, chiefly on prophetical subjects, and all the neighbourhood were invited to hear them'.

The evangelicals did not have it all their own way. The Church of Ireland had been a system of organised outdoor relief for the aristocracy for far too long to jettison the tradition of giving its top jobs to the nobility. Take Lord John George Beresford, appointed Archbishop of Armagh in 1821. Beresford was son of the 1st Marquis of Waterford, and the nephew of John Beresford, who had virtually directed the government of Ireland under the rule of successive Lords-Lieutenant in the 1780s and 1790s. Beresford was made Primate not because of his piety but because he was the descendant of a long line of powerful Planter aristocrats and was hugely rich. When it came to the rebuilding of Armagh cathedral in 1834–37, the Archbishop himself contributed £24,000 of the £34,000 that was required.

Nevertheless, men whose outlook resembled that of Peter Roe much more than Archbishop Beresford were moving into the top positions in the Church. William Magee, made Archbishop of Dublin in 1821, also came from a landed family and, like Beresford, he was a northerner. Magee was not really an evangelical either but he shared many of their attitudes and enthusiasms, particularly for clubs that harnessed the energies of the middle classes and actively targeted the poor. He also shared their almost apocalyptic horror of Rome.

The older generation of bishops had generally been grateful for the fact that ministry in the Established Church entailed few obligations to mingle with the great unwashed. But Magee and Power Le Poer Trench, Archbishop of Tuam from 1819 to 1834, looked out of their palace windows and noted the lack of a Protestant populace with alarm. What was to be done if the Church of Ireland had so few members in the lower classes? For evangelicals there could be only one answer: Go out and get some.

Magee sounded the first blast of the trumpet of what was soon christened the 'Second Reformation' in St Patrick's cathedral in Dublin on 24 October 1822 when he delivered a sermon that was universally interpreted as a declaration of spiritual war on Presbyterians and Catholics. Magee said the Church of Ireland had to shake off its reputation as a civil institution and underline its claim to the Apostolic succession. As it was, it was

> hemmed in by two opposite descriptions of professing Christians. The one possessing a Church without what we can properly call a religion, and the other possessing a religion without what we can properly call a Church. The one so blindly enslaved to a supposed infallible ecclesiastical authority as not to seek in the word of God a reason for the faith they profess; the other so confident in the infallibility of their individual judgement as to the reasons of their faith that they deem it their duty to resist all authority in matters of religion.[12]

Magee's sermon contained nothing new. Ussher would have agreed entirely, and the average sermon preached on the anniversary of the Gunpowder Plot in the eighteenth century was far more strident in tone. The problem was that no bishop in Ireland had used that kind of language for about 20 years. The government was embarrassed and annoyed. A year before Magee's outburst in St Patrick's, the Prime Minister, Lord Liverpool, sternly rebuked Richard Mant, the new Bishop of Killaloe and Kilfenora in Clare, for delivering an address that was far more innocuous than Magee's. Mant had merely reminded his clergy that it was their duty to 'banish away all strange and erroneous doctrine', which was drawn straight from the text of the Anglican ordination service. But it was enough to irritate Lord Liverpool, who warned him of the 'unfavourable impressions created in Ireland by the publication of your first charge' and added that he 'could not but regret that you should have judged it necessary to expose yourself . . . so soon after your settlement in the country and before you could have had sufficient local knowledge of the state of it to hazard anything of a doubtful nature'.[13]

Since the rebellion of 1798, London and Dublin Castle had come to appreciate the Catholic Church as a breakwater against revolution and the only institution that could keep the Irish peasantry in a due state of submission. The fact that the British had failed to deliver political equality made the authorities doubly nervous of picking unnecessary fights with the Catholic Church. Nervousness increased after King George IV visited Ireland in 1821, and parts of the south and south-west were seized by an unprecedented wave of agrarian violence. The co-operation of the Catholic priests was seen as essential if the lid was to be kept on.

The government looked on the Church of Ireland with growing coldness. It expected the clergy to repay the material privileges of Establishment by minding their own flocks and letting the Catholics mind theirs. Archbishop Beresford was content to go along with such an unspoken arrangement. In Armagh, where the flocks were evenly balanced, such an arrangement, in fact, made sense. But it was a lot less attractive a bargain in Dublin and Tuam, where Archbishops Magee and Trench felt the Church of Ireland must grow or die.

Bishop Mant had first-hand experience of the growing disorder in rural Connacht. Not long after his notorious charge, the disturbances in the Killaloe area became so bad that in December 1821 he had to flee to Dublin. He did not judge it safe to return until July 1822 and when soldiers were stationed in the palace grounds. Mant's office guaranteed him state protection. The clergy in remote parishes in the 1820s had to defend themselves. *Saunders's News-Letter* of 27 November 1822 reported a shoot-out between the Reverend McCullough, Vicar of Ogonniloe, near Killaloe, and a group of armed intruders that left the minister gravely wounded. The clergyman had 'instantly discharged a brace of pistols at the ruffians but the gang then fired and wounded Mr McCullough in the arm. He being unable to make further resistance, they ransacked the house and took thereout almost every portable and twenty-five pounds in cash.'[14] It was frustrating for the Church of Ireland. But for evangelicals it was intensely exciting. Schooled in the millenarian passages of the New Testament, their fingers hovered over the texts which foretold that the end of the world would be presaged by a time of chaos. Violence and disorder dismayed, yet energised them. The parable of the bridegroom, about to enter the bridal chamber on the stroke of midnight, had never appeared so real. Irish evangelicals were imbued with a dramatic sense that there was one minute left before the midnight hour. If their Church had squandered earlier opportunities to preach in Irish, distribute Bibles, catechise children and evangelise the poor, it was not too late to start.

The men of the 'Second Reformation' disagreed with the stance the old Whig bishops took on the Irish language. They might not learn it very well, but they abandoned the old notion that men and women needed to speak English if they were to become good Protestants. Archbishop Trench was certainly no intellectual and never got further than reading the Psalms out loud in Irish on the train, but although he found Irish an effort, as a good evangelical he felt he had to try. Irish evangelicals rehabilitated and romanticised the Gael. Men of Boulter's generation had looked on the Gaelic-speaking Irish with distaste. They considered Gaelic culture a barrier to progress and a prop to sedition. The evangelicals turned that axiom on its head. They felt impelled to do so. Since the Reformation, the Church of Ireland had identified its mission strategy with the Pale and with the Old English towns. Long after, the Established Church continued to direct its attention at the urban population: it did not occur to many Church of Ireland bishops to bother about the convictions of illiterate Irish-speaking peasants. The evangelicals sensed that that strategy had failed. It was clear that the English-speaking towns were the most infertile mission territory in the whole country. The Catholics had sewn up the cities. When they pored over maps of Ireland, the evangelicals saw an open window in the neglected peasants of Connacht.

This new interest in the remote west was prompted by their attempt to engage the urban population in highly charged public debates on religion. The evangelicals conducted these debates very much on their own terms. They put up posters in the town chosen for the debate 'inviting' local Catholics to come and defend their beliefs against a series of charges; normally, that they worshipped idols, preached transubstantiation without scriptural warrant and forbade their laity to read the Bible. At Longford in 1827, the 12 topics chosen for the debate in the parish church were the old Protestant favourites. Posters invited 'Roman Catholic friends' to come to the church each Thursday evening at 6.30 p.m. 'where you will have an opportunity of exercising that laudable spirit of enquiry at present existing among you'.[15] They started with papal infallibility and covered the Church, papal supremacy, the role of tradition, the doctrine of transubstantiation, the sacrifice of the mass, the doctrine of merit, the existence of purgatory, indulgences, the number of sacraments, the invocation of saints and whether the liturgy should be in the vernacular. That Catholics might want to debate other aspects of their religion was not considered.

The debates roused widespread interest but the results were disappointing. Some evangelicals hoped that as soon as the Irish clapped eyes on the Bible, they would turn Protestant. This rarely happened. Temporary dissatisfaction with the Catholic Church rarely translated into long-term commitment to Protestantism, because to join the Church of Ireland meant more than abandoning transubstantiation. It implied joining the world of the magistrate, the landlord and the big house.

What the lectures did do was polarise opinion in the towns where they were held and encourage a mob mentality among the partisans of both camps. The Protestants, as the minority, usually came off worse. At Carlow, a debate on 18 February 1824 between four Catholic and three Protestant clergymen ended in a riot and the Protestants required a police escort to leave the church. The British Anglican journal, the *British Critic*, followed the progress of the Second Reformation in Ireland with enthusiasm. But it reported that Catholics who looked like converting as a result of debates were ostracised and threatened by their own community. 'As soon as it was known that an individual entertained an intention of conforming to the Protestant religion, his cow was killed,'[16] it complained. When George Shaw attempted to conduct a mission under Archbishop Trench's auspices in Louisburgh, near Tuam, a hostile crowd almost killed him. 'Mr Potter, the clergyman, had arranged that the service should take place in the open market house where there were porches communicating with public streets,' he recalled.

Presently a crowd assembled, fixed an ass in front of the place where I stood and mounted a boy on it to mimic my gestures till at length the noise increased so much that we were forced to leave off the service. The Revd Lewis Potter who had accompanied me from Westport and I mounted our horses and thought it advisable to pass through a back lane out of the town but we were pursued and pelted with all manner of rubbish and stones and though we galloped our horses, the last missile did not cease flying about our ears till we were a mile from the town.[17]

Most people approached the debates and open-air services like the fans of rival teams at a football pitch. The occasions turned into bear pits where rising Catholic politicians could whip up support and garner a little reputation for themselves by attacking the preachers. It was good to be seen there, which explains why Daniel O'Connell, the great tribune of the Irish in their struggle for representation in parliament, who had risen to prominence in the struggle against the veto, chaired a marathon six-day debate in Dublin from 19 to 25 April 1827.

Another undesirable quality of the debates for the Established Church was their tendency to attract unstable characters, men who, in the opinion of more reserved bishops, added little lustre to the Church of Ireland's reputation. Tresham Gregg, the clerical tribune of working-class Protestants in Dublin, drew large crowds at debates in Dublin in the 1830s, but his war with the Church of Rome either drove him mad or drew out the madness latent within him. To the disgust of Richard Whately, Archbishop Magee's cool and very English successor in Dublin, Gregg broke the law after he burst into a convent on a mission to 'rescue' the inmates and was jailed for a week. By the 1860s he decided he was immortal, in spite of which he died in 1881.

Believers in the Second Reformation did not give up on urban Catholics. It was an article of faith among them that Catholics were simply frightened of their priests and, in spite of appearances to the contrary, were longing to be rescued. Robert McGhee, a Protestant polemicist and convert, told Archbishop Magee in 1831 that only fear held back the tide of converts. There were 'thousands and tens of thousands of poor defenceless Roman Catholics whose cry can never reach the public ear', he wrote, and 'whose complaints can find no vent in the assembly or in the press and who dare no more breathe a word against the spiritual tyranny of the priest than a victim of the Inquisition dare mutter in his dungeon'.[18] McGhee developed an almost pathological hatred of his former religion. He told the great Protestant rally at Exeter Hall in London in June 1835 that if the Catholics ever gained power in Britain, all Protestants would be slaughtered. 'The night would come the latches of our doors should be lifted,' he told the 5,000 audience that included a brace of earls, the Marchioness of Ormond and the young William Gladstone, 'and we should be laid weltering in our blood before the faces of our wives and children.'[19]

Evangelicals believed too strongly in missions to surrender the cities. At the same time, they searched for areas where the Catholic Church was less entrenched. This led them to Achill Island. Before the 1820s, neither the Established Church nor the Catholic Church had paid much attention to this windswept island off the west coast. But in 1831 a young evangelical minister called Edward Nangle planted the Church of Ireland's flag in this virgin territory after visiting the island and starting a mission that attracted enormous attention.

The evangelicals were romantics. They inhabited a Manichaean cosmos in which the powers of darkness and light were engaged in ceaseless warfare. At Exeter Hall, the London centre of English evangelical activity, audiences gasped and thrilled on hearing that the flag of the Gospel had been planted in the wilds of County Mayo, behind Rome's back. The Achill Mission became the symbol of the longed-for Second Reformation in Ireland, and of the attempt to right the wrongs committed in the name of Protestantism since the 1530s. Among these isolated and neglected Gaelic-speaking peasants the evangelicals saw a chance to start afresh with clean hands. Here, they hoped, their creed would not be identi-fied with landlords, squires and tithes. Nangle's missionaries came as teachers, catechisers and social workers. The Irish evangelicals of the 1830s wanted to be loved and believed, rather than feared. A mark of evangelical commitment was to disdain the comforts of middle- or upper-class life. A good evangelical did not mind getting his or her hands dirty, or even looking foolish.

Trench began attending evangelical meetings as Bishop of Elphin in 1817, after being introduced to the movement by William Digby, his archdeacon. The second son of the Earl of Clancarty was an aristocrat and in the early years of his ministry led the life of the stereotypical Ascendancy clergyman. As a country clergyman in County Mayo in the 1790s he was described as 'one of the best horsemen in the county' and in the rebellion of 1798 he 'scoured the country night and day, hunting the rebels'.[20] But at Elphin and Tuam, Trench made his diocese the headquarters of the Second Reformation. Here he started holding Bible meetings with evangelical clergy. His rank as bishop was set aside. As a participant recalled: 'We were brought back at these reunions to primitive days, when bishops took counsel of their presbyters and communed together of the things of God. It was a goodly sight to see the diocesan bending over the sacred volume with his clergy and entering anxiously with them into consideration of all the weighty and momentous subjects which were suggested by the text.'[21] He took a personal hand in catechising poor children in the diocese. Like Peter Roe, Trench saw the fatal illness of his sister, Lady Emily, as an opportunity for proclaiming the Gospel. Another sister, Lady Anne Gregory, recorded Emily's death in a spirit of sublime rapture.

> Never were mortals allowed to behold a more glorious sight – the soul; of an angel escaping to the bosom of its saviour! Surely God was in that place – his hand was conspicuous throughout, strengthening and supporting his faithful servant at the hour of trial. She was anxious to hear every word the bishop said and when he went to administer the sacrament to those in her dressing room, she begged him to speak loud, probably to reckon the number of communicants, that she might know who were participants in her last solemn devotion. When it was over, the bishop stood over her directing her prayers . . . he turned to all and said 'Behold the death of a truly pious Christian! Let us make it our aim to meet our last moments like this beloved young woman.'
>
> The bishop and a sister at times stood over her and repeated pious sentences which she, they could perceive by a motion of her lips, said after them. One sister bent down to her and said 'Into thy hands I commend her spirit for thou hast redeemed her, O Lord God of truth!' She said inarticulately, 'I do not hear you, speak louder'. The sister repeated it and added 'Lord Jesus receive her spirit' and she could be just heard to say 'Receive my spirit, Amen.' Thus died one of the most lovely women at the age of 27, having for the last two years of her life evinced the wonderful change wrought in her heart by the influence of the Holy Spirit.[22]

This was the evangelical revival at work. Here was a privileged Ascendancy family, but one that took religion very seriously. It was not a scene that Bishop Hervey or Archbishop Boulter would have enjoyed.

Evangelicals liked to write and read about wonderful deaths because they inspired the whole movement. 'Precious in the sight of the Lord is the death of his saints,' was the verdict of John Gregg, the Bishop of Cork, who enjoyed writing about the edifying deaths he witnessed as a curate of Kilsallaghan, near Dublin, in the late 1820s. 'Some of the best lessons in instruction are to be learned in conversation with the poor, in the chamber of sickness and at the bed of death.'[23] Bishop Mant's wife, Emma, made as superb an exit from this world as the Archbishop of Tuam's sister, according to her husband, exclaiming 'Holy holy holy, Lord God of Hosts!' just before she died, or, as the Victorians liked to say, 'fell asleep in Christ'. One Irish Protestant clergyman even wrote a book on edifying deaths in the 1840s called *The Happy Death-Bed* which contained a selection of his favourites. The 'most delightful scene' he recalled was the death of Jane Davis, aged 18, who 'exclaimed in a tone of perfect ecstasy, "Oh the joy, oh the glory, oh blessed, blessed saviour, I am ready! Come, Lord Jesus, come, Lord Jesus, come quickly!"' before sinking back on the sheets and expiring.[24]

Broad Church liberals might maintain an eighteenth-century reserve towards death, but evangelicals thought such squeamishness the mark of infidelity. As *The Happy Death-Bed* said, 'true religion is nowhere more evidenced than on the death bed of the believer'.[25] The believer stared death in the eye and rejoiced, while family and friends considered it a privilege to watch the departing Christian's last moments and hear the beating of approaching angels' wings in the sick chamber. The evangelicals reclaimed death from the dreary obscurity to which the Puritans – with their horror of 'popish' funerals – had consigned it. The assault of the Protestant Reformation on the doctrine of purgatory and on the cult of saints had broken the old links between the Christian company on earth and the souls of the departed. Radical Protestants in the seventeenth century reduced the funeral service to the most perfunctory committals. The Puritan doctrine of predestination drove the element of drama from the deathbed scene. The evangelicals restored it.

John Gregg was converted to evangelicalism at the Bethesda chapel in Dublin, which was a Calvinist stronghold. But as a mature man, Bishop Gregg's theology was distinctly Wesleyan. He took pride in his ability to open, 'as well as I knew how, the treasure of grace and mercy' to dying men and women.[26] As a result, evangelicals invested what had been a barren point in Protestant theology with new significance, as well as buckets of emotion, and turned it into a central Christian rite of passage.

Missions to remote places were one part of the evangelicals' strategy in their battle with the Catholics. Another was actively to encourage the defection of Catholic priests, in the hope that they would take their entire flocks with them. The advantages and pitfalls of this were demonstrated at Birr, in County Offaly. Birr was a small town, laid out in the formal, classical style around the walls of the estate of the Parsons, Earls of Rosse. Early in the 1820s the Earl donated land for the erection of a new Catholic chapel. Lord Oxmantown, his son, laid the foundation stone. In April 1821 the town received a new curate, named Michael Crotty. Subsequently, he became priest of the village of Shinrone, County Offaly, but on 14 July 1825 he got involved in a fight with the local Protestant Rector, William Fry as a result of which he was fined. Archbishop O'Shaughnessy of Cashel was furious and decided Crotty was a liability. His fears were confirmed when Crotty began returning to Birr to solicit money for his court case, at the same time embroiling himself in the affairs of the new chapel in Birr by making accusations of corruption against the committee in charge of building the new church. Crotty was a charismatic figure who attracted many supporters in Birr, and in defiance of a letter from the Archbishop ordering him to leave, he staged a *coup d'état* in Birr church on 29 June 1826, when he drove the new priest, Patrick Kennedy, from the altar in the middle of mass to a cacophony of groans and cheers from his various supporters and detractors.[27]

For eight weeks, Father Crotty ruled Birr church. But he reckoned without the Earl of Rosse, who sided with Bishop O'Shaughnessy and Father Kennedy. On the last Sunday in August 1826 troops from the local 66th Regiment were sent to expel Crotty and reinstate Father Kennedy. Amid more groans and hisses, the Archbishop's coadjutor, Bishop McMahon and Father Kennedy, in the presence of the Earl, jointly read out Crotty's suspension from the ministry and his excommunication from the altar. In spite of this show of strength, the Crotty party was back in church the following Sunday; the Earl then deployed two constables to repossess the building on 8 September. For three months Father Kennedy enjoyed possession of Birr Church while Crotty and his supporters retreated to a private house to plot revenge.

On 16 December, days before the opening of the new church building in Birr, unidentified men cut the timbers of the old church, as a result of which the roof fell in, burying Father Kennedy's vestments and chalice in rubble. Crotty, vested and with chalice in hand, turned up at the new church and said the first mass.

From January 1827 the Crotty party and the Kennedy party fought for control of the new church until on 11 March Crotty arrived to say mass only to find the windows and doors had been boarded up. Whether Crotty was personally involved in what happened next is debatable, but Crotty's supporters broke open the door and started brawling with the Kennedy faction inside, after which Crotty was prosecuted for breach of the peace and sentenced to three months' imprisonment for riot at the Spring Assizes. But the irrepressible priest was soon back. After his release he was cheered back into Birr by thousands of his supporters and plaguing Father Kennedy. It was then that Crotty's strange career crossed that of the Second Reformation.

Until the spring of 1827, Crotty's revolt held no doctrinal implications. He had been no more than an unusually rebellious and refractory priest and his quarrel with his diocesan resembled thousands of similar turf wars between secular and religious clergy. But after he emerged from jail Crotty began to introduce Protestant ideas to Birr Catholics. His cousin, William, a curate in Killaloe, resigned his ministry and defected to his cousin's church in 1832. After that the Second Reformation in Birr began in earnest. The Crotty brothers introduced Bible readings and started a Sunday school. They told women to give up scapulars, cords and other traditional and popular Catholic aids to worship. There then followed the most important symbolic break of all. Crotty got married.

On 13 April 1834 the Crotty cousins and their followers made a last attempt to regain physical control of Birr church only to find their path blocked by the police and members of the Kennedy party, who had barricaded the doors and windows. Crotty was back in the courts, was fined again and was sentenced to seven weeks in jail. His breach with the Catholic Church was now absolute. The question remained which way the rebel priest of Birr would turn: to the Church of Ireland or to the Presbyterians. For a while the cousins kept their options open. They placed an appeal in the Dublin press on 1 November 1835 complaining that they were being hunted by 'the bloodhounds of the Inquisition' and professing themselves ready to 'perish in the flames' for the reformed faith like the sixteenth-century English Protestant martyrs, Hugh Latimer and Nicholas Ridley.

The Protestants of Dublin responded and the money the Crottys received enabled them to open a new church in Castle Street on 15 July 1836. However, the future of the Crotty ministry in Birr depended on more than the erection of a building. What they needed was an endowment to give them financial security. Crotty departed for Ulster to prise open the wallets both of Presbyterians like Dr Cooke and of the Church of Ireland community. It was then, however, that the paths of the Crotty cousins diverged and that the Second Reformation in Birr began to unravel. Crotty's instinct was to attach the Castle Street congregation to the Church of Ireland, but his cousin disagreed. William Crotty was more radical in his politics and in his theology and faithful enough to his roots to retain a deep loathing for the Church of Ireland's tithes.

The tithe system was by now in deep crisis. As the hardline opponents of Emancipation had always predicted, the concession of seats in parliament in 1829, and O'Connell's election to represent Clare, stimulated Catholic agitation. O'Connell himself had selected the tithe system as the next object for reform. By the early 1830s, tithes were not being paid across the country. Hysterical clergy-men were calling out the troops to fire on protesters. At Skibbereen in County Cork, the rector famously ordered the police, the 'Peelers', to fire on protesting peasants who were refusing to hand over their crops. About 30 were killed. The Church was heaped in obloquy. 'Brave Peelers, march on with the musket and sword', sang a contemporary doggerel rhyme, 'And fight for my tithes in the name of the Lord.'

While the Church writhed around in its death agonies, Parliament seemed more inclined to listen to the Catholics. Bishop Doyle of Kildare told MPs it would be more sensible if the Church's tithes were taken away and invested in a neutral trust. Richard Whately, the newly appointed Protestant Archbishop of Dublin despaired. Ireland, he predicted, faced a future marked by 'assassination, burning, houghing of cattle, etc,' he told a friend. 'In large parts of Ireland, the Established Church is such as you might establish in Turkey or China – viz, no place of worship, no congregation, no payment.'[28]

At a time when every clergyman of the Established Church was feeling nervous, and many had no certain income, it was unfortunate for Crotty and his fund-raising mission that his cousin delivered a sermon in Limerick in the summer of 1837 that condemned the tithe system as unjust. Crotty duly denounced his brother to the newspapers but found the doors and purses of Ulster's outraged Tory Anglicans closed to him on his second trip to the north that summer. It was the same the following year in England, when a trip to the Midlands and West Country raised a puny sum. The Crottys were now at war with each other as well as with the Catholic Church. In April 1839 Crotty finally attached his Birr congregation to the Church of Ireland, then left Birr for England in May on another fund-raising trip. In his absence, William launched a coup in Castle Street and deposed him. Crotty returned in July to find that the Presbyterians had formally received his church into the Synod of Ulster on 30 May.

Crotty had long since forfeited the allegiance of the thousands who had lined the roads to cheer him back into Birr on his release from prison in 1827. The split between the cousins further depleted their ranks. Crotty left Ireland and took a curacy in the diocese of Ripon. His cousin William fell out with his own flock in Birr and was deposed, after which the Presbyterian Church in Birr settled down to an unremarkable existence as a small congregation of 80.

The rise and fall of the Second Reformation in Birr mirrored the movement's wider failure in Ireland. The landlords were cold. Small pools of converts were established in Sligo, at Ballinasloe in Galway, at Birr, at Askeaton in County Limerick and on Achill Island. But there was no general defection. Protestant activity in remote districts stimulated the Catholic Church into a burst of counter-activity in the same area. At Kilmoe, County Cork, the experience of W. A. Fisher, the Rector for more than 40 years, was typical. 'He saw what seemed to him to be a reformation among the Roman Catholics – so many came out from Rome. He saw them, to his great dismay and grief, return to their former religion in nearly as great numbers.'[29] At Ballymachugh, County Cavan, the interest that the evangelical missionaries stirred in the Bible soon transferred itself to nationalist politics.

The priests adopted a stratagem that alas proved too successful in the issue. They subscribed for seven copies of the Dublin Register, a newspaper then the official organ of the Roman Catholic Association, and arming their emissaries with these sent them to the discussion halls to read the speeches of [the O'Connellite politician Daniel Lalor] Shiel and O'Connell. The Bible was closed that they might drink in sedition and admire the wonderful orations of these great Irishmen. Politics took the place of theology.

The Church of Ireland remained foreign to the poor. In Kilmoe, Fisher found the Protestants would not go to church if they were too poor, or became too poor to buy respectable clothes. He held 'ragged services', aimed at 'those whose clothes were so ragged that they did not like to attend the ordinary service'. But the very name of the service reinforced the glass wall between Protestantism and poverty.

Asenath Nicholson, an American missionary with the Hibernian Bible Society in the 1840s, took a dim view of what evangelical pioneers like the Nangles were up to in Connacht. Nicholson cordially hated the English, so hers is not a totally reliable account. Every inch a rather priggish – and teetotal – daughter of the American revolution, she recorded in fine detail her contempt for the drawling English Protestant women she encountered in Ireland, pouring their goblets of red wine from their *chaises-longues* and keeping battalions of Irish servants dancing in attendance. But her observations of failings in the convert school at Ventry in Kerry were pertinent. She was shocked to find the girls were not being educated at all. 'These are the daughters of the lower orders,' the teacher told her, 'and we do not advance them.' 'But have they not talents to be cultivated?' Nicholson asked. 'I must do as I am bidden,' the teacher answered. 'They are poor and must be educated according to their station.'[30] The local convent, Nicholson added, provided a far better service to the community.

The isolation of the new congregations made it easy for the Catholic majority to subvert them and intimidate clergy and flock alike. George Reade, Rector of Inniskeen, County Monushan, told Archbishop Beresford in 1856 of the price he had paid for adding 18 converts to his previous flock of 52. 'The endeavour to exhibit the beauty and excellence of the Established Church . . . raised up against me the most virulent persecution,' he said. 'We have been denounced from the altar time innumerable, the ladies of my family have been hooted, pelted, spat on, cursed and followed round with readings. One of my sons was fired at from behind a ditch and has also been pelted with stones and much hurt. Two subscriptions were laid by the Ribbonmen to shoot me . . . '[31]

Converts found the hostility of their neighbours so intolerable that they frequently left the country. Evangelical clergy discovered that they were often simply facilitating emigration. A. Miller, Rector of Haynestown, near Dundalk, told Beresford he knew of 40 families in the Ardee region 'who are so persuaded of the falsehood of the Roman system that they intend to emigrate with their families as soon as they possibly can to enable them to worship to the dictates of their conscience'.[32]

By the 1850s, Protestant missionaries confronted a Catholic Church which was rapidly expanding in size and self-confidence. A stalwart of the Irish Church Missions told Beresford in 1856 that Protestant missionaries faced more dangerous obstacles nowadays than physical threats. 'The Church of Rome seems to have recovered much of its influence in the south,' he wrote. 'The people apparently acquiesce in its exactions. Its agency is no longer that of brute force and ruffian violence . . . Agents of the Irish Church Missions who had formerly to contend with nothing more than bodily assaults have now to contend against the influence of missionaries who preach, I am told, with much power and effect . . . for a long time, it may be, the Protestant missions will seem unsuccessful.'[33]

Those fears were confirmed in the 1860s, when evangelical societies began to admit a loss of momentum. In a report to the Anglican bishops in 1863, John

Garrett, the secretary to the West Connaught Church Endowment Society, admitted most of the mission parishes in the west were now in difficulties. 'I leave this district with an extremely anxious heart,' he wrote. 'Rome may possibly be left with a greater triumph than ever.'[34]

A large section of the Church of Ireland was not evangelical and never shared the dream of a Second Reformation. They were sceptical about the chances of dramatically improving the Church of Ireland's position *vis-à-vis* the Catholics, and worried about the damage being inflicted on relations between the Churches by the evangelicals' scathing polemics. In Dublin, Whately proved a very different archbishop to Magee. He courted the loathing of the evangelical party by disdaining missions and sniffing at convert priests, whereas evangelicals were wonderfully optimistic about the qualifications of converts and treated lightly any previous brushes their protégés might have had with the law. Not so Whately. Of one convert he complained: 'He insisted he was a maths tutor but he could not draw a triangle.' Another knew no Greek.[35] These were just the kind of prissy, middle-class objections that evangelicals despised.

Whately disliked allowing converts to preach on Catholicism because he viewed their sermons as inflammatory. He did not want it thought that Catholics would receive material aid from Protestants if they converted. He said one old woman had offered to convert in his diocese in exchange for a leg of mutton and a blanket. 'What leg of mutton and blanket?' the clergyman had apparently asked. 'Why sir,' she said, 'Father Sullivan told us the converts got each a leg of mutton and a blanket, and as I am famished and starving with cold I thought God would forgive me for getting them.'[36] Whately was right to feel alarmed. As famine swept Ireland in the 1840s, evangelicals were to get into a great deal of trouble over the charge that they offered food in exchange for souls.

The Second Reformation failed to arrest the slide towards disestablishment of the Church of Ireland. Its supporters complained that they needed more time to turn the ship round, but the British government was not interested in microscopic advances in Birr or Achill Island. They looked at the big picture: they saw that the countryside was in the grip of a small-scale insurrection against the Church of Ireland. Emancipation had done nothing to pacify rural grievances about tithes. While the Tories were in power the Established Church was safe. But in 1831 the Whigs were returned to office. The long era of Tory rule that had lasted since the French Revolution was over. There were revolutions in France, Poland and Belgium. Although in England there was no revolution, there was a Whig ministry bent on reform. In May 1832 the Reform Bill abolished the rotten boroughs in the English parliament. After that it was inevitable that Whig attention would turn to the rotten bishoprics of the Church of Ireland.

The announcement of a commission entrusted with examining the Irish Church with a view to reform caused near apoplexy among the Tories. A group of Oxford dons, John Henry Newman, John Keble and Edward Pusey, rallied the High Church against the combined assaults of democracy and Erastianism.

Newman, Pusey and Keble knew little about Ireland and what they did know they did not like. Nevertheless, Ireland was the spark that lit the Oxford Movement. Although the Oxford men talked a lot about spoliation and sacrilege, the Whig proposals for the Irish Church were not, in fact, designed to hurt the Church but intended to deploy its resources more efficiently. There was little to fear from a government in which the chief adviser on Irish affairs was Lord Melbourne, the Home Secretary, who distrusted O'Connell, thought almost all change disagreeable and admired Anglicanism as the least fanatical brand of religion available. He was not religious himself and thought the writings of the Fathers of the Early Church 'excellent reading and very amusing'.

The Church Temporalities Act of 1833 was a utilitarian measure. It seemed pointless to maintain four archbishoprics in Ireland when the larger Church in England had only two, and so Cashel and Tuam were sacrificed in order that Dublin and Armagh might be maintained. The tiny sees that lay thick on the ground in the west of Ireland were similarly given up so that each remaining diocese might have a decent Protestant population. Overall, the Whigs cut the number of bishoprics from 20 to 10 and vested the income of the suppressed sees in a Board of Commissioners charged with using the money to repair and build churches. The finances of the board were boosted by a tax on parishes worth more than £300 and the income from parishes with no Church of Ireland population, which were suppressed.

The Act sorted out many absurdities within the Church of Ireland. But the Church never forgave the liberals for tinkering around with their establishment and feeding Catholic appetites for its abolition. Some feared the papists might reclaim their old sees once they were suppressed. Bishop Bisset of Raphoe, in Donegal, confided his worries to the local Presbyterian minister after hearing that his see was to be suppressed. 'I have no pleasure in going through these grounds,' he said. 'I care not to plant a tree here, for I know not who is going to sit under the shadow of it. It may be a Romish bishop.'[37] The immediate history of the Protestant see of Raphoe was melancholy. 'The cathedral took fire, the bishop died; the dean, overwhelmed in debt, fled from the country; the see was suppressed; the castle was reduced to a mass of ruins. One of the curates, who became insane, for a time created a great sensation by his strange utterances in the pulpit and elsewhere.'

The 1833 Act did not, however, solve the tithe crisis. As a result, in 1838 the Whigs passed the Tithe Rent-Charge Act, which sensibly transferred responsibility for paying tithes from the mostly Catholic (or Presbyterian) tenants of the land to the mostly Anglican landowners. But that was the end of the Whig persecution of the Church. Lord Melbourne, Prime Minister since 1834, had had enough. He was 'quite tired of reforming the Church', he said. The Irish Catholics were 'quick and clever but uncertain, false, hypocritical', he told Queen Victoria.[38]

The Whigs reforms left the Church of Ireland in the 1840s less open to ridicule than it had been. Anglican landowners now paid for the upkeep of Anglican clergymen. The Board of Commissioners studded the landscape with hundreds of severe, Gothic churches. Richard Trench, Archbishop of Dublin in the 1860s, was 24 when the tithe war broke out in 1831. He always shivered when he remembered the open graves the peasants dug for him and his family on the lawns of his father's estate at Stradbally, in County Laois. 'Did I possess any property in this country I would sell it at any loss,' he wrote in July 1831.[39] Ten years on, the clergy of the Established Church felt a great deal safer. But state intervention in the affairs of the state Church had one very serious consequence: it gravely undermined the fiction that the Church was an untouchable, autonomous spiritual corporation. Half the strength of the Establishment was that it appeared immutable. Those busy, reforming Whigs broke the spell. If the Established Church was reformed once, it could be reformed again. Or again, it might be disestablished.

In August 1845 William Gladstone wrote to his friend, Samuel Wilberforce, Dean of Westminster, with a list of queries about the Irish Church. In February Gladstone had resigned his position as President of the Board of Trade in Peel's Tory cabinet over the planned increase to the Maynooth grant. In 1838 he had published a large, little-read tome, *The State in its Relations with the Church*, which took the hard, high line on the Church, defending the principle of Establishment and the state's right to impose a religious test on office holders. Since then, Gladstone's opinions had moved to the left but he still felt it necessary to resign as a point of principle. That summer, cooling his heels, he wrote to Wilberforce, asking if the Dean considered the Irish Protestant bishops or the Irish Catholic bishops the true successors of the Apostles. Wilberforce's reply confirmed Gladstone's existing doubts on the question, for on 16 August he wrote back to the Dean, agreeing that when it came to the Church of Ireland, 'title by descent will not uphold her'.[40] Gladstone spoke like a dissatisfied teacher dealing with a failing pupil when he added that the 'working results of the last 10 years have disappointed me. It may be answered: "have faith in the ordinance of God" but then I must see the seal and the signature'. When Church of Ireland Tories accused Gladstone in 1867 of sacrificing the Irish Establishment to unite the Liberal Party behind his leadership, they were wrong. He may have done all that, but the charge of unprincipled behaviour cannot be sustained. He had lost faith in the Irish Establishment's 'divine seal and signature' almost a quarter of a century before.

In the 1830s and 1840s the reform of the tithes, the consolidation of sees and the abolition of the old Protestant town corporations kept the wolf from the door. In the north, Henry Cooke deployed his influence over the Presbyterians to unite them to the Establishment. In 1835 he had proclaimed the 'banns of marriage' between the two great Protestant denominations at a monster meeting in Hillsborough attended by a crowd of at least 20,000. But the marriage remained unconsummated. Cooke's rhetoric and the rise of the evangelical party in the Church of Ireland narrowed the gap between Anglicans and Presbyterians but did not close it. Even as the doctrinal differences faded, Ulster Presbyterians and Anglicans remained separated by a huge social divide. The Establishment was Tory and remained identified with the landlords. Ulster Presbyterians, in spite of Cooke's efforts, were overwhelmingly Liberals and Whigs. Cooke taught Presbyterians to dislike Rome more and the Establishment less. He could not make them love the Establishment.

And English Radicals hated the Irish Church. It was the butt of every mid-Victorian progressive. The Church of Ireland was 'born and cradled amid despotism and corruption', the *North British Review* said in December 1866. The *Morning Star* was positively violent. In January 1867 it urged Liberal England to 'tear down from its pride of place this alien church which perpetuated the memory of detestable tyranny'. 'The abolition of the Church Establishment must come hand in hand with the change in [land] tenure. And it must come soon.'[41]

As well as ameliorating some grievances, the Whig reforms of the 1830s provided British radicals with a great deal of information about Ireland, which proved very serviceable to the Church's critics. A census published in 1834 revealed that of an Irish population of 7.9 million, Catholics made up 6.4 million, the Church of Ireland only 852,000 and the Presbyterians just under 650,000. The Established Church, it was shown, served only about one in 10 of the population. Whig pamphlets put the Irish Establishment at the top of its list of abuses, along with the old corporations and the universities. They made play of the fact that the Bishop of Chester had more parishioners than all the Protestant Irish bishops put together. This head of steam dissipated in the 1840s. Church reform was irrelevant in the Famine years. But after the worst was over in 1849, it inevitably drifted once more to the top of the political agenda as an issue that united Irish Catholics and English Liberals. A statistical survey of Ireland in 1849 deduced from the information supplied to the authorities that while the Anglican archbishops and bishops drew an income of £130,000, their Catholic counterparts made do with £29,700 – less than a quarter of the amount. The Anglicans might insist that the average income of an Irish bishop amounted to no more than the takings of a respectable London shopkeeper but the charge stuck. Liberals complained that property had been conferred on the Established Church for the benefit of all the people and should be taken away if it was being used for the benefit of the few. As one pamphlet complained: 'We have the singular spectacle of an unpopular but wealthy corporation claiming to have the "marks of the true church" in its very feebleness and fewness of numbers, but holding on like grim death to the hard cash!'[42]

The census of 1861 proved that three decades of evangelical missions and revivals had scarcely altered the state of play since the 1830s. The estimated death of a million people and the forced emigration of another million had cut the total population from nearly 8 million to 5,793,967. But the pattern of denominational allegiance was remarkably unchanged. The Catholic population had fallen from 6.4 million to 4.4 million, a drop of almost one-third. But the Protestant population had also dropped. Church of Ireland members were down from 852,000 to 693,000, a decline of almost 20 per cent. The Presbyterians and other dissenters were pretty stable at 595,345.

Irish Protestants had not starved in the same numbers as Catholics, but they had still declined sharply. Protestants in the diocese of Kilfenora now numbered 251 souls. Of the 1,518 benefices, 486 – almost a third – now contained fewer than 100 Church of Ireland parishioners. A spate of hostile pamphleteers pored over these figures and drew acid conclusions. In the minds of English Liberals, the Irish Church was an ecclesiastical 'rotten borough', a symbol of Tory corruption and of unacceptable privilege and wealth.

For the Catholics, the destruction of the Establishment became the litmus test of their new strength. 'As for the Protestant establishment in Ireland, dream no longer of upholding it in Ireland,' John MacHale, the Archbishop of Tuam warned Lord Derby in 1852.[43] 'The axe is already laid to the root.' A few disagreed. David Moriarty, the Bishop of Kerry, was one of the few Unionist Catholic bishops left by the 1860s. In 1867 he suggested the Protestant Establishment form part of the divine plan for Ireland that God had employed as 'a most effectual means of deterring our people from apostasy'. He feared the disestablished clergyman might be nastier than his predecessor, a 'fiery proselytising zealot,' instead of a 'meek unobtrusive parson'.[44]

Moriarty was in a small minority. The Establishment was only 'a nuisance' to Archbishop Paul Cullen in 1860, 'with its mitred dignitaries, its universities, its schools and its enormous wealth, derived from the confiscation of the property of our ancestors'.[45] But by 1864 he, too, was demanding root and branch destruction. Addressing a public meeting in Dublin, Cullen appealed to the census figures of 1861 when he argued that state Protestantism was a failure. He reeled off those embarrassing statistics: that there were no Anglicans at all in almost 10 per cent of the state Church's 2,428 parishes, and that a single Catholic parish in Dublin – St Peter's – contained more Catholics than there were Protestants in the 11 Protestant dioceses of Kilmacdaugh, Kilfenora, Killala, Achonry, Ossory, Cashel, Emly, Waterford, Lismore, Ross and Clonfert. Such figures, Cullen said, 'must convince us at the same time that it is most unreasonable and contrary to the interests of the people and to a sound policy to keep up a vast expensive ecclesiastical establishment for the sake of so small a minority and in opposition to the wishes of the great mass of the population'.[46]

In 1867 the eruption of activity by American-inspired Republican revolutionaries known as Fenians brought matters to a head. So did the need to find an issue to take the Liberals into battle. In July 1866 the Whig-Liberal government of Lord John Russell resigned, divided over proposals to extend the franchise. A minority Tory administration under the Earl of Derby took office until February 1868, when Derby resigned and Benjamin Disraeli took over as Prime Minister.

While the Tories clung to office, the Liberals rallied round Gladstone. In December 1867 he made reform of the Irish Church the centrepiece of a barnstorming speech in Stockport, which carried him to the leadership of the party. After Lord Russell obligingly announced he would not stand again as leader, Gladstone was confirmed as the party's unchallenged head, confronting a weak, Tory minority administration.

In March 1868, a month after Benjamin Disraeli became Prime Minister, Gladstone tested his strength in the Commons by putting forward three resolutions on the Irish Church: abolishing its Established status, halting crown patronage of ecclesiastical offices and asking the Queen to place the crown's interest in the Church's temporalities at parliament's disposal. It was war, but to the horror of Irish churchmen, Disraeli's team declined to put up much of a fight. The *Irish Ecclesiastical Gazette* compared the position of the state Church to that of the British colonists in the Indian Mutiny. The newspaper was incredulous that the Tories were ready to surrender without a shot. 'Shall the Church of God be so afraid of majorities, so afraid of them as to yield before a single blow is struck?' it asked.[47]

The answer, alas, was 'Yes'. The Church of Ireland was Tory and the dominant evangelicals in it were Tory practically to a man, but the English Tories did not repay the devotion of their Irish supporters. They did not want to see the Irish Establishment pulled down, but they were prepared to see it destroyed if it bought them time. They regarded the Irish Church as an outlying bulwark of their regime. It was not, like the Church of England, the Lords or the monarchy, an essential pillar. Instead of denouncing Gladstone for sacrilege and heresy, the Tories started floating compromise suggestions that were almost as unwelcome to the Irish Church as Gladstone's plans. One was to maintain the Establishment on such a small scale that it would no longer be noticeable, let alone objectionable. The Church of Ireland would be shrunk to a single archbishopric. The proposal would inevitably entail massive disendowment and leave a mere skeleton. If this was the best that their friends could come up with, it is not surprising that the Church of Ireland learned to deal with what the *Irish Ecclesiastical Gazette* called 'the arch-spoliator' Gladstone and his 'gigantic scheme of confiscation'.[48] As Richard Trench, Archbishop of Dublin since 1864, said in May 1868, 'instant death at the hands of Gladstone' might be preferable to the 'gradual starvation' Disraeli offered.[49]

Gladstone's battering ram achieved its aim. After only three months in office, Disraeli lost a vote of confidence. The Queen delayed his departure by not dissolving parliament until the autumn of 1868, hoping the gap might give the Tories and her beloved Disraeli time to recover their strength before going to the polls, but the ploy failed. In the general election of November the Liberals swept the country, giving the new Prime Minister a Commons majority of 111. England had spoken, and as Gladstone remarked with satisfaction to the Fishmongers Company in London at a banquet, 'upon no occasion has the country made its meaning more clearly known'.[50] After parliament opened on 16 February 1869, Gladstone made it apparent he would steer through the Irish Church legislation himself.

The Irish clergy were profoundly aware that they were not in a position to do anything except watch events. The *Gazette* could only utter dismal warnings about the folly of believing that 'so-called conciliation will ever appease the deep seated disloyalty of the Irish people'.[51] The paper continued to hope that a champion would arise and subject Ireland to the 'strict and severe rule' that it needed, but they had no illusions that it would happen. At court in March, Trench remarked that he felt 'rather like a ghost about presently to vanish away'.[52]

There was talk of appealing directly to the Queen, and of staging some kind of public protest. There was an entertaining proposal for the bishops and clergy to march in their vestments through the streets of London. Elderly churchmen remembered their success in 1831, when the Irish bishops had presented themselves at court on William IV's birthday and the King had declared his 'fixed purpose, resolution and determination' to maintain the existing Establishment. But there was no chance of extracting such a declaration of war from his niece. Victoria declined to open the 1869 parliament as a mark of her displeasure over disestablishment. She disliked the prospect of surrendering her right to nominate bishops to Irish sees. But she dreaded the fall of the House of Lords much more than the Church of Ireland and was still too much of a practical Whig to sacrifice what remained of the royal prerogative on the altar of Irish Establishment. If the House of Lords wanted to fight for the Irish Establishment she would work for compromise. She told Archibald Tait, the Archbishop of Canterbury, that the Church of England must do nothing to 'prolong a dangerous agitation on the subject'. She urged the English Primate to seek an interview with Gladstone and said: 'He seems to be really moderate in his views and anxious, so far as he can properly and consistently do so, to meet the objections of those who would maintain the Irish Church.' Tait obliged and promised to promote 'that conciliatory policy which Your Majesty has at heart'.[53]

Gladstone was as good as the Queen's word. The Irish Church was to be disestablished but only partly disendowed. He proposed a two-year delay between the passage of the Act and its coming into law, to give the Church time to put its house in order. It would retain all the church buildings currently in use and receive a lump sum in lieu of the life value of the glebes and the life interests of the clergy.

The Irish bishops met their English colleagues at the Archbishop of Canterbury's palace at Lambeth in February to ponder their strategy. But there was nothing they could do. Embarrassed silences punctuated the meeting as the English bishops murmured sympathetic noncommittal noises while the Irish struggled to find a common theme. Archbishop Beresford was an unimpressive figure at Lambeth. He 'wandered and fairly maundered in a feeble way that was actually painful and produced a painful impression on his audience',[54] according to William Magee, Dean of Cork and Bishop-elect of Peterborough.

Magee was equally caustic about Archbishop Trench's action in the Lords, where he spoke in March 1869, urging various amendments to the Irish Church Act. 'The Archbishop of Dublin made a melancholy and almost inaudible "keen" for the Irish Church,' he remarked. 'No one listened to him.'[55] Years later, in the 1930s, Charles D'Arcy, Archbishop of Armagh, recalled the frustrated emotions of the Church of Ireland laity as they passively observed these momentous events. 'Every evening my father used to read out the debates, while my mother sat at her needlework and we children listened. All the things that at other times we enjoyed in our evenings were interrupted that we might follow the progress of the great discussion. How we burned with indignation at the monstrous charges which Gladstone . . . and others brought against our beloved church.'[56]

The Irish church legislation dominated parliament until July. On 23 March, after the Commons passed the second reading of the bill, the battle shifted to the Lords with its large majority of hereditary Tory peers. But with the Queen and Archbishop Tait listing heavily towards compromise, the Irish Church did not find a secure prop even there. When the vote came on 18 June, enough Tory Lords shrank from all-out war to give Gladstone the day and the government won by 179 to 146 votes. For the Irish bishops, that historic vote was something they would never erase from their minds. They had to endure the yells of delight that erupted on the Liberal benches as they were expelled from the house in which their predecessors had sat since the Act of Union. To William Alexander of Derry, it was like 'hearing the crash of a great building'. He stumbled out of Parliament in a daze. 'I can never forget the summer night,' he recalled, 'just after hearing the division when I reeled out into the cool air . . . A kindly touch was laid upon my arm. I turned and saw a Roman Catholic bishop of my acquaintance who had obtained a place to listen to the debate. "I cannot pretend not to be pleased," he said, "though personally, I am sorry for you and the others." Then he patted my arms and added: "Now, my dear lord, you see what these English are".'[57]

The Church of Ireland saw disestablishment as an act not of liberation but of spoliation and humiliation. Bishop Gregg of Cork vowed never to set foot in the British capital again.[58] Many bishops and clergy divided their lives afterwards into a kind of BC and AD, based on this terrible event. With the passage of time memories became fonder and rosier and the nostalgia increased. Churchmen forgot about the hideous tithe wars of the 1820s and 1830s and pretended they had lived in the Garden of Eden. 'For me, the Established Church lies in deep and tender distances,' Bishop Alexander told the Church of Ireland synod in the 1890s.

Unforgotten memories and unforgotten graves present themselves to my memory. Young people were brought up to believe that the relation between Church and State could not be broken without a lowered moral tone as well as peril to Protestantism. Men pronounced the words Church and State, not only as men shout them in their cups but as they breathe them in their prayers.[59]

Not everyone was as sentimental as Alexander. Magee preferred the Church of England to the Church of his birth. He wished himself in England at least once a day, a longing that was gratified when he went to Peterborough in 1868. The grandson of the man who started the Second Reformation had no time for Irish evangelicalism and no sympathy for the disestablished Church. 'The Irish clergy have no principles as a body to fall back on when the outer line of their establishment is gone,' he wrote coldly in May 1867. 'We shall then see what howling the gospel will do.'[60] Magee thought the Church of Ireland's claim to be the 'real' Church of the nation was self-deluding twaddle. 'It is a simple fact that the Irish Church never has been since the Reformation, or indeed long before it, the church of the nation,' he said. 'It has been all along the church of the Pale and the church of the Anglo-Celtic colony in Ireland . . . It remained the Church of the English colony in Ireland and it is that and nothing else.' Magee secretly sympathised with Gladstone and shared the Queen's Whiggish pragmatism. He feared the Tories would propel the country towards a revolution in which the crown, Lords and Church of England would all perish.

William Plunket, Bishop of Meath from 1876 and Trench's successor at Dublin from 1894 to 1897, voiced the aspirations of a new generation. Only 40 at the time of disestablishment, and with many active years ahead of him, he felt less inclined than Alexander to spend his life mourning the past. He was more optimistic about the Church's prospects and less sentimental about England and the Church of England. 'They do not understand us, they never understood us,' he said of his Anglican brothers and sisters over the water. 'Until that heaving channel which frightens them from our shores has been bridged over and its troublesome waves quieted, they will never understand us.' 'His biographer recalled: 'He felt keenly for the honour of Ireland'. Plunket saw disestablishment as a profoundly cynical act. He suspected the Irish Church had been sacrificed to save its English counterpart. 'The wolves were on the track and had to be satisfied with something,' he said. 'The Irish Church was rather overweighting the sledge and so was thrown out with certain decent expressions of sisterly regret.' Plunkett did not look back on establishment with eyes blinded by tears. It had been a 'tottering wall'.[61]

After the Royal Assent on 26 July 1869, the Church was given a grace period of 17 months to put its affairs in order before the Act became law. The task was daunting. An institution that had often functioned as a lifeless appendage of the state had suddenly to acclimatise itself to independence. The Church had no experience in internal self-government. No convocation of the clergy had been held since the reign of Queen Anne. There could be no government by convocation now. The battle over disestablishment hardened the determination of Low Church evangelicals to make sure their 'free' Church was not entrusted to the exclusive care of the clergy. At the Church Convention of 15 February 1870, the question was not whether the laity would be represented in the Church's representative governing body, but to what degree.

When the first General Synod met on 13 April 1871, it was blighted by the vengeful mood of the ultra-Protestant laity who concentrated most of their energy on attacking their own bishops and clergy. There was bitter conflict over proposals to revise the Book of Common Prayer in a more Protestant direction, a row that dragged on until 1878. Some churchmen feared the evangelicals might change the book out of all recognition. The bishops fought off most of the proposed changes to the liturgy but the Low Churchmen forced their anti-papal fetish on the Church's canons. Canon 36 forbade the use of crosses on the communion table. Hostility to ritualism and a morbid suspicion of anything that even smacked of popery became the hallmark of the disestablished Church. This left the Church of Ireland increasingly out of touch with the other branches of the Anglican Communion, all of which were affected to some degree by the theology of the Oxford Movement. In England, a kind of watered down Tractarianism seeped into practically every parish, radically reshaping attitudes to worship. The whitewashed church with its box pews, three-decker pulpit and movable communion table gave way to church interiors consciously appealing to the medieval past. By the end of Victoria's reign, even evangelical clergymen were introducing changes in liturgical practice that an earlier generation would have regarded as rank popery. The Church of Ireland remained aloof from the trend, a dignified Protestant backwater. The Church of England might find its way back to copes, mitres and altars but its Irish counterpart retained a kind of mid-Victorian Puritan austerity. The Church of Ireland's immunity to the Oxford Movement had one beneficial side-effect. It missed the damaging warfare between High and Low Church that plagued the Church of England and which would have been very troublesome for a small Church. From the 1840s, the Church of England had to live with a steady trickle of defectors to Rome that threatened at times to turn into a torrent. The Church of Ireland had no such problem. Much to the annoyance of some Catholics, the Church of Ireland lost few of its sons and daughters to Rome.

After disestablishment, the Church of Ireland perceptibly receded into the background. Its status was now so different from that of its English sister Church that the two bodies had less to do with each other. Inevitably, the Church became more Irish now that there were no Englishmen jostling for Irish bishoprics. The social standing of Church of Ireland clergy declined. In the 1860s and 1870s the bishops still numbered several men from great families. Marcus Beresford, Archbishop of Armagh from 1862 to 1885, belonged to one of the great landed families of Ireland. He had succeeded his cousin, Lord John George Beresford, as Primate. His father, George, had been Bishop of Kilmore. His suffragans, Knox of Down and Bernard of Tuam, were the grandson of a viscount and the brother of an earl respectively. Archbishop Plunket was a baronet after succeeding to the title in 1870. While he was Archbishop, his title and wealth commanded social respect. An observer captured the atmosphere at his home in Bray, Old Connaught, on the days in August and September when the Archbishop and Lady Plunket held their customary garden parties for the clergy of the archdiocese:

> On these gala days crowds filled the house, the lawns, the pleasure grounds and gardens; every clergyman in his wide archdiocese which comprises all the county of Dublin, north Wicklow and nearly all of Kildare and many

clergymen outside his jurisdiction were asked. The black clerical garment perhaps predominated but this was duly diversified by the bright parasols, gay frocks and sweet faces of the bevies of fair women wont to illuminate the garden parties of Ireland. Well-spread marquees were raised to receive and refresh the moving throngs and the host moved through all, making everyone pleasant with a happy word of welcome.[62]

After Marcus Beresford's death in 1885 and Plunkett's in 1897, few bishops came from the great families. The gentry ceased to send their sons into the Church. Archbishop Plunkett was frank about the social consequences of disestablishment, which he listed in 1892 to the *Western Mail*. They included

the disappointed expectations of those who entered the ministry before our disconnection with the state. The miserable incomes of those that have since been appointed to vacant posts. The dependence of a clergyman for his stipend on the precarious and somewhat capricious church offerings of his people . . . the plight of poor and remote parishes being left without the means of grace. The inadequate supply of candidates for Holy Orders and the danger that those who enter the ministry should socially and intellectually fall short of the standard of the past.[63]

The older bishops regretted all this. Orpen of Limerick complained in 1914 that 'very few of the sons of their country gentlemen were to be found in their ranks, while formerly a large proportion of the parishes were served from the ranks of the leading families of the county. Now, with one exception, he believed that not one single case occurred'.[64]

The Church of Ireland was very lucky that at the time of disestablishment its laity still owned most of Ireland. In the 1870s the 250 members of the General Synod were believed to own about a million acres between them. Church of Ireland men still formed the majority of bankers, army officers, barristers and solicitors. Until the local government reforms of 1898, Irish counties were still run by grand juries dominated by Church of Ireland gentry. They were the men who levied the local taxes and spent them, who controlled the boards of guardians, imposed fines and administered the law at petty sessions.

Agitation for land reform soon eroded the power and the bank balances of the landed gentry. The Land Acts of 1881 and 1885 abolished free contracts in rent and gave more rights to tenants. The franchise reform of 1884 greatly reduced the gentry's political power by expanding the Irish franchise by 230 per cent. Landed families began selling their estates. The big houses became shabbier and were shut up for longer and longer periods. Their owners ceased to buy new paintings or furniture.

In the 1860s the Guinness family paid for the restoration of St Patrick's. Henry Roe, a distiller, did the same for Christ Church. In Cork, Bishop Gregg oversaw the erection of a dreamy fantasy in French Romanesque in 1870–79 to a design by Edmund Street. St Finn Barre was a remarkable project. Here a Low Church bishop oversaw the erection of a cathedral whose interior was an essay in almost Byzantine opulence, with dazzling roof paintings and a magnificent marble pulpit. The exterior was an exuberant riot of spires and buttresses, thoroughly continental in inspiration, Catholic in appearance and surmounted by a dazzling gold angel blowing a trumpet. It was, and remains, a thrilling sight. Kildare cathedral was rebuilt in the 1870s and 1880s in another great symbolic undertaking. A roofless shell since the Reformation, the virtually new cathedral was not completed until September 1896, when Edward Benson, the Archbishop of Canterbury, presided over the opening.

The cathedrals in Dublin, Kildare and Cork were defiant statements. They were public proclamations that the Church of Ireland intended to survive disestablishment. In Dublin, there was an additional incentive to rebuild. Dublin Catholics pointedly declined to build a cathedral of their own in the city, designating their metropolitan church a 'pro-cathedral'. The term suggested that the building in Mary Street was very much a temporary stand-in, pending a final settlement of accounts. In 1869 Cardinal Cullen told Gladstone that the Protestants were incapable of filling their two cathedrals in Dublin and that the best way to preserve the buildings was for at least one to be handed back to the Catholics.[65]

Gladstone did not give them the old cathedrals. The Church of Ireland restored the buildings and has them to this day. But it was a humbled Church. During the demolition of the old Christ Church, children of the nearby slums taunted the workmen taking the measurements with the futility of their project. 'Misther, is this goin' to be a [Catholic] chapel?' they asked one of the men working on the project. 'Certainly not,' came the answer. 'Yes it is, we'll have it yet, as we had it before,' they shouted. 'D'ye think we'll let the auld swaddlers have it? Ye needn't be measuring it; it'll be pulled down.'[66] It was not pulled down, but power had shifted in Ireland and even the slum children knew it.

CHAPTER ELEVEN

The Agitating Priest

This clergy with few exceptions are from the ranks of the people; they inherit their feelings; they are not, as formerly, brought up under Despotic governments. They know much more of the principles of the constitution than they do of passive obedience.
(Bishop Doyle, 1824)[1]

In 1835, Alexis de Tocqueville toured Ireland. The Frenchman was struck not only by the populism of the Irish priests but by a new note of triumphalism. At a clerical dinner in Carlow on 20 July, he recalled: 'The feelings expressed were extremely democratic. Distrust and hatred of the great landlords, love of the people and confidence in them. Bitter memories of past oppression. An air of exaltation at present or approaching victory. A profound hatred of the Protestants and above all of their clergy'.[2] He added: 'There is an unbelievable unity between the Irish clergy and the Catholic population. The clergy, rebuffed by Irish society, has turned all its attention to the lower classes; it has the same instincts, the same interests and the same passions as the people . . . in the streets of Carlow I noticed that the people all saluted all the priests who passed'.[3]

De Tocqueville was impressed by the number of new churches dotting the landscape and by the high level of religious observance. The Bishop of Ossory assured him that in Kilkenny, a city of 26,000, there was scarcely a Catholic who had failed to make Easter communion.[4] He noted another significant development – the growth of a free press. In Tuam he watched the labourers waiting to hear the priest reading aloud from the local newspaper at the end of the day.[5] The rise of the radical priest accompanied the rise of the radical press.

Forty years before, the Catholic bishops had shuddered at the kinds of doctrine released into the heady atmosphere of 1798. As Archbishop Troy's biographer wrote: 'Democracy and the rights of man for him and his episcopal contemporaries were abominable aberrations against God and the monarchical state'.[6] Troy and Curtis of Armagh had treated the Protestant Establishment with the deference they naturally accorded to an institution which they believed enjoyed divine sanction. Troy's pastoral letter of 1793, 'On the duties of Christian citizens', had outlined very clearly the limits that Catholics must respect when making 'legitimate complaints' about their station. They must always be 'loyal and deco-rous'.

When they considered what had brought about this unpleasant change in the tone of the Catholic clergy, Protestants came up with several explanations. The Armagh Protestant Association blamed the aristocracy. 'They petted popery and winked at it. They wished to be considered liberal'.[7] But the aristocrats themselves blamed Maynooth. They recalled with nostalgia how the older generation of clergy who had been educated on the Continent had been 'lifted up' by their expo-sure to the aristocracy and made 'mild, amiable, cultivated, learned, polite'.[8] They believed Maynooth had had the opposite effect. The Maynooth man, Henry Inglis in his *Journey throughout Ireland* of 1834 concluded, was 'coarse, vulgar-minded . . . Popish to the backbone . . . it is the Maynooth priest who is the agitat-ing priest'.[9] This was a stereotype. The continental seminaries produced men like William Higgins, Bishop of Ardagh or, as he restyled himself, O'Higgins, a vitriolic anglophobe who hated the aristocracy, while Maynooth nurtured John Healy, Archbishop of Tuam, a learned conservative and one of the most sincere royalists on the bench.

That the tone at Maynooth in its early years was conservative was not surpris-ing. The college was positioned on the estate of the Duke of Leinster, and the front door stood opposite the entrance to the Protestant parish church. It was not an autonomous corporation. The law gave almost unlimited powers over college affairs to 21 trustees, of whom four were Protestants; two others were Troy and Curtis. Then there was the presence within the college walls of conservative French professors, men who had been scalded by personal experience of the Jacobin Revolution. They were not the type of men to encourage their students to question the social order. When James Doyle, Bishop of Kildare, warned the government that the Catholic clergy were becoming more democratic and less deferential than their predecessors, the remarks caused consternation in the college. 'Mon Dieu!' exclaimed L. E. Delahogue, the venerable professor of Dogmatic Theology, 'Est-ce possible qu'il prêche la Revolution?'[10] The professors countered the Bishop's letter with an address of their own, in which they insisted they had always 'uniformly inculcated allegiance to our gracious sovereign, respect for the constituted authorities and obedience to the laws'.[11]

Nevertheless, there was something in the Protestant complaints that Maynooth was failing to produce the type of priest the authorities had hoped for. The old system of dispersing seminarians throughout Europe had exposed them to a world in which absolute monarchy was the norm, and had at the same time prevented the creation of *esprit de corps*. Now, as Archbishop Healy, the college's historian observed, 'Kerry and Donegal, Meath and Connaught, could compare notes'.[12] The old barriers between the provinces melted away as Maynooth helped to forge a clergy who thought in national terms. Another complaint was that the Maynooth seminarians craved 'popularity', and that an excessive number of bursaries and scholarships had stimulated the growth of a plebeian priesthood who naturally identified with the mob. 'The priests who were educated in France had a natural abhorrence of the French Revolution', O'Connell told the House of Commons in 1825, 'but with the priests educated at Maynooth, the anti-Jacobin feeling is gone by and they are more identified with the people . . . '[13]

'The people' in question were not so much the landless cottiers as the priests' own parents, drawn mostly from the petty bourgeoisie. They were shopkeepers, small traders and farmers. These were the shock troops of O'Connell's Repeal movement and of the Catholic revival. In 1808 a survey showed that nearly three-quarters of the 205 seminarians at Maynooth were sons of farmers.[14] It explains why the Catholic clergy almost unreservedly backed the struggles of the tenant farmers against the landlords in Victorian Ireland. In the end, the old French professors gave way to men who did not share their belief in the divine right of kings. Delahogue was succeeded by John MacHale who as Archbishop of Tuam from 1834 to 1881 became known as the 'Lion of the Fold of Judah' for his fervent nationalism and opposition to every British government initiative.

The democratic priests presided over what has been styled a 'devotional revolution', a phrase which comprehends the suppression of looser, laxer, semi-pagan expressions of piety and the imposition of stricter, more regulated, continental practices. The construction of churches enabled the clergy to keep a much closer eye on their flocks. In Dublin, the pro-cathedral Troy had started was complete by 1825. In 1829, the foundation was laid for a new cathedral in Killala. Doyle's new cathedral in Carlow was completed in the same year. Cathedrals in Tuam, Armagh and Killarney followed in 1840. The new churches allowed priests to introduce new devotions, such as benediction, which could be tricky to undertake in the open air. They allowed for elaborate rituals and processions, which hardly made sense in a barn or on an outdoor 'mass rock'. The sacrament could be reserved; incense could be swung. Irish religion moved into the church building, away from the outdoors and away from private homes. This affected the balance of power. The church building was the priest's domain. The fact that religion increasingly took place on his home turf naturally exalted his status.

Bishop Doyle set the tone for the new era in Kildare in the 1820s, popularising retreats and confraternities and reviving the almost abandoned sacrament of confirmation: once the Bishop confirmed a vast crowd of 1,800 at Portarlington.[15] Doyle was the terror of slack clergy, humiliating them in front of their congregations if need be, tearing up their vestments and smashing their chalices if he found them in poor condition. He stopped priests from hunting – including one who said mass with spurs on his boots – and forbade them to attend the bibulous dinners that were customarily given after funerals and at stations. Doyle was a new type of bishop also in his relationship to the Ascendancy. After Archbishop Magee made his notorious sermon in St Patrick's in 1822, Doyle lambasted him with unprecedented boldness, pouring scorn on the Anglican Church's claim to have preserved the Apostolic succession of bishops. Magee had no more claim to be the successor of an apostle than he had to the dukedom of Leeds, Doyle sneered.

'Henry and Elizabeth and Cecil and Burnet and Tillotson and Taylor and Hoadley, these, my Lord, are the Apostles, the Fathers and the supporters of your Church'.[16]

Doyle did not attack abuses in the Establishment: he denied its right to exist. It was 'the scorpion's tail [which] is armed at all points and scourges the peasant through tithes and church rates till it draws his very blood', he said. It was an insulting and anomalous system, which expected peasants 'to feed the parson and his rapacious family and followers, who go about not doing good but vilify and calumniate the religion which this peasant reveres'.[17]

Doyle was Bishop of Kildare at a time when the Catholic clergy was becoming aware of the political power that was dropping into its hands. O'Connell was partly responsible for this. It was not simply that he was a devout Catholic. It was his decision that the campaign for emancipation must be a popular movement and that the clergy must be given a key role if it were to succeed. This was a new idea. Until the early 1820s, the business of lobbying for an improvement in Catholic rights had been the preserve of a handful of mostly aristocratic laymen under the leadership of Ireland's premier Catholic nobleman, the Earl of Fingal. The Catholic Committee that they dominated resisted giving the clergy any role in their proceedings. But O'Connell swept everything before him. In 1823 the Committee gave way to a New Catholic Association, which was under O'Connell's direction. 'Gentlemen,' he told them, 'We have a power that has never yet been called into the field, one that must coerce them [the British] to do us justice, and that is the priesthood of Ireland . . . to succeed we must have them with us, and from this day forward.'[18]

In 1824, O'Connell came up with the idea of raising a subscription from his supporters of a farthing a week. The goal of the 'Catholic rent', as it was called, was to net an annual income of £50,000, to finance petitions by the Association to Parliament, pay for a standing agent in London, set up Catholic newspapers and compensate the poorest and most numerous element in the electorate, the forty-shilling freeholders, when they supported the emancipation campaign against the wishes of their Protestant landlords.

Within weeks, the 'rent' was bringing in £900 a week, the landlords were terrified and O'Connell was on the road to becoming the uncrowned king of Ireland. The subscription was hugely popular, as the lines of the poem 'The New Catholic Rent', one of hundreds of political poems in the early 1820s, suggested:

No matter what critics may say
The Catholic rent we'll cheerfully pay
The heads of our country adopted this plan
And every class should assist who can.

Our King and his laws we'll always obey
And the Catholic rent with honour we'll pay

Our bumpers will be flowing in our native land
And toast to O'Connell with a full bumper in hand.[19]

The clergy were drafted into the whole operation. The Catholic Rent was organised on the basis of Catholic parish boundaries and the collection of the money inevitably devolved onto the clergy. Significantly, even when the government outlawed the Catholic Association in 1825, the Catholic clergy made no attempt to distance themselves from O'Connell.

The whole thrust of O'Connell's movement, which was Catholic, populist and royalist, appealed to the clergy so much more than the United Irishmen had done, with all the latter's atheist overtones and republican ideology. They infinitely preferred the devoutly Catholic Kerry man to the Protestant aristocratic freethinkers of '98.

The following year, O'Connell's supporters suggested that the Bishop of Waterford undertake a religious census of the diocese, with a view to producing some morale-boosting material for the supporters of Catholic Emancipation. The figures the clergy produced underlined the narrow base on which Protestant Ascendancy rested in Waterford. In Ardmore parish there were 7,800 Catholics and only 39 Protestants; at Kilgobbin there were 3,799 Catholics and 4 Protestants; at Ring; 2,464 Catholics lived with 20 Protestants; at Dungarvan 6,592 Catholics shared the parish with 168 Protestants; and in the parish of Trinity, in Waterford city itself, there were 3,755 Catholics and a mere 366 Protestants.[20]

The publication of the clerical survey was the prelude to an unprecedented clerical revolt in Waterford against the dominant Beresford family. That year there was a by-election for the seat in parliament. The family's candidate, Lord George Beresford, saw the contest as a trial of strength against the awakened Roman clergy. In the *Waterford Mirror* he urged electors to vote against 'itinerant orators . . . aided by a portion of the Roman Catholic clergy' who were bent on 'excluding the rank, the Wealth and the Intelligence of the County from a share in its representation'.[21] For his part, O'Connell urged the electors to choose Beresford's opponent, Henry Villiers Stuart. 'On the one side is Stuart, freedom and Catholic emancipation', he said. 'On the other is Beresford, slavery and Ireland's continued degradation.'

The electors defied 'Rank, wealth and intelligence' and followed the lead of O'Connell and the clergy. At the election meeting on 22 June, Beresford endured the humiliation of being booed and losing the seat that his family had held as if by right for generations. He was absolutely furious. The Catholic clergy had 'employed all their influence over a deluded multitude for the establishment of a despotism which threatens to involve our laws and liberties in one common ruin', he complained.[22] The poll was, in fact, a watershed. On one side, as Beresford had put it, stood Property and on the other, the priests. The priests had won.

After the Waterford poll, the Ascendancy looked doomed, though it was not until 1828 that O'Connell decided to test his movement's strength by contesting an election himself. The occasion presented itself when Vesey Fitzgerald, one of the members for the county of Clare, resigned his seat to become President of the Board of Trade. As the angry chronicler of the year 1828 spluttered in the pages of the *Annual Register*,

> From the moment his intention of opposing Mr Fitzgerald was announced, the County of Clare was traversed in every direction by the orators of the Association and the popish parish priests. With unwearied activity they hurried from parish to parish, assembling and haranguing the squalid electors. The places which they chose for their convocations were the popish chapels . . . partly to aid the religious character which their mission instantly assumed. As Mr [Richard Lalor] Shiel, one of their most flowery rhetoricians after wards said, 'Every altar became a tribune'. . . . On the day of the election (30th June) the forty-shilling freeholders were marched into Ennis, the county town, in regular bands, each led to the hustings by the parish priest to vote 'for God and O'Connell'.[23]

The Protestants saw O'Connell's victory in Clare as a repeat of the events in Waterford, and as grim confirmation of the fact that 'rank' and 'property' were being forced onto the defensive in Ireland by the new force of democracy. At the hustings in Ennis, Sir Edward O'Brien, the greatest landlord in Clare wept openly when he heard of O'Connell's victory, and exclaimed that 'the country was not one fit for a gentleman to reside in, when property lost all its influence, and things were brought to such a pass'.[24] The only question was whether the 'ancien régime' would resist, or sue for peace. The sudden proliferaton of Protestant 'Brunswick clubs' in Ireland showed many Irish Protestants trusted the Tory government not to yield an inch. The expectation in their ranks was that a ministry led by the Duke of Wellington would never give in to pressure.

They were totally mistaken. Wellington and the Home Secretary, Robert Peel, MP for Oxford University, had consistently voted against Catholic Emancipation and as late as December 1828 it appeared the Iron Duke had not changed his mind. On 4 December, his old protégé, Archbishop Curtis wrote to him urging a settlement on the question of Emancipation to save Ireland from further agitation. Wellington replied courteously on the 11th, insisting the best course would be to 'bury' the controversy for the foreseeable future. The Protestants were heartened. Primate Curtis forwarded this correspondence to the Marquis of Anglesea, the Lord Lieutenant. Lord Anglesea returned a most encouraging answer to the Catholic Primate, advising the Catholics to continue with the tactics of pacific agitation. The Marquis was abruptly recalled and replaced by the Duke of Northumberland.

The Orange Protestants were again reassured by the administration's display of resolution. But a volte face followed within days. When Parliament reassembled on 5 February 1829, the King's Speech, read out by the Lord Chancellor, contained the explosive information that the government planned to 'review the laws which impose civil disabilities on His Majesty's Roman Catholic Subjects'. Wellington was pilloried in the Tory press as a turncoat. Cartoons depicted the Prime Minister and O'Connell together murdering 'Mrs Constitution', or pulling down a steeple representing the Church of England. Peel was forced to vacate his Oxford seat. But the former stalwarts for Protestant Ascendancy were not dissuaded from the course they had decided on after the Clare election opened up the alarming prospect of 70 Irish Catholic MPs being elected to the next parliament, none of whom would be able to take up their seats. The government's emancipation bill passed the Commons by a majority of 353 to 180 and the Lords by a surprisingly large majority of 213 to 109. The bill received George IV's most unwilling assent on 13 April.

Catholic Emancipation in 1829 and the Reform Bill of 1832, which swept away the rotten boroughs, strengthened the clergy's influence. In the elections in Carlow in 1832, O'Connell's ally, Richard Lalor Sheil, noted that the Tory interest had been broken 'by a single touch of his [Bishop Doyle's] magical crozier'. 'Strange vicissitudes! Who would have conjectured that a bachelor of Coimbra, and afterwards a priest in Wexford should now with a mitre as lofty as Beckett's . . . legislate for the passions of the people . . . and by the simple intimation of his will accomplish that which not a peer in the empire could have effected?'[25]

Doyle did not wholly relish his role as a herald of a new age of church power. He anticipated the new democratic era and to an extent had ushered it in, but he distrusted and occasionally deplored the consequences. He was content to be a British Irishman. In the 1820s he thought it insane that anyone 'in possession of the rights and privileges of a British subject' could want to give them up. He was ambivalent about O'Connell and the agitation he began for repeal of the Union in 1831 and supported the Whig government's decision to respond to the pressure with a coercion bill. The 'despotism of gentlemen', he revealingly declared, was always preferable to the 'brutal canaille composing the Trades' Unions and the Blackfeet [agrarian protesters] confederacies'.[26]

Doyle died in 1834. His successors were less ambivalent about O'Connell or the Church's role in politics. MacHale was made Archbishop of Tuam the year Doyle died. As a professor at Maynooth, he may have worked under Delahogue, and in 1822 he attacked English Whigs for talking lightly of the royal prerogative[27] and spoke of the 'glorious spectacle' of George IV's recent visit to Ireland. But as Archbishop he was an avid Repealer, even addressing O'Connell as 'conqueror'.[28]

MacHale, Cantwell of Meath and Higgins of Ardagh formed the advance guard of radical nationalism in the Irish Church. They employed the fiercely democratic language that Doyle in 1824 had predicted was becoming the norm among the Catholic clergy. They inhabited a different universe from that of Troy and were dedicated supporters of O'Connell's Repeal movement. They took the vast majority of the clergy with them. O'Connell had designated 1843 the Year of Repeal and staged a series of vast rallies to increase pressure on parliament. At the Mullingar meeting on 14 May, Cantwell and Higgins both ascended the platform, while Higgins made an inflammatory speech at the dinner that followed, in which he excoriated the aristocracy. 'I not only belong to the people but I am proud to proclaim it to you', the Bishop declared. 'I belong to the very humblest class of people. I do speak it with pride for to no aristocrat on earth do I owe anything, save for the unbounded contempt I have for the whole class'.[29] Higgins hurled a gauntlet at the authorities and addressed them in ringing tones. 'I for one defy all the ministers of England to put down agitation in the diocese of Ardagh', he said. 'If they attempt, my friends, to rob us of the daylight . . . and to prevent us from assembling in the open fields, we will retire to our chapels and suspend all other instructions in order to devote all our time to teaching the people to be Repealers in spite of them!'

This new discourse was practically the language of class war. Not all bishops used it, but it was significant that none of them denounced it. It was not Higgins and his friends but the conservative and the anti-Repeal bishops, led by Daniel Murray, who had succeeded Troy in Dublin in 1823, who felt on the defensive. By the 1840s, opinions that were customary only a few years previously were now the mark of the 'Castle hack', the 'Castle Catholic', or as Cantwell revealingly put it, the 'bad or Aristocratic Catholics'.[30] Murray thought the Repeal agitation a 'desperate and dangerous infatuation',[31] but only half a dozen, at most, of the 20 bishops shared his opinion. The average priest was far more attracted to the party of MacHale, Cantwell and Higgins than to Murray. They naturally wanted to stand at the head of a movement which commanded the ardent support of millions of their compatriots and which needed and acknowledged their restraining hand. The priests did not impose themselves on the Repeal movement: the Repealers offered them the front seats and the reins.

At the Repeal meeting at Limerick in January 1843, the preponderance of clergy in local leadership positions was striking. O'Connell was surrounded by priests at the dinner afterwards, including the Archdeacon of Limerick and the parish priests of Newcastle, Abbeyfeale, Ashford, Ardagh, Glynn, Monaghan, Tournafulla, Knockaderry and Coolecappe, alongside a host of curates.[32] A priest chaired the Repeal meeting at Louisburgh, County Clare, in February. The clergy were prominent on the platform of the big meeting at Trim on 19 March. The meeting at Fedamore, County Limerick, in March was chaired by a priest, while at the monster meeting at Bellewstown, County Meath, on 9 April, speakers included the priests of the nearby parishes of Duleek and Ardcath in County Meath. At Clones, County Monashan, on 17 April the chair and secretary of the meeting were both clergy as were practically all the speakers. At Kells, County Meath, on 23 March Bishop Cantwell graced the platform of the monster meeting, which drew a crowd of about 150,000. At Mullingar, County

Westmeath besides Bishops Higgins and Cantwell, at least 41 clergy were present at the dinner.

The new assertiveness coursing through the veins of the Church transformed its relationship with the government. A few years earlier it had seemed probable that the Irish Catholic Church and the British state would move into a closer partnership. Now all of that changed and the Church began to treat every initiative of the state with almost hysterical suspicion. The first evidence of this atmosphere of hostility was seen in the battle over education. School reform was a Whig hobby-horse and as soon as the Whigs came into government in 1830 they decided to try out a new system in Ireland. The plan for a state-funded national school system appeared greatly to benefit the Catholic clergy, who stood to gain from a system that would free the Catholic poor from the choice of having no education at all, or attending the proselytising establishments of the Protestant missionaries.

In the previous decade the Tory government had channelled money in Ireland towards a charity, the Kildare Place Society, which did not run schools but supplied funds for the buildings and the teaching staff. The Kildare society was outwardly non-denominational but as the decade progressed Catholics became more wary of it, suspecting large-scale penetration by evangelicals of the Second Reformation variety. In any case, the management was overwhelmingly Protestant. The Whigs proposed to sweep away the voluntary system, withdraw all funds to the Kildare society and the Church of Ireland schools and create a national system controlled by a board on which Catholics would be properly represented. They expected the Catholic clergy to welcome a scheme that was obviously going to benefit their flock more than the Protestants, and cut off government funds to Protestant church schools. But in the increasingly charged, not to say poisoned, atmosphere, nothing was that simple. Like O'Connell, the Repeal bishops viewed all British acts with equal suspicion. The fact that it was a government plan condemned it. Bishop Doyle had deplored such tendencies, voicing his disgust when O'Connell opposed reform of the Irish Poor Laws. But after Doyle's death, the balance of power in the Church tipped towards the radical wing.

It was true that the Catholics at first gained only two of the six seats on the new Board of Education, but it was blindingly obvious that the Established Church was the great loser from the reform. It was certainly obvious to Primate Beresford, who – unlike Whately – protested bitterly against its introduction.

Paul Cullen, Rector of the Irish College in Rome and the Irish hierarchy's agent in Rome, could not fathom why any Catholic should object to the National Schools. The rising star of the Irish Church belonged temperamentally with the Repeal bishops rather than with the men of the old school. He typified the new strain of ultramontane orthodoxy that took a dim view of Murray's genial stance towards Protestants. Yet Cullen pronounced the National School system entirely unobjectionable. 'They could not be more Catholic than they are', he reported to Rome after starting an inspection of schools in Dublin and Kildare in July 1840.

'The teachers are Catholic, the pupils are Catholic and the principal occupation of the children is learning the Christian doctrine. Provided there is a guarantee the system would not be changed, I think things are going pretty well.'[33]

But nothing could assuage the furious opposition of MacHale, Cantwell and Higgins who in company with Bishop Keating of Ferns denounced the entire system to Rome in February 1838 as a wicked trick aimed at robbing the people of their faith. 'We have with us the Catholic feeling of Ireland', Higgins told Cullen, writing off all the supporters of the National Schools as 'Castle-hack Catholics as well as the heretical or Voltairean Liberals of the Empire'.[34]

Murray of Dublin and William Crolly of Armagh both supported the National Schools. But when the Irish bishops assembled on 22 January 1839 to hammer out an agreed strategy on the schools, the primates were able to rally only 15 out of 25 bishops to their side. It was a distinct majority but not a convincing one and the outcome merely emboldened the dissidents to appeal again to Rome, which issued an opaque judgment on the subject in January 1841.

The Whigs had got their fingers burnt in Ireland over education but the Tories fared no better when they returned to office under Peel in 1841. The new administration indicated its wish to forge a working relationship with the Irish Catholic bishops in 1844 by tripling the Maynooth grant to £26,360. There was no opposition to that, yet the gesture brought Peel no goodwill when he decided to complement the Whigs' non-denominational school system in Ireland with a network of non-denominational universities. Peel proposed to build four 'Queen's colleges', one for each of the historic provinces, sited in Dublin, Belfast, Cork and Galway. It was a tremendous project, which would give an enormous boost to each of the cities concerned. Ireland, for so long the laboratory for English experiments of the worst kind, was at last to reap a few benefits. The Belfast Presbyterians were delighted that the government wanted to endow a university they would inevitably dominate. Queen's University Belfast was born. But the Catholic hierarchy ensured the colleges in the south were stifled. The fight ran over exactly the same ground as it had with the National Schools. The Church wanted a denominational system or nothing at all. The only difference was that opinion in the Church had now swung further from the moderates and towards MacHale and the party of confrontation. The two archbishops supported the Queen's Colleges but only four of the bishops joined them and their humiliation was complete when Rome condemned the colleges on 13 July 1846. 'Rejoice, Catholic Ireland', crowed the *Freeman's Journal*. 'Your ancient faith is safe.'[35]

The alienation of the Irish Catholic Church from the British state in the late 1830s and 1840s had momentous consequences when the potatoes – the sole food source of millions – failed in 1845. Crop failures were not new. Ireland had been hit by a disastrous famine in 1741–42, and again as recently as 1822, when wealthy English Protestants contributed enough to stave off total disaster. But conditions since then had worsened. The population climbed remorselessly to a new peak of 8,175,124 in 1841. There was nothing wrong with that in itself; the problem was that in a predominantly rural economy they lived on an increasingly overcrowded land. Some 2.5 million were landless labourers, dependent on seasonal work and the tiny potato patches outside their cabins for survival. The constant subdivision of holdings meant that work was hard to come by. More than 90 per cent of farms now consisted of less than 30 acres.

The crop failed at a time of bitter conflict between the church of the vast majority of victims and the agencies that might have done more to relieve them. The churches and voluntary societies acting on their own, of course, could not have stopped the famine. As the Society of Friends told the government in June 1849, the famine was far beyond the capacity of private institutions to resolve and could only be tackled ultimately by a programme of land reform. But the remorseless free market economics of the Treasury killed a million people, the vast majority between 1846 and 1849, by which time the interventionist Peel had been replaced by the Whigs under Lord John Russell, and Peel's public works schemes had been wound up.

What added to the disaster was the way the famine became a sordid battleground for the Protestant and Catholic Churches over the issue of proselytising. The venom that had invaded relations between priest and rector since the Second Reformation ensured that the biggest catastrophe to befall the country since the Cromwellian transplantation deepened the enmity between the Churches.

The Catholic clergy were not unprovoked. Some Protestant clergymen, like James Morgan of Belfast, transferred to the famine their bitterness at the failure of the Second Reformation. Morgan wrote a short book, *Thoughts on the Famine,* which described the crop failure as an act of divine punishment against the Catholics for their continuing idolatry. God blasted the potato because the Irish Catholics had broken the Second Commandment, he said. Morgan looked on the spectacle of piles of corpses and villages stalked by death and saw the hand of the Almighty. 'God is now asserting his claim to a pure and spiritual worship', he reminded his comfortable audience. 'His Bible has been burned in this land and he is consuming it for so great iniquity'.[36] Lest his congregation feel too complacent, he reminded them that the implacable eye of heaven would not miss the 500 public houses open in Belfast. When the Presbyterians presented the Lord-Lieutenant with an address congratulating the government on its generosity in September 1847, they added that it was 'gratifying to discover that Ulster has been less chargeable to the public than any other of the provinces'.[37] They attributed this to their own 'peaceableness, industry and frugality'. It was the old line. The feckless, rebellious Catholics were reaping the rewards of their rebelliousness and slovenliness.

Archbishop Beresford did not support this view. The Primate told his people to gain the blessing of heaven by helping the victims and in 1846 he set a day (30 October) when Protestants should not only pray for the victims but 'relieve them to the utmost of their power, open their hands wide unto their brethren, deal bread to the hungry and when they see the naked, to cover them'.[38]

The Catholic priests carried by far the greatest load in ministering to the sick and dying. In 1847 the *Cork Examiner* reported on the state of the village of Millstreet, County Cork. 'Fever, dropsy and dysentery are daily increasing in malignity and mowing down the population with frightful rapidity', it said. 'The parish priest's house is from morning to night in a state of siege from crowds of starving people and the Rev. Mr Maginn is now lying down in a bad fever. The parish coffin, a machine so constructed as to hold three bodies, is in constant requisition and may be seen at all hours of the day and night borne through the town towards the grave pit. It is chiefly carried by women.'[39]

In June of that year, the Catholic clergy's half-yearly reports on famine-related deaths showed the extent of the crisis in the villages. There were 150 dead in Kildeysart, County Clare, 95 in Castletownroche, County Cork, 200 in Cloone, County Leitrim, 300 in Carracastle, County Mayo and 186 in Adragool, County Galway. In Adragool, the parish priest reported seeing a man whose jaws had rotted away and literally dropped off with hunger, and other families 'who have nothing but the appearance of spectres actually crawling along on all fours, or stretched out for death'.[40]

The diocese of Elphin produced a detailed survey of the famine in October 1847 in response to a request from the bishops of Connacht. In the parish of Elphin itself, the population had dropped from 8,000 to 5,334, a loss of more than 2,600. Of those 2,600 or so, about 1,000 had died in the parish, 360 from starvation and the rest from dysentery and other famine-related diseases.[41] The rest had emigrated, and their fate was unknown.

John Aylward, parish priest of Clough, near Castlecomer, County Kilkenny, wrote to the *Freeman's Journal* in June 1847, describing the nightmarish scenes he had witnessed in his parish. He said there had been only 16 hunger-related deaths in the village up to June 1846, when the effect of the famine was mitigated by the Tory government's public works schemes. The number of deaths increased tenfold in the year that followed, after the new Whig administration wound up the scheme. 'The people are maddened with hunger,' he wrote. 'They have death in their countenances, marching and counter-marching to and from Comer. The cabins of most of them are without a morsel of food. The deaf, the dumb, the lame and the blind are cut off from the lists and left to perish with hunger'. The priest said he had just finished visiting a boy and a girl whom he found both naked and starving.[42]

At Ballintober, County Mayo, the parish priest in November reported 840 famine deaths in just over a year. Of the 9,000 survivors, he estimated that about 100 families were living in a state of total destitution. 'The families above alluded to are almost naked', he told the *Freeman's Journal*. 'The chapels are almost empty, owing to the want of clothing'.[43]

In Dublin, with its large Protestant population, and in parts of west Cork, the famine claimed Protestant victims as well. But the vast majority of famine victims were Catholics, and it was the Catholic clergy who buried them and in many cases died along with their flocks.

1. The power of shrines: *Pilgrims at Clonmacnoise* by George Petrie, 1828.

Mr Ffordes house rifled. and to make her Confesse where her mony lay. they tooke hot tonges clappinge them to the Soules of her feete & to the Palmes of her handes so tormented her that with the paine thereof shee died.

N

They haue set men & women on hot Grideorns to make them Confesse Where there money was.

O

2. Cromwell's excuse: Irish Catholics torturing English Protestants, a seventeenth-century English school engraving.

3. Catholic martyr: *Oliver Plunkett*, 1625–81 by an unnamed artist.

4. Protestant Jerusalem: Londonderry is besieged by King James II's forces, 1689, an unattributed engraving, 1690.

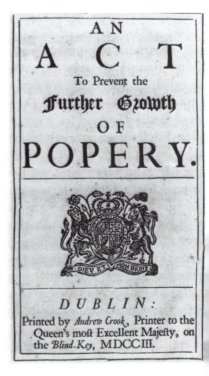

AN

A C T

To Prevent the

Further Growth

OF

POPERY.

DUBLIN:

Printed by *Andrew Crook*, Printer to the Queen's moſt Excellent Majeſty, on the *Blind-Key*, MDCCIII.

5. Penal law: frontispiece of anti-Catholic legislation promulgated by the Dublin Parliament, 1703.

6. Protestant Ascendancy: *Bishop Robert Clayton and his Wife* by James Latham, 1730s.

7. Failed Reformation: Protestant church in ruins in Turmatredy, Co. Galway.

8. English planters: Boyle family tomb at Youghal church, Co. Cork.

9. Church of the Irish College in Paris, with coat of arms defaced in the Revolution.

10. Aristocratic radical: *Frederick Augustus Hervey, Bishop of Derry with his Granddaughter* by Hugh Douglas Hamilton, 1790.

11 a and b. Daniel O'Connell – Liberator?: (*left*) portrait by Bernard Mulrenin, 1836; (*below*) *The Humble Candidate,* an English school lithograph depicting O'Connell kneeling before a Catholic bishop in the 1828 election.

12. Faith driven outdoors: *A Mass in the Mountains of Donegal* by Alexander Ayton, 1867.

13. A nation of prayer: going to church on Sunday morning (in the north), *c.* 1900.

14. Prince of the Church: *His Eminence Paul Cardinal Cullen.*

15. Corpus Christi procession in Tobercurry, Co. Sligo, 1932.

16. Here we stand: Ulster Unionists signing the Covenant on Ulster Day, 1912, Belfast.

17. Clergy at play: priests playing cards on Lough Gill, Co. Sligo, 1929.

18. Triumph of the faith: Children's Mass in Phoenix Park, Dublin, Eucharistic Congress, 1932.

19. View of crowds in
O'Connell Street, Dublin,
Eucharistic Congress, 1932.

20. Church and State:
President Eamon de Valera
talking to Cardinal Hayes,
Archbishop of New York, 1
July 1932.

21 a and b. Pilgrimage to Knock, *c.* 1870 and (*below*) a modern view of the shrine.

22. Crowds leaving Corpus Christi church, Griffith Avenue, Dublin, 1948.

23. Calvin's man: Ian Paisley at an anti-Catholic protest, 1970.

24. Pope John Paul II on his way to Drogheda, 1979.

25. Scandalous priest: Bishop Eamonn Casey, when Bishop of Kerry, *c.* 1971.

26. Grand but empty: St Peter's, Church of Ireland, Drogheda.

27. Orange shrine: Dan Winters' Cottage, Loughsall, Co. Armagh.

28. Feeling besieged: Apprentice Boys' Parade, Derry.

29. Message of hate: Protestant mural, Waterside, Londonderry.

30. Aping the IRA: Protestant paramilitary mural in Shankhill area of West Belfast.

31. Still needed?: 'Priest On Duty', Drogheda.

The Protestant clergy in the southern counties could not stand apart from such a disaster. They joined relief committees, and sponsored and managed soup kitchens. As the wealthiest residents in many parishes, they were the obvious candidates to head local charitable activity. They did so out of a conviction that the job of an Established Church was to serve the community, including those who rejected their religious functions; they had always denied that they existed only to serve Protestants. As the *Plea for the Church in Ireland* put it in patronising terms in 1834, the Established clergy were put in place to serve 'the benighted and ignorant Irish peasant' as well as the true believer.[44] The Rector of Cong in County Mayo made desperate appeals for help to the press on behalf of his Catholic parishioners. 'Fever in all its varied forms is surrounding us and making fearful ravages', he wrote. 'I entreat, I implore in the name of Him who is the silver and gold, your prompt, your liberal assistance'.[45] Some sacrificed their lives. In 1847 alone, 40 Protestant clergy died from famine fever. When Patrick Pounden, the Rector of Westport in County Mayo died, it was found that he had been giving half his stipend to the local relief committee.[46]

There were few reported cases of Protestant clergymen using their role as distributors of food to engineer a change in religious allegiances. The 1848 survey of Elphin diocese produced only one area where this activity was going on. At Killarkin and Eastertown, it said, Protestant clergymen were distributing clothing to the hungry 'on condition of parents sending their children to proselytising schools, or themselves appearing at church or lecture'. The Presbyterians were also involved, according to the priest, and 'every effort is being made to lead our starving people away from the faith'.[47]

Famine proselytisers were a marginal phenomenon. Whately had publicly condemned the notion of 'holding out relief of bodily wants and sufferings as a bribe' in September 1848.[48] This was not countenanced by the other Church of Ireland bishops either. The Protestant clergy had to work with their Catholic counterparts on the relief committees and had few opportunities to tease out converts. But Cullen, who had not been in Ireland during the famine, made great play of the supposed key role of proselytisers in relief work. The 'soupers' were the main focus of his wrath as soon as he was installed as Archbishop of Armagh. It marked a great change from the era of Crolly, who had always tried to see the best in the Protestants and worked happily with their clergy. Cullen issued his first pastoral letter from Rome in February 1850, just as the country was recovering from the worst of the potato blight. The 'apostles of error have availed themselves of the late calamities in Ireland to propagate Protestantism', he told Ireland. These 'emissaries of the enemy of mankind', as he styled them, had endeavoured

to induce them to barter their souls for a mess of pottage held out for them in the hour of hunger . . . If any of them come among you, reverend brethren, and attempt to seduce the poor from the faith, or to poison them with error, be most active and watchful in defeating their schemes, however plausible they may appear . . . if anyone preach to you a gospel besides that which you have received, let him be anathema.[49]

Cullen repeated this theme at the reforming synod he convoked in Thurles,[50] which opened on 9 September, and returned to it once more when he addressed the Catholic Association in Dublin on 29 January 1852. This time, Cullen announced that the proselytisers had, in fact, failed. The Irish Catholics were stronger in the faith than ever, 'even though many of them during the years of Famine underwent all the horrors of a lingering death inflicted by starvation rather than accept the bribe offered them by the tempter'. After his translation from Armagh to Dublin in 1852, Cullen decided his feelings of relief over the failure of the soupers had been premature. By 1855 the danger of proselytising was as bad as ever and in a pastoral letter, 'On the vile system of pecuniary proselytism', he alerted Catholic Ireland to the danger posed by this bogey. 'We are no longer assailed by open persecution and cruel edicts,' he wrote, 'but we have among us wolves in sheep's clothing, lying in wait for the tender lambs of the fold. Confiscation of property, exile, the rack, the sword so often employed against our fathers, are no longer spoken of. Education, charity, the Bible are now inscribed upon the banners of those whose bigotry and fanaticism in past days delighted in persecution and blood.'[51]

Cullen fired off a new pastoral letter on the subject of proselytisers in June 1856.[52] In it he listed 21 missionary societies operating in Dublin alone, including the Society for Defending the Rights of Conscience, which Whately, hardly the friend of soupers, had established.

Where Cullen led, the nation followed. It became an established fact, carved in tablets of stone, that while a million Irish starved to death, droves of Protestants toured the ravaged villages dangling titbits before the salivating mouths of starving peasants on condition that they change their religion. 'These things are so notorious in Ireland,' the Catholic Defence Association complained in 1852, 'it is so well known that multitudes have died of hunger and pestilence who might have saved their lives by a pretended conversion to the Established religion'.[53] Henry Wilberforce, the Association's convert secretary, and brother to the Anglican Bishop of Oxford, cited 'a little girl' from a starving family struck by the famine, who had returned to the true Church after being briefly seduced by soupers. She was 'looking forward to certain starvation from the loss of her former allowance', Wilberforce reported, but had 'conjured her mother not to put into her mouth (when she became too weak to speak) any food which came from the Protestant ministers, fearing lest her mother be tempted to return to her former apostasy in order to preserve the life of her child.'[54]

Was this exposure or calumny? Protestant missionaries in Connacht in the early 1840s generated much of the furore, unwisely popularising trifling victories in books that crowed prematurely about the collapse of Catholicism in MacHale's western fiefdom. In 1845 Mrs Thompson's *Brief Account of the Rise and Progress of the Change in Religious Opinions Now Taking Place in Dingle* had alerted everyone in the Catholic Church to the fact that the evangelical Irish Society had bussed in 20 teachers to the Dingle peninsula in the 1830s, along with a resident pastor.[55]

The high days of the Protestant mission in Dingle were over before the potato crop failed. The Protestant colony there peaked in 1843, when the congregation reached 500. The famine was not a boon but a disaster for the missionaries in the west of Ireland. It mowed down the class of landless peasants that had supplied them with most of their recruits and left in place the shopkeepers and farmers who were their bitterest enemies. In imperial Ireland, as in imperial India, it was the poorest of the poor, not the bourgeoisie, who turned Protestant, often because no one else had previously bothered to instruct them. The famine massively increased the incentive to get out of a country that seemed to labour under a curse, and the Protestant converts left for Canada and America with everyone else. Even in 1844, Mrs Thompson had admitted that many of their converts were emigrating. 'Whole families have been shipped off to America while many of our best-taught converts are acting as school masters and school mistresses throughout the length and breadth of Ireland. This not only prevents the apparent growth of the body but withdraws from it perpetually the best members.'[56] By 1849, Archbishop Beresford heard that a 'passion to emigrate' had gripped the Protestant community in Ulster and that the inevitable consequence would be 'many ruined landlords and many unoccupied farms'.[57]

The last spurt of activity from the missionaries in Connacht came in the 1850s and 1860s, when the Irish Church Mission under Alexander Dallas succeeded in raising funds to set up mission stations at Oughterard, Cornamona, Glengula and Spiddal. But the emigrant ships succeeded in carrying off most of the Protestant converts within a generation and the Irish Church Mission did not profit from the famine; it began its work in 1849, when the worst of the crisis was over.

The Catholic campaign against souperism encouraged Protestants in the comforting conviction that they were better off doing nothing to relieve misery in Ireland. Dallas boasted to Henry Wilberforce in 1852 that his society had not spent one penny on relieving hunger. He told him that his men had 'strongly resisted the pressure of the most distressing emergencies and refused to devote one farthing of their funds to confer temporal advantages or to relieve temporal wants, even when the alternative has been loss of life'.[58] In fact, Dallas was proud of having delivered a lecture on the joys of Protestantism to what he described as a group of 'living skeletons', in Connemara in 1848. 'I never set forth the salvation of Christ under so strong a feeling that my hearers would soon be called to experience the truth of my statement', he marvelled. 'As I stepped into my boat I prayed for them.' There was certainly no question of offering soup.

Cullen deliberately took the war for the souls of the Irish to new heights. Priests who reached out to the community and forgot the importance of the denominational struggle with Protestantism were warned in silken tones to change their style. Theobald Matthew, the 'apostle of temperance' in Cork was one of the first to be slapped down. The temperance campaign tapped into a deep desire to take control over one's life. In the Catholic population it was the spiritual auxiliary to the Repeal movement. They were both, ultimately, about dignity and independence. Matthew's campaign had made him a popular hero and on 30 March 1839, 10,000 Dubliners stood in the rain outside the Custom House to take the Total Abstinence Society pledge, kneeling in the mud and sawdust that had been put down for the occasion to repeat the words after the friar.[59] 'It was delightful to observe the mode in which Father Matthew was always received as he passed through the streets of Cork', an observer wrote in 1840. 'They touched their hats and made way for him; the women curtsied, brightly smiling, apparently deeming it a good omen that they had seen their good shepherd that day.'[60] Asenath Nicholson, the American Protestant missionary who crossed swords with the Nangles in Achill, was utterly won over by him. She wrote of how privileged she felt to sit next to him at dinner.

Cullen opposed this fraternisation across the denominational lines. 'You appear to entertain sentiments too liberal towards Protestants', he wrote to the friar from Rome on 10 October 1841. 'I suppose there is no real foundation for this complaint . . . however it is well to be cautious. We should entertain the most expansive sentiments of charity towards Protestants but at the same time we should let them know that there is but one true Church . . . otherwise we might lull them into a false security in their errors and by doing so we would really violate charity.'[61]

In Armagh, Cullen put a stop to the custom that Archbishop Murray had started of Catholic and Protestant archbishops calling on one another. It was his proud boast that he had never dined with a Protestant and when Beresford paid the expected courtesy call, he found the Catholic Archbishop out and went away confused, having left his card.[62] Naturally, the visit was not returned.

Cullen founded the Catholic Defence Association in September 1851 to put the Catholics on their mettle. It was his aim, he said, to expel 'that spirit of religious indifference, which would abolish every distinction between Catholics and Protestants'.[63] Now, he declared, 'Catholics will be Catholics'.

When he moved to Dublin, the spirit of strife moved to the Irish capital with him. The old, easy relations between the Protestant and Catholic archbishops in Dublin disintegrated at once. Whately was shocked at the difference between Murray and his successor, who at once picked a fight with his Protestant counterpart over the National Schools.

Cullen had supported the National Schools against MacHale and the ultra-nationalists. At that time, he had spotted no problems in the curriculum and had even remarked that the schools were one of the means by which the whole of Ireland was being brought into the true fold. Once in Dublin, he retracted his former good opinions and uncovered a bunch of heresies festering away in the book of scriptural extracts used in the schools, which Whately had compiled in 1837.

Cullen's predecessor, Archbishop Murray, had not found fault with Whately's *Easy Lessons on Christian Evidences*, but Cullen needed a confrontation to test the strength of the reinvigorated Catholic Church. He made the removal of Whately's book the price of his continuing membership of the Education Board. Rather than risk a breach with the Church, the board felt it had no option but to withdraw the volume. Whately could hardly remain now that the board had implicitly accepted Cullen's verdict on his book, and resigned. It was the result Cullen had intended all the time. 'The downfall of the Archbishop is very favourable to us', he exulted to Cardinal Frasconi in August, 'because in the first place he was a very subtle and crafty enemy and in the second because it has shown to the other commissioners that they cannot injure our religion with impunity.'[64]

The sullen, suspicious atmosphere Cullen introduced to Dublin had negative repercussions, however, on his plan to start a Catholic university in the capital. Had the genial Murray headed the scheme, wealthy Protestant purses would have snapped open. Irish Protestants had, after all, bankrolled the construction of many Irish Catholic churches and cathedrals. Cullen's isolationism, and his insistence that every Protestant gesture was deceitful, ensured the university project fell back on to the tighter, smaller purses of the Catholic middle class. No committed Protestant was going to help Cullen after the way he had torpedoed their own Archbishop over the scripture extracts. Nor would many of the Catholic bishops themselves get involved after Cullen selected the English convert John Henry Newman as Rector. MacHale was almost as apoplectic about the university as he had been about the National Schools and the Queen's Colleges. The Pope handed the Catholic University of Dublin a brief in March 1854, Newman was formally installed as Rector on 4 June and the first lectures began on 3 November.

Snug behind its Georgian portals, Trinity could afford to smirk at this upstart. Neither money nor students flowed in. The lower middle-class Catholics of Dublin were not interested in spending their hard-won cash on sending their sons to a university to hear Dr Newman. The upper middle-class Catholics preferred to risk the anger of their bishops and send their sons to Trinity or Oxford. Newman had foreseen a problem with the university's limited catchment and had tried to circumvent it by appealing to a wider English-speaking Catholic audience in Ireland, England and the empire. He failed. Newman grew increasingly miserable. Cullen became curiously elusive. In the spring of 1857 'the hope of the university being English as well as Irish was quite at an end'[65] and Newman resigned. He left Ireland for good on 4 November 1858. Apart from the medical school, almost the only tangible legacy of this once grand project is the university church built in Merrion Square, which today is one of the Dubliners' favourite buildings. But it was built almost entirely at Newman's personal expense.

Cullen raised the prestige of the Catholic Church in Ireland to heights unimagined by his easygoing predecessors. He consigned lingering habits of deference to the dustbin. When he went to Kildare in February 1867, awe-struck newspapers compared the pomp and circumstance to a royal progress. There were vast crowds at the railway station, the Archbishop passed under triumphal arches, and flowery speeches of welcome were delivered to a man referred to revealingly as 'the Prince of Our Church'.[66]

The price of his tactics was a perceptible increase in confessional strife that had huge political consequences as the question of Irish Home Rule loomed on the horizon. Whately had always opposed conversions and the evangelical tendency to demonise Catholics. Licking his wounds after retiring from the Board of Education, he felt very differently. In October 1853 he complained of the 'insolent and overbearing proceedings of Roman Catholics and the disgust and the dread felt by Protestants'. The government, he complained, 'means to allow Roman Catholic "ascendancy" to the same extent as Protestant "ascendancy" formerly prevailed'.

On 28 June 1840, Father John Miley preached in the cathedral in Dublin at a service of thanksgiving held in honour of the 'providential escape of our most gracious Queen Victoria'. It was a great occasion. Although the Queen was unhurt, she had been exposed to the threat of assassination, the first of many bungled attempts throughout her long reign. Thousands packed the cathedral for the service, at which Cardinal Murray presided.

Father Miley preached using language which suggested that the cult of the divine right of kings was still in vogue. It was divine intervention, he said, that had saved the Queen's life, and he went on to dilate in extravagant terms on the wonders of Victoria's reign. 'Scarcely was the diadem of empire placed on her virgin brow when Ireland felt with ecstasy, for the first time after many a dreary century, a smile of pity beam upon her from the tenant on the throne.' In the march of progress outlined from the pulpit of the pro-cathedral before the Cardinal on his throne there was no room for complaint. 'The whole island [had] settled down in the most profound tranquillity as if to enjoy a singular phenomenon never witnessed within the memory of history in the unhappy island before', the preacher said, 'Mercy walking side by side with Justice all around the shores and through every province of the land.'[67] The priest closed with a dig at the so-called loyalists among the Protestants. 'Therefore, most gracious lady, Queen of these mighty islands, your faithful Catholics of Ireland yield to no denomination of Your Majesty's subjects in the fervour of their aspirations to the mercy seat for the security and felicity of your reign. To none will they yield the post of danger in rallying for the throne, and in spending life itself in the defence of your sacred person.'

Father Miley's sermon was a reminder that even at the height of a bitter confessional struggle for the soul of Ireland, a high ultramontane and fiercely anti-Protestant brand of Catholicism was not incompatible with loyalty to the throne. In the 1820s, Bishop Doyle had remarked on the average Irishman's 'strong and almost universal attachment to the person of His Majesty and to the kingly office'.[68] The rise of nationalism and the Repeal movement offered no immediate competition to this old sentiment. When the recently reformed and mostly O'Connellite corporation of Drogheda held a public dinner in 1843, the speaker toasted the Queen using the same language that Father Miley had employed. 'The crown of the British Empire never graced the brow of a sovereign so devotedly anxious that justice should be given to all her people', he began. A royal visit 'would be a great day for Ireland. The shout of joy would vibrate from one end of the kingdom to the other,' he said and he for his part 'would not despair of seeing her Majesty cross the Boyne, surrounded by one hundred thousand of her loyal Irish subjects.'[69]

O'Connell encouraged this kind of talk. He had no wish to resurrect the republicanism of the United Irishmen, and effusive royalism was the order of the day at the vast Repeal meetings he organised in the 1840s. When O'Connell called his Repeal association 'loyal' he meant it. The meeting at Sixmilebridge on 6 January 1843 ended with tremendous cheers for 'the Queen, O'Connell and Repeal'.[70] At Limerick, they toasted the Queen, the Duchess of Kent, the Princess Royal, the Prince of Wales and only then, 'the people'.[71] At Trim, the banners proclaimed 'Victoria our Queen, with her, we'll stand or fall'.[72] At Mullingar, where Higgins made his fiery speech, Cantwell lectured the crowd on the duty of loyalty to the throne. 'History does not furnish an instance of any nation so uniformly distinguished for their loyalty as the Irish people', the Bishop of Meath said. 'They have proved the fidelity of their attachment to the throne under persecutions the most cruel and oppressive and how devoted then should not our attachment be now when we are blessed with a sovereign who reigns and who has declared that she reigns and will govern not for a class but for the benefit of all.'[73]

Yet loyalism and royalism declined among Queen Victoria's Irish Catholic subjects. The crown competed unequally with nationalism in the long term, and the monarch's distant, shimmering figure could not vie indefinitely with the magnetism of a local star such as O'Connell. The Irish respected real power. They saw it in Cardinal Cullen. They did not really understand, or enjoy, as the English did, the strong element of make-believe in Britain's constitutional monarchy.

The Queen assisted the slow but steady erosion of respect for her crown in Catholic Ireland. She had no taste to do for Ireland what the Habsburg Emperor Franz Josef's consort, Elizabeth, achieved in Hungary after 1848, when she wooed the proud nation her husband had humiliated, and in so doing turned the monarchy from a symbol of defeat into a force for reconciliation. The Empress Elizabeth made a point of learning Hungarian, visiting Hungary as often as possible and ostentatiously supporting the cause of Hungarian home rule. Victoria did not imitate her. She did not learn Irish and visited Ireland as little as possible. Her views on Repeal were easy to guess. While Ireland starved, she stayed away. She visited in 1849, after the worst of the famine was over, and returned briefly in 1853 and 1861, to review the troops at the Curragh and take a holiday in County Kerry. A gap of 39 years followed until 1900, when it was widely thought that she had come over only to drum up support for the Boer War.

The vast gaps between fleeting Irish visits were all the more obvious when contrasted with the Queen's assiduous courtship of Scotland. When her beloved John Brown seized Arthur O'Connor, an Irish madman who pointed his pistol at the Queen's passing carriage in March 1872, the event neatly symbolised the relationship between the two peoples in the Queen's imagination. Scotland: Brown, Protestant, plain-spoken, loyal; Ireland: O'Connor, Catholic, dangerous. Brown got a gold medal and an annuity; O'Connor was sent to jail. The courtiers, Brown especially, filled the Queen's head with Irish plots to kidnap her from Osborne or kill her children. Brown certainly believed in them and died in 1883 from a cold he caught when scouring the grounds of Windsor Castle in search of these elusive fiends. The constant alarums fed her horror of the country. Not only would she not go to Ireland herself; she stopped others from going too. When Gladstone tried to strengthen Ireland's bonds with the crown by setting up the Prince of Wales as governor-general, the Queen flatly vetoed the idea.

Catholic royalism was not killed off by her absence, but it withered. The more prescient Protestant churchmen realised that in the new democratic age, royalty needed to be visible. The *Freeman's Journal* commented adversely in 1847 on the royal vacuum in famine-stricken Ireland. 'Her heart is in the Highlands . . . her heart is not here', it noted huffily. 'At all events, Scotland has greater attractions for her than Ireland and she proves her attachment in honouring it a third time, while Ireland is still a stranger to the royal smile.'[74]

The longer they remained strangers to the royal smile, the more the Irish realised they could live without it. Whately fretted over the damage she was inadvertently doing to the cause of the Union. In 1858 he referred to Victoria in caustic terms as 'the great absentee'. He said: 'There can be no loyalty – at least no personal loyalty – to a mere idea, to a person who is never seen.'[75]

In the early decades of the nineteenth century the Irish Catholics celebrated the great rites of passage of the royal family with just as much enthusiasm as English and Scottish Protestants. That sentiment fell away rapidly after the Famine. By the 1860s republicanism was seeping into the country from the Famine emigrants' new home in America, gnawing away at the fibres of loyalism. Cullen presided over this change of heart, almost in spite of himself. The Archbishop had first-hand experience of revolution in 1848, when the Pope was driven from the Vatican by the short-lived Roman republic. It left him with an abiding distaste for the radical nationalists of France, Italy and Hungary who had made life so difficult for the Church. He deplored the way Liberal England encouraged their agitation. Cullen was determined to ensure the Irish Church lent no succour to their domestic equivalents, the men of the Young Ireland movement, who scorned O'Connell's policy of peaceful struggle for Repeal.

In the 1860s, Cullen became increasingly concerned about the imported American menace of revolutionary republicanism known as Fenianism. 'Those who talk of civil war, or resistance to established authorities and revolutionary movements', he told a meeting of Dublin citizens on 29 December 1864, ' are the worst enemies of Ireland and its ancient faith.'[76] In October the following year he addressed a long letter to the Irish clergy on the subject of Fenianism, which he described as 'a compound of folly and wickedness wearing the mask of patriotism to make dupes of the unwary'.[77] He described the Fenians as 'sordid' people whose goal was 'to preach up Socialism, to seize on the property of those who have any and to exterminate both the gentry of the country and the Catholic clergy'. He told the clergy to remind their flocks that anyone joining such a society incurred the instant penalty of excommunication. Cullen agreed wholeheartedly that Irish Catholics had plenty to complain about but insisted the imperial parliament was the proper forum for resolving such grievances; once these were dealt with, Ireland would be 'happy and peaceable and a source of strength to the empire'.[78]

When the Archbishop held a solemn requiem for the Irish soldiers who had volunteered to fight for the Papal States against the Italian nationalists, he rammed home the message that they had died not only for the Pope but for the principle of private property, monarchy and established authority. They had perished in the battle 'against revolutionists, determined to overthrow every lawful government',[79] he said. Cullen hoped the Catholics would join lawful societies such as the National Association, which lobbied for the disendowment of the Established Church, the protection of labourers and Catholic educational projects. Such societies had an important role, he told them in January 1867, in 'turning away the minds of the people from those revolutionary projects and wild undertakings proposed by a wicked and foolish faction which under the pretence of liberty seemed to have no other objects in view but to delude the people'.[80]

Cullen faced the same problem as Troy in the 1790s. The majority of the faithful might obey the bishops but a substantial minority was determined on revolt, whatever the Church said. A small, abortive Fenian rising in February 1867 confirmed all the Archbishop's suspicions about the wicked irresponsibility of nationalist fanatics. Cullen and David Moriarty, the conservative Unionist Bishop of Kerry, rejoiced to see it crushed by the British authorities. Those who acted 'with the avowed object of making war on the Queen of England and of upsetting the British Empire . . . resisted the ordinance of God and by doing so purchased for themselves damnation', Bishop Moriarty declared. 'God's heaviest curse, his withering blighting curse is on them . . . eternity is not long enough nor hell hot enough to punish such miscreants.'[81]

Cullen thought Moriarty's language excessive, but he broke his own rule of rarely attending official functions to appear at a dinner for the incoming Lord Lieutenant, the Marquis of Abercorn, on 19 February, where he spoke in unusually emollient tones about Protestant charity work and denounced the 'false patriotism' of the Fenian rebels.[82] The subject of seditious rebels was one he continually returned to. On the Feast of the Immaculate Conception in November 1869 he painted an awful picture of the Ireland that would have emerged from a successful rebellion against British rule. 'The country would have been deluged with blood. We should have had our guillotines . . . our Robespierres and our Marats or at least our Mazzinis and our Garibaldis,' he said. 'We cannot but be grateful to the public authorities for the humanity they have displayed . . . when suppressing the movements of those by whom they were so recklessly assailed.'[83] He told Gladstone that Fenian agitation was the work of 'adventurers from America who have plenty of money' and he urged the Prime Minister to use his power to crush Ireland's 'infidel and revolutionary press'.[84]

Cullen tried to set limits to what would be tolerated. While he lived, respect for the crown remained part of the Irish Catholic Church's official lexicon. He also tried to divert the nationalists' thwarted feelings of respect for authority into devotion to the papal monarchy, presiding over vast and ardent demonstrations on behalf of the Pope's rule over the papal states in the 1860s, and encouraging Irish soldiers to volunteer for the papal army.

The cult of the papacy, and of a very personal devotion to the Pope, took root. But Cullen was not nearly as successful in inoculating the parish clergy against political agitation as he would have liked. *The Priest in Politics*, by the Tipperary MP, P. J. Smyth, contained an unflattering portrait of the average Catholic clergyman in the 1880s as a meddlesome rabble-rousing politician, intoxicated by power and by the applause of the mob. 'He is a peasant', Smyth said.

He has all the passions, prejudices, instincts and failings of his class. The cries of the platform penetrate the walls of Maynooth and copies of low journals find their way into that seat of learning. He is ordained, he is a curate and his first public appearance is at a political meeting in his parish. Intoxicated by the cheers, he indulges in the wildest extravagance of language and is as illogical and personal as possible. This is the typical political curate.[85]

Cullen died just before the emergence of the Land League. He lived long enough to witness the emergence of the Home Rule movement and to dismiss it as the work of a handful of disaffected Protestant professors from Trinity, backed by 'the editors of half-Fenian or anti-religious newspapers'.[86] His suspicions were not surprising, given that Isaac Butt, the first leader of the 'Home Government Association' in 1870, was a Tory Protestant lawyer who had made a name for himself by defending Fenian suspects in the 1860s. That was just the kind of Orange–Green combination that Cullen both anticipated and most despised. Butt's infinitely more charismatic successor, Charles Stewart Parnell, who seized the reins of the Irish parliamentary party in 1880, was also a Protestant, the descendant of Jacobean land-grabbers and the son of an American. Had Cullen lived to see his rise, his withering comments can be imagined.

But Cullen was dead. The rise of Parnell and the Land League coincided with the election of a new generation of bishops of a very different stamp. They had none of his hatred of revolution, his suspicions about where nationalism ultimately led, or his contempt for popularity. Cullen had taken grim pride in brazening out nationalist fury when in 1861 he refused a Catholic burial to

Terence McManus, one of the leaders of a small, abortive revolt in 1848. He would encounter the hostility of the multitudes, he told Archbishop Ullathorne of Birmingham, 'but nothing will induce me, I trust in God, to go against the dictates of my conscience or to sanction a revolutionary spirit'.[87]

Cullen's successors were more like Smyth's curates, 'intoxicated by the cheers' and more sympathetic to the revolutionary spirit. In the 1880s, the archbishoprics of Dublin and Armagh both fell into the hands of men who were the heirs of MacHale, Cantwell and Higgins, not Cullen. Michael Logue, Bishop of Raphoe from 1879, was elevated to Armagh in 1887. In the south, the whole of national-ist Ireland rejoiced at the appointment of William Walsh to Dublin in June 1885. Walsh repaid the compliment. His first speech as Archbishop on 4 September at Kingstown was a high political homily on Home Rule, which centred on Ireland's right 'to have her own laws made upon Irish soil and by the legally and constitu-tionally chosen representatives of the Irish people'.[88] Under Walsh and Logue there was no more talk of the Queen's august person, or services of thanksgiving in the cathedrals to mark her escape from various assassins. Prayers for the royal family disappeared from the mass. The retiring Lord-Lieutenant, Lord Caernarvon remarked in 1886 on the change in attitude in Ireland to the crown and to the Queen. 'There was no loyalty to the Queen personally,' Victoria recorded him as telling her, merely 'a determination to arrange their own affairs & something would have to be done'.[89] A kind of unconscious republicanism had already pervaded the upper levels of the Irish hierarchy.

Of the two primates, Logue was seen as the more moderate, mainly because he was placid and genial. But Logue's opinions were far more nationalistic than those of Cullen and in 1897 he refused point blank to have anything to do with Victoria's Diamond Jubilee celebrations. Nor would he attend the Queen's funeral service four years later. The contrast between his estimation of the Queen's reign in the 1890s and Father Miley's in the 1840s is revealing. The Jubilee celebrations, Logue complained, were

intended as a laudation of the greatness and prosperity to which England has attained during the 60 years of her reign. As you well know, Ireland has had no share in this progress and prosperity. On the contrary, during that period she has been scourged by famines and oppressive, exceptional laws. Her population has been reduced by half . . .

Hence with the exception of a few Catholic officials and the Protestant minority who are undoubtedly the spoiled children of the country and have nothing to complain of, the Irish people are determined to keep out of the celebrations.'[90]

Logue was simply reading the public mood. By the end of Victoria's reign, participation in royal events was the mark of the southern Protestant, the Ulsterman, or the Catholic 'West Briton', or 'Castle Catholic'.

Loyal, royalist Catholics were still numerous in the last decades of the Queen's reign but they were increasingly ridiculed. The writer George Moore sent the entire class up in his 1886 novel, *A Drama in Muslin*, which portrayed them as hopeless snobs. Moore's particular Castle Catholics, the Bartons of County Galway, were a vapid, vain, socially grasping family who spent their time plotting to snare faded aristocrats for their daughters by haunting the viceregal balls in Dublin. Such people now had few supporters among the Catholic bishops or clergy. Cullen had inaugurated a policy of having as little contact with Dublin Castle as possible. Under his predecessor, the Catholic bishops generally attended the court's levees. By the 1870s, attendance at any government function was the mark of the 'Castle hack' and by the end of the Queen's reign, James Healy, the witty parish priest of Little Bray, County Wicklow, was one of just a handful of cosseted clerics willing to be seen at court. Significantly, court connections by then were seen as a positive hindrance to ecclesiastical promotion in Ireland. Healy blamed his failure to move beyond Little Bray on his high-profile ties to the Ascendancy.

The Land League, founded in 1879, claimed the loyalty of the Irish clergy in the following decade. Aiming to achieve peasant proprietorship and rent reduction by adopting the tactic of rent boycotts, it spread rapidly throughout the country, outside Ulster. The League needed the clergy to act as its local agents, just as much as the Repeal movement had done in the 1840s. James Cantwell, administrator of the Archbishop of Cashel's parish in Thurles, chaired the first Land League meeting in Thurles, County Tipperary, in November 1880, along with his ally, William Power, parish priest of Templetouhy.

The League's targets were landowners, most of whom were Protestant, but not all. On 14 August 1881 Father Power became involved in a Land League battle with a Catholic landowner after the agent of Mary Power Lalor of Longorchard, Templetouhy evicted a non-paying tenant, Edmund Burke, from the farm she owned in Barnalisheen. Land League supporters occupied her pew in Templetouhy church the following Sunday just before the 8 a.m. and 10 a.m. masses. When Mrs Power Lalor's party entered the church they attempted to reoccupy the seats and were jostled. Father Power's curate, Father Graham, significantly asked the Power Lalors, not the Land League supporters, to leave the church. Mrs Power Lalor had worked closely with Father Power to build the church in Templetouhy but his sympathies were entirely on the side of the evicted tenants. The village clergy visited the site where Land League supporters were building a home for the ejected Burkes and encouraged the workmen. According to the *Tipperary Advocate*, 'the chapel bell was tolled as the death knell of slavery and landlord oppression'.[91]

It was just the start of a long conflict between the clergy of Templetouhy and the Power Lalor family. In 1882, the Land League organised a boycott of the local National School after an attempted putsch by Father Power's supporters failed to eject Mrs Power Lalor as school manager.

The priest of Templetouhy was not one of those revolutionary enemies of property that Cullen had dreaded and foretold. He told a meeting of agricultural labourers in Moyne in November 1882 that 'it was the will of God that there should be classes' and that the classes were duty bound to co-operate.[92] However, the classes that the priest listed in this co-operative enterprise were farmers, artisans and labourers. He did not mention aristocrats or landlords.

Father Power died in 1887 but it was not the end of Mrs Power Lalor's battles with the Catholic clergy or with her Catholic tenants. In March 1889, she appointed a Protestant land agent, triggering a fresh confrontation with her tenants. A noisy protest meeting at Longstone ended in two priests, Michael Morris of Newport and John Cunningham of Silvermines, being prosecuted under the Crimes Act for inflammatory speeches. The trial that followed in Nenagh brought thousands of local people into the town, including several priests who attempted to lead their parishioners to the courthouse, accompanied by musical bands. There was no trouble, though this was not surprising as the authorities had deployed 300 police as well as troops from the 3rd Hussars to keep the peace.

The war raging between Mrs Power Lalor and the Catholic priests of north County Tipperary was proof enough that the Land League was not a sectarian, anti-Protestant organisation. It was simply anti-landlord and it was incidental that most landlords were Protestant. When they were not, like Mrs Power Lalor, they got no favours from the priest agitators.

In Templetouhy, the priests clearly did not see their role as that of mediators. Father Power and his clerical allies were tribunes of the tenant farmers and looked forward to the extermination of the landlord system. In July 1885, the conservative *Nenagh Guardian* reported another conflict between Catholics over land in Loughmore after William Fanning, a farmer from Clondotty, defied the Land League by taking a lease from a landlord for a farm which a tenant had been forced to surrender. The League's policy on such cases was rigid. Landlords who ejected non-paying tenants were to be boycotted. The fact that Fanning was a Catholic and that he was also a prominent member of the Land League's successor organisation, the National League, availed him nothing. 'The scene which took place one would scarcely believe capable of being enacted in a Christian community', the *Nenagh Guardian* sniffed.

A very large congregation assembled in the graveyard waiting for divine services to commence . . . [but] on the appearance of Mr Fanning a deafening shout of disapprobation arose from the waiting crowd. There were yells of 'Land grabber, Billy the land grabber' and other epithets of opprobrium . . .

On Mr Fanning's exit from the chapel the offensive shouting was resumed. Females principally took an active part in the performance. On the previous Sunday Mr Fanning's daughter was besmeared with rotten eggs on her way to Divine Service. She did not go to Mass last Sunday being in dread of similar insults.[93]

Fanning soon surrendered the lease on the farm.

Tipperary was a centre of Land League agitation. The priest agitators of the region were encouraged by their diocesan, Thomas Croke, Archbishop of Cashel and Emly from 1875 to 1902. Croke was a crowd-pleasing populist who loved delivering nationalist diatribes from the portals of his residence in Thurles. He also thoroughly enjoyed the business of dispensing political patronage, handing out parliamentary seats in much the same style that he dispensed parishes.

When George Ryan, Mrs Power Lalor's agent, stood against Croke's nominee as a Conservative in the 1886 elections, the Archbishop replied with a rant the sheer vulgarity of which would have appalled Cullen. Ryan was 'a vain pretentious, feather-headed fool from Inch', the Archbishop said. He was a 'mendacious upstart, this country clown, this orange papist, this jackal for the truculent "True Blues of Tipperary" . . . a sneering scurrilous, unsavoury snob, a lazy worthless, illiterate lout'. The unintelligible stream of bile went on. The Archbishop of Cashel had one message for the voters of the newly expanded franchise. '"Up and At them", and let your battle cry at the booths on Monday be "Parnell for ever and down with the ragman of Inch."'[94] Croke had the satisfaction of seeing Ryan crushed by a landslide of 3,804 to 225 votes.

The politicisation of the Irish Catholic Church under Walsh and Logue worried Rome. The general election of December 1885 marked a new period of instability in both kingdoms. In Ireland, the conversion of the Catholics to political nationalism under Parnell was almost total. Gladstone's reward for extending the franchise was the annihilation of the Liberal Party in every constituency with a Catholic majority. In 1880 Ireland had returned 13 Liberals. In 1885 it did not return one. Outside Protestant Ulster, Parnell's supporters swept the country, winning 85 of 103 seats. Gladstone's response was not to confront but to concede. In December, his son Herbert leaked his father's conversion to Home Rule to the *Pall Mall Gazette*. The proposal of an Irish legislature split the Liberal Party and Gladstone introduced the first Home Rule Bill without them. At the division on 8 June 1886 the Liberal Unionists marched into the Tory lobby and the bill fell by 341 to 311.

The Irish Catholic bishops were simply spectators while the English politicians fought over their country's future. At Maynooth on 8 September 1886 they delivered their own verdict on the general election that followed the defeat of Home Rule. The bishops did not conceal their disappointment. 'It is now more than ever the conviction of the bishops and of the clergy that it is only by the recognition of Ireland's right to make and administer her own laws that her miscalled union with England can cease to be a source of trouble and disorder to both countries,' they said. Once that was accomplished, Ireland could fulfil her 'honest desire to live in sisterly union with the rest of the empire'.[95]

One of Gladstone's motives for introducing Home Rule was the hope that the continually worsening struggle over land might be passed to an Irish legislature to deal with. In response to the Land League agitation, the Liberal government passed an Irish Land Bill in 1881 that compensated tenants for improvements they made to their farms and for evictions, setting up a land court to hear appeals. The Act was just the beginning of a raft of laws that within two decades would transfer the vast bulk of the land to the hands of peasant proprietors and unravel the Cromwellian settlement of the 1650s. The Tories had extended the 1881 Act in 1885 to enable tenants to buy their leases through the Land Commission, which was funded by a £5 million grant from parliament. But the nationalists were not bought off easily. After the failure of the first Home Rule Bill in June 1886, the Parnellites launched their proposal for a fresh offensive against the land-lords in the *United Irishman* on 23 October. The 'Plan of Campaign' called on tenants to unilaterally lower their rents or withhold them altogether. The money saved would be diverted to a committee overseeing the whole operation. The Plan went beyond what Parnell privately considered acceptable, but it was a sign of the changing political complexion of the Catholic Church that Croke and Walsh supported a direct assault on the principle of private property, while Logue, about to occupy Armagh, shared their views.

Arthur Ryan, the administrator of Thurles cathedral, told the English Catholic paper the *Tablet* on 25 December 1887 that the Church was united behind the Plan of Campaign. 'Irish priests and bishops bless it and declare it to be high and unassailable morality, a holy war in the cause of the poor and oppressed, a struggle for hearths and homes', he said. 'Rebels we are, almost to a man against the injustice and the misgovernment . . . '[96]

Talk of holy war was strong stuff, but no stronger than Archbishop Croke, who urged the Irish to stop paying their taxes as well as their rents in an interview published on 17 February of the following year. Tax money, he said, went on buying 'bludgeons for policemen to be used in smashing the skulls of our people and generally for the support of a foreign garrison or native slaves who hate and despise everything Irish'.[97]

The Pope was astonished. While Croke was virtually calling for an insurrection and his priests were invoking holy wars, Leo XIII was pondering which gift to select for Ireland's Protestant Queen to mark her Golden Jubilee on 21 June. (He decided on a copy of Raphael's representation of Poetry.) As far back as January 1881, the Pope had communicated his unease at the drift of Irish events to the sympathetic ear of Logue's predecessor, Archbishop McCabe. It was the duty of the Irish, he told the Primate in January 1881, 'not to commit any rash act whereby they may seem to have cast aside the obedience due to their lawful rulers'.[98] The Pope signalled his favour for the conservative McCabe the following year by making him a cardinal.

A papal envoy, Ignatius Persico, was dispatched to Ireland, arriving in Dublin on 7 July 1887. On 26 July he left Dublin for Limerick, Armagh, Dundalk, Tuam, Cashel and Wexford, before returning to Dublin on 26 October and then setting out for Cork on 20 November. He left for Rome in December. The Irish clergy followed the wandering papal envoy with a mixture of hope and suspicion. 'We simply want to manage our own affairs,' Croke told the Pope in his winning, amusing way. 'We are satisfied to live evermore under the sceptre of England's king or queen, yielding all true obedience to the same, providing Ireland's administration is in the hands of the sons and friends of the Irish people. Voila Tout!'[99] The Pope grilled Walsh personally when he was in Rome on 13 February 1888. Walsh told the Pope that Ireland only wanted the same kind of autonomy that the German kingdoms enjoyed in the German empire.[100] The Pope had no objection to Bavarian-style autonomy but he thoroughly disliked what he heard about the war being waged against the landlords. The Plan of Campaign was condemned in April. The papal rescript fell on the Irish Church like a thunderbolt. The bishops felt humiliated and the Parnellite politicians were indignant. Logue had to defend the Pope's right to pronounce on such matters even if he did not like what he heard. He told Croke that the Church could not get round the affair by declining to publicise the decree. 'It is evident that we are required to publish the decision but how this can be done prudently without leading to mischief is another matter', he said. 'It strikes me we have arrived at a very momentous crisis.'[101]

The clergy feared an open rift between the Catholic Church and the Parnellites after the Irish MPs drew up a hostile statement on 17 May, curtly rejecting Rome's right to interfere in Ireland's internal politics. John Dillon, MP for East Mayo and one of the most militant agrarian campaigners, said the Irish knew how to distinguish between the obedience they owed the Church in spiritual matters and absolute independence in temporal matters. The bishops felt caught in a pincer movement. On the one hand the Pope wrote to Logue complaining of how 'deeply pained and grieved'[102] he was by the clamour raised against his decree. On the other hand, the bishops felt exposed to the chilly wind of unpopularity among their flocks. Edward O'Dwyer, Bishop of Limerick, publicly opposed the Plan of Campaign and infuriated the campaigners when he told tenants disputing their rents at Glenharold to accept the landlords' terms. But his colleagues were frightened to back him. Logue told Walsh he feared Rome would think it 'very strange that there is not a single Irish bishop to raise his voice against their [the nationalists'] denunciation of the Holy See – for that is what it comes to – except the Bishop of Limerick'.[103] In October the bishops issued a pastoral address to the nation claiming that their attitude 'on some questions had been misrepresented'.

The furore over the Plan of Campaign left a legacy of bitterness. A certain spirit of anti-clericalism invaded the nationalists. It was not a very serious threat, as men like Dillon combined hostility to clerical leadership with devout Catholicism. There was never a danger in Ireland that mild anti-clericalism among the nationalists would spiral into a rejection of religion. But the affair soured relations and left some of the clergy in a vengeful mood. They felt they had created the nationalist Frankenstein and that it was impertinent of their creation to start offering them criticism.

The Church had an opportunity to take revenge on the nationalists for their insolence in 1890 when the details of Parnell's (unconventional) private life were exposed to the public. On 17 November, a decree nisi was granted to Captain William O'Shea on the grounds of adultery between Parnell and his wife, Katherine. Parnell had met her in 1880, a year after he won the leadership of the Irish parliamentary party, while her husband was Home Rule MP for County Clare. O'Shea kept quiet about his wife's affair. In 1886, he resigned his seat but it was not until 1889 that financial disappointment induced him to begin the divorce petition that would wreck Parnell's career.

At first Parnell was confident of weathering the inevitable storm. A meeting of the National League the day after O'Shea's divorce was granted reaffirmed Parnell's leadership. But then the storm broke. The English Non-conformists on whom Gladstone relied for so many votes were scandalised by the prospect of a continuing alliance between Liberalism and Irish Nationalism under a man of Parnell's moral record. Gladstone told Parnell that his continued leadership of the Irish parliamentary party imperilled his own leadership of the Liberals. He may not have intended this message to be leaked, but when it was, it took on the form of a public ultimatum. Parnell was outraged that an English party leader should dictate the internal affairs of the Irish party and banked on national pride subsuming moral outrage over his conduct with Kitty O'Shea.

But the affair revealed the depth of clerical jealousy over the leadership of the Irish nationalist cause. Henry Manning, Archbishop of Westminster, stoked this resentment. The day after Parnell survived the National League meeting on 18 November, he told Walsh that the Irish Church should have grasped the reins of political leadership for itself, instead of leaving it to laymen like Parnell. 'If ten years ago, the bishops and priests had spoken and acted together, the movement would not have fallen into the hands of laymen', the English Cardinal said. 'There is now both in Ireland and Rome the opportunity of regaining the lead and direction.'[104] The Cardinal's silky suggestion fell on receptive ears. Manning's words were passed down the line from bishop to bishop. On 22 November Croke told Walsh he had thrown Parnell's bust out of his hall. 'I go with you entirely', he told Walsh, 'in thinking that they [the nationalists] make small or no account of the bishops and priests now as independent agents, and only value them as money gatherers and useful auxiliaries . . . We shall have to let them see and feel unmistakably that without us they would simply be nowhere and nobodies.'[105]

A week later, four days after Parnell survived a meeting of the Irish parliamentary party, the Catholic Church broke its ominous silence and declared war on his leadership. The bombshell came in an interview that Walsh granted the Central News agency. 'If the Irish leader would not, or could not, give a public assurance that his honour was still unsullied,' the Archbishop said, 'the party that takes him or retains him as its leader can no longer count on the support of the bishops of Ireland.'[106] On 3 December the Catholic bishops gathered to formally back Walsh's condemnation. 'We cannot regard Mr Parnell in any other light than as a man convicted of one of the gravest offences known to religion and to society,' they said. 'Catholic Ireland, so eminently conspicuous for its virtue and the purity of its social life will not accept as its leader a man thus dishonoured and wholly unworthy of Christian confidence.'[107]

The Catholic Church flattened Parnell. As events in Templetouhy had shown, it was the parish clergy who carried the Home Rule movement against the landlords. But the Catholic Church in the 20 years since disestablishment had learned to savour the sensation of power. Croke in particular had begun to see himself as a kind of oriental pasha, raising up his favourites and destroying them when he pleased. In the provincial backwater of Thurles, it was easy for a man of Croke's quicksilver temperament to grow big-headed. Surrounded by fawning acolytes, his comings and goings assumed an ever more theatrical appearance with the passing of the years. When Croke returned from Rome in May 1883, where it had been expected that the Pope would rebuke him for his radical politics, bands played, fireworks exploded, bells pealed and a vast crowd clapped, knelt and cheered in the streets as the Archbishop processed back to his palace under a triumphal arch that read 'Star of Munster welcome home'.[108] When the Star of Munster conducted a visitation of the diocese the following year, his carriage was pulled by human hands and bands played along the way. Men such as Croke were dangerous allies for any politician.

Parnell tried to counter the bishops' ultimatum by stoking the flames of anti-clericalism. But the Church was not wrong-footed now as it had been over the Plan of Campaign. He was soon made aware of the fact that while he had only one mouth, the bishops had thousands at their disposal, which opened wide in every church on every Sunday. The parliamentary party split on lines that were very unfavourable to Parnell. Three days after the bishops spoke, 26 voted to retain him as chairman of the party while 44 voted against.

Now that they had declared war on Parnell, the bishops had no option but to exterminate him. The Primate devoted his Lenten pastoral on 8 February 1891 to a careful explanation of why nationalist Ireland was duty-bound to renounce its former idol. Logue artfully put the issue into the context of a historic struggle for national integrity that had repeatedly involved renouncing short-term temporal advantages for long-term gain. 'By an act of national apostasy they [the Irish] might have secured for themselves temporal prosperity, political influence, the goodwill of monarchs, the fostering care of an empire, rich powerful and prosperous', he said. 'Did our forefathers consent to that sacrifice? No . . . are we, their descendants, to abandon that inheritance of faith, pity and virtue for which they resisted even unto blood?'[109]

It was a brilliant pastoral letter, free of the vindictive spleen that might have alienated many ordinary people and it left the false impression that the Catholic Church was dispensing with Parnell's services more in sorrow than anger. The crocodile tears were for public consumption. In private, the Primate was venomous. He told Walsh: 'Better fight him now than later, for fight him we must in the long run'.[110]

Croke followed up Logue's pastoral with a confidential circular for the Munster clergy on 2 March that told them exactly how to go about popularising Parnell's destruction. He told his priests to summon their congregations after the last mass on Sunday, 8 March to meetings and instruct them on the nationalist leader's crimes.

> Tell them in what and how shamefully he has sinned against the Christian code without ever having uttered a word of repentance. How he has broken up the great Irish parliamentary party and imperilled if he has not actually wrecked the cause of Home Rule . . . remind them of the never-to-be-forgotten fact that bishops and priests have ever proved themselves their best and staunchest friends.[111]

Arthur Ryan, the priest who had preached on the 'holy war' against the land-lords in the *Tablet* in 1887, led the campaign to destroy the Parnellite faction in Thurles. When Parnell called a meeting of his supporters in Thurles in May 1891, the clergy promptly called a counter-demonstration on the same day that was sufficiently turbulent to force Parnell to call off his rally. Ryan boasted of the way his people had protested against 'the shame of having the Adulterer feted in the Archbishop's cathedral town . . . it was a demonstration of loyalty to the prelate who has made Thurles, despite their petty treason, a fortress of Irish nationality and a monument to the faith.' The Parnellites complained of clergymen armed with cudgels who had 'marched at the head of each contingent; that many of the poor dupes . . . were supplied with drink and asked would they not defend the Archbishop's palace, which they were told was to be attacked'.[112] Parnell died in October 1891, a broken reed. In England, the Tories watched the spectacle of his destruction at the hands of the Church with fascination and envy. 'Nothing in modern history has been shown to equal the influence of Archbishops Croke and Walsh in the recent history of Ireland,' exclaimed Lord Salisbury. 'They have turned the whole of the organisation that seemed to embarrass and baffle the British government – they have turned it clear away from the man in whose hands it was with as much ease as a man turns a boat by leaning on the rudder.'[113] It set the Tories wondering.

In 1885 the Tory maverick Lord Randolph Churchill told Lord Justice Fitzgibbon that he looked to the Catholic Church to save Ireland from Home Rule. The clergy alone, he said, could 'mitigate or postpone the Home Rule onslaught'. The bishops, he went on, 'in their hearts hate Parnell and don't care a scrap for Home Rule'. Give them total control over education and 'the tremendous force of the Catholic Church will gradually come over to the side of the Tory party'.[114]

Churchill was right about the first part and wrong about practically everything else. The bishops did not all hate Parnell, but there was a rivalry and a friction between the Church and the nationalists that had to be resolved after the confusion and embarrassment of the papal condemnation of the Plan of Campaign. Sincere feelings of outrage over Parnell's adultery happily coincided with an opportunity to remind the nationalist politicians that the Catholic Church was the dominant force in Irish society. As for the rest, Churchill misread the bishops. They did care about Home Rule, but were determined to have it on their own terms. Home Rule would be brought about by a man the Church could control, or at least trust, or it would not come at all.

CHAPTER TWELVE

Flags Flying and Drums Beating

We know the wars prepared
On every peaceful home
We know the hell prepared
For such as serve not Rome
The terror threats and dread
In market hearth and field
We know when all is said
We perish if we yield

(Rudyard Kipling, 'Ulster 1912')[1]

On 23 March 1886 the Church of Ireland held a special meeting in the newly completed Synod Hall in Dublin to discuss the crisis over Gladstone's first Home Rule Bill. Archbishop Plunket introduced the meeting. 'The question we have to deal with today – it is no use beating about the bush, is simply this,' he told the gathering of clergy and lay people. 'Whether or not this synod, this synod of the Church of Ireland is in favour of that policy which is known as Home Rule.'[2] After reminding the audience that Gladstone had specifically asked the churches for their opinions, he made his own apparent. 'Undoubtedly, behind the claim for Home Rule – and we should be fools if we did not believe it – there lurks the demand for entire separation and for a very advanced form of Socialism.'

The bishops queued up to repeat Plunkett's opinions. The Bishop of Limerick proposed a motion along the following lines:

We the bishops, clergy and laity of the Church of Ireland . . . representing more than 600,000 of the Irish people, consider it a duty at this present crisis to affirm our constant allegiance to the throne and our unswerving attachment to the legislative union now subsisting between Great Britain and Ireland.

The Bishop thought it important to add that although Protestants comprised only one-quarter of the Irish population, they made up the majority of those 'who form the first rank in education, property and professional eminence'.

The Bishop of Down and Connor described Home Rule as a form of 'living death' for Protestants.[3] In Parnell's kingdom, he said, 'we will be stripped of our rights and liberties and robbed of our very faith'. Bishop William Alexander of Derry painted a horrifying picture of the 'disorder, intimidation and violence' that would prevail under the Home Rule parliament and predicted that the Church of Ireland would be immediately stripped of the property it held after disestablishment. 'What the locust of Disestablishment had spared, the caterpillar and palmerworm of bankruptcy would destroy,' he said gloomily. Irish Protestants, he went on, 'wish to remain an integral part of an imperial people. We and our fathers have lived under the shadow of a great tree, the stately growth of a thousand summers of glory. We will not exchange it for a place under a big tree which sophists and experimentalists have taken a fancy to plant head downwards, whose sure fall will crush us amidst the inextinguishable laughter of the world.' 'Who would be the constituents of this new parliament?' the Provost of Trinity College asked, before answering the question himself. 'They would be the peasantry and the tenant farmers of Ireland.'

The meeting pinpointed the two great Protestant fears about Home Rule. One was that they would be persecuted for their religion. The other was that they would be victimised in a class war against the rich. Class conflict in Ireland did not concern labour and capitalists but peasants and landlords. This affected the Church of Ireland, much of whose revenue came from landlords. When landlords did not get rents from their tenants, the Church of Ireland suffered. In 1885 its income was estimated at £420,000. Of that sum £151,000 came directly from land owned by the Church. Another £136,000 came in donations from landlords. In other words, much more than half the Church's income flowed from land. The Church of Ireland was right to tremble at the prospect of Home Rule and the inevitable extinction of the landlords that would be brought about by a parliament full of small farmers.

The introduction of the bill was a huge shock. It was as if Gladstone had touched Irish Protestants with an electric cattle prod. A week before the Anglicans convened in Dublin, the Presbyterians held a special meeting on 15 March in May Street in Belfast which revealed almost total unanimity between the Anglicans and their own church on Home Rule. Of the 750 delegates present, only half a dozen opposed the Unionists. The handful of Presbyterian Home Rulers was bemused. 'Anyone can understand why landlordism and episcopacy should struggle earnestly to retain the remnants of their Ascendancy, but why the Presbyterian Church should unite with them in the struggle is more than I can understand,'[4] Thomas Macafee, minister of Ardglass, told James Armour of Ballymoney. Armour remained a thorn in the side of the Unionists until his death in 1928. The Presbyterians' democratic instincts and tradition of individualism gave him an honoured place in the Church as a licensed maverick. But he was no prophet. Armour was a throwback to the Presbyterian generation before Henry Cooke, to the men who looked on Catholics as fellow dissenters and on Anglicans as landlords. Most of his colleagues were as opposed to Home Rule as the Anglicans.

The Tories could do little to bolster Unionism in the south of Ireland but in Ulster they spied nationalism's Achilles' heel. The Tory party's erratic star, Lord Randloph Churchill, delivered an inflammatory speech to his Paddington constituents on Home Rule on 13 February 1886. 'It is only Mr Gladstone who could imagine for a moment that the Protestants of Ireland would . . . recognise the power of a parliament in Dublin, a parliament of which Mr Parnell would be the chief speaker and Archbishop Walsh the chief priest,' he said.[5] He then hurried to Belfast to make another oration to the local Protestants, 'Wave, Ulster all thy banners wave,' he shouted, 'and charge with all thy chivalry.'[6] Churchill was unabashedly cynical about his motives. Only months before, he had encouraged speculation about a Tory-Parnellite alliance. Now he noted 'the Orange card would be the one to play. Please God it may turn out the ace of trumps and not the two.'[7]

The Home Rule Bill changed Ulster's political complexion overnight. Before 1885, Ulster Protestants were overwhelmingly Liberal. Cooke had never succeeded in turning flinty Presbyterian farmers and merchants into the tools of Anglican Tory landlords. One of the last acts of the dying man had been to speak at a Protestant rally at Hillsborough in 1867 against the disestablishment of the Church of Ireland. The organisers hoped for a repeat of the great rally he had addressed at Hillsborough in 1835. But this time only a few thousand turned up. The great orator was exhausted and his speech was inaudible. Ulster's tenant farmers would not fight for the Tory Anglican Establishment and they benefited just as much from the provisions of the Land Acts as the Catholics. It was Home Rule that turned them from Liberals into Unionists. 'The immediate cessation of class friction was still more remarkable . . . Their gratitude was wiped out the moment he [Gladstone] hoisted the green flag.'[8]

The Orange Order, which had been moribund for decades, revived as the gentry, clergy and farmers rushed to join. From the moment the bill failed in June 1886 until September, sectarian fighting convulsed Belfast: 32 were killed and 37 wounded. Much of the fighting was between the working-class residents of the Protestant Shankill Road area in west Belfast and the Royal Irish Constabulary, whose ranks were rumoured to have been packed with Catholics to force through Home Rule. The agitation did not cease with the general election of July, which the Liberals lost. On the weekend of 7–8 August alone nine were killed.

The genteel hysteria of the Dublin Protestants in March 1886 and the rawer anger of the working class in Belfast ebbed away after the Irish parliamentary party imploded over the Parnell affair. It was not until 1900 that the party reunited round John Redmond, who offered a very different style of leadership. The Liberals were out of office until 1892, by which time Gladstone was 82. The Protestants were less afraid of his Second Home Rule Bill in 1893, although it passed a third reading in the House of Commons by 34 votes on 1 September.

They knew the Lords would strangle it, which they did on 8 September by 419 votes to 41.

There was almost no reaction. The Irish nationalists remained locked in internecine feuds. The English and Scottish Liberals were bored with being fed on a diet of Irish measures. Gladstone resigned in March 1894. The moderate Irish nationalists mourned the loss of a sincere friend. Logue, who refused to have anything to do with Victoria's Jubilee in 1897, was happy to lend his name to the Gladstone Memorial Committee set up the following year, after his death.[9]

But the southern Protestants were dimly aware they had traded instant execution for death by a thousand cuts. When Edward Benson, Archbishop of Canterbury, visited Ireland to rededicate Kildare cathedral in September 1896, he struck a mournful note. It ought to have been a triumphal occasion, for the restoration of the ruin had cost at least £10,000. But Benson felt that it was not a people's event. One-quarter of the entire sum had come from the Duke of Leinster. The Cooke-Trench family had donated £2,000. Benson wondered how the Irish Church would manage without the aristocracy to prop it up. 'The Church is, I fear, slightly on the ebb,' he wrote. 'The disappearance of the landlords which is steadily going on will leave behind no people willing or able to bear the expense.

'There is much talk of feeble clergy in districts away from the centres – and not one person pretends to think what we hear in England, that the Church is better for Disestablishment – or that it has been anything but a great blow.'[10]

The Anglican Church Congress held in Birmingham in October 1893 heard a similar message. Robert Warren, an Irish delegate, warned the English sister Church against falling for the argument that disestablishment had liberated the Irish Church. 'The landlords as a rule are members of the Church of Ireland,' he said. 'If they shall be deprived of their estates . . . it cannot be supposed that men who shall have ceased to have any connection with a parish will contribute to the support of the church and clergy of that parish.

'There are cases, and not a few, particularly in the south and west of Ireland, in which the discontinuance of the subscription of one resident landlord to the assessment of his parish may be followed by the closing of the church.'[11]

Although the Church was sounding an increasingly pessimistic note in the 1890s, Protestant lay people were not. The land was passing silently and inexorably out of the hands of the families who had held it for almost two and a half centuries, but there was no great crisis of confidence in the community as a whole. In 1903 the Tories crowned the Land Acts of the 1880s with the Land Purchase Act that hastened the death of the landed gentry, but on favourable terms. If landlords and tenants agreed a price and the Estates Commissioner approved it, the government pledged to add a 12 per cent bonus to the value. Moreover the vendors received payment at once, drawn from stock floated on government credit. The purchaser's payments were spread over 68½ years.

In the long term, the Act helped finish off the old Ascendancy. In the short term, it gave a shot in the arm to many landlords who had been struggling to collect their rents for decades and were up to their necks in debt. In Dublin and the other cities, the large and entrenched Protestant middle class breathed a collective sigh of relief that the long and ghastly war over land was over. As the fear of terrorism or outright revolution fizzled out, the dizzy round of galas, balls, exhibitions and races resumed its course with all the old energy. At the Punchestown races, at the Castle, the Viceregal Lodge, the Chief Secretary's lodge, the Commander-in-Chief's residence at Kilmainham and at the palace of the Archbishop of Dublin, the parties whirled on. The Protestants who still dominated Dublin's social life did not feel remotely doomed. The nationalists and their clerical allies might pour scorn on the Castle and on 'Castle hacks', but among the masses the tatty pageantry of the viceregal court lost little of its allure.

'That strange theatrical institution affected everything in the place down to the commonest little tradesman,' Percy Fitzgerald recollected in his bitchy memoir of life at the Victorian viceregal court. He recalled the thrill of excitement that went through the audience at a concert in Dublin when the viceregal court made its hilariously showy entrance.

Everyone rose to his feet. There were agitated cries of 'Here he is'. 'He's coming!' and half a dozen men carrying white wands appeared struggling their way along a very narrow gangway. A dapper-looking clerk-like man came last, wearing a star, following the stewards. This was THE LORD LIEUTENANT, or the Lord 'Liftnant', as he was usually spoken of by the crowd. He came along bowing and smiling and trying to be as gracious as he could. Following him were the aides-du-camps, or 'edukongs', supercilious young men with blue silk facings to their coats – sure and certain seal of their office, the blue being reverenced, even to all but prostration, by the society of Dublin – behind whom slided a number of limp, faded dames, some veterans attired in garments as faded as their persons – the 'Ladies of the Household' . . .

This curious procession was invariably repeated on every public occasion and was ever painfully followed by greedy, admiring eyes . . . The little scene I have been describing is significant, for the same unmeaning adoration permeated every class of society. This theatrical make-believe of a court leavened everything. Everyone played at this sham royalty, and, I am convinced, firmly believed in it, or fancied they did. The 'kestle' was the cynosure. To be asked to the 'kestle', or to know people at the 'kestle', or even to know people who knew people at the 'kestle' was Elysium itself.[12]

The Protestants recalled the Edwardian era as their Indian summer. In the 1930s Charles D'Arcy, Church of Ireland Archbishop of Armagh, sighed over 'the brilliant capital' he remembered from his youth. 'Things were done on a grand scale,' he said. 'Exhibition after exhibition flourished in Earlsfort Terrace. Magnificent loan collections of art were opened to the public from time to time. Great public functions were frequent occurrences.'[13]

Lord Midleton remembered the 'cloudless sky' over Ireland at the turn of the century. 'The "state of Ireland" had long disappeared from British newspapers. Evictions were almost unheard-of. The reduction of the constabulary had begun. A number of prisons had been closed. Crime of all sorts had been largely reduced. Royal visits had been tentatively resumed with marked enthusiasm. Popular local government had gratified local ambition . . . Even the bitterness of the national-ist press was modified.'[14]

The Queen's last visit in 1900 had passed off without much trouble. Nationalists protested by breaking the windows of shops decorated with Union flags, while Maud Gonne and W. B. Yeats staged a mock funeral, using a coffin on which the words 'British Empire' were painted. But the streets were lined with people cheer-ing the royal carriage on its daily rides. The Queen talked confidentially with Cardinal Logue. He had snubbed her Diamond Jubilee celebrations but was too well mannered to snub her in person. When informed that she wished to speak to him he gladly agreed to position himself at the door of the Viceregal Lodge dining room, before dinner, so that she could hold an informal conversation with the Primate. The Archbishop was bashful at their tête-à-tête. Confronted by Victoria's trusting, china-blue gaze he lamely said there were only 'one or two things' wrong with the current situation in Ireland. The Queen was pleased but mystified. What were the one or two things? she asked her officials.[15]

Opponents of the royal visit could claim the crowds who cheered the Queen-Empress in Dublin were stuffed with Protestants, bulked out by Castle Catholic hangers-on. The same excuse could hardly be made in 1903, when the vast figure of Edward VII was seen bouncing along the rocky lanes of Connemara during his post-coronation visit. The King went out of his way to woo the prickly Catholic hierarchy. He ordered his officials to wear mourning clothes in honour of the recent death of the Pope and suggested meeting the Catholic bishops on their home territory at Maynooth. The bishops were charmed by the gesture. Walsh pointed out to Logue that this resolved nationalist qualms about attending levees at Dublin Castle alongside the Protestant bishops and 'takes us out of a cloud of difficulties about court ceremonial etc.'[16]

The King returned to Ireland in 1904, when he stayed with the Ormonds at Kilkenny Castle and at Lismore Castle in County Waterford. There was another visit in 1907, although that was overshadowed by the theft of the regalia confus-ingly known as the Irish crown jewels. There was talk of a new royal residence in Ireland at the hauntingly beautiful lakeside Gothic mansion of Kylemore Abbey, in County Galway. The progresses heartened the diminished ranks of Catholic royalists like Archbishop Healy of Tuam, who lectured schoolteachers at a fund-raising bazaar in Tuam in 1906 on the duty of loyalty to the crown. 'Our fore-fathers were loyal to Charles II,' he said. 'They were loyal in their day to James II . . . We are loyal to King Edward, their descendant, because he is King. We owe him absolute and unconditional loyalty as king de juro and king de facto . . . I hope no teacher and no Irishman will ever fail to pay due homage to the toast of Edward VII.'[17] Such language was old fashioned by then. Few Irish Catholics felt absolute and unconditional loyalty to the House of Saxe-Coburg-Gotha. But the nationalists did feel despondent about the studied calmness of Edwardian Ireland. They fretted that the unifying force of nationalism was giving way to the kind of class conflict that the Church could not control. Bishop O'Dwyer of Limerick complained in 1910 that Ireland was more Anglicised than ever. It was 'subdivided into two British camps, the wealthier classes identifying themselves with English Unionism and the mass of the population . . . being attached to the English Liberals. For any true spirit of nationality, these alliances must be ruinous.'[18] The Bishop moaned that most Irishmen were more interested in English sport than in anything else and took their opinions from English popular newspapers: 'The tide of English opinion, English feeling, English habits, is flowing into every nook and crevice of Irish life.'

The nationalist clergy tried to counteract this trend by reviving the Irish language and indigenous Irish sports. They hoped these would form a barrier to further English penetration. Their predecessors had been indifferent to Gaelic. Cullen never gave it a thought when he was scrutinising the National Schools; it was the intrusion of heresy, not English, that concerned him. In Wales the Nonconformist preachers kept the Welsh language alive in spite of the efforts of the Established clergy and the schools. The Catholic Church under Cullen took no stand on Irish. By the time that a handful of scholars and enthusiasts, most of whom were Protestant, began to revive it, the language was almost extinct outside the extreme west.

Douglas Hyde, the founder of the Gaelic League in July 1893, was the son of a Church of Ireland rector in Roscommon. But Catholic nationalists took the League over almost immediately and denuded it of its non-political and non-denominational quality. The new clerical members erected a whole theology around the lost language as a racially and spiritually purer medium. 'English is the language of revolt, of proud successful rebellion against religious authority,' wrote Father John O'Reilly, an early clerical enthusiast for the League in 1898. 'It is the traditional vehicle of ridicule and scorn for the most sacred practices and functions of religion . . . and latterly English has become for us at least the tongue of passive and aggressive unbelief, to some extent of professed and triumphant immorality.'[19]

The clergy were rapidly and intensely attracted by this kind of Gaelic triumphalism, which ignored the central role played by the Old English community in the preservation of Catholicism in the sixteenth century. Father O'Reilly told an audience at Maynooth in 1900 that the Irish clergy needed to understand that 'the English mind' was intrinsically depraved. 'It is a fleshly spirit, bent towards earth, unmannerly, vulgar, insolent, bigoted, a mind whose belly is its God . . . a mind to which real Christian virtue is incredible.'[20]

Father Patrick Forde told students at Maynooth in December 1899 that Gaelic was a powerful barrier against atheism. In true totalitarian style, he recommended that the Irish be force fed Gaelic, so that they would literally not be able to understand the Anglo-Saxon concept of godlessness. 'The Irish language itself was charged with religious life and no one could speak it from infancy without feeling himself so moulded that to him the act of living faith was the very breath of daily existence,' he said, 'while the development of an infidel mind was not only impossible in itself but inconceivable and incredible.'[21] Father Forde added that speaking English carried the risk of spiritual pollution. 'We Catholics,' the priest warned, 'without consciousness and without offence are ever repeating the half sentences of dissolute playwrights and heretical partisans and preachers.' Father Michael Hickey, Vice-President of the Gaelic League, echoed the sentiment in a more moderate form to a Liverpool Irish audience in 1902. Gaelic was 'the mind, the soul, the great bulwark of Irish nationality,' he said. 'The mission of the Gaelic League is to minister to the soul of the nation.'[22]

The League spread rapidly. The first meeting, on 31 July 1893 in O'Connell Street, fitted comfortably into a single room. The inaugural session in Galway in St Patrick's hall was bigger. By May, League branches had sprouted in Cork, Derry and New Ross, while back in Dublin the Lord Mayor, Valentine Dillon, sponsored an Irish language congress at the Mansion House on 27 March.

The Catholic clergy in the 1890s met the Irish language movement with the unbridled enthusiasm with which they had once greeted the Land League and the Repeal movement. The bishops took the front row, MacCormack in Galway, O'Donnell in Raphoe and O'Callaghan in Cork. One of the Gaelic League's first biographers drew a thumbnail sketch of the type of Catholic most drawn to the League. 'Those who aspire to an upper middle class position fight shy of it,' he remarked. 'The resident magistrate and the district inspector of police of course keep away. The bank manager will at best give it a subscription. But the parish priest gives it either ready support or benevolent tolerance. One of his curates is probably the enthusiast at the back of the enterprise.'[23]

To frustrated priests and curates who shared Bishop O'Dwyer's worries about the corrosive effect on faith of Edwardian prosperity, the Gaelic League was literally a Godsend, and they took the League into every town and village, transforming the specialised interest of a few Protestant professors into a national movement. The priests kick-started the Gaelic revival, but the price tag of clerical involvement in the long term was the injection into the movement of moral puritanism and religious sectarianism – a deadly combination which in the end crippled the whole language project and left the country more anglophone than ever.

The problem was that the extreme tension between the Churches in Ireland invaded every movement that any of them touched. When the Catholic clergy appropriated the Gaelic League, it inevitably became sectarian, almost entirely Catholic and anti-Protestant as well as anti-English. The clergy invested the language movement with their squeamish obsession with moral purity and with their deep distrust of intellectuals. The attempt to yoke Irish to a Catholic outlook and link English speech with depravity alienated many writers, thinkers and poets on whom the movement ultimately depended for success. The intelligentsia instinctively shied away from this Catholic Puritanism, and their defection was a body blow. The leaders of the much more successful language movements among Hungarians, Czechs, Slovenes, Finns, Latvians and Estonians never associated their cause with confessional rivalry or the peculiar moral projects of the clergy. They were less prudish, philistine and anti-intellectual. On the contrary, they were usually associated with a kind of peasant earthiness.

The Irish language could have become the means by which people liberated themselves from the High Victorian stuffiness of the clergy. Instead, the language became the clergy's accomplice. The priests were frightened to unlock the raw, semi-pagan spirit of much of Ireland's Gaelic culture and censored it, sanitising and anaesthetising the literature that emerged. There were many reasons why the Central European nationalities emancipated themselves from German, Swedish and Russian while the Irish failed to re-establish their native tongue as the daily language of the majority. By the time the enthusiasts started to fight for their cause most of the peasants had already forgotten their Irish. The fact that almost all Protestants and many Catholic intellectuals came to dread and to some degree despise Irish was hardly insignificant. From the start, it meant that half the population of Ulster was pulling in the opposite direction.

Among ordinary people, Irish assumed the same status as the temperance movement. It became an object of official veneration, a holy relic to which people resorted on special occasions, but which remained curiously dissociated from the ordinary plane of daily life. Irishmen in their thousands took the pledge and then, with a sigh, went back to the bottle. In the same way, Edwardian Irishmen and women attended language conventions, spoke Irish for the day, signed their letters with the Irish phrase 'Is Mise', bestowed Gaelic names on their patriotic organisations – and continued speaking English. The language in which most people, especially the poor, dreamed in, shopped in, went about their daily business and made love in, remained English. But there was a difference. The language of the Irish working class was invested with a new note of shame as the tongue of conquest. The language movement, intended to free a nation, ended up increasing its self-hatred.

The storm clouds over Ireland reappeared at the end of Edward VII's reign. In January 1906 the Liberals triumphed at the polls, with 377 seats to the Unionists' 157, a huge majority that enabled them to rule without giving much thought to the 83 Irish Nationalists. But on 30 November 1909 Britain lurched into a political crisis after the Tory peers in the Lords threw out the Liberal budget. The election that followed in January 1910 left Conservatives and Liberals neck and neck with 273 and 275 seats. The Labour Party, a relative newcomer, took 40 seats while the Irish Nationalists won 82. The constellation allowed the Liberals to retain power but returned them to their old state of dependency on Irish MPs. On 5 April, Herbert Asquith, the Prime Minister, moved a resolution on removing the veto of the Lords. John Redmond, leader of the reunited Irish parliamentary party since 1900, offered his support. The King died on 6 May. In November, parliament was dissolved. Fresh elections in December failed to break the logjam. The two great parties both emerged with 272 seats, while Labour won 42 and the Nationalists 84. As the Liberals formed a new administration dependent once more on the Irish, Home Rule floated at once to the top of the political agenda.

The first phase, the clipping of the Lords' wings, was over by July 1910. That left Ulster as the last Tory ace to play. John Redmond was the least threatening Irish leader the Tories and their Irish Protestant friends had ever encountered. It was as if a ghost of the long-forgotten Old English of the Pale had crept out of its grave and been reincarnated for one last time. The Redmonds of County Wexford fairly reeked of the toney, Catholic, Old English world of the 'civil' walled towns. Educated at Clongowes Wood, an elite Jesuit academy, Redmond had imbibed the English public school mentality. To enter the portals of Clongowes Wood was to encounter the phenomenon of West Britonism at its most vivid. It is a world recorded in the fading sepia photographs in school albums, of gala days where women dressed like Queen Alexandra in haloes of white ostrich feathers, of cricket matches staffed by bronzed and healthy youths with the imperious faces of those who know they are born to command, of tennis rackets, of scholarly-looking teachers who presided over wonderfully civilised pupils' debates. This was not a different world from that of the red-faced, roaring peasants who staffed the Christian Brothers' schools for the poor. It was a different cosmos.

Redmond was very loyal to his school. Addressing Primate Logue and a phalanx of bishops at the centenary dinner of his alma mater in May 1914, he spoke jovially of the contrast between the Ireland of 1814 and the present. 'We Irish have lived through the night and the centenary of Clongowes is being celebrated at a time of happy promise,' he declared. 'Today, thanks to the God of our fathers, we can say with truth that Clongowes stands in a nation transformed, in a nation filled with hope, confidence and faith, an Ireland whose ideals are beginning to be understood by our neighbours in another island.'[24]

Redmond was correct. The large non-Tory majority on the other island did indeed share his ideals and looked on Redmond as the man to steer Ireland towards a form of self-government that would be compatible with continuing, if undefined, membership of the Empire. Redmond's problem was not so much the other island as the northern segment of his own. The Ulster Protestants were not moved by Redmond's studied moderation, his English wife, or his bourgeois respectability. They saw him as the bespectacled front behind which old Fenians lurked. From the moment that the 1910 election handed the initiative to the Irish MPs, they were on the alert. No matter how amiable and conciliatory Redmond appeared, the northern Protestant churchmen and their laity insisted on seeing the political contest with the Nationalists as a re-enactment of 1689, if not 1641. William McCordie, a former Moderator of the Presbyterian Church, expressed that feeling admirably in January 1914. 'The Protestants of Ireland believe that the old fight is being fought again,' he said, 'the fight on behalf of the principles for which their fathers successfully contended when James the Second was chased from the kingdom.'[25] But the Ulster Protestants did not find their champion among their own ranks. They found him in a middle class barrister and Solicitor-General for Ireland from the south called Edward Carson.

Carson was an unlikely champion of Ulster. His family were Dubliners, while his saturnine features, dark, heavy-lidded eyes, massive jaw and fleshy, sensual lips recalled the family's older Italian origins. He had no connection whatever with the north. His world was that of the drawing rooms of London and Dublin, clubland, the House of Lords and the great houses of the Tory aristocracy. Carson accepted the leadership of the Irish Unionist Party in the House of Commons on 27 February 1910, but it was only in December that he first appeared in Ulster, when he addressed a meeting at Belfast's Ulster Hall. On 31 January 1911 he presided for the first time at a meeting of the new Ulster Unionist Council. It was not until 23 September of that year that he was shown off to the Ulster public at a rally held at Craigavon, the country home of James Craig, MP for East Down.

Carson was a lawyer like Redmond. But he was a bolder man. The Nationalist leader was always afraid his Liberal allies might think him untrustworthy. Carson, who had the Tory leadership within his grasp and the unqualified support of the Tory leader, Bonar Law, could afford to be more cavalier. At the rally at Craigavon he unveiled the trump card he intended to play to bring down Home Rule: partition. 'We must be prepared, in the event of the Home Rule Bill passing, with such measures as will carry on for ourselves the government of those districts of which we have control,' he announced. 'We must be prepared – and time is precious in these things – the moment Home Rule passes, ourselves to become responsible for the government of the Protestant province of Ulster.'[26] The idea of the 'Protestant province of Ulster' sounded absurd but two days later Carson was drawing up a provisional government and organising the import of weapons.

John Crozier, the Protestant Archbishop of Armagh, threw himself into the cause of the 'Protestant province' and the arming of the Unionist population without a backward glance. Two days after the third Home Rule Bill was introduced on 11 April 1912, Crozier and Henry Montgomery, the Presbyterian Moderator, presided at a rally of 100,000 members of the newly formed Ulster Volunteer Force in the Belfast suburb of Balmoral, blessing the inauguration of this insurrectionary movement with prayers and the singing of Psalm 90. It was Bonar Law who appealed most directly to the memories of the siege of Derry at the rally. 'You are a besieged city,' he said. 'The timid have left you, your Lundys have betrayed you; but you have closed your gates. The Government have erected by their Parliament Act a boom against you to shut you off from the help of the British people. You will burst that boom.'[27]

Carson's genius was an instinctive ability to tap the deepest feelings and memories of a people of whom he knew nothing – the working classes and small farmers of Ulster. As the Liberals and Nationalists pushed on with Home Rule, he hit on the idea of reviving the Covenant against popery that the Scots had circulated against Charles I and Archbishop Laud in 1638. The idea came to him – appropriately – in the library of the Constitutional Club in Mayfair.

It was a brilliant stroke. The very word 'covenant' evoked the old struggle of the Ulster Protestants against annihilation in the seventeenth century. Against the manufactured and contrived majorities of parliaments it defiantly hurled the notion of the higher law of God. It captured the imagination of almost all the Protestant population and rallied an instinctively cautious and law-abiding people to the idea of armed resistance to the British government.

The fact that the old covenant had been aimed directly at the Anglican Church did not worry Archbishop Crozier or Charles d'Arcy, Bishop of Down and Connor since 1911. D'Arcy was thrilled by Carson's showmanship and agreed to take a prominent part in 'Ulster Day', the day that Carson had allocated for the grand signing ceremonies of the covenant all over northern Ireland. The drama of Ulster Day on 28 September 1912 began with a solemn service at D'Arcy's cathedral in Belfast at which the Bishop preached. Special services followed at the Ulster Hall and at Presbyterian headquarters in Assembly Hall, at which Moderator Montgomery presided. At midday, the Protestant clergy and the Unionist leaders moved down to the vast new City Hall for the signing ceremony, Carson being preceded by an escort holding the original yellow standard carried in front of William III at the Boyne.

Carson signed first, followed by Lord Londonderry, the Presbyterian Moderator, Bishop D'Arcy, the Dean of Belfast, James Craig, the President of the Methodist conference and a leader of the Congregational Union. All over Ulster the Protestant clergy and the Ascendancy landlords presided over similar ceremonies. The Bishop of Derry signed in his home city. The Bishop of Clogher signed at Enniskillen. Archbishop Crozier did his duty at Armagh along with the Dean. D'Arcy recalled the day that helped blow Ireland to smithereens as 'wonderful'.

> Never have I felt such a sense of solemn and unwavering determination as that which filled the hearts of the vast multitude, which thronged all the approaches to the great central building of the city. We did not doubt the outcome – such faith in the righteousness of the cause animated us – but we felt that whatever happened we were sharing in a most noble endeavour and that it was good to be alive.[28]

The Covenant was a great success. In Ulster, 218,806 men registered as covenanters and 228,991 women signed a similarly worded declaration: only men, it seemed, could sign a covenant. Along with the 2,000 who signed in Dublin and small groups who signed in Edinburgh and elsewhere, Carson could claim the active support of 471,414 people. The only serious threat to Carson's organisation in Ulster was the army. But on 20 March 1914, reports that the

Liberals intended to mobilise troops in the north resulted in the officers based in the Curragh in County Kildare threatening to resign. The so-called 'Curragh Mutiny' ended the military threat to the Unionists. The great weakness of the Liberals was that they were unable to rely on the armed forces in Ireland while the Irish Protestants could. As Carson's biographer wrote, the sons of the Irish Protestant aristocracy were thicker on the ground in the armed forces in 1914 than ever before.

> It was their pride and their livelihood; when the land acts deprived them of their functions as landowners, almost their only occupation. From hundreds of old country houses hidden away among the hills and loughs, green pastures and groves of Ireland, the youth of a fighting stock generation after generation went up to Sandhurst and Woolwich and thence into every branch of the army.
>
> Almost to a man they were loyalists. Home rule was not for them a political question; as in the case of Carson, it touched and revolted an instinct of preservation, a tradition centuries old, something in the blood – even stronger than the ingrained duty of obedience – a matter of life and death.[29]

After the Curragh, Carson had little reason to worry about Asquith. On 24 April, the Ulster Volunteers landed 30,000 Austrian, German and Italian rifles and bayonets at Larne on the Antrim coast and at Bangor in County Down, weapons that had been purchased in Hamburg with impunity. Liberal England was almost as outraged by the mutiny and the gun-running at Larne as the Irish nationalists. Asquith might have gone to the country and secured a fresh mandate to sweep away the old army caste and push through Home Rule once and for all, but on 28 June the assassination of the heir to the throne of Austria-Hungary in Sarajevo sparked a European crisis that rapidly spiralled out of control. The Prime Minister would not take on the army at such a juncture.

The Protestant clergy in the north were as willing as Carson and Bonar Law to go to the end. Personally, Crozier was devoted to Carson. Employing the warlike language that came so naturally to him, the Primate told him in 1915 that if partition hit the rocks, he hoped they would 'go down together with flags flying and drums beating'.[30] The Archbishop and the Presbyterian Moderator both agreed to Carson's invitation to sit in the provisional government of Ulster, a potentially bizarre development for a man who held the title of Primate of All Ireland. The Archbishop expressly approved of the arming of the Ulster Volunteer Force at Larne. Of course, he claimed to have known nothing about it, but other Protestant clergy in the parishes were not so reticent in recalling their role in distributing the weapons by motorcycle. William Forbes Marshall, minister of Aughnacloy in County Tyrone, was a UVF officer in South Tyrone. 'I have never passed the white gate of Aughnacloy Manse,' he recalled later, 'that I have not thought of the night when I sank down on the grass inside it, laden with 1,000 rounds of Mauser cartridges.'[31]

On 6 July 1914 the new Presbyterian Moderator, James Bingham, issued a statement again condemning the establishment of a parliament in Dublin as 'disastrous' and demanding the permanent exclusion from Home Rule of the whole of Ulster. The Presbyterian newspaper, the *Witness*, fortified waverers in the Protestant camp with a strong editorial on the eve of the 12 July celebrations. As Bonar Law had done at Balmoral, the paper insisted that Ulster confronted the siege of Derry all over again. 'The principle now at stake as far as Ulster and Ireland are concerned is the principle that was on trial at Derry and the Boyne, and triumphed,' it said. 'It is the principle of Protestant versus Romish rule over Ulster and Ireland, the principle of civil and religious liberty, which is the hand-maid and birthright of Protestantism . . . it is to placate Roman Catholics and empower them to penalise Protestants or Protestantism that Home Rule has been conceded by the government.'[32]

The battle of Protestant versus Romish rule was temporarily postponed. The ripples from Sarajevo spread outwards, enveloping Britain, France, Russia, Germany and Austria in a European crisis. By August, Home Rule was on the statute book. But its operation had been postponed, for by then Ireland was involved in the First World War.

In February 1916, weeks before the Easter uprising reshaped the course of Irish history, John Redmond penned an emotional portrait of the average Irish soldier fighting in the British army. Ireland was almost two years into the conflict with imperial Germany. Redmond homed in on the soldiers' faith. 'The Irish soldier,' he said, 'with his limpid faith and unaffected piety, his rosary recited on the hill-side, his Mass in the ruined barn under shellfire, his "act of contrition" in the trench before facing the hail of assault, his attitude to women, has mostly been a singular expression.'[33]

Redmond had a job to do, which was to sell the war to a sceptical home audience, and sell the idea of Irish loyalty to an equally sceptical audience in England. After the Herculean effort it had taken to drag Home Rule on to the statute book in 1914, Redmond had decided it was vital to demonstrate Ireland's reliability to make sure the Act was put into operation quickly. At the Mansion House in Dublin, Redmond and Carson appeared on the same platform to appeal for volunteers and agreed to put aside their differences for the duration of the struggle. It was a postponement of the dispute between Nationalists and Unionists over Home Rule, not a resolution. But it was a dramatic moment and as the two old warriors, representing the Orange and the Green, joined together in a noisy rendition of 'God Save the King', it was hard not to believe that war had wrought some kind of miracle in Ireland. The 'dream has come true', enthused the *Church of Ireland Gazette*. 'South and North have sunk their differences in a passionate determination to spend their strength in the crushing of the common enemy of themselves and of all civilisation.'[34]

Protestants, of course, responded to the call of King and country, assured by their militarist Primate that 'no more righteous war has ever been waged'.[35] Cardinal Logue declined to echo this fatuous statement, but many Catholics responded anyway. Of the Irish regiments, the Royal Inniskillin Fusiliers, the Royal Irish Rifles and the Royal Irish Fusiliers were all essentially northern regiments, with their depots at Omagh, Belfast and Armagh. But the Great War was the last hurrah of the grand old regiments of the south: the Royal Irish Regiment, based at Clonmel, the Connaught Rangers, based in Galway, the Leinster Regiment, based at Birr, the Royal Munster Fusiliers, based in Tralee, the Royal Dublin Fusiliers, based at Naas, as well as the 4th Dragoon Guards, the 6th Dragoons, the 5th Lancers and the 8th Hussars.

In the first months of the war, Nationalists were shocked and Protestants delighted by the fighting spirit so many ordinary Catholics displayed. Garret FitzGerald, who served twice as Ireland's prime minister in the 1980s, recalled his father's disappointment at the war fever that gripped Ireland in 1914. 'There were reports of the success of recruiting, of Volunteer bands marching to station to see off their comrades who had volunteered for service in the British army. The movement on which all our dreams had centred seemed merely to have canalised the martial spirit of the Irish people for the defence of England.'[36]

Protestants could hardly believe it. 'There is no longer the old time antipathy to British soldiers. The Army today is the best admired and most popular of institutions,' the *Church of Ireland Gazette* noted in August 1914. 'Not for a generation have the streets of Dublin witnessed such enthusiasm as that evoked by the appearance of soldiers in our midst.'[37] John Bernard, Protestant Bishop of Ossory, spoke of his admiration for Redmond for supporting the war effort. He was 'a true patriot and a wise statesman', the Bishop said.[38]

It was the Royal Dublin Fusiliers who yielded their first Catholic clerical casualty. Father Finn fell at Gallipoli, shortly after the soldiers landed at Sedd-el-Bahr on 25 April 1915. He died with incredible heroism, according to a survivor. 'By the time he had waded to the beach, his clothing was riddled with shot. Yet disabled as he was, and in spite also of the great pain he must have been suffering, he crawled about the beach, affording consolation to the dying Dublins . . . it was while he was in the act of thus blessing one of his men that his skull was broken by a piece of shrapnel.'[39] Father John Gwynn of the 1st Irish Guards died at Béthune in France on 12 October 1915 after being wounded at Loos. 'I saw him just before he died,' a Guardsman wrote.

Shrapnel and bullets were being showered upon us in all directions. Hundreds of our lads dropped. Fr Gwynn was undismayed. He seemed to be all over the place giving the Last Sacrament to the dying. Once I thought he was buried alive, for a shell exploded within a few yards of where he was and the next moment I saw nothing but a great heap of earth.

The plight of the wounded concealed beneath was harrowing. Out of the ground cries of 'Father, father, father' came from those who were in their death agonies. Then as if by a miracle, Fr Gwynn was seen to fight his way through the earth. He must have been severely injured but he went on blessing the wounded and hearing the confessions. The last I saw of him he was kneeling by the side of the German soldier.[40]

It was, of course, the Castle Catholics who responded most keenly to the call, those who dwelt in the no man's land between imperial and Irish nationalism. Upper-class Catholic schools like Redmond's alma mater revelled in their contribution to the war effort. The 1916 school annual of Clongowes Wood listed with pride the 450 old boys engaged in the army or navy, the seven military crosses, the two Legions of Honour and the obituaries: Captain John Dunn, Royal Munster Fusiliers, killed at Gallipoli, 15 August 1915; Captain Michael Fitzgerald, Royal Dublin Fusiliers, also killed at Gallipoli, 15 August 1915; Captain James Smithwick, Royal Irish Regiment, wounded at Le Pelly – visited by the King at Wandsworth hospital. 'He had served with distinction in the South African War,' the paper enthused. 'Physically he was a splendid type of a gallant Irish officer and in Kilkenny, where his family are so highly respected, he was extremely popular amongst all classes.'[41]

The description of the 'respected' family, so popular 'amongst all classes', tacitly revealed much about the Catholic elite from which the school drew its pupils. By 1917 the school had given up 53 of its old boys and by 1918 the death toll had reached 81. One of the teachers died as well. Father Augustine Hartigan fell in Mesopotamia on 16 July 1916. He died marching up the Tigris with the Connaught Rangers. His last letter described a terrible march across the desert in 112 degrees of heat. 'Many of the poor Connaughts, exhausted by hunger, thirst and fatigue succumbed and lay dying on the burning sands.' His obituary continued:

However, their faithful chaplain did not abandon them. He remained behind to administer the consolation of our holy religion long after the marching columns had disappeared. Then he lost his way in the desert and after a few days of wandering about was brought to the Amara hospital ill with jaundice and quite worn out. He wrote to his mother that he was well enough to say Mass and that he hoped soon to return to his regiment. The day after she received this letter she had a telegram from the War Office informing her that he had died . . .[42]

Such valour did not win plaudits from every element in the Irish Catholic Church. It reeked of West Britonism and of the elite who had always cosied up to Protestants. It was the kind of behaviour to be expected from those whom Bishop

Cantwell had long ago dismissed as bad or aristocratic Catholics. Archbishops Logue and Walsh were more in sympathy with the anti-war nationalists than with the soldiers of the Irish regiments, although they held their peace until after Easter 1916.

Primate Crozier revelled in his high-profile visits to the front, handing out pocket hymnals to the troops in the trenches, preaching at vast services of 2,000 or 3,000 soldiers at a time and generally exulting in the cleansing effect of the slaughter on the nation's faith, morals and literature. 'A certain spirit of serious-ness, of solemnity and of service has descended on our country,' he told the clergy of the diocese of Armagh in July 1916, adding that if the war ended now, it would have failed in its object of bringing about national repentance.[43]

The Irish Catholic bishops never went near the front and made few references to the war. 'A great emphasis is laid on prayers for peace,' grumbled the *Church of Ireland Gazette* of the Catholic Lenten pastorals of 1916. 'They are neither black nor white but an indefinite grey.'[44]

There were a few exceptions. Dennis Kelly, Bishop of Ross, was no nationalist. When he addressed Cork people on the war on 10 September 1915, at a meeting of the Irish War Savings Committee chaired by the Lord Mayor, he told people to stop betting and drinking and not to buy foreign clothes. He urged the government to prosecute the war to a successful issue. 'I must declare at the outset that I assume the Allies will win,' he said to the cheers of the audience.[45] Healy of Tuam was of a similar cast of mind. But by 1914 he was a sick man, and he died in 1916. O'Dwyer of Limerick was more typical of the bishops and the population at large. He was openly sceptical about the need for Ireland to fight. The Irish, he wrote to the *Munster News* on 10 November 1915, 'have no burning desire to die for Servia. They would much rather be allowed to till their own potato gardens in peace in Connemara . . . This war may be just or unjust but any fair-minded man will admit it is England's war, not Ireland's.'[46]

O'Dwyer represented the average Catholic cleric. Catholics cooled towards the war after the first year of fighting. They were outraged when Carson, the rock on which a united Home Rule Ireland foundered, was invited to join the cabinet in June 1915. It was one of those moves which was not intended as an insult, but which revealed in a stroke Britain's essentially casual attitude towards Irish opinion. It was 'a horrible scandal and intolerable outrage on Irish sentiment', Bishop Michael Fogarty of Killaloe told Redmond.[47] In November 1917 Logue told his colleagues he had withdrawn from as much contact as he could with the authorities. 'I do not like to have any communication with the local government, or any other government department just at present,' he said.[48] The bishops were simply indifferent to Serbia, or to Belgium, which the *Catholic Bulletin* dismissed as 'a country the size of Munster'.[49] The Catholic hierarchy's coolness towards the war triggered accusations that they were German sympathisers. However, as Bernard explained to the Archbishop of Canterbury: 'They are intensely anti-British at heart, thoroughly disloyal to the King, to Great Britain and to the Empire. That is in their blood . . . but that they are positively pro-German I don't believe, except in two or three instances.'[50]

While the Catholic volunteers heard their masses, made their acts of contrition and died in the mud of Flanders and the deserts of Mesopotamia, the anti-war nationalists planned an act of devotion of another kind. Redmond thought Ireland could prove its manhood in foreign trenches. Sinn Fein planned to achieve the same result by fighting at home. The outbreak of war gave them their great opportunity. As the Bolsheviks were to discover in Russia, simple opposition to the war reaped political dividends as soon as the casualties mounted. Intelligent people were repelled by the crudity with which Redmond's supporters aped British propaganda about supposed German atrocities in Belgium.

Sinn Fein was a relatively recent phenomenon. It was not so much a party as a movement. It expressed all that was latent and extreme in late nineteenth-century Irish Catholic culture, rejecting not just British rule but the English cultural, religious and political experience in entirety. Its attraction was its very extremism – the pledge to erase 700 years of history and begin again. The Sinn Fein propagandist Aodh de Blácam in 1921 foresaw an entirely new type of society developing under its auspices, based on a return to mythical Gaelic models. Ireland would reject the British parliamentary system and the industrial revolution and neatly bypass both capitalism and the class struggle. A new assembly, the Dáil, would contain only 'the good, the wise and the brave, men chosen not for their expertness in economic matters but . . . for kingliness'.[51] These extraordinary beings would hardly ever have to meet, however, as the towns, the ancient centres of English contagion, would disappear along with British rule and Ireland would return to a rural society based on co-operative communes.

What distinguished the Sinn Fein utopians from most of their continental counterparts was their express acknowledgement of Ireland's debt to Catholicism. 'She is peculiar among nations,' De Blácam wrote with pride, 'because in her the most advanced revolutionary spirit is united with the most conservative religious tradition.' Ireland will return to her roots, he prophesied, 'led by the cross and the Catholic banner, amid smoking incense and to the song of canticles'.[52] There was no place in the script for the stately Georgian Ascendancy monument Trinity College, or for Protestants of any shape or form. Everything was to hark back to an exclusively Gaelic Catholic past. The youth of tomorrow was to be taught in the old Celtic monasteries at Clonmacnois, and 'on Tory island, amid storm and under terrific sunset lights, on Inis Catra, where the round towers are reflected in Lough Derg'.[53] How anyone was expected to study in single-sex round towers in that kind of weather was not spelled out.

The 1916 Rising in Dublin was suffused with this kind of Christian inspiration. It was timed to coincide with the most momentous day in the Christian calendar. The chief ideologue of the conspirators, Padraig Pearse, a portly schoolteacher, intentionally thought of the revolt in Catholic terms as a religious sacrifice, freely offered, from which inestimable benefits would flow, though not necessarily in their own time. As the son of an English stonemason and an Irish mother, Pearse was a perfect candidate for the Gaelic League. Celibate, devoted to the Virgin Mary and shunning intimacy with any women except his mother and sisters, in England his fate might have been the dismal one of the repressed homosexual schoolmaster, condemned to a wearying round of common room intrigues and doomed crushes on small boys. In England he might well have shrunk from the hard, knowing glances of the women and the raised eyebrows and mocking leers of their husbands. In the more innocent atmosphere of Catholic Ireland he could float along in a cloud of unknowing. When he asked to sleep in the same bed as the sons of the Gaelic-speaking peasants he visited on the west coast, the parents in question felt honoured by the request. Catholic Ireland's repressive culture protected men like Pearse not only from the scrutiny of other people, but from themselves. When his friends urged him not to publish a poem with paedophile undertones, Pearse was not grateful for the advice, but hurt. He could not understand why anyone could object to a poem celebrating the joys of savouring the kisses of a particularly beautiful boy.[54]

The stuffy piety of the Gaelic League allowed Pearse to unwind and flourish in an atmosphere that was wholly unthreatening. He was comfortable, could expand, in a world of earnest young men and priests, where the only females were the odd not very sexy schoolmistress. After his death nationalist hagiographers sketched out an improbable romance between Pearse and a female friend that would have ended in marriage had she not conveniently perished while swimming. It could never have happened.

The combination of fanaticism and moral probity in the League, and later in Sinn Fein, drew out all that was strongest in Pearse. He 'seemed a reincarnation of the stark Colomban Ireland', De Blácam wrote admiringly. 'He thought in terms of war and stress and sacrifice.'[55] He made his audiences stand up and recite 'I believe in the Irish nation,' in an echo of the Apostles' Creed. In the year of the rising, he published a pamphlet, *The Sovereign People*, which was saturated with religious imagery. The people, he wrote, were those 'who wept in Gethsemane, who trod the sorrowful way, who died naked on a cross, who went down into hell, who will rise again, glorious and immortal, who will sit at the right hand of God and will come again to give judgment, a judgment just and terrible!'[56]

When the rising began on 24 April, Easter Monday, Pearse was designated President of the provisional government of the Irish Republic. By midday he and his little band had captured the General Post Office in the centre of Dublin, and Pearse read out a declaration of independence he had composed. By that night other insurgents had taken up positions on St Stephen's Green, in the College of Surgeons and in the Guinness buildings. The British were slow to react. The Protestant north was the enemy in Ireland for the Liberals, not the south. A revolt in Dublin was hardly what Asquith had expected, still less his emollient and decidedly green-tinged Secretary in Ireland, Augustine Birrell.

By the following Friday, however, General Sir John Maxwell, hurriedly appointed as Commander-in-Chief, Ireland, had 30,000 troops in Ireland compared to the 1,200 under Pearse. The President surrendered at 3.30 p.m. on Saturday and the rising was over.

The Protestants of Dublin did not suffer much in the revolt. Nothing had ever interrupted the flow of services in Christ Church cathedral. But in Easter 1916, the fighting between the rebels and the British forces stopped the show for the first time in centuries. The service books in the cathedral show a red line crossed though the week and in spidery hand the single sentence: 'Services cancelled owing to Sinn Fein rebellion.' The insurgents took over the Synod Hall outside the cathedral and sniped from the windows. The Bishop of Tuam was hijacked in his car on St Stephen's Green, which the Sinn Feiners wheeled away into a barricade they were building beside the Shelbourne hotel.[57] One Dublin cleric, H. Thompson, curate of St Catherine's, was wounded in the leg.

As reigns of terror go, it was a mild affair. But Britain was at war, and the Protestant clergy clamoured for retribution. Archishop Bernard, who had been translated from Ossory to Dublin earlier in 1916, was uncharacteristically vindictive. When Asquith issued a general pardon in an attempt to cool the passions aroused by Maxwell's spate of executions, the Archbishop exploded. 'This is not the time for amnesties and pardons,' he wrote furiously on 3 May. 'It is the time for punishment swift and stern. And no one who lives in Ireland believes that the present Irish government has the courage to punish anybody.'[58] The Archbishop complained that as he wrote, he could see snipers on the rooftops trying to shoot British soldiers. From the loyalist stronghold of Belfast, the Presbyterians hurled their thunderbolts against the rebels. It was 'the most disgraceful and diabolical in the despicable roll of Irish rebellions', spluttered the *Witness*.[59] Ireland had been 'humiliated', the Belfast Presbytery declared. 'It is needless to say that the members of our Presbyterian Church are absolutely loyal to the throne and obedient to the law.'[60] The Assembly in June dispatched a telegram to George V, 'to assure our beloved King . . . that the members of the Irish Presbyterian church remain steadfast in loyalty to the throne and . . . that they deplore and strongly condemn the spirit manifested in the recent outbreak of revolutionary violence in Ireland'.[61]

The Carsonites pointed to the Rising as a portent of the chaos Unionists could expect under a Home Rule parliament. When Carson appeared in person at the Presbyterian General Assembly in June 1916 and spoke of how his heart beat for Ulster, there was huge applause. The *Witness* warned Protestant folk in the north that if they were handed over to 'the wolves of Sinn Feinism and Nationalism', there was only one possible outcome – 'slaughter'. The newspaper said there was no such thing as the Irish nation. 'In the real sense of the term it never was a nation and . . . never was less a nation than at the present time.'[62]

The Rising sundered the brief, shaky alliance between Irish Catholics and Protestants over the war. Protestants condemned the revolt unreservedly and heaped praise on the British troops under Maxwell who put it down. The *Church of Ireland Gazette* only hoped that 'the people of Ireland were worthy of their saviours from the horrors of revolution.'[63] The Catholic Church did not see Maxwell's men as saviours. They found it difficult to dislike the rebels, who were such devoted sons of their own Church and who shared so many of their own cultural enthusiasms.

Sinn Fein men did not revere British Liberalism, which was increasingly agnostic and immoral in Irish Catholic eyes. They did not try to curry favour with Protestants. Cullen had always dreaded an alliance between Irish nationalism and continental radicalism, but Sinn Fein was comfortingly provincial and entirely untainted by French atheism or Spanish anti-clericalism. The Sinn Feiners were as prudish in their morals as they were strict in their religion. They exalted the Irish bishops and made it quite clear that their war posed no threat to episcopal authority.

Between 3 and 11 May, General Maxwell executed 12 rebels and punished thousands of others with jail sentences or deportation orders. No Catholic bishop condemned the Rising. Instead, on 17 May, O'Dwyer of Limerick broke the Church's silence on the matter and savaged the British. 'You took great care that no plea for mercy should interpose on behalf of the poor young fellows who surrendered to you in Dublin,' he replied to Maxwell after the General wrote to him, urging him to restrain two Sinn Fein activists among his clergy. 'The first information we got of their fate was the announcement that they had been shot in cold blood. Personally I regard your action with horror . . . altogether your regime has been one of the blackest chapters in the history of the misgovernment of the country.'[64] The bishop repeated these sentiments in public in September, when he was presented with the freedom of the city of Limerick. Pointing the finger at the Jews the persecution of whom he had actively encouraged in his diocese, he claimed Ireland was ruled by a combination of English barristers and Jews from Shoreditch. 'Sinn Fein is in my judgement the true principle', he said, 'and alliance with English politicians is the alliance of the lamb and the wolf, and it is at that point that I differ from the present political leaders and believe that they have led and are leading the National cause to disaster.'

The Rising left Irish Catholics and Protestants at the opposite ends of a spectrum. But it divided the Irish Protestants as well. As soon as the revolt had been crushed, Asquith sent the Minister of Munitions, David Lloyd George, to Dublin with the brief of lancing the Irish boil. Lloyd George returned with a scheme to pacify the situation through the immediate application of Home Rule, instead of delaying it to the end of hostilities. At the same time, he recommended the exclusion of the Unionist north-east for an indefinite period. Asquith duly made a statement on Ireland in July proposing the rapid introduction of Home Rule outside a six-county Ulster. The plan commended itself to no one. Carson's Unionists would be satisfied only with Ulster's permanent exclusion from Home Rule. Catholic nationalists deeply opposed partition, as did the southern Protestants. The Church of Ireland Synod that met on 20 June 1916 condemned what it called 'a policy of dismemberment with which no Irishman is content'.[65]

The result was a brief alliance of convenience between the Catholic and Protestant bishops of the South against the British government. The Catholic bishops wanted Home Rule for the whole of Ireland; the Protestant bishops wanted continued union with Britain for the whole of Ireland. Their position was a singular one. As the *Church of Ireland Gazette* put it in July 1916: 'We believe that Home Rule without Ulster would have been thoroughly bad. Home Rule with Ulster would have been less bad.'[66] The southern Protestants had an odd, but real convergence of interests with Charles McHugh, Catholic Bishop of Derry, whose city looked likely to be excluded from Home Rule in spite of the fact that it had a narrow Catholic majority. Bishop McHugh was furious with Redmond's parliamentary party for swallowing partition – however reluctantly – as the price of Home Rule and demanded a national convention 'under some great and fearless laymen, chosen by the people'.[67] He urged the nation to disavow 'all connection with doings as despicable as any recorded in the history of the union'. Archbishop Walsh agreed, joining the assault on the parliamentary party, and saying 'he had had no doubt for a long time that the Home Rule cause was being led in parliament along a line that could end only in catastrophe'.[68] O'Dwyer said Ireland 'had been made a thing of truck and barter'.

Southern Protestants were not interested in the Catholic bishops' assault on Redmond in parliament. In fact, they were now much fonder of Redmond than most Catholics, especially as he had lost a son and a brother in the war. But they were not immune to McHugh's suggestion that they should join their names to a petition against partition. To the annoyance of Carson and the northern Protestants, in May 1917 Bishops John Gregg of Ossory, Benjamin Plunket of Tuam and Sterling Barry of Killaloe signed a petition which denounced partition, as did 18 members of the Catholic hierarchy, led by Logue and Walsh.

The three Protestant bishops and the 18 Catholic bishops were looking at Ireland from different ends of the telescope. But at the end of the day the differences between the northern and southern Protestants were greater than those between the southern Catholics and Protestants. There were almost no circumstances in which southern Protestants supported partition. There were almost none in which their northern colleagues supported continued unity.

The same division between the Protestants emerged in the ill-fated 'National Convention on Ireland', which Lloyd George, Prime Minister since Asquith's resignation in December 1916, summoned in August 1917. Of the 96 members, 25 were drawn from Ulster and nine were Southern Unionists, with Archbishop Bernard representing the Church and Viscount Midleton, former Secretary of State for India, the old landed interest.

After the animosity inspired by the reprisals for the Easter Rebellion, the Convention opened in an almost hopeless atmosphere. Redmond was ill and visibly broken. The Catholic bishops' denunciations rang in his ears, and he was losing the battle for public opinion to Sinn Fein. The Catholic Church, of which he was such a faithful son, continually undermined him. In December, the Nationalists and southern Unionists on the Convention reached a fragile compromise that seemed to point a way out of the impasse. The deal conceded the principal Nationalist demands relating to Home Rule, except over customs, which the parties agreed to retain under the imperial parliament. Bishop Patrick O'Donnell of Raphoe, however, made the customs issue the crucial sticking point and withdrew the Church's support. The deal collapsed along with the Convention. An unholy alliance of Catholics and northern Unionists sank it in April 1918, by 47 votes to 41. Redmond's death saved him from further humiliation. Not so his family. When his body was returned to Wexford for burial, the Catholic hierarchy – the same men who had danced attendance on him in his great days – ignored the funeral. Walsh refused even to send a message of condolence, while Denis Hanihan, O'Dwyer's successor in Limerick, refused permission for a requiem mass in his diocese.[69]

The southern Protestants were bitter about the behaviour of their Ulster co-religionists. Archbishop Bernard had expected little from the Catholic bishops, most of whom he considered 'literally peasants', but the selfishness of the northern Protestants rankled. He suspected the role of the southern Protestants was simply 'to hew wood and draw water for Ulster'.[70] Lord Midleton shared his opinion. Ulster had 'preferred to serve in the heaven of Union rather than reign in the hell of Separation', he recalled later. 'She went into the convention in 1917 with stated willingness to consider reasonable terms of settlement; she did not contribute a single concrete proposal in eight months; she ended it by voting against the most advantageous and best-guarded scheme which had yet been devised to keep Ireland united.' He ended with an accurate prophecy. 'If southern Ireland should ever become detached from the empire, the greatest danger will be to Ulster and the responsibility for it will largely lie at Ulster's door.'[71]

The southern Protestant belief that Ireland must remain united was very natural. Their position was precarious. As the *Church of Ireland Gazette* put it in November 1918: 'The life blood of the Church of Ireland is bound up with the unity of Ireland . . . a united Ireland is and must be the first postulate for all Irish churchmen who are churchmen first, for a divided Ireland means death to their Church.'[72] The Catholics were so numerous throughout the country that even a truncated Ulster would still contain a strong Catholic presence. The Presbyterians were practically confined to Ulster anyway. It was the Church of Ireland, thinly spread over 32 counties and with most of its parishes and cathedrals in the South, which had most to fear from partition. The choice was between becoming an insignificant 5 per cent in a 26-county Ireland, or remaining a significant 25 per cent in a 32-county state.

Bernard's special concern was for his beloved Trinity College. In June 1919 he accepted the position of Provost, resigning his archbishopric to Gregg. Bernard divined correctly that the survival of southern Protestantism depended on the retention of institutions – hospitals, schools, newspapers and a university – not church buildings. Trinity's future looked far from assured. There it lay, the bulky symbol of Protestant Ascendancy in the middle of Catholic Dublin, privilege and opulence (so most people thought) oozing from its grey stonework and yet, cap in hand, begging for money. A Royal Commission in 1919–20 recommended an annual subsidy of £49,000 a year and a one-off grant of £113,000 for the buildings. But it soon became clear that such promises were worthless and that British rule in Ireland might not last long.

The British threat to extend conscription to Ireland in the last months of 1918 alienated the Catholic hierarchy and pushed the bishops further into the arms of Sinn Fein. In 1917 there were 349 arrests for political offences and 24 deportations without trial. In 1918 there were 1,107 arrests, 91 deportations, 12 papers were closed and numerous districts put under martial law.[73] In spite of growing disorder, the Catholic bishops refused to be co-opted by the authorities into condemning Sinn Fein. In November 1917, Logue had issued a pastoral letter that was critical of Sinn Fein agitation. He did not denounce it, but said it was 'ill-considered and utopian', and pronounced that it would end in 'disaster, defeat and collapse'. It was pointless, the Primate said, to think of 'hurling an unarmed people against an empire which has five millions of men under arms . . . the thing would be ludicrous if it were not so mischievous'.[74] The Cardinal appealed to common sense and to the common memory of the litany of failed risings that studded Irish history. He did not insult the republicans or the many priests who actively supported Sinn Fein.

Within a month of the armistice in November 1918 the old regime in Dublin collapsed. In the general election held in December, Sinn Fein swept the board outside Ulster, winning 73 seats. The parliamentary party took only six. Some Catholic bishops publicly supported Sinn Fein in the election. In Dublin, Archbishop Walsh received the Sinn Fein candidate for Drumcondra at his palace, and called for 'a working arrangement' between Sinn Fein and the Irish parliamentary party against the Unionist 'common enemy'.[75] On 21 January 1919, the Sinn Fein representatives, those who had not been arrested by the British, gathered in Dublin's Mansion House to proclaim a new source of authority over the country, Dáil Eireann. The new body proclaimed Ireland a republic.

The British authorities tried to ignore the Dáil. But this became impossible after the republicans set up their own courts, police and taxation system and floated a successful loan of £400,000 at home, which was massively boosted by a £10 million contribution from the Irish-American diaspora. When the British held local elections in January 1920 and county council elections in June, Sinn Fein and their Labour allies won 77 per cent and 81 per cent of the votes in Ireland respectively.

By the autumn of 1920 the British faced two choices: forcibly to reintroduce crown rule, or to relinquish even the pretence of authority over the 26 counties in the South. In October, a rash of proclamations closed the shipping links to the United States, cut off government grants to republican local authorities and banned their newspapers and organisations. The revolt against British rule was marked by a wave of terror directed against the mainly Catholic Royal Irish Constabulary. In the first six months of 1920, 51 policemen were killed. By October, the tally had risen to 110 while by the end of 1920 it had reached 165. At Bandon, County Cork, masked gunmen assassinated the chief of the intelligence department for west Cork, Police Sergeant Mulhern, inside a church. The men sprang out from behind the door of St Patrick's and shot him dead, minutes before the start of the 8 a.m. mass, just after he had removed his hat and dipped his fingers in the holy water stoop.[76]

The Catholic hierarchy sent out mixed signals in response to this wave of violence. In March 1919, Logue had released a Lenten pastoral that trod a fine line between denunciations of British repression and warnings about the threat that socialism and Russian Bolshevism posed to family life. The British, he complained, were trying to put Ireland in a strait-jacket 'instead of applying those remedies which got to the root of the disease. This is precisely the treatment to which Ireland has been subjected for beyond the range of living memory, neglect of every remonstrance, reproach or evasion of every just claim, violation of every promise 'til the people were goaded into wild courses.'[77]

The bishops' statement on 24 June from Maynooth denounced Sinn Fein violence but blamed the British for provoking it. 'It is the rule of the sword, utterly unsuited to a civilised nation and supremely provocative of disorder and chronic rebellion,' they said. 'The acts of violence, which we have to deplore, and they are few, spring from this cause and from this cause alone.'[78]

By December 1919, the worsening bloodshed prompted Logue to issue a pastoral letter to be read out in all churches on 21 December, denouncing violence on all sides. It criticised 'the drastic repression' of the British, but still urged Irish Catholics to 'bear these trials in a Christian spirit'. The Cardinal reminded them that 'Holy Ireland, the land of St Patrick, should never be regenerated by deeds of blood or raised up by the hand of the midnight assassin, innocent blood crying to heaven for vengeance and bringing down the divine wrath'.[79] In an interview with the *Armagh Guardian*, the Primate announced he was 'putting up his shutters'; because 'when a person gets to his 80th year he has something else to think about besides politics'.[80]

The bishops' colleagues in the diaspora encouraged them to take a bolder line. In the years after the end of the First World War the Irish ecclesiastical empire brought its strength to bear against the creaking British empire. In December 1918, Cardinal William O'Connell of New York had addressed a huge meeting of Irish-Americans in Madison Square Gardens in which he described Sinn Fein as 'one of the chosen standard bearers of one of the oldest nations in Europe'.[81] In Australia, Daniel Mannix, former President of Maynooth and now the Archbishop of Melbourne, was a militant supporter of the republicans who had presided over large meetings against conscription and involvement in the war. At a rally at the Richmond racecourse in Melbourne he had attacked the Convention and appealed to the memory of the Easter Rising. Ireland, he said, 'claims that the ashes of her brave sons should be given back to her. She claims that Ireland should not be thrown on the dissecting table of the British parliament, that the Dark Rosaleen of all the years should not be hacked up and cut up into sections in order to please an unworthy and disloyal faction in the north. Finally she asks that when the peace conference assembles she should be allowed like the other small nations . . . to plead her own case.'[82]

While the British increased their repression in Ireland in the summer of 1920, Mannix began a mammoth tour of the US and Europe, which took him through San Francisco, Los Angeles, Denver, Omaha, St Louis and Chicago. In New York he was made a freeman of the city and in Madison Square Gardens he denounced Lloyd George to an audience of 18,000 as a 'dying wasp'.[83] The grand tour ended on a note of farce while he was travelling on the high seas from New York to Ireland, after a British destroyer intercepted his passage. A launch party boarded the *Baltic* off Cobh on 8 August and hustled the Archbishop off to Penzance, in Cornwall. The virtual kidnapping of the Sinn Fein Archbishop did the British no good. Mannix revelled in the drama, cracked jokes at every opportunity, gave countless interviews and received a royal welcome when he steamed into London on the train.

Even without bishops like Mannix egging them on, the Irish bishops would have turned more and more resolutely against the authorities as the struggle between the British and the Dáil intensified. The introduction in March 1920 of an auxiliary paramilitary police service composed of British ex-servicemen, the notorious Black and Tans, worsened relations. With the exception of Bishop Kelly of Ross, who told people in Skibbereen that Sinn Fein were no better than the Bolsheviks,[84] the Irish bishops increasingly saw the crown forces and not the rebels as the greater threat. There were still words of criticism for the rebels. In January 1920 Thomas Gilmartin, Archbishop of Tuam, criticised what he called 'undisguised ruffianism'[85] in the rebel ranks while O'Brien of Cashel condemned the Sinn Fein murder of Luke Finnegan, an RIC constable in the Archbishop's cathedral town of Thurles. But on 27 January 1920 the Catholic bishops signed a manifesto at Maynooth that came down unequivocally on the side of Irish independence, condemned the 'iron rule of oppression' of the British and denounced partition. 'The only way to terminate our historic troubles and establish friendly relations between England and Ireland,' the bishops said, 'is to allow undivided Ireland to choose her own form of government.'[86]

The activities of the Black and Tans infuriated them, principally because their tactics of staging bloody reprisals for any assaults on crown forces made the situation more chaotic than ever. 'They have wrecked towns, villages and peaceful homes,' Harty of Cashel wrote on 14 August. 'They have destroyed creameries and been guilty of many robberies. They speak of reprisals, as if reprisals can justify or palliate the murder of innocent men or the destruction of property belonging to innocent people. They speak of outrages "attributed to Sinn Fein" but they do not call to attention the murder of a nation or the depopulation of a country.'[87] On 19 October, the bishops complained of 'countless indiscriminate raids and arrests in the darkness of night, prolonged imprisonments without trial, savage sentences that command no confidence, the burning of houses and town halls, factories, creameries and crops, the destruction of industries to pave the way for want and famine . . . the flogging and massacre of civilians, all perpetrated by the forces of the crown who have established a reign of frightfulness which . . . has a parallel only in . . . the Red Army of Bolshevist Russia.'[88]

The chaos was the signal for a settling of scores. As far as many Catholics were concerned, all Protestants were Unionist enemies of Irish freedom. To be Catholic was almost automatically to proclaim oneself in the eyes of Protestants as a Sinn Fein supporter. In Belfast, Down and Antrim that was bad news for Catholics. Elsewhere, it was Protestants who feared the midnight knock on the door. In July 1920, Catholics in Banbridge, County Down, were attacked after the funeral of a police commissioner who had been killed in County Cork. In Belfast, 18 people were killed in a week of rioting that raged around the Falls Road, Cromac Street, Newtownards Road and Kashmir Road. The victims included a Redemptorist friar, Brother Michael Morgan, killed at the Clonard monastery. Over the course of the year there were 62 civilian deaths in Belfast and 20 in Derry. There was an attempt to burn a convent near Newtownards Road. In Dromore a Catholic club was burned down and the Hibernian hall and convent attacked in Lisburn. In November, after 14 British officers were shot dead in their beds in Dublin, the British retaliated by shooting dead 13 civilians at a Gaelic football match in Dublin's Croke Park. Gregg was outraged by the killing of the British officers and saluted them at their funeral on 21 November 'as brave men who did their duty and died doing it'.[89]

The death toll among the police rose steeply in the autumn of 1920. In August, eight were killed throughout Ireland, in Athlone, Lisburn, Inchigeela, Kilrush, Naas, Dundalk, Gort, Oranmore and Tralee. In Lisburn, a Protestant district inspector was killed while leaving church. By the end of October, more than 100 RIC men had been killed since the beginning of the year.

The *Irish Times* attacked the Catholic bishops for not denouncing the Sinn Fein murders. In fact, Logue was genuinely appalled. One week after the Croke Park massacre he warned the nation that their patriotism must be 'sincere, honourable, just and in accordance with God's laws, otherwise it degenerates into a blind, brutal, reckless passion inspired not by love of country but by Satan . . . God help our poor country, groaning under the infliction of this competition in murders.'[90] It had no effect on the grim round of tit for tat sectarian killings.

In March 1921 it was the turn of the Fleming family of Drumgarra, County Monaghan. The family head, 64-year-old William Fleming, was a marked man after becoming involved in a gun-fight in which he had shot dead a man from

Castleblayney. A crowd of about 40 broke into the Fleming farm and set the house on fire. Fleming's old mother and two of her grandchildren survived by hiding in an outhouse but the intruders shot William and his son Robert dead and threw the bodies into a ditch.[91] In County Kerry it was the turn of Sir Arthur Vicars, Ulster King of Arms and the man blamed for the mysterious loss of the Irish 'crown jewels' during Edward VII's visit in 1907. Dragged from his bed in Kilmorna House in his dressing gown, he was shot and his body was found with a label round his neck reading 'Spy. Informers beware. I.R.A never forgets.'[92] In March, two members of the Good family, Protestant farmers of Balyshall, near Timoleague, County Cork, were shot dead. Mrs Good first buried her husband after he was shot on 10 March. She buried her son after he was killed on 26 March.[93]

Some of the attacks by the Irish Republican Army, as the Dáil's armed supporters were known, had a theatrical aspect. The newspapers recorded a 'startling interruption' in the spring of 1921 to the Hon. Edward O'Brien's lawn tennis party at Roslevin, near Ennis, County Clare.

> While the play was in progress a party of about 40 men, many of them carrying guns, suddenly appeared and calling 'hands up' began to fire shots about the place. Shots were also fired into the luncheon tent. Mr W. H. Ball was wounded in the arm. He also had his head grazed. The motor car of Mr F. N. Stoddart, who was one of the guests, was taken out, set on fire and destroyed. Mr Ball's car was taken away. The guests were terrified and several ladies collapsed.[94]

There was nothing chivalrous about the murder on 12 June of John Finlay, a retired Church of Ireland Dean at Bawnbay, County Cavan. Some IRA soldiers masquerading as British officers called at the deanery and were entertained to supper. While the Dean chattered indiscreetly the soldiers smiled and nodded. Then they dragged him from the dinner table and slashed his throat on the lawn.[95]

The British parliament passed the Government of Ireland Act in December 1920, granting Home Rule to two Irish entities, a 26-county state in the south with its capital in Dublin and a six-county state in the north, with its capital in Belfast. In the south, the Act was a dead letter, as real power had passed into the hands of the Dáil. But in the north Home Rule was now a fact, and, on 22 June 1921, George V came to Belfast City Hall to open the new Northern Ireland parliament. The Catholic Church fulminated helplessly against partition. On 21 June, the bishops called on the Irish to spurn the 'sham settlement' put forward by the British and lambasted the 'special government [which] has been given to one section of her people, remarkable at all times for intolerance . . . a parliament of their own is set up in their midst after a year of continuous and intolerable persecution directed against the Catholics of Belfast. Until repression ceases and the right of Ireland to choose her own government is recognised, there is no prospect that peace will reign among us.'[96] At the end of August, another wave of rioting swept Belfast, killing 16 civilians. In the last week of November there was more fighting, in which 17 Protestants and 15 Catholics were killed.

With no end to the fighting in sight and the threat of a full-scale British invasion, the IRA began inching forwards for a compromise settlement that would secure the principal gains of the armed struggle. On 6 December 1921 a delegation of the Dáil, headed by Michael Collins, signed an Anglo-Irish treaty, ending the war between the Dáil and the crown. The treaty conceded far more than the Protestants had expected. Archbishop Gregg had assumed as a matter of geographical necessity that customs would remain under the British parliament. But the British had conceded almost everything to the Irish except control over the six counties in the north and the symbolically loaded question of a republic. Diplomats would be accredited to the new Irish Free State through George V and the monarch would be represented in Dublin by a governor-general, as he was in the Dominions of Australia, Canada, New Zealand and South Africa.

Swallowing their shock, the southern Protestants decided to give the Free State wholehearted support. As the *Church of Ireland Gazette* pointed out in January 1922, the treaty meant that Unionism had ceased to exist in the south. Protestants 'must remember that when the last British soldier and policeman march out of Ireland, the Provisional government will be the only bulwark against the forces of anarchy'.[97] But hopes of such a respite were premature. The sectarian killings went on, on both sides of the border. A large minority of the Dáil, under the leadership of the American-born Eamon de Valera, denounced Collins and urged continuation of the IRA's armed struggle. They denied the legitimacy of a government that recognised the crown and governed only 26 counties. The Free State immediately found itself in a ferocious 11-month war with the anti-treaty wing of Sinn Fein.

Some Catholic priests actively helped the anti-treaty forces. The Catholic hierarchy did not. They were less panicked by the threat of anarchy than the propertied and salaried Protestants but they supported the Free State against its enemies. If they were hesitant it was because they lacked leadership. Walsh died in 1921. Logue was old and ill, and would die in 1924. On 10 October 1922 the Catholic bishops issued a statement unreservedly supporting the new government and lambasting the IRA in much the same language they had employed against the Black and Tans. The Republicans 'have chosen to attack their country as if it were a foreign power', the bishops said. 'They have deliberately set out to make our Motherland a heap of ruins. They have wrecked Ireland from end to end, burning and destroying national property . . . they have caused more damage to Ireland in three months than can be laid to the charge of the British in so many decades.'[98]

The vast majority of those killed on both sides in the conflict were Catholic soldiers, some 540 from the Free State side and an equivalent or greater number from the Republican side. But Protestants were in a worse position than ever: they became a prime target for the anti-treaty forces. The year before they had been picked off as supporters of the British. Now they paid for loyalty to the Free State.

In his diary, Gregg recorded in his laconic style the chaos that stretched to the centre of Dublin. 'Letters etc till 2.30 – then to club, lunch,' he wrote on 31 May 1922. '2.30. Heard firing on side of [St Stephen's] Green. 3.15 to train, Ambush had just taken place. Saw irregulars under arrest. 4.0 Greystones to see Townsend, Gulf Hotel. Out – saw wife – mistaken by F.F [Free State] troops for De Valera!'[99]

Gregg was in no real danger in Dublin. The danger was far greater in the Republican stronghold of Kerry and Cork, the scene of the worst sectarian killings in the previous two years. Almost a month before Gregg's brush with the troops in Dublin eight Protestants were killed in and around Dunmanway, County Cork. The murders in Dunmanway were particularly brutal. Francis Fitzmaurice, a retired solicitor, was 72. James Buttimer, a retired draper, was 83. A chemist, named Gray, was 34. All three men were dragged from their homes in the middle of the night and shot dead.[100] The next night the insurgents struck 10 miles south at Clonakilty, Collins's home town. This time the victims were Gerald Payton, aged 20, John Chinnery, a farmer aged 32, Robert Howe, a farmer aged 60 and Robert Nagle, aged 18. They were joined a day or two later by John Bradfield, a farmer from Bandon. The result, as intended, was the flight of 100 remaining Protestants from the Bandon area on the next boat train to England.

The Catholic bishops denounced these killings, saying:

> We have seen too many instances . . . of barbarous treatment of our Protestant fellow countrymen. Not only has their property been at times unjustly seized and they themselves occasionally driven from their homes but their lives have in some cases been murderously attacked. We condemn unsparingly these manifestations of savagery . . . our own Catholic people we solemnly warn against associations that might bring any of them to imbrue their hands in the blood of a fellow man.[101]

But the Catholic bishops could not police the countryside and their appeal had little effect. Some 230 Munster Protestants attending the May Synod of the Church of Ireland in Dublin urged Gregg to solicit a meeting with the new government. Gregg and the Bishop of Cashel obliged. After calling on Collins and his deputy, William Cosgrave, the bishops simply asked them whether the Provisional Government wanted any Protestants to remain in the south-west. Collins wanted to protect his new allies among the ex-Unionists but was in no position to guarantee their safety. Skibbereen in County Cork fell to the Republicans in early July and for a month most of the county was under Republican control, a rebel mini-state inside the Free State. The Free State re-took most of the Republican territory by mid-August, but on the 22nd Collins died in an ambush near Bandon. The southern Protestants were devastated. They had forgotten his role in the war of independence against Britain and remembered only the 'big, burly fellow who had the courage of a lion'. The *Church of Ireland Gazette* declared: 'Ireland has lost a son whom she will not be able to replace.'[102]

Munster was the eye of the storm and the scene of the most vicious sectarian attacks. But it was not the only danger spot as far as Protestants were concerned. In June 1922 the *Church of Ireland Gazette* recorded the destruction over the previous two months of virtually the entire Protestant community in Nenagh in Tipperary, Mullingar in Westmeath, as well as in Athenry, Loughrea and Ballinasloe in Galway by Republican terror gangs. The procedure appeared to be the same in each town. Protestants first received anonymous letters ordering them to leave by a certain date. If they ignored the letters, the threat was followed up by bullets through the windows.[103] The other combustible area was the Ulster border. As Catholics were burned out of their homes and killed in inner Ulster, their sympathisers paid back the Protestants in the outer ring. In June, six Protestants were killed in Newry in apparent reprisal for the pogroms in Belfast. The victims included John and Robert Heslip, James Lockhart and Joseph Gray, all of Lisdrumliska, and Thomas Crozier and his wife from Altnaveigh.[104] In Donegal, the Church of Ireland church at Inver was attacked during service time. The Rector locked the door and told everyone to lie down.[105] Fortunately for them, the crowd then moved off to attack the Methodist church. The attacks went on throughout 1922. The situation was so bad in October that the Bishops of Cashel and Ossory publicly appealed to Protestants not to emigrate. But it was too late for many. As one clergyman pointed out, the parishes of Munster and Connacht were mostly deserted. 'There is no use in sticking to Ireland when our parishioners are not any longer with us. If the laity are driven out, why need we stick to Ireland?'[106]

CHAPTER THIRTEEN

Soutaned Bullies of the Lord

Modern forces are not for but against the Church's mission. Today the enemy is invisible and omnipresent. The Irish Catholic is like a soldier who has turned aside the sword but is attacked by a poisonous gas.
(*Irish Monthly*, 1925)[1]

Phoenix Park is Dublin's green lung. More than twice the size of New York's Central Park, it is one of the largest parks in Europe. It started out as a royal deer park under Charles II, and the humble hunting lodge in the middle was transformed in the eighteenth century into an official residence for the Lord-Lieutenant, before being rebuilt in the 1780s and once more in 1849 for the visit of Queen Victoria and Prince Albert. The park's landscape was studded for two and a half centuries with the symbols of British rule. South-west of the Viceregal Lodge stood the Chief Secretary's Lodge. The Royal Military Infirmary lay just inside the main gate. In 1817 a vast, 205-foot-high Wellington Testimonial was begun on the park's south side. The change in ownership in Ireland in 1922 was reflected in the park. Out went the Protestant British lords-lieutenant and chief secretaries. In came Irish Catholic governor-generals and then presidents, along with the American ambassador and – most tellingly of all – the papal nuncio.

When the Irish Catholic Church celebrated the 1,500th anniversary of St Patrick's mission to Ireland in June 1932 with a programme of outdoor masses and processions the like of which had never been seen in Ireland, Phoenix Park was the appropriate setting. The Dublin Eucharistic Congress drew one million people for the final mass in Phoenix Park and the service of benediction delivered by the papal legate. That was more than one-third of the population of the Free State. The world had seen several of these Catholic congresses since the first in Lille, north-eastern France, in 1881, but none attracted anything like so large a percentage of the host population.

The Congress took months of preparation. Leaving aside the stands, crosses and bunting, the nation had to be spiritually prepared. At the beginning of June, parishes in Dublin began organising retreats and devotional exercises. Then, on two successive Sundays, the entire adult Catholic population was encouraged to take communion, while on the evening of the second Sunday devotions were held in every church in the archdiocese for the success of the Congress.

The programme of self-examination and prayer was only an aperitif to the main course on 21 June, when Lorenzo Lauri, the papal legate arrived in Ireland on the SS *Cambria*, serenaded in with as much pomp and ceremony as the impoverished Free State could muster. That did not amount to much, but a formation of Irish army planes did greet the legate's arrival with an air display in the sign of the cross. When the Legate disembarked at Dun Laoghaire port, just south of Dublin, 5,000 children were on hand to meet him, waving yellow-and-white papal flags. Edward Byrne, Walsh's successor as Archbishop of Dublin, received the Legate on Irish soil in the name of the Church. Behind him stood Eamon de Valera, Cosgrave's successor as President of the Executive Council, who greeted him first in Irish and then in Latin. After him stepped forward Sean Lemass, the Minister of Industry and De Valera's successor in 1959, followed by the other members of the Executive Council.

The Legate drove into Dublin through streets lined with people, many of whom sank to their knees as the smiling figure sped past. At 4 p.m. the motorcade reached the outer boundary of the city, where the Lord Mayor and the rest of the corporation waited in their traditional red robes for the sound of a trumpet salute. The Cardinal proceeded through the conquered Protestant bastions of Ballsbridge and Merrion Square in south-central Dublin to the pro-cathedral on the north side of the Liffey, where the Irish bishops had assembled to greet him. That evening there was a state reception at the Royal Dublin Society.

The Congress opened the following day with a vast communion service for the children of Ireland in Phoenix Park and a garden party for about 20,000 guests at Blackrock College, hosted by the college's President, John Charles McQuaid. The women were asked to wear blue and white, the colours of Our Lady of the Immaculate Conception. That evening, the Blessed Sacrament was exposed for veneration in all the city churches from 9 p.m. to midnight, when midnight masses were held. All Catholics, in other words virtually everyone, were asked to place lighted candles 'of Irish manufacture'[2] in their windows as a sign of solidarity with the spiritual proceedings. Thursday began with a Pontifical High Mass in the pro-cathedral followed by a service for men in Phoenix Park at 8 p.m., at which the participants held candles aloft when the Blessed Sacrament was brought up to the open-air altar. Friday followed the same schedule, except that the grand service was for women. The climax of the Congress came on Sunday. At 1 p.m., a Solemn Pontifical High Mass began in the park, sung by a special choir of 500 men and boys. At the end of the service there was a half-hour interval before the gigantic procession of the Blessed Sacrament began moving off at 3 p.m. towards O'Connell Bridge in the centre of the city, initiated by two calls on a bugle.

The huge procession, 'the greatest gathering that ever assembled in Ireland',[3] snaked along for almost five miles. It symbolised the hierarchy and priorities of the new Free State. At the front wobbled the banner of the Blessed Sacrament, followed by the cross-bearer, the acolytes, the choir, the canons of the chapter of the pro-cathedral, the torchbearers and the thurifer. The Blessed Sacrament itself bobbed along under a canopy, followed by the cardinals and their suites, the archbishops and bishops, the members of the Dáil and the Senate. Behind them marched the representatives of the cities, bearers of papal titles, foreign diplomats and the members of Dublin Corporation. At the rear the members of other municipal corporations marched along with the members of county councils and the harbour boards, a 'special group of female singers' and then the vast throng of the congregation. At the bridge, the Legate delivered the final address at around 7 p.m., followed by the papal blessing. There was a final rousing rendition of 'Faith of our Fathers' and the blast of trumpets signalled that the Congress was over. The great crowd dispersed.

The organisation of the Congress was a phenomenal achievement. Never before had such vast numbers been marshalled in and out of the city. It was estimated that at least 100,000 children had attended the children's mass and that at least a million adults witnessed the main event on Sunday. Some 20,000 stewards had been on call, dressed in yellow and white armlets, assisted by 1,500 gardaí, as the police were now called, and 4,000 scouts. This team had marshalled the teeming throng of people at the final High Mass in Phoenix Park into 80 divisions and ensured that everyone wore their congress badge – one shilling for adults and fourpence for children.

The 1930s was an era of vast, open-air processions in Ireland. In June 1929, about half a million people had attended the outdoor mass in Phoenix Park held in commemoration of the hundredth anniversary of Catholic Emancipation. The new political elite of the Free State had jostled for the privilege of holding the monstrance in the procession after the mass. Cosgrave and his rival, De Valera, both took part as canopy bearers to the Blessed Sacrament, flanked by the mayors of Cork, Limerick, Waterford, Drogheda, Wexford, Kilkenny and Clonmel. At least a quarter of a million joined the procession and as Archbishop Byrne raised the monstrance, the huge multitude sank to its knees on the quays and bridges.

The Corpus Christi processions of the 1930s had a particularly monumental quality that struck contemporaries. At Cork, in 1936 benediction was given in front of 40,000 from an altar in the main street. In Limerick, 20,000 marched in a column three miles long. Some 15,000 took part in the biggest procession ever seen in Waterford.[4] There were 40,000 people at the Low Mass which opened the Catholic Truth Society conference held that year in Tuam. 'The Catholic Church has had a blessed year in Ireland', judged the normally staid *Irish Ecclesiastical Record*.[5]

The Catholic Church's confidence in its own ability to rule Ireland was almost limitless; the respect and obedience it drew from its faithful, almost total. In the 1930s there was a sense that the Catholic revolution launched by Cardinal Cullen three-quarters of a century before had finally achieved its potential and that the

Church's influence now permeated each and every village in a way that it had never done since the Middle Ages, if then. Through the Catholic Truth Society, the Church could now touch the thought processes of almost every household in Ireland. By 1918 the society was publishing half a million pamphlets a year. By 1925–26, this figure had ballooned to 1,130,294 pamphlets and 274,202 newspapers and magazines. By the year of the Eucharistic Congress the figure had risen to 1,149,689 pamphlets and 539,967 magazines.[6]

To dissent from the prevailing Catholic ideology in the Free State was almost unthinkable, unless you belonged to the tiny, despised and shrinking Protestant minority. One of the few who did, the writer Liam O'Flaherty, wrote an unflattering account of the Congress in a Kerry village for the American *Spectator*. Before the Congress, O'Flaherty wrote,

> the only pastime permitted to the males was drinking in the fifty-three public houses. The females wandered about with a hungry expression in their eyes.
>
> Then the Eucharistic Congress came along and the populace, exalted by some extraordinary fanaticism, decorated the town with bunting. In the proletarian slum, several altars were erected in the open air. Around these altars some people recited the rosary at night, while others played accordions, danced and drank stout. However, no attempt was made to remove the dung from the streets, nor any fraction of the dirt, which desecrated the walls of the houses and the floors of the taverns. I walked up and down the town pointing from the bunting to the pavement and saying 'Bunting, dung, dung bunting'. It was considered sacrilegious.[7]

This was the view of a tiny, shocking minority. But the Congress was much more than a celebration of Ireland's fidelity to the Holy See. The display of resurgent Catholicism coincided with a momentous shift of power towards the Republican losers in the civil war, and in a sense gave the Church's blessing to this change. To men of De Valera's persuasion, the Cosgrave government had espoused a watered-down brand of Irish nationalism, still tainted with West Britonism and Castle Catholicism. In 1932, the men who had fought against the treaty with Britain came in from the cold. It was a happy coincidence that the Church had chosen that year for its display of militant Catholicism. Ireland, it seemed, was opening a new chapter.

The Congress was also a celebration of empire, the spiritual empire that Cardinal Henry Manning had predicted was to be Ireland's destiny. In 1873 the Archbishop of Westminster had penned an open letter to the Irish hierarchy, which was extraordinary for its adulatory character. The English Primate, a convert, with many ties to the British political establishment, wrote his letter at a time when Britain's wealth, power and influence were at their peak, while Ireland's prospects seemed desultory. But this most English of Catholic archbishops thought he discerned a higher truth behind the tawdry pomp and vainglorious self-congratulation that surrounded him in his own land. Ireland, he pronounced, would be the conqueror. It was the most 'Christian country in the world', besides which England was 'shattered and wasted'. The Archbishop asked:

> What other race on earth since the Apostles has so spread the faith on earth? They are multiplying beyond all other races, founding churches and episcopates, building cathedrals, raising everywhere altars, schools and convents, and covering countries, I may say new continents, with the Catholic faith as fervent, fruitful and pure as in Dublin, Cashel, Tuam and Armagh. I know nothing elsewhere like this in the world, I may say, in Christian history.
>
> I must believe that our divine master has called the Irish nation to a great mission and a great destiny. And this comes out all the more visibly in this time of national apostasy.[8]

In the 1870s, Manning's words seemed exaggerated and somewhat premature. By 1932 they seemed prophetic as Ireland's fervour was contrasted with the collapsed fortunes of the churches in England, France and even Spain, and as the throng of overseas bishops streamed into Dublin from Africa, Australasia and, above all, America, coming 'home' to celebrate the Eucharistic Congress.

The Catholic Church in America had become a vast extension of the Irish Catholic Church. Three of the American archbishoprics were held by men who were Irish born or of Irish descent and who journeyed to Dublin in 1932: Hayes of New York, Dougherty of Philadelphia and O'Connell of Boston. With them in Dublin were Brennan of Richmond, Cantwell of Los Angeles, Curley of Baltimore, Fitzmaurice of Wilmington, Gallagher of Detroit, Glennon of St Louis, Griffin of Springfield, Hanna of San Francisco, McDevitt of Harrisburg, Tooley of Mobile, O'Reilly of Scranton and McMahon of Trenton. From the Philippines, annexed by America after the 1898 war with Spain, came O'Doherty of Manila. They were there in company with many Irish bishops from throughout the British empire, such as O'Reilly of Phoba, in South Africa, O'Leary of the Transvaal, Fitzgerald of Gibraltar, Byrne of Toowoomba in Australia, Kelly of Sydney, Ryan of Sale, Dwyer of Wagga-Wagga, O'Donnell of Halifax, in Canada, McGuigan of Regina and McNally of Hamilton.[9]

Yet the bishops did not feel complacent or self-congratulatory. At a time when its triumph appeared complete, the Irish Church still felt its enemies were legion. In their state of the nation pronouncement of August 1927, the bishops rendered 'fervent praise to God' for the general condition of religion in Ireland, the rate of mass attendance, the membership of sodalities and the fervency of devotion to the Virgin Mary. They spoke of the divine mission of the Irish 'to bear light unto the gentile' and of that 'special destiny of the race' to which Cardinal Manning had alluded in 1873. But there was a stick as well as carrot. 'The evil one is forever setting his snares for unwary feet', the bishops added. 'At the moment his traps for the innocent are chiefly the dance hall, the bad book, the indecent paper, the motion picture, the immodest fashion in female dress, all of which tend to destroy the virtues characteristic of our race.'[10]

The old Protestant enemy could be dealt with quite easily. The remaining heretics could be watched, followed and so hemmed in that they could hardly move. Trinity College was besieged as never before. The Catholic bishops' Synod at Maynooth in 1927 tightened the screws on that 'cesspool of Puritanical secularism',[11] as the *Catholic Bulletin* put it three years later, by imposing a complete ban on Catholics attending the college. The bishops circled round the stone portals of 'Queen Bess's Academy' like sharks, keeping a fierce watch on who came in and out. They could not prevent some renegades from sneaking in. In 1933 Bishop Dignan of Clonfert said he believed about 140 Catholic traitors were on Trinity's books. Dignan reminded Catholics that the bishops' ban was not a symbolic gesture to be trifled with. 'The Pope has condemned Trinity, the Irish bishops have forbidden Catholics to enter it and it remains forbidden. It is for all Catholics to obey.'[12]

The problem was no longer Protestants but the invisible gas of moral turpitude that was seeping in under Ireland's door. The Catholic Church was well aware that Ireland was a small fortress of the faith, easily influenced and tempted to wickedness by the sub-Protestant, immoral and atheist society next door. Much to the Irish Church's disappointment, political independence had not bred a spirit of cultural and intellectual independence. The Church presided over, and encouraged, an atmosphere of moral panic. Under clerical direction, lay Catholics began banding together to form vigilance committees, which patrolled the streets on the watch for filth and backsliding. As the *Irish Rosary* put it:

There are actually on sale in this country periodicals and books (some of the latter printed in Ireland!) so vile with unchastity that their place is not on the shelf but in the boiler fire. In addition people are being tempted to unchastity at cinemas and theatres and to the unsettling of their moral standards, sometimes fatally so. Action by the Catholic body is plainly necessary to quench these unholy fires and make inner moral cleanliness come first.[13]

The idea of vigilance committees was not a Catholic one. It was William Plunket, the evangelical Church of Ireland Archbishop, who had originally fostered lay-run vigilance committees and the Association for the Promotion of Social Purity in the Dublin of the mid-1880s. The Catholic Church took up the idea and developed it. Harmless scientific pictures and innocent advertisements were invested with an evil and dangerous character. In Cork, religious people tore from the walls advertisements for soap that featured naked babies. At the seaports, stacks of popular English newspapers were dumped in the sea to stop their contagion from spreading into Ireland.

The heightened atmosphere of puritanism prompted a great expansion in the membership of sodalities and the creation of a new lay organisation, the Legion of Mary, in December 1921. The Legion began as a small group of workers visiting the poor in the Dublin Union hospital but within a decade it had almost a thousand active members in Dublin alone. Unlike the older charitable societies, such as the St Vincent de Paul Society, the Legion confined its work to combating spiritual evil. Members visited hostels, hospitals and homes, disseminated Catholic literature, encouraged people to join sodalities, checked up on children's mass attendance and encouraged Catholics to 'enthrone' emblems of the Sacred Heart in their homes. They also picketed Protestant institutions, such as the Dublin Medical Mission.

Private initiatives by church members were not enough to win the war for purity. As soon as the Free State put its house in order and stamped out the embers of civil war the bishops began clamouring for a raft of coercive laws to deal with the problems of (lack of) censorship, divorce, contraception and the continuing decline of the Irish language. Bishop McKenna of Clogher, in his Lenten pastoral of 1924, demanded 'imprisonment or the lash' for newsagents selling impure newspapers from Britain and urged 'something more than wailing over this voluntary subjection to the worst English influence'.[14] Bishop Doherty of Galway, speaking at the 1924 Catholic Truth Society Congress, called for a 'great crusade . . . to save the soul of the nation which was being steadily destroyed by filthy publications coming from England'.[15] The bishops demanded the aid of the civil arm to enforce a 'tariff against filth'.

What was the point of political independence, they asked, if the country's spiritual independence was continually undermined by dirty literature steaming nightly towards Ireland on cross-channel steamers? The hope was that Catholics would confine themselves voluntarily to reading the works of people 'who can write in a genuinely Catholic spirit',[16] and whose chaste and holy thoughts could be found in the pages of the *Irish Rosary*, the *Irish Monthly*, the *Irish Messenger*, *Catholic Truth*, the *Irish Catholic Times* and a very few, safe, English Catholic publications, such as the *Tablet*, the *Dublin Review* and *Blackfriars*, the organ of the English Dominicans.

Unfortunately, many Irish Catholics balanced their nationalist and anti-British convictions with subscriptions to the very worst British daily newspapers, including the bishops' *bêtes noires*, the *News of the World* and *Sporting Times*, which between them pumped out a sensationalist diet of society divorces, scandals and murders. In spite of the bishops' denunciations, the *News of the World* had an Irish circulation of about 190,000 in the late 1920s[17] – a huge circulation in a country with a population of 2.75 million.

Dangerous newspapers from England were only one aspect of the moral crisis. The Church was very disappointed in the quality of home-grown writers from Catholic Ireland. The Church's relationship to the Irish intelligentsia was fraught. It had always been a problem in a country where the mass of the population belonged to one Church and the elite belonged to another. The nationalist feelings of the masses could easily be aroused against the works of Protestant writers who seemed to be sneering at them. In 1907 the first performances of John Millington Synge's *Playboy of the Western World*, started a riot at the Abbey Theatre in Dublin as nationalists, encouraged by the Church, protested against the depiction of Catholic peasant women as sex mad and attracted to violence. Synge, however, was a Protestant, and the Church knew what to expect from that quarter.

The greater disappointment came from the rising generation of Catholic writers. The Church had hoped that independent Ireland would produce a new school of Gaelic Catholics. They wanted more Pearses, muscular Christians who would write in a declamatory style about round towers; heroic Celtic warriors devoted to Our Lady and who had a horror of immorality. What they got were men like James Joyce, author of *Ulysses*, which the *Catholic Bulletin* summed up as 'a mass of putrid indecency'.[18] The sedate and far from anglophobic *Irish Rosary* complained that the new generation of Irish writers was failing to reflect the nation in its true light. 'They are no means all zealous that the truth as regards things Catholic and Irish should always see the light. Indeed [they] pander to the cross channel desire for pictures of the country which show us to be mean, drunken, and so forth.'[19] It was a source of embarrassment to the *Irish Rosary* in the year of the Eucharistic Congress that a country as fervently Catholic as Ireland had produced fewer decent Catholic writers than heretical England. Where, it wailed, was Ireland's answer to England's 'Catholic knights of the pen', like G. K. Chesterton, Father Knox and Hilaire Belloc? Casting a cold eye at Yeats and Joyce, it asked 'Why must Ireland, a Catholic country, in the main be represented by writers who are either Protestant or semi-pagan in their outlook?'[20]

Some bishops accused the new 'semi-pagan' Irish Catholic writers of playing the Protestant game. The Irish-born Archbishop Sheehan of Sydney said the Irish school of literature was 'tinged with Protestant rancour'. From far-away Australia he detected a 'current of satanic hatred' in their work. 'Our Dublin school, while professing to be Irish and Catholic, is neither one nor the other; it is but a toadstool growth on the ancient oak, a poisonous thing.'[21]

The Church wanted to crush this toadstool. The bishops wanted censorship on the one hand and compulsory Irish on the other. The first would forensically clean out the bad while the other would nurture all that was good. When Yeats and the *Irish Times* protested against the gathering momentum, the Catholic media were quick to stigmatise the protests as the not-so-hidden hand of the old Protestant Ascendancy. The *Irish Times*, the *Irish Rosary* said in 1928, was well known as an 'anti-Irish and anti-Catholic journal'. It went on: 'They opposed every national movement and every remedy or beneficent measure as long as any of us can remember. They opposed Disestablishment, they opposed the nationalist movement of our boyhood, they opposed the Land Acts . . . and now with a consistent and characteristic perversity they are opposing the censorship of immoral publications.'[22] This was the problem of all liberals in the Free State in the 1920s and 1930s. To protest against any measure proposed by the Catholic Church was to align yourself with the hated landlords, the Penal Laws; even with Cromwell. Yeats and the *Irish Times* pleaded in vain. In 1929, the centenary year of Emancipation, Cosgrave obliged the Catholic Church and passed the Censorship of Publications Act. With the Republican opposition under De Valera breathing down his neck, the Irish leader wanted no cloud passing over his relationship with the Church.

The Act was a victory for the Catholic Church, even if it did not go nearly far enough for some. It banned books that promoted criminal behaviour, advocated abortion or contraception or incited immorality or unnatural vice. The Act set up a board of five members, responsible to the Minister of Justice. Not exclusively Catholic, it included a few Protestants at various periods. In practice, the Act passed the enforcement of censorship to the Catholic Church, as there was hardly a bookshop in Ireland that would dare stock works that drew disapproving frowns from priests.

Benedict Kiely, one of the many writers who fell foul of the system, recalled how the business of censorship worked. 'The Catholic Truth Society had a group of people reading books and marking passages in them, and they would send them into the censorship board,' he said.[23] As Kiely recalled, although the buck stopped at the board, the real work of censorship fell on these self-appointed committees of Catholic lay people. The devolution of power to such groups meant that the criteria for censorship were rudimentary and philistine. The self-appointed, petty bourgeois censors rarely had any taste for complicated theological arguments and invariably concentrated on what they considered 'smut'. 'What they went for was something relating to sex,' Kiely said. 'You could have put in every heresy from Albigensianism fore and aft ten times over and nobody would notice the differ- ence.' The writer John Broderick reached the same conclusion: 'You could publish a book attacking the Church through Thomist philosophy . . . [and] it would not be banned. It wasn't intellectually biased, but it was biased as regards sex, which was the *verboten*, forbidden thing in Ireland.'[24] 'It was a young insecure state without any traditions, without any manners and there was this notion that to be Irish was good. Nobody took any time to understand what to be Irish was. There was this slogan and fanaticism and a lot of emotion, but there wasn't any clear idea except what you were against; you were against sexuality, you were against the English.'[25]

Over the longer term, this cack-handed censorship system rebounded on the Church, reinforcing an anti-clerical alliance among the intelligentsia and pushing Catholic writers into the ranks of the Church's avowed enemies. The *Irish Times* warned that censorship would become a badge of honour, not of shame. The newspaper mocked the banning of the first 13 books in May 1930. 'Our first thought is that the authors of the condemned books will receive hearty congratu- lations from their friends,' it remarked cheekily. 'The legend "banned by the Irish Free State" in a publisher's notice will make the fortune of novels which without this aid might fall still-born from the press.'[26] The prediction was accurate. Irish writers became more, and not less, hostile to the Catholic Church. O'Flaherty railed at the 'soutaned bullies of the Lord, fortressed in their dung-encrusted towns [who] hurl the accusation of sexual indecency at any book that might plant the desire for civilisation and freedom in the breasts of their wretched victims'.[27] The Eucharistic Congress was the Church's last hurrah, he prophesied. 'The militant puritans in Ireland have in my opinion staged the last great parade.'

Evil literature was only one of the dragons that the Church was determined to slay. The bishops were equally concerned with other undesirable manifestations of sexual desire, namely short skirts on women, dance halls and the cinema. The bishops' statement in October 1925 homed in on the evils of dances, demanded 'proper supervision' of such events and called for a time limit of 11 p.m. at the latest. They wanted sensual American dances replaced by good old-fashioned Irish jigs. The bishops feared that at such events 'the world, not God's world but that which he uncompromisingly denounced, is encountered at its strongest and worst, and the Christian soul tossed to and fro like a tiny barque on wild and stormy waters'.[28]

The annual statements of the hierarchy at Maynooth were models of moderation compared to the individual utterances of some of the bishops and parish clergy. The Bishop of Achonry's Lenten pastoral of 1929 spoke of 'midnight orgies' and speculated about 'dark rites'. 'There is one agency which Satan has set up here and there in recent years that does incalculably more harm than all the others,' he said. 'We have in mind the rural dance hall.'[29] The parish priest of Newbridge in County Kildare called dances the 'synagogues of Satan'.[30] Father Devane, author of 'The dance hall – a moral and national menace' in 1931, quoted a senior judge's horrifying report on a village where religion had been all but superseded by dancing. 'For a day and a night in the village of Killorglin on August 15th, which used to be one of the great church holidays of the country, the whole place was abandoned to an orgy of drink and dissipation.'[31]

Archbishop Gilmartin of Tuam led the campaign against jazz music which he criticised as a 'mesmeric rhythm of sensuality'. He urged a return to 'the old Irish national life of innocent mirth, of stories round the fireside, and all the better if the fires are of turf, of music expressive of the smile and the tear in Erin's eye'.[32] In 1937 he complained that life in some senses had been purer under the 'alien' rule of the British. 'Neighbours visited each other and told stories around the hearth and discussed local affairs while the women plied their knitting needles to make socks and stockings out of Irish wool. Instead of keeping late hours, all returned home in good time to recite the family rosary . . . ' The Archbishop asked: 'were they going to have a free Catholic Ireland with their own language, their own games, their own music, their own food, their own clothes and their own souls, or were they going to lose their distinctive nationality in the dread materialism which was now invading the world?'[33]

The cinema was another wholly unwelcome development. It did not entirely replace the Church in the South, as it often did among Protestants in the North, but it was an uncontrollable source of information, was foreign and the message it purveyed was often immoral. Its arrival in country areas was an inauspicious sign of the penetration of what were seen as urban Anglo-Jewish values into the last bastions of the Celts. The Primate, Joseph MacRory in 1934 urged Catholics to boycott the cinema. Making it quite clear he had never visited one of these dens of iniquity in person, he said: 'Judging from what I hear, it is often no place for Catholics, even outside Lent. I understand the pictures are frequently suggestive, if not indecent . . . above all, keep your children away from the cinema.'[34]

The best defence against cinemas, dances, dirty books, English newspapers and Protestants was the Irish language. Back in the 1890s and 1900s, the apostles of the Gaelic League had propagated the idea that the native language was a spiritually purer medium of communication than heretical English, thereby investing the movement with the aura of a religious crusade. The rapid spread of the Gaelic League had promised much, but the first decade of independence did not see the language advance in the expected way. Alone of all the European nations that gained independence after the First World War, Ireland remained in hock to the language of the old imperial power. In 1924 the Cosgrave government had encouraged the Gaelic movement by making Irish a compulsory subject in examinations. The government also established regions, known as the Gaeltacht, where Irish was actively promoted as the first language of education and communication. But compulsory Gaelic exams did not arrest the decline of the language and in the 1930s Catholic periodicals began to carry alarming articles on 'The ruin of the Gaeltacht'.[35]

The Catholic Church strained every fibre to promote the language. In Galway, which lay at the heart of the largest Irish-speaking area, the bishops promoted an annual language *feis*, spoke the language and provided Gaelic-speaking clergy for every parish where the language was spoken. Speaking at the 1929 Connacht Feis, O'Doherty of Galway crowed over Protestant dismay at the extension of compulsory Irish. He attacked 'the small minority' who 'tell you in honeyed tones that Irish is beautiful in itself but they want no compulsion. That was not the tune of their forefathers when they forced the English language on the Irish people. That would not be their tune today, I am convinced, if they had any longer the power to keep the English language as the spoken language of Ireland.'[36] But the optimism was not sustained. English did remain the spoken language of the overwhelming majority. 'This facing of the facts shatters a great dream, a great idea,'[37] the *Irish Monthly* commented gloomily in 1934. It was suddenly apparent that freedom from Britain did not mean the realisation of the dream of an agrarian, Gaelic Ireland governed by wise chiefs who sent their children to Gaelic seats of learning by the banks of the Shannon. English did not disappear. Nor did those English constructions, the cities.

Many churchmen felt profoundly disappointed by these developments. The language question was a lowering cloud that hovered over the apparent triumphs of the decade. Some clergymen began to see the very existence of towns as a threat to their religion. 'Machinedom is proving more deadly than alien landlords,' complained Father H. Rope in the *Irish Monthly* in 1932. 'To go into the town is not a sin per se but it is often the occasion of sin, and sinful indeed is the prevalent contempt of those homely conditions that enabled Ireland to stand fast in the evil day and to bear witness as a martyr nation to the Faith through the long centuries of Protestant tyranny.' Father Rope hoped Ireland would hold out against 'the flashy glitter of American-yiddish progress' but did not sound too optimistic.[38]

The Church's fears about being silently undermined by invisible enemies led to an intensified search for visible scapegoats. The *Irish Rosary*, which snorted at the Gaelic movement and disdained the anti-English tone of some other Catholic publications, preferred to see Communism as the great danger to Catholic Ireland. As a political force, Communists were negligible, but the *Rosary* was convinced they lurked under every bed. It devoted much of the Congress year of 1932 to dark warnings about their silent infiltration of society, insisting with an intriguing lack of evidence that 'Soviet moles' were active even 'in our most select convent schools'.[39]

The more populist, pro-De Valera publications picked on Jews, Freemasons and Protestants. The Free State was perhaps the most homogeneous society in Europe outside Scandinavia. But the tiny size of Ireland's minorities did not save them: it simply made them more visible and vulnerable. The Jews had already experienced bouts of persecution at the hands of Catholic nationalists. In Limerick, Bishop O'Dwyer had overseen a vicious campaign in 1904 against a small, defenceless population of 171 immigrants from Lithuania.[40] The Limerick Jews numbered 35 families and were mostly poor shopkeepers who had fled persecution in Tsarist Russia. In January 1904, John Creagh, a Redemptorist preacher and spiritual director of the powerful Arch-confraternity of the Holy Family, preached a violent sermon against the Jews, denouncing them as enemies of the Catholic Church and ritual child murderers. The community's rabbi, Elias Levin, tried to visit O'Dwyer to get him to call off the dogs. The Bishop refused to see him, which was in itself an immensely important symbolic gesture that gave a green light to a Church-run campaign against them. The Catholic nationalists of Limerick trained the same weapon against the Jews that they had used against the Protestant landlords: the boycott. The goal was to destroy the Jews economically, but physical force was also involved. On 4 April a 12-year-old boy, John Raleigh, stoned the rabbi in the street and was detained by the British authorities for a month. On his return, he was fêted by the city as a great son of Ireland and of the Church.

Anti-Semitism remained intertwined with hard line Irish nationalism. It was no accident that the *Catholic Bulletin*, the most ultra-nationalistic Catholic publication, was also obsessed with Jewish conspiracies. The paper carried lurid articles on Jewish ritual murder in places it knew nothing about, such as the Ukraine, or Bessarabia, and it referred to Britain as a 'Jew-cum-mason' state. Recommending its readers to read Father Cahill's book *Freemasonry and the Anti-Christian Movement*, published in 1929, the *Bulletin* complained: 'The great capitalistic press of the United States, England, Germany and France is now almost entirely controlled by the great Jewish international financiers. Even among the journalistic writers themselves the Jewish element is predominant. Even the Socialistic press of the world is owned and controlled by Jewish financiers.'[41] Cahill's book made similar claims. Freemasonry, it said was almost single-handedly responsible for the de-Catholicisation of France, German unification, the fall of the Papal States, the Paris Commune, the anti-clerical riots of 1909 in Barcelona, the Russian Revolution and the partition of Ireland.[42] 'The organisation of the Orange rebel army in 1919–20 and the hideous pogroms perpetrated in Belfast . . . were supported by the whole weight of Masonic influence,'[43] Cahill wrote. Good Catholics were expected to blanch as Father Cahill revealed that there were 530 lodges belonging to this organisation in Ireland, and 59 in Dublin alone. Masons were also responsible for partition.

The *Irish Rosary* detected the dark hand of the Jew in the recent jazz craze. There was a great danger, it said in 1929, from 'lascivious Jewish jazz dances . . . from the imported cinema films, mostly Jewish [and] . . . from the immodest fashions for women, mostly invented by Jewish men'.[44] The *Irish Rosary* talked up a bogus panic about an influx of Jews into Ireland, and of pure Catholic Celts having to 'make way for the Russian Jew and his class, breed, creed and country. We want to keep our blood pure and our morals equally so', it insisted. 'They are, above all, parasites as a race, living off the follies and weaknesses of their weaker Christian brethren whom they love to spoil and plunder.'[45]

The anti-Semitic character of Irish Catholic propaganda in the 1930s conditioned Ireland's response to foreign affairs. It was inevitable, given the domestic climate of near hysteria over racial and spiritual enemies, that the Church would engage frantically in support of Franco's war against the left-wing Republicans in Spain and show scant sympathy for Hitler's Jewish victims. De Valera, for all his piety, remained aloof from the Church's foolish flirtation with Fascism. In a masterly speech to the nation on St Patrick's Day in 1935, he reminded the country that Ireland had been a Catholic nation for 1,500 years. 'She remains a Catholic nation and as such she sets the eternal destiny of man high above the "isms" and idols of the day. Her people accepted no system which denies or imperils that destiny. While that is their attitude, none of the forms of state worship prevalent in our time can flourish in this land.'[46] The Irish leader made the same point on the same date two years later, when he remarked that the Irish way did not lead through Communism or Fascism and that no solution to the country's problems would ever be sought along the lines of any form of state absolutism.[47]

De Valera remained the Church's dutiful and sincere son and he consulted extensively, though not exclusively, with Catholic leaders while remodelling the Free State constitution that was promulgated in 1937, especially with McQuaid, who succeeded Byrne in Dublin in 1940. The new document incorporated a number of clauses reflecting Catholic social teaching, while the preamble made a direct reference to the country's Christian character by invoking the Holy Trinity. Clause 44.1.2 singled out the Catholic Church for particular mention and accorded it a vague 'special position' in the nation's life. Clause 41.3.2 forbade the passage of laws dissolving marriage. Clause 41.2.2 committed the state to endeavouring to ensure that mothers would not be obliged to engage in labour to the neglect of their duties in the home. McQuaid had reason enough to be satisfied with the inroads Catholicism had made into the secular character of the 1922 document even if he was a little disappointed that the role of the Catholic Church was not given greater pre-eminence. He had to be satisfied with what he was given, as De Valera had also consulted Archbishop Gregg to solicit the Protestant viewpoint.

De Valera retained complete independence from the Catholic bishops over foreign affairs. He condemned the Italian invasion of Abyssinia, which the Pope lauded. It was 'aggression pure and simple', he told the Dáil on 18 June 1936, and he insisted Ireland would remain neutral in the Spanish civil war, in spite of the Irish bishops' hollering for Franco. The bishops took their cue from Rome, not from De Valera. From the start of the war in Spain in July 1936, the Vatican openly proclaimed its support for the rebellion against the deeply anti-clerical Republican government. As the two sides dug in for what was clearly going to be a long conflict, the Irish bishops became convinced that the British and American media were spreading lies about the Spanish Fascists to the Irish public, who were forced to rely on Anglo-American news agencies for information. In a message to the Spanish bishops in October 1937 Archbishop MacRory launched a blistering attack on the 'cruel injustice that has been done to the Catholics of Spain by the world press . . . by cunning and malevolent distortion of the facts and by giving full publicity to the mendacious propaganda of your enemies'. Primate MacRory assured the Spanish rebels that the truth was getting through to Ireland, in spite of the media blockade: 'Our faithful Irish people have had the true state of the case laid before them by the Catholic and nationalist press in Ireland, as well as by pamphlets and public addresses.'[48]

Some lay Catholics had problems accepting the 'true state of the case' as presented by the bishops. When Father Arthur Ryan gave a lecture on the war to the Catholics of Belfast on 19 October 1936, he had to disabuse his audience of the suspicion that the rebel cause was tied up with an assortment of monarchists, political conservatives and capitalists. The idea that Franco supported Fascism was 'Communist propaganda', Ryan assured the audience. He insisted that Franco aimed at no more than a dose of 'mild authoritarian rule' in Spain and characterised the conflict as 'a struggle for decency against barbarism, for civilisation against chaos, for humanity against savagery, for Christ against anti-Christ'. He ended: 'No lover of liberty and no believer in spiritual values can do other than salute the insurgents' flag and say with the soldiers of Franco, "Viva España!"'[49]

The nationalist writer, De Blácam, took the opportunity provided by the civil war to rail at the treacherous Catholic intelligentsia at home. The 'dirty literature brigade' in Ireland had rendered Franco's cause unpopular in Ireland with their 'cant about freedom of speech', he said.[50] It was the dirty literature brigade who accused the Fascists of bombing the Basque town of Guernica 'so that common men were misled and even some generous young Irishmen sent out to Spain to die fighting against all that their race had defended in better days'. The *Irish Monthly* agreed. It complained of the spread of 'a false philosophy that democracy (meaning the English system of government) is of more consequence than tradition, spiritual freedom or culture'.[51]

Archbishop MacRory encountered the same problem of scepticism as Father Ryan. He assured pilgrims in Drogheda that the Spanish civil war was 'not a question of the army versus the people, nor of the aristocracy plus the army and the Church against labour. Not at all. It is a question of whether Spain will remain, as she has for so long, a Christian and Catholic country or a Bolshevist and anti-God one'. The Spanish Republican government, he added, aimed 'to destroy every Catholic state in the world'.[52] The other bishops described the war from the pulpits in the same terms. Bishop Mulhern of Dromore said it was a contest between God and his enemies. 'The heart of Catholicism is with the noble Spanish', gushed Bishop Fogarty of Killaloe in his 1938 Lenten pastoral, 'that under General Franco are now fighting at tremendous cost to themselves the sacred cause of Christianity against the anti-God ferocity of the Reds.'[53]

The *Irish Monthly* followed up thrilling accounts of the slaughter of the Reds with sycophantic articles about the Franco family's inspiring piety. It reported in honeyed tones in 1937 on the ceremonial induction of Dona Carmen Franco into the Sodality of Our Lady, in Salamanca. 'The whole city shared their joy,' the magazine gushed, 'and immense crowds took part in the picturesque ceremony. It is interesting to note that the members of Franco's family meet together to recite the Rosary daily . . .'[54]

Northern Catholics like Father Ryan might pretend the Nationalist cause had no connection with right-wing politics or Fascism, but the *Irish Monthly* felt no such need to economise with facts. 'The truth is, of course, that we must support Fascism if it is the alternative to Communism, or else we must stand over the horrors of the Spanish persecution,' it said. 'Whoever opposes the Right opposes the freedom of the faith. More, he lends his support to the most terrible persecution Western Europe ever has seen.'[55] The *Irish Ecclesiastical Record* put the same case in more moderate terms. 'It is not that she [the Church] hates Fascism less but that she hates Communism more,' Cornelius Lucey wrote in 1939, 'and consequently where no alternative except Fascism or Communism is practical politics, she will certainly prefer the former . . . At its worst . . . she can carry on somehow in Fascist-land, whereas in Communist-land she is crushed out of existence altogether.'[56]

As the Fascists slowly vanquished Spain's republican government, the Irish Catholic media could hardly find words to express its euphoria. 'It must be joyous to live in liberated Spain today,' the *Irish Monthly* burbled, 'feeling that the spirit of the Cid is exultant in Burgos, that the sons of Santiago are freemen in Galicia again, and that the daughters of Aragon may give thanks for victory before the Virgin del Pilar in Saragosa.'[57]

In the 1860s, Archbishop Cullen had encouraged Catholics to fight in the Pope's army against the Italian nationalists. In the 1930s, under the former Garda Commissioner (and organiser of the Eucharistic Congress) General Eion O'Duffy, right-wing Catholics, known as Blueshirts, volunteered for Franco. Francis McCullagh, a journalist, followed them to Spain to write about their exploits. McCullagh toed the Catholic Church's line on the Spanish war. 'This is not a civil war, it is a holy war, a crusade', he wrote. 'And these are not soldiers, they are fighting monks, Knights Templars.'[58] But he had to admit that the Irish 'fighting monks' contributed little or nothing to the Fascist war effort. Much to his anger and embarrassment, he wrote that the Irish soldiers were addicted to clowning around in the streets in a most undignified fashion, playing for laughs and exciting the deep scorn of their proud Spanish colleagues. The Irish fighters saw little action. Of the seven casualties, four were shot by accident by their Spanish Fascist allies. McCullagh thought the only decent fighter among them – ironically – was a young English Protestant killing machine called John Peel, who curiously renamed himself 'Captain O'Biffin'. 'Although still a youth, he has so far sent more than 150 Reds into eternity,' McCullagh wrote admiringly, 'while the whole O'Duffy outfit, which has cost Franco £170,000 and an infinite amount of worry, failed to bag a single militiaman. Moreover the O'Duffy outfit has gone home whereas Don Jon . . . is still on the job, as cool, deadly and inexpensive as ever.'[59]

Not all the bishops were swept away on a tide of emotion about Fascism. Michael Browne of Galway was a voice of moderation amidst the shrieking about Spain. In February 1938 he said Catholics had always refused, to adore the state as divine and absolute, 'as unfortunately the Japanese and Nazis adored it in the present day'.[60] In his Lenten pastoral of 1939, he launched an uncompromising attack on state worship in Italy as well as Germany. 'Unfortunately there are in our midst some admirers of Nazi methods,' he said.[61] The most sedate of journals, the *Irish Ecclesiastical Record*, also maintained a cool distance from the European dictators, criticising Fascism as a movement that was almost as totalitarian as Communism and denouncing the state it implied.

The admirers of Nazi methods that Bishop Browne referred to included, naturally, the *Catholic Bulletin*, which lauded Hitler's annexation of Austria as a welcome precedent for Ulster and called for an 'Irish Anschluss'.[62] Later it chortled over the destruction of the 'masonic conglomerate' known to the world as Czechoslovakia.[63] The Czechs were guilty on several counts as their land was apparently full of Jews, Masons and Protestants, and was traditionally pro-British to boot. It was 'the ulcer of Europe'. The *Catholic Bulletin* hoped the Irish universities would emulate the Nazi students by burning unsavoury literature. 'They should chuck their Anglo-Jewish books of up-to-date economics into the yard to be burnt,' it demanded and 'hold their conferences in the village forge where they could hear the voice of the race. To save the race – that is nationhood.'[64]

The *Irish Rosary* did not welcome the start of organised Nazi persecution of the Jews but it concluded with much shedding of crocodile tears that the Jews were only reaping what they had sown. Drawing heavily on the prevailing cult of the 'pure' Celtic countryside, it accused the German Jews of cutting themselves off from agriculture. It was their lack of rural roots that had 'engendered in them a proclivity towards usury and trickery and getting rich quickly, to profiteering, pawn broking and buying up slum tenements so as to get rich quickly by fleecing impoverished gentiles'.[65] All this, it concluded pompously, 'inevitably and rightly begets antipathy and opposition'.

The Irish Church did feel equivocal about Germany. Although it was bitterly anti-liberal and often espoused fairly anti-democratic opinions, outside Ireland at any rate, it could not but feel queasy about sheer Nazi godlessness and 'race and blood deified to the point of worship'.[66] Churchmen felt far more comfortable with Mussolini, who was 'only opposed by freemasons, liberals and democrats'[67] and still more with the Portuguese dictatorship of Dr Salazar, which had abolished political parties and given the Church total control over religious education in the school. Here was the kind of partnership many Irish Catholics yearned for. 'He has eliminated the poison of liberalism from the body corporate of Portugal,' wrote the Jesuit priest Richard Devane in 1938. 'Salazar is the saviour of Portugal, the saviour of the Church, the saviour of the state, the saviour of his people.'

Devane was certain that Salazar had pointed the way for Ireland. 'How long have Irish patriotic dreamers looked through tear-dimmed eyes with despairing hope at the ever elusive mirage and dream of the resurrection of our crushed and broken nation! . . . Today Portugal has risen with dignity from the dust in which she has so long lain – while Ireland is still on her knees.'[68]

The tone of the Irish Catholic publications was crucial in a country where the Church had a direct say on the political agenda. It meant that shrill anti-Semitism remained politically respectable in Ireland. Primate MacRory was not sympathetic to Hitler's Germany. But he was not remotely sympathetic to the Jews either. When MacRory and Byrne launched a Christmas appeal for Ireland to take in refugees in 1938, they specifically stated that their appeal referred only to Christians, the least vulnerable victims of the German annexation of Austria and the Sudetenland. As the international crisis deepened in 1938, MacRory publicly attacked Germany, but only over Hitler's persecution of the Catholic Church. Catholic Ireland remained blind to the vastly greater suffering of the Jews. Following an appeal by the tiny Jewish community in Ireland, the Free State grudgingly admitted 35 Jewish refugees on condition that their stay was temporary. Belgium, another strongly Catholic country, smaller in size though richer and larger in population, admitted 12,000 Jews. Yugoslavia, which was larger but little wealthier than Ireland, accepted 7,000.

MacRory remained bitterly hostile to the British. On the eve of war between Britain and Germany he denounced London for taking no action to dismantle the Ulster state. In May 1939, along with the other Ulster bishops he signed a furious letter warning the British not to impose conscription on Catholics in Northern Ireland. Any attempt to compel northern Catholics to fight for their oppressor would be likely to rouse them to indignation and resistance, they said.[69] The bishops scuppered conscription in Northern Ireland, much to the annoyance of its Protestant rulers. On 11 October, more than a month after Britain and Germany had gone to war, the Catholic hierarchy released an opaque statement from Maynooth. It scarcely touched on the war and on the titanic struggle that had been unleashed on the Continent. The bishops briefly mentioned the invasion of Poland but attached no great urgency to dealing with the German occupation of one of the great Catholic states of Europe, a country which had quite a lot in common with their own. Parochial to the last, the bishops urged the Irish Catholics to increase their adoration of the Blessed Sacrament. Whether the Catholic Church aided the anti-partition cause by their action is debatable.

CHAPTER FOURTEEN

A Tendency towards Defeatism

I feel convinced that you'll swamp us yet. Your people breed and ours don't. Anyone who thinks we'll be got in any other way is a fool.
(William Marshall, minister of Castlerock, 1933)[1]

The parish church of St Peter's in Bandon, County Cork, is full of memorials to the Bernard Earls of Bandon. Countess Georgina Dorothea put up the reredos in 1893, in memory of her father, Lord Carbery. Two years later she had the bells hung in memory of her mother. The interior is dominated by the splendid white marble tomb of James, the 2nd Earl, Lord-Lieutenant of the County of Cork, who died in 1856. Near it lies an equally imposing tomb, the final resting place of Richard Boyle Bernard, Dean of Leighlin, who died in 1853.

The interiors of such churches illustrate at a glance the cosy and dependent relationship between the Church of Ireland and the landed gentry. The umbilical link between St Peter's and Bernard Castle ended abruptly after the First World War. The castle was burned down in June 1921. Countess Dorothea, known as Doty, survived the trauma better than her husband, who was briefly kidnapped. But the power and influence of the Bernards over Bandon were gone for ever. When Dorothea died in 1942, there was no question of marble effigies or new roofs. The church benefited this time to the tune of a small clock.

The 'Big Houses' were sitting ducks all over Ireland in the crisis years of the 1920s, squat symbols of social injustice and emblems in the popular mind of all that was wrong in Ireland, and had been wrong since William III's reign, or possibly Henry II's. Hundreds went the way of Castle Bernard, though loss of life was mercifully rare. It was what the Big House stood for that the arsonists resented. The owners' opinions were irrelevant, as the nationalist writer George Moore discovered in 1923, when Moore Hall in County Mayo went up in flames.

By the end of the decade it was clear that the Protestant population in the 26 counties had collapsed. During the fighting from 1921 to 1923 the Protestants knew their numbers were falling but did not know by how much. The Bishop of Killaloe had warned in the summer of 1921 that the Church of Ireland population of his diocese had slumped to 5,876 – down by two-thirds from its Victorian heyday and a decline that the Bishop described as 'almost staggering'.[2] But his report was an isolated one. The first Free State census, published in 1926, came as a shock. The Church of Ireland population in the 26 counties had dropped by 34 per cent since 1911 from 249,535 to 164,215 – a massive fall. By contrast, the Catholics had contracted only fractionally during the same period from 2,812,509 to 2,751,269. 'That we had lost so heavily in recent years was well known,' the *Church of Ireland Gazette* said. 'But the extent of the loss was until now a matter of surmise.'[3] Not surprisingly, the biggest fall was registered in Munster, where the Protestant community was sliced in half. In Connacht and Leinster the decline was in the range of 33 to 34 per cent.

By 1936, long after peace had returned to Ireland, the Protestant community had shrunk again, to 145,034. Seen over a longer perspective, the collapse of southern Protestantism was stupendous. In 1861, the 26 southern counties had contained 372,702 Church of Ireland Protestants. By 1936, that figure had plummeted by a stunning 61 per cent. Almost two-thirds of the Protestants were gone.

The withdrawal of the British army and the Castle bureaucracy counted for only a quarter of the loss. Practically the whole of the Protestant working class – perhaps 10,000 – fled from Dublin in the early 1920s. In parts of Munster, entire local communities had been driven out. A large percentage of the lower middle classes, shop workers, shopkeepers, hospital matrons, governesses, schoolteachers and local government officials, had left Ireland, an emigration of youth, money and mercantile know-how that contributed to the listless, fly-blown character of so many Irish provincial towns in the 1920s and 1930s.

Their story went largely unreported. It lacked the drama of the Greeks' tumultuous exodus from Smyrna ahead of Atatürk's army in 1922. Most Irish Protestants left the country to safeguard their savings, their chances of employment and their children's future, rather than their lives. The numbers involved were not huge and they were easily dispersed throughout Britain's vast empire. They were drawn from an inarticulate section of society, used to taking orders, with no tradition of public protest.

Only a few fled to the new Protestant state in the North. A census carried out for the Boundary Commission between the two entities in 1925 showed that 2,100 southern Protestants had emigrated to County Fermanagh. From the list of occupations, which is incomplete, it is clear that few of them were ex-policemen or were drawn from the higher professional classes. Robert King, his wife and five children, were from Waterford, where he had managed a co-operative store.[4] Lily Carson, from Castleblayney in County Monaghan, was a servant. Ruby Brown, from Sligo, was a teacher. John McClure, from County Clare, was a coachman. Robert Bell, from Longford, was a 'pensioner'. Jane Armstrong, from Dublin, was a former prison matron. The professional middle classes were least affected. They depended less on government patronage and were not beholden to landlords. At the end of the 1920s, Protestants still made up 38 per cent of the Free State barristers, 21 per cent of the doctors, 37 per cent of the solicitors, 45 per cent of chartered accountants and 30 per cent of civil engineers.[5] In the old Pale,

Protestants held their own. It was not like the old days, but they still formed a large portion of the population of the once almost entirely Protestant suburbs of south Dublin. In the mid-1920s they made up one-third of the population of Rathmines and Rathgar, a quarter of that of Dun Laoghaire and more than one-fifth of the population of Pembroke and Blackrock. And for Protestants who could not bear being in the minority there was always the minute seaside hamlet of Greystones, south of Dublin, where 979 Protestants narrowly outnumbered the 915 Catholics.[6]

The change was much more marked in the countryside. In rural Munster and Connacht the destruction of the Big Houses and the flight of the landed families ended the Protestant presence in many areas. The departure of the landlord deprived the local church of the only important patron. Often he took the congregation with him. It was not just the landlord's family that went but his employees, many of whom were Scots or English, brought over to Ireland during the land agitation of the 1880s to replace the politically unreliable locals. As John Waddall, Presbyterian Moderator for 1938, reported:

> The break-up of the great estates, where many Protestants, particularly Scottish Presbyterians used to be employed and the transfer of army, police and government officials as well as many businesses of various kinds to the North, or across the water to Great Britain, have diminished our numbers and depleted the strength of our congregations. To those who knew the Ireland of the last century . . . the contrast is at once startling and depressing.[7]

For Presbyterianism, always a delicate plant in the south, it was the end of the road for many congregations. The Presbyterians numbered 66,172 in 1861 in the 26 counties. They had already declined substantially by 1911, to 45,486. By 1926 this number had slid to 32,429, falling rather more gently to 28,007 in 1936. The Munster Presbyterians were hit hardest. Between 1916 and 1927 the two Cork congregations dropped from 403 to 267 families.[8]

A report on the home mission to the Presbyterian General Assembly in 1927 noted: 'In almost every part of the country in which Protestants are a minority there has been a serious shrinkage of the Protestant population.' Athlone Presbytery was down by 30 per cent in seven years, it said, Cork by 45 per cent, Connacht by 36 per cent, Munster by 44 per cent. The embattled Cork congregation, clinging on in one of the fiercely Republican strongholds in the country, told the assembly it took consolation from the fact that 'in the midst of trying and dark experiences, with trenched roads and flying bullets and grim death dogging their footsteps, it is indeed gratifying to record that our people have preserved their faith in God undimmed, stood nobly by the standards of their church and with unfailing regularity attended Divine Service.'[9] The treaty Collins signed with the British in December 1921 brought no respite. The Presbyterian Church's report on 1923 was the gloomiest yet. The previous 12 months had been 'a time of unutterable sadness, of lawlessness and confusion and in some parts even of persecution,' it said. 'In more than one congregation members have received threatening notices and have been compelled to abandon their homes . . . church property has been stolen, burned, or otherwise destroyed. A very large number of Protestants was compelled to leave the country, in some cases, nothing being left to them but their lives and the smoking ruin of their homes.'[10]

When peace returned, Protestants woke up in a different country. The arbitrary violence of the civil war years was over. But Ireland's new rulers were devoted children of the Catholic Church. Presbyterians now found themselves operating in a society that was self-consciously Catholic, nationalist and Gaelic. The Protestants were reminded that their religion was the creed of a politically discredited minority of one in 20. There were aware of an instant loss of precedence at public ceremonies, of influence in government, over local appointments and over school books. There was no question of even fantasising about converting the broad mass of the people. That battle for the soul of Ireland was over. Missionary activity in the South had to be redefined in the humblest, meekest terms, as a means of keeping scattered pockets of Protestants alive, in good spirits and in touch. The most that could be hoped for was that isolated Protestants could be visited and encouraged to maintain the evangelical tradition.

In 1927 the Presbyterian Church admitted that its mission work in many parts of the South had been suspended. It was no longer possible, the Church said, now that the Catholic Truth Society 'has a branch in practically every parish . . . and a Vigilance Committee to watch all Protestant activities within the bounds of the parish'.[11]

Despair deepened throughout the 1930s. On the eve of the Second World War, the *Christian Irishman*, the paper of the Home Mission, wrote: 'Protestants enjoy toleration at the moment but that is very largely because they no longer possess anything, either power or property, which others want. It is the toleration we all accord to the dead.'[12]

The Church of Ireland was better off in the South than the Presbyterians. They had more members left. They also had more to maintain. They had the burden of upholding a national church. For four centuries, the Church of Ireland had been competing with the Catholic Church for the title of Ireland's national church. It had lost that war but it still strove with all its diminished might to maintain a presence in every community. 'In the past, the Church of Ireland had been the church of the whole country,' wrote the authors of a study of Protestant demographic trends, published in 1942. 'But if the present processes were to continue, there would be a danger of it becoming a church of the North with a Southern appendix. The awareness of all Ireland as its environment . . . might weaken to the point of extinction. A Church of Ireland that had undergone a mutation so profound would be something very different from the church of Ussher, Bramhall and Taylor, of King, Berkeley and Swift.'[13]

With the ghosts of great dead archbishops hovering over them, the Church of Ireland could not shut up shop easily in far-flung towns and villages. Many of its parish churches had been built at the end of driveways that led up to the Big Houses, a geographical position that expressed only too graphically the dependent relationship of the Protestant Rector on the Protestant landlord. The church buildings were full of memorials to their aristocratic patrons. At Adare, in County Limerick, eight of the 10 monuments in the chancel were dedicated to members of the Wyndham Quin family, earls and countesses of Dunraven, who had paid for the church's restoration in 1854.

Deprived of their aristocratic patrons, Protestant rural parishes took on the seedy, decayed look many have retained to this day – where they survive at all. W. B. Stanford shuddered over the 'mouldering' parish libraries he encountered while writing a book on the church in the 1940s.[14] The writer Molly Keane referred obliquely to the decline in *Good Behaviour*, a fictional portrait of a southern Protestant family that has survived the dramas of war and partition only to find itself becalmed in the 1920s. The church of the St Charles family demesne in Temple Alice was a 'stark little Protestant church at our gates, endowed long ago by the family and visited only for funerals, and christenings and weddings . . . it was chilly and stuffy and dead birds usually lay about in the aisle'.[15]

To be a Protestant clergyman in the Free State, outside the old Pale, among dust and dead birds, was to encounter dreadful loneliness. A report on the state of the Church in October 1932 innocently described the church conference that year as a 'happy reunion of those who naturally feel isolated'.[16]

While the Catholic Church flexed its rippling muscles at the Eucharistic Congress, the Church of Ireland could only stare at its withered sinews and arthritic hands. The contrast between the two Churches was highlighted by their responses to the 1,500th anniversary celebrations of Patrick's mission. While the Catholics staged their imperial processions and million-strong masses, attended by virtually all the members of government, the Church of Ireland contented itself with a humble thanksgiving. In Northern Ireland, the Archbishop of Armagh held that most Anglican of summer rites, a garden party. Thus was Patrick's earth-shattering mission to Ireland commemorated – with tea and sandwiches. The event was too much for the Archbishop's wife, who collapsed and died soon after. As a result the Primate was too upset to attend the 'festivities' in Dublin.

In the Free State, the Church of Ireland mustered a service in Christ Church cathedral and another at St Patrick's. The Low Church ethos of the Church of Ireland forbade even an attempt to emulate the Catholics' gorgeous pomp, but even the delights of a rousing sermon failed them. The hoped-for star turn at Christ Church, Hensley Henson, the controversial Bishop of Durham, fell ill and did not turn up. It was widely agreed that the service in St Patrick's was flat, marked by 'melancholy or unknown hymns, unknown chants and services'.[17]

The Church organised a series of conference papers to be read out in the Dublin Mansion House. They hardly sent the blood racing in those ancient

Protestant veins. A lecture on cathedrals cheerfully reminded the audience that the Church of Ireland had built very little since the 1860s, the decade when much of the audience was born. The chilly new cathedral dedicated to St Anne in Belfast did not count, as this lay in what was now another state. Since Disestablishment, 216 church buildings had been closed – 45 in the dioceses of Cork, Ross and Leighlin and 47 in Ossory, Ferns and Leighlin. It was also true that 80 churches had been built – but these were nearly all in Northern Ireland, 26 of them in Down and Connor, which included Belfast. The Protestant 'celebration' closed with a pageant play, staged in the conference room of the Mansion House on Saturday, 15 October.

The Church of Ireland countered the avalanche of Catholic Truth Society booklets with their own booklets that rehearsed the old, tired arguments over the Apostolic Succession of bishops and the marks of the 'true' Church. A tedious propaganda war over St Patrick was waged between Archbishops Gregg and MacRory in the columns of the *Irish Times*. The two primates slugged it out like gladiators, hurling mountains of useless information at each other about general councils, forgotten schisms, bits of various gospels and the epistles of St Clement.

The Irish Protestants and the Irish Catholics celebrated St Patrick in their own tents. There was no question of erecting a common monument to a saint that each claimed as their own exclusive property. The Catholics flung up a hideous statue that anticipated the Soviet style, constructed of imperishable grey granite on a hill near Saul in County Down, close to where Patrick is said to have landed. The Church of Ireland trumped this grim sentinel with a marginally less offensive looking church, in the kitsch 'Celtic' style, a mile distant, complete with a miniature round tower. The Catholic statue was inscribed only in Irish; the church only in English.

A Church weighted so heavily towards old people, spinsters and bachelors was naturally very short of children. The Catholic Church was conspicuously young; the Protestant Church obviously old. The contrast struck everyone. Bishop John Day of Ossory complained in July 1935 of what seemed a virtual cult of celibacy among Protestants. 'Many of our young men seem strangely reluctant to enter the holy state of matrimony,' he said. 'A leading clergyman said to me that in his parish there were several middle aged men with good farms who seemed to have no intention of getting married. I would suggest that here is field where the clergy might profitably exercise their powers of influence or persuasion.'[18] It was a common complaint that even the few of marriageable age were not tying the knot. It hinted at a great communal weariness, if not a death wish.

Protestant schools were closing fast in the west and south, especially in Galway, Waterford, Wexford, Clare and Limerick. The future of the remaining 55 Protestant secondary schools was far from bright. Twenty had fewer than 40 pupils and 12 fewer than 30. Ballymote, in County Sligo, was a case in point. The school had put all the Protestant children of the area under one roof – but that only amounted to eight Presbyterians, five Church of Ireland and one Methodist.

The Irish government was scrupulously correct towards the remaining Protestant schools, offering to pay the salaries of teachers even in tiny establishments. But the government would not pay for the children's transport. With the best will in the world, it was clear that in the end there was no future for such places.

The Church of Ireland was pietistic and socially and politically conservative. It lost members to the grave and to the British empire, not to Rome. Much to the disappointment of some Catholics, converts were almost unknown. The Church strongly disliked the growing pressure to learn Irish. Protestants had long been alienated from the language by the politicisation of the Gaelic League and its association with Sinn Fein. Bishop White of Limerick in 1930 complained that 'many of them (Protestants) viewed with dismay the unnecessary forcing of a language upon their people'.[19]

The Church of Ireland did not much like the Censorship Bill of 1929. The *Church of Ireland Gazette* worried that 'the appetite for prohibition may grow by eating' and suggested the best way to combat bad literature was 'the freest circulation of good literature'.[20] But, much to the annoyance of the *Irish Times*, the Protestant bishops declined to criticise censorship or compulsory Irish at the General Synod in Dublin on 14–17 May 1929. 'The Primate's address was silent on all the political developments of recent years and the whole synod took refuge in a little silence,' it noted bitterly.[21] It was left to secular Protestant intellectuals, and to the *Irish Times*, to criticise the Catholic authoritarianism of the Free State. After the government outlawed divorce in 1925, W. B. Yeats lambasted the bill in the upper house of parliament, the Senate, as an attack on Protestant liberty. 'We are no petty people,' he said in a celebrated speech. 'We are one of the great stocks of Europe. There is no more famous stock in Europe.'

The memory of the speech outlasted the bill he attacked. But it did not impress contemporary Catholics. The following day, Joseph Byrne, Provincial of the Holy Ghost Fathers in Rathmines, slapped him down in language that suggested the Catholic Church would no longer indulge this 'great stock'. 'In spite of all that men like Senator Yeats may think,' Father Byrne sneered, 'Anglo-Saxon culture is not a model for the world today. Far from it. The world needs modesty, humility and self-denial and in none of these does the Anglo-Saxon race or any of its "great stocks" shine.'[22]

By the late 1930s, Yeats's generation of self-confident Protestant secular intellectuals was dead or dying. Yeats himself died in 1939. His friend, Lady Gregory, the redoubtable director of the Abbey Theatre, had died in 1932. After their passing, the Protestants fell increasingly silent. The clergy had no stomach, or desire, to make a fuss on behalf of divorcees or the writers of banned books. A handful of activists longed for the Church of Ireland to become more Irish and at the same time more assertive. W. B. Stanford urged a Dublin youth conference in November 1943 to protest when they saw Protestant rights infringed, warning that 'drastic action would be needed' in the form of large protest meetings if church buildings were seized or Protestants forced to attend Catholic schools.

Stanford suggested that even a dose of outright persecution might be more beneficial than a lingering death through the present 'cold shouldering, such as we often have to bear'. He urged the Church of Ireland to identify itself more closely with the nation. 'If we imply that England or the British Commonwealth has our loyalty above Eire, our fellow countrymen can only regard us as resident aliens,'[23] he insisted.

The Church of Ireland in the South did not take either of those messages to heart. The respectable old men and women who dominated the laity now wanted to be left alone, not persecuted. The Church remained respectful of the new order on the outside and incorrigibly British on the inside. It was the absolute reverse of what Stanford recommended. The bishops talked of 'our army' in India.[24] They did not sing the new national anthem, 'The Soldiers' Song', but 'God Save the King'. They were very loyal to the monarchy while George V lived. When the Primate read out a statement from the King at the 1929 General Synod, thanking them for a resolution they had passed on his recent health scare, the entire assembly rose to its feet and applauded. Stanford recalled being asked by a curious southern Protestant in 1933 whether he was 'a Home-Ruler?'[25] The archaic phrase revealed the stunningly reactionary mindset of his questioner. Probably few families went to the lengths of the fictional Dublin characters in Barbara Fitzgerald's 1946 novel, *We Are Besieged*, who refused to use postboxes because they had been repainted green. But most continued to think of Britain as 'home'.

As Provost of Trinity College from 1919 to his death in 1927, Bernard set a tone for the inter-war period, resolutely, if almost apologetically, hoisting the Union flag over the college roof on the King's birthday and on Armistice Day. 'You must forgive me,' he told his friend Violet White, 'but I am one of those who prefer to walk in the old paths.'[26]

Relations between the Protestant University and the Catholic city were uneasy and small sparks easily touched off brush fires. In June 1933 some students caused an affray by pulling the cap off a garda in Grafton Street. The affray escalated after the students then pulled the wires off some of the tramcars, causing a traffic jam all the way to the O'Connell Bridge. That night there were more antics in the upper circle of the Theatre Royal, which ended with bread, tomatoes and oranges being hurled on to the stage.[27] This was standard student behaviour in Oxford and Cambridge. Transferred to the outpost of Dublin it was an unwise exercise, now that the college was marooned in an unfriendly state in which all power lay with the college's enemies, the Catholic bishops.

One by one the Protestant landmarks in the South were removed. The royal arms disappeared from shop fronts. The statues were taken away. In 1928 the statue of William III on College Green, which had stood there since 1701, was taken down. The Diamond Jubilee monument in once-Protestant Bray was demolished in 1933. The statue of George II on St Stephen's Green was destroyed in 1937.

In November 1929 the first papal nuncio to Ireland was appointed since Rinuccini in the 1640s. It was seen as a great diplomatic advance, confirming

Ireland's independence on the world stage. But it was a specifically Catholic, rather than an Irish, triumph. Protestant alarm was heightened when the government announced in November of that year that it would abolish the right of appeal to the Privy Council. Both the Protestant archbishops published letters of protest in the *Irish Times*, referring obliquely to Protestant difficulties in Ireland. 'The position of a minority, a minority viewed with jealous hostility by elements of the population far from negligible, needs the protection of such a safeguard,'[28] they said. The archbishops called on Cosgrave and were careful to describe themselves as representatives of 'the minority in this country who were formerly Unionists but are now loyal citizens of the Irish Free State, upholders of the Treaty and constitution and supporters of the present government'. They got nowhere. The Cosgrave government could afford to take Protestant support for granted.

Almost all southern Protestants supported Cosgrave's party, Cumann na nGaedhal. They were angry about the language laws, sceptical about censorship and disappointed by the continual paring away of the British connection. But Cumann na nGaedhal had restored order, financial prudence and respectability. The alternative was Fianna Fáil, the 'Soldiers of Destiny', the party De Valera created after he split with Sinn Fein over the policy of abstentionism. Populist, nationalist and isolationist, it was not a party with obvious attraction for a Protestant. In the elections of March 1932 Cosgrave lost power. The victory of Fianna Fáil ushered in a new tone, more militantly anti-British, more republican and more Catholic. Demonstrations of Unionist sympathy now became much more risky.

A cold wind had been blowing even before this watershed election. In 1930 attention was aroused by the case of Letitia Dunbar-Harrison, a Trinity graduate who was rejected for the post of county librarian in Clare basically because she was a Protestant. The Cosgrave government had supported Dunbar-Harrison. But the Catholic Dean and Bishop of Killala publicly supported a noisy campaign to block her appointment. Although the Free State Minister for Local Government dissolved the County Council after it refused to back down, the government backed away from a confrontation with the Catholic Church. Dunbar-Harrison was forced to seek employment elsewhere. Nine years later, the Presbyterian newspaper, the *Christian Irishman*, complained of the conscious exclusion of Protestants from state employment. 'In positions which are of public appointment and which are paid out of public monies, the Protestant now has no chance,' it said.[29]

The case of the Mayo librarian received a great deal of publicity. Less attention was paid to the piecemeal suppression of Orange Order processions in the Free State, which gathered momentum in the summer of 1931. Orange marches had continued in reduced numbers in the South since partition, and at first encountered little popular opposition in the climate of tolerance that Cosgrave fostered. When Cosgrave addressed an election meeting in Monaghan in August 1923 the

Deputy Grand Master of the County Orange Order stood on the platform beside him.[30] In the 1930s such a scene would have been impossible as the wave of intolerant Catholic nationalism swept the country. The action against the Orangemen was invariably the work of pro-government thugs who simply forced them off the road. At Cootehill, in the border county of Cavan, the intimidation began the day before the march on 11 August with an IRA proclamation against the annual procession. The following day,

> there was an invasion of the meeting place by hundreds of young men armed with hurley sticks and other weapons. All were determined that the meeting of the Orangemen should not take place. And to this end railways were put out of commission, telegraph and telephone lines were cut down and main roads were blocked by highly built walls and felled trees and trenches. The invaders held up motor cars, buses and lorries on the roads and commandeered them for their own use.[31]

That was the end of that.

The last Orange march in Dublin took place in July 1937. It was very much a side-street affair, a 'feeder' procession, heading for the railway station at Amiens Street, in north Dublin, to join the big parade in Belfast. But it was attacked and driven out all the same. The authorities murmured regrets but did nothing. The Orange Order virtually disappeared from the Free State outside a few villages in Donegal.

The new government cut the remaining ties with the crown. In the spring of 1939 references to the King disappeared from Irish passports. Out went the old request 'in the name of His Majesty, the King of Great Britain, Ireland and the British Dominions beyond the Seas, Emperor of India'. Many Protestants felt the loss of the royal connection keenly. Dudley Fletcher, Rector of Old Leighlin, told the *Irish Times* of 17 November 1939 that it was the principal reason why so many Protestants had given up and left the country. 'Many heads of families with private means or pensions who are free to live where they like and who were loyally attached to the King and the empire refused to remain in a country which the King or any member of the royal family dare not visit nor the imperial flag be flown nor the imperial anthem sung,' he said.[32]

Archbishop Gregg did his best to preside over a gentle *rapprochement* between the Protestants and independent Ireland, but he was hardly enthusiastic. Like his predecessor, he remained committed to the old ways. 'In 1922 he felt that he had been banished from the Garden of Eden,' his daughter recalled. 'The British government was in his view sacrosanct and he could not imagine it acting except in the most lofty and humane motives . . . he envisaged the British as the trustees of Christianity in a pagan world.'[33] For all that, he was pragmatically resigned to making the best of the disagreeable reality of Irish independence and impatient of those who just grumbled. 'To many of us these changes have been changes difficult to accept,' he said, on being presented with two portraits of himself by the Vice-Provost of Trinity in 1936.

> But . . . one of those things that one has to do is try to learn to accept facts with as good grace as you can . . . There is a tendency towards defeatism, which is exactly what we have got to fight against. I have heard people say: 'I might as well get out of this country'. Why not stay in it and make the best of it? I find some people saying they do not want their children growing up here. But why? If you live in this country, do you not owe a duty to it?[34]

There was a slow but steady reconciliation between southern Protestants and Irish nationalism, based on the idea of duty to Ireland, not affection for the Free State, let alone the form it took under De Valera. The death of George V in 1936 ended an era. He had known Ireland in his youth and the Irish Protestants felt they had known him. They knew nothing of Edward VIII and were distanced by the Wallis Simpson affair. In 1929 they had protested about the loss of appeals to the Privy Council. There was no equivalent protest in 1937, when De Valera used the abdication crisis to cut all references to the crown out of the constitution.

The Protestants forgot their hostility to compulsory Irish. It had been a bitter pill to swallow in the early 1920s. But Gregg had told his flock to stop making such a drama about it. 'If the path to those [government] positions is along the thorny track of Irish grammar,' he said in March 1927, 'Irish cannot be altogether an uneconomic subject of study when it makes the difference between employment and unemployment.'[35] By 1937 the Dean of St Patrick's was boasting of his pupils' proficiency in the language. 'We teach Irish here and we are proud to do so,' he said at the annual prize distribution at St Patrick's cathedral grammar school.[36]

In 1936, the Presbyterian Moderator, Andrew Moody, toured the Free State. He was struck by the transformation of the 26 counties in the few short years since independence. 'The dominant impression produced by travelling in the Free State is that of being in a foreign country, where a violent recoil from English rule is the master key to policy and popular sentiment,' he wrote. 'One is everywhere confronted with the unintelligible characters of an unknown language.'[37]

Moody's reaction to the changes was a sign of how the South and the North were pulling away from each other. Partition was becoming more of a reality and Protestants on either side of the border were becoming slightly estranged from each other. Among the northern Protestants, the memory of the First World War hung over the new state like a pall, a source of infinite regret mingled with a certain consolation. On 19 November 1921 a 70-foot-high memorial tower was opened in Thiepval in France, dedicated to the memory of the men of the 36th (Ulster) Division who had perished at the Somme. Archbishop D'Arcy was joined by Dr Lowe of the Presbyterian Church, W. H. Smyth of the Methodists, Field

Marshal Sir Henry Wilson, the Duchess of Abercorn, the Marquis and Marchioness of Londonderry, the Marquis and Marchioness of Dufferin, a host of Belgian mayors and General Weygand of France.

After the General had unveiled the tablet, Dr Lowe and Archbishop D'Arcy led the singing of 'O God, our help in ages past'. In the address, Dr Lowe compared the Irish Protestants who had fought in the war to the men of Derry who had closed the gates against James II. 'They fought and alas many of them fell in the cause of freedom, the cause of the empire and the cause of Ulster, because the cause of Ulster is the cause of freedom and the cause of the Empire.' They sang 'God save the King', the Duchess of Abercorn unfurled the Union flag and the French tricolour from the tower and a yew tree was planted on behalf of the women of Ulster. At lunch in a low-key hut before the party motored back to Amiens, 'the proceedings had a quiet dignity,' the newspapers reported. 'Even when one of the seats gave way, no one dreamt of laughing.'[38]

In the South, the humbled Protestants discreetly hid their memorials in their church porches and churchyards, yielding the centre of town to statues that commemorated the heroes of the Easter Rising. In Northern Ireland, public war memorials were one of the symbols of partition and in the Protestant citadel of Portadown, they commandeered the most impressive site possible in the high street.

The Ulstermen had many dead to mourn. About 5,000 men from the 36th (Ulster) Division had perished on the first terrible day of the Battle of the Somme. But whereas in England the war dead were a source of almost unrelieved sorrow, here the memory was bitter-sweet, for the blood sacrifice had given birth to partition. It was the blood of the dead that had finally liberated them from Home Rule.

The 20th anniversary of the Battle of the Somme on 1 July 1936 was celebrated in Northern Ireland with particular fervour. The Presbyterian Moderator, Andrew Moody, recalled the tremendous awe he felt at taking part in the event. 'At 11.30a.m.,' he wrote,

the Lord Mayor, aldermen and councillors accompanied by the representative of the Governor of Northern Ireland, His Majesty's lieutenant for the city, the heads of the churches, representatives of the Navy, Army and Air Force, all wearing ceremonial robes or full uniform, proceeded to the Garden of Remembrance, where the resolution of the corporation was read, the Union Jack lowered to half mast and the last post sounded. The ceremony of wreath-laying followed, the band meanwhile playing Chopin's Funeral March. Then, as the flag was run up again, Reveille was sounded and the national anthem brought the ceremony to a close. Remembering the wet cheeks and stifled sobs in that dense mass of silent onlookers, we unrobed and stole away with a little lump in the throat.[39]

There were class and geographical differences between the Protestant churches in the North. The Church of Ireland dominated both the top and the bottom of the social pyramid. They had the landowners and the poorest Protestant workers in Belfast and Londonderry in their keep. The Presbyterians and Methodists held the middle ground. The Presbyterians remained concentrated in their old heartland in the area of the first Scots plantation, in Down and Antrim. The Anglicans were more spread out, reflecting the settlement pattern of the English 'undertakers' in the second plantation. They made up the overwhelming majority of Protestants in English-settled Fermanagh, in the south-west of Ulster. War commemorations were occasions to celebrate a generic tribal Protestantism that was vague and undenominational. The cult of the war welded Protestants together. So did fear. Protestants huddled together like king penguins when they reflected on the fact that demographic trends were all operating in favour of the Catholic minority.

The Church of Ireland population was holding its own, reflecting the relatively high birth rate of its large working-class population. In 1861 they had numbered 320,634 in the six counties of Northern Ireland. The figure dipped a little in the 1880s and 1890s but it recovered, reaching 338,724 in 1926 and 345,474 ten years later. But the overwhelmingly middle-class Presbyterian community was decreasing, as families shrank in size and ambitious children left the fusty, decaying world of Ulster for Britain and the dominions. In 1861 the Presbyterians had numbered 457,119 in the six counties that would later comprise Northern Ireland, and been by far the largest denomination. By 1926 this figure had slid to 393,374 while in 1936 it was down to 390,930.

The Protestants had been too greedy. A smaller Ulster would have been more homogeneous. As it was, they made up a convincing majority in only two of the six counties. In Antrim, the 38,619 Catholics of the northern coastal villages were easily outweighed by the 153,024 Protestants of the interior and the south of the county. In Down, the 63,589 Catholics of Newry and the south confronted 145,639 Protestants in the north. In the Borough of Belfast there were 95,682 Catholics, mostly in the west of the city, and 319,469 Protestants. Elsewhere, the Protestant majority was precarious or non-existent. In Armagh county there were 50,000 Catholics in the south and 60,080 Protestants in the north. In County Londonderry there were about 40,000 Catholics and 50,000 Protestants. In Fermanagh and Tyrone the influx of Protestant refugees from the South briefly reversed a slight pre-war nationalist majority in the 1920s: in Fermanagh, 32,455 Protestants jockeyed with 25,529 Catholics, while in Tyrone the ratio was 73,683 Catholics to 59,109 Protestants. Londonderry borough had a Catholic majority of 27,062 to 18,097.

While the number of Presbyterians declined and the Church of Ireland population remained static, the number of Catholics grew constantly. By 1936, they numbered 428,290, or 33.4 per cent of the Northern Ireland population. But they comprised a substantially higher percentage of the population of young children: 38 per cent of the under-five-year-olds, for example, and the differential was set to widen. For every 1,000 Catholic women of child-bearing age there were

746 children aged three or under. Among the same number of Presbyterian women there were only 463.[40] William Marshall, Presbyterian minister of Castlerock between the wars, told a nationalist friend that his own side was doomed. 'I feel convinced that you'll swamp us yet,' he wrote in 1933. 'Your people breed and ours don't. Anyone who thinks we'll be got in any other way is a fool.'[41]

Protestant newspapers such as the *Christian Irishman* fuelled their readers' fears about a secret Catholic plot to take over Ulster by means of buying up Protestant land. In June 1945 the paper was less interested in the defeat of Nazi Germany than in revealing details of a diabolical papal plot to destroy Protestants in Ulster. 'A deliberate and carefully sustained campaign is being pursued in Northern Ireland,' it said, 'the object of which is the acquiring of Protestant property with a view to the ultimate numerical ascendancy of Roman Catholicism in the six counties.' The newspaper left readers in no doubt about the horrors in store for those who now slept soundly in their beds.

> By every means in her power and with all the resources at her disposal, slowly, insidiously but surely the Church of Rome is working day and night, knowing that every farm or residence that passes from the possession of a Protestant to a Roman Catholic . . . is helping to bring about the day when our present majority shall be wiped out, placing our Protestant rights and liberties at the mercy of a power that is determined to destroy them.[42]

It was a theme repeated at every opportunity for at least another decade. In 1949 the newspaper implored Presbyterians not to forget the real enemy that lurked behind political Republicanism. The IRA, it said, were 'mere actors strolling across the stage of Irish political life . . . No, our one never-sleeping foe is the papacy, ever waiting patiently and watching silently to seize the opportunity that such circumstances give for the advancement of its totalitarian aims.'[43]

The *Christian Irishman* was a church paper and its writers, especially the indefatigable Fred Gibson, Superintendent of the Irish Mission, were much more fixated on ecclesiastical subjects than the average layman. Nevertheless, its paranoid world view was not unrepresentative of the Presbyterian community. Many Ulster Protestants in the 1940s and 1950s saw the world in terms that would have been very familiar to English Protestants of the 1620s, as a struggle between the contending principles of Romanism and Protestantism. It was the wide spread of such views that paved the way for the rise in politics in the 1960s of a Protestant fundamentalist pastor called Ian Paisley.

Protestant church leaders did not speak of plots and conspiracies in the same way, but they strongly encouraged Protestants of all classes to stick together and vote together. When the Church of Ireland clergy clashed with the new Northern Ireland government over its plans for education in the mid-1920s, Primate D'Arcy went against his clergy and told them to support the authorities. Even on his deathbed in 1938, the Archbishop rallied to issue an hysterical appeal to voters to back the government of James Craig, now Lord Craigavon, in the elections that the Ulster premier called for January of that year. On the British mainland a bishop who interfered so obviously in an election would probably have been forced to resign. In Northern Ireland, a close identification of the Church with the government was seen as normal. 'Never for one moment have I regretted our action at that time,' D'Arcy said in 1938, recalling his support for the Covenant of 1912. 'It is my belief that the present crisis is just as serious and the need for unity is just as urgent. United we stand, divided we fall. Support our great leader, Lord Craigavon.'[44]

The constant atmosphere of low-level alarm kept the old Ascendancy in place. The little people felt secure with these craggy old titans, whose families had seen off assorted Catholic threats over the centuries. The northern Protestant state was run along patrician lines by the scions of great Anglican landed families dating back to the Ulster Plantation. Their helpers and supporters were the Church of Ireland, Presbyterian and Methodist farmers and middle classes. The southern state in the 1930s rested on the four pillars of the Fianna Fáil, the Catholic Church, the farmers and the Gaelic Athletic Association, the sporting counterpart to the Gaelic League. Its northern counterpart was run by the aristocracy, the Ulster Unionist Party and the Orange Order.

Basil Brooke, Lord Brookeborough, who succeeded Craigavon as Prime Minister in 1943, epitomised this Ascendancy tone. The Brookes had owned their estate at Colebrooke in County Fermanagh since the seventeenth century. 'They came to Ireland with swords in their hands unashamedly,' wrote Brooke's biographer. 'They tenaciously defended the British crown and the Protestant succession with which their fortunes as a family had been intertwined.'[45] The Brookes epitomised the Ascendancy's martial qualities. They had taken part in the Williamite war, defending Donegal against the Jacobite army, the siege of Derry, the firing of Washington in 1812, a clutch of Indian campaigns and, naturally, the First World War. Brookeborough's own education at Winchester and Sandhurst had imparted a thoroughly British outlook. One strand in the make-up of the Brookes was imperial service. Another was Protestantism. Brooke's grandfather, Sir Arthur, had led the opposition to the extension of the Maynooth grant in 1845 and had championed the revival of the Orange Order. His son, Victor, who died in 1891, was an equally fervent Tory and an opponent of Disestablishment and Home Rule. This was the heritage Brooke brought to government. It explained why, in the words of his successor, Terence O'Neill, 'in twenty years as Prime Minister he never crossed the border, never visited a Catholic school and was never received or sought a civic reception from a Catholic town'.[46] A third strand in Brooke was a love of sport, the natural pastime of the warrior in repose. It was significant that on being made Prime Minister in May 1943, he noted: 'Caught 1 pound 6 ounce trout in the Narrow . . . '[47]

The flip side to such Ascendancy warriors was a dilatory attitude to government, a slight feeling of bewilderment about what they were supposed to do when there was no fighting. O'Neill came from the same class, for all the family's distant origins as a Gaelic clan, but was far more intelligent and critical. Stormont, the neo-classical parliament, opened in 1932, was 'reminiscent of a London theatre', he recalled.

> One entered a hall where the messengers made their tea, then went on into another hall, which looked like a dentists' waiting room with all the stuffing come out of the chairs. One then clattered on down a brown linoleum-covered passage past a gurgling lavatory into the Prime Minister's study. All the staff were on the first floor and one's only form of communication was a bell either for the messenger or the permanent secretary. The evidence of its former use as a country house was all too clear.[48]

The religion of Carson, Craigavon and Brooke and, indeed, that of Archbishops Crozier and D'Arcy (though not Gregg, who went to Armagh reluctantly) was a vague, tribal Protestantism. They were all Church of Ireland members but their outward beliefs appeared unconnected with dogmatic formulas or narrow denominational allegiances. They found their perfect focus in the propagation of the Orange cult, in commemorations of the First World War and in jamborees connected with royal weddings and jubilees. Craigavon told the Stormont parliament on 24 April 1934 that the Orange Order was the most important element in his make-up. 'I am as high up in the order as anyone, being Grand Master of the Loyal County Down, of which I am very proud. I prize that far more than being prime minister. I have often said I am an Orangeman first and a member of parliament afterwards.'[49] When he departed for London to take part in George V's Silver Jubilee in 1935, he urged young Protestant boys to put on their Orange sashes as soon as possible. 'It was fitting,' he said, speaking at Dromore, County Down, 'that at a time when they are paying tribute to His Majesty the King on the occasion of his silver jubilee they should remember the tribute they owed to the glorious pious and immortal memory of the great and good King William of Orange.'[50]

The Jubilee was Ulster's Protestant riposte to the 1932 Eucharistic Congress, celebrated with lighted beacons and special church services. Instead of a papal legate, Northern Ireland got the Duke of Gloucester, who toured Belfast and Londonderry on behalf of the King. Another riposte was the funeral of Lord Carson. The old patriarch died at Minster, in Kent, on 22 October 1935. Four days later the remains left Cleve Court for the long journey 'home' to Northern Ireland. From Kent they travelled to the Princess landing stage in Liverpool before being taken on HMS *Broke* to Donegall Quay in Belfast.

The workers of Dublin knelt for Archbishop Byrne's blessing at the centenary celebrations of Catholic Emancipation in 1929. The Belfast people got their chance in 1935, when thousands of shipyard workers lined the quays to watch Carson's last journey. There was absolute silence as the ship moved to the landing stage and the body was brought ashore and placed on a gun carriage provided by HMS *Caroline*. With a guard of honour from the RUC, the successors in Ulster to the old RIC, the procession wound its way through Queen's Square Victoria Street, Chichester Street, Donegall Place and Donegall Street to the cathedral. The crowds in the streets were dense, ten or twelve deep.

The procession halted outside the old town hall, the former headquarters of the UVF in the stirring days of 1912–14, and again outside the City Hall, where the Covenant had been signed. At the cathedral, Primate D'Arcy, John McNeice, Bishop of Down, Dean Kerr of Belfast, the Presbyterian Moderator Moody and Methodist church leaders were waiting to conduct the burial service. Earth from the six counties and from the city of Londonderry, the Maiden City, was dropped into the grave.

Since the great days of the Home Rule crisis Carson had enjoyed remarkably little contact with 'his' people. He resigned as leader of the Ulster Unionists in 1921 and had scarcely been seen in Northern Ireland since. It was not altogether surprising. Carson's aim had never been partition – but use of the threat of partition to keep the whole of Ireland in the Union. Even as late as 1921, when the game was up for the British in Ireland, he was predicting to an audience in Torquay that without Ulster, the Free State would soon come back crawling on its knees to the British empire. In a sense, Carson was reluctant to acknowledge paternity of his Ulster baby. But if the father felt embarrassed by the child, the child had only adoration for the father. In Northern Ireland, the memory of Carson, like that of the First World War, lingered on and if anything gained an extra sweetness with the passing of the years. Vast crowds turned out to applaud him when he opened the new parliament at Stormont in 1932. A year later his statue was unveiled in the grounds. To many Protestants, Carson was a semi-deity and while he breathed, if only in Kent, they could sleep soundly in their beds. It became important to assume that he kept them uppermost in his thoughts in retirement amid the hop fields and oast houses. At his death, Lord Craigavon assured Northern Ireland that 'during his last hours he must have experienced consolation in the knowledge that the North was safe'.[51]

To northern Protestants, Carson was a Moses figure. He had led the chosen people out from under the noses of the Catholic pharaohs of the South and into the Promised Land. James Little, preaching after Carson's funeral in Belfast's Ulster Hall, drew on the Old Testament prophets to create the right image. 'The call of the people of Ulster was the call of God to be leader in a campaign to preserve Protestantism and liberty in the Northern land where God had planted their forefathers to be witnesses . . . against the errors of Romanism,' he said. Carson had 'marched breast forward, ever keeping his face towards the light, never for a single moment doubting that whatever baffling forces might be in the way, right would eventually triumph, and through the favour of God it surely did.'[52] The sermon hit an appropriate note for a people with a strong notion of itself as the elect, raised up by God to be a witness against the heathen multitude.

While the Brookes of Colebrooke stood at the apex of the Protestant pyramid in the Northern Irish state, men like Robert Harbinson, author of *No Surrender: An Ulster Childhood,* were at the bottom, inhabiting the gently decaying landscape of industrial Belfast. Working-class Presbyterians like the Harbinsons were acutely aware of their religious heritage. Protestant history was dinned into their heads in the state-funded schools. Where Catholics were inculcated in their beliefs by Irish Catholic Truth Society pamphlets, many working-class Ulster Protestant homes contained short, popular books such as *How We Differ from Rome,* or possibly the two-volume *Orangeism in Ireland and throughout the Empire,* which revealed that the Pope had started the First World War.[53] Their homes were furnished differently from those of their Catholic neighbours and were instantly recognisable. There were no statues. There might be a copy of the Lord's Prayer, or, as in the Harbinson home, a few biblical texts in Gothic letters entwined with roses, in huge wooden frames.

Just as Catholic lives revolved around the annual cycle of church feasts and fasts, Protestant lives in the North revolved around the liturgical cycle created from the Irish life and times of William III, which reached its climax on 12 July and 12 August. The anniversary of the siege of Derry was a kind of alternative crucifixion, followed by resurrection at the Battle of the Boyne. Although only a month separated the two high days in the Protestant calendar, the preparation of the bands and the elaborate street decorations consumed months of activity beforehand.

The Orange lodges had a sacral quality, which, if only temporarily, made priests and shamans of the masters. Harbinson recalled the atmosphere of religious awe at his induction ceremony, a classic rite of passage marking his transition from childhood to adulthood and his entry into the world of the grown-up, male Protestant. 'I had to stand outside the sacred locked door of the inner chamber,' he remembered, 'trembling and waiting in a gloomy passage. Then before the whole assembly wearing its glittering regalia my name was put forward and approved. The doors opened and my sponsors emerged to lead me in, keeping position on both sides of me. I was marched through the columns of Loyal Sons. I was now shaking physically and almost incoherent as I swore to keep the Lodge password.'[54]

The world of the Ulster Protestant working man was infinitely more religious than that of his counterpart in England or Scotland. But it was far less so than that of his Catholic neighbour. The Northern state was a joint-stock operation of several Protestant churches and one consequence was that clerical authority was broken down and dispersed. Northern Ireland was never an Anglican or a Presbyterian state; it was a condominium. This state of affairs gave enormous power to the believing Protestant to pick and choose his or her denomination and place of worship. Inevitably, Protestants belonged to a society that was less cohesive and more individualistic. The ecclesiastical geography of south Belfast, where dozens of Victorian churches crowd a small area, is a memorial to the intense competition that raged between the churches for congregations. Harbinson recalled a society which was close to the churches, but which had none of the spirit of reverence that Catholics bestowed on their priests. Harvest festivals were 'a chance to steal marrows and crispy loafs', while Christmas was a time to mend fences with the Church of Ireland, because it was the Rector who supplied poor families with a joint from the poor-box. There was little denominational loyalty. Missionaries of all shapes and sizes were popular in a world that was starved of amusements and attractions. They had an exotic star quality, because 'the steam of tropical forests had hardly dried out of their clothes'. Crowds of children attended baptisms by immersion conducted by evangelical ministers because of the 'comedy and thrills spiced with the possibility of an accident'.[55]

It was a cheerfully casual and opportunistic attitude to worship, which paved the way for a rapid decline in church attendance in the 1930s when radio and cinema supplanted church and chapel as sources of 'comedy and thrills'. Secularisation had been making inroads into the Ulster Protestant way of life for a long time. In the First World War, the *Irish Presbyterian* newspaper noted a striking decline in the once fiercely strict observation of the Sabbath. It traced the decline to the first appearance of music bands on Sunday in Belfast in 1855, the first Sunday concerts in 1858, the opening of museums on Sunday in 1896 and the spread of Sunday newspapers. It noted with grim satisfaction that when the pride of the Belfast shipyards, the *Titanic*, went down in 1912, it had been on a Sunday and the 'sacred hours of that Sabbath evening had been spent on board in dancing, card playing and other gaieties'.[56]

One reason why the Protestant clergy had been so enthusiastic about the First World War had been their genuine, if entirely misguided, conviction that the carnage would recall their wavering congregations to a knowledge of God. In 1915 the *Irish Presbyterian* had approvingly noted that the war had 'effected a solemnising of men's thoughts and a great movement towards God'. Archbishop Crozier had told the Armagh clergy meeting at Dungannon, County Tyrone, in August 1916 that 'God must have permitted this war for some great good cause'. He said one of its first fruits was the 'spirit of seriousness, of solemnity and of service for others that has descended on our country'.[57]

To the disappointment of Protestant Church leaders, the war ended by boosting atheism and socialism rather than belief in God. The Protestant churches found themselves struggling for influence as never before, competing not only with Sunday concerts and museums but with the cinema and the Sunday outing in the family motor car. Secularism was a problem even in a society where sectarian tension kept the churches in a state of feverish activity. In 1936, Presbyterian ministers complained that church attendance was fast becoming a minority pursuit. Some were reaching for desperate solutions, such as the conversion of the evening service into a discussion group. J. K. Elliot, minister of Islandmagee, thought secularisation had bitten deep into the northern Presbyterian community and that 'outside a few favoured congregations in the cities or large towns the proportion of church members who attend with reasonable regularity is lamentably small'.[58] The 1938 Assembly in Belfast heard a report on the state of religion that proclaimed family prayers to be 'almost extinct'.[59] The decay of organised religion did not create a new kind of politics in the North. Religious Protestants evolved into less religious or irreligious Protestants. They did not evolve into some new, third category of Irishmen or women, or occupy an equidistant position between nationalism and Unionism.

Many Northern Catholics had accepted the new order in the North because they expected it to be short-lived. Nationalist politicians, like English Liberals, had traditionally dealt with the objections of northern Protestants by ignoring them. The result was that northern Catholics fatally underestimated the determination of the Protestants to create a permanently separate state. The dawning knowledge that Northern Ireland was there to stay – and that the South had learned to live without them – came as a crushing blow. In 1929 Archbishop MacRory voiced the continuing hope that the Ulster state would evaporate, peacefully and painlessly.

I pray that Ireland will be before long united in one common state, an undivided motherland . . . I believe that would be good for all Irishmen . . . I believe it would be good for those who insisted on partition, but I can understand their fears. I can respect their fears . . . we cannot bring it about by anything like force or pressure . . . the best and surest way to bring it about is for the Free State to build itself up in prosperity and strength.[60]

As the Craigavon regime rolled on and on, he adopted a bitterer tone. In 1932, Northern pilgrims were pelted with rocks on the trains taking them to the Eucharistic Congress. It was a forceful reminder that in one corner of Ireland, the 'Irish' were still in a state of subjection. There was no apology. The matter was referred to the Belfast Corporation, which forgot all about it.

As Minister of Agriculture in the 1930s, Brooke reinforced the notion that Northern Ireland was run exclusively by and for the Protestant population. At Newtownbutler in County Fermanagh on 12 July 1933, he made a speech that attracted particular notoriety both north and south of the border when he complained about Protestants who employed Catholics. 'He felt he could speak freely on the subject as he had not a Roman Catholic about his own place,' he said. 'He would point out that the Roman Catholics were endeavouring to get in everywhere and were out with all their force and might to destroy the power and constitution of Ulster. There was a definite plot to overpower the vote of Unionists in the north. He would appeal to loyalists therefore wherever possible, to employ Protestant lads and lassies (cheers).'[61]

The speech caused uproar and reinforced the comforting perception in the South that their state was a haven of democracy compared to the bigoted North. Brooke was entirely unrepentant. A month later, at the celebrations in

Londonderry, he repeated his words, warning that Protestants would be 'drawn and quartered' if they lost power in Northern Ireland. Rejecting the charge of religious bigotry, Brooke repeated the old formula that it was not the religion of Catholics that he objected to but their politics. Once more he repeated his plea for Protestants not to employ Catholics because 'their religion is so politically minded . . . [that they are] out to destroy us as a body'.[62] Southern Protestants were embarrassed by this kind of language. A few northern ones were too, calling him 'the Colebrooke Hitler'.[63]

Catholic frustration with their position and with the permanence of partition exploded in July 1935, when Belfast saw violence on a scale that had not been experienced since the partition years. The match was lit by an Orange procession returning from Belmont over the Queen's Bridge to the city centre. Fighting began from the direction of North Street. At Donegall Street, the procession divided, some going down Clifton Street to their headquarters, the rest going along York Street, where another riot started. At the end of the day there were 40 wounded and one dead, a Protestant. The following day, a Tuesday, and on Wednesday, worse rioting left seven dead, 70 houses burnt down and 100 people injured. By the end of the affray, Daniel Mageean, Catholic Bishop of Down and Connor, claimed that 384 Catholic families had been driven from their homes, totalling 1,646 individuals. On 18 July a ban on further processions was announced, which was not lifted until the 27th.

To the Protestant clergy, such displays of sectarian hatred were an embarrassment to the northern state and a stain on their own honour. The 1935 riots briefly brought Catholics and Protestants together. On behalf of the Protestants, Bishop MacNeice of Down and Dean Kerr of Belfast issued statements denouncing the violence, while 18 clergy handed out handbills at the shipyard – always a focus for the trouble – urging the workers to keep the peace. Bishop Mageean similarly insisted there must be no reprisals, saying it was not his Protestant clerical counterparts but the local authorities who were to blame. The Ulster premier characteristically suggested the attacks had been directed against people who were disloyal to the crown and the constitution. 'Was it on account of their disloyalty that ex-servicemen were evicted from their homes?' Bishop Mageean asked, addressing the Maynooth Union on 16 October in London. 'Was it on account of its disloyalty that a baby two days old was thrown onto the street?'[64]

As always, a brief truce was followed by a return to mutual recrimination. Protestant embarrassment over the Belfast riots evaporated after the southern Catholics destroyed the Presbyterian church in Henry Street, Limerick, the Methodist church at Boyle, County Roscommon, a Church of Ireland church in Kilnagoolagh, Newmarket-on-Fergus, County Clare, as well as Protestant shops in Letterkenny in Donegal, and at Trim, County Meath. Days before Dean Kerr had been urging Protestants to keep the peace. Now he was exchanging insults with Bishop Mageean, accusing him of deliberately misrepresenting affairs. The Northern Catholic bishops, Mageean of Down, and MacRory, fulminated against this state of affairs, especially after the introduction of the new 'all Ireland' constitution in the South failed to bring down the walls of Jericho. In his 1938 Lenten pastoral, Mageean condemned Stormont's 'long record of partisan and bigoted discrimination'.[65]

The outbreak of war revealed that the chasm between Irish Protestants and Catholics was as wide as ever. Protestants, north and south, rallied to the empire. 'The long suspense is over,' said Archbishop Gregg, who had moved from Dublin to Armagh the year before, 'and our country is at war.'[66] Our country was, of course, Britain. The Catholics, north and south of the border, thought of their country as Ireland and they supported De Valera's policy of neutrality; some even supported Germany. The Catholic clergy used the opportunity of the crisis to clamour for an end to partition. When the Germans bombed Belfast, De Valera famously sent fire engines to help put out the blazes. But there was no reconciliation between the two states. Many Protestants claimed their Catholic neighbours lit fires to guide the German bomber planes to their targets. The accusation said much about relations between the communities.

Although the southern Protestants supported the British cause, there were far fewer of them to volunteer in 1939 than there had been in 1914. A glance at any of the war memorials in the Republic today confirms it. The parishes and cathedrals recorded the names of those who died, beside the older list of casualties from the First World War. The difference in size is striking. The memorial in the porch of St Canice's cathedral in Kilkenny records the names of 68 local Protestants who died in the First World War, and 22 who died in the Second. Some northern and southern Catholics fought alongside the Irish Protestants. But those who did, especially if they came from the embittered North, were seen as traitors to their communities, not heroes. The Irish Catholics were not fighting for Britain, in any case. They were fighting against Nazism. The Protestants were fighting for the mother country, too. There was a difference.

The Northern Protestants returned to an Ulster that felt its membership of the United Kingdom had been tested and validated. There had been a nasty scare under Churchill, when it seemed the British might trade Ulster for Ireland's participation on the Allied side. It came to nothing. Fortunately for the Unionists, De Valera chose neutrality over reunification.

The Southern Protestants returned to a country that had remained aggressively neutral, where the dominant Church had been pro-Fascist in the 1930s and where Catholic opinion was overwhelmingly anti-British. When the Trinity students hoisted the Union flag on VE Day in Dublin in 1945 and started singing 'God save the King', there was uproar. As the *Irish Times* recorded, 'A section of the crowd took exception to the [subordinate] position of the Eire flag and three attempts, frustrated by the Guards, were made to effect an entrance into the university. The Guards had to make repeated baton charges in College Green last night to disperse large crowds of young men and women demonstrating in front of Trinity College.'[67] Later, it went on, a crowd of 50 men attacked the Wicklow

Hotel, shouting: 'Give us the West Britons', only to be repelled by the bell-boys. The crowd retired to Nassau Street. They were carrying Vatican as well as Irish flags. To many Dubliners, the British victory was a Protestant victory and all the more unwelcome.

It was not Fianna Fáil, or De Valera, who rolled up the last slender rope bridge linking southern Protestants to the empire. To the surprise of some of its supporters, it was the inter-party coalition government under John Costello that declared Ireland would pull out of the Commonwealth and become a Republic in 1949. Protestants could no longer pretend they were part of the empire and still, however tenuously, subjects of the British King. 'The hard facts,' the Rector of Askeaton, county Limerick told his colleagues in 1949, 'are that the 26 counties, whether one likes it or not, have become a Republic, a Republic outside the Commonwealth, in whose affairs George VI has no say.'[68] Amid a few grumbles about 'liturgical regicide', the Church of Ireland had to withdraw the prayer for the royal family from the state prayers in the liturgy south of the border. Archbishop Gregg, still able to pray for his King from the safety of Armagh, found it distasteful but accepted the situation. 'We meet today under strange conditions,' he told the 1949 Church Synod, 'with the Republic of Ireland an established fact. Many dwellers in the Republic will regret the loss of the familiar words, but what other way out is there? In our prayers, above all, there must be reality.'[69] The Protestants had to turn south, face Dublin and adopt a more Irish identity.

CHAPTER FIFTEEN

Most Fruitful of Mothers

*One thing is clear: we have the ear of the people, the children in schools
and the adults at mass.*
(Fr Kevin Smyth, 1958)[1]

At Maynooth, in the summer of 1956, the Catholic bishops assembled to bestow their blessing on the wonderful state of religion in the country. The panic about the nation's faith and morals in the 1920s seemed light years away. England and America had succumbed to atheism and Eastern Europe to Communism. But in Ireland, faith was undimmed. 'Our country is deeply conscioous of its duty to God and religion,' the bishops said.

> We have witnessed a wonderful expansion of missionary effort in Ireland at a time when religion is being cruelly repressed or persecuted in so many other parts of the world. Communistic or anti-religious influences, once they have been recognised as such, have gained little support here. We have had an impressive demonstration of the faith and piety inspiring these developments, in the unprecedented attendances at the Holy Week ceremonies this year.[2]

The Catholic Church had more vocations than ever. In 1940 there were 3,354 diocesan clergy in Ireland and another 1,024 clergy in religious orders. In 1950 the figures were 3,563 and 1,481 respectively. In 1956 they were 3,772 and 1,717. The trend was relentlessly upwards. As Ireland had a total Catholic population, North and South, of 3,257,400 in 1956, this meant one priest per 593 Catholics. Beyond the ranks of secular priests and priests in religious orders stood the battalions of nuns and brothers who were not ordained. Together they boosted the army of God to a total of 18,300 in 1956.

The number of priests, brothers and nuns told only half the story. Irish vocations were so high that between one-third and one-half of the clergy went abroad to serve in Ireland's overseas spiritual empire in England, Nigeria, South Africa, Kenya, Uganda, Trinidad or India. The 1950s was an era of growth for all the Irish missionary societies. The Irish province of the Holy Ghost Fathers had expanded from 143 in 1920 to 620 in 1959. The province of the Society for African

Missions grew from 40 to 400 in the same period. The Legion of Mary, which was a kind of internal, lay-run missionary society, continued to expand.

Rome was astonished at the fecundity of its Irish daughter. 'Any Christian nation will produce a greater or lesser number of priests,' Pope John XXIII told Archbishop D'Alton of Armagh in 1961. 'But Ireland, that beloved country, is the most fruitful of mothers in this respect. In the number of priests, diocesan and regular, and in the number of nuns and sisters to which she has given birth, she is second to none. To no other nation does she yield this palm.'[3]

The Catholic Church could take pride in the fidelity of the people. It could claim credit also for the peace that reigned in the land. The old accusation of the Church's Protestant enemies had been that Catholicism left people unregenerate. Victorian Protestants complained that the façade of religion among Catholics not only concealed vice but at the same time aided and encouraged it. A glance at the Ireland of the 1950s seemed to disprove the charge. Now the British and the landlords had been removed, Catholic Ireland found a kind of peace it had never before experienced in recorded history. Victorian Ireland lumbered from one 'outrage' to another and at times it seemed the whole land was locked in a perpetual state of emergency; in De Valera's Ireland, the crime rate was extraordinarily low. In neighbouring Britain, the 1950s figured as a law-abiding decade. Even so, Britain's 125 murders a year in the middle years of the decade compared unfavourably with the Irish Republic's three, even taking into account the disparity in population. The rate of illegitimate births in the Irish Republic was only 1.8 per cent, compared to 4.7 per cent in Britain. Throughout Ireland the impression was that church attendance had actually increased during the 1950s. Most urban churches held at least six masses on Sundays to cope with the numbers.

Why was the Church in Ireland so strong? Jeremiah Newman, Bishop of Limerick, looked to the continuing, rock-solid alliance between religion and nationalism. 'For centuries, religion and patriotism went hand in hand in Ireland,' he said in October 1958. 'The priests were leaders of the people in many national movements. They helped the country rise from political and social depression. The memory of this is still fresh in Irish minds and accords the priest a high place in the public estimation.'[4] The idea that this situation might ever change appeared remote well into the next decade. When Desmond Fennell published an essay in May 1962 in the periodical *Doctrine and Life*, entitled 'Will the Irish stay Christian?', the publishers thought the title so absurd that they renamed it 'Ireland and Christianity'.

Emigration and poverty were the great blots on this landscape. The departure of the British had brought peace but not prosperity. Life was better than it had been, but desperately frugal by the standards of the Western democracies. In 1949–50 just half of the households in the Republic had an inside lavatory. Fewer than half had piped water. Only the privileged elite possessed a bathroom or a shower. Cars and telephones were rare. There were only about 15,000 telephones in private hands at the time.

Fianna Fáil and De Valera dominated the political landscape. De Valera was Prime Minister with only two interruptions from 1932 to 1959. He brought the country stability, but his vision of Ireland was as a Gaelic, agrarian society. In practice, he left economic policy to Séan Lemass, who had a more urban outlook. But, economically the country stagnated.

There was a strange, almost ghastly, contrast between the seemingly limitless growth of the Irish Church and the shrinking secular society. While the number of clergy climbed steadily upwards, the population declined remorselessly. It was as if the Church had evolved into a vast cancerous lump that was steadily sucking the life blood out of the society from which it drew nourishment. The visible decline imbued many Irishmen, including thoughtful Catholic churchmen, with deep pessimism. In the 1990s it became common to call Northern Ireland a 'failed entity'. In the 1950s many Irish people regarded their own state in the same way. When Denis Meehan, a priest in Elphin diocese and a Maynooth professor, wrote an article in 1960 in which he spoke of the eventual collapse of the Republic of Ireland, he suggested the question was not whether it would happen but when. 'Even if one accepts the ultimate demise of the Republic as an inevitable fact and the desirability of merging with some sort of larger entity,' he said, 'there remains the question of what is going to happen in the meantime.'[5]

To Frank Duff, founder of the Legion of Mary, the remorseless decline of the Irish population could only be comprehended in the context of a larger divine dispensation. Like Cardinal Manning in the 1870s, Duff was convinced that God had singled out the Irish nation to carry the cross to a fallen world and in doing so, endure immense privation. The De Valera government was wrong to treat emigration as a mere economic problem, he wrote in 1957. 'The fact is that the entire Catholic population of Ireland is caught up in that Divine campaign.' Duff was careful to insist that it was God who had elected Ireland as his torchbearer, not Ireland that had presented itself because of its intrinsic virtues. 'We are not fitted for that role of a campaigning army which God has forced upon us,' he said. 'But he had to assign us to it for the elemental reason that in a decayed world he has nowhere else to look for the manpower for this manoeuvre. In heaven itself echo the old words of Fontenoy: "The Irish troops remain".'[6]

Compared to the steely ranks of Catholic priests, religious brothers and nuns, the Church of Ireland in the 26 counties was a ravaged force. Beside the Catholic Church's testosterone-loaded thousands, the old Established Church could only muster 640 tottering legs. Wasted and ageing, southern Protestants maintained a kind of discreet apartheid from the Catholic majority in those businesses that they still controlled. The *Irish Times*, Protestant run and still very much with a Protestant ethos, was their noticeboard and house journal. It still carried advertisements for positions that were reserved to their own creed, whatever their qualifications. 'Junior assistant, ladies wear, Protestant, two or three years experience, smart appearance, good at sales,' was a typical advertisement which appeared on

8 May 1957. Or again, on 22 May, 'Young lady assistant (Protestant) required for sweets, confectionery and ice-cream department, high-class trade, Midlands.'

The Protestants had got used to the Republic and De Valera. They felt less uncomfortable than they had done in the 1920s, when the arguments over censorship and the language were at their height. Middle-class Protestants in the relatively cosmopolitan atmosphere of Dublin felt least uncomfortable of all. Growing up in the slightly down-at-heel south Dublin suburb of Harold's Cross in the 1950s, Hugh Maxton recalled no special feeling of isolation from his neighbours. Unlike the situation in the countryside, the differences between city Catholics and Protestants were very slight. The typical rural Catholic listened to Radio Eireann, took the *Irish Independent* or the *Irish News* and voted for Fianna Fáil. The Maxtons tuned their wireless to the BBC, read the *Irish Times* and voted Labour, a party whose conspicuous hostility to sectarianism made it a natural, if somewhat unlikely, repository of many Protestant votes. At his grandparents' parish church in rural Aughrim, County Wicklow, Maxton was surprised to find the words 'Protestant fucks' scrawled on the door on one occasion. But it was an isolated blip, a poltergeist memory of the old intolerance. What struck Maxton in the Wicklow countryside was the similarity between his Protestant grandmother and her Catholic neighbours. 'There was no trace of nostalgia for the regime under which she and her older children were born,'[7] he recalled. Other Dublin Protestants growing up at the same time made the same observation. Vague clues around the house might point to different ancestral allegiances – a faded picture of Victoria's Diamond Jubilee, perhaps. But the heart had gone out of it. As Edith Newman Devlin recalled of the royal portrait that hung in her father's parlour in Dublin, 'She might have been the Queen of China for all that she meant for us.'[8]

The Maxtons were unaware of any feelings of hostility on the part of their neighbours. But Protestants like the Maxtons may simply have been ignorant of their neighbours' real feelings about them. Brendan Hoban recalled being taught as a child in the 1950s to look on the local Protestant church with fear and scorn.

> To go inside was to commit a mortal sin. Sometimes for a dare we crept down the inside of the stone wall and pretended to touch the ground. You could touch the grass, an older boy said, there was no harm as long as you didn't touch the ground. As kids we felt the Protestants were different. They hadn't the true faith like us Catholics. God alone knew the horrible things they got up to inside the church and when they died they would all go to hell.[9]

The best-selling author Frank McCourt recalled much the same atmosphere in Limerick in the late 1940s. As a paper-boy, his duty was to distribute copies of the *Irish Times* to members of the small Protestant community. But as a Catholic, he was forbidden even to glance at the contents and his Catholic boss handled the business of delivering the paper with repulsion. When McCourt's bicycle skidded on the winter ice, 'Shops complain to Mr McCaffrey that *The Irish Times* is coming in decorated with bits of ice and dog shit and he mutters to us that's the way that paper should be delivered, Protestant rag that it is.'[10] This was not a society that had let go of the old hatreds. In the Irish countryside, the old sectarian barriers were very much in place and it took little to ignite the persecutory instincts of the majority community if and when Protestants tested the limits of Catholic tolerance.

In the village of Fethard-on-Sea, in County Wexford, a small rural Protestant community of a few dozen families was subjected to a collective punishment of extraordinary viciousness, organised and maintained over many months by the local clergy and with the total support of the Bishop, James Staunton of Ferns. The 'Fethard-on-Sea controversy', as it became known, had its origins in a mixed marriage. Sean Cloney, a local Catholic farmer, married Sheila Kelly, daughter of Thomas Kelly, a local Protestant farmer. They got married in London in 1949. Their problems began when they returned to Wexford, started a family and were forced to confront the issue of their children's education. The Ne temere decree of 1908 had left mixed-faith couples with little room to manoeuvre over their children's schooling. The Catholic Church tolerated marriages between Catholics and Protestants on condition that the children were brought up as Catholics. If they had been like most other families, little Mary and Eileen Cloney would have been sent off to the local Catholic school with no more ado. However, Sheila Cloney was unusually obstinate and insisted that the question was still an open one. The only local alternative was a small Church of Ireland school in the village with 11 pupils, which like many tiny Protestant schools in Ireland depended on the services of a Catholic schoolteacher. Early in 1957 the Protestant Bishop of Ossory, Leighlin and Ferns had warned that there was a danger of the school closing. For the moment, it lingered on.

The future education of Mary and Eileen Cloney was an internal affair involving the family and the local priest, James Stafford. But on 27 April 1957, to the surprise of her husband and the rest of the village, Mrs Cloney and her two children disappeared from Fethard-on-Sea. It transpired that they had moved to an undisclosed location in the North. The lawyers moved in. Mr Cloney was granted a writ of habeas corpus in the Northern Ireland High Court for the production of the children. At the same time, a lawyer representing Mrs Cloney offered terms for a settlement of the dispute which involved bringing up the children as Protestants.

Under Father Stafford's hot-headed stewardship, the Catholics of Fethard-on-Sea reacted militantly. Without much evidence, the entire local Protestant community of the parish, including Sheila Cloney's parents, was pronounced collectively guilty of aiding and abetting what was called the 'kidnapping' of the Cloney children and their 'theft' from their father and from the Church. The method the militants chose was the tried and trusted tactic used against the Jews of Limerick in 1904 and the landlords before them – the boycott. Catholics were told not to go to Protestant shops, work for Protestant farmers, purchase Protestant goods or milk, or continue in the employment of Protestant institutions, such as schools. The teacher at the small Protestant school was ordered to cease educating her charges on Saturday, 11 May. In fact, she turned up on Monday. But by Tuesday afternoon she had been 'persuaded' to withdraw her services. Adrian Fisher, the Protestant Rector, found himself embroiled in a national controversy within a week of his arrival. Bishop Phair had instituted him to the living as recently as 9 May.

Within weeks, Fethard's Protestants were experiencing what the Limerick Jews had gone through under Bishop O'Dwyer – slow economic strangulation. Shopkeepers like Betty Cooper, owner of the local newsagent's, told the *Irish Times* that even children had stopped buying her sweets.[11] After a month, Bishop Phair was back in Fethard. Only weeks before he had been inducting Adrian Fisher to St Mague's; now he addressed a flock that faced economic and social annihilation. 'These people have not the remotest idea where this woman has gone,' he declared afterwards. But he could offer no words of consolation except to advise the local community not to contemplate marrying 'out'. 'I think people should marry into their own faith and church,' the Bishop said. 'Then these things would not happen.'[12]

The Irish government was in the hands of men who had no intention of quarrelling with the Catholic Church, least of all over the Ne temere decree. When Owen Sheehy Skeffington attempted to raise the subject in the Senate, the Education Minister did not even turn up to hear the debate and a ministerial spokesman was quoted as saying: 'There is no issue as far as we are concerned here.'[13] By the end of June, all Catholic workers had quit from Protestant farms, some local Protestants had applied for police protection and others complained they were being put under pressure to emigrate to the North.

If the Fethard Protestants entertained any hopes of the Catholic bishops reining in Father Stafford, they were mistaken. At the annual congress of the Catholic Truth Society in Wexford town in June, Bishop Browne of Galway tore into the victims of the boycott, using language that was tantamount to an invitation to violence. All the local Protestants, he said, were guilty of 'the crime of conspiring to steal the children of a Catholic father. But they try to make political capital when a Catholic people make a peaceful and moderate protest.'[14]

Bishop Browne may have thought that what his boys were getting up to in Wexford could be passed off as a 'moderate protest', but De Valera disagreed. The government had taken no notice of the Fethard-on-Sea controversy when Sheehy Skeffington raised the subject, but by the middle of July, international journalists were descending on the village in south-east Ireland and sending reports on an outbreak of Counter-Reformation-style intolerance in a modern Western democracy. De Valera was embarrassed by a furore that cast a poor light on the Republic's claim to be a more tolerant society than bigoted Ulster. In July he described the events in Wexford as 'this deplorable affair'.[15] It was a cautious phrase, which did not take the side of the embattled Protestants, but it took some of the wind out of Catholic claims to be fighting for justice.

In the South, the Fethard controversy left the Protestant remnant more humbled and fearful than before. 'There are areas in Ireland where the minority is smaller and therefore more vulnerable to intimidatory action than in south Wexford,' the *Church of Ireland Gazette* commented. 'Such may well ask themselves if this is to be the pattern of "Catholic Action" in the future.'[16] In the North, where the police were wrestling with a sudden upsurge of IRA violence, the Fethard-on-Sea story was manna from heaven, final proof, as if any was needed, of the justice of Northern Ireland's separate status. The *Belfast Telegraph*, the fairly moderate voice of Unionism, commented: 'The people of Northern Ireland would not be human if they did not raise an eyebrow at the contemporary application of Article 44 of the Eire Constitution which is at present being applied at Fethard.'[17] That was putting it mildly. Most Northern Protestants did more than raise their eyebrows. The Fethard case loomed large in the speeches and banners of the Twelfth of July celebrations throughout the province.

The Fethard-on-Sea boycott faded away after Mrs Cloney returned to her husband and the two of them decided to educate their children at home. But from the Catholic Church's point of view, the campaign was not a failure. The boycott was a sharp reminder to Protestants of how far they could go in the Republic. Some Catholics were disgusted by the controversy. Not all went along with the hyper-ventilated language about spiritual robbery. The *Irish Times* was inundated with letters from indignant Protestants urging their co-religionists to send money to the boycotted shopkeepers of Fethard. But there was a fair sprinkling of letters from Catholics, too, complaining of their own Church's tactics. Daniel Barrington, a young lawyer, told a Ballsbridge conference of the Catholic Social Study Conference that the boycott was 'the most terrible thing that had happened in this part of the country since the Civil War'.[18] But such voices were a small minority. The *Irish Times* also printed letters from Catholics who wholeheartedly supported the boycott. It aroused no general crisis of conscience.

Victor Griffin, who was a controversial Dean of St Patrick's in the 1950s and 1960s, recalled the atmosphere of fear and self-censorship inside the southern Protestant community, at a time when the Irish authorities regularly contrasted their much-vaunted liberty with the supposed reign of Orange terror in the North. 'You'll get us all burnt out if you go on saying things like that,' Griffin recalled his mother saying, not as a joke, every time he opened his mouth about the inferior position of his own community.[19]

Fethard-on-Sea exposed the cutting edge of Ireland's climate of religious intolerance. Events there had got out of hand, but the Fethard boycott was only one example of the atmosphere of religious apartheid that existed in much of the island. In Londonderry, where Griffin was sent in 1947, Protestants and Catholics lived in hermetically sealed communities. Each had its own churches, political parties, newspapers and social clubs. Protestants were Unionists, Catholics were

Nationalists. Protestants read the *Belfast Newsletter*, the *Northern Whig*, the *Londonderry Sentinel* and the *Belfast Telegraph*. Catholics read the *Irish News* and the *Derry Journal*.

The sectarian rivalry was so fierce that churches still resorted to deathbed conversions of 'the other side' to boost their side in the local cemetery and in heaven. The Presbyterian Moderator John Barkley recalled the kidnapping of one of his father's parishioners in Derry in the 1940s. Isabella Baird was a lifelong Presbyterian but for a fatal 48 hours before her death at the age of 68, Barkley's father, a Presbyterian minister, neglected to visit her, as a result of which the Catholics moved in and filled the breach. Barkley turned up to be confronted by a woman neighbour of Baird's who told him in a triumphant voice that his visit had come too late. Baird had 'converted' to Catholicism with hours of life left and been buried in the Catholic cemetery.[20]

The television broadcaster Gay Byrne, who grew up in working-class Dublin, recalled the atmosphere of communal shame in the 1950s over mixed marriages. 'If the couple could get a dispensation they could not be married in front of the high altar in the church but in a side-chapel. The whole thing was rushed, grudging, with no flowers. And then the whole neighbour-hood waited with bated breath for news as to whether the Protestant partner would "turn".'[21]

The Catholic blockade of Trinity College was rigorously upheld by Archbishop McQuaid. It left the institution increasingly reliant on students from Northern Ireland and the British mainland. Not all bishops were as rigid as McQuaid and, even in Dublin, some Catholics defied their archbishop and went to Trinity. Gay Byrne recalled the tragicomic ballyhoo that erupted when his brother insisted on going to Trinity, and which ended in his parish priest performing a diplomatic shuttle to-and-fro from McQuaid's palace in Drumcondra. Al Byrne's obstinacy led to the Church backing down. He was allowed to go on condition that he did not join any social clubs, or the apparently lethal Historical Society. But the Byrnes were tough Dubliners. Most Catholics had no stomach for defying the clergy.

Opponents of the Catholic Church's domination had no political channels through which they could express their dissent. Unlike the Catholic countries on the Continent, or countries with a large Catholic population, there was no division of the political spoils in Ireland between a party of centre-right 'Christian Democrat' views, which transmitted the Church's social teaching, and a more secular, left-wing alternative. In Ireland, all the political parties, with the exception of the tiny Labour Party, vied for the privilege of carrying the Church's banner. As the party of the countryside and the ultra-Catholic west, Fianna Fáil naturally enjoyed close ties to the hierarchy. But the opposition Fine Gael, successor to Cosgrave's Cumann na nGaedhal, was equally loyal, as was the breakaway Republican party, Clann na Phoblachta, under Sean MacBride.

MacBride's party was the most militantly Republican and anti-partitionist party of the three and its initial success in the local elections of 1947 was attributed to the backing of the old IRA constituency, which had become impatient with De Valera's gradualist approach on the North. But the Clann's fervent belief in Irish unity was not matched by an original approach to the country's religious divisions. MacBride acted and spoke as if all Irishmen and women were Catholic and that the problem of partition was simply one of British military presence.

The elections of 1948 gave the Clann its first taste of government. For the first time since 1932, Fianna Fáil lost office to an inter-party coalition of Fine Gael and Clann na Phoblachta under John Costello. The new government immediately displayed its Catholic credentials, sending a telegram to Rome assuring Pius XII that the new ministry wished only 'to repose at the feet of your Holiness'. When President O'Kelly visited Rome in 1950, which the Pope had proclaimed a Holy Year, he used the same filial tone, announcing that he had come 'to place my personal homage and that of my people at the feet of his Holiness'.[22] MacBride, who had been appointed Foreign Minister in the coalition, had already flown to Rome to be present at the ceremony of the opening of the Holy Door. After the 1948 elections in which the Clann won 10 seats, he had written to McQuaid in obsequious terms to inform him that his 'first official act' was to tell the Archbishop of his determination to act as the Church's mouthpiece. He hoped the Archbishop would 'not hesitate to summon me' if he wished to discuss any matter with the Clann leader. MacBride added that he would 'deem it a favour to be given the opportunity to place myself at Your Grace's disposal'.[23] It was curious language for a Republican, all-Ireland party.

There were a few dissenters, and Noel Browne, the Clann minister with the health portfolio, was one of them. Browne was a true outsider. His background was one of almost numbing poverty and brutality. Both his parents and two of his sisters had died of tuberculosis, one of the many poverty-related diseases that raged through the slums of the Free State. One of his brothers was physically handicapped. Browne's education at the hands of the Christian Brothers left him with a permanent loathing of their notoriously savage disciplinary methods. Years later, he was able to recall the flogging exploits of one of his Christian Brother teachers as if they had taken place the previous day.

The Brother would grip my desk tightly with his hand until his fingers were blanched white in order to give himself support and added power. Then he carefully took hold of the visibly trembling fingertips of the defenceless victim and opened the dirty hand firmly. He took careful aim and slashed out without restraint or pity. Each time, increasingly excited, beads of sweat gathering on his pale forehead he raised the cane higher over his shoulder like an old-time thrashing flail; down it came again and again, increasing in speed in ferocity until it seemed to us that the tip of the cane appeared to whistle around in a full circle.[24]

The Christian Brothers excited contempt in Browne. He despised their crude nationalism, their 'obsessive hatred for and of the English', their 'hatred for Protestants because their faith was of English origin'.[25] But the time he subsequently spent in England did not turn him into an anglophile. The British class system repelled him and the country's creaking snobbery only honed his radical, Republican instincts. At the same time, he returned to Ireland distanced and alienated from Ireland's priggish Catholic society. It was significant that he married a left-wing Irish Protestant.

For Browne, the Church conjured up a series of exclusively negative memories: his mother, dying of TB, shunned by the petty bourgeois clerical sons of grasping shopkeepers and smug farmers; the excited face of the thrashing Christian Brother, beads of sweat rolling down his cheeks; the hot, probing tongue of the priest who hungrily kissed him in the corridor before sailing into the classroom to teach as if nothing had happened.

Browne became the advocate of the desperately poor, atheists, homosexuals, single mothers, Protestants – anyone, in fact, who felt shut out of the new establishment. He conceived a particular hatred for McQuaid, the iron-willed prince of the Church who stood at the apex of a system Browne increasingly resented. Behind a prickly, severe exterior, volcanic passions were slowly building up. He was a time bomb waiting to explode in the heart of the Irish government.

McQuaid was at the height of his powers when he clashed with Browne. By the time the Archbishop retired in 1972, the monolith had begun to crack, censorship was collapsing and politicians were beginning to ask loud questions about the Catholic Church's right to set the political and educational agenda. But in the high days of McQuaid's episcopate in the 1950s it was agreeable to be a bishop, to observe the obedient crowds trudging to and from mass, to bestow one's favour on one politician and then another, to watch ambitious men scrabble for the privilege of kissing the episcopal ring, to exalt them from the mud to the pinnacle of fame and then, if it was sadly necessary, hurl them into outer darkness.

Browne left a famous pen-portrait of McQuaid in action:

> The Archbishop approached in procession with all the panoply of the Church 'en fete'; the demure child acolytes, the robed clerical students, the shining gilt crucifix carried by its tall student bearer. Scented incense rose from the gently moving thurible . . .
>
> A broad white silk shawl covered his frail, bent shoulders, falling down on each side to cover his hands in which he clasped the glinting gold processional monstrance. His dark eyes, glittering in a mask-like face, were transfixed on the shimmering white sacred host. He had a long straight thin nose and a saturnine appearance, with an awesome fixity of expression and the strong mouth of an obsessional.
>
> Drowsily fanatasising on the imposing and fearful procession in a mixture of dream and nightmare, I was nudged into wakefulness by [British ambassador

Sir Gilbert] Braithwaite. 'What an impressive figure, Noel! Would he not make a notable addition to the distinguished company of Spanish Inquisitors?'[26]

Browne's portrait was, of course, a hostile one. There were other critics who thought the Archbishop, a Cavan man, imported the sectarianism of the Ulster border counties to Dublin. But the Archbishop had many admirers. He certainly wanted people to live better. Within a short time of his translation to the see of Dublin in 1940 he had set up the Catholic Social Service Conference as an umbrella group to co-ordinate Catholic charity work. He also set up the Catholic Social Welfare Bureau, charged with looking after war workers heading off for factories in Britain. He was active in promoting the construction of new housing estates in Dublin and set up the Magnificat Family Guild to help poor families buy their own homes. Brendan Behan's family loathed being transferred from the sordid intimacy of the old inner city tenements to the sterile, antisceptic suburbs,[27] but most people were probably delighted by the change. The Archbishop campaigned for better care for the elderly, the sick and the handicapped. In industrial disputes, he was more often on the side of the strikers than the employers and his support for the teachers' strike in March 1946 annoyed De Valera. McQuaid believed strongly in the dignity of labour and that the test of a Christian society was its willingness to pool its resources to benefit the least well off.

Pastorally, McQuaid was a man of great energy. Dublin was rapidly expanding during his period in office, with 60 new parishes established in the suburbs, and the Archbishop made sure the Church kept pace with the spiritual needs of a growing population. On the negative side, his religious intolerance forced the closure of societies that brought Catholics and Protestants together, such as the ecumenical Mercier Society. He devoted great energy to maintaining the ban on Catholics attending Trinity. In public he was civil to his Church of Ireland counterpart, George Simms, and to the Archbishop's wife, Mercy. But some of his own associates were convinced he nursed a hatred for Protestants in private, and when the Archbishop of Canterbury visited Ireland in 1961, he refused to meet him.[28]

Personally, McQuaid was not vain. His style was that of the *éminence grise*. His pride was in his exalted office, not in himself. Like Cardinal Manning, a man he resembled in many ways, he was severe, modest, shy and abstemious. His meals were frugal: he ate a light breakfast, poached eggs for lunch, tea and a biscuit in the afternoon, soup, meat and fruit for supper. He did not drink. Noel Browne noted with contempt the epicurean tastes of Bishop Michael Browne of Galway, who boasted of his taste for expensive foreign cigars. No such complaint could be laid at McQuaid's door.

He inherited and exemplified the Church's phobia about sex. Outwardly he was an ultra-puritan, horrified even by the sight of undressed manikins in shop windows and by relatively innocuous lyrics in songs he heard on the radio. He thought nothing of telephoning radio stations to demand assurances they would not be played again.

Some of his seminarians recalled a peculiar obsession with impure thoughts and with male genitalia. According to his recent biographer, John Cooney, the Archbishop took an interest even in the type of underwear his seminarians wore and grilled them on their sexual thoughts. Patrick Buckley, a student at the Clonliffe seminary in Dublin the early 1970s, recalled being interrogated for two hours by the Archbishop

'almost exclusively about sex and the facts of life'. He said: 'He drew diagrams for me of the male and female genitalia and used his hands and fingers to show me what happened in intercourse. He also presented me with a pocket crucifix to be used to ward off any temptation to masturbate.

'For the whole of those two hours Dr McQuaid had me at the corner of his desk with his knees touching and nudging my knees and with his feet on top of my feet. When he made sensitive points he pressed his feet enough down on mine for it to be painful.'[29]

This side of the Archbishop's character was probably more relevant to his political clash with Browne than the Minister acknowledged. Browne might have felt very differently towards a bluffer, more manly bishop, like MacRory. As it was, McQuaid was the distillation of everything Browne had encountered in the Church and most disliked and feared. The stage was set, therefore, for the clash that was to result in Browne's humiliation, and in a dramatic exposure of the extent to which the Church ruled the country.

The battle took place over health. The 1945 election victory of the Labour Party in Britain led to the introduction of a free, cradle-to-grave National Health Service. Browne had seen it in action when working as a doctor in Britain and was determined Ireland should follow suit. In September 1949 the minister announced what was known as the 'Mother and Child' scheme, which he submitted in June 1950 to the Irish Medical Association. The Mother and Child scheme proposed to incorporate the core elements of the British National Health Service, centring on free ante-natal and post-natal care for women and free medical attention for children up to the age of 16. There would be no means tests and no financial contributions.

Browne's self-imposed isolation from his own country's Catholic culture blinded him to the extent to which his proposals were bound to excite opposition. When the danger was apparent, it made him inflexible and obstinate. The displays of flattery and craven submission that the Irish bishops had come to expect, and which might have deflated the crisis, were not forthcoming. Instead, Browne insisted on behaving as if Ireland was a secular republic on the French or American pattern, when all the world, and all his colleagues, knew that it was nothing of the kind.

The Church was wholly opposed to universal free medicine. Back in 1947, Fianna Fáil had put forward an outline of a welfare scheme that had put the bishops and the Irish Medical Association on the alert. That scheme had disappeared when the government fell. Browne's plan revived it in full. The problem for the Church was that it implicitly struck at the roots of ecclesiastical authority by nudging the clergy from their control over women's bodies during the vital period of childbirth. If the scheme had succeeded, the whole system of denominational, and overwhelmingly Catholic, hospitals would have been displaced and nuns would have been edged out of the hospital wards by lay nurses. The scheme threatened to establish an entirely secular source of sexual education for women over which nuns and priests would have no supervision or veto. For all his concern for the disadvantaged, McQuaid did not want a health system that subverted the state within a state that the Church had built up since the era of Cardinal Cullen. Hospitals, as much as schools and churches, were one of the great props of church authority in Ireland. It had taken a century to build up this empire and McQuaid and the other bishops had no intention of meekly surrendering their hard-won position. Moreover, the Church was not alone in its fight. While the clergy wanted control of the agenda, the doctors wanted fees. The IMA overwhelmingly opposed any limit on their right to set whatever charges they felt were appropriate.

Over the summer of 1950, a coalition of hostile forces mustered in the drawing rooms, doctors' surgeries and clerical presbyteries of Dublin, before the Health Minister, tellingly, was summoned on 10 October to Drumcondra. There, McQuaid, Michael Browne of Galway and the bishops' secretary, James Staunton of Ferns, handed him an ultimatum. It was uncompromising. The bishops complained that the state planned to invade the rights of the Church and those of the family in relation to women's sex education and gynaecological care. The bishops said the state had no need to provide free medical care to reward the laziness, profligacy and incompetence of the poor. On the question of sex education, the bishops said: 'We regard with the greatest apprehension the proposal to give local medical officers the right to tell Catholic girls and women how they should behave in a sphere of conduct at once so delicate and sacred.'[30]

There were only two possible outcomes after Browne left the palace in Drumcondra. Either the minister or the bishops would have to back down. It was obvious which of the two parties was in the weaker position. Browne's political colleagues, including his own party leader, rushed to dissociate themselves from a man who had incurred the bishops' displeasure. In a country where more than 90 per cent of the population attended mass on Sunday, scalding criticism in a pastoral letter was a grave business. The end came after the bishops published their final condemnation of the Mother and Child scheme on 6 April 1951, following a series of unproductive meetings between Browne, Bishop Browne and Cardinal D'Alton of Armagh, and an exchange of letters between McQuaid, Brown and Costello. McQuaid had repeated the bishops' objections on 8 March, extracting a humiliating reply from the embattled minister. 'I hope I need not assure you,' Browne told the Archbishop on 21 March, 'that as a Catholic I will unhesitatingly and immediately accept any pronouncement from the Hierarchy as to what is Catholic moral teaching in reference to this matter.'

It was too late for such formulas. The bishops were out to crush Browne, *pour encourager les autres*, and on 4 April they had gathered at Maynooth to compose their public condemnation of the scheme. The letter was careful to emphasise the supposed threat to the family rather than to the Church. 'The Hierarchy cannot approve of any scheme which in its general tendency must foster undue control by the state in a sphere so delicately and so intimately concerned with morals as that which deals with gynaecology or obstetrics,' it said. 'Neither can the bishops approve of any scheme which must have for practical result the undue lessening of the proper initiative of individuals and the undermining of self-reliance.'[31]

After the publication of the bishops' condemnation, Browne was summoned to the cabinet by Costello, who read out the bishops' letter. He recalled: 'He [Costello] then looked at me and said. "This must mean the end of the Mother and Child scheme".'[32] His last meeting with the executive of Clann na Phoblachta was even more unpleasant. Browne, displaying that naivety that seems to have been a hallmark of his political career, was genuinely perplexed to be reminded just how clericalist his supposedly radical Republican colleagues in the Clann really were. He was roasted for having been photographed in the company of the Protestant Archbishop of Dublin at the Dublin Rotunda hospital, an act that MacBride said 'had done great damage to the party and to the coalition government'.[33] MacBride demanded his resignation on 10 April.

In the Dáil debate on 12 April, Costello remarked on the folly of proposing policies that the bishops opposed. 'I said to him,' the Prime Minister said, 'whatever about fighting the doctors, I am not going to fight the bishops. And whatever about fighting the bishops I am not going to fight the bishops and doctors together.'[34] Dumped by his party as well as by the Prime Minister, Browne resigned. The Mother and Child scheme sank without trace, as did the inter-party coalition, which lost the election to Fianna Fáil on 30 May. He was still only 32.

Noel Browne was offered up as a sacrifice on the altar of Catholic Ireland. No other single political drama revealed quite so startlingly and starkly the extent to which the Church could call on the secular power to bolster its authority over the life of the nation. It was a real victory, not a Pyrrhic one. Over the water in England, the Tory English Catholic writers of the *Tablet* could only gasp with admiration at the sight of the Irish ecclesiastical juggernaut flattening its opponent with such ease. The *Tablet* saw the Irish bishops as heroic warriors in an international struggle against the forces of Socialism. 'We are profoundly grateful to the Irish hierarchy,' the paper wrote, 'for their plain speaking at a time when it is the fashion of the hour to present as "social justice" a succession of policies which are in effect repugnant to justice.'[35]

The Mother and Child battle and the Fethard-on-Sea controversy offered convincing proof of the Catholic Church's desire, and ability, to dominate

Irish society. A rural Protestant woman and an urban Catholic man had both challenged the bishops and been visibly humiliated. In neither case was there the slightest sign of the mass of the people taking the side of the Church's enemies.

Yet, the apparent triumphs left a bad taste. The irony of these victories was that they occurred at precisely the same time that the old feeling of total self-confidence was draining out of the clergy. The mood in the Irish ecclesiastical establishment at the close of the decade was one of deflation. Uncertainty and even gloom invaded the Church's own discussions. The Browne case revealed that the Church really did rule Ireland. But the Catholic Church did not revel in this public scrutiny. They did not like having a torch shone in their eyes.

There was a strange loss of confidence, an end-of-empire feeling. The brighter, younger clergy began complaining that their Church had purchased the outward conformity of the public at the price of a certain spiritual hollowness. Clerical writers in the liberal Catholic periodical, the *Furrow*, began carping about the Church's insularity and alleged philistinism. They wrote sharp essays on the quality of Irish worship. There were grumbles that the Irish went to church, but took no part in, or even interest in, the liturgy. They were overwhelmingly 'detached, silent spectators' in their churches, Michael O'Dwyer, a priest from Thurles, complained in the issue of May 1954.[36] He blamed his fellow clergy for inculcating 'that strange clericalism in some of us which makes us afraid of the laity, distrustful of them'.

There were grim warnings that a Church with so little apparent internal dynamism could easily follow the awful example of England, where religion had decayed. The Irish Catholic periodicals documented the decline in religious observation among the Irish-born community in Britain with morbid fascination. They noted that they had a far lower level of church attendance than the population at home and that up to 60 per cent had married non-Catholics, which was never a good sign. In 1958, the *Furrow* published a prophetic 'Letter from Ireland', fancifully dated from the year 2060, which purported to explain the death of Irish Catholicism by the end of the twentieth century. 'Catholicism became a religion of "do not" rather than "do",' it said.

> While a great deal of time and energy was spent on censoring books and plays and 'dangerous thinking', and while schools continued to teach religious knowledge in routine, mechanical manner, little or nothing was done in the creative fields of literature or art.
>
> It was a quite fantastic experience to read the kind of literature which was produced for the Catholic people of Ireland. It was the kind of stuff a modern child would find sickening and silly.
>
> The whole country slept on, secure in its title of being a truly Catholic nation while all the time it was stagnating, sickening and inwardly dying. It was a very easy, painless death. Catholic Ireland, in fact, died in its sleep.[37]

The Church became a little less certain about sex. John O'Brien, an Irish-American writer, attracted considerable attention with a book entitled *The Vanishing Irish*, which painted a stark portrait of a nation 'on the brink of near extinction'[38] owing to a combination of late marriage and emigration. The book blamed a clerically inspired culture of puritanism for what it considered an unnatural horror of sex. The Irish Catholic media attacked the book, but there were also tentative calls for the Church to adopt a less squeamish view about sex. A nun writing in the *Furrow* in 1959 said it was foolish to teach girls that every time they whistled, Our Lady blushed. If the clergy were to win the war against divorce and contraception, they must learn about rock and roll music and nuns must know about make-up.[39]

Censorship was attacked as never before. In the 1940s clerical writers had defended a censorship system they controlled with total confidence. Father P. J. Gannon, writing in *Studies* in 1942, took it for granted. All or most Hollywood films, he wrote, were 'moral deformities, as repulsive as leprosy', while all towns were 'moral sewers . . . divorced from the healing influence of nature and now very often, of religion'. Art, he concluded, had no right whatever to regulate itself. 'The state has the right and the duty to protect [people] from the manifold evils which spring inevitably from moral decline among its subjects.'[40]

There was no let-up in the rate of banning books in the 1950s, but opposition was growing and the clergy had lost much of Father Gannon's conviction. It seemed that the country had never produced so many writers of international distinction and that no state outside the Soviet Union held its prophets in so little honour. Almost every well-known Irish author, except the Protestant Elizabeth Bowen, had been banned at some point. The Church was blamed for this; McQuaid in particular.

The more the Irish wrote, the more they were banned. Kate O'Brien's *Land of Spices* was banned in 1941 for a line that appeared to hint at a homosexual embrace. Liam O'Flaherty's *Land* was banned in 1946; Benedict Kiely's *In a Harbour Green* in 1949. His book *Honey Seems Bitter* followed suit in 1952, as did *There Was an Ancient House* in 1955. Brian Moore's *Judith Hearne* was banned in 1956, *The Feast of Lupercal* in 1957, *The Luck of Ginger Coffey* in 1960 and *An Answer from Limbo* in 1962. Samuel Beckett's *Watt* was banned in 1953 and *Molloy* in 1954. Edna O'Brien's *The Country Girls* was banned in 1960, *The Girl with Green Eyes* in 1964, *Girls in their Married Bliss* in 1963 and *August is a Wicked Month* in 1964.

It was not that the criteria for banning had been changed or tightened. In fact, the system had been relaxed in 1946 after the introduction of an appeal board. But increasingly it was seen as a complete joke. The younger generation of Irish writers, mainly Catholic and working class, were far less gentlemanly about the censors and their clerical backers than the old school of upper-class, Anglo-Irish Protestants had been. The Ascendancy feared to throw mud at the Catholic Church and in any case, Protestant writers like Molly Keane were more interested in writing about their own tribe than about the Catholic clergy.

Not so the Catholic Young Turks. Dublin's new prodigy in the 1950s, Brendan Behan, aimed a solid stream of bile at the clergy. 'To hell with you, you fat bastard,' he shouts at the prison chaplain in *Borstal Boy*, an account of his imprisonment in Walton jail for IRA activities in 1940, 'and to hell with England and to hell with Rome, up the Republic . . . '[41]

To Behan, a slum child and youthful IRA supporter, the Catholic clergy were the handmaidens of British imperialism. From a totally different standpoint, the clergy were excoriated as the bigoted and self-interested propagators of philistine, anglophobic nationalism, forever dinning into the heads of their unhappy charges an almost cretinous and counter-productive loathing of the land over the water.

Moore's *Lonely Passion of Judith Hearne* was a particularly damaging work, a horrific portrait of a woman driven mad by the stultifying hypocrisy of the Catholic lower middle class in Belfast. The picture Moore painted of this Catholic minority as Hitler-worshipping genteel snobs was highly unflattering and far from the image that the Church had attempted to convey of a suffering people. The Catholics creeping round Hearne's sepulchral boarding house are a miserable, life-denying, self-righteous bunch, wearing their Pioneer Total Abstinence pins with thin-lipped pride and nursing a secret nostalgia for the Nazi victory that never came. Hearne's 'friends' boast of their total ignorance of any books that had been placed on the papal Index. The parish priest is a legalistic, insensitive blockhead. Moore depicted Hearne as a woman enduring a pain that is all the more unbearable for its being unconscious. Unable to locate her real oppressor, the Church, and unable to rationalise her predicament, she can only fling herself at the end with animal-like fury at the tabernacle in an orgy of destruction.

The Church hierarchy was indifferent to these literary blow-pipes fired into its elephantine rear from Paris, London and New York. But what was changing in spite of them was ordinary people's uncontrolled access to sources of information. In the 1920s and 1930s the Church had worried about the influx of British newspapers and American films. Censorship was introduced to contain Ireland from these corrupting influences. But by the 1950s the Church was losing its grip on the sources of popular knowledge. MacRory's campaign to discourage cinema attendance had petered out: in the early 1950s almost a million people in the Republic went to the cinema every week out of an entire population of only 2.5 million. In other words, the Irish went to the cinema with the same regularity that they went to mass. The films they saw were not very sexually explicit, but as the bishops in the 1920s correctly identified, they were not Catholic either. They did not inculcate the virtues of restraint and sexual discipline and they glamorised a lifestyle that was far from the Catholic ideal.

Radio was another a problem. The Catholic Church had entertained high hopes of Radio Eireann as a weapon of Catholic propaganda against British Protestant secularism and, after the 1940s, against Russian Communism. In the 1950s it was still seen as 'a great centre of cultural and missionary activity, a Christian counterpart of Moscow'.[42] What the bishops had not foreseen was the vast extension and multiplication of frequencies and the ease with which people could tune in to foreign stations. By the mid-1950s, contamination by the BBC was only one danger. An additional threat came from new 'pop' music stations further afield, such as Radio Luxembourg. According to one survey in 1954 it was attracting more Irish listeners in the evenings than either the BBC or Radio Eireann.[43]

It was soon clear that the Church was going to have to deal with another potentially hazardous source of information. Television had spread rapidly through England in the early 1950s, boosted by a rush to acquire sets to watch the 1953 coronation of Queen Elizabeth II. By 1955 there were 3.5 million sets and the spread to Ireland was inevitable. Catholics hoped it could be turned to good effect. Bernard Smyth, a priest in Navan, made the bold suggestion in 1959 that a truly Christian Irish television station might act as a bridgehead between the estranged religious communities in the North.[44] Smyth's great fear was that Irish television might end up a pale copy of the BBC. 'Paganism is often there [in the BBC],' he wrote in 1960, 'sometimes open, sometimes wrapped up in a plot or a play. It is dripping steadily on our Catholic home.'[45]

The fact that Pope Pius XII was known to be enthusiastic about the new medium soothed some of the Church's worries. McQuaid shared his enthusiasm. On 6 June 1955 scenes of a papal benediction were broadcast to an estimated 15 million viewers in Italy, France, Britain, Germany, Switzerland and Holland. On 22 June a Franciscan priest told the Maynooth Union that Irish television might turn out to be a boon for the Church. 'Television,' he informed his fellow clergy, 'enables us to see the glory of the Mass in the magnificent basilica of St Denis in Paris; it takes us with the pilgrims to the tombs of the Apostles in St Peters' Rome and it takes us along the galleries and loggias of the Vatican.'[46]

The bishops saluted the inauguration of Irish television in 1961 and MacQuaid appeared on the screen in person to bless the new medium. At the same time, the bishops sounded a warning on 10 October from Maynooth. Unlike the theatre, they said, television 'penetrates the very sanctuary of the home where anything which offends purity or modesty is particularly abhorrent and where the innocent souls of children should be safe from poisonous influences'. The bishops ended with a call for the public to ensure that 'the currency in un-Christian ideas in other countries' was not extended to Ireland.[47]

The bishops were concerned. But they had no idea of the force that had just been unleashed on them and still hoped television might turn out to be an agency that they could control, as they had controlled so much of the print media in Ireland for a century and a quarter. They were not to know that as the decade advanced, Irish television would take the viewers a lot further than the tombs of the Apostles, still less that television would in the end usher in a kind of secular Reformation, which would practically sweep away the old Catholic Ireland.

CHAPTER SIXTEEN

Till Boyne Rivers Run Red

Ireland is entering on a new phase in her history which may be critical . . .
Among the churches there are cautious moves towards co-operation and unity.
Ireland is changing and during the next twenty years it looks like being an
exciting place in which to live.
(*Presbyterian Herald,* September 1965)[1]

In the autumn of 1958 Pope Pius XII died. In his place, the cardinals chose
Angelo Roncalli, an elderly, fat Italian in indifferent health and of known conservative views. Archbishop Heenan of Westminster recalled the prevailing
impression of Roncalli, who chose the title John XXIII. He was a 'garden of the
soul type of Catholic . . . not an original thinker . . . I doubt if he read many books
of contemporary theologians.'[2]

The man many hoped would be no more than a caretaker turned the Catholic
Church upside down in his short reign. Within months of becoming Pope, in
January 1959, he summoned an Ecumenical Council, the first since 1870. The
calling of the Council was in itself a revolutionary act. As one Anglican observer
wrote, it was 'a trumpet blast, which shattered the Vatican wall, for there were
many inside who had predicted and hoped there would never be a council again'.[3]

From then on, changes followed quick and fast. In June 1960 the Pope
established a a Secretariat for Unity among Christians, a body whose very title
expressed a novel approach by Catholics to those outside the fold. In December,
Archbishop Geoffrey Fisher of Canterbury paid a courtesy call on the Pope, the
first time an Anglican Primate had visited what used to be enemy headquarters.

The Council fathers began work in Rome in October 1962. Over three years,
they cleared away a vast amount of ideological baggage that had alienated the
Reformed churches from the Catholic Church over the previous four centuries. The
liturgy was to be translated into the vernacular. The Council restated that the Bible
was the ultimate point of reference for all Christian doctrine. The position of the
laity was affirmed and raised up. Conservative hopes that the Council might pile
more honours on the Virgin Mary were shattered. The Council instead ordered the
Church to 'avoid the falsity of exaggeration' and locate the Mother of God's office
within her relationship to Christ as 'the source of all truth, sanctity and piety'.[4]

The more old-fashioned Protestants scoffed at this as superficial tinkering, but the mainstream Protestant churches were astonished at the pace and quality of the Catholic Church's transformation. It was not simply the content of the decrees that impressed them but the tone. They warmed to the note of humility and self-questioning. The new emphasis on the Catholic Church as a 'pilgrim church' dovetailed with what most Protestants thought the Church ought to be – a wagon on the road rather than a destination.

In the third session in the autumn of 1964, the Council made a leap towards putting inter-church relations on an entirely new footing with the *Decree on Ecumenism*. The document contained ground-breaking material. It abandoned the old discourse about Protestants as heretics and schismatics, which the Catholic Church had been using since the Council of Trent. Instead, the decree spoke of the Protestants as 'separated brethren', and far from stigmatising them, told Catholics to acknowledge and value their common Christian heritage. The decree placed a wholly new emphasis on the common baptism of all Christians, by which it said all must be accepted as brothers by the children of the Catholic Church.

Over time, Protestants came to realise that the decree perhaps did not go quite as far as they imagined. Lurking under the scented petals of the many roses in the text were a few doctrinal thorns. The decree did not recognise Protestant churches as 'churches' but qualified them as 'ecclesial communities', which possessed some of the 'marks' of the true Church. It was a massive advance on previous thinking but it was not equality. Then again, while Catholics recognised Protestant baptisms, they came no nearer to recognising the Protestant Eucharist, and as the communion service lay at the centre of the life of most Reformed churches, this was a serious shortfall. A separated brother or sister clearly was not someone in possession of the full truth.

Overall, Protestants were astonished and moved by the Council's acts. The Synod of Thurles Cullen had summoned in 1850 had explicitly forbidden Catholics from 'visiting the churches of heretics in order to assist at their worship'. The decrees, reinforced in 1875 and 1900, banned Catholics in Ireland from attending Protestant prayers, hearing their sermons, or reading their books. Now they were suddenly invited to explore their churches, to look benignly on their liturgies and think of them as co-workers in God's vineyard.

The Irish Protestants responded eagerly. In 1962, even before the Council began, the Church of Ireland released a statement that breathed a spirit of good-will. It urged its members to pray for 'our brethren, members of the Roman Catholic Church who are about to assemble in Council to consult for the good governing and unity of thy church'.[5] Probably a good number of Church of Ireland people, especially in the North, had no intention of doing any such thing. But it set a tone. Robert Nelson spoke in stronger words for the Methodists. It was clearly time for Protestants to get down on their knees, 'recognising with fear and trembling that God is speaking to our Roman brothers', he said.[6] The Catholics in turn responded to the overture. In November 1962 the future Catholic

Archbishop of Dublin, Kevin McNamara, broke the mould when he addressed a Methodist ministers' conference at Cloughjordan, County Tipperary, following an invitation from the chairman of the Methodist Conference to the Catholic Bishop of Killaloe to send them a speaker.

When Cardinal D'Alton died in the spring of 1963, Irish Protestant reaction was unprecedentedly warm. Noel Browne might not have remembered him with any sorrow but the Protestants fell over each other in their desire to sing his praises. 'Charity and kindliness characterised his attitude towards those of communions different from his own,' the *Church of Ireland Gazette* wrote. 'It is, we believe, such men who pave the way for more overt steps towards unity.'[7]

The liberal Catholics on the *Furrow* then invited three Irish Protestant leaders, Dean Emerson of Christ Church, John Cairns from the Methodists and J. L. Haire of the Presbyterians, to describe their reactions to the Vatican Council in their periodical. This was another milestone. The editors of the *Furrow* may have been on the liberal wing of the Church, but it was still almost unheard-of for Protestants to write articles for the Catholic media in the early 1960s.

It was an exciting time for the churches, especially for the younger priests and ministers who were bored and frustrated by the sterile controversies of the past. 'The pristine simplicity which our faith inherited from Penal Times is both exposed and stimulated by the draught of new ideas brought from the Council,' wrote David Thornley in *Studies* in 1964, 'and from the theologians of Europe, by the press, by television and by publications like the *Furrow* [and] *Studies*'.[8]

In June 1964, as the Presbyterian General Assembly met in Belfast, it was clear that the decision of the Council in Rome called for an official response. A slightly waspish statement on Catholic–Presbyterian relations in February had warned Protestants against premature rejoicing. 'The spirit of Ireland is such that progress must be slow and the building up of a spirit of co-operation and trust after centuries of suspicion and mistrust will take time,' it said. But by the summer the debate had already moved on and there was a feeling that Presbyterians needed to say something much more positive. A debate held by the Church on inter-church relations in the Crescent Church in Belfast was packed, as the public piled into the galleries to watch the assembly back resolutions welcoming the changes in the Catholic Church, registering 'deep appreciation' of the ecumenism decree and saying they were moved by 'the note of penitence and humility'. Presbyterians also shared the guilt for the historic rupture between the churches, they declared, and they condemned their own side for 'absolutising the doctrinal formulations of a particular historical period'.[9]

That summer, everything seemed to be up for grabs. Almost overnight the mainstream churches appeared ready to subject their most tenaciously held theological positions to examination. The Church of Ireland suddenly looked embarrassed by the Low Church anti-popery of its canons, which in the 1870s had forbidden crosses to be placed on altars, and in 1964 it lifted the old prohibition. At the Irish Methodist annual conference, which opened on 5 June in Belfast, delegates voted overwhelmingly to open discussions with the Catholic Church on social and religious questions. They frankly acknowledged the implications of ecumenism on the Northern Irish political situation and announced it was time for Northern Protestants to be in the forefront of the campaign for social justice for Northern Catholics. Their community, they said, 'deplores any uncharitable discriminatory attitude to another person and . . . welcomes the call of the government of Northern Ireland upon all citizens . . . to use their influence to create a better atmosphere and discourage discrimination in all its forms'.[10]

This tentative desire among Protestants, North and South, to reach out to the former enemy gained strength in 1965. In an editorial entitled 'Forward', the *Presbyterian Herald* noted that the government of Brookeborough's successor since 1963, Terence O'Neill, had changed the atmosphere in Northern Ireland. The newspaper urged Presbyterians to embrace the mood. 'There are signs that Ireland is entering on a phase in her history which may be critical,' it said. 'Tentative efforts are being made to end old hostilities . . . among the churches there are cautious moves towards co-operation and unity. Ireland is changing and during the next twenty years it looks like being an exciting place in which to live.'[11]

Men who had been brought up to regard popery and all its works as virtually satanic underwent dramatic personal conversions. At the 1965 Presbyterian General Assembly, Rupert Gibson presented the report of the Irish Mission Committee. The Mission's Superintendent spoke movingly of the 'new spirit of friendship [as] barriers of hatred, misconception and misunderstanding are being broken down in a new spirit of brotherhood'. As he spoke, Gibson found it difficult to restrain feelings of strong emotion. His father, Fred, Superintendent of the Mission from 1931 to 1953, had seen himself as one of God's generals leading the army of the righteous against the forces of the Antichrist, and Rupert recalled standing on the steps of his father's church on Ormond Quay in Dublin and watching the funeral of the 14 British officers murdered in their beds in November 1919 on 'Bloody Sunday'. 'I have stood and watched an Irishman dying, shot down, not by British soldiers but by Irishmen, his blood staining the ground,' he said. 'In spite of all this, my father prophesied there would be a Reformation in Ireland. His words are coming true today, because today men are prepared to meet each other and discuss their differences in a reasonable manner . . . To seek to understand the things in which they differ.'[12]

Men like Gibson were converted almost overnight to the conviction that the long night of religious warfare in Ireland was over, and that a new day was dawning in which Catholics and Protestants would wake as if from a bad dream and discover they were not enemies, as they had conceived, but estranged brothers and sisters. The Presbyterians followed the example the Methodists had set a few weeks earlier by formally acknowledging their own responsibility for reducing Catholics to second-class status in Northern Ireland. The assembly adopted a crucial motion, urging Presbyterians 'humbly and frankly to acknowledge and to ask forgiveness for any attitudes and actions which have been unworthy of our calling as followers of Jesus Christ'.[13] One of the speakers explained why he had supported the motion. 'Have we never spoken disparagingly of "papishes" and "Fenians?"' he asked the General Assembly. 'Even when we have refrained from the more blatant outward expressions of prejudice and contempt, have we attempted sincerely to understand the fears and insecurity of the minority community in Northern Ireland?'[14]

The ferment inside the Irish churches was intimately linked to seismic political changes in both Irish states. In the South, De Valera had finally relinquished control. In 1959 he had been shunted aside by Sean Lemass to the symbolic post of President. The new leader had fought both in the Easter Rising and on the anti-treaty side in the civil war. Yet his reputation was as a technocrat and a moderniser, not a nationalist ideologue, and he promptly took steps to dismantle the protectionist economy, encourage investment and go for growth. There was talk of joining the European Economic Community. Wages rose, as did the number of cars on the roads. Immigration from the country into the cities increased. The pace of urbanisation in Ireland accelerated and Dublin expanded faster than the rest of the towns. By the early 1960s, almost 700,000 of the Republic's 2.8 million inhabitants lived in the capital, a quarter of the population. Back in 1874, Dublin had contained only 265,000 of the 5.5 million in the 32 counties. Now little more than half the population lived in rural areas, down from 66 per cent in the 1920s and 83 per cent in the mid-nineteenth century.

The economic transformation Lemass set in place had as big a knock-on effect on religious practice as the Vatican Council. A generation living mainly in cities, with more opportunities to travel and read, was bound to think more independently than their parents had done. Television began to exert an enormous impact. It was crucial, because it penetrated much further than any dangerous book or film. The Church found they had an uncontrollable force on their hands. The rot started in 1962 with a seminal flagship programme, *The Late Late Show*. Under the stewardship of its popular presenter, Gay 'Gaybo' Byrne, it rapidly seized a high profile, taking the highest television ratings of any programme in Irish history. At a time when the country had only one station, a programme that occupied three hours of airtime every Friday was bound to set the agenda.

The format of *The Late Late Show* was safe and comfortable enough. 'Gaybo' was a cosy, homely presenter. He looked like Ireland's tweedy uncle, not its seducer. But Gaybo relentlessly probed the boundaries of accepted taste and Catholic morality. Before his show hit the screen, most Irish people, especially in the countryside, knew relatively little about sex and nothing about such shocking phenomena as lesbianism. What they did know about such things filtered down through the pulpit, or the odd, daring film. Gaybo introduced a new and very foreign world to the bemused, but far from indifferent, inhabitants of lonely farmhouses and isolated villages. The views of people holding moral codes very different from the Church's were beamed into living rooms the length and breadth of the country. The bishops, naturally, were perplexed. A rumpus ensued when a certain Mrs Fox appeared on the show in February 1966, and was asked what kind of nightie she had worn on her wedding night. When she daringly confessed she had not worn anything, clerical viewers were scandalised. Thomas Ryan, the Bishop of Clonfert, launched a furious diatribe about this affront to Catholic decency and the Director-General of RTE, the television company, ordered Byrne to apologise.[15] On that occasion, Byrne was the loser. But the new television elite was not afraid of Catholic bishops any more. Only a month after the bishop and the nightie affair, Gaybo interviewed a Trinity student Brian Trevaskis who described Bishop Browne of Galway as 'a moron', attacked McQuaid, the Christian Brothers and compulsory Irish.[16] The Bishop responded huffily but the programme did not noticeably tone down as a result.

The year 1966 marked the end of an era when Catholic bishops could set boundaries on the march of the media. It was not long before homosexuals and lesbian nuns were trooping on to the set and setting new standards in confessional journalism. Television was on the loose and would become progressively more insolent towards the institution that had once sought to control it. Nationalists, as well as devout Catholics, often hated Byrne. He was a 'half-baked, arse-licking, West British slave-minded avaricious poor product of the Rialto ghetto of King-lovers and Poppy wearers',[17] one outraged patriot spluttered. But the show went on relentlessly. Week in, week out, it provided an alternative pulpit for the nation. Under a headier, edgier presenter the programme might have lost its nerve, or gone over the top. But Byrne was a kind of alternative bishop himself, so soothing and unthreatening that his many fans among the conservative housewives of Ireland hardly noticed that he had subtly changed the way they looked at the world.

The media, both in print and on air, increasingly challenged and eroded ecclesiastical authority in the 1960s and 1970s. It ceased to defer. It was not exactly aggressive but there was a new note of nonchalance and scepticism. It undercut the Church by omission. Pop music edged out the informative programmes in which clergy had once been prominent. Like the American film industry, the new Irish television blessed and legitimised the culture of desire. For decades, the priest had been the principal source of information for most people about the outside world, and self-denial, abstinence and patient endurance had formed a large part of his message. Television bypassed the parish church and preached a different doctrine.

> Almost overnight there was a box in the corner of most Irish homes whose screen portrayed a sophisticated, glossy lifestyle that was far removed from the quiet, conservative community life that existed in and around them. Not only did these people in these foreign provided programmes move about in smooth slick cars and homes but they portrayed a lifestyle based on individual satisfaction, fun, sex and violence. Few of these programmes had any reference to priests or religion.[18]

Northern Ireland was changing as fast as the Republic. O'Neill was a scion of one of Ulster's old Ascendancy families, but, like Lemass, he was critical of the conservatism of the old regime. He, too, was a technocrat. Lemass's priority was to tackle the Republic's hidebound protectionism and bring in foreign competition and investment. O'Neill wanted to open up a dialogue between Protestants and Catholics in Ulster and between Ulster and the Republic. Whereas Brookeborough had ignored the Northern Catholics, the new Prime Minister started widely publicised visits to Catholic schools after a historic trip in April 1964 to one in Ballymoney, County Antrim. On 14 January 1965, he hosted the first ever meeting of the prime ministers of the two Irish states at Stormont.

O'Neill's initiatives were not really welcomed by the Protestant clergy, he complained, 'with a few shining exceptions'.[19] In fact, his autobiography was waspish about the contribution of the Protestant leaders to his doomed attempt to put communal relations in the North on a new footing.

In the general election held in Northern Ireland in October 1965, the public endorsed his policy of *détente* with the South. Catholics welcomed him into their areas, not exactly as a liberator but as that rarest of known birds, a Northern Protestant leader who was genuinely interested in their welfare. At the same time, he did not lose the trust of the mainstream Unionists. At the end of the year it seemed as if Ireland was on the brink of an extraordinary change that would close the door on the centuries of hatred and mistrust. The two states were edging closer to one another and the churches that had for centuries stood as landmarks and emblems of division were for the first time working as friends.

Within a few years the hopes of those times had faded. There were more obstacles on the road to a new understanding than people had realised. One was the sluggish attitude of the Irish Catholic bishops to the Vatican decrees, which communicated itself to the wider public. A second was the startling revival of fundamentalist Protestantism in Ulster under a firebrand minister called Ian Paisley. The last and largest was Ulster's descent into virtual civil war.

The Irish bishops executed the Vatican decrees obediently. The transition from Latin to the vernacular was carried out smoothly. The hierarchy published the vernacular text in January 1965. In June 1966 the Irish hierarchy formally gave permission for Catholics to attend non-Catholic baptisms, marriages and funerals. They might even attend Protestant services 'on official occasions'. But they acted without visible enthusiasm. Cornelius Lucey, Bishop of Cork and Ross, in May 1964 made a landmark call for Catholics to forget their historic quarrels with Irish Protestants. In the Irish mind, he said, the words 'Irish Protestant' were 'associated with the dark past of the Ascendancy and Penal times. Our immediate contribution to the ecumenical movement should be to forget the past and see our Protestant neighbours not as descendants of landlords, planters and the rest, but as Irishmen like ourselves, differing from us in religion but not one hundred per cent or even fifty per cent.'

Lucey was unusual. Such talk never emanated from the lips of Archbishop McQuaid. His Church was not in crisis, so why change it? McQuaid had spent a lifetime censoring books and trying to stop Catholics from going to Trinity. He was not the man to oversee a cultural revolution in Catholic attitudes towards Protestants. After the Council in 1965 he had returned to Ireland and informed the Irish they could sleep soundly in their beds. 'Allow me to reassure you,' he said in the pro-cathedral. 'No change will worry the tranquillity of your Christian lives'.[20] The bishops obeyed Rome. But they sometimes gave the impression that they were being dragged along by the Vatican Council rather than set free. Some lay Catholics were frankly disappointed. The convert writer, Daphne Mould, blamed the Irish bishops for what she thought a tardy reception of the conciliar changes. She told them 'we must stop patting ourselves on the back for having kept the faith for all these past centuries'. She accused them of keeping the laity 'impotent' and 'inarticulate' and said if things were allowed to drift, 'the youth of this country will be lost to the Church'.[21]

The Council gave birth to a more democratic perception of the Church. The Fathers had downplayed the monarchical prerogatives of the Pope, emphasised the collegial status of all the bishops and upgraded the status of the laity. Irish Catholics soon complained that their Church was not following suit by becoming more transparent in its workings. In America, the bishops had made their meetings public, but at Maynooth, the old atmosphere of secrecy and skulduggery remained intact. In an article entitled 'Ireland and the Council', Donall O'Morain, chairman of the National University Convocation, accused the clergy of maintaining a 'claustrophobic atmosphere in the parishes'.[22] There was a sudden focus on the deficiencies of seminary education and on the status of the clergy. Socially, culturally and materially, the Catholic clergy were starting to 'slide down the ladder', Ignatius McQuillan, a priest in Derry diocese, complained.[23] A report in *Studies* in 1967 said many lay Catholics were irritated at the slow pace of change in the Irish Church. They thought the clergy 'too slow to move with the times, too cautious, too old fashioned. On relations with other churches, official Catholic attitudes are inadequate, insulting to Protestants, frustrating for Christians who want to give expression to the generous instincts of the age.'[24]

If the lethargy of the Catholic hierarchy was one obstacle on the road to ecumenical harmony, a more serious one was the emergence of Protestant fundamentalism. The man who took centre stage in this campaign was Ian Paisley. Born to James and Isabella Paisley in 1926 in Armagh, Paisley's childhood was steeped in the traditions of the sixteenth-century Scottish Calvinist opponents of episcopacy who had signed the original Covenant against Archbishop Laud and Charles I. Paisley's daughter, Rhonda, was to recall happy times spent with her parents rooting around in the hills of south-west Scotland and looking for their graves: 'Many a holiday we spent trekking over the moors to be photographed at some Covenanter's grave in Scotland.'[25]

The vignette Rhonda provided was an illustrative one, for it suggested a man remarkably unaffected by any cultural movements and fashions since the eighteenth-century Scottish Enlightenment. Paisley was no more touched by modern ecumenism than he had been by teddy boys, hippies, the Beatles or free love. His politics, theology and entire thought processes appeared to be located in the ecclesiastical battlegrounds of the sixteenth century. His critics failed to comprehend this essential fact about his personality and it often led them to underestimate his resolve and place anachronistic interpretations on his motives. To many on the British Left, Paisley was a Fascist. In fact, his was the Fascism of Cranmer, Zwingli or Knox.

Paisley was born and brought up inside the narrow, fenced field of Irish Calvinism. He accepted his father's belief system in its entirety and his children did the same. Filial loyalty has been a consistent characteristic of the Paisley family. Ian Paisley went home after a hard day's bruising encounters with popery as his father had done, confident in the knowledge that when he closed the front door he could count on the unquestioning support of wife and children. The calmness at the centre of his private life reinforced a total lack of self-doubt. Neither of the Paisley men had to cope with questioning or quizzical looks in the domestic sanctuary, let alone arguments.

Both the Paisley men were splitters. Paisley senior had been born into the Church of Ireland before joining the Baptists and becoming a Baptist pastor in Armagh in 1918. Fifteen years later he left to form his own independent congregation. Paisley junior was cut from the same cloth. He too had no qualms about swapping churches and dividing congregations. Like most Protestants on the theological extreme left of the Reformation, the Paisleys believed Man constantly corrupted the Church, and that God kept faith with his chosen ones by sending prophets and preachers to lead the minority out of this bondage and into the truth. Splitting, therefore, was not a crime but an obligation to the true Christian. As an adult, Ian Paisley was to be accused of dividing every church and party he joined against itself. It was an insult which had no impact on Paisley, whose religious education gave a very low priority to preserving church establishments.

There was never any question that Paisley would follow his father into the ministry. After training at a school of evangelism near Cardiff, in Wales, and at the Reformed Presbyterian Theological Hall, on Grosvenor Road, Belfast, he was ordained in 1946 to the pastorate of the Ravenhill Evangelical Mission. Five years later, after splitting that congregation, he led his flock of supporters out into his own organisation, the Free Presbyterian Church, of which he was to become permanent Moderator.

A decade or two earlier, Paisley might have spent his pastorate without really noticing events on the political stage. What brought this tall, massively built young man to the forefront was the gauntlet that Terence O'Neill unwittingly hurled in his face. The first insult came only weeks after O'Neill took over the helm on 25 March 1963, when Pope John XXIII died. The breezy new premier decided to demonstrate the inclusive style of his leadership by ordering flags to be flown at half mast on the City Hall in Belfast in honour of the man who had initiated the Vatican Council and impressed the world with his humanity and piety.

Paisley was outraged by the gesture, and by the telegram of condolence O'Neill sent to Archbishop William Conway. After assuring a meeting that the former Pope was burning in hell as he spoke, he staged an unauthorised protest rally outside Belfast City Hall. The £10 fine he received marked the beginning of his political activities. On 27 September 1964 he was up in arms again over an Irish tricolour seen fluttering from Sinn Fein headquarters in the nationalist Divis flats, at the bottom of the Falls Road in west Belfast. After Paisley threatened to march his supporters on the flats and remove it himself, the RUC agreed to move in. According to the future Sinn Fein leader Gerry Adams, they 'sledge-hammered their way into the premises and seized the flag' on 1 October and stirred into life the young Adams's political interests; he recalled his satisfaction at the sight of a crowd replacing the flag the following day.[26] Paisley never drew the obvious lesson from so many of his protests: that they were entirely counter-productive. His thought processes were linear. If an insult was offered to his beliefs, he charged.

Flags at half-mast and tricolours flying from council flats were mere bagatelles compared to the furore he generated over Lemass's ground-breaking trip to Stormont in January 1965. Paisley's supporters marched on the Northern Ireland parliament the day after Lemass had gone back to Dublin, holding placards that read NO MASS NO LEMASS – a fairly concise summary of Paisley's political and religious beliefs. He led a larger demonstration when O'Neill staged a return visit to Dublin on 25 February. This time the watchword was 'King William crossed the Boyne to save us – O'Neill crossed it to sell us.'[27]

Paisleyism might have remained a peripheral phenomenon if O'Neill had kept a tight grip on the affections of the Protestant community. But his Ascendancy background isolated the Ulster premier from his constituency. The mellifluous, upper-class voice, more English than Northern Irish, instinctively alienated working-class Protestants, among whom he cut a distant, patronising figure. Had he been able to communicate his new ideas in a populist fashion, he might have kept the broad mass of Protestants on his side. As it was, Paisley mined a suspicion among lower middle-class and working-class people that they were being talked down to. By the time that elections were held again in the province in 1969, when Paisley first contested a seat, it was clear that the old Unionist monolith was breaking up and splitting on class lines. The comfortably off mostly went along with O'Neill. But the poorer sort of Protestants had lost the thread by then.

Real trouble began in 1966. Until then, O'Neill had made all the right noises to the Catholic community but little had really changed on the ground. Northern Ireland remained a Protestant state, run by a Protestant parliament, guarded by a Protestant police force. A number of insensitive decisions brought the brewing frustration of the Catholics to the surface. One was transport. When the government announced cuts to the railway network, it became apparent they were

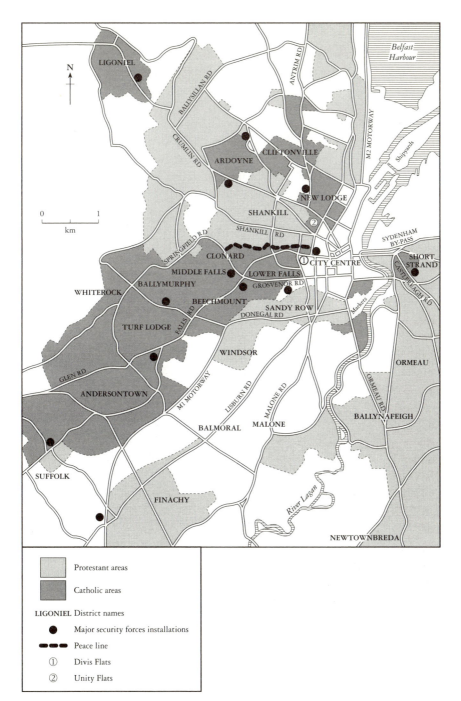

Map 5   Catholic West Belfast

almost all in the west of the province. The Beeching plan affected the whole of rural Britain, but in Northern Ireland the cuts had other implications as the west was predominatly Catholic and the plan threatened to isolate them even further from the economic heartland of the north-east. There was another row over education. Perhaps even more than wealth itself, Catholics wanted access to higher education after years of feeling excluded from Ireland's two great Protestant universities, Trinity and Queen's. They expected the promised expansion of university-level education, which was proceeding apace in Britain, to result in the upgrading of Derry's Magee College. Much to their disappointment, Stormont decided to pitch the New University of Ulster in the small, mostly Protestant town of Coleraine, County Londonderry. The planned new town also seemed like a snub to the Catholics. The government announced that Craigavon (the very name was off-putting) would be sited outside the Protestant fortress of Portadown, supplementing the industrial muscle of the Protestant east, not the Catholic west. None of these issues was decisive on its own, but taken together on top of a fizzing crisis in housing, they were dangerously inflammable.

Londonderry was the eye of the coming storm. The Maiden City of Protestants was an infernal city as far as Catholics were concerned, the symbol of all that was rotten in the state of Ulster. It had become steadily more Catholic in composition over the decades but through some mysterious alchemy in the electoral process, it remained under the control of a Protestant corporation. By the mid-1960s, about 10,000 Protestants were still electing 12 Unionists councillor, while 20,490 Catholics elected only eight Nationalists. The trick was in the judicious management of the boundaries of the electoral wards and the retention of the business vote, which mainland Britain abolished after the Labour victory of 1945. A small Protestant ward enjoyed the same clout as a large Catholic one. New social housing was confined to the Catholic wards, so that it did not dilute the Unionist vote. The Protestants were accused of conniving in the city's stunted growth, out of a fear that immigration would increase the Catholic majority. The suspicion was unfair. One of the most memorable press photographs of Northern Ireland in the 1960s was the joint protest of Derry's Protestants and Catholics against the decision to locate the new university in Coleraine. The photograph was revealing. There was the Unionist mayor, looking wooden and impassive in his spectacles and Orange Order bowler hat. Beside him stood the Catholic civil rights leader John Hume, all youthful passion and brio.

O'Neill's ecumenical gestures had raised expectations he could not fulfil. James Coulter, a schoolteacher in Derry, voiced the complaint of many Ulster Catholics, when he said that O'Neill 'speaks reason, appeals for moderation and does nothing'. 'Catholics in the North have important things to do,' he said, 'and they intend to do them – if permitted – within the framework of the Northern Ireland state. It is here they want to work out the better life for themselves and for their children.'[28] The old Unionist power structure was proving resistant to change. It was brittle and could not be stretched: it had to be left alone, or broken entirely.

O'Neill put more blame on the Protestant extremists than the Catholic militants for the crisis. 'It was the Protestant extremists yearning for the days of the Protestant Ascendancy who lit the flame which blew us up,' he said.[29]

The year 1966 saw the fiftieth anniversary of the Easter Rising. It was a red-letter day in the calendar of Irish Catholicism and the Northern Catholics noisily celebrated the uprising against British rule. When the RUC refused to clamp down on celebrations, Paisley decided to take action. His first response was to set up his own newspaper, the *Protestant Telegraph*. An amateur scissors-and-paste job that looked as if it was compiled by students, the paper was a mishmash of crude cartoons, columns on the Bible by Paisley's American fundamentalist mate, Bob Jones, and potted biographies of assorted great Protestants, called 'Their Faith Lives On'. The column 'Did You Know?' was a sequence of gasp-inducing facts designed to make Protestants choke on their breakfast cornflakes. It revealed, among other things, that Catholic schools in Northern Ireland received an annual subsidy of £8 million and that nuns were now in charge of the laundry at the Queen's University halls of residence. Other 'facts' were that papal blessings had a history of turning the recipients insane, including the Empress Carlotta of Mexico, who turned into 'a hopeless maniac' immediately after receiving one in the 1860s.[30] Another 'fact' was that the Vatican had organised the assassination of a prime minister of Ceylon.

The *Protestant Telegraph* wore its cap at a jaunty angle. It reflected Paisley's robust, one-track, sense of humour. It was, as the masthead, said, 'the paper with a punch'. One cartoon showed O'Neill stuffing a Union Jack into the dustbin while priests in soutanes merrily waved their Irish tricolours beside him.[31] Another showed the Pope in bed with a fork waiting to eat a turkey labelled 'Free Presbyterians'. None the less, the paper was deadly serious at heart. It served notice on the O'Neill government that Paisley was determined to mobilise Protestant public opinion against ecumenism in the churches and O'Neillism in government. The first edition, on 28 May 1966, set out the Paisleyite agenda. 'To the task of combatting the combined forces of Tyranny in our province this paper has dedicated itself,' it read.

> Not with tongue in cheek or with kid gloves will we fight this battle. Giving no quarter and begging for none we enter the conflict, confident that the God of battles will enable us to defend the right. We invite every true and faithful Protestant to make this paper their paper and so ensure for the coming generation the same liberties which our fathers bequeathed to us.[32]

The next few weeks saw Paisley in a whirlwind of activity. On 26 May he had been in Belfast's Ulster Hall, presiding over the foundation of his newspaper. Two days later he was preaching in Newtownards, County Down. On 1 June he was in Castlederg. The following day the faithful of Ballymena were treated to a sermon on 'the true colours of the papal anti-Christ'. On 6 June he was back in Belfast, leading a protest against the 'Romanising tendencies' of the Presbyterian Church outside the headquarters of the General Assembly. On 9 June he was back in the Ulster Hall, on 12 June he was in Lisburn, while on 15 June he was in Ballymoney. On the 19th he was in Dromore before holding a meeting in the Ulster Hall that evening. On 27 June he was in Belfast's Shankill Road.

Paisley's religious take on Unionism meant he devoted as much time and energy to combating ecumenism as he did to Catholic nationalism. For that reason the agenda of the 1966 General Assembly of the Presbyterian Church was of particular concern to him. The conference was due to debate a keynote report by the Church on discrimination and prejudice against Catholics in Northern Ireland, which would be seen as Irish Presbyterianism's considered response to the 1964 Vatican decree on ecumenism. It represented 18 months of Protestant soul-searching on the background to the political logjam in the North. Paisley and his growing band of supporters decided this was crucial evidence of a sell-out in the Protestant camp. The mainline Protestant leaders needed to be exposed as Lundies, men who were pretending to defend the City while working secretly on the side of the besiegers.

Paisley's church in Ravenhill Road was located on the eastern edge of the Ormeau Park, in east Belfast. The route to the headquarters of the Presbyterian Church in the centre took him and his supporters across the River Lagan through the Catholic Markets area and a riot broke out before they had even reached church headquarters. The stunt gained them enormous publicity as the governor of Northern Ireland, Lord Erskine and his wife were attending the Assembly's opening session and were heckled and jostled as they entered the building. Paisley was charged with unlawful assembly, but after he refused to enter a bail bond, he was rewarded with a brief spell in Crumlin Road prison, providing another boon to his political career. By the time he was out in October, sectarian tension had claimed the lives of three Catholics who were shot dead drinking in a pub in the Shankill area. One of the three Protestants charged with murder claimed that Paisley's message had inspired his action. 'I'm sorry I ever heard of that man Paisley, or decided to follow him,' he said.[33] Paisley himself had occupied his jail term composing a series of addresses with the heart-rending title, 'Messages from the Prison Cell'. His friend Bob Jones greeted the martyr's release with a gift – a doctorate from his own Bob Jones University in Greenville, South Carolina.

The rumpus over the Easter Rising celebrations and the General Assembly paved the way for the emergence of a more militant brand of Catholic politics in the following year. Galvanised by the anti-imperialist rhetoric of the Vietnam War and by Martin Luther King and the Civil Rights movement in the US, northern Catholics began forming a plethora of organisations aimed at applying the civil rights agenda to Northern Ireland. These new groups all had a modern, urgent, secular ring about them. People's Democracy was based among the recent Catholic intake into Queen's University. The Derry Citizens' Action Committee focused on the housing crisis in the north-west. The Northern Ireland Civil

Rights Association (NICRA) and the Campaign for Social Justice were umbrella organisations covering the whole province. The parallels with Martin Luther King's movement were attractive. For the Ku-Klux-Klan, read the Orange Order. For the brutal law enforcement agencies of America's Deep South, read the RUC and its B-Specials auxiliary. For white supremacy, read Protestant Ascendancy. For Black, read Catholic.

As in the United States, the campaigners staged marches to get the message across. In August 1967, NICRA and the Campaign for Social Justice announced a joint march on 24 August in County Tyrone from Coalisland to Dungannon. Paisley insisted on a counter-protest by his own supporters, who called themselves the Ulster Protestant Volunteers. The police kept the two marches apart. But in November, events took a more violent turn after 400 NICRA supporters marched from Duke Street to the Diamond in Derry, which lies at the centre of the walled city and houses the war memorial. This was like trampling through the shrine as far as Protestants were concerned, and the Home Ministry slapped a ban on the march. It took place anyway and sparked two days of disorder in the Catholic Bogside. Sensing that the province was on the brink of a widespread breakdown in law and order, O'Neill announced a package of five key reforms, including the abolition of the old company vote and the suspension of the Londonderry Corporation. A few months earlier these would have seemed generous. Not for the first time in Ulster's drawn-out crisis, it was now too little and too late.

The birth pangs of the crisis did not derail the ecumenical movement in the Irish churches. They did the opposite. The anticipation of trouble in the Six Counties, as they were known in the Republic and to nationalists throughout Ireland, prodded the mainline Protestant denominations into peering over the ecclesiastical wall into the heart of the Catholic community. What they saw convinced them that they must support the urgent calls for an end to discrimination in housing, employment and voting.

The Catholic and Protestant churches moved in step. At the Presbyterian General Assembly in June 1968, the incoming Moderator, J. H. Withers, launched a devastating attack on religious bigotry, which underlined the Church's support for the civil rights movement and its rejection of the failed policies of the past. Withers referred obliquely to Paisley, promising he would do all in his power to 'contribute to the spirit of good will and tolerance, which is just waiting for expression. I shall speak boldly if discrimination or intolerance rears its ugly head.'[34] There were unprecedented attacks at the Assembly on the Orange Order's unofficial ascendancy in Ulster. People were being denied jobs, one speaker said, 'by the machinations of certain secret societies'.[35]

Far from drawing back, the distant beat of sectarian war drums induced Presbyterians to hurry on and the delegates approved calls for the Church to carry out a thorough study of relations with the Catholic Church and empowered the Doctrine Committee to go back to the Church's title deeds in the 1646 Westminster Confession and remove references to the Pope as the Antichrist.

There was wild talk of holding the next General Assembly in 1969 in the former enemy capital of Dublin and strong support for a motion calling for Catholic priests to be invited to address Presbyterian candidates for ministry.

The Presbyterian stance was backed by the interdenominational Industrial Churches' Council, which included most of the main Protestant churches. On 21 October 1968 this body called for an impartial examination of the principal complaints of the civil rights movement. The Council opposed bans by the Northern Ireland Home Secretary on planned civil rights marches scheduled for November and remained involved in mediating between the RUC and the Catholic residents of Derry's Bogside until spring of the following year.

The Catholic bishops were careful in their first public comments on the crisis to limit themselves to demands for reform, rather than resurrect the old campaign against partition. By demanding changes in the internal workings of the Ulster state they appeared to give it a legitimacy it had never previously enjoyed among Catholics. A pastoral released in June 1968 by the Northern Catholic bishops mainly pointed to the 'bias against Catholics'[36] in Northern Ireland's local government. The Primate, Cardinal Conway, took the same line when he spoke out on 5 October. 'The immediate causes of these events are social,' he said. 'They grow out of the frustration of the ordinary people who want houses and a fair chance of jobs and equitable representation . . . I believe that the broad spectrum of public opinion throughout the community would welcome concrete action now.'[37]

The Protestant clergy were grateful for this self-imposed restraint. The Protestant Primate and the Presbyterians and Methodist leaders echoed Conway's line in a joint statement on 14 October and called on the O'Neill government 'fearlessly to analyse the causes of unrest'. Conway, in turn, praised the Reformed churches for their contribution. He called for an unthreatening 're-examination of conscience by everyone into the significance of recent events'. The Catholic community, Conway predicted, 'will respond to any credible sign that their position is going to be remedied soon'.[38]

In November 1968, NICRA announced two more marches: in Derry on 15 November and in Armagh a fortnight later. The first passed off peacefully. The two primates then issued a joint appeal against violence in the ecclesiastical capital of both churches during the second. A few days later, O'Neill went on television. On 9 December 1968 he delivered a personal appeal for the people to back his reforms. 'Ulster stands at the crossroads,' he said, in what would be the most famous speech of his career. Within days, it was clear what direction the province had taken and it was not the one that O'Neill had recommended in his 'crossroads' speech. Paisley lambasted the premier's appeal in the *Protestant Telegraph* and predicted Armageddon. 'Historically the blood of Ulster's youth has run till Boyne rivers run red,' he said, his rhetoric, as usual, returning to the great days of the sixteenth and seventeenth centuries. 'Today the battle is not yet won and sacrifices will have to be made. Now is the time for Ulster to prepare for the final conflict to come.'[39]

On the other side of the divide, 'People's Democracy' began a four-day march on 1 January across the province from Belfast to Derry, a distance of 73 miles. The police gave permission for the march. In a normal society it would have been possible for the march's opponents to close their front curtains for an hour and ignore the demonstrators as they plodded through their towns and villages. But in Ulster's contested landscape, where turf and territory have stronger connotations, it was inevitable that the overwhelmingly Catholic marchers would be regarded as enemies invading Protestant areas. The expected clash erupted outside Derry at Burntollet bridge, where an eccentric maths teacher, Major Ronald Bunting and a group of Paisleyite extremists ambushed the marchers, pelting them with stones and other missiles. To the fury of the marchers, the RUC intervened more on the side of the armed assailants than the unarmed marchers, and news of the attack immediately triggered an eruption of street fighting between the police and population in Derry's increasingly tense Bogside area.

The affray at Burntollet bridge wrong-footed O'Neill. He delivered a head-masterly ticking-off to the marchers, addressing them as if they were naughty schoolchildren. It was 'high time that certain students returned to their studies, for which they have the support of the tax-payer, and learned a little more about the nature of our society before displaying such arrogance towards those who have built up the faculties they enjoy,' he remarked.[40] It was an inappropriate comment on a bloody and dangerous confrontation.

The Burntollet episode put the first real strain on relations between the churches. The Catholic bishops released a pastoral letter in January 1969, which referred directly to the episode, strongly defending the integrity of the civil rights movement and lambasting the police as well as the Paisleyites. The bishops complained of 'the activity of people who despite their almost cynical disregard for community peace were allowed to impede lawful and peaceful demonstrations with the threat of force'.[41] But the bishops were careful to praise their new friends among the Protestant clergy and said they wished 'to pay tribute to the service in the cause of social justice which has been rendered in recent months by many Protestant members of the community, including leading churchmen. Their voice has given consolation and encouragement to those who have suffered from injustice for a very long time.' It had also been a very long time since Irish Catholics had addressed Irish Protestants in that kind of language, possibly not since the emancipation struggle of the 1820s.

O'Neill decided he had to have a clearer mandate from the electorate to push through fresh reforms, so he summoned an election at the end of February. The result was not clarification but confusion. If O'Neill had expected the still, small voice of common sense to rise above the smoke of battle he was mistaken. The O'Neillite candidates scraped home but they were badly bruised by a combination of Paisleyites and other Unionists who opposed his reforms. The premier endured the indignity of almost losing his formerly impregnable Bannside seat to Paisley himself. O'Neill clung on by less than 1,500 votes. As his authority over the Ulster

Unionist machine unravelled, he had almost no option but to resign, which he did on 28 April. The attempt to reform the Ulster state from within had failed. Subsequent reforms would be much more rigorous and would be enforced from the outside.

The Presbyterians gathered in 1969 with the debris of O'Neill's failure lying around them. The experiment in political ecumenism had collapsed. At Stormont, the hand on the tiller had listed to the right following O'Neill's succession by James Chichester-Clark as the new premier. The June General Assembly had the responsibility of giving some kind of measured verdict on the turmoil, as well as on the civil rights movement in general.

The Church drew a deep breath and there was no return to the old-style anti-Catholic polemics. In its report on the increasingly muddled situation, the Church blamed hard-line Unionists for the violence at Burntollet and defended the rights of Catholic nationalists to protest. 'Such a treatment of those who were protesting against what they believed to be wrong has been a grievous betrayal of the Protestant and Presbyterian principle of civil and religious liberty,' the report said. 'We believe many still do not realise the irreparable damage which has been done to the witness of the gospel and to the Protestant and Presbyterian name, both in Ireland and overseas. Avowed enemies of Christianity could not have done more damage to the faith . . . '[42]

The Presbyterian statement showed that Northern Ireland's Catholic and Protestant churches were still singing more or less from the same hymn sheet. But 1969 marked a parting of the ways over politics, if not over the wider ecumenical experiment. As the once moribund IRA revived and steadily penetrated the civil rights movement, the agenda inevitably moved on from reform of the Northern Irish state to Irish reunification. That was a road most Protestants would not go down. They were alienated by the wave of violence that followed the July 1969 marching season, which they thought unjustified. By 14 August, the RUC was fighting running battles with crowds of youths in Derry and Belfast. Responding to an urgent request from the Northern Ireland government, the British Prime Minister, Harold Wilson, sent British troops into the Bogside, and the following day into the Ardoyne and Falls areas of north and west Belfast. Conway was scathing about the RUC's handling of the escalation. 'The Catholic districts of Falls and Ardoyne were invaded by mobs equipped with machine guns and other fire arms,' he said. 'Streets of Catholic houses were set on fire. We ask all to realise that among Roman Catholics belief in the impartiality of the Ulster Special Constabulary is virtually non-existent.'[43]

As the leadership of the Catholic Church began tentatively to probe the continuing viability of the Northern Irish state, the chasm reopened between themselves and the Protestant clergy. Underneath all the ecumenical gestures, Protestants and Catholics remained more divided than perhaps they realised over the question of a united Ireland. While this lurked in the background, ecumenism could proceed. But when Irish unity moved to the centre ground, the new friendship between the churches was tested to the limit, for however much Catholic leaders opposed the means employed by the IRA, they were not prepared to disavow its goal. In 1968 the issue had been discrimination. After the summer of 1969, the issue was Northern Ireland's position inside the United Kingdom.

Conway remained a restraining figure. While church leaders were still in a position to guide political events, he did his best to rein in extremists without forfeiting the confidence of his community. The Labour government in Britain believed his support for political reform was crucial and the Home Secretary, James Callaghan, artfully courted his goodwill after a fact-finding visit to the province at the end of August 1969. The Home Secretary's visit was the prelude to a new package of reforms which Westminster was determined to force through, whether or not the Unionists liked it. They included the disbanding of the B-Specials, an armed wing of the police made up of part-time unpaid volunteers which many Catholics saw as a particularly oppressive force,[44] and a new police authority, the creation of a new housing authority, which would take the sensitive matter of council house allocation out of local government hands. Funding for the province as a whole was to be increased. Like O'Neill's earlier reforms, they came late in the day and followed, rather than preceded, the outbreak of violence, but Callaghan made a point of drawing Conway into the process. 'I told the Cardinal the principal points in the communiqué and that apart from the GOC he was the first man to know because it was his community which was in trouble,' Callaghan recalled. 'I said I had a request to make of him. I wanted him to give his blessing to the communiqué as soon as it was announced on television. The Cardinal said that from what I had told him it sounded a very good agreement . . . I thanked him very much and said I was now going to get on to the press.'[45]

It was an important gesture to a Church that the Northern Ireland authorities had virtually ignored since 1922. The Home Secretary's diplomatic footwork with the Primate kept Conway on side throughout the year. At heart, he remained a moderate nationalist, committed to eventual Irish unity, but Callaghan's gesture left him feeling bound to talk favourably of British reforms to the province even if, as the IRA suspected, such reforms only propped up the six-county state and delayed its hoped-for collapse. The Cardinal gave a positive response to the report on policing in October that recommended disarming the RUC. Much to the anger of the IRA, the Primate urged Catholics to join a reformed police force. 'I imagine many policemen themselves will welcome the changes,' he said, 'and I anticipate Catholics will be willing and anxious to join the new force in consider-able numbers.'[46]

But Presbyterian goodwill fell away. Violence continued in the Bogside and west Belfast, and Presbyterians felt less generous and more anxious than they had about earlier protests. Their official statements began to reflect fears for the future of the Northern Irish state and to deal less with Catholic grievances. In October 1969, while Conway was welcoming the Hunt Report on the police, the Presbyterian Church warned dolefully 'of the very great danger now facing

Northern Ireland out of the violence, disorder and rebellion of recent weeks'.[47] While Conway was holding out hopes for a reformed police force, the Presbyterians were pointedly praising the RUC as it was constituted. The Church said it wished to 'acknowledge with gratitude in this situation the peace-keeping service of the RUC and of the army'. It complained bitterly of the 'partial and misleading' propaganda about Northern Ireland in the British and foreign media.

There was a growing resentment among the Protestant clergy that after Rome's initial spadework at the Vatican Council, Irish Catholics had done less than the Protestants to remove old sectarian barriers. They complained that in spite of the political reforms at home, Catholics remained abstentionists in politics, would not join social organisations such as the Young Farmers' Club, or the British Red Cross Society, did not attend public meetings and put all the blame for the Ulster crisis on Protestants. J. H. Withers had led the attack on discrimination as Presbyterian Moderator in 1968. One year on, he was more critical of the Catholic position. 'The Roman Catholic hierarchy,' he said on leaving office, 'have felt unable to acknowledge that their people, too, have contributed to the malaise of Ulster and have seemed unwilling or unable to understand the genuine fears and grievances of Protestants.'[48]

The Presbyterian Church was swayed by the rise of Paisleyism as a political force. This had little to do with the coincidence that Paisley incorporated the word 'Presbyterian' in the title deeds of his little denomination. On the contrary, the widespread confusion this caused in Ireland and overseas irritated mainstream Presbyterians. Paisley had never been a member of their Church. But the Church was affected by Paisleyite politics, which became a force to be reckoned with after he won O'Neill's Bannside constituency in the by-election that followed the premier's resignation in 1969. It was undeniable that Paisley had won the seat with Presbyterian votes: the Bannside seat encompassed much of the Presbyterian Church's heartland, including the rolling villages and small towns the Presbyterians had settled in the seventeenth century. Paisley's blasts at Rome, the World Council of Churches, ecumenism and pussy-footing Unionists had tapped into a build-up of steam that was not being expressed in the Presbyterian General Assembly.

Paisleyism did not take over the Presbyterian Church, but it moved the goalposts a little and boosted conservative forces inside the Church in their internal fight against the liberal agenda. However, they were not strong enough to engineer a return to the old confrontational sectarianism and direct criticism of the Catholic Church. The Presbyterian Church continued to support measures that aimed to soothe Catholic nationalist discontent. But at the same time, the Presbyterians began to set limits on its relations with other churches. The ecumenical juggernaut slowed down, rolled to a halt. Then slid steadily backwards, culminating in the Church's withdrawal in 1980 from the World Council of Churches, an organisation that Paisley particularly loathed for the leftward slant of its political statements as well as for its theology. At the same time, the

Presbyterians began to defend the existence of the Northern Irish state more vigorously. They continued to praise the security forces and to rebut what they saw as Catholic propaganda against the state in Britain and overseas.

The gap between the churches widened in the new decade, after the introduction of internment of prisoners without trial in August 1971 and the 'Bloody Sunday' disaster in Derry in January 1972, when rioting resulted in British troops shooting dead 13 apparently unarmed civilians. None of the churches was ready to throw in the towel and start denouncing the others. That much the Irish ecumenical movement had achieved over the previous 10 years. But the fact was that ordinary Catholics and Protestants increasingly wanted their clergy to voice the anger of their polarised communities. Whatever their personal feelings, the clergy could not opt out of their appointed role as 'chaplains to the warring tribes'.

The Catholic Church strongly opposed internment and the bishops condemned it on 30 September 1971. The Protestant churches were either ambivalent, or supported the policy. The Catholic clergy were outraged by Bloody Sunday: one of the abiding images of the Northern Irish conflict is the photograph of a priest, Edward Daly, later Bishop of Derry, waving a white handkerchief as he attempted to shepherd a group of Catholic civilians through the tear gas and mayhem.

But Protestants felt very differently about Bloody Sunday. Two Northern Church of Ireland bishops issued a statement that placed most of the blame for the bloodshed on the protesters. 'Amid serious and mounting pressures aimed at altering the status, institutions and structures of Northern Ireland,' they said, 'we feel obliged to state that . . . the majority of members of the Church in our diocese will not be coerced into the society and community of the Republic of Ireland.'[49] The Presbyterians took the lead among the mainline Protestant denominations in accusing southern politicians of misrepresenting the northern crisis to the all-important American public. In February 1972, weeks after the bloodshed in Derry, the Presbyterians issued a statement that condemned the Irish government for 'a persistent lack of any real understanding of the position of the great majority of our people and, we believe, of Northern Protestants generally'.

Protestant anger was heightened when Edward Heath, the Conservative Prime Minister who replaced Wilson in 1970, prorogued Stormont on 24 March 1972 and put the province under direct rule from Westminster. They were shocked that such a seemingly hostile act could come from the Conservative and Unionist Party. The Presbyterian Church had been intimately involved in the creation of a northern state 50 years before and they refused to keep silent as it dissolved in front of their eyes. 'We speak for a people in Northern Ireland who without consent are now suffering a massive deprivation of their constitutional and civil rights,' the Church complained after Stormont was closed down, 'exceeding any previous curtailment of local voting rights such as have caused such widespread protests in the past.'[50]

Presbyterians did not come out of the closet and stand up for the Northern Irish state just because Paisley prodded them in that direction. Their Church had little to lose in the Republic by the 1970s. Though still an all-Ireland Church in name, it was an all-Ulster Church in practice by the 1970s after the slow process of inter-marriage and emigration had wiped out one scattered congregation after another. The Presbyterian Church was more willing to risk Catholic hostility than the Church of Ireland because it had no hostages to worry about in the South, or very few. In 1971 the city of Belfast alone numbered 48,000 Presbyterian households. The entire united presbyteries of Dublin and Munster numbered 2,095 families. There were only 80 Presbyterian households left in the city of Cork, which had once been a southern stronghold, seven in Wexford, four in Carlow and one in Roscommon. Three Presbyterian families lingered on in Tralee, County Kerry, down from 14 in 1953 and 29 in 1890. The Presbyterian Church had no reason to worry about persecution in the Republic, whatever it said in the North. There was nothing left to persecute.

The Protestant churches, and Presbyterians in particular, became increasingly critical of nationalist demands as the spiralling violence sparked an exodus of Protestants from the west of the province. In Londonderry, the overwhelming bulk of Protestants in the city fled west of the River Foyle to the suburb of Waterside. The Protestant population on the east bank fell from 18,000 in 1968 to a derisory 2,800 by 1994. Most left between 1970 and 1974. The remnant still encamped on the city side of the Craigavon bridge was confined to a single, tiny housing estate, the Fountain. A similar emptying out of the Protestant population took place in parts of north and west Belfast, such as the New Barnsley estate, as well as in Newry, in south County Down, and in the rural border lands of Fermanagh and south Armagh, where an IRA policy of 'greening' the frontier resulted in the enforced flight of all but a handful of Protestants. The result was that from 1970, Ulster Protestants and Catholics lived increasingly segregated lives in watertight enclaves. The river that flowed through Derry now formed a religious frontier. In Belfast, the clergy now had to shout their ecumenical discussions over the so-called 'peace walls' that were flung up to segregate the Catholic Falls district from the Protestant Shankill.

Conway trod a lonely path from 1970. After the Presbyterians emerged as shrill champions of the Northern Irish state, pressure from the Catholic public throughout Ireland grew on the Church to attack Britain's right to govern the North. Priests in west Belfast and Derry were spokesmen of communities that saw themselves as virtually at war with the British state.

The Irish Labour Party politician and diplomat Conor Cruise O'Brien was shocked by the emergence of these clerical militants on a visit to Northern Ireland in July 1970, shortly after the IRA shot dead two Protestants who had attacked St Matthew's Catholic church in east Belfast. O'Brien noted in his diary:

To 12'o clock Mass at St Peter's, Falls Road. Father P.M. preaches. Natural right to self-defence. Troops proved incapable of defending our people. Example;

heroic defenders of St Matthew's. Concluding appeal for calm and restraint. No hint that right of self-defence might be abused. No word at which any Provisional might jib.

Coffee with Father M in his office after Mass. Says he was edified to see me in his congregation. I tell him I have sat in Paisley's congregation too. Sharp look. I ask him: 'Do you think it right to shoot to kill to stop people from burning down a church?' He answers calmly: 'No, I don't. That would not be right. But this was an attack against a community, their homes and their lives. The church grounds were used in the defence of the people . . .

Afterwards out in the Falls Road itself a small crowd gathers around us. One or two men are angry, almost hysterical, as well as the women. 'What is the Dublin government doing?' 'What are you doing?' 'Isn't this our country?' 'Aren't you our government?'[51]

O'Brien represented the patrician liberal elite of the Republic, which felt deeply uncomfortable in the whole drama. Catholic Whigs, such people were far closer in spirit to the old southern Protestants than to the rancorous marginalised northern Catholics.

The Northern Catholic bishops had to reconcile conflicting pressures in their statements. Every word had to have one eye on the British, another on the people O'Brien had encountered in the Falls Road, and a third, if that was possible, on the southern Catholics O'Brien spoke for, who wanted justice, but not necessarily triumph, for the Northern Catholics. As the Protestants became increasingly critical of the Catholic Church's supposed ambivalence towards violence, Conway and the northern bishops delivered a statement on 12 September 1971 that aimed to set clear blue water between the forces of consti-tutional nationalism and the Provisional IRA. 'In Northern Ireland at the present time there is a small group of people who are trying to secure a united Ireland by the use of force,' the bishops said.

One has only to state this fact in all its stark simplicity to see the absurdity of the idea. Who in his sane senses wants to bomb a million Protestants into a united Ireland? At times, the people behind this campaign will talk of defence. But . . . their bombs have killed innocent people, including women and girls. Their campaign is bringing shame and disgrace on noble and just causes . . . This is the way to postpone a really united Ireland until long after all Irish men and women living are dead.[52]

In 1972, the Northern bishops were careful not to crow about the suspension of Stormont, knowing the outrage it had caused among the Protestants. In November, the Northern bishops balanced the above statement with a strong condemnation of internment. Conway's moderation showed through in the way the statement appealed to mainland British public opinion. The bishops had criticised the practice of keeping men 'hooded and kept standing with arms and legs outstretched practically continuously for days and nights on end', and described it as 'unworthy of the British people', hardly a qualification that was likely to please the IRA.[53] The Northern bishops opposed internment precisely because they believed it was feeding support for the nationalist paramilitaries. Speaking in Longford, on New Year's Day in 1972, Cahal Daly, Bishop of Ardagh, said internment 'with all its accompanying and inherent inhumanity, raids, house searches, harassment of entire Catholic communities, cratering of border roads [was] daily advancing the cause of violence'.[54] Daly pointed to a growing revulsion against bloodshed and praised the historians engaged in a critique of the cult of violence that had always surrounded the Easter Rising.

Conway backed the British White Paper on Northern Ireland released in March 1973, which led the way to the return of limited self-government in the form of a power-sharing executive. In place of what had been seen by Catholics as a Protestant parliament for a Protestant people, the new arrangement proposed an executive comprising mainstream Unionists, the constitutional nationalists of the Social Democratic and Labour Party and the non-confessional Alliance Party. The executive offered the best hope for the containment of the violence that was to plague Ulster until the mid-1990s. But power-sharing foundered like O'Neillism on the rocks of hardline Protestant intransigence. Shortly after the British devolved authority to the executive on 1 January 1974 a general strike by Protestant workers in May brought the province to a halt and the experiment came to an end.

The Protestant clergy were as divided over power-sharing as their political colleagues in the Unionist Party. Broadly, the Church of Ireland and the Methodists welcomed the agreement. Most Presbyterians opposed it and their Church declined to condemn the strikers who brought it down. At the 1974 General Assembly, weeks after the strike, a motion was forwarded criticising the use of intimidation in the strike. It gained some support but still lost by 209 votes to 191. At Christmas, the leaders of all the main Churches, Catholic, Anglican, Methodist and Presbyterian, united to launch an appeal for a Christmas truce in the violence. 'Think, pray and talk peace' was the campaign slogan. It may have helped propel the IRA towards the 11-day ceasefire that the paramilitaries called in December, and which sputtered on into the spring of 1975, but there was no escaping the fact that the Irish Churches were no longer even superficially united over the way that peace in Northern Ireland should be secured.

Conway's death in 1977 signalled the end of an era. The leaders of the Church of Ireland, the Presbyterians and the Methodists were prominent among the mourners. They had every reason to regret the passing of a man who never allowed the passions aroused by the conflict in Ulster to overwhelm his judgement. As hopes faded for a political solution to the crisis, the election of Tomás O'Fiaich as Conway's successor inaugurated a very different epoch. O'Fiaich was a great bull of a man. With the coarse, fleshy features of a peasant, he resembled a prize fighter more than a cleric. His roots were in the fiercely Republican heartland of south Armagh, a region the British army christened 'bandit country' on account of the number of shootings at the security forces. He was a folk leader and a worthy successor to the warrior bishops of sixteenth-century Ulster who had perished on the battlefield against the Elizabethan invaders. O'Fiaich loved tramping over the wild heaths of south Armagh, around the villages of Crossmaglen and Creggan, and visiting the graves of the Gaelic 'poets of the Fews' who had kept alive the Irish language against the English in the seventeenth and eighteenth centuries. He was an excellent historian. But he said his prayers in Irish and his political passions overshadowed and dominated his ministry. 'He could best be described as an ethnicist,' said Monsignor Denis Faul. 'He was for the ethnic groups, in reality the clan with its history, its genealogy its graves . . . The Irishness of the faith was as important to him as the faith itself.'[55]

O'Fiaich did not halt the ecumenical dialogue that his two predecessors in Armagh had started, but he offered political leadership of a very different kind to that of D'Alton or Conway. As the Presbyterians pulled back from their earlier support of civil rights to defence of the Ulster state, O'Fiaich began to champion the Republican nationalist cause. 'I think the British should withdraw from Ireland,' he told the Northern Irish nationalist newspaper, the *Irish News*, in January 1978.

> I believe in a declaration of intent. I know it is a coloured phrase but I think it is the only thing which will get things moving. I regret that it didn't happen after the collapse of Stormont. There were Protestants looking round in frustration for a friendly hand to grasp and a declaration, coupled with sincere gestures from the South, would have done much good. I don't see any solution for the Northern Ireland problem save in an All-Ireland context.[56]

This was the note on which O'Fiaich conducted his archepiscopate. He looked on Britain as a colonial power, which stood in exactly the same relation to Ulster as it did to Ghana, or to Cyprus. The solution to the crisis was British withdrawal. 'I would like them to say "Just as we brought British colonialism to an end in other parts of the world, we are not going to be in Northern Ireland ad infinitum . . . ultimately we would like to see all Ireland ruled by the Irish."'[57]

Individual clergy continued to work for peace. The most bizarre initiative involved a group of brave and far-sighted Protestant clerics who decided to engage the leadership of the Republican paramilitaries in direct talks. The contacts began in 1971 and in December 1974 the two sides met at Smyth's hotel, in Feakle, in County Clare. Eric Gallagher, in *Christians in Ulster*, which he co-wrote with Stanley Worrall, described the surreal atmosphere of this encounter between ministers and men of war as the Irish Special Branch police arrived. Four of the seven 'Provos' had left before then.

The eight of us sat in silence as a good deal of uneasy shuffling was heard at the foot of the stairs. The first thing to appear above the floor line was the muzzle of a sub-machine gun followed a moment later by the tense face of the policeman holding it. When he saw no guns covering him he advanced more confidently and soon the room was full of policemen. The officer in charge demanded our names. 'Arthur Butler, Bishop of Connor.' 'Henry Morton, General Secretary of the British Council of Churches.' 'Jack Weir, Clerk of the Presbyterian General Assembly.' 'Eric Gallagher, former President of the Methodist Church in Ireland'. Blank bewilderment and disbelief! Downstairs they had found Rory O'Brady, president of Provisional Sinn Fein, reading by the fire. He was not on the wanted list and is reputed to have said: 'You will find the men you are looking for upstairs.'[58]

Gallagher and the others got nowhere in their attempt to persuade Republicans to stop their war. But they set a pattern for other private initiatives by Catholic and Protestant clergy to make chinks in the walls separating the communities and plant the idea of peace in the gunmen's heads.

The churches were not to blame for failing to stop the violence. From the early 1970s, they had little restraining power over the Republican and Loyalist militants. Individual gunmen might be devout Catholics and Protestants. The Sinn Fein leader, Gerry Adams, was a case in point, a devout Catholic regularly to be found at prayer in west Belfast's Clonard monastery. But the sight of Sinn Fein or Loyalist leaders on their knees did not mean any of them heeded the monotonous ecclesiastical appeals for peace. Cahal Daly, now Bishop of Derry, commented in 1975 on the Republican militants' growing indifference to their pastors. Visiting 400 Republican prisoners at Magilligan jail that year, Bishop Daly was struck by the hostile 'wall of silence'. The Bishop observed that while the Irish clergy were still inching towards each other, their congregations were moving in the opposite direction.[59] By the end of the 1970s the churches were passive spectators of Ulster's seemingly unending agony. Even Pope John Paul II's personal appeal for peace delivered on his historic trip to Ireland at Drogheda in 1979 had no effect.

By 1990, Republican fighters had killed about 1,500 people during 20 years of fighting. Their Loyalist opponents had killed about 800. In November, Daly who succeeded O'Fiaich at Armagh, told Radio Ulster that the churches had saved Northern Ireland from becoming another Lebanon.[60] Was it true? By the time the Archbishop made this claim the general impression was that Irish ecumenism had run out of steam and that the churches had retired to their own tents. The hopes raised in the early 1960s had manifestly not been fulfilled. It had become fashionable to deride ecumenism as a 'mild hobby', practised discreetly between consenting adults in the comfortable Dublin suburbs. Andy Pollack, the *Irish Times'* highly respected religious affairs correspondent, wrote an obituary of the ecumenical movement in 1992, which pinpointed why the enthusiasm of the 1970s had withered away. Pollack blamed the alienation of Irish opinion on

Ulster's internecine strife, a conservative theological trend within Protestantism, the failure of various ecumenical conferences to set up any new structures for ecumenical growth and the failure of the churches to provide any theological education on ecumenism.[61] Clergymen had talked about this and that theological point, but there had been no fusion among the laity. As Gerry O'Hanlon sarcastically remarked in 1992, Protestants prayed at their services for the security forces, Catholics prayed for Republican prisoners and everyone prayed for the Third World.[62]

The Irish clergy were their own worst critics. Their expectations were the highest. When the history of Northern Ireland is compared to that of Lebanon and Cyprus in the 1970s and 1980s, and to Rwanda and Yugoslavia in the 1990s, it is clear that the refusal of the Irish church leaders to demonise their rivals played a crucial role. Overwhelmingly, they declined to disinter their old grudges and parade past wounds and atrocities as a justification for recent violence. Paramilitary violence tested the churches' willingness to talk to each other to the limit, and the slender rope bridge never snapped.

The churches helped defuse the fury over Bloody Sunday and in December 1974 fomented a movement against violence with the 'Let Peace Begin at Christmas' campaign. Individual clerics had met the men of violence face to face at the secret talks at Feakle. The churches tried listing the areas they could agree on in order to reduce the causes of violence. In 1976 they drew up a joint report, which came up with 16 specific recommendations to resolve communal strife. Against a background of gruesome sectarian atrocities, church leaders continued to meet and promote theological dialogue. They supported the establishment of the ecumenical Corrymeela Community in County Antrim in the North in the 1960s and the ecumenical conference near Dundalk in the Republic at Ballymascanlan in 1973, which led to a series of meetings between theologians.

The clergy channelled and contained the anger and grief of their people when they buried the victims of violence. Few exploited this most sensitive of church services to sanction, let alone encourage, revenge. Perhaps they had not escaped the role of chaplains to the warring tribes. But most of them had restrained their troops as much as they could. It was not a bad record.

CHAPTER SEVENTEEN

I Never Asked for a Pedestal

Many people feel justifiably betrayed by the Church which they loved and trusted.
Many are shocked and bewildered by it all. We bishops share all those feelings and
we wish to reach out to all the hurt ones and assure them that we grieve with them.
(Cardinal Daly, February 1995)[1]

At four minutes past ten on a gloriously sunny morning on 29 September 1979, Pope John Paul II touched down at Dublin airport, the first Pontiff to visit St Patrick's island. After the Pope marched briskly down the gangway of the Aer Lingus plane, white robes billowing in the wind, he knelt and kissed the ground in the symbolic salute that was to become the hallmark of all his foreign visits.

The Pope rose to his feet and after acknowledging the waves and cheers of the 20,000 men, women, soldiers, bishops and officials who had crowded round the airport runway, and clasping Cardinal O'Fiaich, he stepped towards the microphone. He had come to walk in the footsteps of St Patrick, he said, praying in the words of St Peter, 'Peace to all of you in Christ.'[2]

The three-day whirlwind tour of Ireland, which would have taxed the strength of a man half his age – he was 59 – began in Phoenix Park, site of the great Catholic jamborees of 1929 and 1932, when crowds of half a million and a million had attended the centenary of Catholic Emancipation and the Eucharistic Congress. Those vast crowds paled in comparison to the numbers who flocked to see the first Pope on Irish soil in 1979. By midday, one and a quarter million people had assembled, waiting for the Pope to arrive by helicopter. Thousands had moved into the park the previous night to be sure of a good view. The following day they were joined by one-third of their fellow countrymen and women.

Everything about the mass in Phoenix Park was on a grand scale. The steel cross over the purpose-built altar towered 120 feet into the sky. Behind it 60 gold-and-white papal banners flapped in the breeze. A battalion of 200 cardinals from all around the world joined the Pope at the altar to concelebrate the mass. Some 2,000 priests were on hand to distribute the host to the more than a million communicants. If there was a living God, he could hardly fail to have noticed what was going on in Phoenix Park.

At the climax of the liturgy, the Pope lifted up the chalice. It was the same one that the papal legate had used in 1932. But comparisons with the Eucharistic Congress, though inevitable, were misleading. The Church had conducted the Eucharistic Congress in an atmosphere of intense triumphalism and with maximum imperial pomp. It had been a dark celebration of the war of independence, the growth of Ireland's spiritual empire and of the crushing defeat that she had inflicted on the forces of English Protestantism. Compared to that ghoulish festival, the Pope's visit in 1979 was a sunny, joyous affair. There was nothing triumphal about Rome's smiling sovereign and the crowds, singing 'He's got the whole world in his hands', were not in the least like the awe-struck masses of 1929 and 1932. The Pope was fresh in his pontificate and had the mien of a man in his prime. Years of resistance to Communist pressure in his native Poland had made him an idol in the Western media. Yet he seemed to sit nonchalantly on the throne of popularity that would have turned the head of a lesser man. Everyone basked in the golden glow of his smile, while the ripples of pleasure spread outwards. This time there was no snarling about Protestants, as there had been in 1929, nor any return to vengeful, self-pitying moans about the Penal Laws. Even though the Pontiff's time was measured out to the last minute, he insisted on meeting Protestant church leaders and holding out the hand of friendship, for which the Presbyterians rewarded him with a distinctly grumpy statement.[3]

The Pope displayed sure-footedness at every turn, targeting each homily at a different audience and dealing each time with a different aspect of Christian life. At Phoenix Park the accent was on celebration, pure and simple. This was the day when Catholics were entitled to savour and give thanks for the painful centuries of fidelity to the Holy See and the mass. But if Dublin was a time for congratulation, the next stop showed the Pope was not afraid to address the dark side of Ireland's religious heritage.

The Pope needed no reminder of what that included. A month before his visit, the IRA assassinated Lord Mountbatten in a boat off the coast of Sligo. Two teenage boys died in the explosion. The assassination of the last British Viceroy of India and a close relative of Britain's royal family threw an immediate question mark over the Pope's planned visit to Northern Ireland. Nationalists throughout Ireland and Northern Catholics in particular were desperate for the visit to include at least a stop-over in Ulster. But the Pope was loath to offend the Northern Protestants and the British while the wound of Mountbatten's death was so fresh and journeyed instead to Drogheda, which lay on the southern tip of the diocese of Armagh inside the Republic. There, he delivered a tremendous plea for an end to what he called the 'lie of violence'. The Pope did not mince his words:

'Christianity is decisively opposed to fomenting hatred or to promoting or provoking violence or struggle for the sake of struggle,' he said. 'The command: "Thou shalt not kill" must be binding on the conscience of humanity if the terrible tragedy and destiny of Cain is not to be repeated . . . to all of you who are listening, I say: do not believe in violence, do not support violence. It is not the Christian way.'[4]

It was majestic, statesmanlike stuff and included a ringing endorsement of Ireland's wobbly march towards Christian unity. Irish Protestants must not see him as an enemy, he said, but as 'a friend and a brother in Christ'.

The Pope flew from Drogheda to the western capital of Galway for a mass for Ireland's youth. About 280,000 youngsters along with 800 priests from the lands west of the Shannon had gathered on the Ballybrit racecourse outside the city to see the figure in dazzling white robes arrive. Two of Ireland's star turns among the clergy, Eamonn Casey, the portly, moonfaced Bishop of Galway and his huge gangly friend, Michael Cleary, a popular priest in Dublin, were on the platform to greet him and warm up the crowds before his arrival. These two were charismatic characters with a large following among the young. Casey had devoted his ministry to the homeless in England as well as Ireland and had earned a reputation as a left-wing firebrand for his trenchant views on Third World development and rich people in general. Cleary was equally well known for his work with the poor. He was the Catholic Church's greatest media star, hosting an hour-long radio show five nights a week and penning columns for the *Sunday Independent* and the *Star*. The two priests looked like men after the Pope's heart, celibate but masculine, humane but unimpeachably orthodox. They seemed exemplars of a Church wholly at ease with its past, but also embracing the changed priorities of a new generation.

From Galway it was back to Maynooth on 1 October to address seminarians and the Religious. 'The degree of religious practice in Ireland is high,' the Pope told the priests of the new era. 'But,' he asked, 'will the next generation of young Irishmen and Irish women still be as faithful as their fathers were? After two days in Ireland and after my meeting with Ireland's youth at Galway I am confident that they will . . . '[5]

To Tony Flannery, a Redemptorist priest in Limerick, the 1970s were the Indian summer of the Irish Catholic Church. Archbishop McQuaid had gone and taken his Victorian stuffiness and queasy obsession with sex with him. The Church remained rock solid about its core beliefs but was loosening up at the edges. It was the era of the groovy television priest, the priest who could boogie, the left-wing priest who liked a pint, had long hair and was big on the Third World and homelessness. It seemed that in Ireland the Church was enjoying a new lease of life, marrying a growing concern for the socially excluded with its undiluted old doctrinal conviction.

Flannery recalled the atmosphere after his ordination in 1974 by Bishop Tom Ryan of Clonfert. 'Bonfires were lit, the village was bedecked with bunting, a platform was erected beside my parents' house and everybody gathered,' he said.

The following day I said my first mass in the local church and after that it was open house, open turf shed (equipped with a temporary timber floor for dancing) and open hay shed (with a keg of Guinness and a keg of lager from which my uncle doled liberal measures) for the rest of the day. Everybody queued up for my first blessing and handed me a fairly generous donation.

The faith of these people told them that I was special, that because of what had taken place that morning I was now in some way more holy than they were, that I had great and mysterious powers, that I had blessed hands. A mixture of faith and superstition told them that I had the power to do many wonderful things, to bring healing, to impose and lift curses, to choose whom to bless and whom not to bless, even, on occasions, to tell the future.[6]

Flannery was beginning his ministry in a country that took its faith more seriously than any nation in Europe. The East and Central European Catholics, the Pope's own Poles, as well as the Slovaks, Croats and Slovenes, were much more loyal to the Church than their counterparts in the old Catholic heartlands of France, Spain and Italy. But measured in terms of daily and weekly commitment, their piety paled in comparison to the Irish. At a time when not more than a fifth of the population in most West European countries attended church on a regular basis, 86 per cent of the Irish Catholics attended mass each week while a large percentage attended mass daily, or more than once a week. Two-thirds of the Irish population claimed to have no difficulty accepting any of the Church's teachings.[7] About 47 per cent of the population went to confession at least once a month. The Church seemed as secure under Cardinal O'Fiaich as it had been under Cardinal Cullen. As the authors of a report on Irish values wrote a few years after the Pope's visit: 'The first and correct impression when religious beliefs and practice in Ireland are compared with those in Britain or Europe is that Ireland remains an outstandingly religious country.'[8]

But change was in the air. After the bunting from the Pope's visit came down and the great altar at Phoenix Park was dismantled, there was a dawning sense that the Pope's visit had been a last hurrah rather than the dawning of a new era. 'Somewhere along the way the dream died,' Flannery wrote later about that crucial decade. 'The promise of new growth, of a new style of religious life that would speak powerfully to the modern world never quite materialised.'[9]

The Pope's dynamism and his ecumenical gestures obscured the extent to which he was bent on tying the Church to a more conservative agenda than most people realised. After the talk at Maynooth, the Pope delivered his least-reported speech at Limerick. Foreign reporters scarcely noticed it after the sensational and deeply moving appeal against violence in Drogheda. At Limerick, the Pontiff inveighed against abortion, contraception and divorce in the strongest terms. He had also pleaded with Irish women not to desert the joys of motherhood and their place at home for the illusory satisfaction of a job. It was an old-fashioned menu that was to place the Church on a collision course with women's rising expectations and their new emphasis on choice.

Even before the Pope's visit, the first rumblings of discontent over the Church's pre-eminence in Irish life had become audible. The IRA bombing campaign in the North encouraged the intelligentsia in the South to examine the foundations of the Republic to look for clues to all this horror. The mayhem encouraged a great deal of soul-searching and while most Irish people still blamed the British connection for the mess, a growing minority, including many writers and opinion-formers in the media, were coming to the conclusion that the Republic shared the responsibility. Conor Cruise O'Brien was a prodigious and effective communicator on Northern affairs. Long sojourns on the streets of Belfast and Derry had left him deeply worried about the fate of Irish democracy. More volubly and more persuasively than any other individual, he contested the rose-tinted view of 'the struggle' and took up the hitherto unheard and unpopular views of the Protestants. O'Brien's view did not prevail but he shifted the goalposts of the debate. Many people still supported the IRA, but they were no longer automatically unchallenged. IRA violence made it permissible to question the motives of the Easter Rising and criticise the cult of bloodshed in the writings of nationalist icons like Pearse. Some people wondered if the IRA bombers were not Pearse's spiritual children. Had the Catholic school system produced a generation that hated Protestants? The process of self-examination was not in itself anti-Catholic but it inevitably encouraged a greater distance from the Church and dovetailed with a new tendency to champion the rights of the state against the Church and to decry clericalism.

Part of the soul-searching sprang from a premature and unrealistic belief, encouraged by O'Fiaich, and by the *Irish Times*, that Britain was about to withdraw unilaterally from the North. The expectation contained more wishful thinking than substance but generated a debate about what needed to be done to accommodate the Republic's million or so future Protestant citizens. If the Protestants were going to surrender their place in the United Kingdom, secular nationalists in Ireland wanted changes to be made at home. They wanted to discuss compulsory Irish, the invocation of the Holy Trinity in the Irish constitution, the hazy 'special position' the constitution accorded the Catholic Church and the ban on laws that promoted divorce or contraception.

The reference to the Catholic Church in the Republic's constitution was scrapped in 1972 with barely a murmur of opposition. With Irish reunification round the corner, no one wanted to be seen putting spokes in that chariot. It was a curious postscript to the long reign of Archbishop McQuaid. He had wanted a greater emphasis on the Catholic Church to be incorporated into the 1937 document. Instead, his 32-year reign in Dublin concluded with the expunging of all mention of his Church from the constitution.

This symbolic change was not enough for the critics. The new liberal nationalists were not satisfied with lopping off a word here and there: they wanted substantive changes. Garret FitzGerald, Foreign Minister in the new Fine Gael/ Labour coalition, announced, in April 1976, that the state would take steps 'to eliminate legal anomalies that are damaging to respect for law and . . . remove such basis as may now exist for the charge that the Constitution and laws of the Republic are unduly influenced by the teachings of one Church'.[10] The changes were to include support for mixed-faith schools, the repeal of the articles in the constitution that forbade divorce, and reform of the laws on contraception. Nothing much happened about divorce for a while but by the end of the decade the ban on the sale of condoms had been dropped. Donal Barrington, a constitutional lawyer, voiced the complaints of Ireland's impatient liberals in 1977 when he accused the Catholic Church of creating a sectarian society that put the goal of a united Ireland beyond their reach. It was thanks to the Church, he said, that 'the law and institutions of government in 1969 were further from those appropriate to a united Ireland than they had been in 1920.'[11] He insisted the Church had forced a moral code on the South which they knew the Northern Protestants would never accept.

Dark clouds began to pass over the once rock-solid ties between the Church and Irish women. Mothers had been the props and allies of the priests for centuries. Elizabeth I's Protestant bishops had spotted the key role women played in inducing their men to withdraw from contact with the Reformed Church in the sixteenth century. Women had preceded men in withdrawing from the state Church and the hatred so many children of the time displayed towards Protestant clergymen came from their mothers. They had imbibed the Counter-Reformation with their mothers' milk.

The alliance between Irish priests and Irish women had withstood the challenge of time, but in the 1970s and 1980s this alliance for the first time began to fray at the edge. The lack of a language barrier between Ireland, England and America meant Anglo-American ideas quickly washed up on Ireland's shores. The feminist critique of Western capitalist society as an oppressive patriarchy altered the perceptions of many Irish women of their environment and focused attention on those parts of the 1937 constitution relating to the family, especially Article 41:2, which stated a woman's place was within the home and that 'the state should therefore endeavour to ensure that mothers shall not be obliged by economic necessity to engage in labour to the neglect of their duties in the home'. Women were changing their attitudes. Edna O'Brien's 1960 novel, *The Country Girls*, had damaged the old image of the Irish Catholic woman as a 'shy colleen' possessed of a very modest appetite for, and expectation of, sex. The books horrified Archbishop McQuaid, who gave a copy of *The Country Girls* to the rising Fianna Fáil politician and future Prime Minister, Charlie Haughey. Haughey, whose vocabulary was notoriously colourful, made appropriate noises of disgust. 'Like so many decent Catholic men with growing families, he was just beaten by the outlook and descriptions,' McQuaid recorded naively.[12] O'Brien was something of a pattern for a new brand of Irish womanhood, even if she was in exile in Britain. Her publicity photographs did not show her looking meekly downwards or coyly to one side but staring straight back at the camera. She was a woman who visibly revelled in her sexuality and who obviously did not conform to the prescribed models of shy virgin, or serene mother. Her books were, naturally, banned at home. But the O'Brien version of Irish womanhood gained increasing acceptance over the older, Catholic model.

A growing number of women had jobs. In the 1970s and 1980s the percentage of women in the workforce rose from about a quarter to one-third of the total. The state acknowledged the impact this change had on the workplace, and in 1973 the Fine Gael/Labour coalition began introducing legislation to improve women's status. The government set up a council on the status of women and in 1974 it passed an Act against discrimination in pay, followed three years later by another Employment Equality Act and an Unfair Dismissals Act. The first Minister for Women followed suit in 1982, and in 1985 Ireland signed the United Nations convention on the elimination of all forms of discrimination against women.

With its eternal message about the joys of hearth and home, the Church began to look out of step with the progress of women in Irish society. While Ireland's secular institutions accommodated themselves to women's changing expectations, the Church remained a society of middle-aged men. Even among the Church's most loyal supporters, the feminist analysis of male chauvinism was beginning to have an impact. Even nuns began to complain that the Church was excessively male dominated and had ignored women's contribution. When it came to a test of strength in 1983, with the first referendum on divorce, the Church found it could still rely on the majority. But as child abuse scandals began to rock the Church a decade later, many women began to see it as an enemy.

Women were not the only problem area for the Church in the 1980s. Another was youth. If the Church was starting to lose its old cosy alliance with women, it was facing an even worse crisis of confidence with young people. Philip Fogarty, author of *Why Don't They Believe Us?*, wrote that the younger generation in Ireland was fast drifting out of the Church's orbit. They prayed only in times of panic, found the Eucharist 'meaningless and boring'[13] and saw confession as 'a non-starter'. It was pretty familiar stuff for any Church in any European country, but it was not until the early 1990s that the Catholic Church in Ireland really alerted itself to the defection of the younger generation.

The sea-change in public attitudes towards homosexuality was another sign of a silent revolt against the Catholic Church's right to set the rules on sexual behaviour. Homosexuality had been an invisible presence in Holy Ireland. No one referred to it. Kate O'Brien's 1941 novel *The Land of Spices* had contained a passage in which the heroine saw her father in 'an embrace of love' with another man; this had ensured that the book was banned. Protestant Dublin had produced an infamous homosexual in the shape of Oscar Wilde, but before the 1960s, few Irishmen took pride or notice of their country's connection with him. Public ignorance about homosexuality was so complete that a certain kind of flamboy-antly camp queen found Ireland the ideal backdrop. Behaviour went undetected or misinterpreted in Ireland which would have attracted harsher, more knowing glances in Britain. The dramatist Micheál MacLiammóir wore makeup off stage and on and lived for decades with his male partner Hilton Edwards in south Dublin without raising an eyebrow. The repressive nature of Irish Catholic society provided cover for a homosexual who was willing to remain silent about his real orientation. Rouged, dyed and powdered, MacLiammóir flounced around Dublin and went to his grave in 1978 without breathing a word in public about his sexuality. Official Ireland might have left it at that. Instead, President Hillery made the remarkable gesture at his funeral of publicly commiserating his partner. 'I'm sorry for your trouble, Hilton,' he said, employing a form of words traditionally bestowed on grieving widows. It was a small but significant gesture and in the 1980s the laws on homosexuality ceased to be enforced, although decriminalisation did not take place until 1993.

The Church too seemed increasingly alien from the *Zeitgeist* in the 1980s. Until then, its reputation as the patron of the Gaelic revival had been secure, based on the role of countless clergy and bishops in promoting the Gaelic League and the Gaelic Athletic Association over many decades. The GAA was one of the great pillars of post-1922 society in the South, along with Fianna Fáil and the Church itself. Its ethos was profoundly Catholic, bishops were *ex officio* presidents and its most famous stadium in Dublin, Croke Park, was named after the famous nationalist Archbishop.

But the upsurge in interest in Ireland's pre-Christian Gaelic culture threatened the Church's reputation as the guardian of all things Gaelic. As the censorship system crumbled away, inquisitive intellectuals began delving deeper into the field of sexually explicit Gaelic literature, which the Gaelic League had suppressed out of deference to the Church's sensibilities. Suddenly, it began to be suggested that the Catholic Church had crushed the life out of Gaelic Ireland, instead of reviv-ing it. It had helped to kill off the native culture by pasteurising it, rendering it dreary and puritanical. The new historical fashion was to present pagan Irish society as sexually liberated and egalitarian towards women. Catholic Ireland, especially in its post-famine, post-Cullen, incarnation, was portrayed as frumpish, dumpy and repressive. It was not even a native phenomenon, apparently. The trend now was to portray 'modern' Catholicism as a grim fusion of fussy conti-nental French and Italian devotions with Anglo-Saxon Puritanism. The idea rapidly gained currency that the Catholic Church had robbed the Irish people of an older, freer, more authentic, way of life, in which sex had been almost guilt free.

If the clergy had united in defence of the Church, the argument might have been more nuanced. But no group in society agreed with the Church's most caustic critics more than the disappointed clerical children of the Second Vatican Council. When Brendan Hoban, a priest in Killala diocese, said: 'The media have declared open season on us', he appeared to revel in this state of affairs. 'We are presented variously as a motley band of power-hungry semi-politicians, manipulators of civil legislation, self-appointed moral policemen, and latterly closet sexual deviants,' he said in the early 1990s.[14] Hoban likened the Irish Catholic Church to a vast ship that was sinking in the harbour before a huge audience. 'Around us are crafts trying to navigate the choppy waters, some waving cheerfully from the deck, others releasing torpedoes under water, still others cajoling, patronising, criticising, and the occasional female crew drawing alongside offering to help us integrate our sexuality.'

Clergy like Hoban filled the columns of the *Furrow, Studies* and the Dublin diocesan magazine *Intercom*, not to mention the secular press, with indignant and sarcastic analysis. Often they seemed engaged in a competition to find the best and most demeaning metaphors to encapsulate the Church's troubles. It was a sinking ship, or a burnt-out volcano, or a dinosaur, or even the *Titanic*. These were the young clergy of the Vatican Council, now middle aged and, in some cases, furious about what they saw as their wasted years.

The Religious orders were the first to feel the chilly wind of decline. Before the Vatican Council they had been the Church's favourite sons and daughters. The council fathers took this status away. They wanted to correct the perceived evils of clericalism by restoring the status of the laity. As Tom Cahill, a priest at Maynooth put it, 'Opting for religious life to derive still more abundant fruit from the grace of baptism seems to be self-seeking . . . and condoning such vested interests implies a God with favourites.'[15] The concept of God having favourites was out. The Council distinguished between two types of religious life, the monastic and enclosed life, and the active religious life – and aimed for a renewal of both types. What happened was that the active orders cast off their old vestments and, in many cases, their old convictions. There was no revival. Instead, many brothers and sisters felt uncertain what the religious life now meant. 'Everybody now knows it is not necessary to join us to make a commitment to serve the Church,' Sister Helena O'Donoghue, told *Intercom*. 'So what are we for?'[16]

No one really knew the answer. In the decade after the Council the orders experimented with new lifestyles and activities, breaking up the old, large communities and in some cases going to live in blocks of flats and engaging in social work. By the early 1980s it was obvious that the change had not attracted a new generation into the ranks. Individual nuns, like Stanislaus Kennedy, gained national respect for their work with the homeless but this respect did not translate into recruits. The Religious orders got smaller and older. The decline had enormous implications in Ireland. Since Cardinal Cullen's time, the orders had jealously guarded their right to supervise the nation's welfare, health and education. Irish Catholics did not only encounter the clergy at Sunday mass in a church, they met them in the schoolroom from Monday to Friday and in hospital when they were giving birth, or when they were sick or dying.

By the 1980s the empire of the Irish orders was slipping out of their hands as falling numbers made the burden of sustaining a welfare state impossible. To the new generation in Ireland, born in the 1960s and 1970s, nuns and monks would be much more distant figures than they had been to their parents. They might be a headmaster or headmistress seen on a distant platform. Most often they would be old people, occasionally encountered on the street. In 1992 Tony Flannery made a grim prediction: 'In 15 years' time,' he said, 'the Religious will be a small group of people occupied with the following tasks: caring for large groups of infirm men and women; closing apostolates; selling off convents; dealing with teachers and nurses in off-loading schools and hospitals; coping with Religious whose lives have disintegrated; digging up cemeteries.'[17] It was a terrifying prospect. But by 2000 it appeared largely to have come true.

As the Church's life blood dribbled away, men and women of conservative opinions began to fear an all-out secular assault on what they thought of as the Irish way of life. Opposition to any relaxation of the ban on abortion was the issue that rallied them. Like the civil rights movement in the 1960s, it was an American import. The Society for the Protection of the Unborn Child (SPUC) arrived in Ireland from the United States, via Britain, in 1980 and in April 1981 a home-grown body devoted to pressing for a constitutional amendment in Ireland, the Pro-Life Amendment Campaign (PLAC), launched its campaign.

The Irish political establishment responded to the sudden rise of this lobby group by agreeing to insert an amendment to the constitution, tightening up any remaining loopholes. SPUC and PLAC had no direct connection to the Catholic hierarchy but their message enthused the Catholic bishops and put both main political parties on the defensive. Neither Fine Gael nor Fianna Fáil wanted to forfeit the electoral support of such a powerful and well-organised special interest group and both entered a bidding war for PLAC's backing.

The Fianna Fáil government put forward the wording of a proposed amendment on abortion on 2 November 1982. The formula was: 'The state acknowledges the right to life of the unborn and with due regard to the equal right to life of the mother guarantees in its law to respect and as far as practicable by its laws to defend and vindicate that right.' However, the government fell only days later and in January 1982 Garret FitzGerald, now Fine Gael leader, became Prime Minister in coalition with the Labour Party's Dick Spring. FitzGerald immediately tried to wriggle out of the commitment to an amendment, partly because his Labour allies were the Irish party least reactive to Church pressure. At the same time, Peter Sutherland, the Attorney-General, alerted FitzGerald to ambiguities and pitfalls in the amendment's current wording. The new government tried to sell a vaguer, alternative form of words to the Dáil, but failed. Not even all the Fine Gael members supported the new phraseology, while Fianna Fáil members naturally rallied to their original formula. The Dáil voted to keep the old wording and set a date for the nation to vote on the issue on 7 September 1983.

The campaign was bitter and divisive, pitting Catholics against liberal Catholics and Protestants. Ray Kavanagh, chairman of the anti-amendment campaign, urged all the churches to stay out of the fray, but the priests were having none of that. At Rochestown, in County Cork, at a mass celebrated by the papal nuncio Gaetano Alibrandi, the preacher Sean Cunningham compared the vote to the Battle of Lepanto in 1571, when the Christian Spanish vanquished the Muslim Turks and saved Europe from invasion.[18] Father Cunningham's sermon set the tone. On 16 August the Bishop of Kerry, Kevin McNamara, claimed to have spotted a powerful pro-abortion clique in the ranks of the anti-amendment people 'with powerful backing in the media and very substantial support from the international pro-abortion movement'.[19] Defeat, he warned, would lead to abortion on demand. The Archbishop of Cashel and the Bishop of Raphoe spoke mostly in a similar vein. At Knock shrine the Bishop of Elphin urged the nation to 'support the absolute rights of God and of the unborn child, since abortion is an abominable crime'.[20] Some priests used language that was so graphic that members of their flock complained of feeling sick. At Sligo, a priest at Sunday mass on 31 July described the spectre of unborn foetuses being shredded with hooked knives with such force that some people walked out of church.[21] Other clergy told their congregations that their chances of getting to heaven depended on their voting 'yes' to the abortion amendment. The papal nuncio announced he would offer midnight mass in the course of a 24-hour vigil against abortion to be held in the south Dublin suburb of Stillorgan.

The hierarchy released a statement on 22 August 1983 that tried to undo some of the damage caused by the clergy's more extreme statements. The bishops conceded that not all their opponents were necessarily 'pro' abortion, but insisted that the faithful must vote for the amendment. 'The direct taking of innocent human life is always gravely wrong,' they said. 'We are convinced that a clear majority in favour of the amendment will greatly contribute to the continued protection of unborn human life in the laws of our country.'[22] FitzGerald was furious. It was 'a remarkable excursion by the bishops into the field of constitutional law in the course of which they clearly had no qualms about flatly contradicting the view of the Attorney-General'.[23]

The issue divided the churches. The Protestants disliked being tarred as pro-abortionists and although they were fewer than ever in number, they were bolder than they had been in the 1920s in the arguments over divorce and censorship. They were adamant that legislation on abortion ought to be the prerogative of the Irish legislature, the Oireachtas, and had no place in the constitution.

A day after the Catholic hierarchy threw its support behind PLAC the Church of Ireland insisted that the vote must be a matter of conscience. The amendment, it said, 'will not alter the human situation as it exists in the country, contribute to its amelioration, or promote a responsible and informed attitude to the issue of abortion'.[24] The *Church of Ireland Gazette* insisted that whole business had more than a whiff of sectarianism about it. 'It has profoundly shaken many members of Protestant churches in their confidence of the separation of Church and State . . . there has been a nasty smell of the early 1950s about the whole business.'[25] The Dublin Council of Churches, which represented all the main Protestant groups in the capital, agreed, but went further, saying it was 'profoundly disturbed' by what it called PLAC's 'uncaring attitude to women'.[26]

Victor Griffin, Dean of Christ Church, was one of the few Protestant clergy to campaign actively for the anti-amendment movement, addressing a rally at New Ross, County Wexford, and insisting forthrightly that he believed a mother's life took priority over that of the child she carried. Ireland, he said, had to choose between republicanism and confessionalism.

In the final days before the vote the atmosphere became more poisonous than ever. The newspapers denounced Griffin as a Paisleyite and an Orangeman who had upheld Protestant bigotry in his native Ulster and had deliberately sabotaged the career prospects in Derry of the popular SDLP leader, John Hume.[27] It was a fabrication, which typified the direction that the campaign was taking. PLAC convenor Teresa O'Reilly detected the hand of a 'pro-British' element in the opposition camp.[28] The Catholic bishops pumped out pastorals urging a 'yes' vote. On the other side, bitter jokes circulated which likened the PLAC to the IRA. They were carrying 'a Carmelite in one hand and a ballot box in the other', the 'no' people joked. The Labour Party chairman Michael Higgins charged the Catholic hierarchy with a massive abuse of their authority. Fine Gael's Monica Barnes complained of a war conducted from the pulpits.

On the day of the vote, the Catholic bishops and the PLAC decisively defeated FitzGerald, the liberal Catholics, the *Irish Times* and the Protestants. On a relatively low turnout of 53.67 per cent, 60.45 per cent voted for the amendment. The west crushed the east and the country overrode the city. The 'no' campaign did best in the old Pale counties of Dublin, Kildare and Wexford and fared reasonably well in Cork city, Galway city and County Wicklow. But the 'yes' vote swept the board in the Ulster border counties of Cavan, Monaghan and Donegal, in the western counties of Mayo and Roscommon and in Kerry and Tipperary in the south.

The campaign did not divide the population on watertight confessional lines. Robert Townsley, Protestant Dean of Ross, urged a 'yes' vote, while a couple of risky Catholic priests, such as Martin Cogan, a Dominican friar in Tallaght, Dublin, and Finbarr Healy, the Dublin Redemptorist preacher, urged a 'no' vote. The 12 per cent of Donegal voters who were Protestant, and in many cases Orangemen, voted 'yes', alongside their Catholic neighbours. The Galway West constituency, which had next to no Protestants, produced a substantial 'no' vote of 35.61 per cent.

It was not the Protestants but liberal or secular Catholics who emerged from the referendum with the biggest grudge against the Catholic hierarchy. The tiny Protestant community had no hope or ambition to shape Ireland's agenda. The liberal metropolitan Catholics did. They felt tomorrow belonged to them and fiercely resented the Church for postponing their inevitable take-over. The columnist Mary Holland took away memories of rosary-waving fanatics, holding banners that read 'murderer' and screaming at them at rallies[29] and stored away the bellicose comments of the bishops. The liberal Catholics retired into their tents and brooded over this setback. 'The groups promoting this legislation have promoted what never existed before,' the Dáil deputy, John Kelly, warned on the day of the referendum. 'That is, a large secular platform from which in the future repeated attacks will be launched.'[30] It was an accurate prediction, though the liberals would suffer another referendum defeat in 1986 on proposals to permit divorce before Kelly's prediction was fulfilled. The modernisers were defeated but unbowed by the votes against abortion and divorce. They talked of a 'new partition' of Ireland – this time between liberals and conservative Catholics. But for all the talk of partition, they assumed Ireland would be reunified before long and on their terms.

The presidential election of 1990 was the most highly charged since the office was created. The post had always been held by a Fianna Fáil nominee. The president exercised purely symbolic functions, which meant there had never been much controversy over – or interest in – the occupant of the old Viceregal Lodge in Phoenix Park. But that changed when the Labour Party nominated Mary Robinson as their candidate against the presumed Fianna Fáil shoo-in, Brian Lenihan, and Fine Gael's Austin Currie. Robinson, the daughter of a wealthy Catholic family in County Mayo, became the mascot of all the forces who had fought – and lost – the referendum battles of the 1980s. She was a woman, for one thing. She was married to a Protestant. But there had been Protestant presidents before, and none had ruffled any feathers. Robinson's career, on other hand, was like a red rag waved at the Holy Catholic Irish bull. From the start of her political life in the early 1970s, when she became Ireland's youngest senator, she championed bills proposing to end the ban on contraception. She had been involved in the first environmentalist protests against developers in Dublin in 1979, when plans to rebuild the historic Wood Quay area of the city ignited the country's first 'green' protest. She had consistently supported homosexual law reform. She was sympathetic to Northern Protestants, so much so that she resigned from the Labour Party in 1985 in protest against its support for the 1985 Anglo-Irish Agreement, which she believed rode roughshod over Unionist sensibilities. In short, she was a homo-loving, poppy-wearing, woman president in the making and it seemed an absurdity that she could win, especially after the unguarded statements she made in the course of her campaign. When the Dublin listings magazine *Hot Press* asked if she would lend her support to the opening of a stall in a music shop selling contraceptives, she simply answered 'Yes.' She attacked what she called the 'whole patriarchal, male-dominated presence of the Catholic Church' and said it was 'an awful pity the Catholic Church hasn't grasped the importance of being on the side of equality and opportunity'.[31] She said she would like to see a woman Pope. Was she even a Catholic? Her answer to the *Enniscorthy Echo* was evasive. 'I am not a non-practising Catholic,' she said, whatever that meant.[32]

The idea that any person holding views like that, and with a record like that, might win in straight competition with Fianna Fáil seemed improbable and the general wisdom was that her *Hot Press* interview in October had torpedoed the Left's chances. But when it came to the vote on 7 November, New Ireland won and the old Holy Ireland went down to defeat for the first time. Robinson took 47.5 per cent of the vote in comparison to 39 per cent for Lenihan. The victor attributed her astonishing triumph to women. It was 'the women of Ireland – mna na hEireann – who instead of rocking the cradle, rocked the system', she said.

The presidential election of 1990 was a milestone in the history of the decay of Catholic Ireland. The powerlessness of the Irish president was irrelevant: what mattered was that in a head count, that constellation of restive forces loosely bracketed as 'New Ireland' had for the first time outvoted the old. The city had for the first time tipped the scales against the country and for all the fact that she came from Mayo, it was a victory of east over west, and Dublin over the rest. Secular, liberal, agnostic Ireland had beaten Catholic Ireland. Her Aunt Ivy may have been a nun, but no faithful conservative Catholic could possibly entertain the illusion that this President would 'repose at the feet of his Holiness', as Costello had offered to do in 1948.[33]

Robinson's election triumph set the scene for the battle over the 1983 constitutional amendment. Liberals had been waiting for the case that would expose what they saw as its folly, and it duly presented itself at Christmas 1991. The case concerned a 14-year-old girl, known for legal reasons simply as X, who had been repeatedly raped by the father of a friend since the beginning of the year and who became pregnant as the result of non-consensual intercourse in December. The girl's parents decided the foetus should be aborted and on 4 February went to England. The purpose of the journey was not kept a secret and after the Gardaí informed the Director of Public Prosecutions, Harry Whelehan, the Attorney-General, issued an injunction prohibiting the termination of the pregnancy.

The family returned immediately to Ireland amid a blaze of media publicity without having accomplished anything. The question was now whether the girl was entitled to leave Ireland and terminate the pregnancy or not. On 17 February the High Court ruled that she was not entitled, and Justice Declan Costello forbade girl X from leaving Ireland for a period of nine months. A thrill of horror ran down the collective backbone of liberal Ireland as the entire secular coalition mustered itself for a bellow of outrage. The *Irish Times* was incandescent. The newspaper compared the Republic of Ireland to Nicolae Ceaucescu's prison-like regime in Romania,[34] while a cartoon entitled 'Internment in Ireland' depicted a girl holding a toy, trapped behind a high barbed wire fence that ran around the Irish frontier.

The Fianna Fáil government was hugely embarrassed. They did not want to be associated with a hate-filled, Brit-filled word like 'internment' or be thought of as a bunch of callous men who had placed a ball and chain around the feet of an abused teenager. The ruling was the work of a secular judge interpreting the law of the state. The Catholic hierarchy remained in the background. But the spotlight of public opinion inevitably descended on the Church more than it did on the judiciary. Who had saddled the Republic with a law that resulted in this ludicrous affair? Why, the Church! Liberals and some Protestants were not slow in recalling the bitter words of the referendum campaign and all the foolish comments of 1983 were raked up. However much they shrank back in the shadows, the bishops could not escape the liberals' righteous indignation. They were held responsible for the whole wretched amendment. The bishops had set themselves up as constitutional experts, Garret FitzGerald reminded them, contrasting what he saw as the calm wording of the Vatican's 1974 declaration on abortion with the 'strident utterances of some self-appointed lay Catholic spokesmen on this issue'.[35]

The few clerical interventions into the furore over X's case were disastrous. The best known was that of Michael Cleary, the popular Dublin priest who had carried out an extraordinarily successful ministry among the poor of Dublin's grim housing estates, in Finglas. He was the priest who had warmed up the crowds at the Pope's youth mass in Galway in 1979 and who in the 1980s had exemplified the successful and uniquely Irish marriage of conservative theology and left-wing politics. But he tripped up over the abortion row. On *The Late Late Show*, Cleary suggested the family could have got on with the abortion without responding quite so precipitately to the Attorney-General's injunction and returning to Ireland. The X case affair had been 'got up', he said, in order to 'test' the 1983 amendment.[36] Critics of the amendment were quick to point out the implications of the priest's remark, which appeared to advocate hypocrisy as well as accusing girl X's family of being cunning actors in a sinister liberal plot.

Cleary did not mean that. He was simply expressing his anger at the way the case was being used to tar what he saw as a perfectly good law. But the damage was done and the Church, in the person of one of its favourite sons, had been heard to endorse abortions – as long as they were done on the sly in England. Cleary entered the lists as an enemy of the liberals, and they remembered his intervention.

Another blunder followed from Jeremiah Newman, the eccentric Bishop of Limerick. Newman was a conservative intellectual whose harsh views published in cold print belied an essentially kind nature. At a confirmation service, Newman criticised the Protestant contribution to the abortion debate, saying that 'no issue was absolutely right or wrong' for them.[37] A few years previously such a remark would have gone totally unnoticed; it was hardly a declaration of war, but in the polarised climate engendered by the abortion row the newspapers seized on this evidence of Church bigotry.

Much to the government's relief, girl X's parents appealed to the Supreme Court against Justice Costello's ruling on 20 February. The agony for the Church and the government ended six days later when the Supreme Court, under Chief Justice Thomas Finlay, overturned the ruling and lifted the travel injunction. The Catholic Church released the briefest and most neutral of statements. Far from complaining, the bishops seemed relieved that the Supreme Court had got them off the hook, commenting that 'it can only be a matter of satisfaction that the legal issues in this case have been resolved with the minimum of delay'.[38]

But the bitterness did not end there. The Church would not let the issue alone. Desmond Connell, the new Archbishop of Dublin, issued a pastoral letter linking the growth of permissiveness on abortion to Nazism,[39] while one of the lay champions of the Church, Don Lydon, a Fianna Fáil senator, said the Supreme Court had 'spat in the face of Christ'.[40]

The Church-baiters, gathered round those twin peaks of secular Ireland, RTE and the *Irish Times*, seized happily on this ludicrous language, highly inappropriate when used by the Church, which had not been in the forefront of the campaign against either Nazism or Fascism. The more the Catholic Church lashed out blindly, the more they danced nimbly out of range and parried the blows. The *Times* columnist, Fintan O'Toole, one of the high priests of the liberal elite, teased the bishops over the implications of their statements. Why were they not at the airports questioning women over their reasons for travelling abroad, he mocked? Why was the Irish army not bombing abortion clinics in London?[41]

The opponents of the amendment felt the wind of public opinion in their sails. Newspapers reported polls in which 60 per cent backed either an alteration to the ban on abortion, or its removal. A growing number of people, said FitzGerald, saw the Catholic Church 'in an increasingly negative light'.[42] It was anti-intellectual, he said, tarnished by association with its extreme lay supporters and vaguely associated in the public mind with the violence in the North. When the hierarchy delegated Bishop Joseph Duffy to give an extensive interview to RTE on their position over abortion, RTE made use of the interview to humiliate the Church by not airing a minute of it.[43] The bishops were apoplectic, but there was nothing to be done.

The fallout over the abortion row of the spring of 1992 was a test for both Catholic primates. Cardinal O'Fiaich had died on a pilgrimage to Lourdes, his favourite shrine, in 1990, raising a cackle from Paisley, whose old newspaper, the *Protestant Telegraph*, had been full of stories about people who died or went insane after they visited shrines or received papal blessings. Cahal Daly had been installed in Armagh on 16 December, less than a fortnight after Robinson's inauguration as President in Dublin. So there were new men in Church and state, or rather, a new man and a new woman. Daly brought a striking a change of mood to Patrick's see, as O'Fiaich had done. An elf-like figure, with twinkling eyes and an otherworldly mien, he contrasted very favourably in the eyes of most Protestants with his predecessor. O'Fiaich had been very earthbound, rooted in the clammy soil of his beloved south Armagh. It was possible to imagine him wielding a machine-gun. Daly seemed to inhabit a higher plane and carried with him the pure oxygen of the cloister. He offered a more theological leadership, with less of the old tribal and racial overtones. He dropped the bald appeals for the British to 'get out' of Ireland and told Catholics that the challenge to unity was not the British military presence but the fears of a million Irish people. Daly said the real unfinished business of which Republicans spoke was to persuade Northern Protestants that their future home was Ireland.[44]

In every sense, Daly's promotion to Patrick's see was timely. O'Fiaich, a scholarly historian, would have been confused by the issues that confronted the Church in the 1990s, and which could not be solved by appeals to blood, bones, history and Irish unity. Daly's cautious, delicate and febrile mind seemed to suit the demands of the times. But the new Primate of All Ireland was wrong-footed by events. He wanted to be a peacemaker between the two tribes in Ulster, about which he knew a great deal. Instead, he found himself dragged almost weekly into a very different war in the South about which he knew little. He was less deft at handling the secular Catholics of the Republic than the gritty Protestants of the North or, for that matter, the southern Protestants. The man who ought to have been the best loved Irish primate since MacRory found himself stumbling over one issue after another, as his Church was dragged down into the gutter by a series of revelations that became known simply as 'the scandals'.

On 7 May 1992 Ireland woke up to the news that Eamon Casey, Bishop of Galway, had resigned. A front-page story in the *Irish Times* said the Bishop had travelled to Rome over the weekend to tender his resignation 'for personal reasons' and that he intended, as he put it, to 'to devote the remainder of my active life to work on the missions'.[45] The sudden departure of the most popular member of the hierarchy was surprising enough, but the newspaper hinted that more momentous revelations were in store. It referred to reports that the Bishop had paid $115,000 over a number of years 'to a woman in Connecticut' and it said the unnamed woman had instructed a firm of Dublin solicitors to initiate proceedings against the Bishop in the summer of 1991.

The reports shocked and confused the public. If any bishop seemed to point the way towards a successful pattern of future ministry, that man was Casey. During the 1980s his brand of left-wing politics and conservative theology – like that of his friend, Father Cleary – provided the model for reconciling church teaching with the needs of a fast-modernising, youth-orientated society. Like Cleary, he had a commanding physical presence. Cleary was a vast man, his big head made even bigger by a shaggy mop of curly hair. His huge hands were stained yellow from the cigarettes that he chain-smoked. Casey made up for his lesser stature in girth. He looked like a Hollywood image of Friar Tuck: rotund, good humoured, and – like Cleary – thoroughly masculine.

Casey did not soft-pedal the thornier points of Catholic moral teaching but he conveyed the strong impression that he was the kind of man who understood the ways of the world and the pitfalls that befell Christians composed of flesh and blood. As Ireland's youngest bishop – he was 42 when he was appointed to his native Kerry in 1969 – he had scrapped the ban on Saturday night dances in church halls. At the same time, he fought for the development of the Shannon airport near Limerick. There was nothing parochial, retiring or introverted about Casey. He had worked in England, pioneering the creation in 1968 of Shelter, an organisation set up to help the homeless, and in Ireland in the 1970s he had chaired the Catholic Church's Third World development agency, Trocaire. He cajoled the government over its aid to the world's poorest countries. His episcopal hero was Oscar Romero, the left-wing Archbishop of El Salvador who was assassinated by right-wing terrorists in 1980. He urged Ireland to break off relations with the United States in protest against its involvement in that country's civil war. He was not afraid of challenging Ireland's traditional pro-Americanism and when Ronald Reagan visited Ireland in 1984 he refused to meet him.

Among a people who took fierce pride in their rebellions, Casey struck a chord. He embodied a long tradition in Ireland and stirred distant memories of bishops like MacHale and Croke, who had combined doctrinal loyalty to Rome with the pursuit of radical politics at home. No one had forgotten the sight of his rotund figure on the platform in Galway when the Pope had visited Connacht in 1979, or the fact that he believed 'any clergyman with more than four figures in the bank has lost the faith'.[46]

Within 24 hours of the news of Casey's resignation, the vague details about 'a woman in Connecticut' had been firmed up. The name of 44-year-old Annie Murphy, of Ridgefield, Connecticut, had entered the public domain, along with that of her son, Peter, now 17, whose features bore a marked resemblance to those of the Bishop of Galway.

The first reaction of the public to the news of Bishop Casey's plight was over-whelmingly sympathetic. His work with the travelling community, battered wives and the homeless commanded respect. His love of a drink, and the fact that he had been caught driving under the influence of alcohol in England, commanded affection. If he had been one of those thin-lipped, skull-faced, anathematising bishops, the whole scandal might have played very differently. But what people remembered about Casey was his humanity. Now it appeared that he was, indeed, all too human.

Within 48 hours of the story breaking, the wave of public sympathy for Casey began to turn. As Ms Murphy began presenting her side of the story to the news-papers, a picture emerged of Bishop Casey as not merely human but deceitful, selfish and hypocritical. He was a man who had been determined to sacrifice the happiness of the child he had fathered to save his episcopal career. Ms Murphy claimed the Bishop had tried bullying her into giving up her child for adoption, saying it would bring her closer to God. He had shouted and waved adoption papers in her face. Fortunately, the Bishop had not tried to persuade Murphy to have an abortion.

Hard on the heels of her revelation came the question of where the money had come from. In the initial wave of sympathy for Casey no one had bothered to ask where a man on a bishop's salary, a man moreover who believed no Christian should have more than four figures in the bank, could have found $115,000. On 10 May Emmanuel Garada, the papal nuncio, told the press it would be 'useful' to know where Casey had found the cash. Casey replied with an eight-paragraph statement admitting he had authorised payment of £70,669.20 IR as a loan 'to a third party' from Galway's diocesan funds. He had repaid the loan, he said, but only after his resignation.

The scandal of Bishop Casey punctured the ecclesiastical balloon at a very inopportune moment. Days before it broke the Catholic hierarchy had been piling pressure on the government to hold another referendum on abortion prior to Ireland's accession to the Maastricht Treaty, which the bishops feared might open up new avenues for judicial appeals in Europe against the 1983 constitutional amendment. The revelations of the Bishop of Galway's sex life knocked the whole campaign sideways. The bishops were totally uncoordinated. Brendan Comiskey, Bishop of Ferns, had known of the affair back in Holy Week and it was Comiskey who had informed the papal nuncio on 1 May. What was extraordinary was that neither the nuncio nor the Bishop of Ferns had seen fit to warn Primate Daly of the coming explosion for another four days, while the rest of the hierarchy only got wind of the affair when they watched the news on RTE.[47] The *Irish Times*, by contrast, had been sitting gleefully on the story since mid-January, when Murphy's companion, Arthur Pennell, first contacted the paper's Washington correspondent, Conor O'Clery, over Casey's paternity. The *Irish Times* and RTE were able to ride into the story with all guns blazing. The Catholic Church, by contrast, looked almost painfully disorganised. It was payback time for Ireland's liberals and the assorted enemies of the Catholic Church, and few of the snubbed politicians, humiliated writers, ignored women, feminists, gays, left-wing intellectuals and journalists wanted to pass up the opportunity to harpoon the whale.

The Casey affair left the Church winded and wounded. There was a palpable loss of prestige among the bishops. People now looked at them with different eyes – with Annie Murphy's eyes. To be a bishop had been to belong to a mysterious category of humanity. But Murphy's partner had filmed Bishop Casey arguing with his ex-lover in a New York hotel over their son. She had told him over the telephone afterwards that if he did not shape up she was going to come over to Galway and 'pull his damn hat off'. His hat? Bishops wore mitres, exotic emblems that marked them out as a separate caste. More than any other single dress item it was the mitre that placed the Bishop apart from the common run of humanity. Now it appeared a bishop was just another guy in a funny hat. It was all very well for the Bishop's supporters to say that the affair showed he was only human. But this was a form of defence that came with a price tag. If a bishop was just like the next man, why should anyone sit up (let alone kneel) to listen to what he had to say on abortion, Northern Ireland, or the Third World?

The interventions of bishops in Irish social and industrial affairs once commanded hushed reverence. When McQuaid had sided with strikers against the government, De Valera blanched. Now they were told to mind their own business, and the attempts of John Magee, Bishop of Cloyne, to intervene in the Irish steel dispute at Cobh in 1994 merely resulted in a snub from the unions.[48] A constant stream of niggling criticism was directed against the bishops. Archbishop

Connell was attacked for removing a popular left-wing priest from the grim Dublin suburb of Tallaght. Casey's successor in Galway, James McGoughlin, was lambasted as colourless and churchy.

But at least Casey was a regular guy. The next affair was to cause far greater shock, outrage and revulsion. This harpoon was fired from the television, not from RTE but from its northern sister, Ulster Television. It took the form of an hour-long documentary for the programme *Counterpoint*, which detailed the life and the crimes of a Belfast priest named Brendan Smyth. The Casey affair was a firecracker compared to this atomic bomb. Nothing as damaging to the Church had been seen on Irish television. Chris Moore's programme portrayed the activities of an aggressive paedophile who had terrorised and destroyed children's lives over a period of almost 40 years in two continents.

Smyth had rattled round the grim streets of west Belfast in his little car, the boot loaded with sweets, waiting until parents went out of their houses before he descended salivating on the hunt for children to molest. In the Catholic ghetto of west Belfast, people felt honoured by visits from the clergy and as a result, the door had rarely been closed to him. The ordeal for the children started with what was euphemistically described as 'tickling', but frequently ended up much, much worse. 'Don't look at me!' he was heard to roar at his battered charges as his feverish hands jabbed and fumbled away. 'Look away!'[49] In one family he abused several members – two brothers and a sister.

Smyth cherry-picked his victims from the range of schools and orphanages that he visited in his pastoral duties, such as the Nazareth House children's home on Belfast's nationalist Ormeau Road. Others were selected at mass and kept behind after the service was over. The worst violence took place on the children's holidays he organised away, where children were forced to masturbate each other as well as the priest.

The spotlight the programme shed on clerical paedophilia was disturbing enough. Worse was the revelation that children had been raped in the schools they attended, practically under the noses of the nuns and priests who were in charge of them. Smyth's abusive career had, in fact, been an open secret. These were not hidden crimes. The Catholic Church in Ireland had known all about Father Smyth for decades but when any of his victims had complained, the Church had punished them instead of the offender. One woman who was abused over a period of eight years in Nazareth House told Moore what happened when she tried to explain her predicament to a nun. 'She ripped the hair out of me and beat me over the head with a bunch of keys and made me kneel outside the door all night and pray.'[50]

Much of Smyth's abuse had taken place in the diocese of Down and Connor, where Cahal Daly had been Bishop from 1982 to 1990. But the Bishop had taken no concrete steps to have him removed on the grounds that he was a Religious and not a secular priest and therefore did not come under a bishop's jurisdiction. As a member of the Norbertine Order, Smyth was not responsible to Daly but to Kevin

Smith, the Norbertine Abbot at Ballyjamesduff, County Cavan. Instead of expelling him, Abbot Smith had shuffled Smyth around the country, at one point sending him off to Tralee, in County Kerry, to work as a hospital chaplain with unlimited access to children for several summers from 1990 to 1993. Another locum job was at the Mercy Hospital in Cork. Occasionally, Abbot Smith had sent him for therapy at institutions in Dublin, Belfast and Stroud, in Gloucestershire, in the west of England. But then he was offloaded once more on a series of unsuspecting parishes in Ireland, Wales, Rhode Island and North Dakota. Crossing the Atlantic did not help Smyth to start again. A three-year sojourn in Providence, Rhode Island, from 1965 to 1968, ended in the predictable disaster. The *Providence Journal* of 25 February 1968 wrote that Smyth would 'leave behind him the memory of a man whose love of children and lilting r's and e's brightened the town and the lives of many in it'.[51] But Moore interviewed Abbot Smyth's former secretary, Bruno Mulvihill, who claimed he had seen a letter to the Abbot from Russell McVinney, the Bishop of Providence, complaining that Smyth was being sent home after assaulting children at Our Lady of Mercy church in East Greenwich.[52] 'If this is true,' commented Fintan O'Toole, 'then awareness of Father Smyth's crimes went all the way to the heart of church power.'[53] Moore's own indictment of Abbot Smith was damning.

> For a quarter of a century Abbot Smith was Fr Smyth's religious superior, the man most likely to be aware of Fr Smyth's unnatural sexual interest in children. Yet, rather than hand him over to the forces of justice, for the most part he simply kept moving the priest around. This was in line with Church policy at the time: frequent reassignment of offenders in an effort to keep them from forming attachments to families and children.[54]

Both Abbot Smith and Father Smyth had profited from Ulster's convoluted religious politics. The police got wind of Smyth in 1990. But the fact that the overwhelmingly Protestant RUC kept out of the Republican ghetto of west Belfast meant Smyth was able to move in and out of the province undetected, shifting south of the border to Ballyjamesduff when he needed to. No wonder Father Smyth was a diehard Republican, for the stand-off between the Catholics and the British police in the province was very convenient. It was not until the spring of 1993 that the RUC pounced, signing an extradition order for Smyth's arrest in the Republic. But then nothing happened: the authorities in Dublin sat on the request for seven months. Eventually Smyth pleaded guilty to 17 charges before being sentenced to four years jail in 1994.

The IRA ended its quarter-of-a-century war with the British state at the end of August 1994 with an announcement of a complete cessation of military operations. The Loyalist paramilitaries hung back for a while but followed suit on 12 October. It was not the end of the violence in Northern Ireland. The Omagh bomb of 1998, the work of an IRA splinter group, which killed 29 people, and the battles over the Orange march in Drumcree, showed that real peace was far off. But the IRA announcement marked a sea-change in Ulster politics and was a triumph for those individuals who had been brave and far sighted enough to grasp the need to bring armed Republicans and Loyalists into a future peace settlement. The IRA had made war – famously – with a ballot box in one hand and an Armalite rifle in the other. Now they seemed to recognise they would have to settle for the ballot box on its own.

The churches were not the main factor in bringing about the cessation of warfare. The struggle had, simply, failed to drive the British out of the North. The attempt to bomb the Protestants into submission had also failed. Some areas, especially in the west and on the border, had been 'greened' but there was no mass exodus from the province. In 1992, for the first time, Loyalist killings began to outnumber Republican killings. That was the stick driving the Republicans into dialogue. The carrot was a demographic trend which suggested that a Catholic majority in Ulster early in the new century might render the war against the British state unnecessary.

Nevertheless, the churches had played an honourable role in creating the conditions that made peace between the communities possible. They had kept the idea of common humanity alive and for the most part refrained from employing the powerful symbolism at their disposal in the service of extremism. They had, for the most part, declined to give succour to gunmen or praise their deeds. In some cases they had infuriated their flocks and risked their lives by delivering anti-war sermons at terrorist funerals. Both the Catholic and Church of Ireland Primates had taken risks in urging peace on their communities. But of the two men, Daly had stepped out of line more often than Archbishop Robin Eames. The Protestant Archbishop of Armagh was a safe pair of hands, a practical, hard-headed Unionist whose patriarchal air enabled the Church of Ireland to punch above its weight throughout the years of the conflict. Eames was to endure a great deal of flak over the Drumcree dispute the following year, but he never said anything that risked offending moderate middle-class Protestants. Daly had had a more difficult job. His community had far less ballast and the middle ground was smaller. Northern Irish Catholics were almost hopelessly split between the silent 15 per cent who in most polls supported the Union with Britain and the 30 per cent who supported the IRA with all its baggage of murder and mayhem. The job of speaking for a community like that was enough to give anyone multiple personality disorder. The temptation was to retreat to the lowest common denominator and peddle milksop clichés. Instead, Daly led from the front. He constantly urged both communities to 'chance their arm' for peace, as the medieval Earl of Kildare had famously done quite literally with his Ormond rival in Dublin's St Patrick's cathedral in 1492.[55] He told the Irish-American community in Washington there would be no long-term advantage for nationalists if their concerns were addressed at the expense of all others. When Daly said the solution in Northern Ireland was to find institutions Catholics could identify with without becoming Unionists, he pinpointed an avenue that both the British and Irish governments were to explore in their peace strategy towards the divided people of the North after the IRA ceasefire.

At 77 in 1994, Cardinal Daly might have expected the tributes of a grateful nation as he eased his way towards retirement. Instead, he was to find himself constantly under media sniper fire over his handling of clerical paedophiles. He gave a disastrous interview on the subject of Smyth on RTE's news review programme *This Week* in mid-October 1994. The previous few days had brought more bad news items. Tralee General Hospital had expressed 'outrage' over the fact that Smyth's Abbot had approved his employment as a hospital chaplain. Also in October there was more trouble over an interview the former papal nuncio had given to the journalist John Cooney. The garrulous Galibrandi had clearly opened up to the avuncular-looking reporter of Scots Catholic-Irish background, unaware that Cooney was not quite the loyal son of the Church he might appear to be. Cooney had his own agenda. Five years later he produced a scabrous biography of Archbishop McQuaid. Whether it was the hot Italian sun or a glass of wine too many, Galibrandi prattled away, releasing one appalling indiscretion after another and heaping up trouble for the Church at home at the worst time possible. Galibrandi crowed into Cooney's waiting ear about the political influence he had wielded as nuncio from 1969 to 1989, savaging the record of FitzGerald's Fine Gael government in the 1980s and boasting of his decisive role in tipping the scales against him in the 1983 referendum on abortion. 'I fought very hard against Mr FitzGerald,' he said.[56]

To ordinary people the Galibrandi interview was hardly a 'scandal'. But it made waves among the politically active and infuriated all those who thought the Church enjoyed an excessive influence in Irish politics. In secular and liberal circles, FitzGerald was 'Garret the good' and the revelation that the papal nuncio had spent much of his time plotting against Ireland's elected government damaged the standing of the Church as a whole. Daly went on to RTE's *This Week* with the reports of Galibrandi's machinations hanging over his head and public fury over the Smyth scandal still running at full tilt. The only thing to do was to harness the fury and announce substantive policy initiatives aimed at ensuring such things would never happen again. Instead, the Cardinal ran for cover and explained that as Bishop of Down and Connor in the 1980s he had had no jurisdiction over Smyth. It was a technical point that experts in ecclesiastical organisation might have appreciated. Among the public at large it went down like a lead balloon. 'Children were sacrificed to keep the truth about a priest hidden,' wrote the commentator Nuala O'Faolain.[57]

The Cardinal had failed to assuage public concern and it was clear that the case was not going to end with Smyth's imprisonment in Magilligan prison in County Londonderry. Two days after the Archbishop's interview, one of Smyth's victims, now aged 22, announced she was planning legal action against the Church. The news sent a shiver down many ecclesiastical spines. In the United States, a spate of civil actions by victims of clerical abuse had brought several American Catholic dioceses to the brink of bankruptcy. The Chicago archdiocese had spent $1.9 million fending off abuse cases in 1992 alone and the Church in America had spent an estimated $500 million since the landmark jailing of Father Gilbert Gauthe, of New Orleans diocese, in 1984. Compensation claims were soon lodged by three of Smyth's victims, against Smyth, Abbot Smith and Cardinal Daly. Whatever he might say about the Abbot's jurisdiction, Smyth's victims insisted the buck stopped with the Cardinal.

The Smyth scandal opened up public debate on issues that were not going to go away. It increased the pressure on defenders of clerical celibacy and clerical authority. For many people, the two points were conflated. The revelations were an achievement of Ireland's modern secular society, not the Church, said Sean O'Conaill, a teacher in Coleraine. The clergy's claims of ignorance were 'devastatingly damaging for a Church which claimed until this event that it knew everything, especially about sex'.[58]

The trickle of clerical child abuse cases continued. Apart from Smyth, these concerned a priest in Galway, a priest of the Servite Order from County Tyrone who had pleaded guily to assaulting three 11-year-old girls, another priest from Belfast accused of assaulting nine boys aged from nine to 15 and a brother who was appealing against an 18-year sentence for the rape of six schoolboys in the west. The fear in church circles was that this trickle would turn into a flood with potentially devastating consequences for the Church's finances as well as its prestige. There were reports that at least 100 children had been abused in the church-run Madonna House residential care centre in the south Dublin suburb of Blackrock and that the Sisters of Mercy, the Order that ran the centre, was trying to suppress a hostile report by the Ministry of Health. There were claims that two priests in the diocese of Kerry had been removed as a result of child abuse allegations, and a report that a Dublin priest was to be investigated by the Director of Public Prosecutions for assaulting a 13-year-old boy in a hotel lavatory after a funeral.

On 12 November 1994 Liam Cosgrave, the 68-year-old curate of Baldoyle parish, in north Dublin, collapsed and died of a heart attack in the 'Incognito' gay sauna club in the backstreets of central Dublin. Another priest in the club had administered the last rites. If that was not embarrassing enough for Archbishop Connell, who dutifully murmured how 'shocked and saddened' he was by the media report, the club's owner handed the see of Dublin an unsolicited compliment by saying it supplied him with at least 20 of his most regular patrons.[59]

The bishops assembled in Maynooth for a meeting on 15 November in a mood of despondency. The previous day, Michael Carrey, a respected former president of St Mary's College in Gort, County Mayo, had received a 15-month suspended sentence for assaulting a hitch-hiker. The Fianna Fáil–Labour government of Albert Reynolds, meanwhile, was writhing in its death throes over the Brendan

Smyth affair. The question of why there had been a seven-month delay in dealing with the RUC's extradition warrant in April 1993 was tearing the coalition apart. The battlements of Maynooth offered the bishops no security. The seminary that had symbolised the pride and the power of Catholic Ireland for 200 years was in a state of acute financial crisis caused by falling enrolment.

Slowly the Smyth scandal died away. The Church dealt with the most serious criticism of its handling of the priest by introducing new guidelines on sexual abuse, headed by a pledge to refer all cases of suspected or alleged abuse without delay to the relevant secular authorities. But the affair left the Church with gaping wounds and following so shortly after the Casey affair, it massively impaired the Church's ability to pronounce with authority on moral and sexual issues. It did not, perhaps, undermine the average Irishman or woman's belief in God, or turn them into Protestants, but it certainly dented his or her belief in the Catholic Church as an infallible barometer of the divine will. An RTE poll in spring 1995 showed that 60 per cent of Catholics thought the Smyth affair had undermined the Catholic Church's authority on matters such as divorce and abortion. Almost the same number now favoured the ordination of women to the priesthood while 71 per cent wanted an end to the rule on clerical celibacy.[60]

The Church went into its next legislative battle with one arm tied behind its back. Also in the spring of 1995, the government announced the first step towards the repeal of the ban on abortion. The proposed bill did not countenance terminations inside the Republic of Ireland but repealed existing prohibitions on the provision of information about abortion services outside the state by Irish health authorities. The bill was plainly a front: it was an advertisement for repeal of the abortion ban in the future. As such, the information bill constituted the most direct assault on Catholic social teaching in the history of the Free State and the Republic. But with the Casey and Smyth affairs behind them, the Irish clergy proved lethargic defenders of this cornerstone of Catholic legislation. Archbishop Connell publicly led opposition to the change and the bishops' meeting at Maynooth in March 1995 produced a tough statement saying the bill was tantamount to aiding abortion. But there was no repeat of the events of 1983, when the clergy had successfully marshalled their flocks against the metropolitan liberals. Most parish priests avoided the issue altogether in their sermons on the eve of the Dáil vote on 8 March and the deputies rejected the Church's advice by nodding through the measure with a comfortable margin of 85 to 67.

Clerical abuse cases continued to drip on the Church's head throughout the summer of 1995. Most attention fell on Daniel Curran, like Smyth a northerner, who was sentenced to seven years' imprisonment on 14 June for 13 offences committed against boys in the early 1990s. As a priest in Belfast and then Ballymena, Curran had plied boys with drink and hustled them to his little cottage at Rathmullan, County Down, five miles from Downpatrick. His dismal, lonely world caved in one night in March 1994 when one of the boys had run screaming from the cottage into the arms of the neighbours, followed by another boy with a split lip. Cardinal Daly was suitably 'horrified' by the case,[61] but many people wondered out loud what kind of Church it was that offered sanctuary to such misfits. Like Smyth, Curran had been unpopular and friendless, chronically unable to relate to his peers and propelled predictably towards bouts of frantic sexual activity with minors.

The Curran scandal, like the Smyth case, seemed an indictment of a whole system as much as of one man. Under the pressure of public anger, the bishops began to break ranks and publicly dispute Rome's rulings. Comiskey of Ferns and Willie Walsh, the Bishop of Killaloe, who had already gained a reputation as someone prepared to speak forthrightly, both disputed the official line on celibacy in separate interviews in June. Walsh said ending the celibacy rule was the only way to stem the catastrophic fall in vocations that threatened to sink the entire Church. It was widely thought that the two bishops represented the tip of the iceberg and that at least two others, John Kirby of Clonfert and Laurence Ryan of Kildare, took the same line.

The celibacy row threatened to set the bishops at loggerheads with each other. Rome was annoyed by these unexpected signs of revolt from her most faithful daughter Church and the Bishop of Ferns was summoned to the Vatican for a dressing down over the remarks he had made to the media on 11 June. Cardinal Daly tried to repair the damage by making the Church's traditional teaching on celibacy the keynote of his address to pilgrims visiting Knock shrine in County Mayo on 26 June. But events tripped up the Cardinal once more. Those Knock pilgrims who made it to the village newsagent's the following morning found the front pages plastered with the news that Ireland's favourite priest had lived with a woman for 26 years and fathered a family.

Father Cleary had died at Christmas 1993 from cancer, probably brought on by his incessant smoking. A crowd of at least 1,000 had attended the funeral of the best known and possibly best loved priest of his generation, including the papal nuncio and leaders of the pro-life campaign. Father Cleary had gone to his grave with a reputation for strict theological orthodoxy and his claim that the X-case had been manipulated to test the 1983 abortion amendment was widely remembered. Now, however, it appeared that Cleary had not applied the same moral code to himself that he applied to others. The newspapers revealed that the woman many thought of as his housekeeper was the mother of his two sons, born in 1970 and 1977. Cleary's 45-year-old partner, Phyllis, recalled his justification of their odd union. 'Michael explained that in the time before Jesus there was no marriage ceremony and that this was all that was required for a man and woman to become husband and wife . . . Michael warned me that this was to be "our secret" and that no one else should know.'[62] Her book on the affair was a catalogue of horrors. When she had confessed to a priest that one of his colleagues had made her pregnant, he had apparently called her 'a lying whore'.[63] She had been forced to hand over for adoption the first baby fathered by Cleary and had been sexually assaulted by another priest in Finglas. As Michael Pollack, the *Irish Times* religious affairs correspondent noted, Cleary had been a role model. Like his friend Bishop Casey, he had been conservative in theology but pastorally sensitive. 'His passionate and even triumphant defence of the Church's hard line on contraception, abortion and divorce were a feature of the retreats he used to give to Maynooth seminarians.'

There was more embarrassment ahead for the bishops. On 17 June, Ryan of Kildare had the humiliating task of offering an official apology to the husband of Sinead Flower, of Newbridge, County Dublin, who had gone to see Patrick Henlon, 34-year-old curate of Newbridge, for marriage guidance counselling, and had come out pregnant. The child was born in August 1993.[64]

At the same time, the diocese of Down and Connor was in hot water over Alphonsus Reid, who was charged with committing offences against boys in a County Down home run by his De la Salle Order. On 3 November 1995, episcopal prestige reached an all-time low when Cardinal Daly was interrupted and heckled on *The Late, Late Show*, while defending the ban on women priests and clerical marriage. The Primate was contrite and said the scandals had made the Church 'a repentant church that realises the strength of sin within its own membership'.[65] But the studio audience was visibly hostile.

Some members of the hierarchy began to crack up over the strain. In September 1995 Bishop Comiskey of Ferns quietly slipped away from his County Wexford diocese. He had not, in the end, had to travel to Rome after the summons for his remarks on celibacy, but the Bishop was a depressed man, apparently suffering from alcohol addiction and pursued by accusations of mishandling child abuse allegations in the Ferns diocese. While the rest of the hierarchy rolled around in agony his absence was scarcely noted for weeks. But by New Year, Wexford people were asking where their bishop was. There were queries over the sale of his Dublin flat before he left for the United States and curious reports that he had been detained at Bangkok airport in a state of confused inebriation. On 17 February the Bishop staged an emotional crash landing in the diocese amid a blaze of media flashlights, another case of a church showman come to grief. Bishop Comiskey was a born communicator, popular on local radio and possessing the common touch. Whether he pulled it off on his return to Wexford was another matter, as he delivered a series of public pleas and apologies that some found heart-rending and others found excruciating. He had never stood in the way of investigations into paedophilia, he said. 'I was born in a little house in the middle of nowhere,' he said plaintively, 'and I never asked for a pedestal.'[66] How much more of this could the Church take? To the columnist John Waters, the Irish Catholic Church was going the same way as the Communist parties of Eastern Europe:

> Irish Catholicism is like a rotten tree which stands there day after day, dozing and rotting away until one day someone will think to touch it with a little finger and then . . . crash!

One day everything will be proceeding as normal – the faithful will be listening to the empty blathering from the pulpit – and the next they will open their church doors and find that no one at all wants to come in.[67]

Waters's caustic indictment was more significant than the usual pat condemnation of one of the media liberals of RTE or the *Irish Times*. Waters was a nationalist who spent much of his column inches railing at liberals for giving up on the old war against the Brits and the Prods. An admirer of the peasantry and a devotee of the Famine cult, he made no secret of his almost obsessive loathing of the chattering classes of south Dublin and their bland 'New Ireland' of pasteurised nationalism, condom machines, Chardonnay and cappuccino. If men like Waters were giving up on the Church, the priests were really in trouble.

The problem with the Church was that it was no longer in favour with either the groovy new Ireland of RTE or the grumpy old Ireland of John Waters. The nationalists yearned for the days when the Irish spat fury at the enemy over the water, crooned over their Fenian dead and shook knobbly fists at the Orange North. Mirror images of the Orangemen for whom they professed such visceral loathing, they did not want to stop history in its tracks so much as roll it back a century or three. But the Catholic Church was no longer a reliable spokesman for this constituency. The bishops were not at ease with the cappuccino drinkers, but they did not much like the ultra-nationalists either. They were too into the ecumenical gig for that. Years of trotting down to Ballymascanlan or up to Corrymeela to chat with the Protestants had made them uncomfortable with high-octane nationalism and its dripping hatred. Daly had devoted much of his adult life to trying to understand and get alongside Ulster's permanently nettled Protestants. While he was Primate there was no question of returning to the age when the Catholic cat had prowled round the Ulster cage, licking its lips at the Protestant canary twittering nervously inside. The Cardinal's insistence that a peace that left either community dissatisfied was no peace at all earned him the respect of many Irish Protestants and was one reason why the mainstream Irish Protestant churches refused to make capital out of the Catholic Church's difficulties in the 1990s. The 'scandals' pitted the Catholic clergy against their own alienated flock. They did not revive the ancient conflict with the Protestants over soul control.

While Bishop Comiskey was in rehab in America, the bishops stumbled into their next major battle. This time it was divorce. Having prised open the abortion question, the government announced a November referendum on a proposal to amend Article 40.3.2 of the constitution to enable the courts to grant a dissolution where the couple had lived apart for four years from the commencement of proceedings. Like the abortion information bill, it was a moderate change, but one that paved the way for further reform. As with abortion reform, the clergy proved lacklustre in repelling this organised attack on the Catholic elements of the 1937 constitution. There was not much unity among the bishops. Bishop

McLoughlin of Galway merely urged people to vote. Bishop Murphy of Cork said Catholics might even vote 'yes', as the poll was 'a civil matter and the state has to do what it feels is best for the people'.[68] The Bishop of Limerick told Catholics to vote 'no'. Dermot Clifford, Archbishop of Cashel, courted more ridicule than anger when he warned a congregation at Holy Cross abbey, County Tipperary, that divorcees smoked and drank more than married people and were more liable to be involved in car accidents.[69]

In the event, the muddled and sometimes foolish-sounding interventions of the clergy did the 'no' camp little good. The government got the endorsement it sought in the referendum, albeit by a wafer-thin majority of 1 per cent. Altogether, 818,841 voters supported lifting the 58-year-old ban while 809,731 voted for its retention. As in 1983, the country split on geographical lines. It was Dublin and the old Pale versus the west. Town voted against country. The capital's 10 constituencies all supported change, as did the cities of Cork and Limerick and the Pale counties of Louth, Kildare and Wicklow. It was much the same line-up of forces as in 1983, only this time the country had failed to overawe the town. To some, it was 'another serious weakening of the Catholic hierarchy's authority as the once unquestioned fount of wisdom on moral issues for most Irish people'. But it was perhaps better seen as the victory of Dublin over rural Ireland. In that sense it could be said that De Valera's Ireland was finally dead and buried.

The 'scandals' of the 1990s were a blight that affected first one part of the plant and then another. The first stages involved bishops, parish priests and the Religious orders. Thus far, a large portion of the Church's manpower, or rather womanpower, was left unaffected by the furore of Bishops Casey and Comiskey, Fathers Smyth and Curran, Brother Alphonsus and all the other lesser-known clerical miscreants. But now the great searchlight of public opinion turned towards the nuns.

The first blast of the media trumpet against the convents came from RTE in a devastating indictment of the Sisters of Mercy's management of the Goldenbridge orphanage near Dublin in the 1960s. The programme *Dear Daughter*, shown in April 1996, portrayed a regime of daily beatings and virtual starvation of the children under the care of Sister Xaviera, the Reverend Mother of Goldenbridge for a decade until her transfer in 1963 to the orphanage at Rathdrum in County Wicklow. Sister Xaviera was accused of striking one girl so hard that she had to have more than 100 stitches. She was also accused of pushing a girl into a tumble dryer and then turning it on. The onslaught on the nuns in *Dear Daughter* did not have quite the same effect as the UTV's exposé of Brendan Smyth. For one thing, some former inmates of Goldenbridge had fond memories of the Xaviera regime and the establishment of the 'Sister Xaviera Support Group' took some of the wind out of the sails of her accusers. There was no attempt to institute legal proceedings.

Nevertheless, it was the start of an open season on the nuns. It marked the beginning of an extensive media investigation of the often brutal conditions in church-run schools, orphanages, homes for single women and so-called 'industrial schools', where children from allegedly problem families were dumped in their thousands in the 1940s and 1950s. This brutality was not exactly front-page news. There was hardly an Irish writer of note who had not excoriated the Religious orders, especially the Christian Brothers, for the notorious ease with which they resorted to the whip and the cane. But the exposure of cruelty by nuns was a new issue and it was a deadly assault on the most numerous representatives and advocates of the celibate life in Irish society. *Dear Daughter* followed allegations about the Sisters of Mercy orphanage at Rathdrum, and at St Anne's, in Booterstown, south Dublin, where former inmates claimed they were forced to drink from lavatory bowls and eat from pig bins. 'They beat you senseless,' Madeline Hopkins told the press on 7 March.[70]

The nuns fumbled around to find the appropriate reaction, but by alternating between coy expressions of regret and the odd snarl of defiance, they riled a public that would settle for nothing less than total contrition. Helena O'Donoghue, Provincial of the Sisters of Mercy for the Dublin-Midlands area, tripped up even more crassly than the bishops had with Father Smyth. She was roundly roasted by the audience on RTE's radio programme, *The Pat Kenny Show*. The now-standard 'victims' hotlines' were set up. The fact was that Irish society as a whole had been harsh and punitive towards children in the 1950s and 1960s. That kind of behaviour had since become wildly unfashionable among the elite who now set the agenda in Ireland. The nuns took the rap for the whole country. By May 1996 the Sisters of Charity were embroiled in a separate row over their conduct in Madonna House in Stillorgan, south Dublin, where 15 former children were complaining of abuse, not by the nuns, but by a maintenance man in their employment.

The biggest blow to the reputation of the Sisters of Mercy involved the nuns' treatment not of children but of grown women. In 1993 the Order sold the High Park convent on Grace Park Road, near the Archbishop's palace in Drumcondra, for demolition. But when they moved out, they inadvertently called attention to the forgotten graves of 133 women lying in a small cemetery behind the convent walls. These were not the bodies of nuns but of 'maggies', unmarried women who had been sent to the convent after becoming pregnant and who in many cases had spent the rest of their lives atoning for their disgrace by working in the laundry. The word 'maggie' referred to the nickname of these institutions – Magdalen laundries, after Mary Magdalene, the prostitute whose sins Jesus forgave.

Public interest in the Magdalen laundries at first concerned only the relatives of dead 'maggies', who clamoured for the dead women to be reburied in a fitting environment. But in 1995 and 1996 as the media combed through the hitherto unexplored hinterland of the Catholic Church, its full beam turned on the prison-like regime in Ireland's dozen or so 'Magdalen laundries'. The newspapers interviewed women who said they had lived in virtual slave-labour conditions and had been separated by force from their children, who in some cases were brought up only a stone's throw away in other church-run institutions. The *Irish Times* reported on one woman who had been incarcerated in one of these institutions because she was thought too pretty, and therefore at risk. The Republican newspaper *An Poblacht* in April 1996 interviewed Patricia McDonnell, a campaigner for a memorial to the Magdalen women, who said a girl from her Galway village had been locked up in a laundry aged 16 on the orders of her parish priest simply because she was an orphan. When her brother tried to find her, McDonnell said, the priest told him she had gone to work in Dublin and was best left alone. 'When she came out nearly 20 years later she was really in quite a disgusting condition and weighed about four stone.'

The anguish over the Magdalen laundry scandal peaked after Pat Tierney, a fellow campaigner for a memorial to the women, killed himself on 4 January 1996 in Drumcondra. A victim of the harsh regime in the industrial schools, which had left him permanently scarred, he had telephoned McDonnell hours before he took his life. On Saturday, 20 April, Tierney's wish was fulfilled even though he was no longer alive to see it. A bench was dedicated to the Magdalen laundry women in Dublin's St Stephen's Green beside a magnolia tree. The metal plaque on the side read: 'To the women who worked in the Magdalen laundry institutions and to the children born to some members of those communities – reflect here upon their lives.' The Catholic Church was invited to send a representative to the ceremony, but no one came.

CHAPTER EIGHTEEN

A Family Quarrel

*It is the media, and particularly television, which brought to an end the long
19th century tradition of Irish Catholicism.*
(Tom Inglis)[1]

Clonliffe seminary in north Dublin on a winter's day at the end of the twentieth
century was a gloomy sight. Buildings that once were busy and now are virtually
empty always have a peculiarly depressing air about them, like abandoned schools,
and Clonliffe was no exception. A few decades ago those portals echoed to the
tramp of hundreds of young men's feet, bustling to and from studies, chapel and
their work placements. There was energy then, and a sense that the seminary was
a great turbine in the engine of the Irish Catholic Church. To have any part in it,
however lowly, was to have a part in the most important institution in Ireland.
That air has certainly departed from Clonliffe. Weeds have grown up through the
paths and pavements. The seminarians have gone, replaced by mature students
and trainee teachers. When I visited, the chapel was locked and a large rusting
chain bound the gates together.

Maynooth is still a functioning seminary, but the streets of the village are no
longer full of soutaned seminarians. The clerical seminary is dwarfed by the
secular university that has grown up beside it. The chapel is still open. John Healy
of Tuam preached there in 1891 on the theme of Ireland's religious destiny.
Echoing the words of Cardinal Manning, the Archbishop of the west spoke of
Catholic Ireland's divine mission to hold the lamp of faith aloft at a time when the
light seemed to be going out all over Europe. Healy said the Irish were 'a nation
that seems to have been chosen, as visibly as were the Hebrews of old, and that
mission seems to be the preservation and propagation of Catholic truth. Its work
is to preach, and if needs be, to suffer . . . '[2]

A century later, the Irish appeared to have had enough of suffering. Was this the
end of Catholic Ireland? To Mary Kenny, who wrote a book with that title, it was,
more or less, though she regretted it. The word priest, she wrote, was now
popularly associated with the word paedophile. 'A native anti-clericalism has
arisen in Ireland which is new in tone and ferocity.' Kenny cited, disapprovingly,
the scabrous remark of Nell McCafferty in the popular listings magazine, *Hot*

Press. 'Beware the local priest. He is a danger to your mental, physical and sexual health. Never leave one alone with a child. Not ever.'[3] The ecclesiastical historian Parick Corish sounded a similar pessimistic note at the end of his exhaustive history of Maynooth. 'Discrimination of almost any kind seems to be the only thing that (now) passes for sin,' he wrote, bleakly.[4]

Catholic Ireland was not dead, though it was certainly declining. Cardinal Daly, so sure-footed on northern questions and ecumenism, had never struck the right chord on the Church's internal failings. He would say, as he told *Intercom* in February 1995, that the Church had been disgraced. But then he ruined the effect by comparing this disgrace to Christ's humiliation on the Cross.[5] It was well meant but it failed to appease the public's frustration. Many people did not feel that the Catholic Church was suffering in the way that Christ suffered on the Cross and found the comparison offensive. It implied that the Church was an innocent victim of nothing more than rage and spite.

The scandals highlighted, rather than provoked, the Church's fall in esteem. Vocations to the ministry practically dried up. In 1967 the Irish Church boasted 34,000 clergy. At the start of the new millennium that number had fallen to 20,000. More importantly, the age profile had risen alarmingly. The average priest was well over 60. The number of diocesan clergy had shrunk little, dropping from 4,000 to 3,500, but the number of men in Religious orders had shrunk by far more. They were down by 45 per cent, while the number of nuns was down by 41 per cent. Very few men were putting themselves forward for ordination. In 1965 there were 412; in 1998 there were 44.[6] It was the same with the orders. Death carried away many and few were joining. In the late 1960s about 1,000 men and women entered the orders each year. In 1990, only 52 women put themselves forward to become nuns. Just 33 followed suit in 1994. The number of new brothers was eight in 1990 and four in 1994.

The effect on an individual diocese was striking. In Dublin diocese 16 men were ordained to the priesthood in the year of the Pope's visit. There were eight in 1989. In 1999 there was one – 30-year-old Rory Brady. By then his career choice seemed so curious that the Irish edition of the *Sunday Times* devoted an entire page to him.[7]

If a diocese that normally employed 550 people in parish ministry was only ordaining one new man a year in the 1990s, an acute manpower shortage was inescapable by the end of the first decade of the twenty-first century. At the least, the Catholic Church would have to amalgamate parishes on a grand scale, place many parishes under the effective management of lay men and women and scale down the number of eucharistic services. The few men who put themselves forward for ministry no longer worried about being regarded with exclusive awe, as Tony Flannery had done in the 1970s. When the *Sunday Times* interviewed a young priest, Damian McNeice, in August 1999 about his vocation, the first subject he mentioned was the widespread suspicion of clerical paedophilia. 'When people conclude that you cannot be trusted with children or that your vow of celibacy inevitably leads to sexual deviancy, it hurts,' he said.[8]

Irish mothers no longer earmarked one – let alone more than one – of their children for the priesthood or the convent. Clerical scandals were not the only reason for this change. The decline in the birth rate meant it was no longer practical. In De Valera's Ireland the Catholic Church had soaked up many of the surplus children of farming families. The alternative to such celibacy was emigration or enforced celibacy without the prestige of a soutane or a wimple. Now there were fewer farmers and families were becoming smaller. In 1980 there were 74,400 live births in the Republic. By 1993 this had dropped to only 49,456 – a sharp fall of one-third in little more than a decade. The old stereotype of the sprawling Irish family with half a dozen or a dozen children no longer matched reality. Families with only two children – or single mothers with one – even if they were committed Catholics – were going to think very hard before encouraging their offspring to join the celibate ministry of the Church.

The job of priest no longer brought much money, honour or prestige. In the 1950s poorer families felt honoured to donate a son to the priesthood. It still had a certain cachet in the 1960s, 1970s and 1980s, as the careers of Father Cleary and Bishop Casey had shown. By the 1990s it simply looked freakish. The Ireland of the 1990s was, as the media tirelessly reminded everyone, a 'Tiger Economy', with an annual growth rate of about 8 per cent – more than double the rate of neighbouring Britain and far ahead of the European average. Unemployment was below 5 per cent. Salaries were rising so fast that the greatest danger was a bout of high inflation. For the first time in at least 150 years, a clerical career was an option for relative poverty and the income of about £11,500 a year was now well below the national average.

For centuries, English Protestants had tried to break the connection between the ordinary Irish people and the Religious orders and failed miserably. The collapse in vocations succeeded where fire, sword and bowls of soup had failed. All over Ireland in the 1990s 'For Sale' signs went up outside the nation's convents and monasteries. A change in ownership was taking place every bit as momentous as that which took place during the Reformation. Where monks and nuns had worked and prayed, hotel guests now reclined in their rooms watching satellite television and the children of the Celtic Tiger lived in converted loft-style apartments.

The Protestants sold their property off as well. The Archbishop of Cashel's palace became an upmarket hotel. The Archbishop of Armagh's palace was converted into the headquarters of local government. In the year 2000 the Georgian palace of the Bishop of Ossory in Kilkenny looked set to be handed over to a preservation society. As the Church of a small minority in the Republic, the Church of Ireland's secularisation of its property had less emotional or psychological impact on the mass of the population. They might protest on aesthetic grounds, as they did when the Presbyterians demolished a church in the salubrious south Dublin suburb of Sandymount. But they rarely went inside these Protestant churches or their deaneries and palaces, so if the building was not knocked down they might hardly notice the change in function. It was a different matter with the Catholic convents and monasteries. This was snapping an umbilical cord. It was a rite of passage in the history of the nation which in some cases ended a connection that had lasted many centuries. When the Franciscans closed their doors in Drogheda in August 2000 it was noted that the Order was ending an era in the town that dated back to 1245. Ulic Troy, Franciscan Provincial of Ireland, blamed the fall in vocations. Since 1987, he said, the Order had lost more than 100 friars in Ireland and only two had been ordained.[9]

Catholic lay societies faced the same crisis in manpower. The old societies that had wielded so much power behind the scenes faded away. Limerick was no longer the infamous 'City of the Confraternity', all rain, poverty and socialised Catholicism. It still had the rain, but the old Georgian centre had been refurbished and much of the city torn down and rebuilt.

All over Ireland those two great pillars of lay Catholic piety, the Legion of Mary and Our Lady's Sodality, withered away. In the early 1960s, the Legion of Mary counted 24,000 members while the Sodality boasted 250,000. By the mid-1990s, the Sodality had lost 90 per cent of its members, while the Legion was down by two-thirds, to about 8,000 members.[10]

As its man – and woman – power declined and aged, the Church silently relinquished its tight grip on the nation's social fabric. In the 1950s the blighted career of Noel Browne showed just how determined the Church was to retain control over the nation's health. A generation later the fall in the number of nuns made their withdrawal from schools and hospitals inevitable. Ever since the Whigs introduced the National Schools in the 1830s, priests and nuns had educated most people in Ireland. They saw who came into the world and who went out of it, supervising women in childbirth and dealing harshly but efficiently with the women who became pregnant outside marriage.

By the 1990s, lay teachers and nurses had taken over. They might have no religious beliefs at all and even if they did, they took their orders from government ministries, not from priests or from bishops' pastorals. The withdrawal of the clergy from the day-to-day management of schools was matched by a resolve on the part of government to trim the clergy's power on the boards. A government White Paper on education in 1995 recommended depriving the Church of the right to nominate most members of the boards of the country's 3,000 Catholic primary schools. The era of the 'Magdalen laundry' was over. There was no longer a stigma attached to being a single mother. The old prejudice, much stronger in Ireland than in most European countries, collapsed with extraordinary speed. Before the 1950s, births outside marriage were practically unknown. By the 1990s, at least one-third of all live new babies in Ireland were born out of wedlock.

The enfeeblement of the Church was not much lamented. A few people shared Mary Kenny's sorrow, but not that many. Even the clergy often seemed relieved that they were no longer the centre of national attention. Some of their lay people seemed discreetly pleased that the clergy had been humbled a little.

The Catholic Church remained part of the furniture of Ireland. But was it a precious heirloom or a smelly old armchair no one had the heart to chuck out? For the new elite of writers and filmscript writers, it was payback time for the years of censorship, when government ministers had courted the smiles of archbishops and politicians waited anxiously in the ante-rooms of their palaces for make-or-break interviews. Irish Catholicism took a roasting in film and in print in the 1990s. Irish-made films revisited the past and found the Church guilty on most counts. *A Love Divided*, released in 1999, mined the claustrophobic horror of the Fethard-on-Sea controversy and came down heavily on the side of Sheila Cloney, the Protestant mother who had not wanted her two children to be sent to the local Catholic school. Orla Brady's Mrs Cloney – shown as a kind of supermodel with the convictions of Martin Luther and the conscience of Martin Luther King – was the obvious heroine against the thuggish Father Stafford and the sinister, Machiavellian Bishop Staunton. The real hero of the film was not Mrs Cloney but Peter Caffrey's village publican – the only atheist in town. The message of *A Love Divided* was that Catholicism equals fanaticism and bigotry, a past from which the nation needs to escape.

David Keating's *The Last of the High Kings* in 1997 was another snapshot of Ireland's religious divide filmed from a different angle. Set in the present, it centred on a Catholic family living next door to Protestants in the middle-class suburbs of Dublin. Once more, Catholicism took the rap. Catherine O'Hara as the mother of the teenage hero Frankie Griffin is given to hurling nationalist diatribes over the garden wall at her peaceable Protestant neighbours. Frankie knows better and forms a crush on some of the local Protestant girls. The message: sexual urges will triumph over our ancient tribal divisions.

The biggest-selling books by Irish authors at the end of the century took a similar line. Frank McCourt's two-part blockbuster autobiography, *Angela's Ashes*, published in 1996, and *'Tis*, published in 1999, explored the life of a deadbeat family in the Limerick of the 1940s. McCourt's first page set the tone:

When I look back on my childhood I wonder how I survived at all. It was, of course, a miserable childhood: the happy childhood is hardly worth your while. Worse than the ordinary miserable childhood is the miserable Irish childhood, and worse yet is the miserable Irish Catholic childhood.

People everywhere brag and whimper about the woes of their early years, but nothing can compare with the Irish version: the poverty; the shiftless loquacious alcoholic father; the pious defeated mother moaning by the fire: pompous priests; bullying schoolmasters; the English and the terrible things they did to us for eight hundred long years.[11]

McCourt in his account of his young life spent under the involuntary tutelage of these 'pompous priests and bullying schoolmasters' probably did more to shape foreign perceptions of Ireland than any writer of his generation. The book was an international publishing phenomenon. It was as if the whole world had been waiting to hear a definitive account of what it meant to be Irish, and that this was it. The first print run for *Angela's Ashes* was 27,000. By the time its sequel *'Tis* came out it had sold more than 4 million copies and been translated into 22 languages, including Estonian and Serbo-Croat. Everybody wanted a share of McCourt's take on Irish Catholic misery, including nations who one might have thought had suffered worse experiences. By 2001 the book was available in 32 languages, although, significantly, Irish was not one of them. The Estonians who had lived through Stalinism, the Bosnians who had survived a horrific civil war and the Chinese victims of Chairman Mao's Cultural Revolution all sank their teeth into *Angela's Ashes*.

Maeve Binchy was the other great Irish literary success of the 1990s. The former *Irish Times* columnist became one of the most popular authors in the world, thanks in part to the sheer size of her output. While McCourt cornered the soggy, grey, priest-ridden Limerick of the 1940s, Binchy marketed the sunny, spruced-up and apparently priest-free Ireland of the present. Binchy's novels were a commentary on Ireland as much because of what they left out. No Catholic writer from the generation before Binchy ignored the Catholic Church. It dominated the landscape and you either loved it or railed against it. Binchy airbrushed religion out of the picture. Her characters were cogs in the Celtic Tiger economy and children of the secular age who started businesses, went on foreign holidays and spent a lot of time shopping. Their dilemmas were those of bored middle-class consumers in any Western country. Vaguely unsatisfied by the trappings of prosperity, they start affairs, divorce, take drugs and get pregnant unexpectedly, or by the wrong man. The odd religious thought flits across the stage. An occasional house is called Fatima. But there is no assumption in Binchy-land that the Irish live under a moral or religious code that differs substantially from that of post-Protestant England or America.

A great Irish cultural export of the 1990s was the musical extravaganza, *Riverdance*. Dreamed up to fill the gaps during the 1994 Eurovision Song Contest, which Ireland hosted, it started life as a traditional hard-shoe dance routine lasting only a few minutes before spawning a music single, a video and then a show lasting two hours. The show went from Dublin to London and then split into three companies, which toured the world simultaneously. By the end of the decade, *Riverdance* had notched up audience figures of more than 11 million.

Both *Angela's Ashes* and *Riverdance* marketed versions of the Irish past. *Riverdance* was a blast of Irish essence that left out what had been the central component – the Church. As Thomas Casey, a Jesuit priest, observed, the show presented the Celtic experience as 'a river which gushed from a pre-Christian past to a post-Christian future'.[12] Casey thought that in the eyes of most young people, the *Zeitgeist* was with the eco-warrior rather than the priest and based on this observation, he drew up lists of attributes of the two figures. The word 'eco-warrior', he wrote, conjured up positive images: happy and young; creative and experimental; exotic and marginal; confident and audacious; strong sense of identity; egalitarian; recovering a golden past. The word 'priest' conjured up a rather different set: depressed and elderly; unimaginative and cautious; boring and mainstream; perplexed and apologetic; self-questioning; hierarchical; chained to a burdensome past.

Inside the Catholic Church, lay Catholics took over the ecumenical movement in the 1990s and left the clergy behind. In the first 20 years after the Vatican Council, it was the clergy who complained they were making all the running. Priests were interested in discussing theological differences with Protestant ministers, but their congregations were not. By the 1990s this had changed. Catholic lay people were attending Protestant services and even taking their sacraments, much to the annoyance of the Catholic clergy, who now had become a restraining force. What worried the priests most was that some of these law-breakers were the most intellectual, committed and outwardly conservative people left in the Church. Mary McAleese, elected President after Robinson's term expired in November 1997, was a northerner and a strong Catholic. Unlike Robinson, she totally upheld orthodox Catholic teaching on the touchstone question of abortion. But no sooner was she in office than she attended a service in honour of her inauguration at Christ Church cathedral and took the sacrament, the first Catholic head of the Irish state ever to do so. The city's Catholic Lord Mayor went up to the altar rail with her. MacQuaid would have been aghast, and priests lined up to denounce her. She was 'a scandal to its [the Church's] members', said James McEvoy, a Maynooth professor.[13] Archbishop Connell said she had taken part in 'a sham'.[14]

A quarter of a century previously the Archbishop's choice of words would have passed without comment. At that time most Irish people thought Protestant services were indeed a sham. At the inauguration of the Protestant Erskine Hamilton Childers as President in 1973, Archbishops Conway and Ryan had attended the Church of Ireland service but declined the invitation to read out any prayers or lessons because the service included the Eucharist.[15]

By the 1990s the Catholic bishops had remained where they were, but the laity had moved on, and outside the Catholic press Connell's use of the word 'sham' was roundly condemned. Yet again, the Catholic clergy seemed out of step with the New Ireland. The row over the President's fake Eucharist was a storm in a teacup but it touched a raw nerve. On 21 December 1997 the Archbishop issued an abject apology. 'It was very unfortunate that I used the word "sham",' he said.

The staccato sound of media gunfire obscured the degree to which Catholic and Protestant clergy were, in fact, working together in Ireland on a raft of issues ranging from homelessness to racism. There was no more striking and symbolic example of this than Ferns, the diocese that included Fethard-on-Sea. The two bishops of Ferns were great friends and often appeared together in spite of the enormous disparity in the size of their flocks and in 1998 Bishop Comiskey made a moving public apology to the Protestant community for the Fethard-on-Sea boycott. In Kerry the Catholic Bishop, William Murphy, attended the opening of the first new Church of Ireland church in the Republic for 30 years in October 1997, at Killorglin. In Cork, John Buckley, the Catholic Bishop, led the public appeal for funds for the restoration of the Protestant cathedral. Laurence Ryan, his colleague in Kildare, did the same for the Protestant cathedral in Kildare. In June 1997 Bishop Walsh of Killaloe had attacked the Ne temere decree as 'contrary to the spirit of generosity and love'.

After so long in the dark, the Protestant clergy in the Republic of Ireland, much to their surprise, basked in the warm glow of media approbation. Donald Caird, Archbishop of Dublin, told his synod in October 1995: 'The Church of Ireland today stands high in the esteem of the nation, both north and south of the border and is in a position to speak on issues of national importance without the suspicion of prejudice, self-interest or of being controlled by any ecclesiastical authority outside its own elected structure.'[16] The *Church of Ireland Gazette* agreed. 'The Church of Ireland has found itself at the centre of a new pluralism in recent years,' an editorial concluded in August 1998. 'A Church which was very uncertain about its future now has a confidence and optimism inconceivable 20 years ago . . .'[17]

The Protestants were still declining for all that. In the 1950s, a visitor to Dublin entered a city that was strewn with grandiose monuments to Protestant Ascendancy. At the western end of the high street the turrets of Christ Church cathedral reared up. Beside them rose the massive hulk of the Synod Hall. At the other end of Dame Street squatted the dove-grey ramparts of Trinity College, next door to the classical splendour of the Bank of Ireland. A few minutes' walk from Trinity College up Grafton Street brought the visitor to the headquarters of the Church of Ireland on St Stephen's Green. A few minutes' walk in the opposite direction brought one to the front door of the Irish Times building. Physically, the old Established Church commanded the heights of the Irish capital decades after all political power had passed to the Catholics. A Protestant wandering through the city could comfort him or herself with the thought: 'So much of this is still ours'.

By the end of the century, the Protestants had surrendered most of their strongholds. They still had the two cathedrals, but Synod Hall was a Viking museum and the Church had sold its headquarters on St Stephen's Green and moved out to the suburbs. Trinity College, the Bank of Ireland and the *Irish Times* were still there, but none was a Protestant preserve.

The shrinkage of southern Protestants made all these losses inevitable. The Church of Ireland was a shadow of its old self. In 1861 its members had numbered 372,000 in the 26 counties, alongside 66,000 Presbyterians. By the 1990s the Presbyterians had practically vanished – they numbered only 14,000. The Church of Ireland was down to 135,000 members in the South by 1961. A decade later, they had dropped to 125,000. By 1991 there were only 90,000 – less than a quarter of the 1861 figure. By contrast, the Northern population was relatively stable. The Church of Ireland had about 320,000 members in 1861 and about 270,000 at the end of the next century, a drop of about one-sixth. The Presbyterians had lost rather more ground. They numbered 457,000 in the 1860s and about 340,000 in the 1990s. At the beginning of the century they were the first faith of Ulster. At the end they were only the third in size, behind both Catholics and Anglicans.

In the South, a community so pitifully reduced in size and with relatively few children could not hope to fill universities, staff banks and maintain a national newspaper. The Catholic intelligentsia had colonised and appropriated the *Irish Times* after the Second World War. Dissatisfied with its lowbrow Catholic rivals, the *Irish Independent* and the *Irish Press*, they found the *Times's* liberalism on social questions and censorship more to their taste. In the early 1950s the Arnott family who had owned the paper since the 1870s relinquished control to a trust, and the *Irish Times* drifted out of the orbit of the old closed circle of clergymen, dons and Protestant gentry. Robert Smyllie, editor from 1934 to 1954, courted the new readership and commissioned the young and then virtually unknown Brendan Behan to write columns. His predecessor would hardly have considered an ex-IRA prisoner from the slums of Dublin a suitable object of patronage. In the 1960s the paper – symbolically – introduced an Irish language column. At the end of the twentieth century a few fossilised columns in the newspaper bore witness to its Protestant roots. The Saturday edition still provided a full menu of Protestant church services in the capital, and an incoming Protestant dean could still rely on a decent-sized interview in the *Irish Times*. But the newspaper had by then become a paper written by, and for, liberal Catholics. It was their mouthpiece, espousing their secular brand of Irish nationalism, their views on Irish unity (good idea in principle, tricky idea in practice) and their self-consciously progressive views on Europe, divorce, abortion, sexual freedom, race and homosexuality. In the 1980s it was a journal of the supporters of 'Garret the Good' and his crusade for constitutional reform. In the 1990s it was a journal for the loft-livers and second car and home owners who had done well out of the Tiger Economy. Its adoration of money was almost touchingly lacking in guile or irony.

The Church of Ireland's own media shrank to almost nothing. At the turn of the century, the *Church of Ireland Gazette* had been a magnificently reactionary organ, a superb she-elephant at bay, trumpeting and bellowing with rage at the spear-throwing hordes of English Liberals and Irish Home Rulers. Densely written and covering several pages, it presupposed an age of relative leisure when the average clergyman had time on his hands and several servants. The *Gazette* began to shrivel in the 1930s, but it was only after the Second World War that it dwindled into a bite-seized pamphlet with a few tabloid articles and scraps of information. Catholics still had the *Furrow* and *Studies* to conduct their debates in. The Irish Protestants had nothing. It was a pathetic end for a Church that had produced Archbishop Ussher, and which had once prided itself on its knowledge and love of history.

Trinity College shrugged off its Protestant inheritance at much the same time as the *Irish Times*. In 1939 over 60 per cent of the student body were from the Free State, 25 per cent were from the North and 5 per cent from Britain.[18] Twenty years later the percentage of students from the Republic of Ireland was down to 43 per cent, 14 per cent came from Northern Ireland and more than one-quarter of the student body was from Britain. The violence in the North in the 1960s and 1970s frightened off the British and Northern Irish Protestants. Meanwhile a government plan in 1967 to merge Trinity with its Catholic rival UCD had prompted a dash for growth.

The merger plan came to nothing. But it revealed the abiding animosity of Ireland's Catholic rulers towards the Protestant college. At the same time, the ban on Catholic students attending the college lapsed, causing a marked change in the nature of the student body. Out went the British Protestants. In came the Irish Catholics. By 1990 over 90 per cent of the students were from the Republic, and at least 80 per cent were from a Catholic background. In 1991 Thomas Mitchell became the first Catholic Provost since Michael Moore's brief sojourn under James II. The college did not disown its past. Portraits of proud deans and portly bishops who had strained every sinew to erect, and then maintain, the Penal Laws, still graced the halls and walls. But the students who strolled underneath them were the distant descendants of those whom the Penal Laws were designed to destroy as a politically active class. The chapel had been open to all denominations since 1973. Almost four hundred years after its foundation, Dublin had finally claimed the university at its heart for itself.

The Irish Protestants gracefully ceded control over Trinity in the 1960s and 1970s. They lost control of Queen's University, Belfast in more acrimonious circumstances a decade or so later. As recently as 1968, Catholics had comprised only 10 per cent of the student body at Queen's. Educational changes in Britain, as well as demographic changes in Northern Ireland, transformed the situation. The massive expansion of tertiary education in Britain brought the sons and daughters of people who had never dreamed of going to university into the new so-called 'red-brick' colleges and polytechnics. In the North this change had religious as well as social implications. It was not simply, as in Britain, a case of working-class students invading an upper middle-class preserve. It involved Catholics claiming a place in the sun, in what had been Protestant territory.

The change in Belfast was accentuated by an exodus of Protestant students to universities on the British mainland. They did not leave only because of 'the troubles'. Emigration dovetailed with a growing trend among students to 'go away' from home to university; the net result was a rapid change in the student body from a Protestant Unionist to a Catholic nationalist majority by the 1990s. In such a polarised society the change could only cause conflict, as the new

Catholic majority engaged in trials of strength with the old guard over the emotive symbols of flag, anthem and language. Catholic students deliberately disrupted graduation day ceremonies, when 'God Save the Queen' was played, and the anthem was withdrawn in 1994. A transition was made in Queen's to a kind of no man's land, but it was neither graceful nor settled. At the start of the new millennium the identity of Queen's still seemed up for grabs.

Irish Protestantism at the end of the century was more fashionable among the opinion-forming classes than it had been for a long time. In the 1940s the very name 'Church of Ireland' had angered Catholics. It was seen then as a presumption, if not a lie. That sentiment was dead half a century later. Catholics now accepted the Church of Ireland at face value, and many of its distinguishing characteristics, especially the married priesthood, now appeared a bonus. But while Catholics appreciated the distinct contribution of the Church of Ireland, very few joined, and converts were usually the result of mixed marriages. The Church of Ireland was the Church of the Pale, as it had always been. Its Dublin cathedrals had taken on a new lease of life as centres of liturgical excellence, bulked out on Sundays by ever increasing numbers of tourists and foreign residents. But to visit the churches in the west of Ireland was to see a Church near the end of its life. There were broken spires, smashed windows and overgrown churchyards. At Askeaton, the centre of the Second Reformation in County Limerick, where Bishop John Jebb had confirmed hundreds of converts in the 1820s, trees grew through the church roof. At Tourmakeady, the grave of Bishop Plunket, leader of the Second Reformation in Connacht, had disappeared under a forest of weeds and the nearby church was an impenetrable, ivy-clad ruin. When Peig Sayers wrote her popular account of life on Great Blasket Island, off the coast of Kerry, she recalled a time when the Protestants of Dingle had been numerous enough to constitute a threat to Catholics.[19] When I attended a Sunday service in Dingle it might not have taken place had I not turned up.

'We are no petty people,' W.B. Yeats had said of the southern Protestants in 1925. 'We are one of the great stocks of Europe.' Yeats was no prophet. By the year 2000 the southern Protestants were a very petty people, almost entirely confined to the Dublin–Kildare–Wicklow area, with a few outposts in Wexford, Kilkenny and the holiday-cum-retirement home of Kerry. Beyond that, Irish Protestantism was almost extinct. Where they had buildings of any size and splendour, as in Cork, they depended on the charity of local Catholics to maintain them. There was no end in sight to this decline. The number of conversions could not possibly keep pace with the depletion of the ranks caused by intermarriage. The raw fact was that since the 1980s two in every five Protestants married outside the faith, well up on the percentage in the 1950s. In spite of the relaxation of the Ne temere decree, the majority of children of such unions were still brought up as Catholics, even if a growing minority was not. It may be that Protestants in the South have fallen below the threshold of a sustainable community in the long term.

For five centuries the Church of Ireland tried to keep the old Catholic diocesan structure going by amalgamating bishoprics. By 2000 the process had gone as far as it could. Some bishops now held up to six old bishoprics, entailing half a dozen enthronement ceremonies at the start of their turn of office and almost countless deanery and diocesan synods after that. It could not stagger on. The abolition of the patchwork of ancient bishoprics and their replacement by two or three bishops in charge of 'the midlands', 'the west' and 'the south' was increasingly discussed as the only way ahead. For a Church with even a vague memory of the past, the idea of having no Bishop of Cork or Limerick was galling. It marked the final chapter in the long struggle against the Catholics to be the national Church. Now at last the Anglicans were having to settle for the same role as the Methodists and Presbyterians – just another sect, one of many.

The change was not a simple administrative matter. If the Church cut the number of dioceses in the Republic, the number in Northern Ireland would remain the same, shifting the balance of power towards the British end of the organisation. What then of the Church's hopes of positioning itself 'at the centre of the new pluralism' in the Republic?

Since partition, the Church of Ireland primates had engaged in a high-wire act. In the 1980s and 1990s this worked well enough. In Armagh, Primate Eames was an authoritative voice for moderate northern Unionism. In Dublin, Walton Empey was the equally respected voice of moderate Irish nationalists. Each Primate belonged to the Church as a whole, while at the same time representing their respective camps. In the past some archbishops of Armagh had been too 'green' for Ulster tastes and some archbishops of Dublin had never shaken off a faintly foreign aura. But Eames looked every inch a solid Ulsterman, while Empey was the most authentically Irish Archbishop the Protestant see of Dublin had seen in generations. He was the first Protestant Primate truly to belong to the Republic, having served in the Irish army. It gave him a certain confidence to criticise the Tiger Economy's shortcomings, lambasting the rise in racism, corruption in high office and mean-mindedness to asylum-seekers.

But the double act performed by Eames and Empey would not necessarily commend itself to their successors. Although the Church of Ireland looked unlikely to split into two, there was a danger that the Church in Northern Ireland and the Church in the Republic would effectively go their own ways. The Church in the Republic was increasingly ecumenical and liberal in its theology and moderately nationalistic in its politics. It had not become anti-British but was keen to capitalise on its new popularity as an authentically Irish institution. It was hostile to the Orange Order. The Church in the North was largely evangelical in theology and the laity were sturdily and unrepentantly Orange. In most rural parishes, membership of the Orange Order was virtually conterminous with membership of the Church. For most of the time these two sections of the Church, North and South, British and Irish, could happily coexist in one institution. Evangelical clergy went down to Dublin for their training, grumbled about the ecumenical flavour of Dublin Anglicanism but put up with it. The Church deliberately encouraged clergy to spend part of their ministry in the North and part in the Republic. But once in a while an issue blew up that exposed the rift in all its glory and in the 1990s that issue was Drumcree.

Drumcree is an old parish. For many years it encompassed the neighbouring hamlet of Portadown. The industrial revolution changed the balance. Drumcree remained a village while its neighbour expanded into one of the largest manufacturing towns in the North. Years of commercial decline have taken the edge off Portadown, but there is still a lot of old Protestant money washing around the town and it is the natural hub and shopping centre for north County Armagh. While the Catholics of south Armagh go to Dundalk or Newry for their business, Protestants go to Portadown. It remains a defiantly Protestant community, physically dominated by the First World War memorial and the Church of Ireland parish church in the centre. It was always a centre of Orangeism. Dan Winter's cottage, the birthplace of the movement in the sectarian squabbles of the 1790s, is situated only a few miles away in Loughgall, in the appleseed heart of Ulster's orchard. Mrs Winter, the cottage's custodian and Dan's descendant by marriage, is often to be seen there doing her weekly shop.

The parish church of Drumcree has been an Orange shrine since the Order's foundation and members have attended the movement's high days and holy days there since 1807. The proximity of Drumcree church to Portadown has allowed marchers for generations to make an easy loop from the church to the town and back again. In recent years the agreed route formed a rough circle. After the service in the church they headed down the Dungannon Road into town, marched up the high street and returned to Drumcree by the most direct route, the Garvaghy Road.

Until the 1960s the Garvaghy Road ran through fields with only a few houses. The construction of several large new housing developments in the 1960s and 1970s, Garvaghy Park, Churchill Park and Ballyoran, changed all that. What originally had been a sparsely settled and denominationally mixed area quickly evolved into a Catholic nationalist stronghold of about 1,000 houses. Protestants left and now hold only the bottom end of the Garvaghy Road nearest the town centre. Relatively quickly, the Orange Order found itself marching back to Drumcree on the last leg of the walk through hostile urban territory. This was not an infrequent development, owing to the steady change in the province's demographic composition, but it was a fraught one in a town with such a history of militant Unionism.

Orange spokesmen were quick to spot Sinn Fein's involvement in the protests against the march. But the protests would have taken place at some stage, as the Catholic community became increasingly conscious of its numerical strength and consequently less willing to give way on such symbolic issues. Although Orange people invariably said the attacks were orchestrated by a minority, a 1997 survey showed that opposition to the march was not a minority pursuit and that about 69 per cent of the Garvaghy Road residents considered the issue very important.[20]

The saga of the Drumcree conflict was the Church of Ireland's 'scandal' in the 1990s. The protest gathered steam in 1995, following the formation of a pressure group, the Garvaghy Road Association (GRA), which was dedicated to blocking the parade or imposing a list of conditions. The RUC Chief, Sir Hugh Annesley, responded by sealing off the road that year to prevent the march. The police move united the Orangemen in protest and about 50,000 of them descended on Drumcree, accompanied by Ian Paisley and David Trimble, Ulster Unionist MP for Bannside. The first Drumcree 'stand-off' lasted two nights before the pressure of numbers prevailed and 800 of the Orangemen, accompanied by a visibly elated Trimble and Paisley, marched down the road. Trimble's militant stance helped ensure his election to the leadership of the Unionist party that year. He was not seen again at Drumcree. Apart from Trimble, the real beneficiaries of the stand-off were Sinn Fein and the GRA. Force had been seen to prevail over the wishes of the local population. Coverage of the story around the world, as well as in the Irish Republic, was overwhelmingly hostile to the Order, and predictably in the American media comparisons were drawn with the Ku-Klux-Klan.

The Order's unconvincing triumph at 'Drumcree One' paved the way for a far worse confrontation at 'Drumcree Two', the following year. Again, the police at first sided with the wishes of the GRA and agreed to block the parade. The decision was then reversed after three days of rioting in which there were 156 arrests and 90 civilian and 50 RUC injuries. Annesley's apparent surrender to Orange muscle by allowing 1,200 Orangemen to march down the road in silence in turn triggered Republican riots in Derry and Armagh. About 1,000 petrol bombs were thrown, a Catholic protester was killed on Belfast's Strand Road and Protestants as far away as Donegal found themselves paying for the Protestant 'victory' at 'Drumcree Two'. It was 'a black day', said Cardinal Daly, a 'disastrous decision', and the Orange Order took a pasting from the world's media. There were even complaints from the Netherlands that the word 'Orange' was being besmirched by the Northern Irish.[21]

Drumcree Two turned out to be a last, chaotic hurrah for the Portadown Lodge in the Garvaghy Road. The British government would not again preside over such a débâcle and the scale of the mess in 1996 ensured that when the police blocked the road in future, it would stay blocked.

The scenes of Orange chaos at Drumcree in 1996 and the boycotts and evictions applied by both communities on minorities in their areas brought strong pressure on Archbishop Eames from the Church's southern wing to sever ties with the Order. The Primate said this was impossible. 'There is hardly a Church of Ireland parish in Northern Ireland which does not contain members of those [Loyalist] institutions,' he told the Armagh Synod in October 1996. 'They view their membership as part of their culture . . . Their fathers and grandfathers before them were members. They do not see any conflict between Church allegiance and

Orange membership.' Far from hinting at such a break, he warned against a tendency to demonise the Orange Order.[22]

That was not how the story played in Dublin. The southern Primate wanted to shore up the Church of Ireland's new-found prestige in the Republic, push for a higher Protestant role in such traditionally Catholic preserves as the Gardaí and the army and raise the Church's profile on the issues of homelessness and asylum-seekers. Empey did not welcome reminders that the Church of Ireland was coloured bright orange north of the border, and far from complaining about the demonisation of the Orange Order, in November he delivered a cool broadside against what he called 'parades of an offensively triumphalist nature'.[23] The two Protestant primates were too statesmanlike to cross swords with each other directly, but there was no concealing the tension that Drumcree injected into the Church of Ireland's own North–South relationship. As the *Church of Ireland Gazette* noted in the spring of 1997, the southern wing felt chipper and wondered why the northerners were not moving with the times. 'The southern . . . community feels itself to be moving with new confidence, well integrated into a rapidly developing society,' it wrote. 'It wonders why the Northern church has been unable to divest itself of what looks like uncomfortable and anachronistic sectarian baggage.'[24]

That summer there was a respite from what was turning into an annual crisis, after the Orangemen agreed to re-route the march away from the Garvaghy Road area. But it was a reprieve, not a solution. In 1998, the Portadown Lodge and the Garvaghy Road Association failed to reach an agreement and as a result, the annual service in the little Church of the Ascension was followed by a tense confrontation between the marchers and the RUC only yards from the church porch. The RUC did not back down this time. In 1997 a Labour government with a massive majority took power in Westminster. Tony Blair's administration had no need of Unionist votes and was determined to seek an inclusive settlement in the North. The way down the Garvaghy Road was securely blocked.

In the ensuing violence a policeman was killed. Then, in a malicious act of arson, came the shocking deaths of three Catholic children and their mother in Ballymoney, County Antrim. The deaths of Jason, Mark and Richard Quinn took the wind out of what was a declining force. The more cautious wing of the Orange Order saw it as a verdict on the annual Drumcree protests and withdrew from an event that had attracted an uncontrollable element, seemingly spoiling for a fight. The scenes of Orange mayhem in July 1998 embarrassed the Church of Ireland. It was a double humiliation for Eames, as he had stuck his neck out in defence of the 'moderate' Orangemen over the previous two years and tried to stave off violence in 1998 by intervening in July to extract a promise of good conduct from the marchers. The Archbishop had asked all the Orangemen attending morning service under John Pickering to promise to avoid any action before or after the service that diminished the sanctity of worship. He had called on them to obey the law of the land and show respect for the Church by word and action. The days were long gone when militants from either side had much time for clerical pronouncements and the Portadown Lodge did not even reply to the Archbishop's three-point letter.

On 23 October 1998, Eames reflected on the damage done and on his own feelings of disappointment. 'Across the world the images of Drumcree church . . . have been portrayed as the scene of violence, sectarianism, mass gatherings and disorder,' he told the Armagh Synod. Mr Pickering, he went on, had become a virtual hostage in his neat little rectory. The Archbishop described the Drumcree disaster as 'a defining moment for all of us within the Church'.[25] But he still refused to condemn the Orange Order. The good Orange must not be thrown in the same basket as the bad Orange. Down south, all Oranges looked the same colour.

It seemed as if Drumcree might wrench the Church of Ireland apart. More than any other Church, it was vulnerable to the conflict between Catholic nationalism and Protestant isolationism. Until the 'troubles' it could hide behind the fact that both communities considered themselves 'Irish' but by the 1990s even that was no longer the case. Few Northern Protestants defined themselves in even a limited sense as Irish by the turn of the twenty-first century. In 1969 a survey showed about 20 per cent of northern Protestants thought of themselves as primarily Irish. By 1993 that had dropped to 8 per cent. As Northern Protestants lost power, and lost the demographic battle in Ulster, they recoiled from the Irish advance and reaffirmed their separateness. They called themselves Ulstermen, Ulster people, Ulster Scots or simply British. When referring to both communities they would say 'the people of Northern Ireland'. What did all this have to do with the Church of Ireland? A lot. If almost three-quarters of its members belonged to a community that was increasingly British, while one-quarter belonged to a community that was increasingly Irish, how long could it present a coherent message? The answer was: for a long time, as long as Britishness and Irishness were not seen as mutually exclusive; but not for so long if, as in Drumcree, the two identities collided like express trains.

In 1934, the nationalist writer Aodh de Blácam wrote that the Ulster problem was founded on religion. 'The Ulster Protestants are mainly Gaelic in blood. Their ethos is that of the Scottish Protestants. They have the same traits of character as Catholic Gaels but inverted. An Orange procession is utterly un-English; it is like a parody of a Catholic procession. Perverted kinsmen are the hardest to reconcile and the revolt in the North-east has all the bitterness of a family quarrel.'[26]

De Blácam's analysis would be vigorously contested today. Churchmen of all denominations, the political Left in England and Ireland and Republicans and all but the most diehard Unionists would all unite in denouncing the idea that the conflict in Northern Ireland is a religious war. It is certainly not a war of churchmen and women. As in the Balkans, religion and national identity are hard to unpick. Religion has created the national identities and is no respecter of blood.

Gaelic blood flowed through the veins of some of the stoutest Drumcree marchers, while some Republicans have Old English blood in their veins. Even the surname of the Sinn Fein leader, Gerry Adams, hints at distant ancestors among the medieval English settlers. In the North, as in the Republic, the nationalisms which religion forged have outgrown the churches that gave birth to them. The British marchers at Drumcree do not now need or even notice the advice of Church of Ireland archbishops. The men behind the Omagh bomb of 1998 certainly did not heed the Catholic Church. Protestantism and Catholicism created two nations in the North, and Unionism and Republicanism are their children. Unionists look back to the Covenant of 1912, and Republicans to the Easter Rising of 1916. Neither side needs clerical guides any more. The voices of the clergy on the peace process are hardly heard, let alone heeded. In the Republican heartland of west Belfast, teenagers on the street taunt the Catholic clergy about Brendan Smyth and the other child sex scandals in a way that would have been unthinkable in the 1960s and 1970s. There has never been a time in Irish history when clergy of different denominations were so ready to reach out to one another – and never a time when it mattered so little whether they did or not. Ecumenism is now a purely religious issue, devoid of wider political significance. Paisley was almost certainly the last major Protestant politician to be seriously worried about 'Rome rule'.

As religion separates out from religious-based nationalism, the churches have become less political. Outside Northern Ireland, many people believe that Paisley is an important religious leader as well as a politician. He may be the leader of his own denomination, but on the Sunday when I attended Paisley's mother church off the Ormeau Park in east Belfast I found it virtually empty. Only a small group of very respectable, elderly, old-fashioned looking people in Sunday hats were there to hear the word. The daughter churches of the Martyrs' Memorial church possibly do better business than their parent but no one attending a service there could possibly come away with the impression that Paisley's brand of religious Unionism holds any appeal outside a small circle.

By contrast, that evening I watched about 3,000 people stream into Pastor James McConnell's Metropolitan Tabernacle in north Belfast for the evening service. Cars and coaches queued bumper to bumper to get into the car park. The road running alongside this vast modern church, which looks like a cross between a supermarket and a small airport, was clogged with buses coming from towns all over the province. At the entrance, uniformed stewards were on hand to conduct the throng in the direction of the huge balcony area or the stalls. As the service started, cameras whirred into life, panning the congregation; they were there to tape each of the services for the pastor's 'outreach' ministry.

McConnell has many critics in the world of Belfast Protestantism, who feel his giant temple will not outlast his own lifetime and that he is a one-man church. They dislike the tone of his biography, which recounts his frequent encounters with devils and a direct meeting with an angel in September 1973 on the balcony of his church.[27] His message is extreme biblical fundamentalism, a no-holds-barred, no-quarter-given gospel of heaven or hell, salvation or damnation. He is convinced the world is living through the 'last days' mentioned in the New Testament, a message that has struck a chord with many people in Belfast's bomb-blasted landscape.

What marks out the Metropolitan Tabernacle from the old-fashioned Protestant sects is not just the size and fervency of the congregation or its super-modern premises, but the lack of politics. Pastor McConnell has discarded the baggage of history and divorced nationalism from worship. McConnell may have started out preaching to an audience of ten in an Orange hall but no Orange or Union flags are seen in the Tabernacle and there are no slogans about God and Ulster on the walls. When Pastor McConnell claims, as he did the evening I was there, that ex-IRA people sit in that vast throng, I feel inclined to believe him.

At the Tabernacle I sat back in the comfy cinema-style seat and let the pastor's sermon wash over me. The torrent of words about God, the Devil, heaven and hell harked back to a world whose cosmology had not changed since Ussher's time. But these modern-day Puritans are quite at home with modern technology. At the end of the service the pastor announced that seats were still available on the Tabernacle's specially chartered plane to Bucharest to visit the Church's orphanage. I couldn't help smiling, thinking of the earnest sons and daughters of Ulster whizzing across Europe to the Balkans in their jet.

The Belfast Tabernacle is one example of a new direction in Irish religion, which involves uncoupling the old ties between faith and nationality. But there are others. In the village of Lucan, outside Dublin, the local Presbyterian community has expanded sevenfold in recent years, bringing an entirely new type of person into the church. These are not Protestants in the former sense of the word, and certainly not Unionists. They are the orphans of secularism – mostly non-practising Catholics – who have little knowledge of, or interest in, the battles Presbyterians fought long ago. They are not Ulster Scots, know nothing of 1642 or the Covenant of 1912 and are wholly Irish in their culture, politics and allegiances.

In the summer of 2000 I drove to the National Novena at the Marian shrine of Knock in County Mayo. The west is famous for its wet weather and I expected sheets of rain. Instead the Irish climate played tricks on us all. The Mayo countryside was bathed in a bosky evening glow as I reached Knock while the sky turned a deep indigo blue. As night fell, the sky remained clear and I could see the stars.

The shrine was packed with people, several thousand, mostly in the older age group and mostly women. But there was a fair contingent of younger families and even the occasional black- or brown-skinned worshipper. As the communion service ended we were invited to pick up our candlelit paper lanterns and form a solemn procession, heading round the stations of the cross in the landscaped park outside the shrine. At the front of the procession the white illuminated statue of the Virgin bobbed along, lit up against the night sky. Behind me snaked the long, winding column of pilgrims. The stream of softly lit lanterns rippling along the path gave a ghostly effect. The priest intoning the rosary through a loudspeaker as we wended our way around the park was not Irish. He sounded Spanish and constantly made small grammatical mistakes. 'Hail Mary, full of the grace,' he said. 'Blessed art thy among women . . . '

We ended up at the east end wall of the old parish church at Knock, where a group of visionaries had seen an image of the Virgin in the poor old, sad old Ireland of 1879. When they had that vision, MacHale was Archbishop of Tuam, the embers of the Second Reformation were still smouldering in Connacht and the priests were in the front line of the war against the Ascendancy landlords.

Knock has changed as much as Ireland has changed. The back wall of the old church has been covered in glass. Next door lies the splendid new shrine complex. In the village, thatched cottages with mud walls have given way to the ubiquitous 'hacienda-style' bungalows that now cover so much of the Irish countryside. The literature at the shrine bookshop, which dwells on the horrors of the 1870s, and on the famine, evictions, hunger and death, seemed curiously at odds with the sanatorium-like flavour of the modern shrine complex. It is a testament to the New Ireland, with its manicured lawns and banks of low-maintenance cotoneaster bushes. I had expected everyone in Knock to live their lives around the shrine. But when I returned to my hotel at the end of the Novena, my head still ringing with the refrain 'Hail Mary, full of the grace', I found a dance going at full strength in the dining room and satellite television blaring sports news in the packed bar. Even at Knock, the old Ireland has to compete with the new.

The process of secularisation in Ireland is relentless and has reached every corner. In the year that the Pope visited Ireland, the rate of mass attendance was around 90 per cent. By the 1980s, it was about 86 per cent. By 1992, weekly mass attendance had dipped to 78 per cent and by the end of that disastrous decade it had dropped to around 60 per cent. By the end of the first decade of the twenty-first century, at the same time that the Catholic population is expected to exceed 50 per cent of the Northern Ireland population, the practising Catholic population of the South may dip below 50 per cent.

In Northern Ireland, the change will finally bury Brookeborough's dream of a Protestant parliament for a Protestant people. In the year 2000 the only way forward for what has often been called 'a failed entity' appeared to be a neutral state with neutral emblems, whose public institutions avoided all, or nearly all, references to either Britain or Ireland. In the Republic, the change means the old assumption that an Irish man or woman was a Catholic, either of the practising or of the guilt-ridden lapsed variety, no longer applies.

In 1996, the Minister of Finance, Ruari Quinn, memorably described Ireland as a 'post-Catholic, pluralist republic'.[28] A country in which half the adult population regularly attends religious services and in which a book of prayers compiled by the Cistercian monks of Elenstal, near Limerick, tops the best-seller list,[29] is not accurately described as post-Catholic. There are even signs of a mild reaction setting in. When the Dublin Corporation fined a group of Redemptorist Missioners £50 in spring 2000 for putting up an advertisement for their mission on a lamp-post – in breach of the litter laws – people felt the Catholic Church was becoming the victim, rather than the perpetrator, of bullying. There was a new wave of scepticism about some of the people who were demanding compensation for alleged clerical sexual abuse. A corner was turned, perhaps, in the Nora Wall case. In June 1999 the courts gave Wall, a former Sister of Mercy, a life sentence for abusing a 10-year-old girl in the 1980s in a convent-run children's home in Cappoquin, County Waterford. But in July the Director of Public Prosecutions set Wall free on bail because of fears about the quality of the evidence. When the DPP announced in November of that year that it would not proceed with a retrial, the media concentrated on the former Sister Dominick's 'three years of silent pain and torment'.[30]

The Wall case drew a line under a certain phase of Ireland's reckoning with the Catholic Church. The dribble of cases against alleged clerical abusers continued, but they evoked more scepticism and less passion. Ireland in the early 1990s was transfixed by the revelation of abuse in the Church. At the end of the decade the spotlight had shifted entirely to revelations about bribery and corruption in the state.

The secularisation of Irish society did not bring as much liberty to people's lives as many had expected. Greater freedom was also greater freedom to be lonely. The suicide rate rose sharply in Ireland in the 1990s, along with the murder rate. The New Ireland looked a less cohesive society than the old. The papers carried regular reports on previously unknown phenomena, especially random violence inflicted on strangers, and old women and men who died in their homes without their neighbours noticing for days or even weeks. Secularism did not bring tolerance. At the turn of the century Ireland faced a race problem, which could not be blamed on the Catholic Church. From nowhere it suddenly achieved extraordinary prominence. Alongside the question of the unredeemed land Ulster, the immigration and asylum question seemed set to become a significant issue on Ireland's political landscape in the first decades of the new millennium.

In the early 1990s, Dubliners knew the city's non-white population practically by name. The cod wisdom of the Irish intelligentsia was that the Irish, as the colonised and enslaved 'blacks of Europe', were destined to remain immune from what was seen as an English or American disease. The decade disproved that hollow boast, as an influx of economic migrants and asylum-seekers fuelled a sudden upsurge in racial animosity, leading to attacks on non-whites in the streets of the capital and shrill campaigns in towns and villages against foreigners being allowed into their communities. The change began in 1992 with the arrival of Muslim Bosnian refugees from the Yugoslav conflict. As much as the Robinson election, the arrival of the Bosnians was a landmark, an adieu to the old Ireland. Holy Ireland did not take in foreigners. In the 1930s Ireland had refused to take in more than a handful of Jews. A much larger number of Hungarian refugees arrived after the Budapest uprising of 1956, but there had been no question of their permanent settlement. The advent of the Bosnians marked a new chapter: ten years after their arrival 1,200 were still in Ireland and they had been augmented by 12,000 Muslims in the capital alone from the Horn of Africa and the Middle East. There were two mosques in Dublin by 2000 and four more elsewhere in the Republic. The Muslim community rapidly equalled and then dwarfed the shrinking, ageing Jewish and Methodist communities. Muslims are destined to overtake the Church of Ireland population in the city within a decade or two, unless the Muslim community's present growth rate slows dramatically.

Immigration changed the face of parts of Dublin, especially the northern part of the city centre, in a very short time. According to the *Irish Times*, non-Irish nationals accounted for at least 10 per cent of maternity patients in the Rotunda city centre hospital in the late 1990s and a large proportion were African asylum-seekers. Their concentration in the streets around Parnell Square in north Dublin led locals to nickname the area 'Little Africa'.

The change aroused resentment. Liberal columnists on the *Irish Times* railed at this embarrassing display of provincial racism, so at odds with their own vision of the New Ireland. Their pious calls went mostly unheeded. Ireland was a country with no recent tradition of immigration, where a dominant nationalist ideology had for generations centred on the struggle to rid Ireland of foreigners and foreign influence. Staff at the Irish Islamic Centre complained of furious hostility to children in headscarves in some schools, as well as stone throwing and verbal abuse.

Even if many of the asylum-seekers are eventually expelled, the skills shortage created by the economic boom means the percentage of black and brown Irish-born people will rise. It poses an entirely new and unexpected question over what it means to be Irish, a question the Irish political establishment has scarcely begun to address. Until the 1530s, all Irish men and women were Catholic. It was the one force that bound the Old English and native Irish together. England's failed religious experiment in Ireland involved the country over the next three centuries in a confessional battle that the Catholics won hands down throughout the country, with the exception of the Protestant north-east. From then on, Irishness has been a matter of white Catholic versus white Protestant. The identities formed around those ideas were rigid and inflexible. To be Catholic was to be Gaelic in blood, Irish-speaking by culture, nationalist by politics, Green in sentiment. To be Protestant was to be Scots or English in blood, English-speaking, Unionist in politics, Orange in sentiment. Each side had its offshoots – the pro-British Castle Catholics, and the radical Protestant United Irish. But both groups were alien to the mainstream of their own community. The rise of a multi-cultural and multi-racial Ireland, which seems irresistible in the absence of a massive economic slump, challenges all the old certainties. It will do what decades of ecumenism failed to achieve: render the struggle between Catholics and Protestants for the soul of Ireland redundant once and for all.

Notes

INTRODUCTION
If Stones Could Speake

1. George Bernard Shaw, *John Bull's Other Island. In Four Acts*, London 1909, pp. xvi–xvii.
2. Bernadette Devlin, or McAliskey, as she became known after her marriage, was born in 1947 in Cookstown, Co. Tyrone. Elected MP for Mid-Ulster in 1969, she was imprisoned for her part in the conflicts in Derry, in 1969, and in 1972 after Bloody Sunday. In 1996 German police applied for extradition of her daughter Roisin to face charges over an IRA mortar bomb defused outside Osnabrück barracks in June.
3. The Red Hand is the emblem of the O'Neill clan. According to legend, the clan's founder was engaged in a race with a rival to reach land. They agreed that the first to touch land would claim it as his kingdom, whereupon O'Neill, who was losing the race, cut off his left hand and threw it ashore. More recently the symbol has been appropriated by Protestant paramilitary groups, who now sometimes portray it as a clenched fist rather than an open hand.
4. Mythical Queen of Connacht, her forces vanquished those of the warrior hero Cuchulain after an epic four-day fight.
5. The name Londonderry was adopted after James I's royal charter to the city in 1613. It was known as Derry before that date, and Derry is the preferred term of Irish Catholics. In 1984 the City Council renamed the city Derry, although Londonderry remains in official use by the British government for both the city and the surrounding county. Protestant reaction against the term Derry is relatively recent and reflects the politicisation of the language since the 1960s. Some radio announcers have taken to using the term Derry-stroke-Londonderry, giving rise to the nickname 'Stroke City.' Both the Protestant and Catholic dioceses use the older term, Derry, and that is the term I have generally employed here, except where I am specifically referring to the Protestant community.
6. There were no exact statistics until the 1890s but as the ratio seems to have been roughly 70:30 in the Albanians' favour by 1870, it seems likely that the Albanians took the lead at least several decades earlier. For a full discussion of the row see N. Malcolm, *Kosovo: A Short History*, London, 1998, pp. 194–201.
7. The Unionists lost control of the corporation to a combined Irish Parliamentary Party and Sinn Fein coalition in January 1920. See J. Bardon, *A History of Ulster*, Belfast, 1992, p. 467.
8. The cathedral, built in a style known as 'Planters' Gothic', was begun on the site of a medieval ruin. The foundations were laid in 1628 and the cathedral was completed in 1633 at a cost of £4,000. See P. Galloway, *The Cathedrals of Ireland*, Belfast, 1992, pp. 65–9.

9. This was hotly disputed, naturally, by most Church of Ireland theologians and historians, especially in the seventeenth and nineteenth centuries, who insisted on the identification of the Reformed Church with the supposedly pure church of the Celtic saints and stigmatised the Catholic Church as an alien implant. A gentler modern interpretation of this idea is contained in R. B. MacCarthy, *Ancient and Modern: A Short History of the Church of Ireland*, Dublin, 1995, pp. 28–37.

10. The thirteen apprentice boys shut the gates of the city on 7 December 1688 against Catholic troops under Lord Antrim. The cult of the Apprentice Boys dates from 1814 when the association was founded to commemorate the shutting of the gates and the lifting of the siege in August. Calendar changes have shifted the dates of the celebration to 18 December and 12 July respectively

11. George Walker (1646–91) was Rector of Donaghmore, Co. Tyrone and joint governor of Derry during the siege. He was killed at the Battle of the Boyne. Contemporary Presbyterian attacks on Walker as a self-promoting champion of Anglican exclusivism failed to prevent his subsequent elevation to cult status among Ulster Protestants of all denominations.

12. *The Relief of Derry*, by G. Folingsby, painted in 1861. A reproduction hangs in the Guildhall while the blackened original is in the Derry Harbour Museum.

13. For an account of the relative strengths of the city denominations, see J. O'Neill, *My Faith, Our Faith, Inter-Faith Practice – an Overview: An Examination of Various Religious-based Initiatives and Religious Faiths within Derry/Londonderry*, Derry, 1999, p. 6.

14. A British government review of parades and marches in August 1996 ended in a report in January 1997 and the establishment of the Independent Parades Commission on 26 March 1997. In October the government formalised the Commission's powers to re-route and prohibit parades.

15. The Royal Ulster Constabulary, formed on 5 April 1922, was modelled on the old Royal Irish Constabulary that policed the whole of British-ruled Ireland. From the start of partition the minority saw it as the great bulwark of Protestant and British domination. Attempts to reform the force to make it more inclusive have repeatedly run up against resistance from both sides, a fate that seems likely to overwhelm the recent report of the Commission set up under the former Hong Kong governor Chris Patten. This report, released in September 1999, urged radical reforms, including the abolition of the RUC's name, badge and other emblems.

16. A bomb in the centre of Omagh, the main town in Co. Tyrone, exploded at 3.10 p.m. on 15 August 1998, killing 21 people immediately. The final death toll was 29. An offshoot of the IRA, the 'Real' IRA, admitted responsibility on 18 August. The worst single atrocity in 30 years of conflict, it took place 13 weeks after the signing of the Good Friday Agreement between the British and Irish governments raised hopes of an end to paramilitary violence.

17. Lower Ormeau Concerned Community was founded in March 1992, a pressure group to co-ordinate Republican and nationalist opposition to Orange parades through this mainly Catholic area of central Belfast.

18. Born in 1660; Queen 1689 to 1694. A sincere and devout Protestant, she never attracted the devotion Irish Protestants accorded her husband, although she was undoubtedly more interested in improving the status and quality of the Church of Ireland than he was.

19. Widely seen until recently as the Belfast of England, Liverpool saw sectarian riots in 1909 and 1910, and until the 1920s the main opposition to the Conservatives and Liberals was not Labour but the Irish nationalists, who for years boasted a Liverpool MP. Sectarian tension drove many working-class Protestants to vote Conservative, as a result of which

Labour was kept out of control of the City Hall until 1955. Church leaders, especially Derek Warlock, Catholic Archbishop from 1971 to 1996 and David Sheppard, Anglican Bishop from 1975 to 1997 did much to dampen down the old tradition of confessional rivalry.

20. Drumcree is a mainly Catholic area of modern housing estates lying between the parish church of Drumcree village and the centre of the strongly Protestant town of Portadown, Co. Armagh. The road has been at the centre of a struggle over an Orange parade since 1995, pitting the Order and its Unionist allies against a coalition of Republicans and nationalists. The decision of the government's Parades Commission to prohibit the march in 1998 sparked violence that split Unionist ranks. Restoring the right to march down the Garvaghy Road has assumed cardinal importance among hard-line Orangemen and Unionists.

21. P. Collinson discusses the exposure to Swiss theology on the first generation of Anglican bishops in 'A Germanical nature', a chapter in *Archbishop Grindal: The Struggle for a Reformed Church*, London, 1979, pp. 67–82.

22. James I and VI. Born 1566, he was crowned James VI of Scotland at age of 13 months, after the abdication of his mother, Mary Stuart. He became James I of England 36 years later after Elizabeth's death in 1603. He died in 1625.

23. John Knox (1513–72) was born in Haddington. A convinced reformer since the 1540s, he became chaplain to Edward VI in 1551 and pastor of the English refugees at Frankfurt under Queen Mary. In 1558 he published an infamous diatribe against her and Mary of Guise, Regent of Scotland, called *The First Blast of the Trumpet against the Monstrous Regiment of Women*. Returning to Scotland in 1559 he became leader of the reforming party, coming into repeated conflict with Mary Stuart after her return from France in 1561. Mary's abdication in 1567 sealed his triumph.

24. Collinson, 'Germanical nature', p. 289.

25. The Confederate Catholics of Kilkenny, established in June 1642 to govern Ireland after the rising of 1641, was an uneasy alliance of Old English and Irish elements. It set up a supreme council, a mint, collected taxes and raised armies. Splits between lay and clerical factions weakened its ability to resist Oliver Cromwell's English Puritan army which invaded in August 1649 and subdued the country within nine months. For all its short-comings, nationalists have mostly praised the Confederation as a positive experiment in Irish self-determination. See J. Ohlmeyer (ed.), *Ireland from Independence to Occupation, 1641–60*, Dublin, 1993.

26. See D. Graham, 'The Scullabogue massacre, 1798', *History Ireland*, Autumn 1996, pp. 27–31.

27. An exclusive Protestant fraternity, the Loyal Orange Institution was founded in September 1795 after a sectarian skirmish in County Armagh. In Ireland today it comprises 1,400 private lodges organised into 125 district lodges and 12 county lodges. An unofficial organ of government in Northern Ireland for half a century after partition, it has suffered a decline in prestige and numbers while its annual parades in memory of the Williamite revolution have attracted increasing opposition from the Catholic community. Widely criticised as sectarian, it received a rare, sympathetic study from Ruth Dudley Edwards, in *The Faithful Tribe: an Intimate Portrait of the Loyal Institutions*, London, 1999.

28. See P. Compton, 'Religious demography in Northern Ireland', *Studies*, 78, 1989. Compton suggests that Catholics, at that time numbering 650,000 out of a total population of 1,575,000 in Northern Ireland, will form a numerical majority by 2020 and a voting majority by 2030.

CHAPTER ONE
The Hart of the English Pale

1. D. Quinn, 'Edward Walshe's "Conjectures" concerning the state of Ireland', in *Irish Historical Studies*, 5 (Dublin, 1947), p. 303.

2. Between 1520 and 1534 there were nine changes of regime at Dublin Castle, for example. The Earl of Surrey, Lord Deputy 1520–22, was followed by Piers Butler, 1522–24, the Earl of Kildare, 1524–26, Richard Nugent, 1527–28, Piers Butler again, 1528–29, a 'secret council', 1529–30, Sir William Skeffington, 1530–32 and the Earl of Kildare again, 1532–34. S. Ellis, 'Tudor policy in Ireland 1496–1534,' *Irish Historical Studies*, 20 (Dublin, 1977).

3. R. Stanihurst, 'A Treatise containing a plaine and perfect description of Ireland', in *Holinshed's Chronicles of England, Scotland and Ireland*, London, 1586, p. 20.

4. For a description of the surroundings of medieval Dublin, see H. B. Clarke, '*Urbs et Suburbum*: beyond the walls of medieval Dublin,' in C. Manning (ed.), *Dublin and beyond the Pale*, Bray, 1998.

5. Holy Trinity and St Patrick's were both styled cathedrals but Holy Trinity was the seat of the archbishops and was where their crosses, mitres and rings were interred. After various quarrels over precedence an agreement in 1300 provided that the former should be recognised as the mother church of the archdiocese.

6. J. A. Carr, *The Life and Times of James Ussher, Archbishop of Armagh*, London, 1895, p. 21.

7. Stanihurst, *Treatise ... of Ireland*, p. 21.

8. Ibid., p. 23.

9. Ibid., p. 20.

10. Ibid., p. 33.

11. Quinn, 'Walshe's "Conjectures"', p. 317.

12. E. Spenser, 'A View of the State of Ireland, written dialogue-wise between Eudox and Iranaeus, by Edmund Spenser ... in 1596' in J. Ware (ed.) *The History of Ireland*, Dublin, 1633, p. 64.

13. J. Brewer and W. Bullen (eds), *Calendar of the Carew Manuscripts Preserved in the Archepiscopal Library at Lambeth 1515–1574*, London 1867, p. 258.

14. J. Morrin (ed.), *Calendar of the Patent and Close Rolls of Chancery in Ireland*, Vol. I, Dublin, 1861, p. 371.

15. Brewer and Bullen, *Carew Manuscripts 1515–1574* p. 285.

16. *The Letter Book of Lord Deputy Sir John Perrot between 9 July 1584 and 26 May 1586, Analecta Hibernica*, 12, Dublin, 1943, p. 58.

17. Gerald Fitzgerald (Gearoid Og), 1487–1534, Lord Deputy 1513–20, 1524–28, 1532–34.

18. From 1540 to 1548, when he was replaced by Sir Edward Bellingham, from 1550 to 1551, when he was replaced by Sir James Croft, and from 1552 to 1554. See C. O'Mahoney, *The Viceroys of Ireland*, London, 1912.

19. Stanihurst, *Treatise ... of Ireland*, p. 110.

20. Brewer and Bullen, *Carew Manuscripts 1515–1574*, pp. 252–3.

21. From David Wolfe's description of Ireland, dated 25 March 1574, in J. M. Rigg (ed.), *Calendar of State Papers Relating to English Affairs Preserved Principally at Rome in the Vatican Archives and Library*, London, 1916, Vol. II, p. 163.

22. F. Moryson, 'A Description of Ireland', in H. Morley (ed.), *Ireland under Elizabeth and*

James the First, Described by Edmund Spenser, by Sir John Davies and by Fynes Moryson, London, 1890, p. 425.

23. J. Gilbert, *Calendar of the Ancient Records of Dublin*, Vol. I, Dublin, 1889, p. 375.
24. Rudolf von Munchhausen, 1570–1640, a Lutheran, visited Ireland in 1591, sailing from Bristol to Waterford.
25. D. O'Riain-Raedel, 'A German visitor to Monaincha in 1591', *Tipperary Historical Journal*, 1998, p. 229.
26. Morley (ed.), Moryson's *Description of Ireland*, p. 426.
27. Ibid., p. 428.
28. J. Gilbert, *A History of the City of Dublin*, Vol. I, Dublin, 1861, p. 110.
29. Ibid., pp. 151–2.
30. Morley, Moryson's *Description of Ireland*, p. 425.
31. Ibid.
32. N. Canny, 'Rowland White's *The Dysorders of the Irisshery*, 1571', *Studia Hibernica*, 19 (Dublin, 1979), p. 156.
33. Stanihurst, *Treatise … of Ireland*, p. 44.
34. Brewer and Bullen, *Carew Manuscripts 1515–1574*, p. 275.
35. Ibid., p. 277.
36. E. McEneaney (ed.), *A History of Waterford and its Mayors from the 12th Century to the 20th Century*, Waterford, 1995, p. 118.
37. Derived from the Irish *sliocht*, meaning offspring.
38. See D. Quinn's essay, 'Henry VIII and Ireland 1509–1534', *Irish Historical Studies*, 12, Dublin, 1961.
39. Brewer and Bullen, *Carew Manuscripts 1515–1574*, pp. 276–7.
40. The Irish parliament passed the Act declaring Henry King of Ireland on 26 June 1541.
41. Sir John Davies, b. 1569, Tisbury, Wiltshire, d. 1626. Solicitor-General for Ireland in 1603 and Attorney-General in 1606, he was responsible for the Plantation of Ulster. He became Speaker in the Irish parliament in 1613 and resigned in 1619.
42. Morley (ed.), Moryson's *Description of Ireland*, p. 219.
43. J. Otway-Ruthven, 'The character of Norman settlement in Ireland', in J. L. McCracken (ed.), *Historical Studies*, Vol. V, London, 1965, p. 77.
44. The earldom dated back to 1329. Piers Butler succeeded to the earldom in 1515. He died in 1539 and was succeeded by James (1539–46) and Thomas 'Black Tom' (1564–1614). The earldomthen passed to Walter Butler of Kilcash (1614–33), who was succeeded by his grandson, James, 1st Duke (1633–88). The flight of his Jacobite grandson, the 2nd Duke in 1715, ended the dominant role of the Ormonds, although the family retained their great castle at Kilkenny until the 1960s.
45. J. Dymmok, *A Treatise of Ireland*, 1599 (app) p. 14, in *Tracts Relating to Ireland*, Vol. II, Irish Archaeological Society, Dublin, 1843.
46. Ibid., p. 13.
47. E. Hogan, *The Description of Ireland and the State thereof as it is at This Present in Anno 1598*, Dublin and London, 1878, p. 55.
48. Stanihurst, *Treatise … of Ireland*, p. 24.
49. B. Bradshaw 'Fr Wolfe's description of Limerick city, 1574', *North Munster Antiquarian Journal*, 17 (1975), p. 47.
50. J. Hardiman, *The History of the Town and County of the Town of Galway*, Dublin, 1820, p. 22.
51. Ibid., p. 56.
52. W. G. Neely, *Kilkenny: An Urban History 1391–1843*, Belfast, 1989, p. 28.
53. Ibid., p. 29.
54. Hardiman, *Galway*, p. 201.

55. S. O'Cathain, 'Galway, ancient colonie of Englishe', *Studies*, 3 (1942), p. 459.
56. Gilbert, *Ancient Records of Dublin*, I, p. 281.
57. Ibid., p. 287.
58. Stanihurst in his treatise complains that there are no longer any woods in the Pale, which suggests the deforestation had taken place within living memory. 'Now the English pale is too naked,' *Treatise … of Ireland*, p. 13.
59. Brewer and Bullen, *Carew Manuscripts 1515–1574*, p. 50.
60. From Irish 'breitheamh', a judge.
61. Hogan, *Description of Ireland*, p. 27.
62. Brewer and Bullen, *Carew Manuscripts 1515–1574*, p. 41.
63. Stanihurst, *Treatise … of Ireland*, p. 24.
64. Hogan, *Description of Ireland*, p. 76.
65. *State Papers, Henry VIII, Part iii, Vol. II* [*SP VIII, iii, II*], London, 1834, p. 503.
66. Ibid., p. 12.
67. See E. McEneaney, 'Mayors and merchants in medieval Waterford 1169–1495', in W. Nolan, T. Power and D. Cowman (eds), *Waterford, History and Society: Interdisciplinary Essays on the History of an Irish County*, Dublin, 1992.
68. *Carew Manuscripts 1589–1600*, p. 44.
69. M. Gill (ed.), '*The Description of Ireland and the State Therof as it is at This Present in Anno 1598,' from a Manuscript Preserved in Clongowes-wood College, Dublin*, London, 1878, p. 40.
70. Ibid., p. 42.
71. J. F. Lydon, 'Medieval Wicklow – "a land of war"', in K. Hannigan and W. Nolan (eds), *Wicklow History and Society*, Dublin, 1994, p. 188.
72. Ibid, p. 173.
73. The phenomenon of degeneracy 'beganne about the xxxth yeare of the sayd king Edward the third his raigne', 'Lord Chancellor Gerrard's "Notes of his report on Ireland"', in *Analecta Hibernica*, 2 (Dublin 1931), pp. 95–6.
74. A. Bliss, *Spoken English in Ireland 1600–1740*, Dublin, 1979, p. 15.
75. Quinn, 'Walshe's "Conjectures"', p. 303.
76. The Munster Plantation was hatched in 1585 on lands of the attainted earls of Desmond. By 1594 there may have been about 3,000 settlers. Hampered by red tape, uncertain titles to land, and local hostility, the experiment collapsed when Munster rose in 1598. Much of the land ended up in the hands of the Boyle family. See D. Quinn, 'The Munster Plantation', *Journal of the Cork Historical and Archaeological Society*, 71 (1966).
77. W. Males, 'The Supplication of the blood of the English most lamentably murdered in Ireland, crying out of the earth for revenge, 1598', *Analecta Hibernica*, 36 (Dublin 1995), p. 72.
78. Quinn, 'Walshe's "Conjectures"', p. 316.
79. R. Krueger (ed.), *The Poems of Sir John Davies*, Oxford, 1975, p. xxvi.
80. Sir J. Davies, 'A discovery of the true causes why Ireland was never entirely subdued and brought under obedience', in Morley, *Ireland under Elizabeth*, p. 266.
81. J. O'Donovan 'Physical characteristics of the ancient Irish', *Ulster Journal of Archaeology*, 6 (Belfast, 1858), p. 199.
82. Gerald of Wales, 1146–1223, Archdeacon of Brecon, visited Ireland in 1180s after which he wrote *Topographia* and *Expugnatio Hibernica*, in which he excoriated the Irish as savages.
83. J. Watt, 'Negotiations between Edward II and John XXII concerning Ireland', *Irish Historical Studies*, 10 (1956), Dublin, 1957, p. 6.
84. Davies, 'A discovery of the true causes …' in Morley, *Ireland under Elizabeth*, p. 297.
85. Perrot, *The Chronicle of Ireland 1584–1608*, ed. Wood, p. 17.
86. G. Kew, *The Irish Sections of Fynes Moryson's Unpublished 'Itinerary'*, Dublin, 1998, p. 111.

87. Sir William Herbert, 1553–93, disciple of the Puritan theologian Lawrence Humphrey, was undertaker in the Munster Plantation 1586–90.

88. A. Keaveney and J. Madden (eds), *Sir William Herbert: Croftus sive de Hiberniae Liber*, Dublin, 1992, p. 109.

89. Ibid., p. 45.

90. Quinn, 'Walshe's "Conjectures"', p. 318.

91. Stanihurst, *Treatise … of Ireland*, p. 45.

92. Davies 'Discovery of the true causes', p. 298.

93. Males (ed.), *Supplication of the Blood of the English*.

94. *SP VIII, iii, II*, p. 8.

95. Brewer and Bullen, *Carew Manuscripts 1575–1588*, p. 39.

96. H. C. Hamilton (ed.), *Calendar of State Papers relating to Ireland 1509–1573*, London, 1860, p. 170.

97. 'The Description of Ireland as the present state thereof as it is at this present in anno 1598', from a manuscript preserved in Clongowes-wood College, Dublin and London, 1878, p. 55.

98. Kew, *Moryson's 'Itinerary'*, p. 50.

99. *SP VIII, iii, II*, p. 338.

CHAPTER TWO
It is Necessary that we Eradicate Them

1. E. Curtis and R. McDowell (eds), *Irish Historical Documents 1172–1922*, New York and London, 1968, pp. 33–4; also M. Sheehy, 'Ireland and the Holy See', *Irish Ecclesiastical Record*, 97, 1962, p. 13.

2. E. McEneaney (ed.), *A History of Waterford and its Mayors from the 12th to the 20th Century*, Waterford, 1995, p. 88.

3. Ibid., p. 87.

4. Ibid.

5. Ibid., p. 92.

6. Ibid., p. 95.

7. Ibid.

8. The fourth house of the Cistercian order, founded by St Bernard in 1115.

9. B. O'Dwyer, *Letters from Ireland 1228–1229. Stephen of Lexington*, Kalamazoo, Mich., 1982, p. 68.

10. Ibid., p. 35.

11. Ibid., p. 44.

12. Ibid.

13. Ibid., p. 188.

14. D. O'Sullivan, 'The Franciscan Friary of medieval Cork', *Journal of the Cork Historical and Archaeological Society*,45 (1940), p. 7.

15. F. J. Cotter, *The Friars Minor in Ireland from their Arrival to 1400*, New York, 1994, p. 41.

16. E. Curtis and R. McDowell *Irish Historical Documents 1172–1922*, New York and London, 1968, pp. 38–43.

17. K. Simms, 'The Archbishops of Armagh and the O'Neills 1347–1471', *Irish Historical Studies*, 19 (Dublin, 1975), p. 44.

18. Cotter, *The Friars Minor in Ireland*, p. 43.

19. J. Watt, 'Negotiations between Edward II and John XXII concerning Ireland', *Irish*

Historical Studies 10 (1956–7), p. 7.

20. P. O'Dwyer, 'The Carmelite Order in pre-Reformation Ireland,' *Irish Ecclesiastical Record*, 110 (Dublin, 1968), p. 362.

21. Cotter, *The Friars Minor in Ireland*, p. 132.

22. Ibid., p. 50.

23. H. Berry, *Statutes and Ordinances and Acts of the Parliament of Ireland*, Vol. I, Dublin, 1907, p. 273.

24. Curtis and McDowell, *Irish Historical Documents 1172–1922*, pp. 52–9.

25. Berry, *Acts of the Parliament of Ireland*, p. 447.

26. J. Fahey, 'The collegiate church of St Nicholas, Galway', *Irish Ecclesiastical Record*, 16 (Dublin, 1895), p. 704.

27. Ibid., p. 705.

28. The crown ceased issuing licences for elections to Achonry, for example, in the thirteenth century. W. H. Grattan Flood, 'The episcopal succession of Achonry 1219–1561,' *Irish Ecclesiastical Record*, 20 (Dublin, 1922) pp. 475–6.

29. English but not English born, like the archbishops of Dublin. J. Watt, 'The Church and the two nations in late medieval Armagh', in W. J. Sheils and D. Wood (eds), *The Churches, Ireland and the Irish*, Oxford, 1989, p. 42.

30. See Simms, 'The Archbishops of Armagh and the O'Neills 1347–1471'.

31. The six were John Artilburgh, 1405–8, Nicholas FitzMaurice, 1408–9, Maurice Stack, 1449–51, Maurice MacConcubhair, 1451–55, John Stack, 1458–88 and Philip Stack, 1488–95. See J. O'Connell, 'The Church in Ireland in the fifteenth century', in *Proceedings of the Irish Catholic Historical Committee 1956*, Dublin, 1956, pp. 2–3.

32. See H. Jefferies, 'The Church among two nations. Armagh on the eve of the Tudor Reformations', *History Ireland*, 6 (1998).

33. M. Ronan, *The Reformation in Dublin 1536–58*, London, 1926, p. 118.

34. J. Mills (ed.), *Account Roll of the Priors of the Priory of the Holy Trinity, Dublin 1337–1346*, Dublin, 1996, p. xvii.

35. Ronan, *Reformation in Dublin 1538–58*, p. 118.

36. Mills (ed.), *Account Roll of . . . the Priory of the Holy Trinity, Dublin*, p. xv.

37. G. Carville, *The Heritage of Holy Cross*, Belfast ,1973, pp 116–18.

38. D. Murphy (ed.), *Triumphalia Chronologica Monasterii Sanctae Crucis in Hibernia*, Dublin, 1895, p. 133.

39. Ibid., p. 149.

40. Ibid., p. 131.

41. St Coemgen, or Kevin, built a hermitage in the valley in the fifth century. After his death in 618 the monastery grew into a centre of pilgrimage. Destroyed in 1398, it fell into disuse after the Reformation.

42. J. Lydon, 'Medieval Wicklow – a land of war', in K. Hannigan and W. Nolan (eds), *Wicklow History and Society*, Dublin, 1994, p. 155.

43. 'The diocese of Dublin in the year 1630', *Irish Ecclesiastical Record*, 5 (Dublin, 1869), p. 162.

44. M. Purcell, 'St Patrick's Purgatory: Francesco Chiericati's letter to Isabella d'Este', *Seancas Ard Mhacha*, 12 (1987), pp. 9–10.

45. Ibid., p. 8.

46. D. O'Riain-Raedel, 'A German visitor to Monaincha in 1591', *Tipperary Historical Journal*, 1998, p. 231.

47. P. O'Mordha, 'Saint Patrick's well Clonfad', *Clogher Record*, 8 (1975), p. 284.

48. D. O'hEaluighthe, 'Saint Gobnet of Ballyvourney', *Journal of the Cork Historical and Archaeological Society*, 57 (1952), p. 49.

49. G. Lynch, 'The holy wells of county Wicklow: traditions and legends' in Hannigan and

Nolan (eds), *Wicklow History and Society.*

50. Produced in the seventeenth century, *The Four Masters: Annals of the Kingdom of Ireland* drew on earlier works, such as the *Annals of Connacht* and the *Annals of Loch Ce*, which were compiled in monasteries and contained material dating back to the eleventh century.

51. J. O'Donovan (ed.), *The Four Masters: Annals of the Kingdom of Ireland from the Earliest Times to the Year 1616*, 3rd edition, Vol. V, Dublin, 1990, pp. 1447–9.

52. J. M. Rigg (ed.) *Calendar of State Papers Relating to English Affairs Preserved Principally at Rome*, Vol. II, London, 1916, 1572–78, p. 49.

53. Grattan Flood, 'Episcopal succession of Achonry', p. 483.

54. M. Hares, 'A description of Clogher Cathedral in the early sixteenth century', *Clogher Record* 12 (1985), p. 52.

55. R. Stalley, *The Cistercian Monasteries of Ireland*, London and New Haven, 1987, pp. 23–4.

56. M. Ronan, *The Reformation in Dublin 1536–1668*, London, 1926, p. 184.

57. Ronan, *Reformation in Dublin*, p. 187–9.

58. T. O'Keefe, *An Anglo-Norman Monastery: Bridgetown Priory and the Architecture of the Augustinian Cannons Regular in Ireland*, Cork, 1999, p. 43.

59. *Calendar of the Patent and Close Rolls of Chancery in Ireland of the Reigns of Henry VIII, Edward VI, Mary, and Elizabeth*, Vol. I, ed., J. Morrin, Dublin, 1861, p. 55.

60. B. Bradshaw, *The Dissolution of the Religious Orders in Ireland under Henry VIII*, Cambridge, 1974, p. 22.

61. Ibid., p. 23.

62. Canice Mooney produces several examples in 'The Irish Church in the sixteenth century', in *Proceedings of the Irish Catholic Historical Committee 1962*, Dublin, 1963.

63. J. Watt, 'The Church and the two nations in late medieval Armagh', in Sheils and Wood, *The Churches, Ireland and the Irish* p. 45.

64. P. Happe and J. King (eds), *The Vocacyon of John Bale to the Bishoprick of Ossory*, New York, 1990, p. 55.

65. See A. O'Connell, 'Edmund Butler, Archbishop of Cashel 1524–51 and the Reformation', *Irish Ecclesiastical Record*, 100 (Dublin, 1963).

66. H. Walshe, 'Enforcing the Elizabethan settlement. The vicissitudes of Hugh Brady, Bishop of Meath 1563–84', *Irish Historical Studies*, 26 (1989), p. 354.

67. N. Canny, 'Rowland White's *The Dysorders of the Irissherye* 1571', *Studia Hibernica* 19, Dublin, 1979, p. 156.

68. Happe and King (eds), *Vocacyon*, p. 52.

69. M. Mahoney, 'The Scottish hierarchy 1513–1565', in D. McRoberts (ed.), *Essays on the Scottish Reformation 1513–1625*, Glasgow, 1962, pp. 60–1.

70. T. Flynn, *The Irish Dominicans 1536–1641*, Dublin, 1993, p. 5.

71. F. Martin, 'The Irish friars and the Observant movement in the fifteenth century', *Proceedings of the Irish Catholic Historical Committee 1960*, Dublin, 1961, p. 12.

72. Ibid., p. 11.

73. J. Silke 'Some aspects of the Reformation in Armagh province', *Clogher Record*, 11 (1984), p. 347.

74. Flynn, *The Irish Dominicans 1536–1641*, pp. 1–5.

CHAPTER THREE

Myn Auctoritie is Litle Regarded

1. *State Papers, Henry VIII, Part iii, Vol. II [SP VIII, iii, II]*, London, 1834, p. 316.

2. 1776–1848, Bishop of Killaloe 1820–23 and of Down and Connor, 1823–48.

3. R. Mant, *History of the Church of Ireland from the Reformation to the Revolution*, London, 1841, p. 111.

4. B. Bradshaw, 'George Browne, first Reformation Archbishop of Dublin, 1530–1554', *Journal of Ecclesiastical History*, 21 (Cambridge, 1970), p. 309.

5. P. Happe and J. King (eds), *The Vocacyon of John Bale to the Bishoprick of Ossorie*, New York, 1990, p. 68.

6. The Imperial ambassador Chapuys in April 1533 noted Browne's new prominence as a preacher in favour of the King's marriage to Anne Boyleyn. J. Gairdner (ed.), *Letters and Papers, Foreign and Domestic, of the Reign of Henry VIII*, London, 1882, p. 179. For an account of Browne's progress in England in 1534 and 1535, see M. Ronan, *The Reformation in Dublin 1536–58*, London, 1926, pp. 5–16.

7. Ronan, *Reformation in Dublin*, p. 11.

8. Anne was executed on 19 May 1536.

9. *SP VIII, iii, II*, p. 316.

10. R. Dudley Edwards, 'The Irish Reformation Parliament of Henry VIII 1537–7' in T. W. Moody (ed.), *Studies in Irish History*, Vol. VI, London, 1968.

11. *SP VIII, iii, II*, p. 371.

12. For an account of this see B. Bradshaw, 'Opposition to the ecclesiastical legislation of the Irish Reformation parliament', *Irish Historical Studies*, 16 (Dublin, 1969).

13. *SP VIII, iii, II*, p. 439.

14. Ibid., p. 425.

15. Ibid., p. 465.

16. Ronan, *Reformation in Dublin*, pp. 67–8.

17. *SP VIII, iii, II*, p. 513.

18. Ibid., p. 539.

19. Ibid., p. 540.

20. See A. O'Donnell, 'Edmund Butler, Archbishop of Cashel 1524–51 and the Reformation', *Irish Ecclesiastical Record*, 100 (Dublin, 1963).

21. Mant, *History of the Church of Ireland*, p. 137.

22. Ibid.

23. *SP VIII iii, II*, p. 35. Cited in A. Cogan, *The Diocese of Meath, Ancient and Modern*, Dublin, 1862–70, pp. 92–3.

24. *SP VIII, iii, II*, p. 103.

25. Mant, *History of the Church of Ireland*, p. 160.

26. Ibid., pp. 145–6.

27. *SP VIII, iii, II*, p. 6–7.

28. Ibid., pp. 8–9.

29. Ibid., p. 30.

30. Cogan, *Diocese of Meath*, p. 93.

31. Ibid., p. 91, citing *SP VIII, iii, II*, p. 1.

32. Ibid.

33. R. Dudley Edwards, 'The Irish bishops and the Anglican schism 1934–1947', *Irish Ecclesiastical Record*, 45, Dublin 1935, p. 43.

34. A statement produced by Convocation: they drew on the earlier Wittenberg Articles drawn up by a team of German Lutheran and English churchmen. Principally they endorsed the Lutheran doctrine of justification by faith alone. See D. MacCulloch, *Thomas Cranmer*, London and New Haven, 1996, p. 161.

35. Dudley Edwards, 'Irish Bishops', p. 43, citing *SP VIII, iii, II*, p. 117.

36. Bishop of Waterford 1519–51, succeeded by Patrick Walsh, 1551–66, Peter White, 1566–70, David Cleere, 1570–? It was only under Marmaduke Middleton (1579–82) that Protestantism really reached Waterford.

37. Dudley Edwards, 'Irish Bishops', p. 43.
38. *SP VIII, iii, II*, p. 123.
39. Cogan, *Diocese of Meath*, p. 97.
40. Ibid., p. 96, citing *SP VIII, iii, II*, p. 130.
41. B. Bradshaw, *The Dissolution of the Religious Orders in Ireland under Henry VIII*, Cambridge, 1974, p. 68.
42. *SP VIII, iii, II*, pp. 142–3.
43. J. Mills (ed.), *Account Rolls of the Priors of the Priory of the Holy Trinity, Dublin, 1337–1346*, Dublin, 1996, p. xiv.
44. Reproduced in K. Nicholls, 'A list of monasteries in Connacht 1577', *Journal of the Galway Archaeological and Historical Society*, 33 (1963–7).
45. Ibid., p. 31.
46. F. Bigger, 'Kilkonnel Abbey', *Journal of the Galway Archaeological and Historical Society*, 2 (1902), p. 8.
47. M. Ryan, 'The Franciscan houses of Thomond in 1616', *North Munster Antiquarian Journal*, 10 (1967), p. 113.
48. Ibid.
49. Nicholas Blake's will in September 1568 left money for the friars with the proviso that 'in case the friars should be put out of the abbeys about Galway then that the legacies made to them should return to the heirs of the testator'. B. Jennings, 'The Abbey of St Francis Galway', *Journal of the Galway Archaeological and Historical Society*, 22 (1947), p. 106.
50. B. Jennings, 'The Abbey of St Francis, Galway', *Journal of the Galway Archaeological and Historical Society*, Vol. 22, 1947.
51. Ibid.
52. P. F. Moran, *History of the Catholic Archbishops of Dublin since the Reformation*, Vol. 1, Dublin, 1864, pp. 104; see also P. O'Dwyer, *The Irish Carmelites*, Dublin, 1988.
53. B. Jennings, 'The Abbey of Muckross', *Journal of the Cork Historical and Archaeological Society*, 45 (1940), p. 82.
54. J. Ware, *The Antiquities and History of Ireland*, London, 1705, pp. 76–116.
55. N. White (ed.), *Extent of Irish Monastic Possessions 1540–1541 from Manuscripts in the Public Record Office, London*, Dublin, 1943. The list details 12 houses in County Dublin, six in Carlow, 20 in Cork, 18 in Kildare, 14 in Kilkenny, nine in Limerick, 17 in Louth, 37 in Meath, 19 in Tipperary, eight in Waterford and 12 in Wexford.
56. J. Morrin (ed.), *Calendar of the Patent and Close Rolls of Chancery in Ireland*, Vol. 1, Dublin, 1861, p. 57.
57. White, *Irish Monastic Possessions*, p. 302.
58. Abbot of Holy Cross from 1538 to 1563.
59. R. Gillespie and B. Cunningham, 'Holy Cross Abbey and the Counter-Reformation in Tipperary', *Tipperary Historical Journal* (Thurles, 1991), p. 177.
60. The only surviving collection of pre-Reformation vestments in Ireland was found when the building was knocked down in the 1770s. It is now housed in the National Museum of Ireland in Dublin. C. MacLeod, 'Fifteenth century vestments in Waterford', *Journal of the Royal Society of Antiquaries of Ireland*, 1952.
61. White, *Monastic Possessions 1540–1541*, p. 59.
62. *SP VIII, iii, II*, p. 9.
63. Ronan, *Reformation in Dublin*, p. 149.
64. Bradshaw, *Dissolution of the Religious Orders*, p. 106.
65. Morrin, *Calendar of the Patent and Close Rolls*, Vol. I, p. 57. Also Ronan, *Reformation in Dublin*, pp. 170–7.
66. Ronan, *Reformation in Dublin*, p. 196–7.
67. White, *Monastic Possessions 1540–1541*, p. 155.

68. Morrin, *Calendar of the Patent and Close Rolls*, Vol. I, p. 90.
69. Ibid., p. 73. White, *Monastic Possessions 1540–1541*, p. 302. Also, Ronan, *Reformation in Dublin*, p. 185.
70. J. Brewer and W. Bullen (eds), *Calendar of the Carew Manuscripts Preserved in the Archepiscopal Library at Lambeth 1515–74*, London, 1867, p. 200; also White, *Monastic Possessions 1540–1541*, p. 121.
71. White, *Monastic Possessions 1540–1541*, p. 352.
72. Ibid., p. 184.
73. Morrin, *Patent and Close Rolls*, p. 75.
74. Ibid., p. 62.
75. Cogan, *Diocese of Meath*, p. 320.
76. Morrin, *Patent and Close Rolls*, p. 59.
77. Cogan, *Diocese of Meath*, p. 225.
78. Morrin, *Patent and Close Rolls*, p. 64.
79. Ibid., p. 60.
80. The name is written 'Habarde', ibid., p. 61.
81. White, '*Monastic Possessions 1540–1541*, p. 235.
82. Cogan, *Diocese of Meath*, p. 91.
83. St John's Hospital, Naas, was turned into a barn: White, *Monastic Possessions 1540–1541*, p. 155.
84. St Mary de Hoggles, Dublin, was used to repair Dublin Castle: ibid., p. 121.
85. *SP VIII, iii, II*, pp. 304–5.
86. Brewer and Bullen (eds), *Carew Manuscripts 1515–1574*, pp. 183–207.
87. O'Donnell's indenture, for example, recognised Henry VIII as 'in terris immediate sub Christo Anglicane et Hibernicane Ecclesiae Supremi Capitis'. *SP VIII, iii, II*, p. 318.
88. Dudley Edwards, 'Irish bishops', p. 53.
89. See 'Documents concerning Primate Dowdall', *Archivium Hibernicum*, 1 (Dublin, 1912).
90. For a description of the mission, F. O'Donoghue, 'The Jesuits come to Ireland', *Studies* 80 (1991).
91. *SP VIII, iii, II*, p. 123.
92. 'Documents concerning Primate Dowdall', p. 258.
93. According to Ruth Dudley Edwards in 'Irish bishops', only two of Henry VIII's nominations to Irish sees were convinced Protestants, Browne and Nangle.

CHAPTER FOUR
The Kings Most Godlie Procedings

1. M. Ronan, 'Booke oute in Latten', *Irish Ecclesiastical Record*, 25 (L) p. 505.
2. J. Bradley 'The medieval tombs of St Canice's cathedral', in S. Barry, J. Bradley and A. Empey, *A Worthy Foundation: The Cathedral Church of St Canice Kilkenny 1285–1985*, Mountrath, Leix, 1985, p 74.
3. H. C. Hamilton *Calendar of State Papers Relating to Ireland, 1509–1573*, London, 1860, p. 94.
4. 'Documents concerning Primate Dowdall', *Archivium Hibernicum*, I, (Dublin 1912), p. 260.
5. Ronan, 'Booke oute in Latten', p. 505.
6. Ibid., p. 502.
7. Ibid.
8. J. Bale, *The Vocacyon of John Bale to the Bishoprick of Ossorie in Irelande, his Persecucions in*

the same, and Finall Delyveraunce, Harleian Miscellany, 6, London, 1810, p. 452.

9. P. F. Moran, *History of the Catholic Archbishops of Dublin since the Reformation*, Vol. I, Dublin, 1864, p. 40.

10. Ronan, 'Booke oute in Latten', p. 505.

11. D. MacCulloch, *Thomas Cranmer: A Life*, New Haven and London, 1996, p. 227. MacCulloch suggests the production may have been Bales's *On the Treasons of Becket*.

12. Bale, *Vocacyon*, p. 446.

13. Ibid., p. 447.

14. Ibid., pp. 454–5.

15. Ibid., p. 447.

16. Ibid., p. 452.

17. Ibid., p. 452.

18. Ibid., p. 453.

19. J. Morrin (ed.), *Calendar of Patent and Close Rolls of Chancery in Ireland*, Vol. I, Dublin, 1861, p. 302; also p. 315.

20. Ibid., pp. 327–8.

21. Moran, *Catholic Archbishops*.

22. J. Brewer and W. Bullen (eds), *Calendar of the Carew Manuscripts Preserved in the Archepiscopal Library at Lambeth 1515–1574*, London, 1867, pp. 252–3.

23. Cranmer died at the stake on 21 March 1556, six months after Latimer and Ridley.

24. Roland Baron of Cashel: Morrin, *Patent and Close Rolls*, p. 310.

25. J. O'Flanagan, *The Lives of the Lord Chancellors and Keepers of the Great Seal of Ireland from the Earliest Times to the Reign of Queen Victoria*, Vol. I, London, 1870, p. 240.

26. A former Cistercian monk at Bective Abbey, he was sent to Meath in 1554. After deprivation in 1560 he escaped arrest by moving to Spain, where he died at the Cistercian house in Alcala in 1577. See A. Cogan, *The Diocese of Meath, Ancient and Modern*, Vol. II, Dublin, 1862, p. 109.

27. Archbishop from 1559 to 1574. Although a convinced Protestant he evolved into a bitter opponent of the Puritan wing of the Church as it emerged in the 1560s, fiercely defending the existing Book of Common Prayer, vestments and the episcopal hierarchy. His stance placed him at odds with a number of his fellow bishops.

28. Tunstall died in Parker's custody, soon after Elizabeth's accession. Bonner died in the Marshalsea prison 10 years later.

29. Writs were sent to 20 bishops and 23 peers, 20 shires and 29 boroughs and towns. See H. Jefferies, 'The Irish parliament of 1560: the Anglican reforms authorised', *Irish Historical Studies*, 26 (1989).

30. See ibid.

31. J. Rigg (ed.), *Calendar of State Papers Relating to English Affairs Preserved Principally at Rome*, Vol. I, London, 1916, p. 483.

32. Richard Creagh, 1522–1586 (app.). See W. H. Grattan Flood, 'Pre-Reformation Archbishops of Cashel', *Irish Ecclesiastical Record*, 29 (1911).

33. C. Lennon, *Richard Stanihurst the Dubliner 1547–1618 a Biography with Stanihurst's Text on Ireland's Past*, Dublin, 1981, p. 21, citing P. F. Moran (ed.), *Analecta*, Dublin, 1884, pp. 235–6.

34. Hugh Brady, 1527–84. Educated at Oxford, he served in London. His episcopate was a failure. The local great families, the Plunketts, Berminghams, Flemings and Nettervilles remained Catholic. He was unable to attract educated English clergy to serve in his diocese and few of the Meath livings were in the Bishop's hands. By the time he died he was deeply in debt. H. Walshe, 'Enforcing the Elizabethan settlement: the vicissitudes of Hugh Brady, Bishop of Meath 1563–84', *Irish Historical Studies*, 26 (1989).

35. Moran, *Catholic Archbishops*, Vol. I, p. 72.

36. R. Jackson, *Archbishop Magrath, the Scoundrel of Cashel*, Dublin and Cork, 1974, p. 10.

37. Ibid., pp. 38–9.

CHAPTER FIVE
The Devil's Service

1. From 'A Discourse of Ireland, wherein it is conjectured that if the Spaniards do invade Ireland, they will make their descent in Munster', in J. Brewer and W. Bullen (eds), *Calendar of the Carew Manuscripts preserved in the Archiepiscopal Library at Lambeth 1589–1600*, London, 1869, p. 129.

2. Edmund Campion was born in 1540 and executed at Tyburn on 1 December 1581. For a description of his Irish sojourn, see E. Reynolds, *Campion and Parsons: the Jesuit Mission of 1580–1*, London, 1980.

3. C. Lennon provides details of the history of the family in *Richard Stanihurst the Dubliner 1547–1618, a Biography with Stanihurst's Text on Ireland's Past*, Dublin, 1981, p. 17.

4. Reynolds, *Campion and Parsons*, p. 40.

5. Ibid.

6. W. Trimble, *The Catholic Laity of Elizabethan England 1558–1603*, Cambridge, Mass., 1964, p. 11.

7. Ibid., p. 26.

8. Ibid., p. 123.

9. P. Collinson, *Archbishop Grindal 1519–1583: the Struggle for a Reformed Church*, London, 1979, pp. 187–95.

10. G. Kew, *The Irish Sections of Fynes Moryson's Unpublished 'Itinerary'*, Dublin, 1998, p. 92.

11. P. F. Moran, *History of the Catholic Archbishops of Dublin since the Reformation*, Vol. I, Dublin, 1864, p. 63.

12. J. Brewer and W. Bullen (eds), *Calendar of the Carew Manuscripts Preserved in the Archiepiscopal Library at Lambeth 1575–1588*, p. 143.

13. 'An Irish diocese in the seventeenth century', *Irish Ecclesiastical Record*, 1 (Dublin, 1897), p. 3.

14. E. G. Atkinson (ed.), *Calendar of State Papers Relating to Ireland, July 1596–December 1597*, London, 1893, p. 14.

15. W. G. Neely, *Kilkenny, an Urban History 1391–1843*, Belfast, 1989, p. 44.

16. B. Bradshaw, 'Fr Wolfe's description of Limerick city, 1574', *North Munster Antiquarian Journal*, 17 (1975), p. 47.

17. C. Lennon, *Sixteenth-century Ireland the Incomplete Conquest*, Dublin, 1994, p. 7. Lennon suggests it was probably below this figure.

18. Brewer and Bullen (eds), *Carew Manuscripts 1589–1600*, Intro. pp. lxxviii–lxxx.

19. Moran, *Catholic Archbishops*, p. 151. See also *Calendar of State Papers … Ireland, 1588–1592*, p. 312.

20. J. M. Rigg (ed.) *Calendar of State Papers Relating to English Affairs Preserved Principally at Rome*, London, 1916, Vol. I, p. 347.

21. Brewer and Bullen (eds), *Carew Manuscripts 1575–1588*, p. 174.

22. Some writers have suggested the bishop was Patrick O'Healy of Mayo, citing a reference to him in the State Papers in Rome. B. Millet states definitively that O'Healy did not join Fitzmaurice's expedition and that the bishop was O'Gallagher. See 'The beatified martyrs of Ireland: Bishop Patrick O'Hurley and Conn O'Rourcke', *Irish Theological Quarterly*, 64 (Maynooth, 1999).

23. A key feature of Elizabeth's more ambitious Irish policy was the establishment of presi-

dency councils in the provinces of Munster, Connacht and Ulster. Lennon, *Sixteenth-century Ireland*, pp. 208–36. Based on the expansion of the Welsh Marches, the plan was for the presidents to control a small armed force, set rents, collect taxes or function as a court. Drury was the second president of Munster, following Sir John Perrot, who had been appointed in 1570.

24. Millet, 'Beatified martyrs of Ireland'.
25. E. Spenser, *A View of the Present State of Ireland*, ed. R. L. Renwick, Oxford, 1970, p. 104.
26. J. Hogan and M. O'Farrell (eds), *Walsingham Letter Book*, Dublin, 1959, p. 245. See also Sr M. Benvenuta, 'The Geraldine wars – rebellion or crusade?', *Irish Ecclesiastical Record*, 103 (Dublin, 1965), p. 153.
27. *Kerry Archaeological Magazine*, 4 (1916–18), p. 60.
28. 'All the cities and towns cry out against the victualling of our soldiers in garrisons', Pelham to Irish Privy Council, Brewer and Bullen (eds), *Carew Manuscripts, 1589–1600*, p. 239.
29. Ibid., p. 289.
30. K. C. Hamilton (ed.), *Calendar of State Papers Relating to Ireland, 1588–1592*, London, 1885, p. 366.
31. See Note 1.
32. J. Silke, 'The Irish appeal of 1593 to Spain', *Irish Ecclesiastical Record*, 92 (1959), p. 287.
33. Lennon, *Richard Stanihurst the Dubliner*, p. 49.
34. C. W. Russell and J. P. Prendergast (eds), *Calendar of State Papers relating to Ireland, 1603–1606*, London, 1872, p. 28.
35. Ibid.
36. Russell and Prendergast (eds) . . . *Calendar of State Papers 1603–1606*, p. 179.
37. Kew, *Moryson's 'Itinerary'*, p. 52.
38. C. Lennon, 'The rise of recusancy among the Dublin patricians, 1580–1613', in W. Sheils and D. Wood (eds), *The Churches, Ireland and the Irish*, Oxford, 1989, p. 129.
39. Miscellaneous documents, *Archivium Hibernicum* (Dublin, 1917), p. 65.

CHAPTER SIX
Seminaries beyond the Seas

1. W. Males, 'The Supplication of the blood of the English most lamentably murdered in Ireland crying out of the yearth for revenge, 1598', *Analecta Hibernica* 36, Dublin, 1995, p. 43.
2. See L. Swords, *Collège des Irlandais de Paris*, Dublin, 1986.
3. J. Brady, 'The Irish colleges in Europe', in *Proceedings of the Irish Catholic Historical Committee 1957*, Dublin, 1957, pp. 7–9.
4. P. F. Moran, *History of the Catholic Archbishops of Dublin since the Reformation*, Vol. I, Dublin, 1864, p. 221.
5. W. Burke, *History of Clonmel*, Waterford, 1907, p. 49.
6. P. Corish outlines Wadding's life and family connections in 'Father Luke Wadding and the Irish nation', *Irish Ecclesiastical Record*, 88 (Dublin, 1957).
7. T. O'Connor, 'Towards the invention of the Irish Catholic "Nation"', *Irish Theological Quarterly*, 64, Maynooth, 1999, p. 161.
8. 'Irish colleges on the continent', *Irish Theology Quarterly*, 64 (Maynooth, 1999), p. 138.
9. 'Irish colleges since the Reformation', *Irish Ecclesiastical Record*, 9 (Dublin, 1873), p. 210.
10. Ibid., p. 217.
11. See J. Niles, 'The Irish College, Antwerp', *Clogher Record*, 15 (Enniskillen, 1996).
12. Anon. 'Irish Colleges since the Reformation', *Irish Ecclesiastical Record*, 9, Dublin, 1873,

pp. 210–11.

13. See F. Bigger 'The Irish in Rome in the 17th century', *Ulster Journal of Archaeology*, 5 (Belfast, 1899).

14. M. Walsh, 'The Irish College at Madrid', *Seanchas Ard Mhacha*, 15, Armagh, 1993, p. 44.

15. Niles, 'The Irish College, Antwerp', p. 16.

16. J. Silke, 'The Irish College, Seville', *Archivium Hibernicum*, 24 (Maynooth, 1961), p. 112.

17. These are described by P. Corish in 'The Irish College, Rome', in *Father Luke Wadding*, edited by the Franciscan fathers, Killiney, Dublin, 1957.

18. 'Irish colleges since the Reformation', p. 545.

19. Brady, 'The Irish colleges in Europe', p. 4.

20. Richard Creagh, b. 1522, d. 1586 (app). For a sketch of his life, see W. H. Grattan Flood, 'Pre-Reformation Archbishops of Cashel', *Irish Ecclesiastical Record*, 29 (Dublin, 1911).

21. A. Ford, *The Protestant Reformation in Ireland, 1590–1641*, Frankfurt, 1985, p. 44.

22. W. Hayes, 'Dermot O'Hurley's last visit to Tipperary', *Tipperary Historical Journal*, 1992, p. 172.

23. Henry Fitzsimon was born in Dublin in 1567, educated at Hart Hall and Christ Church, Oxford. He then left for Douai. In 1598 he was selected along with James Archer of Kilkenny for a Jesuit mission to Ireland. Jailed in 1599, he was released in 1604.

24. 'The diocese of Dublin in the year 1630', *Irish Ecclesiastical Record*, 5 (Dublin, 1869), p. 150.

25. Ibid., p. 160.

26. Ibid., p. 158.

27. 'Irish colleges since the Reformation', p. 433.

28. Ibid., p. 434.

29. Ibid., p. 438.

30. J. M. Rigg (ed.), *Calendar of State Papers Relating to English Affairs Preserved Principally at Rome 1558–1571*, Vol. 1, London, 1916, pp. 467–8. In J. Silke 'Some aspects of the Reformation in Armagh Province', *Clogher Record*, 11 (1984), p. 354.

31. 'An Irish diocese in the 17th century', *Irish Ecclesiastical Record*, 1 (Dublin, 1897), p. 6.

32. M. D. O'Sullivan, 'The lay school at Galway in the sixteenth and seventeenth centuries', *Journal of the Galway Archaeological and Historical Society*, 15 (1931–33), p. 30.

33. Rigg (ed.), *Calendar of State Papers at Rome . . . 1558–1571*, p. 483.

34. E. Spenser, *A View of the Present State of Ireland*, ed. W. L. Renwick, Oxford, 1970, p. 162.

35. O'Sullivan, 'The lay school at Galway', p. 15.

36. 'The Letter Book of Lord Deputy Sir John Perrot between 9 July 1584 and 20 May 1586', *Analecta Hibernica*, 12 (Dublin, 1943), p. 23.

37. Ibid., p. 29.

38. H. Murphy, *A History of Trinity College Dublin from its Foundation to 1702*, Dublin, 1951, p. 12.

39. J. W. Stubbs, *Archbishop Adam Loftus and the Foundation of Trinity College Dublin, as Preserved in a Manuscript in the Library of Armagh*, London and Dublin, 1892, pp. 3–5.

40. 'Irish colleges since the Reformation', p. 315.

41. Murphy, *History of Trinity*, p. 62.

42. B. Jennings (ed.), *Wadding Papers 1614–1638*, Dublin, 1953, p. 609.

43. J. Ussher, *The Religion Professed by the Ancient Irish*, London, 1631, p. 77.

44. G. D. Burtchaell and J. M. Rigg (eds), *Report on Franciscan Manuscripts Preserved at the Convent, Merchants Quay, Dublin*, Dublin, 1906, p. 16.

45. T. McKenna, 'Church of Ireland clergy in Cork: an analysis of the 1615 regal visitation', *Journal of Cork History*, 77 (1972).

46. P. Dwyer, *The Diocese of Killaloe from the Reformation to the Close of the Eighteenth Century*, Dublin, 1887, p. 144.

47. P. Egan, 'The royal visitation of Clonfert and Kilmacdaugh, 1615', *Journal of the Galway Archaeological and Historical Society*, 35 (Galway, 1976), p. 68–70.
48. C. Moore, 'William Lithgow's tour of Ireland in 1619', *Journal of the Cork Historical and Archaeological Society*, 8 (1902), p. 105.

CHAPTER SEVEN
The Scum of Both Nations

1. C. Hanna, *The Scotch-Irish or the Scot in North Britain, North Ireland and North America*, Vol. I, New York and London, 1902, p. 550.
2. G. Benn, *A History of the Town of Belfast from the Earliest Times to the Close of the Eighteenth Century*, London, 1877, p. 79.
3. Ibid., p. 86.
4. Hanna, *Scotch-Irish*, p. 545.
5. Ibid.
6. J. S. Curl, *The Londonderry Plantation 1609–1914*, Chichester, 1986, p. 79.
7. Hanna, *Scotch-Irish*, p. 549.
8. Ibid., p. 550.
9. Ibid., p. 551.
10. T. McCrie (ed.), *The Life of Mr Robert Blair, Minister of St Andrews containing his Autobiography from 1593 to 1636*, Edinburgh, 1848, p. 15.
11. Ibid., p. 27.
12. Ibid., p. 54.
13. Ibid., p. 59.
14. Hanna, *Scotch-Irish*, p. 552.
15. Ibid., p. 553.
16. P. Adair, *A True Narrative of the Rise and Progress of the Presbyterian Church in Ireland 1623–1670*, Belfast, London and Edinburgh, 1866, p. 17.
17. Hanna, *Scotch-Irish*, p. 554.
18. Adair, *A True Narrative*, p. 24.
19. Ibid., p. 25.
20. Letter from the Bishop of Derry to the Bishop of Down of 31 May 1698. Benn, *History of the Town of Belfast*, p. 378.
21. J. S. Reid, *History of the Presbyterian Church in Ireland . . .* Vol. I, Belfast, 1867, p. 118.
22. J. McCafferty, 'John Bramhall and the Church of Ireland in the 1630s', in A. Ford, J. McGuire and K. Milne (eds), *As by Law Established: the Church of Ireland since the Reformation*, Dublin, 1995, p. 106.
23. Ford, 'A Puritan church?', in Ford, McGuire and Milne, *As by Law Established*, pp. 57–8.
24. McCafferty, 'John Bramhall', in Ford, McGuire and Milne, *As by Law Established*, p. 100.
25. Ibid., p. 104.
26. R. P. Mahaffy (ed.), *Calendar of State Papers Relating to Ireland 1633–1647*, London, 1901, p. 17.
27. D. Townshend, *The Life and Letters of the Great Earl of Cork*, London, 1904, p. 212.
28. Reid, *Presbyterian Church in Ireland*, Vol. I, p. 188.
29. Ibid., p. 235.
30. Ibid., p. 239.
31. Ibid., p. 244.
32. Ibid., p. 183.
33. Hanna, *Scotch-Irish*, p. 566.
34. T. Macaulay, *The History of England from the accession of James II*, Leipzig, 1849, Vol. III,

pp. 70–4.

35. Reid, *Presbyterian Church*, pp. 331–2.

36. *Bloody Newes from Ireland, or the barbarous Crueltie By the papists used in that Kingdome by putting men to the sword, deflouring women and dragging them up and downe the Streets and cruelly murdering them and thrusting their Speeres through their little Infants before their eyes*, London, 1641.

37. Adair, *A True Narrative*, p. 74.

38. W. Hamilton, *The Dangers of Popery and the Blessings arising from the Late Revolution*, Dublin, 1723, p. 24.

39. H. Simms, 'Violence in County Armagh', in B Mac Cuarta (ed.), *Ulster 1641: Aspects of the Rising*, Belfast, 1993, p. 134.

40. Ibid., p. 137.

41. Reid, *Presbyterian Church*, p. 385.

42. M. Hickson, *Ireland in the Seventeenth Century, or the Massacres of 1641–2*, Vol. I, London, 1884, p. 191.

43. Ibid., p. 40.

44. Ibid., pp. 292–3.

45. Ibid., p. 228.

46. Ibid., p. 194.

47. H. Jones, *A Remonstrance of Divers Remarkable Passages concerninge the Church and Kingdome of Ireland*, London, 1642, p. 61.

48. Hickson, *Massacres*, p. 204.

49. Ibid., p. 186.

50. Ibid., pp. 177–8.

51. Ibid., p. 199.

52. B. S. Shuckburgh (ed.), *Two Biographies of William Bedell, Bishop of Kilmore, with a Selection of his Letters and an Unpublished Treatise*, Cambridge, 1902, p. 295.

53. Mahaffy (ed.), *Calendar of State Papers Relating to Ireland 1633–1647*, p. 205.

54. 'Speculum Episcoporum, or the Apostolick Bishop, being a brief account of the life and death of the Most Revd Father in God Dr William Bedell', in Shuckburgh, *Two Biographies of William Bedell*, p. 133.

55. Jones, *Remonstrance*, p. 49.

56. Ibid. p. 58.

57. J. Froude, *The English in Ireland in the Eighteenth Century*, Vol. I, London, 1884, pp. 94–5.

58. Townshend, *Earl of Cork*, p. 391.

59. G. B. Rinuccini, *The Embassy in Ireland in the Years 1645–1649*, trans. A. Hutton, Dublin, 1873, pp. 90–7.

60. Ibid., p. xlix.

61. Ibid., p. 144.

62. Rinuccini *Embassy in Ireland*, p. 21.

63. *Report of the Manuscripts of the Earl of Egmont*, Vol. I, pt 1, London, 1905, p. 472.

64. Rinuccini, *Embassy in Ireland*, p. 404.

65. *The Present State of Ireland with Some Remarques upon the Antient State thereof*, London, 1673, p. 70.

66. J. Begley, *The Diocese of Limerick in the Sixteenth and Seventeenth Centuries*, Dublin and London, 1927, pp. 239–60.

67. *Calendar of the Manuscripts of the Marquis of Ormonde Preserved at Kilkenny Castle*, Vol. II, London, 1899, p. 157.

68. Ibid., p. 119.

69. W. Gostelow, *Charles Stuart and Oliver Cromwell* [London], 1655.

70. W. Burke, *A History of Clonmel*, Waterford, 1907.

CHAPTER EIGHT
Such Dangerous Persons

1. C. S. King (ed.), *A Great Archbishop of Dublin: William King 1650–1729*, London, 1908, pp. 207–8.
2. G. Williams, *Seven Treatises Very Necessary to be Observed in These Very Bad Dayes*, London, 1662, Preface.
3. Ibid.
4. *The Proceedings Observed in Order to, and in the Consecration of the Twelve Bishops at St Patrick's Church, Dublin*, London, 1661, p. 8.
5. J. S. Reid, *History of the Presbyterian Church in Ireland*, Vol. II, Belfast, 1867, p. 273.
6. Ibid.
7. Ibid., p. 391. also, L. Landa, *Swift and the Church of Ireland*, Oxford, 1954, p. 21.
8. W. Burke, *The Irish Priests in Penal Times 1660–1760*, Waterford, 1914, p. 42.
9. R. Burnet, *History of His Own Time*, Vol. I, London, 1724, p. 502.
10. R. P. Mahaffy (ed.), *Calendar of the State Papers Relating to Ireland September 1669–December 1670*, London, 1910.
11. Burke, *Priests in Penal Times*, p. 81.
12. *The Last Speech of Mr Oliver Plunket, Titular Primate of Ireland*, London, 1681, in *The Harleian Miscellany*, ed. W. Oldys, T. Park, Vol. VI, London, 1810, p. 192.
13. *Report on the Manuscripts of the Earl of Egmont*, Vol. II, London, 1909, p. 112.
14. *Manuscripts of the Marquess of Ormonde, Preserved at Kilkenny Castle*, Vol. 7, London, 1912, p. 491.
15. [W. King], *The State of the Protestants of Ireland under the Late King James's Government*, London, 1691, p. 210.
16. Ibid., p. 395.
17. Ibid., p. 398.
18. Ibid., p. 22.
19. Ibid., p. 26.
20. R. Doherty, *The Williamite War in Ireland 1688–1691*, Dublin, 1998, p. 71.
21. Doherty suggests James' army numbered 10,000, rather than the 20,000 Walker referred to, *Williamite War*, p. 56.
22. G. Walker, *A True Account of the Siege of London-derry*, Dublin, 1736, p. 148.
23. Ibid., p. 135.
24. Ibid., p. 150.
25. *A Sermon Preached on the Day of Thanksgiving for Peace at St Ann's Church in Dungannon*, Dublin, 1698, pp. 1–7.
26. P. Dwyer, *The Diocese of Killaloe from the Reformation to the Close of the Eighteenth Century*, Dublin, 1878, p. 401, citing Mason's *Parochial Survey*, Vol. II, p. 461.
27. J. Simms, 'The bishops' banishment act of 1697', *Irish Historical Studies*, 18 (1970), p. 194.
28. F. Bickley (ed.), *Manuscripts of the Late Allan George Finch*, Vol. 3, London, 1957, p. 304.
29. T. O'Fiaich, 'The registration of the clergy in 1704', *Seanchas Ard Mhacha*, 6 (1971), p. 47.
30. J. Swift, *The Presbyterians Place of Merit*, in *Jonathan Swift's Irish Tracts 1728–1733*, Oxford, 1955, p. 273.
31. Letter of Bishop King of Derry to the Archbishop of Armagh, undated (1700?), in 'Visitation of Armagh' by William King, 1693, 1694, 1702, Robinson Library Mss.
32. Ibid.
33. *The Insolence of the Dissenters against the Establish'd Church … by His Grace the Lord Primate and the Lord Bishop of Down and Connor*, London, 1716, p. 4.

34. King, *A Great Archbishop of Dublin*, p. 90.
35. Ibid., p. 295.
36. E. O'Byrne, *The Convert Rolls*, Dublin, 1981, p. xvii.
37. Ibid., p. 62.
38. M. Quare, 'Bishop Foy School, Waterford', *Journal of the Cork Historical and Archaeological Society*, 71 (1966), p. 104.
39. J. Richardson, *The Great Folly, Superstition and Idolatry of Pilgrimages in Ireland especially of that to St Patrick's Purgatory*, Dublin, 1727.
40. King, *A Great Archbishop*, p. 294.
41. Letter to Charles Irvine, 20 June 1727, ibid., p. 258.
42. H. Boulter, *Letters written by His Excellency Hugh Boulter, Lord Primate of Ireland to Several Ministers of State in England*, Vol. I, Oxford, 1769, p. 46.
43. Ibid., p. 133.
44. Ibid., Vol. II, 1770, p. 128.
45. 'A sermon preached in Christ-Church cathedral Dublin before the Incorporated Society for Promoting English Protestant Schools in Ireland', Dublin 1738, Robinson Library Mss, p. 23.
46. G. Stone, 'A sermon preached at Christ-Church Dublin on the 28 March 1742 before the Incorporated Society for Promoting English Protestant Schools in Ireland', Dublin 1742, Robinson Library Mss, p. 12.
47. *Philosophical Survey of the South of Ireland*, Dublin, 1778, p. 271.
48. Ibid.
49. K. Milne, *The Irish Charter Schools, 1730–1830*, Dublin, 1997, p. 199.
50. 'A sermon preached at Christ-Church on the 5th of November 1743, before his grace William Duke of Devonshire ... and the Lords spiritual and temporal in Parliament assembled', Dublin, 1743, Robinson Library Mss, pp. 11–13.
51. Boulter, *Letters written by ... Boulter*, Vol. I, p. 223.
52. King, *A Great Archbishop*, pp. 207–8.
53. Boulter, *Letters written by ... Boulter*, Vol. I, p. 250; also p. 261.
54. 'Report on the state of popery in Ireland 1731, *North Munster Antiquarian Journal*, 17 (1975), p. 124.
55. Thirty clergy were registered in Ossory even though there were only 23 parishes. See F. O'Fearghail, 'The Catholic Church in County Kilkenny 1600–1800', in W. Nolan and K. Whelan (eds), *Kilkenny, History and Society*, Dublin, 1990, p. 231.
56. G. Benn, *A History of the Town of Belfast from the Earliest Times to the Close of the Eighteenth Century*, London, 1877, p. 416.
57. Burke, *Priests in Penal Times*, p. 282.
58. Ibid., p. 320.
59. W. Burke, *A History of Clonmel*, Waterford, 1907, p. 139.
60. Burke, *Priests in Penal Times*, p. 253.
61. *Manuscripts of the Marquis of Ormonde Preserved at Kilkenny Castle*, Vol. 4, London, 1966, p. 352.
62. King, *A Great Archbishop*, p. 208.
63. Whelan, *Archbishop Blake*, p. 293.
64. 'Report on the state of popery in Ireland 1781', *North Munster Antiquarian Journal*, 17 (1975), p. 131.
65. Burke, *Priests in Penal Times*, p. 361.
66. J. Brady, 'Aspects of the Irish Church in the 18th century', *Irish Ecclesiastical Record*, 70 (Dublin, 1948), p. 517.
67. Burke, *Priests in Penal Times*, p. 222.
68. Brady, 'Aspects', p. 519.

69. *The Flying Post, or The Post-Master's News*, 14 June 1739.

70. Ibid., 15 August 1739.

71. Burke, *History of Clonmel*, p. 147.

72. *The Public Register, or Freeman's Journal*, 1 July 1767.

73. Ibid., 7 February 1764.

CHAPTER NINE
Furious Demagogues of Rebellion

1. R. Woodward, *The Present State of the Church of Ireland, containing a Description of its Precarious Situation; and the Consequent Danger to the Public*, London, 1787, p. 14.

2. H. Rennison, *Historical Sketch of Drumcree Parish*, Belfast, 1927, p. 8.

3. W. Neely, 'Archbishops Robinson, Stuart and Newcombe', Robinson Library Mss, 1994, citing Cumberland's memoirs, supplement, pp. 37–8.

4. C. Motion, 'Archbishop Robinson, builder of Armagh', *Seanchas Ard Mhacha*, 6 (1971), p. 98, citing Froude, *The English in Ireland in the Eighteenth Century*, Vol. II, p. 490.

5. F. Elrington Hall (ed.), *The Correspondence of Jonathan Swift*, Vol. 3, London, 1912, pp. 309–10.

6. H. Boulter, *Letters written by His Excellency Hugh Boulter, Lord Primate of Ireland to Several Ministers of State in England*, Vol. II, Oxford, 1770, p. 236.

7. The population rose from 1,910 in 1770 to 6,699 in 1814: Motion, 'Archbishop Robinson', p. 119.

8. J. D'Arcy Sirr, *Memoir of the Honourable and Most Reverend Power Le Poer Trench, the Last Archbishop of Tuam*, Dublin, 1845, p. 97.

9. C. Forster, *The Life of John Jebb, Bishop of Limerick, Ardagd and Aghadoe*, Vol. I, London, 1836, p. 231.

10. *Saunders's News-Letter and Daily Advertiser*, 7 July 1786.

11. Woodward, *State of the Church of Ireland*, p. 104.

12. *A Letter from the Most Revd Doctor Butler, Titular Archbishop of Cashel to the Right Honourable Lord Viscount Kenmare*, Kilkenny, 1787, p. 2.

13. *Saunders's News-Letter and Daily Advertiser*, 7 July 1786.

14. W. Childe-Pemberton, *The Earl Bishop, The Life of Frederick Hervey, Bishop of Derry, Earl of Bristol*, Vol. II, 1925, p. 381.

15. Ibid., pp. 640–1.

16. P. Cunningham (ed.), *The Letters of Horace Walpole, Fourth Earl of Oxford*, Vol. VIII, London, 1891, p. 506.

17. D. Bowen, *The History and Shaping of Irish Protestantism*, New York, Washington, 1995, p. 162.

18. 'Report on the state of popery in Ireland 1731,' *North Munster Antiquarian Journal*, 17 (1975), p. 173.

19. W. Burke, *A History of Clonmel*, Waterford, 1907, p. 278.

20. 'Report on the State of Popery in Ireland 1731', p. 15.

21. T. Campbell, *Philosophical Survey of the South of Ireland in a Series of Letters to John Watkinson*, Dublin, 1778, p. 29.

22. Ibid., p. 179.

23. Ibid., p. 181.

24. Ibid., p. 132.

25. D. Bowen, *History and the Shaping of Irish Protestantism*, New York, 1995, p. 155.

26. W. Hayes, *Thurles, a Guide to the Cathedral Town*, Thurles, 1999, pp. 6–7.

27. *Letter of Todd Jones MP for Borough of Lisburne to the Volunteers reviewed at Belfast on the 12th of July 1784*, p. 19.

28. *Plain Arguments in Defence of the People's Absolute Dominion over the Constitution*, Dublin, 1784, p. 34.

29. *Declaration of the Catholic Society of Dublin: Resolutions and Oath of the United Irishmen*, Dublin, 1791.

30. G. Benn, *A History of the Town of Belfast from the Earliest Times to the Close of the Eighteenth Century*, London, 1877, p. 645.

31. W. McMillan, 'Presbyterian ministers and the Ulster rising', in *Protestant, Catholic and Dissenter: the Clergy and 1798*, ed. L. Swords, Dublin, 1997 p. 109.

32. *The Flying Post, or The Post-Master's News*, 7 May 1739.

33. *The Flying Post*, 22 March 1739.

34. For this detail and much of the information on the Battle of the Diamond, see B McEvoy, 'Peep of Day Boys and Defenders in the County Armagh, Part I, II', *Seanchas Ard Mhacha*, 12 (1986).

35. *Manuscripts of James, First Earl of Charlemont, Vol. 2, 1784–99*, London, 1894, p. 279.

36. B. McEvoy, 'Father James Quigley, priest of Armagh and United Irishman', *Seanchas Ard Mhacha*, 5 (1970), p. 254, citing *Life of Revd James Quigley*, London, 1798.

37. L. Tute, *Letter written in England in August 1813 Explaining the Rise, Progress and Principles of the Orange Institution in Ireland*, Dublin, 1814, p. 8.

38. Benn, *History of the Town of Belfast*, p. 659.

39. J. Niles, 'The Irish College, Antwerp', *Clogher Record*, 15, Enniskillen 1996, pp. 29–30.

40. J. Troy, *Pastoral Instructions Addressed to the Roman Catholics of the Archdiocese of Dublin on the Duties of Christian Citizens*, Dublin, 1793, p. 19.

41. *Records of the General Synod of Ulster 1691–1820*, Vol. III, Belfast, 1898, p. 137.

42. Ibid., p. 157.

43. T. O'Beirne, 'A sermon preached in the church of Longford on 28 February 1794 being the day appointed for a general fast', Dublin 1794, Robinson Library Mss, pp. 11–13.

44. 'A sermon preached in the chapel of Trinity College on Thursday 16th February 1797 being the day appointed for a national thanksgiving on account of the providential deliverance of this kingdom from the late threatened invasion', Dublin 1797, Robinson Library Mss, p. 14.

45. Ibid., p. 21.

46. W. Newcome, 'The duty of Christian subjects: a pastoral letter to the inhabitants of the diocese of Armagh', Dublin 1797, Robinson Library Mss.

47. *Saunders's News-Letter and Daily Advertiser*, 6 January 1797.

48. Ibid., 16 January 1797.

49. Ibid., 21 December 1797.

50. T. Hussey, *A Pastoral Letter to the Catholic Clergy of the United Diocese of Waterford and Lismore, Waterford*, London, 1797, p. 10.

51. *Saunders's News-Letter and Daily Advertiser*, 15 January 1798.

52. Ibid., 14 April 1797.

53. Ibid., 17 April 1797.

54. Ibid., 11 April 1797.

55. Ibid., 10 April 1797.

56. Ibid., 4 May 1797.

57. Ibid., 29 May 1797.

58. Ibid., 28 May 1797. See also *A History of the Irish Rebellion in the Year 1798*, Dublin, 1799, p. 77.

59. For an account of the established clergy in the rising, see P. Comerford, 'Church of

Ireland clergy and the 1798 rising', in L. Swords, ed. *Protestant, Catholic and Dissenter: the clergy in 1798*, Columba Press, 1997.

60. D. Gahan, 'The Scullabogue massacre', *History Ireland*, Autumn 1996, p. 30.
61. *Saunders's News-Letter and Daily Advertiser*, 25 July 1798.
62. K. Whelan, 'The Wexford priests in 1798', in L. Swords (ed.), *Protestant, Catholic and Dissenter*, p. 172.
63. Ibid., p. 171.
64. [J. Stock] *A Narrative of What Passed at Killala in the County of Mayo during the French Invasion in the Summer of 1798, by an Eyewitness*, London, 1800, p. 79.
65. Ibid., p. 24.
66. See P. Hogan, 'Bishop Dominick Bellew (1745–1813)', *Seanchas Ard Mhacha*, 10 (1982), p. 420.
67. Whelan, 'Wexford priests', p. 186.
68. *Records of the General Synod*, pp. 208–9.
69. Ibid., pp. 209–10.
70. Ibid., p. 221.
71. W. D. Bailie, 'William Steel Dickson', in L. Swords (ed.), *Protestant, Catholic and Dissenter*, p. 65, citing *Narrative of the Confinement of William Steel*, Dublin, 1817, p. 39.
72. Bailie, 'William Steel Dickson', p. 70.
73. J. Porter, *The Life and Times of Henry Cooke*, London, 1871, p. 14.
74. Ibid., p. 223.
75. Ibid., p. 341.
76. Ibid., p. 338.
77. Ibid., p. 79.
78. Ibid., p. 276.

CHAPTER TEN
The Crash of a Great Building

1. Letter to the National Association, *Freeman's Journal*, 9 January 1867.
2. S. Madden, *Life of Peter Roe*, Dublin, 1842, p. 213.
3. Ibid., p. 130.
4. Ibid., p. 230.
5. 'Report on a debate in the House of Commons on Mr Fox's motion for the House to resolve itself into committee on the Catholic petition on Monday 13th and Tuesday 14th of May 1805', Dublin, 1805, Marsh's Library, Dublin.
6. 'A Statement of the Penal Laws which Aggrieve the Catholics of Ireland,' 1812, Marsh's Library, Dublin. Intro, pp. i–ii.
7. C. Keogh, *The Veto: a Commentary on the Greville Manifesto*, London, 1810, p. 68.
8. 'An answer to Lord Granville's letter to the Earl of Fingal on the subject of the veto, By a Fingalian', London, 1810, Marsh's Library, Dublin, p. 26.
9. 'The address of the Roman Catholic prelates assembled in Dublin on the 26 February 1809 to the clergy and laity of the Roman Catholic churches in Ireland', 1810, Marsh's Library, Dublin.
10. Keogh, *Veto*, p. 56.
11. C. Forster, *The Life of John Jebb, Bishop of Limerick, Ardfert and Aghadoe*, Vol. I, London, 1836, pp. 182–3.
12. *The Archbishop of Dublin's Charge on 24 October 1822 in St Patrick's Cathedral to which is added a Letter to His Grace by a Dignitary of the Roman Catholic Church*, Dublin, 1822, p. 7.

13. W. Mant, *Bishop Mant and his Dioceses: Memoirs of the Right Revd Richard Mant, Lord Bishop of Down and Connor, and of Dromore*, Dublin, 1857, p. 142.

14. Cited Ibid., p. 146.

15. J. D'Arcy Sirr, *Memoir of the Honourable and Most Revd Power Le Poer Trench, Last Archbishop of Tuam*, Dublin, 1845, p. 546.

16. Ibid., p. 535.

17. Ibid., pp. 612–13.

18. *Letters addressed to His Grace the Lord Archbishop of Dublin by the Revd Robert Mghee, and to the Right Hon. E. Stanley by Revd Robert Daly*, Dublin, 1831, p. 10.

19. *Authentic Report of the Great Protestant Meeting Held at Exeter Hall on Saturday June 20 1835*, Dublin, 1835.

20. Sirr, *Power Le Poer Trench*, p. 12.

21. Ibid., p. 120.

22. Ibid., p. 59.

23. R. S. Gregg, '*Faithful unto Death*'. *Memorials of the Life of John Gregg*, Dublin, 1879, p. 30.

24. Lady Ferguson, *Life of the Revd William Reeves, Lord Bishop of Down, Connor and Dismore*, Dublin, 1893, pp. 42.

25. A. Crawford, *The Happy Death-Bed*, Belfast, 1846, p. 24.

26. Gregg, *Life of John Gregg*, p. 31.

27. M. Crotty, *A Narrative of the Reformation at Birr*, London, 1847, p. 105.

28. E. J. Whately, *Life and Correspondence of Richard Whately, Late Archbishop of Dublin*, I, London, 1860, p. 111.

29. Anon. [W. Fisher] *Forty Years in the Church of Ireland, or the Pastor, the Parish and its People*, London, 1882, p. 7.

30. A. Nicholson, *Ireland's Welcome to the Stranger, or Excursions through Ireland in 1844 and 1845*, London, 1847, p. 356.

31. Beresford Correspondence, Robinson Library Mss, Armagh, Vol. II, pp. 358–63.

32. Ibid., p. 28.

33. Ibid., Vol. I, pp. 149–52.

34. J. Garrett, *Good News from Ireland: an Address to the Archbishops and Bishops of the Church of England*, London, 1863, p. 104.

35. E. Whately, *Life and Correspondence of Richard Whately, Late Archbishop of Dublin*, London, 1866, Vol. I, pp. 362–3.

36. Ibid., Vol. II, p. 241.

37. W. D. Killen, *Reminiscences of a Long Life*, London, 1901, p. 56.

38. L. Mitchell, *Lord Melbourne, 1779–1848*, Oxford, 1997, pp. 178–80.

39. M. Trench, *Richard Chevenix Trench, Archbishop, Letters and Memorials*, Vol. I, London, 1888, p. 97.

40. A. R. Ashwell, *The Life of the Right Reverend Samuel Wilberforce with Selections from his Diary and Correspondence*, Vol. I, London, 1880, p. 272.

41. Cited in *Freeman's Journal*, 9 January 1867.

42. Ibid., 16 January 1867.

43. *Apostolic letter from His Grace the Most Revd Dr McHale to the Earl of Derby, taken from the Daily Freeman of 2 September 1852*, Dublin, 1852, p. 12.

44. *Allocations to the Clergy and Pastorals of the Late Right Revd Dr Moriarty, Bishop of Kerry*, London and Dublin, 1884, pp. 315–16.

45. 'Discharge of the Archbishop of Dublin in the cathedral, 9 January 1860, to express sympathy with His Holiness', in P. F. Moran, *The Pastoral Letters and Other Writings of Cardinal Cullen*, Vol. I, Dublin, 1882, p. 731.

46. Ibid., Vol. II, p. 317.

47. *Irish Ecclesiastical Gazette*, 11 (21 January 1869), p. 5.

48. Ibid., 19 March 1869, p. 53.
49. Trench, *Richard Chevenix Trench*, Vol. II, p. 55.
50. *Annual Register*, 1869, p. 3.
51. *Irish Ecclesiastical Gazette*.
52. Trench, *Richard Chevenix Trench*, Vol. II, p. 88.
53. R. Davidson and W. Benham, *Life of Archibald Campbell Tait, Archbishop of Canterbury*, Vol. II, London, 1891, p. 26.
54. J. C. MacDonnell, *The Life and Correspondence of William Connor Magee, Archbishop of York, Bishop of Peterborough*, Vol. I, London, 1896, p. 217.
55. Ibid., p. 228.
56. C. F. D'Arcy, *The Adventures of a Bishop*, London, 1934, p. 28.
57. E. Alexander, *Primate Alexander, Archbishop of Armagh*, London, 1913, p. 173.
58. Gregg, *Life of John Gregg*, pp. 250–1.
59. Alexander, *Primate Alexander*, p. 166.
60. MacDonnell, *Life of William Connor Magee*, p. 155.
61. F. D. How, *William Conyngham Plunket, Fourth Baron Plunket and Sixty-first Archbishop of Dublin*, London, 1900, p. 179.
62. Ibid., p. 364.
63. Ibid., pp. 84–5.
64. *Church of Ireland Gazette*, 56 (3 July 1914), p. 578.
65. P. MacSuibhne, *Paul Cullen and his Contemporaries*, Vol. IV, Naas, 1974, p. 245.
66. W. Butler, *Christchurch Cathedral, Dublin*, Dublin, 1874, p. 8.

CHAPTER ELEVEN
The Agitating Priest

1. 'Letter from the Rt Rev Dr Doyle, Roman Catholic Bishop of Kildare, to A Robertson MP, Carlow 13 May 1824', in D. O'Croly, *Address to the Lower Orders of the Roman Catholics of Ireland*, Cork, 1835, cited in Anon., *The Case of Maynooth considered, with a History of the First Establishment of That Seminary*, Dublin, 1836, p. 55.
2. A. de Tocqueville, *Journeys to England and Ireland*, ed. J. Mayer, London, 1958, p. 130.
3. Ibid., p. 136.
4. Ibid., p. 142.
5. Ibid., p. 167.
6. V. McNally, *Reform, Revolution and Reaction, Archbishop John Thomas Troy and the Catholic Church in Ireland 1787–1817*, New York and London, 1995, p. 5.
7. E. Rogers, *The Present and Past Policy of the British Government towards Protestantism in Ireland, Lecture Delivered at a meeting of the Armagh Protestant Association, Monday 22 April 1861*, Armagh, 1861, p. 15.
8. *The Case of Maynooth Considered*, p. 69–70.
9. H. Inglis, *A Journey throughout Ireland in 1834*, Vol. II, London, 1834, p. 339.
10. J. Fitzpatrick, *The Life, Times and Correspondence of the Right Revd Dr Doyle, Bishop of Kildare and Leighlin*, Dublin, 1861, Vol. I, p. 351.
11. Ibid., p. 350.
12. J. Healy, *Maynooth College: its Centenary History*, Dublin, 1895, p. 240.
13. *The Case of Maynooth considered*, p. 55.
14. In 1808, 148 of 205 seminarians were sons of farmers. S. J. Connolly, *Priests and People in Pre-Famine Ireland 1780–1845*, New York, 1982, p. 39.
15. Fitzpatrick, *Life … of the Right Revd Dr Doyle*, p. 118.

16. J. Doyle, *The Archbishop of Dublin's charge on 24 October 1822 in St Patrick's Cathedral to which is added a letter to His Grace by a dignitary of the Roman Catholic Church*, Dublin, 1822.

17. J. Doyle, *Letters on the State of Ireland addressed by JKL to a Friend in England*, Dublin, 1825, p. 104.

18. W. Fagan, *The Life and Times of Daniel O'Connell*, Cork, 1847–8, Vol. I, p. 284.

19. Anon., *The Young Man's Dream, to which are added ... The New Catholic Rent*, Limerick 1824.

20. *Waterford Mirror*, 21 January 1826.

21. Ibid., 10 June 1826.

22. Ibid., 4 July 1826.

23. *The Annual Register, or a View of the History, Politics and Literature for the Year 1828*, London, 1829, pp. 124–5.

24. R. Huish, *The Memoirs Private and Political of Daniel O'Connell, His Times and Contemporaries*, London, 1835, p. 455.

25. Fitzpatrick, *Life ... of the Right Revd Dr Doyle*, Vol. II, p. 295.

26. Ibid., p. 459.

27. [J. MacHale] *Letters of Hierophilus to the English People on the Moral and Political State of Ireland*, London, 1822, p. 8.

28. U. Bourke, *The Life and Times of the Most Rev John MacHale*, New York, 1902, p. 141.

29. *Freeman's Journal*, 16 May 1826.

30. A. Macaulay, *William Crolly, Archbishop of Armagh 1835–1849*, Dublin, 1994, p. 323.

31. Ibid., p. 285.

32. *Freeman's Journal*, 23 January 1843.

33. P. MacSuibhne, *Paul Cullen and his Contemporaries*, Vol. I, Naas, 1961 and 1962, p. 230.

34. Macaulay, *William Crolly*, p. 182.

35. *Freeman's Journal* 23 October 1846. Cited in Macaulay, *William Crolly*, p. 405.

36. J. Morgan, *Thoughts on the Famine*, Belfast 1848, p. 7.

37. *Freeman's Journal*, 1 October 1847.

38. Beresford Correspondence, Robinson Library, Mss Armagh, Vol. I, p. 56.

39. *Freeman's Journal*, 31 May 1847.

40. Ibid., 2 June 1847.

41. Ibid., 28 October 1847.

42. Ibid., 5 June 1847.

43. Ibid., 17 November 1847.

44. Anon., *A Plea for the Church in Ireland*, London, 1834, p. 19.

45. *Freeman's Journal*, 3 June 1847.

46. D. Bowen, *Souperism: Myth or Reality? A Study in Souperism*, Cork, 1970, p. 12.

47. *Freeman's Journal*, 28 October 1847.

48. R. Whately, *The Right Use of National Afflictions, being a Charge Delivered on the Annual Visitation of the Dioceses of Dublin and Kildare, 19 and 22 September 1848*, Dublin, 1848, p. 4.

49. Pastoral letter to Armagh on the occasion of his consecration, from Rome, 24 February 1850, in P. F. Moran, *The Pastoral Letters and Other Writings of Cardinal Cullen*, 3 vols, Dublin, 1882, pp. 17–20.

50. Synodical address to the fathers of the National Council of Thurles, 9 September 1850, p. 41.

51. *Pastoral letter of His Grace the Most Revd. Dr Cullen, Archbishop of Dublin, on the Vile System of Pecuniary Prosleytism*, Dublin, 1855, p. 3.

52. Ibid.

53. A. Dallas, *Proselytism in Ireland. The Catholic Defence Association Versus the Irish Church*

Missions on the charge of Bribery and intimidation, London, 1832, p. 7.

54. Ibid., p. 20.
55. D. P. Thompson, *A Brief Account of the Rise and Progress of the Change in Religious Opinion now taking Place in Dingle and the West of the County of Kerry, Ireland*, London, 1845, p. 46.
56. Ibid., p. 139.
57. Beresford Correspondence, Robinson Library Mss, Vol. XI, p. 195.
58. Dallas, *Proselytism in Ireland*, p. 12.
59. 'Temperance movement', *Dublin Review*, 16, (1840), p. 472.
60. Ibid., p. 467.
61. E. Malcolm, 'The Catholic Church and the Irish temperance movement 1838–1901', *Irish Historical Studies*, 23 (May 1982), p. 4, citing MacSuibhne, *Cullen*, Vol. II, p. 11.
62. MacSuibhne, *Cullen*, Vol. II, p. 52.
63. Ibid., Vol. III, p. 92.
64. Ibid., p. 181.
65. L. McKenna, 'Catholic University of Ireland', *Irish Ecclesiastical Record*, 31 (1928), p. 354.
66. *Freeman's Journal*, 12 February 1867.
67. *Sermon Preached by John Miley in the Metropolitan Church on Sunday 28 June 1840… in Thanksgiving for the Providential Escape of our Most Gracious Queen Victoria*, Dublin, 1860.
68. Doyle, *Letters on the State of Ireland*, p. 47.
69. *Freeman's Journal*, 12 January 1843.
70. Ibid., 10 January 1843.
71. Ibid.
72. Ibid., 21 March 1846.
73. Ibid., 16 May 1846.
74. Ibid., 23 August 1847.
75. E. J. Whately, *Life and Correspondence of Richard Whately, Late Archbishop of Dublin*, Vol. II, London, 1866, p. 365.
76. Discourse delivered at a meeting of the citizens of Dublin, 29 December 1864, in Moran, *Pastoral Letters … of Cardinal Cullen*, Vol. II, p. 302.
77. Moran, *Pastoral Letters … of Cardinal Cullen*, Vol. II, p. 390.
78. Ibid.
79. 'Discourse of the Archbishop of Dublin in cathedral, 9 January 1860 to express sympathy with His Holiness', in ibid., Vol. I, p. 713.
80. *Freeman's Journal*, 9 January 1867.
81. Ibid., 18 February 1867.
82. Ibid., 20 February 1867.
83. Letter to the clergy and laity on the feast of the Immaculate Conception, 24 November 1869, in Moran, *Pastoral Letters … of Cardinal Cullen*, Vol. III, p. 279.
84. MacSuibhne, *Cullen*, Vol. V, p. 79.
85. P. J. Smyth, *The Priest in Politics*, Dublin, 1885, p. 11.
86. MacSuibhne, *Cullen*, Vol. V, p. 167.
87. S. O. Rafferty, 'Cardinal Cullen, early Fenianism and the McManus funeral affair', *Recusant History*, 22 (1995), p. 551.
88. P. Walsh, *William J. Walsh, Archbishop of Dublin*, Dublin and Cork, 1928, p. 181.
89. Queen Victoria's Journal of 23 November 1885 cited in E. Longford, *Victoria RI, 1840–1924*, London, 1964, p. 484.
90. A. Walsh, 'Michael, Cardinal Logue, 1840–1924', *Seanchas Ard Mhacha, Journal of the Armagh Diocesan Historical Society*, 17 (1996–97), p. 151.

91. *Tipperary Advocate*, 20 August 1881.
92. *Tipperary Leader*, 1 November 1882.
93. *Nenagh Guardian*, 22 July 1885.
94. *Freeman's Journal*, 12 December 1885; also in Croke Papers, Cashel Archdiocesan Archives Thurles, 1885, no. 39.
95. 'Resolutions of the Irish bishops adopted at their meeting held at Maynooth College 8 September 1886', *Irish Ecclesiastical Record*, 1886, p. 1054. Also M. Tierney, *Croke of Cashel: the Life of Archbishop Thomas William Croke 1823–1902*, Dublin, 1976, p. 188.
96. Walsh, *Archbishop Walsh*, pp. 247–8.
97. Ibid., p. 270.
98. Ibid., p. 109.
99. Ibid., p. 320.
100. Ibid., p. 323.
101. Walsh, 'Cardinal Logue', p. 127.
102. Letter of Pope Leo XII to the Irish bishops, 24 June 1888, Logue Letters, Box 1, O'Fiaich Library, Armagh.
103. 31 July 1890, Letters of Logue to Archbishop Walsh 1882–1921, Logue Letters, ibid.
104. Walsh, *Archbishop Walsh*, p. 409.
105. Ibid.
106. Ibid., p. 416.
107. Ibid., p. 419.
108. *Tipperary Leader*, 26 May 1993.
109. Walsh, 'Cardinal Logue', p. 138.
110. Ibid., p. 137.
111. Confidential Circular to the Clergy of Cashel, 2 March 1891, Croke Papers, 1891, no. 23.
112. *Freeman's Journal*, 30 April 1891.
113. Tierney, *Croke of Cashel*, p. 246.
114. Walsh, *Archbishop Walsh*, p. 483.

CHAPTER TWELVE
Flags Flying and Drums Beating

1. R. Kipling, 'Ulster 1912', from A. Lycett, *Rudyard Kipling*, London, 1999.
2. *The Church of Ireland and the Present Crisis: Report of the Special Meeting of the General Synod holden at Dublin 23 March 1886*, Dublin, 1886, p. 7.
3. Ibid., p. 22.
4. J. McMinn, *Against the Tide: a Calendar of the Papers of Rev J. B. Armour, Irish Presbyterian Minister and Home Ruler 1869–1914*, Belfast, 1985, p. xlii.
5. *The Annual Register, A review of public events at home and abroad for the year 1886*, London, 1887, p. 50.
6. Ibid., p. 308.
7. R. R. James, *Lord Randolph Churchill*, London, 1959, p. 233.
8. R. McNeill, *Ulster's Stand for Union*, London, 1922, p. 12.
9. Logue told Walsh on 13 July 1898 he had joined the Gladstone Memorial Committee, 'considering what Mr Gladstone did for Ireland and the sacrifices he made for her'. Letters of Logue to Archbishop Walsh 1882–1921, Logue Letters, Box I, O'Fiaich Library, Armagh.
10. R. Murray, *Archbishop Bernard: Professor, Prelate and Provost*, London, 1931, p. 124.
11. R. Warren, *The Church of Ireland since 1868*, Paper Read at the Church Congress,

Birmingham, October 1893, p. 8.

12. P. Fitzgerald, *Recollections of Dublin Castle and of Dublin Society*, London, 1902, pp. 4–7.

13. C. D'Arcy, *The Adventures of a Bishop*, London, 1934, p. 28.

14. Earl of Midleton, *Ireland – Dupe or Heroine*, London, 1932, p. 83.

15. A. Walsh, 'Michael, Cardinal Logue 1840–1924', *Seanchas Ard Mhacha, Journal of the Armagh Diocesan Historical Society*, 17 (1996–97), p. 154.

16. Letters of Walsh to Logue, 16 July 1903, Logue Letters, Box I, O'Fiaich Library.

17. P. J. Joyce, *John Healy, Archbishop of Tuam*, Dublin, 1931, p. 275.

18. Pastoral letter by Edward Thomas, Bishop of Limerick 1910, pp. 9–10.

19. J. O'Reilly, 'What religion has lost by the decay of the Irish language', *New Ireland Review*, 3 (1897–98), p. 366.

20. J. O'Reilly, *The threatening metapsychosis of a nation, read to the Maynooth union 21 June 1900*, Gaelic League pamphlets 24, National Library of Ireland, Dublin.

21. P. Forde, 'The Irish language movement', read at Maynooth College, 6 December 1899, p. 27.

22. M. Hickey, *The Irish language movement*, Gaelic League pamphlets 29, National Library of Ireland, Dublin.

23. A. Cleary, 'Gaelic League', *Studies*, 8 (1919), p. 402.

24. *Clongownian*, 1914, p. 124.

25. *Witness*, 9 January 1914, p. 5.

26. I. Colvin, *The Life of Lord Carson*, Vol. II, London, 1934, p. 79.

27. Ibid., p. 111.

28. D'Arcy, *Adventures of a Bishop*, p. 190.

29. Colvin, *Lord Carson*, Vol. II, p. 244.

30. Ibid., Vol. III, p. 118.

31. S. A. Blair, 'Rev. W. F. Marshall: profile of an Ulsterman', *Bulletin of the Presbyterian Historical Society of Ireland*, 24 (1995), p. 15.

32. *Witness*, 10 July 1914, p. 4.

33. M. Macdonagh, *The Irish at the Front*, London, New York and Toronto, 1916, p. 11.

34. *Church of Ireland Gazette*, 56 (2 October 1914), p. 804.

35. Ibid., 4 September 1914, p. 737.

36. G. Fitzgerald, 'The significance of 1916', *Studies*, 55 (1966), p. 31.

37. *Church of Ireland Gazette*, 56 (21 August 1914), p. 704.

38. Ibid., p. 689.

39. Macdonagh, *Irish at the Front*, p. 110.

40. Ibid., p. 113.

41. *Freeman's Journal*, 9 November 1915.

42. *Clongownian*, 1917, p. 32.

43. Address to the clergy of the diocese of Armagh at Dundalk, 6 July, 1916, Dungannon, 7 July, Armagh, 11 July, by the Lord Primate, John Crozier.

44. *Church of Ireland Gazette*, 58 (10 March 1916), p. 180.

45. Address on National Thrift, delivered by the Most Rev. Dennis Kelly, Bishop of Ross, at City Hall, Cork, Friday 10 September 1915, p. 2.

46. Correspondence and unpublished letters and full speech at Limerick, September 1916, complete, of the late Dr. O'Dwyer, Bishop of Limerick, p. 15.

47. A. de Blácam, *What Sinn Fein Stands For*, Dublin and London, 1921, p. 244.

48. Letters of Logue, to the Bishop of Down and Connor, 26 November 1917, Logue Letters, Box I, O'Fiaich Library.

49. *Catholic Bulletin*, 5 (June 1915), pp. 401–3.

50. Murray, *Archbishop Bernard*, p. 325.

51. de Blácam, *Sinn Fein*, p. 141.

52. Ibid., p. 144.
53. Ibid., p. 147.
54. See R. Dudley Edwards, *Patrick Pearse: The Triumph of Failure*, London, 1977.
55. De Blácam, *Sinn Fein*, p. 59.
56. Ibid., p. 63.
57. *Church of Ireland Gazette*, 58 (28 April 1916), p. 320.
58. *Witness*, 12 May 1916, p. 5.
59. Ibid., 5 May 1916, p. 4.
60. Ibid., p. 7.
61. *Minutes of the Proceedings of the General Assembly of the Presbyterian Church in Ireland*, 1916–1920, Vol. XIII, Belfast, p. 20.
62. *Witness*, 15 June 1917, p. 4.
63. *Church of Ireland Gazette*, 58 (28 April 1916), p. 320.
64. 'The bishops' reaction to 1916', *The Furrow*, May 1975; also, *Correspondence and unpublished letters ... of the late Dr. O'Dwyer*, pp. 11–12.
65. *Church of Ireland Gazette*, 23 June 1916, p. 486.
66. Ibid., 58 (28 July 1916), p. 542.
67. *Witness*, 14 July 1916, p. 1.
68. Ibid., 28 July 1916, p. 7.
69. T. Morrissey, *William J. Walsh, Archbishop of Dublin 1841–1922*, Dublin 2000, p. 307.
70. Murray, *Archbishop Bernard*, p. 316.
71. Midleton, *Ireland*, pp. 107–9.
72. *Church of Ireland Gazette*, 60 (22 November 1918), p. 772.
73. J. Horgan, 'Precepts and practices in Ireland 1914–1919', *Studies*, 8 (1919), pp. 220–1.
74. Sinn Fein, What Cardinal Logue says of it. Dublin, (1917, 1918?).
75. Morrissey, *William Walsh*, pp. 316–17.
76. *Witness*, 30 July 1920, p. 8.
77. K. McMahon, 'The time of the Trouble, 1919–1921: Armagh, South Down and North Louth', *Seanchas Ard Mhacha*, 15, 1992, p. 228, citing *Armagh Guardian*, 7 March 1919.
78. 'Irish bishops' statement at Maynooth 24 June 1919', *Irish Ecclesiastical Record*, 14, pp. 328–9.
79. McMahon, 'The time of the Trouble', *Seancas Ard Mhacha*, 15 (1972), p. 270, citing *Armagh Guardian*, 26 December 1919.
80. Ibid., p. 271, citing *Armagh Guardian*, 26 December 1919.
81. *Catholic Bulletin*, 9 (January 1919), p. 2.
82. Ibid., 8 (March 1918), p. 117.
83. F. Murphy, *Daniel Mannix, Archbishop of Melbourne*, Melbourne, 1948, p. 98.
84. *Catholic Bulletin*, 9 (April 1919), p. 218.
85. *Witness*, 2 January 1920, p. 8.
86. Ibid., 20 January 1920.
87. *Catholic Bulletin*, 9 (September 1920), p. 530.
88. *Statement issued by the Cardinal Primate and the Archbishops and Bishops of Ireland on the Present Condition of their Country*, Maynooth, 1920, p. 4.
89. G. Seaver, *John Fitzallen Gregg, Archbishop*, Leighton Buzzard, 1963, p. 118.
90. Pastoral letter of Cardinal Logue, read out on 28 November 1920.
91. *Witness*, 1 April 1921, p. 7.
92. Ibid., 22 April 1922, p. 8.
93. Ibid., 6 May 1921, p. 7.
94. Ibid., 8 June 1921, p. 7.
95. Seaver, *John Fitzallen Gregg*, p. 114. *Church of Ireland Gazette*, 17 June 1921, p. 373.

96. 'State of the Hierarchy', 21 June 1921, *Irish Ecclesiastical Record*, 18, 1921, p. 87.
97. *Church of Ireland Gazette*, 22 January 1922, p. 46.
98. Pastoral letter of 10 October 1922, *Irish Ecclesiastical Record*, 20, p. 547.
99. Seaver, *John Fitzallen Gregg*, p. 123.
100. *Witness* 5 May 1922, p. 8.
101. 'State of the Hierarchy', p. 82.
102. *Church of Ireland Gazette*, 23 August 1922, p. 490.
103. Ibid., 22 June 1922, p. 363.
104. *Witness*, 23 June 1922.
105. Ibid., 30 June 1922, p. 8.
106. *Church of Ireland Gazette*, 13 October 1922, p. 630.

CHAPTER THIRTEEN
Soutaned Bullies of the Lord

1. *Irish Monthly*, 53 (1925), p. 350.
2. *Handbook of the Eucharistic Congress*, Dublin, 1932, p. 13.
3. *Irish Independent* Eucharistic Congress souvenir number, Dublin, 1932, p. 34.
4. *Catholic Bulletin*, 26 (1936), p. 561.
5. J. O'Doherty, 'The Catholic Church in 1936, *Irish Ecclesiastical Record*, 49 (1937), p. 4.
6. Anstruther, G., and Hallett, P. E., *Catholic Truth Society: the First 50 Years*, London, 1934, p. 59.
7. Cited in J. Carlson (ed.), *Banned in Ireland: Censorship and the Irish Writer*, London, 1990, p. 140.
8. 'The Archbishop of Westminster on Ireland', *Irish Ecclesiastical Record*, 10 (1873), p. 3.
9. Information taken from the *Irish Independent* Eucharistic Congress souvenir number.
10. Pastoral address of the archbishops and bishops at plenary synod, Maynooth, 15 August 1927, *Irish Ecclesiastical Record*, 30 (1927), p. 526.
11. *Catholic Bulletin*, 20 (1930), p. 914.
12. Ibid., 23 (1933), p. 667.
13. 'Unclean books', *Irish Rosary*, 42 (1938), p. 566.
14. *Irish Rosary*, 29 (1925), p. 235.
15. *Catholic Bulletin*, 15 (1925), pp. 865–6.
16. *Irish Rosary*, 29 (1925), p. 637.
17. Ibid., 30 (1926), p. 298.
18. *Catholic Bulletin*, 19 (1929), p. 100.
19. *Irish Rosary*, 27 (1923), p. 805.
20. Ibid., 36 (1932), p. 883.
21. Ibid., 30 (1926), p. 803.
22. Ibid., 32 (1928), p. 793.
23. Carlson, *Banned in Ireland*, p. 25.
24. Ibid., p. 39.
25. Ibid., p. 63.
26. *Irish Times*, 14 May 1930, p. 6.
27. Carlson, *Banned in Ireland*, pp. 140–1.
28. Bishops' statement of 6 October 1925, *Irish Rosary*, 30 (1926), p. 90.
29. R. Devane, 'The dance hall – a moral and national menace', *Irish Ecclesiastical Record*, 37 (1931), p. 173.
30. Ibid., p. 175.

31. Ibid., p. 176.
32. *Catholic Bulletin*, 26 (1936), p. 461.
33. Ibid., 27 (1937), pp. 407–8.
34. Ibid., 24 (1934), p. 182.
35. H. E. Rope, 'The ruin of the Gaeltacht', *Irish Monthly*, 60 (1932).
36. *Catholic Bulletin*, 19 (1929), p. 696.
37. 'Is Irish being revived?', *Irish Monthly*, 62 (1934), p. 17.
38. Rope, 'Ruin of the Gaeltacht', pp. 236–41.
39. *Irish Rosary*, 36 (1932), p. 807.
40. Information taken from the Irish Jewish Museum, Walworth Road, Dublin.
41. *Catholic Bulletin*, 20 (1930), p. 1137.
42. E. Cahill, *Freemasonry and the Anti-Christian Movement*, Dublin, 1929, p. vi.
43. Ibid., p. 42.
44. *Irish Rosary*, 33 (1929), p. 309.
45. Ibid., 31 (1927), pp. 313–15.
46. *Catholic Bulletin*, 25 (1935), p. 274.
47. Ibid., 27 (1937), p. 258.
48. Ibid., p. 828.
49. A. Ryan, 'Spain, the Church and Europe', *Irish Ecclesiastical Record*, 48 (1936), p. 576.
50. A. de Blácam, 'The secrets of propaganda', *Irish Monthly*, 65 (1937), p. 781.
51. 'Spain Arises – But We?' *Irish Monthly*, 66 (1938). p. 110.
52. *Witness*, 25 September 1936, p. 7.
53. *Catholic Bulletin*, 28 (1938).
54. 'Truth about Spain', *Irish Monthly*, 65 (1937), p. 150.
55. 'Should Irish Labour Support Franco?', *Irish Monthly*, 63 (1937), p. 310.
56. C. Lucey, 'The principles of Fascism', *Irish Ecclesiastical Record*, 53 (1939), p. 371.
57. 'Spain towards the Second Glory', *Irish Monthly*, 66 (1938), p. 467.
58. F. McCullagh, *In Franco's Spain*, London, 1937, p. 40.
59. Ibid., p. 306.
60. *Catholic Bulletin*, 28 (1938), p. 174.
61. Ibid., 29 (1939), p. 143.
62. Ibid., p. 225.
63. Ibid., 28 (1939), p. 741.
64. Ibid., 29 (1939), p. 311.
65. *Irish Rosary*, 42 (1938), p. 85.
66. Anon., 'Whither Germany?' *Irish Ecclesiastical Record*, 49 (1937).
67. T. O'Herlihy, 'Italy', *Irish Ecclesiastical Record*, 37 (1931), p. 226.
68. R. Devane, 'The religious revival under Salazar', *Irish Ecclesiastical Record*, 51 (1938), p. 41.
69. J. Murphy, *The People's Primate: A Memoir of Joseph Cardinal MacRory*, Dublin, 1945, pp. 37–8; also, *Catholic Bulletin*, 29 (1939), pp. 299–300.

CHAPTER FOURTEEN
A Tendency towards Defeatism

1. S. Blair, 'Rev. W. F. Marshall: profile of an Ulsterman', *Bulletin of the Presbyterian Historical Society of Ireland*, 24 (1995), p. 16.
2. *Church of Ireland Gazette*, 12 August 1921, p. 483.
3. Ibid., 22 February 1929, p126.

4. T. Dooley, 'Protestant migration from the Free State to Northern Ireland 1920–25', *Clogher Record*, 15 (Enniskillen, 1996), p. 121.

5. *Catholic Bulletin*, 19 (April 1929), p. 300.

6. J. White, *The Protestant Community in the Irish Republic*, Dublin, 1975, p. 5.

7. *Witness*, 8 June 1938, p. 8.

8. *Minutes of the proceedings of the General Assembly of the Presbyterian Church in Ireland*, 1916 (Vol Xiii, 1916–20, Belfast), *Reports and Accounts*, p. 6; ibid., 1927 *Reports and Accounts*, p. 146.

9. Ibid., 1922, *Reports and Accounts*, p. 19.

10. Ibid., 1923, *Reports and Accounts*, pp. 1, 3.

11. Ibid., 1927, p. 4.

12. *Christian Irishman*, June 1939, p. 109.

13. R. P. McDermott and D. A. Webb, *Irish Protestantism Today and Tomorrow*, Dublin and Belfast, 1942, p. 23.

14. W. B. Stanford, *A Recognised Church: The Church of Ireland in Eire*, Dublin and Belfast, 1944, p. 23.

15. M. Keane, *Good Behaviour*, London, 1981, p. 111.

16. W. Bell (ed.), *The Church of Ireland AD432–1932. The Report of the Church of Ireland Conference Held in Dublin 11–14 October 1932*, Dublin, 1932, p. 15.

17. *Church of Ireland Gazette*, 21 October 1932, p. 642.

18. *Catholic Bulletin*, 25 (1935), p. 680.

19. *Irish Times*, 19 May 1930, p. 7.

20. *Church of Ireland Gazette*, 18 February 1927, p. 102.

21. *Irish Times* quoted in *Catholic Bulletin*, 19 (June 1929), p. 493.

22. Ibid., 15 (1925), p. 685.

23. Stanford, *A Recognised Church*, p. 27.

24. *Church of Ireland Gazette*, 10 May 1929, p. 262.

25. Stanford, *A Recognised Church*, p. 16.

26. R. Murray, *Archbishop Bernard: Professor, Prelate and Provost*, London, 1931, p. 347.

27. *Catholic Bulletin*, 23 (July 1933), p. 537.

28. Ibid., 20 (December 1930), p. 1106.

29. *Christian Irishman*, June 1939, p. 109.

30. K. O'Shiel, 'The problem of partitioned Ireland', *Studies*, 12 (1923), p. 637.

31. *Catholic Bulletin*, 22 (March 1932), p. 181.

32. Ibid., 29 (1939), p. 765.

33. G. Seaver, *John Fitzallen Gregg, Archbishop*, Leighton Buzzard, 1963, p. 126.

34. *Church of Ireland Gazette*, 14 February 1936, p. 106.

35. Seaver, *John Fitzallen Gregg*, p. 190.

36. *Catholic Bulletin*, 28 (1938), p. 12.

37. A. F. Moody, *Memoirs and Musings of a Moderator*, London, 1937, p. 208.

38. *Witness*, 21 October 1921, p. 7.

39. Moody, *Memoirs*, p. 38.

40. Figures taken from the *Christian Irishman*, June 1945, pp. 42–3.

41. See note 1.

42. *Christian Irishman*, June 1945, p. 45.

43. Ibid., February 1949, p. 13.

44. *Witness*, 4 February 1938, p. 1.

45. B. Barton, *Brookeborough: the making of a Prime Minister*, Belfast, 1988, p. 4.

46. T. O'Neill, *The Autobiography of Terence O'Neill, Prime Minister of Northern Ireland 1963–69*, London, 1972, p. 47.

47. Barton, *Brookeborough*, p. 15.

48. O'Neill, *Autobiography*, p. 46.
49. Anon, 'The present position of Catholics in Northern Ireland', *Studies*, 25, 1936, p. 585; also J. Bardon, *A History of Ulster*, Belfast, 1992, p. 538–9, citing *Parliamentary Debates* (Northern Ireland House of Commons, Vol. 16, cols 1091–5).
50. *Witness*, 26 April 1935, p. 1.
51. Ibid., 25 October 1935, p. 7.
52. Ibid., 8 November 1935, p. 7.
53. R. M. Sibbett, *Orangeism in Ireland and throughout the Empire*, Vol. II, Belfast, 1914, p. 637.
54. R. Harbinson, *No Surrender: an Ulster childhood*, London, 1960, p. 127.
55. Ibid., p. 57.
56. *Irish Presbyterian*, 24 (April 1915), p. 50.
57. Address to the Clergy of the Diocese of Armagh at Dundalk, 6 July, Dungannon, 7 July, Armagh, 11 July, by the Lord Primate John B Armagh, August 1916, p. 27.
58. *Witness*, 3 April 1936.
59. Ibid., 25 March 1938, p. 5.
60. J. Murphy, *The People's Primate: a Memoir of Joseph, Cardinal MacRory*, Dublin, 1945, pp. 36–7.
61. Barton, *Brookeborough*, p. 78.
62. Ibid., p. 79.
63. Ibid.
64. 'Documents on the Belfast pogrom of July 1935', *Catholic Bulletin*, 25 (1935), p. 869.
65. *Catholic Bulletin*, 28 (1938), p. 263.
66. *Church of Ireland Gazette*, 15 September 1939, p. 490. The letter is dated 8 September.
67. *Irish Times*, 8 May 1945, p. 1.
68. *Church of Ireland Gazette*, 28 January 1949, p. 9.
69. Ibid., 22 April 1949, p. 6.

CHAPTER FIFTEEN
Most Fruitful of Mothers

1. K. Smyth, 'Priests and people in Ireland,' *Furrow*, March 1958, p. 150.
2. 'Statement of the hierarchy at the conclusion of the plenary synod at Maynooth, 7–15 August 1956', *Furrow*, September 1956, p. 555.
3. 'John XXII's message to Cardinal D'Alton', *Furrow*, April 1961, p. 234.
4. J. Newman, 'Priestly vocations in Ireland', paper read in Vienna, 10 October 1958, ibid., November 1958, p. 711.
5. D. Meehan, 'Views about the Irish', *Furrow*, August 1960, p. 506.
6. F. Duff, 'Emigration and providence', *Furrow*, 8 (1957), p. 566.
7. H. Maxton, *Waking: an Irish Protestant Upbringing*, Belfast, 1997, p. 68.
8. *Irish Times*, 16 March 1999, p. 15.
9. *Intercom*, May 1994, p. 11.
10. F. McCourt, *Angela's Ashes: a Memoir of a Childhood*, New York, 1996, p. 414.
11. *Irish Times*, 3 June 1957, p. 7.
12. Ibid., 7 June 1957, p. 1.
13. Ibid., 6 June 1957, p. 9.
14. *Church of Ireland Gazette*, 5 July 1957.
15. Ibid., 12 July 1957, p. 1.
16. Ibid., 14 June 1957, p. 1.

17. *Belfast Telegraph*, 11 June 1957.
18. *Irish Times*, 26 June, 1957, p. 1.
19. V. Griffin, *Mark of Protest: an Autobiography*, Dublin 1993, p. 27.
20. J. Barkley, *Blackmouth and Dissenter*, Belfast, 1991, p. 68.
21. G. Byrne with D. Purcell, *The Time of my Life*, Dublin 1989, p. 57.
22. J. Cooney, *John Charles McQuaid, ruler of Catholic Ireland*, Dublin, 1999, p. 216.
23. Ibid., p. 248.
24. N. Browne, *Against the Tide*, Dublin, 1986, p. 31.
25. Ibid., p. 30.
26. Ibid., p. 151.
27. M. O'Sullivan, *Brendan Behan: a Life*, Dublin, 1997, pp. 30–1. O'Sullivan cites Brian Behan: 'De Valera pulled down [the] slums only to break up the anarchistic blocks of people who lived so communally that they oft times found themselves in one another's beds (something the puritanical politician would hardly have approved of).'
28. Cooney, *McQuaid*, p. 374.
29. *Irish Times*, 10 November 1999, p. 15.
30. Browne, *Against the Tide*, p. 158.
31. *Tablet*, 21 April 1951, p. 308.
32. Browne, *Against the Tide*, p. 176.
33. Ibid., p. 182.
34. *Tablet*, 21 April 1951, p. 307.
35. Ibid., p. 303.
36. M. O'Dwyer, 'The liturgy in a rural parish', *Furrow*, May 1954, pp. 686–95.
37. J. Scott, 'A letter from Ireland, 1 April 2060', *Furrow*, May 1958, pp. 300–1.
38. A Curtayne, review of John O'Brien, *The Vanishing Irish*, *Furrow*, May 1954, p. 331.
39. Mother Mary Michael of the Convent of the Holy Child Edgbaston, near Birmingham, writing in *Furrow*, March 1959, p. 180.
40. P. J. Gannon, 'Art, morality and censorship', *Studies*, 31 (1942), p. 412.
41. B. Behan, *Borstal Boy*, London, 1958, p. 76; see O'Sullivan, *Brendan Behan: a Life*, p. 47.
42. *Furrow*, January 1954, p. 42.
43. Ibid., March 1954, p. 169.
44. B. Smyth, 'Catholic programmes on Irish television', ibid., December 1959, p. 772.
45. B. Smyth, 'Problems posed by British television', ibid., August 1960, p. 496.
46. Father Agnellus Andrew, 'Television and religion', *Irish Ecclesiastical Record*, 1955, p. 22.
47. 'Statement on television: the bishops of Ireland, Maynooth 10 October 1961', *Furrow*, November 1961, pp. 695–6.

CHAPTER SIXTEEN

Till Boyne Rivers Run Red

1. *Presbyterian Herald*, September 1965, p. 243.
2. *Westminster Cathedral Journal*, July 1964, cited in B. and M. Pawley, *Rome and Canterbury through Four Centuries*, London and Oxford, 1974, p. 312.
3. Ibid., p. 320.
4. Ibid., p. 326.
5. *Furrow*, January 1962, p. 569.
6. Ibid., p. 19.
7. Ibid., March 1963, p. 140.
8. *Studies*, 53 (1964), p. 15.

9. *Furrow*, January 1965, p. 10.
10. Ibid., July 1964, p. 475.
11. *Presbyterian Herald*, September 1965, p. 243.
12. *Christian Irishman*, November 1965, p. 122.
13. *Furrow* (January 1965), p. 434.
14. Ibid., p. 493.
15. G. Byrne, *The Time of my Life*, Dublin, 1989, p. 162.
16. Ibid., p. 164.
17. Ibid., p. 232.
18. T. Inglis, 'Sacred and secular in Catholic Ireland', *Studies*, 74 (1985), p. 44.
19. T. O'Neill, *The Autobiography of Terence O'Neill, Prime Minister of Northern Ireland 1963–1969*, London, 1972, p. 75.
20. J. Cooney, *John Charles McQuaid, ruler of Catholic Ireland*, Dublin, 1999, p. 371.
21. *Furrow*, February 1964, pp. 92–3.
22. Ibid., July 1966, p. 432.
23. Ibid., November 1966, p. 687.
24. *Studies*, 57 (1967), p. 2.
25. R. Paisley, *Ian Paisley, My Father*, Basingstoke, 1988, p. 136.
26. D. Cooke, *Persecuting Zeal: a Portrait of Ian Paisley*, Dingle, 1996, p. 142.
27. Ibid., p. 144.
28. *Furrow*, December 1968, p. 715.
29. O'Neill, *Autobiography*, p. 87.
30. *Protestant Telegraph*, 2 July 1966, p. 10.
31. Ibid., 28 May 1966, p. 2.
32. Ibid.
33. Cooke, *Paisley*, p. 149.
34. *Furrow*, June 1968, p. 401.
35. Ibid., p. 403.
36. *Irish Catholic*, 25 January 1968, p. 1.
37. *Irish News*, 14 October 1968, p. 1.
38. E. Gallagher and S. Worrall, *Christians in Ulster 1968–1980*, Oxford, 1982, p. 41.
39. Cooke, *Paisley*, p. 159.
40. *Tablet*, 11 January 1969, p. 26.
41. G. McElroy, *The Catholic Church and the Northern Ireland Crisis 1968–1986*, Dublin, 1991, pp. 23–4.
42. *Minutes of the Proceedings of the General Assembly of the Presbyterian Church in Ireland*, 1969, p. 6.
43. Gallagher and Worrall, *Christians in Ulster*, p. 51.
44. The Ulster Special Constabulary set up in 1920 comprised three categories. Class A was paid and served full-time. Class B, or the 'B-Specials' was part-time and unpaid and Class C was a reserve force. See T. Hennessey, *A History of Northern Ireland, 1920–1996*, London, 1997, p. 15.
45. McElroy, *Catholic Church and the Northern Ireland Crisis*, p. 28.
46. Ibid., p. 29.
47. *Minutes of the Proceedings of the General Assembly of the Presbyterian Church in Ireland*, Belfast, 1970, p. 3.
48. *Furrow*, August 1969, p. 401.
49. Gallagher and Worrall, *Christians in Ulster*, p. 65.
50. *Minutes of the Proceedings of the General Assembly of the Presbyterian Church in Ireland*, Belfast, 1972, p. 7.
51. C. O'Brien, *States of Ireland*, St Albans, 1974, pp. 217–18.

52. 'Bishops of Northern Ireland on the situation in Northern Ireland, 12 September 1971', *Furrow*, October 1971, p. 664.
53. 'Violence in Northern Ireland: statement by the Northern Ireland bishops, 21 November 1971', ibid., January 1972, p. 60.
54. Ibid., February 1972, p. 104.
55. D. Faul, 'The repose of Cardinal O'Fiaich', ibid., September 1991, pp. 481–2.
56. McElroy, *Catholic Church and the Northern Ireland Crisis*, p. 57.
57. *Studies*, 81 (1992), p. 180.
58. Gallagher and Worrall, *Christians in Ulster*, p. 1.
59. *Furrow*, October 1975, p. 596.
60. *Studies*, 80 (1991), p. 173.
61. *Irish Times*, 31 January 1992.
62. *Studies*, 81 (1992).

CHAPTER SEVENTEEN
I Never Asked for a Pedestal

1. *Irish Times*, 19 February 1996, p. 11.
2. S. Noonan and J. Hourigan, *A Pilgrim for Peace: Pope John Paul II in Ireland*, Dublin, 1979, p. 1.
3. 'Presbyterian Church in Ireland: church statements 1980', 29 September 1979, p. 5. 'The Church complained that their own courtesy to the Pope has not been matched on the part of prominent members of the Roman Catholic Church by similar courtesies to leaders held in honour and loyalty by so many in our own community.'
4. John Paul II, *The Pope in Ireland: Addresses and Homilies*, Dublin, 1979, pp. 22–4.
5. Ibid., p. 70.
6. T. Flannery, *From the Inside, A Priest's View of the Catholic Church*, Cork and Dublin, 1999, p. 12.
7. T. Inglis, 'Sacred and secular in Catholic Ireland', *Studies*, 74 (1985) p. 39. Original quotation from M. Nic Ghilla Phadraig, 'Religion in Ireland: preliminary analysis, *Social Studies*, 5, 1976, p. 129.
8. M. Fogarty, L. Ryan and J. Lee, *Irish Values and Attitudes: The Irish Report of the European Value Systems Study*, Dublin, 1984, p. 8.
9. T. Flannery, 'Religious in decline', *Furrow*, January 1992, p. 32.
10. *Irish Times*, 29 April 1976, p. 10.
11. D. Barrington, 'Violence in Northern Ireland', *Furrow*, February 1977, p. 70.
12 J. Cooney, 'Was he a saint or a sinner?' *Sunday Times* (Irish edn), 7 November 1999, p. 2.
13. K. Hegarty, 'Handing on the faith in a changing society', *Intercom*, May 1994, p. 5.
14. B. Hoban 'What are we at?' *Furrow*, September 1992, p. 495.
15. T. Cahill, 'Is religious decline a lot of nonsense?' ibid., May 1992, p. 272.
16. H. O'Donoghue, 'Where have all the flowers gone?', *Intercom*, April 1994, p. 7.
17. Flannery, 'Religious in decline', pp. 33–4.
18. *Irish Times*, 16 August 1983, p. 7.
19. Ibid., 17 August 1983, p. 4.
20. Ibid., 22 August 1983, p. 1.
21. Ibid., p. 6.
22. Ibid., 23 August 1983, p. 1.
23. G. Fitzgerald, *All in a Life: an autobiography*, Dublin, 1991, p. 445.

24. *Irish Times*, 24 August 1983, p. 1.
25. *Church of Ireland Gazette*, 13 May 1983, p. 6.
26. *Irish Times*, 26 August 1983, p. 1.
27. V. Griffin, *Mark of Protest: an Autobiography*, Dublin, 1993, pp. 197–8.
28. *Irish Times*, 9 September 1983, p. 5.
29. Ibid., 20 February 1982, p. 12.
30. Ibid., 8 September 1983, p. 6.
31. L. Siggins, *Mary Robinson, The Woman Who Took Power in the Park*, London and Edinburgh, 1997, p. 136.
32. Ibid., p. 132.
33. *Irish Times*, 10 March 1995, p. 2.
34. Ibid., 18 February 1992, p. 13.
35. Ibid., 22 February 1992, p. 8.
36. Ibid., 24 February 1992, p. 7.
37. Ibid., 2 March 1992, p. 4.
38. Ibid., 27 February 1992, p. 6.
39. Ibid., 2 March 1992, p. 4
40. Ibid., 12 March 1992, p. 6.
41. Ibid., 4 March 1992, p. 12.
42. Ibid., 21 March 1992, p. 10.
43. Ibid., 19 March 1992, p. 1.
44. Ibid., 27 March 1992, p. 2.
45. Ibid., 7 May 1992, p. 1.
46. Ibid., p. 10.
47. Ibid., 13 May 1992, p. 6.
48. Ibid., 26 September 1994, p. 4.
49. C. Moore, *Betrayal of Trust: the Father Brendan Smyth Affair and the Catholic Church*, Dublin, 1995, p. 29.
50. Ibid., p. 124.
51. Ibid., p. 207.
52. Ibid., p. 205.
53. *Irish Times*, 8 October p. 5.
54. Moore, *Brendan Smyth*, p. 173.
55. The hole through which the quarrelling noblemen chanced their arms and were reconciled was made in the Chapter House door. 'Ormond surmising that this drift was intended for some further treacherie, that if he would stretch out his hand, it had been perchance chopt off, refused that proffer; until Kildare stretcht in his hand to him, and so the doore was opened, they both embraced'. J. Bernard, *History of St Patrick's Cathedral, Dublin*, Dublin, 1903, p. 10.
56. *Irish Times*, 14 October 1994, p. 14.
57. Ibid., 17 October 1994, p. 12.
58. S. O'Conaill, 'Scandals in the Church', *Studies*, 84 (Spring 1995), p. 24.
59. *Irish Times*, 14 November 1994, p. 1.
60. Ibid., 1 March 1995, p. 47.
61. Ibid., 15 June 1995, p. 1.
62. Ibid., 26 June 1995, p. 7.
63. P. Hamilton, *Secret Love: My Life with Father Michael Cleary*, London and Edinburgh, 1995, p. 55.
64. *Irish Times*, 18 June 1995, p. 2.
65. Ibid., 4 November 1995, p. 10.
66. Ibid., 19 February 1996, p. 11.

67. Ibid., 8 August 1995, p. 12.
68. Ibid., 14 November 1995, p. 7.
69. Ibid., 28 August 1995, p. 1.
70. Ibid., 8 March 1996, p. 9.

CHAPTER EIGHTEEN
A Family Quarrel

1. T. Inglis, cited in K. Hegarty, 'The Church and the media', *Furrow*, February 1996, p. 78.
2. P. J. Joyce, *John Healy, Archbishop of Tuam*, Dublin, 1931, p. 109.
3. M. Kenny, 'Is this the end of Catholic Ireland?' *Tablet*, 26 November 1994, p. 1503.
4. P. Corish, *Maynooth College 1795–1995*, Dublin, 1995, p. 437.
5. C. Daly, 'Needing forgiveness', *Intercom*, February 1995.
6. J. Donnelly, 'A Church in crisis: the Irish Catholic Church today,' *History Ireland*, Autumn 2000, p. 17.
7. P. McAleer and D. McNeice, 'Lonely soul', *Sunday Times* (Irish edn), 1 August 1999, p. 16.
8. 'The tough but rewarding job of serving God', *Sunday Times* (Irish edn), 1 August 1999, p. 16.
9. *Catholic Times*, 20 August 2000, p. 6.
10. Donnelly, 'A Church in crisis', p. 13.
11. F. McCourt, *Angela's Ashes: a Memoir of a Childhood*, New York, 1996, p. 1.
12. T. Casey, 'Old yarns and new stories', in E. Conway and C. Kilcoyne (eds), *The Splintered Heart: Conversations with a Church in Crisis*, Dublin, 1998.
13. *Irish Times*, 13 December 1997, p. 1.
14. Ibid., 17 December 1997, p. 9.
15. Ibid., 18 December 1997, p. 10.
16. *Church of Ireland Gazette*, 20 October 1995, p. 5.
17. Ibid., 7 August 1998, p. 2.
18. J. V. Luce, *Trinity College Dublin: the First 400 Years*, Dublin 1992, p. 154.
19. 'At that time … an immense throng of people attended the Protestant church in those days, although neither trace nor tidings of them there today.' From P. Sayers, *The Autobiography of Peig Sayers of the Great Blasket Island*, translated by B. MacMahon, Dublin 1973, p.44.
20. P. Ward and D. McDade, *Public Attitudes to Parades and Marches in Northern Ireland, Area Survey: Garvaghy Road*, Research and Evaluation Services, London, 1997, p. 1.
21. R. Dudley Edwards, *The Faithful Tribe: an Intimate Portrait of the Loyal Institutions*, London, 1999, p. 348.
22. *Church of Ireland Gazette*, 11 October 1996, p. 5.
23. Ibid., 1 November 1996, p. 12.
24. Ibid., 18 April 1997, p. 2.
25. Ibid., 30 October 1998, p. 8-9.
26. A. de Blácam, 'Some thoughts on partition', *Studies*, 23 (1934), p. 570.
27. J. McCreedy, *The Seer's House: the Remarkable Story of James McConnell and the Whitewell Metropolitan Tabernacle*, Belfast and Greenville, 1997, p. 74.
28. T. Inglis, *Moral Monopoly: the Rise and Fall of the Catholic Church in Modern Ireland*, Dublin, 1998, p. 223.
29. F. Gibbons, Divinely guided missal hits target', *Guardian*, 28 July 2001, Review, p. 3.
30. K. Moore, 'Nora Wall desperate for fresh start', *Sunday Independent*, 21 November 1999, p. 6.

Select Bibliography

Secondary sources

(Anon.), *An authentic report of the discussions which took place at Carrick-on-Shannon on the 9th November 1824 between three Roman Catholic priests and three clergymen of the Established Church*, Dublin, 1824.

(Anon.), *Authentic report of the great Protestant meeting held at Exeter Hall on Saturday June 20th 1835*, Dublin, 1835.

(Anon.), *Bloody Newes from Ireland, or the barbarous crueltie By the papists used in that kingdome by putting men to the sword, deflouring women … and cruelly murdering them …*, London, 1641.

(Anon.), *The Case of Maynooth considered with a History of the First Establishment of That Seminary*, Dublin, 1836.

(Anon.), *Historical notices of the several Rebellions, Disturbances and Illegal Associations in Ireland from the earliest period to the year 1822*, Dublin, 1822.

(Anon.), *A History of the Irish Rebellion in the Year 1798*, Dublin, 1799.

(Anon.), *Late and Lamentable Newes from Ireland wherein are truly related the Rebellious and Cruell Proceedings of the Papists*, London, 1641.

(Anon.), *The State of His Majesty's Subjects in Ireland professing the Roman Catholic Religion*, Dublin, 1799.

(Anon.), *A Treatise of Irelande*, 1588.

(Anon.), *A Vindication of the Roman Catholic Clergy of the Town of Wexford during the Late Unhappy Rebellion*, Dublin, 1798.

Akenson, D., *God's Peoples: Covenant and Land in South Africa, Israel and Ulster*, New York and London, 1992.

Alexander, E., *Primate Alexander, Archbishop of Armagh*, London, 1913.

Anstruther, G., and Hallett, P. E, *Catholic Truth Society: the First 50 Years*, London, 1934.

Ardagh, J., *Ireland and the Irish: Portrait of a Changing Society*, London, 1995.

Arwaker, E., *A Sermon Preached on the day of Thanksgiving for Peace at St Ann's church in the Diocese of Armagh, by Edmund Arwaker, Rector of Drumglass and Chaplain to the Duke of Ormonde*, Dublin, 1698.

Ashwell, A. R., *The Life of the Right Reverend Samuel Wilberforce with Selections from his Diary and Correspondence*, 3 vols, London, 1880–2.

Bailey, K., *A History of Trinity College Dublin, 1892–1945*, Dublin, 1947.

Bale, J., *The Vocacyon of John Bale to the Bishoprick of Ossorie in Irelande, his Persecucions in the same, and Finall Delyveraunce*, Harleian Miscellany, 6, London, 1810.

Ball, J., *The Reformed Church in Ireland (1537–1886)*, London and Dublin, 1886.

Bardon, J., *A History of Ulster*, Belfast, 1992.

Barkely, J., *Blackmouth and Dissenter*, Belfast, 1991.

Barry, S., Bradley, J., and Empey, A. (eds), *A Worthy Foundation: The Cathedral Church of St Canice Kilkenny 1285–1985*, Mountrath, Leix, 1985.

Barton, B., *Brookeborough: the making of a prime minister*, Belfast, 1988.

Beckett, J.C., *The Making of Modern Ireland 1603–1923*, London, 1966.

Begley, J., *The Diocese of Limerick in the Sixteenth and Seventeenth Centuries*, Dublin and London, 1927.

Bence-Jones, M., *Twilight of the Ascendancy*, London, 1987.

Benn, G., *A History of the Town of Belfast from the Earliest Times to the Close of the Eighteenth Century*, London, 1877.

Bliss, A., *Spoken English in Ireland 1600–1740*, Dublin, 1979.

Bolster, E., *A History of the Diocese of Cork from the Earliest Times to the Reformation*, Dublin, 1972.

Bolton, F., *The Caroline Tradition of the Church of Ireland*, London, 1958.

Boulter, H., *Letters written by His Excellency Hugh Boulter, Lord Primate of Ireland to several Ministers of State in England*, 2 vols, Oxford, 1765–70.

Bourke, U., *The Life and Times of the Most Revd John MacHale*, New York, 1902.

Bowen, D., *Souperism: Myth or Reality? A Study in Souperism*, Cork, 1970.

Bowen, D., *The Protestant Crusade in Ireland 1800–1870*, Montreal, 1978.

Bowen, D., *Paul Cardinal Cullen and the Shaping of Modern Irish Catholicism*, Dublin, 1983.

Bowen, D., *The History and Shaping of Irish Protestantism*, New York and Washington, 1995.

Bradshaw, B., *The Dissolution of the Religious Orders in Ireland under Henry VIII*, Cambridge, 1974.

Briollay, S., *Ireland in Rebellion*, Dublin, 1922.

Brown, S., and Miller, D. (eds), *Piety and Power in Ireland 1760–1960. Essays in Honour of Emmet Larkin*, Belfast and Notre Dame, Ind., 2000.

Browne, N., *Against the Tide*, Dublin, 1986.

Bruce, S., *The Red Hand: Protestant Paramilitaries in Northern Ireland*, Oxford and New York, 1902.

Burke, E., *Some Reflections on the Operation of the Popery Laws in Ireland*, Dublin, 1777.

Burke, W., *A History of Clonmel*, Waterford, 1907.

Burke W., *The Irish Priests in Penal Times 1660–1760*, from the State Papers in HM Record Offices... Waterford, 1914.

Bush, J., *A Letter from a Gentleman in Dublin to his friend at Dover in Kent*, London, 1764.

Byrne, G. with Purcell, D., *The Time of my Life*, Dublin, 1989.

Cahill, E., *Freemasonry and the Anti-Christian Movement*, Dublin, 1929.

Campbell, W., *A Vindication of the Principles and Character of the Presbyterians of Ireland, Addressed to the Bishop of Cloyne in answer to his book, entitled The Present State of the Church of Ireland*, London, 1787.

Carlson, J. (ed.), *Banned in Ireland: Censorship and the Irish Writer*, London, 1990.

Carlyle, T., *Reminiscences of my Irish Journey in 1849*, London, 1852.

Carr, J., *The Life and Times of James Ussher, Archbishop of Armagh*, London, 1895.

Carrigan, W., *The History and Antiquities of the Diocese of Ossory*, 4 vols, Dublin, 1905.

Carville, G., *The Heritage of Holy Cross*, Belfast, 1973.

Casey, E., *Young People of Ireland I Love You*, ?Dublin, 1979.

Childe-Pemberton, P., *The Earl Bishop, The Life of Frederick Hervey, Bishop of Derry, Earl of Bristol*, 2 vols, London, 1925.

Christmas, H. (ed.), *Select Works of John Bale, Bishop of Ossory*, Cambridge, 1849.

Cogan, A., *The Diocese of Meath, Ancient and Modern*, 3 vols, Dublin, 1862–70.

Coldrey, B., *Most Unenviable Reputation, the Christian Brothers and School Discipline over Two Centuries*, Perth, 1991.

Colvin, I., *The Life of Lord Carson*, 2 vols, London, 1934.

Connolly, S. J., *Priests and People in Pre-Famine Ireland 1780–1845*, New York, 1982.

Conway, E., and Kilcoyne, C., *Twin Pulpits: Church and Media in Modern Ireland*, Dublin, 1997.

Conway, E., and Kilcoyne, C. (eds), *The Splintered Heart: Conversations with a Church in Crisis*, Dublin, 1998.

Cooke, D., *Persecuting Zeal: a Portrait of Ian Paisley*, Dingle, 1996.

Cooney, J., *John Charles McQuaid, ruler of Catholic Ireland*, Dublin, 1999.

Corish, P., *Maynooth College 1795–1995*, Dublin, 1995.

Cotter, F., *The Friars Minor in Ireland from their Arrival to 1400*, New York, 1994.

Crawford, A., *The Happy Death-Bed*, Belfast, 1846.

Crotty, M., *A Narrative of the Reformation at Birr*, London, 1847.

Cunningham, P. (ed.), *The Letters of Horace Walpole, Fourth Earl of Oxford*, 9 vols, London, 1891.

Curl, J. S., *The Londonderry Plantation 1609–1914*, Chichester, 1986.

Curtis, E., *A History of Ireland*, London, 1936.

Curtis, E., and McDowell, R. (eds), *Irish Historical Documents 1172–1922*, New York and London, 1968.

D'Arcy, C. F., *The Adventures of a Bishop*, London, 1934.

Dallas, C., *Prosleytism in Ireland. The Catholic Defence Association Versus the Irish Church Missions on the charge of Bribery and Intimidation*, London, 1832.

Davidson, R., and Benham, W., *Life of Archibald Campbell Tait, Archbishop of Canterbury*, 2 vols, London, 1891.

de Blácam, A., *What Sinn Fein Stands For*, Dublin and London, 1921.

Dillon, J., *The Question as to the Admission of Catholics to Parliament considered upon the Principles of Existing Laws*, London, 1801.

Doherty, R., *The Williamite War in Ireland 1688–1691*, Dublin, 1998.

Doyle, J., *Address to the lower orders of the Roman Catholics of Ireland, Carlow, May 13 1824*, Cork, 1835.

Doyle, R., *The Archbishop of Dublin's charge on 24 October 1822 in St Patrick's Cathedral to which is added a letter to His Grace by a dignitary of the Roman Catholic Church*, Dublin, 1822.

Dudley Edwards, R., *Patrick Pearse: The Triumph of Failure*, London, 1977.

Dudley Edwards, R., *The Faithful Tribe: an Intimate Portrait of the Loyal Institutions*, London, 1999.

Dunlop, J., *A Precarious Belonging: Presbyterians and the Conflict in Ireland*, Belfast, 1995.

Dwyer, P., *The Diocese of Killaloe from the Reformation to the Close of the Eighteenth Century*, Dublin, 1878.

Dymmok, J., *A Treatise of Ireland*, in *Tracts Relating to Ireland*, Irish Archeological Society, vol. 2, Dublin, 1843.

Fagan, P., *Dublin's Turbulent Priest, Cornelius Nary (1658–1738)*, Dublin, 1991.

Fagan, W., *The Life and Times of Daniel O'Connell*, 2 vols, Cork, 1847–8.

Falls, C., *The Birth of Ulster*, London, 1936.

Fennell, D., *The Changing Face of Catholic Ireland*, London, Dublin, Melbourne, 1968.

Fitzgerald, B., *We are Besieged*, London, 1946.

Fitzgerald, G., *All in a Life: an autobiography*, Dublin, 1991.

Fitzgerald, P., *Recollections of Dublin Castle and of Dublin Society*, London, 1902.

Fitzgibbon, G., *Roman Catholic Priests and National Schools*, Dublin, 1872.

Fitzpatrick, H., *A Statement of the Penal Laws which aggrieve the Catholics of Ireland*, Dublin, 1812.

Fitzpatrick, J., *The Life, Times and Correspondence of the Right Revd Dr Doyle, Bishop of Kildare and Leighlin*, 2 vols, Dublin, 1861.

Fitzpatrick, W., *Memories of Father Healy of Little Bray*, London, 1899.

Flannery, T., *From the Inside, A Priest's View of the Catholic Church*, Cork and Dublin, 1999.

Flynn, T., *The Irish Dominicans 1536–1641*, Dublin, 1993.

Fogarty, M., Ryan, L., and Lee, J., *Irish Values and Attitudes: The Irish Report of the European Value Systems Study*, Dublin, 1984.

Ford, A., *The Protestant Reformation in Ireland, 1590–1641*, Frankfurt, 1985.

Ford, A., McGuire, J., and Milne, K. (eds), *As by Law Established: the Church of Ireland since the Reformation*, Dublin, 1995.

Forster, C., *The Life of John Jebb, Bishop of Limerick, Ardfert and Aghadoe*, 2 vols, London, 1836.

Foster, R., *Modern Ireland 1600–1972*, London, 1988.

Fothergill, B., *The Mitred Earl, an Eighteenth-century Eccentric*, London, 1974.

Froude, J., *The English in Ireland in the Eighteenth Century*, Vol. 1, London, 1884.

Gallagher, E., and Worrall, S., *Christians in Ulster, 1968–1980*, Oxford, 1982.

Galloway, P., *The Cathedrals of Ireland*, Belfast, 1992.

Garrett, J., *Good News from Ireland: an Address to the Archbishops and Bishops of the Church of England*, London, 1863.

Gilbert, J., *A History of the City of Dublin*, Vol. 1, Dublin, 1861.

Gilbert, J. (ed.), *Calendar of the Ancient Records of Dublin*, Vol. 1, Dublin, 1889.

Gill, M. (ed.), '*The Description of Ireland and the State Therof as it is at this Present in Anno 1598,' from a Manuscript Preserved in Clongowes-Wood College, Dublin*, London, 1878.

Gostelow, W., *Charles Stuart and Oliver Cromwell United*, London, 1655.

Gregg, R. S., '*Faithful unto Death*'. *Memorials of the Life of John Gregg, Bishop of Cork*, Dublin, 1879.

Griffin, V., *Mark of Protest: an Autobiography*, Dublin, 1993.

Hall, F. (ed.), *The Correspondence of Jonathan Swift*, Vol. 3, London, 1912.

Hamilton, P., *Secret Love: My Life with Father Michael Cleary*, London and Edinburgh, 1995.

Hamilton, W., *The Dangers of Popery and the Blessings arising from the Late Revolution*, Dublin, 1723.

Hammond, J., *Gladstone and the Irish Nation*, London, 1938.

Hanna, C., *The Scotch-Irish, or the Scot in North Britain, North Ireland and North America*, 2 vols, New York and London, 1902.

Hannigan, K., and Nolan, W. (eds), *Wicklow History and Society*, Dublin, 1994.

Harbinson, R., *No Surrender: an Ulster childhood*, London, 1960.

Hardiman, J., *The History of the Town and County of the Town of Galway*, Dublin, 1820.

Harris, M., *The Catholic Church and the Foundation of the Northern Irish State*, Cork, 1993.

Harrison, J., *The Scot in Ulster*, Edinburgh and London, 1888.

Hayes, W., *Thurles, a Guide to the Cathedral Town*, Thurles, 1999.

Healy, J., *Maynooth College: its Centenary History*, Dublin, 1895.

Hennessey, T., *A History of Northern Ireland, 1920–1996*, Basingstoke, 1997.

Hennessy, W., *The Annals of Loche Ce, A chronicle of Irish affairs from 1014 to AD 1590*, Vol. II, London, 1871.

Hickson, M., *Ireland in the Seventeenth Century, or the Massacres of 1641–2*, 2 vols, London, 1884.

Holinshed, R., *Holinshed's Chronicles of England, Scotland and Ireland*, 2 vols, London, 1586.

Holmes, F., *Our Irish Presbyterian Heritage*, Belfast, 1985.

How, F., *William Conygham Plunket, Fourth Baron Plunket and Sixty-first Archbishop of Dublin*, London, 1900.

Huish, R., *The Memoirs Private and Political of Daniel O'Connell, His Times and Contemporaries*, London, 1835.

Hussey, T., *A Pastoral Letter to the Catholic Clergy of the United Diocese of Waterford and Lismore, Waterford*, London, 1797.

Inglis, H., *A Journey throughout Ireland in 1834*, 2 vols, London, 1834.

Inglis, T., *Moral Monopoly: the Rise and Fall of the Catholic Church in Modern Ireland*, Dublin, 1998.

Jackson, R., *Jonathan Swift, Dean and Pastor*, London, 1939.

Jackson, R., *Archbishop Magrath, the Scoundrel of Cashel*, Dublin and Cork, 1974.

James, R. R., *Lord Randolph Churchill*, London, 1959.

Jefferies, H., *Priests and Prelates of Armagh in the Age of Reformations 1518–1558*, Dublin, 1997.

Jones, H., *A Remonstrance of Divers Remarkable Passages concerning the Church and Kingdome of Ireland*, London, 1642.

Jones, L., *The New Reformation in Ireland*, Dublin, 1852.

Joyce, P. J., *John Healy, Archbishop of Tuam*, Dublin, 1931.

Keaveney, A., and Madden, J. (eds), *Sir William Herbert: Croftus sive de Hibernia Liber*, Dublin, 1992.

Kelly, J., Keogh, D., and McMahon, C. (eds), *History of the Catholic Diocese of Dublin*, Dublin, 2000.

Keogh, C., *The Veto: a Commentary on the Greville Manifesto*, London, 1810.

Kernohan, J., *Rosemary Street Presbyterian church: a record of the last 200 years*, Belfast, 1923.

Kew, G., *The Irish Sections of Fynes Moryson's Unpublished 'Itinerary'*, Dublin, 1998.

Killen, W., *Reminiscences of a Long Life*, London, 1901.

Killen, W. (ed.), *Mackenzie's Memorials of the Siege of Derry*, Belfast, 1861.

Killen, W. (ed.), *A true narrative of the rise and progress of the Presbyterian Church in Ireland 1623–70*, by the Revd Patrick Adair, Belfast, London, Edinburgh, 1866.

King, C. S. (ed.), *A Great Archbishop of Dublin, William King 1650–1729*, London, 1908.

King, W., *The State of the Protestants of Ireland under the Late King James's Government*, London, 1691.

King, W., *An answer to the considerations which obliged Peter Manby (as he pretends) to embrace what he calls the Catholick Religion*, Dublin, 1687.

Krueger, R., *The Poems of Sir John Davies*, Oxford, 1975.

Landa, L., *Swift and the Church of Ireland*, Oxford, 1954.

Lawlor, H., *The Reformation and the Irish Episcopate*, London, 1932.

Leland, T., *The History of Ireland, from the invasion of Henry II …*, 3 vols, London, 1773.

Lennon, C., *Richard Stanihurst the Dubliner 1547–1618, A Biography with Stanihurst's Text on Ireland's Past*, Dublin, 1981.

Lennon, C., *Sixteenth-century Ireland: The Incomplete Conquest*, Dublin, 1994.

Lockington, J., *Robert Blair of Bangor*, Belfast, 1996.

Luce, J. V., *Trinity College Dublin: the First 400 Years*, Dublin, 1992.

Lydon, J., *The Making of Ireland, from Ancient Times to the Present*, London and New York, 1998.

Macaulay, A., *William Crolly, Archbishop of Armagh 1835–1849*, Dublin, 1994.

MacCarthy, R. B., *Ancient and Modern: A Short History of the Church of Ireland*, Dublin, 1995.

McCreedy, J., *The Seer's House: the Remarkable Story of James McConell and the Whitewell Metropolitan Tabernacle*, Belfast and Greenville, 1997.

McCrie, T. (ed.), *The Life of Mr Robert Blair, Minister of St Andrews, containing his Autobiography from 1593 to 1636*, Edinburgh, 1848.

Mac Cuarta, B. (ed.), *Ulster 1641: Aspects of the Rising*, Belfast, 1993.

McCullagh, F., *In Franco's Spain*, London, 1937.

McDermott, R. P., and Webb, D. A., *Irish Protestantism Today and Tomorrow*, Dublin and Belfast, 1942.

Macdonagh, M., *The Irish at the Front*, London, New York and Toronto, 1916.

MacDonnell, J., *The Life and Correspondence of William Connor Magee, Archbishop of York, Bishop of Peterborough*, 2 vols, London, 1896.

McDowell, R., *The Church of Ireland 1869–1969*, London and Boston, 1975.

McDowell, R., *Crisis and Decline: the Future of the Southern Unionists*, Dublin, 1997.

McElroy, G., *The Catholic Church and the Northern Ireland Crisis 1968–1986*, Dublin, 1991.

McEneaney, E. (ed.), *A History of Waterford and its Mayors from the 12th Century to the 20th Century*, Waterford, 1995.

MacHale, J., *Letters of Hierophilus to the English People on the Moral and Political State of Ireland*, London, 1822.

MacKnight, T., *Ulster as it is*, 2 vols, Belfast, New York and London, 1896.

McNally, V., *Reform, Revolution and Reaction, Archbishop Thomas Troy and the Catholic Church in Ireland 1787–1817*, New York and London, 1995.

McNeill, R., *Ulster's Stand for Union*, London, 1922.

MacSuibhne, P., *Paul Cullen and his Contemporaries*, 5 vols, Naas, 1961–77.

McVittie, R., *Details of the restoration of Christs Church cathedral Dublin*, Dublin, 1878.

Madden, S., *Life of Peter Roe*, Dublin, 1842.

Manning, C. (ed.), *Dublin and beyond the Pale*, Bray, 1998.

Manning, H., *Letter written to His Grace the Archbishop of Armagh, Primate of All Ireland, by Henry Edward, Archbishop of Westminster*, London, 1873.

Mant, R., *History of the Church of Ireland from the Reformation to the Revolution*, London, 1841.

Mason, W., *A Statistical Account or Parochial Survey of Ireland*, 3 vols, Dublin, 1814–19.

Maxton, H., *Waking: an Irish Protestant Upbringing*, Belfast, 1997.

Meigs, S., *The Reformations in Ireland, Tradition and Confessionalism 1400–1690*, London and New York, 1997.

M'Ghee, R., *Maynooth, its sayings and doings*, London, 1856.

Miley, J., *A sermon preached by John Miley in the metropolitan church on Sunday 28 June 1840… in thanksgiving for the providential escape of our most gracious Queen Victoria*, Dublin, 1840.

Mills, J. (ed.), *Account Roll of the Priors of the Priory of the Holy Trinity, Dublin, 1337–1346*, Dublin, 1996.

Milne, K., *The Irish Charter Schools, 1730–1830*, Dublin, 1997.

Moody, A. F., *Memories and Musings of a Moderator*, London, 1937.

Moore, C., *Betrayal of Trust: the Father Brendan Smyth Affair and the Catholic Church*, Dublin, 1995.

Moran, P. F., *History of the Catholic Archbishops of Dublin since the Reformation*, Vol. I, Dublin, 1864.

Moran, P. F., *The Pastoral Letters and Other Writings of Cardinal Cullen*, 3 vols, Dublin, 1882.

Morgan, J., *Thoughts on the Famine*, Belfast, 1848.

Moriarty, D., *Allocations to the clergy and pastorals of the late Rev Dr Moriarty, Bishop of Kerry*, Dublin and London, 1884.

Morley, H. (ed.), *Ireland under Elizabeth and James the First, Described by Edmund Spenser, by Sir John Davies and by Fynes Moryson*, London, 1890.

Morrissey, T., *William J. Walsh, Archbishop of Dublin 1841–1922*, Dublin, 2000.

Murphy, D. (ed.), *Triumphalia Chronologia Monasterii Sanctae Crucis in Hibernia*, Dublin, 1895.

Murphy, F., *Daniel Mannix, Archbishop of Melbourne*, Melbourne, 1948.

Murphy, H., *A History of Trinity College Dublin from its Foundation to 1702*, Dublin, 1951.

Murphy, J., *The People's Primate: A Memoir of Joseph Cardinal MacRory*, Dublin, 1945.

Murray, R., *Archbishop Bernard: Professor, Prelate and Provost*, London, 1931.

Nangle, E., *The Origins, Progress and Difficulties of the Achill Mission*, Dublin, 1839.

Nangle, E., *Fifteenth Report of the Achill Mission for the year ending December 31 1848*, Achill, 1849.

Neely, W. G., *Kilkenny: An Urban History 1391–1843*, Belfast, 1989.

Nelson, S., *Ulster's Uncertain Defenders: Protestant paramilitaries and community groups in the*

Northern Ireland conflict, Belfast, 1984.

Nicholson, A., *Ireland's Welcome to the Stranger, or Excursions through Ireland in 1844 and 1845*, London, 1847.

Nolan, W., Power, T. and Cowman, D. (eds), *Waterford, History and Society: Interdisciplinary Essays on the History of an Irish County*, Dublin, 1992.

Nolan, W., and Whelan, K. (eds), *Kilkenny, History and Society*, Dublin, 1990.

Noonan, S. and Hourigan, Fr J., *A Pilgrim for Peace: Pope John Paul II in Ireland*, Dublin, 1979.

O'Boyle, J., *The Irish Colleges on the Continent*, Dublin, Belfast, Cork and Waterford, 1935.

O'Brien, C. Cruise, *States of Ireland*, St Albans, 1974.

O'Byrne, E. (ed.), *The Convert Rolls*, Dublin, 1981.

O'Connor, F., *In Search of a State: Catholics in Northern Ireland*, Belfast, 1993.

O'Donnell, C., *Outraged Ulster: Why Ireland is Rebellious*, London, 1932.

O'Dwyer, B., *Letters from Ireland 1228–1229. Stephen of Lexington.* Kalamazoo, Mich., 1982.

O'Dwyer, E., *Correspondence and unpublished letters … of the late Dr O'Dwyer, Bishop of Limerick*, Limerick, n.d., *c.* 1917.

O'Dwyer, P., *The Irish Carmelites*, Dublin, 1988.

O'Faolain, S., *Vive Moi! An Autobiography*, London, 1965.

O'Fiaich, T., 'The registration of the clergy in 1704', *Seanchas Ard Mhacha* 6, 1971.

O'Flanagan, J., *The Lives of the Lord Chancellors and Keepers of the Great Seal of Ireland, from the Earliest Times to the Reign of Queen Victoria*, 2 vols, London, 1870.

O'Keefe, T., *An Anglo-Norman Monastery: Bridgetown Priory and the Architecture of the Augustinian Canons Regular in Ireland*, Cork, 1999.

O'Mahony, C., *The Viceroys of Ireland*, London, 1912.

O'Neill, J., *My Faith, Our Faith, Inter-Faith Practice – An Overview: An examination of various Religious-based initiatives and Religious faiths within Derry/Londonderry*, Derry, 1999.

O'Neill, T., *The Autobiography of Terence O'Neill, Prime Minister of Northern Ireland 1963–69*, London, 1972.

Otway-Ruthven, A., *A History of Medieval Ireland*, London and New York, 1968.

Payne, R., *A Brife description of Ireland Made in this yeere 1589, By Robert Payne unto xxv of his partners for whom he is undertaker there*, London, 1590.

Phoenix, E., *Northern Nationalism, Nationalist Politics, Partition and the Catholic Minority in Northern Ireland 1890–1914*, Belfast, 1994.

Porter, J., *The Life and Times of Henry Cooke*, London, 1871.

Rafferty, O. P., *Catholicism in Ulster 1603–1983, An Interpretative History*, London, 1994.

Reid, J. S., *History of the Presbyterian Church in Ireland, comprising the Civil History of the Province of Ulster from the Accession of James the First … to the Present Time*, 3 vols, Belfast, 1867 (first edition 1834–53).

Rennison, H., *Historical Sketch of Drumcree Parish*, Belfast, 1927.

Reynolds, E., *Campion and Parsons: the Jesuit Mission of 1580–1*, London, 1980.

Richardson, J., *A Short History of the Attempts that have been made to convert the Popish Natives of Ireland to the Establish'd Religion*, London, 1712.

Richardson, J., *The Great Folly, Superstition and Idolatry of Pilgrimages in Ireland, especially of that to St Patrick's Purgatory*, Dublin, 1727.

Rinuccini, G. B., *The Embassy in Ireland in the Years 1645–1649*, trans., A. Hutton, Dublin, 1873.

Rogers, E., *The Past and Present Policy of the British Government towards Protestantism in Ireland, Lecture Delivered at a meeting of the Armagh Protestant Association, Monday 22 April 1861*, Armagh, 1861.

Ronan, M., *The Reformation in Dublin 1536–1558*, London, 1926.

Sayers, P., *The Autobiography of Peig Sayers of the Great Blasket Island*, trans. B. MacMahon, Dublin, 1973.

Seaver, G., *John Fitzallen Gregg, Archbishop*, Leighton Buzzard, 1963.

Sheehy, M., *Is Ireland Dying? Culture and the Church in Modern Ireland*, London, Sydney and Toronto, 1968.

Sheils, W., and Wood, D. (eds), *The Churches, Ireland and the Irish*, Oxford, 1989.

Shuckburgh, E. (ed.), *Two Biographies of William Bedell, Bishop of Kilmore, with a Selection of his Letters and an Unpublished Treatise*, Cambridge, 1902.

Siggins, L., *Mary Robinson, The Woman Who Took Power in the Park*, London and Edinburgh, 1997.

Sirr, J. D'Arcy, *Memoir of the Honourable and Most Reverend Power Le Poer Trench, Last Archbishop of Tuam*, Dublin, 1845.

Smith, W., *The Battle for Northern Ireland*, Belfast, 1972.

Smyth, G., *Ireland, Historical and Statistical*, 3 vols, London, 1849.

Smyth, P .J., *The Priest in Politics*, Dublin, 1885.

Spenser, Edmund, 'A View of the State of Ireland, written dialogue-wise between Eudox and Iranaeus by Edmund Spenser . . . in 1596', in J. Ware, *The History of Ireland*, Dublin, 1633.

Spenser, Edmund, *A View of the Present State of Ireland*, ed. R. L. Renwick, Oxford, 1970.

Stalley, R., *The Cistercian Monasteries of Ireland*, London and New Haven, 1987.

Stanford, W. B., *A Recognised Church: The Church of Ireland in Eire*, Dublin and Belfast, 1944.

[Stock, J.], *A Narrative of What Passed at Killala in the County of Mayo during the French Invasion in the Summer of 1798, by an Eyewitness*, London, 1800.

Stubbs, J. W., *Archbishop Adam Loftus and the Foundation of Trinity College Dublin, as Preserved in a Manuscript in the Library of Armagh*, London and Dublin, 1892.

Swords, L., *Collège des Irlandais de Paris*, Dublin, 1986.

Swords, L. (ed.), *Protestant, Catholic and Dissenter: the Clergy and 1798*, Dublin, 1997.

Temple, J., *The Irish rebellion, or, an history of the beginning and first progress of the generall rebellion raised within the kingdom of Ireland upon the... 23 October 1641*, London, 1646.

Thompson, D., *A Brief Account of the Rise and Progress of the Change in Religious Opinion now taking Place in Dingle and the West of the County of Kerry, Ireland*, London, 1845.

Tierney, M., *Croke of Cashel: the Life of Archbishop Thomas William Croke 1823–1902*, Dublin, 1976.

Tocqueville, Alexis de, *Journeys to England and Ireland*, ed. J. Mayer, London, 1958.

Townshend, D., *The Life and Letters of the Great Earl of Cork*, London, 1904.

Trench, M., *Richard Chevenix Trench, Archbishop, Letters and Memorials*, 2 vols, London, 1888.

Troy, J., *Pastoral Instructions Addressed to the Roman Catholics of the Archdiocese of Dublin on the Duties of Christian Citizens*, Dublin, 1793.

Tute, L., *Letters written in England in August 1813 Explaining the Rise, Progress and Principles of the Orange Institution in Ireland*, Dublin, 1814.

Ussher, J., *The Religion Professed by the Ancient Irish*, London, 1631.

Walker, G., *A True Account of the Siege of London-derry by the Reverend Mr George Walker, Rector of Donoughmoore in the County of Tyrone, and the Late Governor of Derry in Ireland*, Dublin, 1736.

Walsh, L., *The home mission unmasked, or, a full and complete exposure of the frauds, deceptions and falsehoods practised by the agents of the home mission of the general assembly of the Presbyterian Church in Ireland*, Belfast, 1844.

Walsh, P., *William J. Walsh, Archbishop of Dublin*, Dublin and Cork, 1928.

Ware, J., *The Antiquities and History of Ireland*, London, 1705.

Watters, J., *What an Orangeman is: His duties and obligations*, Armagh, 1857.

Whately, E. J., *Life and Correspondence of Richard Whately, Late Archbishop of Dublin*, 2 vols, London, 1866.

Whately, R., *The Right Use of National Afflictions, being a Charge Delivered on the Annual Visitation of the Dioceses of Dublin and Kildare, 19 and 22 September 1848*, Dublin, 1848.

Wheeler, H., and Craig, M., *The Dublin City churches of the Church of Ireland*, Dublin, 1948.

White, J., *The Protestant Community in the Irish Republic*, Dublin, 1975.

White, N. (ed.) *Extent of Irish Monastic Possessions 1540–1541 from Manuscripts in the Public Record Office, London*, Dublin, 1943.

Williams, G., *Seven Treatises Very Necessary to be Observed in These Very Bad Dayes*, London, 1662.

Williams, H. (ed.), *The Correspondence of Jonathan Swift*, Vol. IV, 1732–1736, Oxford, 1965.

Wood, H. (ed.), *The Chronicle of Ireland 1584–1608 by Sir James Perrott*, Dublin, 1933.

Woodward, R., *The Present State of the Church of Ireland containing a Description of its Precarious Situation; and the Consequent Danger to the Public*, London, 1787.

Yeats, W. B., *Memoirs: autobiography [and] first draft journal*, ed. D. Donoghue, London, 1988 (first edition 1972).

Articles

(Anon.), 'The diocese of Dublin in the year 1630', *Irish Ecclesiastical Record* 5, Dublin, 1869.

Agnellus, Fr A. 'Television and Religion', *Irish Ecclesiastical Record* 82, 1955.

Barber, N., 'The Religious Orders – the end?', *Studies* 85, 1996.

Barrington, D., 'Uniting Ireland', *Studies* 46, 1957.

Bell, W., and Emerson, N., 'The Church of Ireland AD432–1932', *Report of the Church of Ireland Conference held in Dublin 11th–14th October 1932*, Dublin, 1932.

Berman, D., Lalor, S., and Torode, B., 'The theology of the IRA', *Studies* 72, 1983.

Bigger, F., 'The Irish in Rome in the 17th Century', *Ulster Journal of Archaeology* 5, Belfast, 1899.

Bigger, F., 'Kilconnel Abbey', *Journal of the Galway Archaeological and Historical Society* 2, Galway, 1902.

Blair, S., 'Rev. W. F. Marshall: profile of an Ulsterman', *Bulletin of the Presbyterian Historical Society of Ireland* 24, 1995.

Bossy, J., 'The Counter-Reformation and the people of Ireland, 1596–1641', *Historical Studies* 8, London, 1971.

Bottigheimer, K., 'The failure of the Reformation in Ireland: Une question bien posée', *Journal of Ecclesiastical History* 36, Cambridge, 1985.

Bradshaw, B., 'Opposition to the ecclesiastical legislation of the Irish Reformation parliament', *Irish Historical Studies* 16, Dublin, 1969.

Bradshaw, B., 'George Browne, first Reformation Archbishop of Dublin, 1530–1554', *Journal of Ecclesiastical History* 21, Cambridge, 1970.

Bradshaw, B., 'Fr Wolfe's description of Limerick city, 1574', *North Munster Antiquarian Journal* 17, 1975.

Brady, J., 'The Irish colleges in Europe', *Proceedings of the Irish Catholic Historical Committee, 1957*, Dublin, 1957.

Brady, J., 'Aspects of the Irish Church in the 18th Century', *Irish Ecclesiastical Record* 70, Dublin, 1948.

Brown, S., 'The Dublin newspaper press', *Studies* 25, Dublin, 1936.

Burns, G., 'The people back Franco', *Irish Monthly* 65, Dublin, 1937.

Cahill, T., 'Is religious decline a lot of nonsense?', *Furrow*, May 1992.

Canny, N., 'Why the Reformation failed in Ireland: Une question mal posée', *Journal of Ecclesiastical History* 30, Cambridge, 1979.

Canny, N., 'Rowland White's *The Dysorders of the Irissherye, 1571*', *Studia Hibernica* 19, Dublin, 1979.

Cleary, A., 'Gaelic League', *Studies* 8, Dublin, 1919.

Compton, P., 'Religious demography in Northern Ireland', *Studies* 78, 1989.

Comyn, A., 'Censorship in Ireland', *Studies* 58, 1969.

Corish, P., 'Ireland's first papal nuncio', *Irish Ecclesiastical Record* 81, Dublin, 1954.

Corish, P., 'Father Luke Wadding and the Irish nation', *Irish Ecclesiastical Record* 88, Dublin, 1957.

Coulter, J., 'The meaning of Derry', *Furrow*, December 1968.

Coulter, J., 'The problems of the Church in Northern Ireland', *Furrow*, August 1969.

Curtayne, A., Review of John O'Brien, *The Vanishing Irish*, *Furrow*, May 1954.

Daly, C., 'Violence or non-violence?', *Furrow*, February 1972.

Daly, C., 'In place of terrorism', *Furrow*, October 1975.

Daly, C., 'Needing forgiveness', *Intercom*, February 1995.

Deane, D., 'Ecumenism in Ireland', *Studies* 72, 1983.

de Blacam, A., 'The secrets of propaganda', *Irish Monthly* 65, 1937.

de Blacam, A., 'Some thoughts on partition', *Studies* 23, Dublin, 1934.

Devane, R., 'The religious revival under Salazar', *Irish Ecclesiastical Record* 51, 1938.

Devane, R., 'The dance hall – a moral and national menace', *Irish Ecclesiastical Record* 37, 1931.

'Documents concerning Primate Dowdall', *Archivium Hibernicum*, I, 1912.

Donnelly, J., 'A Church in crisis: the Irish Catholic Church today', *History Ireland*, Autumn 2000.

Dooley, T., 'Protestant migration from the Free State to Northern Ireland 1920–25', *Clogher Record* 15, Enniskillen, 1996.

Dudley Edwards, R., 'The Irish bishops and the Anglican schism 1534–1547', *Irish Ecclesiastical Record* 45, Dublin, 1935.

Duff, F., 'Emigration and providence', *Furrow* 8, 1957.

Egan, R., 'The royal visitation of Clonfert and Kilmacdaugh, 1615', *Journal of the Galway Archaeological and Historical Society* 35, Galway, 1976.

Fahey, J., 'The collegiate church of St Nicholas Galway', *Irish Ecclesiastical Record* 16, Dublin, 1895.

Faul, D., 'Catholic ecumenical activity', *Furrow*, January 1963.

Fennell, D., 'Propositions on Irish Catholicism', *Furrow*, October 1964.

Ferguson, H., 'The paedophile priest: a deconstruction', *Studies* 84, 1995.

Finegan, F., 'The Irish Catholic convert rolls', *Studies* 38, Dublin, 1949.

Fitzgerald, G., 'The significance of 1916', *Studies* 55, 1966.

Gallagher, E., 'Northern Ireland, the record of the churches', *Studies* 80, 1991.

Gannon, P., 'The latest phase in the Spanish civil war', *Studies* 26, Dublin, 1937.

Gannon, P. J., 'Art, morality and censorship', *Studies* 31, London 1942.

Gillespie, R., and Cunningham, B., 'Holy Cross Abbey and the Counter-Reformation in Tipperary', *Tipperary Historical Journal*, Thurles, 1991.

Grattan Flood, W. H., 'Pre-Reformation Archbishops of Cashel', *Irish Ecclesiastical Record* 29, Dublin, 1911.

Grattan Flood, W. H., 'The episcopal succession of Achonry 1219–1561', *Irish Ecclesiastical Record* 20, Dublin, 1922.

Grattan Flood, W. H., 'The episcopal succession of Killaloe', *Irish Ecclesiastical Record* 22, Dublin, 1923.

Griffin, S., 'Archbishop Murray and the episcopal clash on the interdenominational school scripture lessons controversy, 1835–1841', *Recusant History* 22, 1995.

Hayes, W., 'Dermot O'Hurley's last visit to Tipperary', *Tipperary Historical Journal*, Thurles, 1992.

Hegarty, K., 'The Church and the media', *Furrow*, February 1996.

Henley, A., 'Near dramatic trends in Irish Church personnel', *Intercom*, January 1995.

Hoban, B., 'What are we at?', *Furrow*, September 1992.

Inglis, T., 'Sacred and secular in Catholic Ireland', *Studies* 74, 1985.

Jefferies, H., 'The Irish parliament of 1560: the Anglican reforms authorised', *Irish Historical Studies* 26, 1989.

Jefferies, H., 'The Church among two nations, Armagh on the eve of the Tudor Reformations', *History Ireland* 6, 1998.

Jennings, B., 'The Abbey of Muckross', *Journal of the Cork Historical and Archaeological Society* 45, Cork, 1940.

Joy, J., 'Catholic action in Ireland', *Irish Monthly* 59, 1931.

Lawler, B., 'Dolfuss and his work', *Studies* 26, Dublin, 1937.

Lennon, C., 'Richard Stanihurst (1547–1618) and Old English identity', *Irish Historical Studies* 21, Dublin, 1978.

'The letter book of Lord Deputy Sir John Perrot between 9 July 1584 and 20 May 1586', *Analecta Hibernica* 12, 1943.

Linehan, M., 'Catholic social order for Ireland', *Irish Monthly* 63, 1935.

Lucey, C., 'The principles of Fascism', *Irish Ecclesiastical Record* 53, 1939.

Macaulay, A., 'The appointments of Patrick Curtis and Thomas Kelly as Archbishop and coadjutor Archbishop of Armagh', *Seanchas Ard Mhacha, Journal of the Armagh Diocesan Historical Society* 10, Armagh, 1982.

MacCurtain, M., 'The fall of the House of Desmond', *Journal of the Kerry Archaeological and Historical Society* 8, Naas, 1975.

MacCurtain, M., 'Moving statues and Irishwomen', *Studies* 76, 1987.

McEvoy, B. 'Father James Quigley, priest of Armagh and United Irishman', *Seanchas Ard Mhacha* 5, 1970.

McEvoy, B., 'Peepe of Day Boys and Defenders in the County Armagh', *Seanchas Ard Mhacha* 12, Armagh, 1986.

McKenna, T., 'Church of Ireland clergy in Cork: an analysis of the 1615 regal visitation', *Journal of Cork History* 77, 1972.

McKenna, L., 'Catholic University of Ireland', *Irish Ecclesiastical Record* 31, 1928.

McKevitt, P., 'The Jews in Christendom', *Irish Ecclesiastical Record* 46, 1935.

McMahon, K., 'The time of the Trouble 1919–1921: Armagh, South Down and North Louth', *Seanchas Ard Mhacha* 15, 1992.

McQuillan, I., 'Vocations crisis?' *Furrow*, November 1966.

McRedmond, L., 'Some deficiencies of lay Catholicism in Ireland', *Studies* 56, 1967.

Malcolm, E., 'The Catholic Church and the Irish temperance movement 1838–1901', *Irish Historical Studies* 23, Dublin, 1982.

Males, W., 'The Supplication of the Blood of the English most lamentably murdered in Ireland, crying out of the yearth for revenge, (1598)', *Analecta Hibernica* 36, Dublin, 1995.

Martin, F., 'The Irish friars and the Observant movement in the fifteenth century', *Proceedings of the Irish Catholic Historical Committee 1960*, Dublin, 1961.

Michael, M., 'Sex education for girls', *Furrow*, March 1959.

Millet, B., 'The beatified martyrs of Ireland: Bishop Patrick O'Hurley and Conn O'Rourcke', *Irish Theological Quarterly* 64, Maynooth, 1999.

Moody, T., 'The Irish parliaments under Elizabeth and James I', *Proceedings of the Royal Irish Academy* 45, 1940.

Moody, T. 'The Irish Reformation parliament of Henry VIII 1536–7', *Historical Studies* 6, London, 1968.

Mooney, C., 'The Irish Church in the sixteenth century', *Proceedings of the Irish Catholic Historical Committee 1962*, Dublin, 1963.

Mooney, C., 'The Franciscans in County Mayo', *Journal of the Galway Archaeological and Historical Society* 28, Galway, 1959.

Moore, C., 'William Lithgow's tour of Ireland in 1619', *Journal of the Cork Historical and*

Archaeological Society 8, 1902.

Mould, D., 'Ireland's opportunity', *Furrow*, March 1964.

Murphy, M., 'The suppression of Ireland's monasteries', *Irish Ecclesiastical Record* 25, 1925.

Murphy, M., 'The Irish Church: Its need of re-assessment', *Furrow*, January 1996.

Murphy, S., 'I don't support the IRA, but...', *Studies* 82, 1983.

Neely, W., 'The Protestant community of south Tipperary 1660–1815', *Tipperary Historical Journal*, Thurles, 1991.

Newman, J., 'Priestly vocations in Ireland', *Furrow*, November 1958.

Nicholls, K., 'A list of monasteries in Connacht 1577', *Journal of the Galway Archaeological and Historical Society* 33, Galway, 1963–7.

Niles, J., 'The Irish College, Antwerp', *Clogher Record* 15, Enniskillen, 1996.

O'Brien, C. Cruise, 'Church, State and Nation', *Furrow*, February 1975.

O'Brien, R., 'Ireland in the general elections (1826–1911)', *Irish Ecclesiastical Record* 29, 1911.

O'Cathain, S., 'Galway, ancient colonie of Englishe', *Studies* 31, Dublin, 1942.

O'Conaill, S., 'Scandals in the Church', *Studies* 84, 1995.

O'Connell, J., 'The Church in Ireland in the fifteenth century', *Proceedings of the Irish Catholic Historical Committee 1956*, Dublin, 1956.

O'Connor, E., 'Our Lady's Sodalities in parish life', *Furrow*, February 1960.

O'Connor, P., 'How religious news is reported', *Furrow*, August 1957.

O'Doherty, J., 'The Catholic Church in 1936', *Irish Ecclesiastical Record* 49, 1937.

O'Donnell, A., 'Edmund Butler, Archbishop of Cashel, 1524–51 and the Reformation', *Irish Ecclesiastical Record* 100, Dublin, 1963.

O'Donoghue, F., 'The Jesuits come to Ireland', *Studies* 80, Dublin, 1991.

O'Donoghue, H., 'Where have all the flowers gone?', *Intercom*, April 1994.

O'Donovan, J., 'Physical characteristics of the ancient Irish', *Ulster Journal of Archaeology* 6, Belfast, 1858.

O'Dwyer, M., 'The liturgy in a rural parish', *Furrow*, May 1954.

O'Dwyer, P., 'The Carmelite Order in pre-Reformation Ireland', *Irish Ecclesiastical Record* 110, Dublin, 1968.

O'hEaluighthe, D., 'Saint Gobnet of Ballyvourney', *Journal of the Cork Historical and Archaeological Society*, 57, Cork, 1952.

O'Herlihy, T., 'Fascist Italy', *Irish Ecclesiastical Record* 31, 1928.

O'Herlihy, T., 'Spain,' *Irish Ecclesiastical Record* 37, 1931.

O'Morarin, D., 'Ireland and the Council', *Furrow*, July 1966.

O'Reilly, J., 'What religion lost by the death of the Irish language', *New Ireland Review* 3, 1897–8.

O'Riain-Raedel, D., 'A German visitor to Monaincha in 1591', *Tipperary Historical Journal*, Thurles, 1998.

O'Riordan, S., 'Rinuccini in Galway, 1647–1649' *Journal of the Galway Archaeological and Historical Society* 23, Galway, 1949.

O'Riordan, S., 'Protestantism in Ireland', *Furrow*, February 1958.

O'Riordan, S., 'Catholic–Protestant relations in Ireland', *Furrow*, January 1961.

O'Shiel, K., 'The problem of partitioned Ireland', *Studies* 12, Dublin, 1923.

O'Sullivan, M. D., 'The lay school at Galway in the sixteenth and seventeenth centuries', *Journal of the Galway Archaeological and Historical Society* 15, Galway, 1933.

Otway-Ruthven, J., 'The character of Norman settlement in Ireland', *Historical Studies* 5, London, 1965.

Perceval-Maxwell, M., 'The Ulster rising of 1641 and the depositions', *Irish Historical Studies* 21, Dublin, 1978.

Purcell, M., 'St Patrick's Purgatory: Francesco Chiericati's letter to Isabelle d'Este', *Seanchas Ard Mhacha* 12, Armagh, 1987.

Quare, M., 'Bishop Foy School, Waterford', *Journal of the Cork Historical and Archaeological Society* 71, 1966.

Quinn, D., 'Edward Walshe's "Conjectures" concerning the state of Ireland', *Irish Historical Studies* 5, Dublin, 1947.

Quinn, D., 'Henry VIII and Ireland 1509–1534', *Irish Historical Studies* 12, Dublin, 1961.

Quinn, D., 'The Munster Plantation', *Journal of the Cork Historical and Archaeological Society* 71, 1966.

Quinn, D., 'An icon for the new Ireland: An assessment of President Robinson', *Studies*, Autumn 1997.

Rafferty, O., 'Cardinal Cullen, early Fenianism and the McManus funeral affair', *Recusant History* 22, 1995.

Ronan, M., 'Booke oute of Ireland in Latten', *Irish Ecclesiastical Record* 25, 1925.

Rope, H. E., 'The ruin of the Gaeltacht', *Irish Monthly* 60, 1932.

Rossetti, S. 'Child sexual abuse and power', *Furrow*, December 1995.

Ryan, A., 'Spain, the Church and Europe', *Irish Ecclesiastical Record* 48, 1936.

Ryan, M., 'The Franciscan houses of Thomond in 1616', *North Munster Antiquarian Journal* 10, 1967.

Scott, J., 'A letter from Ireland, 1 April 2060', *Furrow*, May 1958.

Sheehy, M., 'Ireland and the Holy See', *Irish Ecclesiastical Record* 97, Dublin, 1962.

Silke, J., 'The Irish appeal of 1593 to Spain', *Irish Ecclesiastical Record* 92, Dublin, 1959.

Silke, J., 'The Irish College, Seville', *Archivium Hibernicum* 24, Maynooth, 1961.

Silke, J., 'Hugh O'Neill, the Catholic Question and the papacy', *Irish Ecclesiastical Record* 104, Dublin, 1965.

Silke, J., 'Some aspects of the Reformation in Armagh province', *Clogher Record* 11, Enniskillen, 1984.

Simms, J., 'The bishops' banishment act of 1697', *Irish Historical Studies* 18, 1970.

Simms, J., 'Remembering 1690', *Studies* 63, 1974.

Simms, K., 'The Archbishops of Armagh and the O'Neills 1347–1471', *Irish Historical Studies* 19, Dublin 1975.

Smyth, B., 'Catholic programmes on Irish television', *Furrow*, December 1959.

Smyth, B., 'Problems posed by British television', *Furrow*, August 1960.

Smyth K., 'Priests and people in Ireland', *Furrow*, March 1958.

Smyth, W., 'Towns and town life in mid-17th century County Tipperary', *Tipperary Historical Journal*, Thurles, 1991.

Steele, E., 'Cardinal Cullen and Irish nationality', *Irish Historical Studies* 14, Dublin, 1975.

Thompson, J., 'The churches in Northern Ireland – problem or solution? A Presbyterian perspective', *Irish Theological Quarterly* 58, 1992.

Tierney, M., 'The problem of Partition', *Studies* 26, Dublin 1937.

Wall, M. 'The rise of a Catholic middle class in eighteenth-century Ireland', *Irish Historical Studies* 11, Dublin, 1958.

Walsh, A., 'Michael Cardinal Logue, 1840–1924', *Seanchas Ard Mhacha, Journal of the Armagh Diocesan Historical Society* 17, 1997.

Walsh, M., 'The Irish College at Madrid', *Seanchas Ard Mhacha* 15, 1993.

Walsh, W., 'Challenges to the Irish Church', *Furrow*, June 1996.

Walshe, H., 'Enforcing the Elizabethan settlement: the vicissitudes of Hugh Brady, Bishop of Meath 1563–84', *Irish Historical Studies* 26, 1989.

Warren, R., 'The Church of Ireland since 1868', Paper read at the Church Congress, Birmingham, 1893.

Watt, J., 'Negotiations between Edward II and John XXII concerning Ireland', *Irish Historical Studies* 10, Dublin, 1956–7.

Whelan, P., 'Anthony Blake, Archbishop of Armagh 1758–1787', *Seanchas Ard Mhacha* 5, 1970.

Primary Sources

Atkinson, G., (ed.), *Calendar of State Papers Relating to Ireland, July 1596 – December 1597*, London, 1893.

Beresford Correspondence, Robinson Library, Armagh.

Brewer, J., and Bullen, W. (eds), *Calendar of the Carew Manuscripts Preserved in the Archiepiscopal Library at Lambeth 1515–1574*, London, 1867.

Brewer, J., and Bullen, W. (eds), *Calendar of the Carew Manuscripts Preserved in the Archiepiscopal Library at Lambeth 1575–1588*, London, 1868.

Brewer, J., and Bullen, W. (eds), *Calendar of the Carew Manuscripts Preserved in the Archiepiscopal Library at Lambeth 1589–1600*, London, 1869.

Boulter, H., *A charge given by Hugh Boulter, lord Archbishop of Armagh and Primate of all Ireland to his clergy at his primary visitation of his diocese, begun at Drogheda July 16 and continued at Armagh July 22 1725*, Dublin, 1725.

Burtchaell, G. D., and Rigg, J. M. (eds), *Report on Franciscan Manuscripts at Merchants Quay, Dublin*, Dublin, 1906.

Calendar of the Manuscripts of the Marquis of Ormonde Preserved at Kilkenny Castle, Vol. 2, London, 1899; Vol. 6, London, 1911; Vol. 7, London, 1912.

The Church of Ireland and the Present Crisis, Report of the special meeting of the General Synod holden at Dublin 23 March 1886, Dublin, 1886.

Franciscan Fathers Killiney, *Father Luke Wadding*, Dublin, 1957.

Hamiltion, K. C. (ed.), *Calendar of State Papers Relating to Ireland 1509–1573*, London, 1860.

Hamilton, K. C. (ed.), *Calendar of State Papers Relating to Ireland August 1588 – September 1599*, London, 1885.

Jennings, B. (ed.), *Wadding papers 1614–1638*, Dublin, 1953.

John Paul II, *The Pope in Ireland, Addresses and Homilies*, Dublin, 1979.

King, W., 'Visitation of Armagh, 1693, 1694, 1700–2 by William King, for the Lord Primate, with Bishop King's letter to the same', Robinson Library Mss, Armagh.

Lindsay, T., *The Insolence of Dissenters against the Establish'd Church exemplified in a Memorial given in to the Lords Justices of Ireland by His Grace the Lord Primate and the Lord Bishop of Down and Connor*, London, 1716.

Logue letters, O'Fiaich Library, Armagh.

Mahaffy, R. (ed.), *Calendar of State Papers Relating to Ireland 1633–1647*, London, 1901.

Manuscripts and Correspondence of James, first Earl of Charlemont, I, 1745–1783, London 1891.

McMinn, J. (ed.), *A Calendar of the papers of the Rev T. B. Armoour, Irish Presbyterian Minister and Home Ruler, 1869–1914*, Belfast, 1985.

Minutes of the Proceedings of the General Assembly of the Presbyterian Church in Ireland, 13, 1916–20, Belfast.

Minutes of the Proceedings of the General Assembly of the Presbyterian Church in Ireland, 13, 1922, Belfast.

Minutes of the Proceedings of the General Assembly of the Presbyterian Church in Ireland, 13, 1923, Belfast.

Minutes of the Proceedings of the General Assembly of the Presbyterian Church in Ireland, 1928, Belfast.

Morrin, J. (ed.), *Calendar of the Patent and Close Rolls of Chancery in Ireland of the Reigns of Henry VIII, Edward VI, Mary, and Elizabeth*, Vol. I, Dublin, 1861.

Records of the General Synod of Ulster 1691–1820, III, Belfast, 1898.

Report of the Church of Ireland conference on youth held in the Wellington Hall, Belfast, 18–23 September 1944, Belfast and Dublin, 1944.

Report of the Manuscripts of the Earl of Egmont, 1, London, 1905.

Rigg, J. (ed.), *Calendar of State Papers Relating to English Affairs Preserved Principally at Rome, in the Vatican Archives*, I, 1558–1571, London, 1916.

Rigg, J. (ed.), *Calendar of State Papers Relating to English Affairs Preserved Principally at Rome, in the Vatican Archives and Library*, II, 1572–1578, London, 1916.

Russell, C., and Prendergast, J. (eds), *Calendar of State Papers Relating to Ireland 1603–1606*, London, 1872.

State Papers of Henry VIII, Part III, Correspondence between the governments of England and Ireland 1538–1546, London, 1834.

Index